REA

AFRICAN AMERICAN AUTOBIOGRAPHERS

AFRICAN AMERICAN AUTOBIOGRAPHERS

A Sourcebook

Edited by
EMMANUEL S. NELSON

Greenwood Press
Westport, Connecticut • London

Library of Congress Cataloging-in-Publication Data

African American autobiographers : a sourcebook / edited by
Emmanuel S. Nelson.
    p. cm.
  Includes bibliographical references and index.
  ISBN 0–313–31409–8 (alk. paper)
  1. American prose literature—African American
authors—Bio-bibliography—Dictionaries. 2. Autobiography—African American
authors—Bio-bibliography—Dictionaries. 3. African American
authors—Bio-bibliography—Dictionaries. 4. African
Americans—Bio-bibliography—Dictionaries. I. Nelson, Emmanuel S. (Emmanuel
Sampath), 1954—
PS366.A35A36   2002
818'.08—dc21   2001050104

British Library Cataloguing in Publication Data is available.

Library of Congress Catalog Card Number: 2001050104
ISBN: 0–313–31409–8

First published in 2002

Greenwood Press, 88 Post Road West, Westport, CT 06881
An imprint of Greenwood Publishing Group, Inc.
www.greenwood.com

Printed in the United States of America

The paper used in this book complies with the
Permanent Paper Standard issued by the National
Information Standards Organization (Z39.48–1984).

10 9 8 7 6 5 4 3 2 1

FOR TREVOR, WITH LOVE

CONTENTS

PREFACE

The earliest cultural conflict between blacks and whites in the United States can be framed partly as a conflict between orality and literacy. As a preindustrial people systematically denied access even to the rudimentary tools of literacy in the New World, the imaginative texts created by African Americans during the seventeenth and much of the eighteenth centuries remained exclusively in oral form. Blending their West African cultural memories and their harsh American experiences, the early preliterate African American artists pioneered a unique Afro New World idiom that found expression in their work songs, folktales, spirituals, sermons, and other verbal structures that were orally transmitted across generations. In political terms, however, those cultural productions were no match for the power of the written texts produced by the literate segments of white America. Books, after all, are not innocent entities; they are repositories of ideology. Inscribed in an overwhelming majority of early American political, legal, religious, medical, and literary texts were racist, sexist, and elitist ideologies that empowered the white male ruling class. Even when African Americans were the subject of white discourse, they were powerless — because of their preliterate status — to intervene and resist. The very absence of textual challenge from African Americans ensured the pseudolegitimization and perpetuation of white assumptions and representations. The written texts, which constitute a most potent manifestation of literacy, thus crucially helped establish and maintain white hegemony and functioned as powerful instruments of domination.

Beginning in the late eighteenth century, however, the terms of the racial encounter were gradually rearranged. African Americans began to write. Soon autobiographical narration emerged as a preferred mode of creative self expression. To a large extent, this privileging of self representational writing over other textual forms was a result of encouragement by Northern white abolition

ists. The antislavery activists sponsored the production and circulation of autobiographical narratives by fugitive slaves because they realized that those
poignant first-person accounts of life in inhuman bondage in the South could be
used effectively to advance the abolitionist cause. For the fugitive slave, too, the
act of self-creation implied in the autobiographical role had enormous personal
and political significance. Autobiographies indeed are narratives of selfhood; the
narrator lays claim to the power and authority of self-definition. For an African
American autobiographer, in the antebellum era, to claim her subjectivity was
inherently a revolutionary act. It was a profoundly political gesture because she
dared, in effect, to insist on her selfhood and agency in a society that refused to
recognize her humanity and viewed her instead as commodity. Moreover, the
autobiographical form offered her an exemplary opportunity to fuse the power of
personal testimony with trenchant social observation. It granted her a communal
voice that allowed her not only to tell her life story but also to expose the various
forms and structures of oppression that maimed her life and the lives of others
in her community. The early African American autobiographies, therefore, were
more than life stories; they were carefully crafted instruments of resistance.

This melding of personal, communal, and sociopolitical concerns continues to
be a salient feature of African American lifewriting. Moreover, the autobiographical tradition, which originated in the antebellum slave narratives, still occupies
a position of primary in African American expressive culture. The project of
claiming and defining the self—an enabling act that defies the racist logic of the
dominant culture—still remains at the heart of the African American autobiographical enterprise.

The central objective of this reference volume is to provide a wide-ranging
introduction to the autobiographical tradition in African American writing from
the mid-eighteenth century to the late 1990s: from the early captivity narratives,
antebellum fugitive slave narratives, spiritual autobiographies, and travelogues to
the sleek, self-reflexive autobiographies of the late twentieth century that reveal
their authors' postmodern awareness of the fictionality of all constructed selves.
Included in this sourcebook are sixty-seven representative autobiographers;
thirty-five of them are women. The works of major authors, such as Frederick
Douglass, W.E.B. Du Bois, Richard Wright, Zora Neale Hurston, Langston
Hughes, James Baldwin, Audre Lorde, Maya Angelou, and Malcolm X, receive
careful and extensive attention. But I have also included numerous lesser-known
authors—such as Julia A.J. Foote, Sarah Rice, Hilton Als, Marita Golden, and
Toi Derricotte—whose compelling works deserve greater academic attention.
Though my goal is not to define the African American autobiographical canon,
I am acutely conscious of the fact that a reference volume such as this is likely
to be implicated in canon formation.

My primary purpose, rather, is to offer reliable, thorough, and up-to-date biographical, critical, and bibliographic information on the authors included. Advanced scholars will find this volume a useful research tool; its user-friendly style,
format, and level of complexity, however, make it accessible to a wider audience

that includes undergraduate students and even general readers. Each chapter begins with relevant biographical information on the writer, offers an interpretative commentary on his or her major autobiographical work(s), provides an overview of the critical reception accorded, and concludes with a bibliography that lists, separately, the autobiographical work(s) and the available secondary material. To facilitate cross-referencing, whenever a writer who is also the subject of a chapter in this volume is mentioned, an asterisk appears next to his or her name.

Let me take this opportunity to thank the contributors to this volume; my work as the editor was considerably eased by their professionalism and promptness. I would also like to thank Dr. George Butler, senior editor at Greenwood Press, for his unfailing support for this as well as other projects.

ELIZABETH LAURA ADAMS
(1909–?)

Heather Rellihan

BIOGRAPHY

Elizabeth Laura Adams is one of the first female African Americans to have been recognized within the body of writings in and around the Catholic Church, and her autobiography *Dark Symphony* has remained an integral piece of this literature up to the present time. Adams was born in Santa Barbara, California, to Daniel Henderson and Lula Joseph Holden Adams, both of whom had a love for the arts. Daniel was a waiter with a deep appreciation for visual art and music, and Lula, who had decided against pursuing art studies in Paris so she could get married, was an artist and architect. Adams spent her early years in California where she enjoyed a rather idyllic lifestyle.

As an only child, she had a particularly close relationship with her parents, although her father's love seemed to shelter more than nourish. Her father was the unquestioned patriarch and seems to have been more oppressive than Adams cares to admit. Her mother seemed to counter these conservatisms with fancy and fairy tale. Modeling herself after her mother, Adams learned to use art as an escape from the oppressiveness of her father and the community race dynamics. Adams's parents played an important role in her development; not only did her mother foster an appreciation for art and music, but the specific ways that Adams's parents interacted with their primarily white community — for example, how her parents coped with racism — provided important instruction that contributed in significant ways to Adams's emerging sense of self, who she was in relation to the world. Her parents taught her to deal with discrimination and other forms of hatred with passive understanding and dismissal rather than anger and aggression. Adams's mother, for example, admonished her to pray for, rather than get angry with, the little girls that taunted her at school. Learning these doctrines of forgiveness and understanding helped prepare Adams to find and accept religion as her primary calling—her view of the world blended effortlessly into her religious avocation. Ironically, even though her parents played an important role in the development of Adams's moral philosophies, her father was adamantly opposed to her conversion to Catholicism. Adams credits her father's opinion to religious conservatism, but one might wonder if gender dynamics didn't contribute to his thinking. Adams accepts her father's lifelong objections even though they interfered with her religious calling. In fact, Adams couldn't fully embrace religion until after her father's death—only then did her mother allow her to convert to Catholicism. Adams wanted to join a convent to dedicate herself to God fully. Although she never gets this opportunity, Adams experiences this time in her life with great excitement. She feels self-actualized in the Catholic Church as her burgeoning spirituality finally finds its home.

Troublingly, though, once fully immersed in Catholicism, Adams begins to recognize the subtle racisms of the Church. She begins to notice, for example, that African Americans are often ignored or slighted during Communion and Confession. Certainly this behavior is troubling to Adams on several levels, but racism was an omnipresent variable in her life, one that she had unfortunately learned to live with, if not accept. But here, in the Church, Adams experiences a new and more deeply felt offense. She feels a profound hypocrisy, although she deals with it in a characteristic fashion: She turns to God for help. She prays that the Church will come to see that these practices work against God and that the Church will, therefore, devote its efforts to combating racism, rather than supporting it.

Although religion was arguably Adams's principal calling, she flirted with a literary career throughout her life. At several points she endeavored to turn this passion into a career. Before the publication of *Dark Symphony*, Adams had poems, essays, and reviews published in both literary and religious journals. Ultimately, her desire to work as a journalist was never fully realized, and she had to turn to other means to make a living, especially before the publication of her autobiography. Adams did, however, receive a modest amount of public recognition and praise prior to the remarkable success of *Dark Symphony*. For example, *The Morning Star* awarded her prizes for some of her work, and years later she had a feature article published in the *Sentinel of the Blessed Sacrament*, a Catholic magazine of the day. Following that, one of Adams's poems, "Consecrated," was recognized favorably by a literary club. This particular praise proved somewhat dubious, however: Exposing their racist assumptions, the judges noted their surprise when they realized that Adams was a black woman. In fact, the publication of her work was delayed for years until *Westward* eventually published one of her poems in its magazine. Adams presumes that prejudice was responsible for the deferment. Just as racism had surfaced in the Church, mitigating Adams's feelings of acceptance, similar prejudices restricted her success as a poet. Beginning in October 1940, *Dark Symphony* was serialized in *Torch*, a national Catholic magazine of the day. This marked a pivotal moment in her career as this text would allow her widespread popularity among the Catholic community and a lasting recognition in the literary world.

AUTOBIOGRAPHICAL WORK AND THEMES

Adams's major autobiographical work is *Dark Symphony*, which was published in 1942, a year after her narrative first appeared in the serialized essay "There Must Be a God . . . Somewhere: A True Story of a Convert's Search for God." Her work focused on the search for peace and purity through religion. *Dark Symphony* works as a spiritual *Bildungsroman*—taking the reader on a religious journey that transcends the realities of racism, death, and physical frailty. While her autobiography discusses the importance of poetry and music in her life, religion—and specifically Catholicism—structures the text thematically. Adams's message is clear: Faith brings peace and salvation. Interestingly, secondary narrative strains seep through the principal story line and imbue her writing with other, and more complex, meanings. That is, Adams maintains that her religious focus and, particularly, her commitment to certain ideals of forgiveness and acceptance have helped her find happiness, but, and somewhat paradoxically, her narrative reveals the basic inability for faith to cure all her evils: Adams seems unfulfilled despite her fervent commentary to the contrary. At times her narrative smacks with disappointment over her literary endeavors and her chronic career frustrations. And further, while a modern reader certainly wants to read more into her commentary on racism, there does seem some innate tension that Adams herself recognizes, however subconsciously. For example, in recalling her mother's effort to contain Adams's childhood anger—which grew in reaction to her early encounters with prejudice—there seems some resentment—some frustrated recognition—that her mother's solution was problematic. The tone of the Adams story expresses victory—Adams marks her spiritual journey a success—but the reader can't help but question the all or nothingness of this branding while simultaneously hoping that Adams herself experienced more questioning than she voiced publicly.

CRITICAL RECEPTION

Dark Symphony has met with marked appreciation for the last fifty years. The initial reviews, written primarily by white Catholic writers, were overwhelmingly positive. The reviewers of her day seemed to appreciate Adams both for her writing style and for her politics. Notably, the two reviews that stand out in contradistinction to this trend are both written by African Americans: Ellen Tarry and Theophilus Lewis both seem uncomfortable with Adams's unyielding patience vis à vis her experiences with racism. Adams's autobiography was a popular text within the Catholic community, selling approximately 15,000 copies and thereby earning Adams enough royalties to make her living after 1942. The text was republished in Great Britain and underwent several translations, in cluding editions in Dutch and Italian. Within the Catholic community of her time, Adams's text was well known, and her autobiography was, and still is, considered a seminal text on African Americans and Catholicism.

BIBLIOGRAPHY

Autobiographical Work by Elizabeth Laura Adams

"There Must Be a God . . . Somewhere: A True Story of a Convert's Search for God." *Torch* (October 1940): 4–6; (November 1940): 19–20, 30; (December 1940): 9–10; (January 1941): 16–18; (February 1941): 10–11; (March 1941): 23–24, 29. (Serialized)
Dark Symphony. New York: Sheed and Ward, 1942.

Studies of Elizabeth Laura Adams's Autobiographical Work

"The Art of Living Joyfully." Rev. of *Dark Symphony. Torch* (December 1942): 29.
Barton, Rebecca Chalmers. *Witnesses for Freedom: Negro Americans in Autobiography.* New York: Harper and Brothers, 1948. 123–34.
Braxton, Joanne M. *Black Women Writing Autobiography: A Tradition within a Tradition.* Philadelphia: Temple University Press, 1989. 140.
Brignano, Russel A. *Black Americans in Autobiography.* Rev. and exp. ed. Durham, NC: Duke University Press, 1984. 3.
"Children under Fire." Rev. of *Dark Symphony. Torch* (November 1943): 29.
David, Jay. *Growing Up Black.* New York: William Morrow, 1968. 60–70.
Dwyer, Joseph. Rev. of *Dark Symphony. Torch* (June 1942): 27.
Kaplan, Carla. "I Wanna March." Introduction. *Dark Symphony and Other Works.* Ed. Henry Louis Gates Jr. and Jennifer Burton. New York: G.K. Hall, 1996. xvii–lvii.
Lewis, Theophilus. Rev. of *Dark Symphony. Interracial Review* (May 1942): 20–21.
Mathews, Geraldine O. *Black American Writers, 1773–1949: A Bibliography and Union List.* Boston: G.K. Hall, 1975.
Scally, Mary Anthony. *Negro Catholic Writers 1900–1943: A Bio-Biography.* Detroit: Walter Romig, 1945. 19–23.
Tarry, Ellen. Rev. of *Dark Symphony. Catholic World* (July 1942): 504–5.

HILTON ALS
(1961–   )

Jacqueline C. Jones

BIOGRAPHY

Cultural critic, literary critic, journalist, and screenwriter, Hilton Als was born in Barbados in 1961 to Cyprian Williams and Marie Als. He described his absent father as irresponsible, childlike, and beautiful. Als's father did not live with the family, and the femaleness of his household had a great impact on him. Als has four sisters and a younger brother. A female cousin was raised in his immediate family, and he considers her to be a sister as well. He grew up in Brooklyn in a predominantly West Indian and African American neighborhood. His tenure at a white high school in Manhattan was his first prolonged association with whites. Als was greatly influenced by one of his sisters' stints as a model when he was a teenager. At age sixteen he attended the State University of New York at Purchase for one year. After a three-year break Als studied art history at Columbia University. A voracious reader, Als lists his literary influences as Marcel Proust, Jane Bowles, and James Baldwin.* He later took a job at *The Village Voice* as a secretary. Writer Ian Frazier helped Als in getting published in *The New Yorker*. He began writing "Talk of the Town" pieces in 1989 and currently writes literary circles, fashion reviews, and cultural criticism as a staff writer for *The New Yorker*. He is also a contributor to *Grand Street* and *The New York Times Magazine*. His work has also appeared in *Art Forum International*, *The Village Voice*, and *Vibe*, among other publications. Als has written introductions for *Strange Fruit: Billie Holiday, Café Society, and an Early Cry for Civil Rights* and *Without Sanctuary*. *The Group*, his book on James Baldwin and the Jewish intellectual circle, will be published in late 2001. He is also a screenwriter, with *Looking for Langston* (1988) and *Swoon* (1992) to his credit. Als is making his directorial debut with the film *Fine and Mellow*.

AUTOBIOGRAPHICAL WORKS AND THEMES

Much of Als's published work is an interesting mix of autobiography, literary criticism, and cultural criticism. Visibility, silence, and gaining voice are key themes in Als's work. His only published book is a collection of three essays entitled *The Women*. Published in 1996, each essay in *The Women* examines an aspect of gender construction or identity. At 145 pages, the book is brief. The themes in Als's book are primarily related to identity and self-acceptance. The book is also a record of his own journey to acknowledging the impact of his relationship with his mother and Owen Dodson—a poet, playwright, and academic—on his own development and the necessary casting off of those experiences on his road to selfhood.

The Women also charts Als's journey to becoming a writer. It allows him a voice when he is often silenced. "When I was eight I told her I wanted to be a writer. Writing things down was the only way I understood how to be heard, there being so many women in my mother's house at various times, talking" (24). In an interview with Coco Fusco, Als explains his impetus for writing the book. "I had to write about these people so that I could leave them—in order to speak" (51). By coming to terms with his understanding of his mother, Owen Dodson, and Dorothy Dean—an iconic figure in gay New York—Als creates a new identity for himself. Thus the writing of the book is a liberatory act.

The first essay explores Als's struggle to define himself in relation to his mother and the concept of the Negress. He seeks to understand and reconcile his conflicting feelings toward his mother and his own self-image. Beneath Als's commentary on the Negress lurks a longing for his father or another male figure. He describes his father as a grown child who is dependent on women to take care of him. Without a male in the household Als turned to his mother and sisters for identification. "For years before and after her death, I referred to myself as a Negress: it was what I was conditioned to be. And yet I have come no closer to defining it. . . . I have expressed my Negressity by living, fully, the prescribed life of an auntie man—what Barbadians call a faggot" (8–9). His first homosexual experiences entail Als "seducing [his partners] into performing acts defined as male" (18). Thus if his partner acts "male," then Als can be the female or the auntie man. Ross Posnock finds that Als cannot separate himself from his Negressity. "Not simply is Als absorbed in his 'Negressity,' he flaunts it as the lens of his cultural criticism" (130). Being a Negress allowed Als to redefine himself, to resist the definitions of his body by others. It permits Als to be a rebel.

Als's feelings about his homosexuality are as complicated as his feelings toward his mother. "Had she had access to other people besides her children, lover, employer, doctors, she might have been a fag hag, fond of auntie men, music, and movies" (29). Sex becomes another form of escape for him. He equates the Negress with need, emotional and physical need for affection, touch. "I avoided mentioning how the men I seduced were almost always white, because I did not visually associate their color with anything that mattered, such as Negressity, home, my mother" (60). Thus Als's literal and figurative flight from blackness are embodied in his sexual experimentation.

He goes on to examine the portrait of the Negress in the fiction of African American women writers Alice Walker,* John Edgar Wideman,* Gayl Jones, Toni Cade Bambara, and Terry McMillan. Als states that the Negress in fiction is a symbol of both oppression and blackness (48). She is large, ugly, servile, and silent. He argues that the writers' egos distract them from sufficiently probing or representing the essence of the Negress.

The second essay in *The Women* examines the life and significance of Dorothy Dean (1933–1987). The essay appeared in a different form in *The New Yorker*. Dean, a 1954 graduate of Radcliffe who received her master's from Harvard in 1958, grew up as a member of the black middle class in White Plains, New York. She was employed by the Boston Museum of Fine Arts and Brandeis University as a slide curator/librarian. Dean moved to New York City in 1962 where she worked as a fact checker at *The New Yorker* and later as a copy editor at *Shout*, *Vogue*, and *Essence* magazines. She was fired from *The New Yorker* in 1964, an act she expected and even courted.

Dean's social life revolved around her circle of gay white men. "As a socially authoritative figure, Dean took control of a group of [gay] men who had largely grown up in environments where everything was allowed and encouraged, and never controlled by women" (79). With her "Lavender Brotherhood" Dean was able to transcend her physical being and become the person she envisioned herself. Her feelings of self-hatred seemed to stem from her racial and gender identities. Dean was also very class conscious. "What Dean believed was that intellectual life was a function of being European and male. And one way of ensuring that her identification would be taken seriously was to deny her body everything while indulging in behavior that was gay-male-identified" (81). She was "candid about her reverence of white people" (73).

Als seeks to investigate the source of Dean's allure for audience. Her eloquence and witty exchanges kept her friends/fans enraptured. Yet she was also acerbic, sarcastic, and bitter. He asserts that "she was a symbol whose death signaled an end to *then* era, which . . . has come to represent a time of highly aestheticized waste" (70). Yet what is Dean's allure for Als? He sees her as another form of the Negress. Als argues that Dean was in essence a Negress as evidenced by her adherence to a WASP (White Anglo-Saxon Protestant) style of dress and her belief in the rightness of whiteness.

Als describes Dean as a fag hag who maintained a disgust for fellow African Americans and adored whiteness and white gay men. He offers a brief meditation on the fag hag. "She becomes a star attraction among men who have limited, if any, sexual response to her (a fact she eventually, inevitably, resents). . . . The fag hag operates on the premise that social ambition in the gay world is her only power" (92). Although he laments that she did not develop her writing voice, Als locates some of Dean's power in her journalism. Dean wrote and published

The All Lavender Cinema Courier, a newsletter in which she reviewed films and skewered people.

Dean's fall from favor was precipitated by her fondness for malicious language, alcohol, and the arrival of a more attractive form of fag hag. Dean's audience, infatuated with sex and infected by AIDS, dwindled. She relocated to Boulder, Colorado, where she died of lung cancer in 1987.

The last essay explores Als's relationship with Owen Dodson. Als's connection to Dodson is quite clear: The two men were lovers. Als even remarks on their similar physical resemblance. Dodson was, in fact, Als's first lover; he seems to discount the sexual experience that he had with a male janitor at the age of ten. Characterizing Dodson as his "first woman," Als refers to the circumstances surrounding their sexual relationship throughout the essay (132). "Entering his mouth with my tongue was like entering the atmosphere of another age" (134). Als began a relationship with Dodson when he was fifteen, and it continued for four years. Dodson was a middle-aged man in decline, according to Als's portrait. Yet there was genuine affection for the older writer. "[I]t was my first experience of love—and of the will I have sometimes exercised in avoiding it" (136).

Ambition fueled Als's desire to spend time with Dodson. He acknowledges that Dodson taught him to think (129). Yet he found little inspiration in Dodson's own work or in the work of Dodson's Harlem Renaissance contemporaries. Als identifies the meaning of the Harlem Renaissance as "the moment when Negro social life devolved from Negro to black" (121). He describes Dodson as "intellectually lazy" and found little truth in his work (126). He felt that Dodson was too much aware of the expectations of his audience and that he sacrificed his artistic vision in exchange for moderate success. He also belittles writers for a lack of talent and publishers for their lack of criticism. Interestingly, he neglects to mention the writers by name.

Ultimately Als acknowledges the difficulties posed by his merging of genres in his book. The question of the veracity of Als's memory and the relationship between autobiography, confession, and fiction are addressed by Als: "[T]his is my story, finally, or, rather, a story I fight to own, since it is not independent of any and all of the people I have known" (136). *The Women* is indeed Als's story; his memoir is subtly woven through the three essays, and one leaves the book wishing that he had used a mirror instead of a veil.

CRITICAL RECEPTION

Given that it is a work that refuses categorization, *The Women* clearly presents a challenge to reviewers. Most comment on the book's brevity and its innate refusal to be classified by one genre or style. Two reviews in the *New York Times* typify responses to Als's book. Andrea Lee finds that the book has "an almost magical cohesiveness [that] is due to the peculiar talents of the visual and psychological description worthy of a novelist" (7). Although he states that the three essays "represent a fascinating sensibility," Richard Bernstein concludes that the "book is too fragmentary and episodic." James Hatch, author of the biography of Owen Dodson titled *Sorrow Is the Only Faithful One*, takes great exception to the way in which Als denigrates others. "It is sad that Als, now a middle aged man of some talent, has to destroy others' reputations in an attempt to achieve one of his own." Generally it appears as if *The Women* led reviewers to identify Als as a writer with great promise.

BIBLIOGRAPHY

Autobiographical Works by Hilton Als

"The First Steps of Becoming an Art Historian." *Black American Literature Forum* 19.1 (Spring 1985): 28–30.
The Women. New York: Farrar, Straus and Giroux, 1996.
"Notes on My Mother." In *Best American Essays 1997*. Ed. Ian Frazier. Boston: Houghton Mifflin, 1997.
"Notes on My Mother." In *Contemporary Creative Non Fiction: The Art of Truth*. Ed. Bill Roorbach. New York: Oxford University Press, 1999. 113–18.

Studies of Hilton Als's Autobiographical Works

Bernstein, Richard. "Feminine Mystique in the Eyes of an 'Auntie Man.'" *New York Times*, January 1, 1997, 33.
Cunningham, Al. Rev. of *The Women*. *Lambda Book Report* 5.7 (January 1997): 25.
Fusco, Coco. Interview with Hilton Als. *Bomb* (Winter 1997): 48–51.
Hatch, James. Rev. of *The Women*. www.amazon.com
Lee, Andrea. "Fatal Limitations: Review of *The Women*." *New York Times Book Review* (January 5, 1997): 7.
Posnock, Ross. "Race and Responsibility." *Raritan* 17.3 (Winter 1998): 120–36.
Schulman, Sara. "A Woman's Soul: Review of *The Women*." *Advocate* 722 (December 10, 1996): 79.

MAYA ANGELOU
(1928–   )

Eileen O. Jaquin

BIOGRAPHY

The author of five autobiographies and numerous volumes of poetry, Maya Angelou's literary talents have earned her a reputation in contemporary literature
as one of America's most candid and inspirational authors. In addition to her
literary achievements, Maya Angelou has had a prolific career as a singer, dancer,
actress, playwright, director, editor, lecturer, and civil rights activist. Born Mar-
guerite Johnson on April 4, 1928, in St. Louis, Missouri, Angelou was called
"Maya" by her brother Bailey as a shortened version of "My sister" (Angelou,
Singin' and Swingin' 84). At the age of three, Maya and four-year-old Bailey
crisscrossed the country, unescorted, by train from Long Beach, California, to
the home of their paternal grandmother, Mrs. Annie Henderson, in Stamps,
Arkansas, after their parents, Bailey Johnson Sr. and Vivian Baxter, decided to
end their calamitous marriage. "Momma," Maya's name for her Grandmother
Henderson, was a religious, economically independent woman with a larger-
than-life presence. A true enigma in the rural South of the 1930s, not only did
Annie Henderson own property, which she rented to the "powhitetrash," but
she also owned and operated the Wm. Johnson General Merchandise Store,
which served as a social center for the poor blacks of Stamps. Angelou's early
memories of her Grandmother Henderson were those of a woman whose "world
was bordered on all sides with work, duty, religion and 'her place' " (Angelou,
Caged Bird 57) and "who came to stand for all the courage and stability she ever
knew as a child" (Neubauer, "Self" in Bloom, *Maya Angelou* 193). She also
remembers that her grandmother never "knew that a deep-brooding love hung
over everything she touched," and Angelou "saw only her power and strength"
(Angelou, *Caged Bird* 46). Grandmother Henderson's resiliency and immense

personal pride embodied strength in the face of severe economic depression and racial bigotry. From her example, Angelou learned that she had the power to control her own destiny and to take pride in herself despite the negative effects of the poverty and racism she experienced while growing up in the segregated South.

Most of Angelou's childhood was spent in Stamps, except for a brief period of time in 1936 when she and Bailey were sent to St. Louis to live with their mother. In St. Louis, the Johnson children found themselves more academically advanced than their schoolmates. They skipped ahead a grade because they did "arithmetic at a mature level" from working in their grandmother's store and "read well because in Stamps there wasn't anything else to do" (Angelou, *Caged Bird* 63). Maya took out her first library card in St. Louis and "read more than ever" (75). She greatly admired the strong heroes of Horatio Alger and the Sunday funnies "who always conquered in the end" (76).

However, Angelou's stay in St. Louis turned into a nightmare when she was raped by her mother's boyfriend, Mr. Freeman. As an eight-year-old child devoid of true affection, Maya became confused by Freeman's attentions and the true nature of his activities prior to the rape. Traumatized by the belief of her complicity in the crime and with her accusation against Freeman leading to a trial and his subsequent murder, Maya retreated into a world of silence. Burdened with guilt over Freeman's death, she believed her words had the power to kill and if she "talked to anyone else that person might die too" (Angelou, *Caged Bird* 87).

The stress of these events caused Maya and Bailey to once again be sent back to their Grandmother Henderson. "For nearly a year," Angelou wrote, "I sopped around the house, the Store, the school and the church, like an old biscuit, dirty and inedible" (Angelou, *Caged Bird* 93). The familiarity and quietness of Stamps, coupled with the love of her grandmother and the attentions of Mrs. Bertha Flowers, an elegant black woman whom Angelou viewed as an aristocrat amidst the poverty of Stamps, helped Angelou regain her voice. Mrs. Flowers told Maya: "Words mean more than what is set down on paper. It takes the human voice to infuse them with the shades of deeper meaning" (98). Sharing afternoons of reading literary classics in her home, Mrs. Flowers introduced Maya not only to a love of books but to a world of imagination, creativity, and the power of the written word, as well as teaching her that she "must always be intolerant of ignorance but understanding of illiteracy" (99). Elizabeth Fox Genovese contends in "Myth and History" that Mrs. Flowers "joined the world of Stamps to the world of literature, [and] embodied in [Angelou's] person the dreams that shaped Marguerite's imagination" (232). Through the inner strength and deep personal pride of her grandmother and the imperturbable dignity and wisdom of Mrs. Flowers, Angelou gained positive life affirming values while also learning to appreciate the strength found in a black community bonded together by faith and adversity. Despite her painful childhood experiences and the effects of the racial prejudice she encountered growing up in the Jim Crow South, the years

Angelou lived in Stamps, Arkansas, provided her with the fertile ground of imagination for the first volume of her most popular autobiography, *I Know Why the Caged Bird Sings*.

In 1940, after graduating from the Lafayette Training School in Stamps, Angelou and Bailey were once again uprooted from their grandmother's home and sent to live with their mother in San Francisco. She skipped ahead two semesters at George Washington High School and won a scholarship to attend evening classes at the California Labor School, where she studied drama and dance. According to Miles Shapiro, Angelou told an interviewer: "The only two things I've ever loved in my life are dancing and writing" (67). Surprisingly, Angelou's relationship with her mother began to improve as she grew to see her mother's positive qualities, and she no longer harbored bitterness toward her mother's past abandonment. Shapiro notes that "the daughter was better able to understand the spirit and independence of her mother" and that "much of her own philosophy is derived from her mother's approach" (69).

However, her relationship with her father remained chaotic. An invitation to spend a summer vacation with him and his girlfriend ended with Maya running away to spend several weeks in an automobile junkyard, sleeping in abandoned cars as "the newest member of an egalitarian, multiracial commune of young ragamuffins" (Shapiro 71). According to Sidonie Ann Smith, the experience provided "her with a knowledge of self-determination and a confirmation of her self-worth" (in Bloom, *Maya Angelou* 11) as well as the importance of community. These feelings led Angelou to recall in *Caged Bird* that the "unquestioning acceptance by my peers had dislodged the familiar insecurity" and that the "lack of criticism evidenced by our ad hoc community influenced me, and set a tone of tolerance for my life" (254). Even though Angelou viewed this experience in a positive light, after a month, she called her mother for help to return home.

Before returning to school in 1944, Angelou "decided to take a job as a demonstration of her newfound self-reliance" (Shapiro 73). Despite many obstacles, one of which was the company's policy of refusing to hire blacks, Angelou became the first black woman trolley car conductor for San Francisco's Market Street Railway. But this was also a time of confusion for the teenager. She began to grow concerned about her sexual attractiveness and questioned her sexuality. In *Caged Bird*, Angelou wrote: "I was being crushed by two unrelenting forces: the uneasy suspicion that I might not be a normal female and my newly awakening sexual appetite" (280). The only answer for Angelou was to confront these mysteries head-on through sexual experimentation. A loveless, sexual encounter left her pregnant at the age of sixteen. The year she graduated from high school, she gave birth to a son, Clyde (Guy) Johnson, and left childhood behind.

For the next few years, determined to be on her own and support herself and her infant son, Angelou worked at a string of dead-end jobs: a cook at the Creole Cafe, a cocktail waitress at the High Hat Club in San Diego, and the owner of a small brothel. Despite her chaotic lifestyle, she continued her love affair with books, especially the nineteenth- and twentieth-century Russian authors Dostoyevsky, Turgenev, Chekhov, and Gorky. She was again on the move from city to city, with a brief visit to her grandmother in Stamps, still unchanged and "halved by racial prejudice [and] the smell of old fears, and hate, and guilt" (Angelou, *Gather Together* 61, 62), and attempted to settle back in California with her mother. Unhappy with her life, Angelou tried to enlist in the army but was rejected, worked briefly as a dancer, and in an attempt to aid a lover, became a prostitute for a short time. She became aware of the dangers of her lifestyle and the negative effect it had on her young son after a baby-sitter abducted him, and she almost lost him. Later, a friend's exposure to the brutality of the under-world prevented Angelou from sinking deeper into the dark world of drugs. Angelou writes in *Gather Together*: "No one had ever cared for me so much . . . one man's generosity pushed me safely away from the edge" (181). Angelou chronicles these events and her relationships in the second volume of her autobiography, *Gather Together in My Name*.

In 1952, Angelou married a white ex-sailor, Tosh Angelos, but the marriage failed due in part to Angelou's fear that her son's pride in his black ancestry might be compromised with a white stepfather. In addition, her husband's athe-ism influenced the dissolution of the marriage. According to Shapiro, Angelou "regarded the church as a defining element of her black heritage that she did not wish to relinquish" (87). During her marriage, however, Angelou's dance career took a promising turn. And it was in 1953, while performing at the Purple Onion, a cabaret in San Francisco, that she first used the stage name of Maya Angelou. Her dancing and singing at the Purple Onion attracted the attention of the producers of the touring company of *Porgy and Bess*, an opera with an all-black cast. Maya Angelou was chosen for the role of Ruby, and during 1954 and 1955 she toured twenty-two European nations with the opera, which Angelou felt had "the greatest array of Negro talent [she] had ever seen" (*Singin' and Swingin'* 113). In her autobiography *Singin' and Swingin' and Gettin' Merry Like Christmas*, she writes about the awe she felt while on tour: "I was really in Italy . . . me, Mar-guerite Johnson, who had read 'bout Verona and the sad lovers while growing up in a dusty Southern village" (140). For Angelou, performing at the Paris night-clubs, the Mars Club and the Rose Rouge, was also a personal highlight. In spite of her successes, she missed her son and felt guilty when she learned he had suffered in her absence. After being informed of an untreatable skin ailment that Guy had contracted, she left *Porgy and Bess* to return home.

Angelou reunited with her son but was still interested in pursuing a career in show business. In *The Heart of a Woman*, she describes how her singing/acting career and writing career blossom. While working as a calypso dancer in the past, she had composed the lyrics to songs from poems she had written. Her interest in writing poetry evolved into short story writing. This interest in writing was encouraged by a black novelist, John Oliver Killens, who encouraged Angelou to pursue her literary talents by moving to New York City and joining the Harlem Writers Guild. In 1959, Angelou moved to Brooklyn with her son and renewed her love of writing. She became an active member of the Harlem Writers Guild, who critiqued her literary skills and offered valuable advice, such as "Write each sentence over and over again, until it seems you've used every combination possible, then write it again" (*Heart of a Woman* 44).

It was an exciting time in New York, and Angelou met several famous people, such as Bayard Rustin, a leader in Martin Luther King's civil rights organization, the Southern Christian Leadership Conference (SCLC). Angelou's deep concern about the "hating and fearing" (Angelou, *Heart of a Woman* 211) of blacks by whites led to her involvement in the civil rights movement. First, she helped organize and performed in the *Cabaret for Freedom*, an off-Broadway musical revue produced for the benefit of the SCLC. She also performed in another off-Broadway play, *The Blacks*, Jean Genet's dramatic indictment of colonial imperialism, which "reflected the real-life confrontations that were occurring daily in America's streets" between whites and blacks (211). Angelou was then chosen to succeed Rustin as northern coordinator for the SCLC. Her involvement in the civil rights struggle also led to her introduction to Dr. Martin Luther King Jr., Malcolm X,* and Vusumzi Make, a South African freedom fighter who became her second husband.

Two years after her marriage, in 1959, Angelou moved to Cairo, Egypt, with Make and her son. Although Angelou did not have experience as a journalist, she became associate editor of the *Arab Observer*, an English-language news weekly in Cairo. In 1962, after her marriage to Make ended, due in part to his philandering, Angelou remained in Africa and, with her son, moved to Accra, Ghana. Two days after arriving in Ghana, her son Guy was critically injured in an automobile accident. While Guy recovered from his injuries, Angelou became involved in a group of black American expatriates who had a desire to return to their roots. In the fifth volume of her autobiography, *All God's Children Need Traveling Shoes*, she states: "We had come home . . . we knew that we were mostly unwanted in the land of our birth and saw promise on our ancestral continent" (19, 20). During this time, Angelou became an assistant administrator at the University of Ghana's School of Music and Dance at the Institute of African Studies. She also continued her career in journalism at the *Ghanaian Times* and as a feature editor of the *African Review*. Angelou felt welcome in Africa where for the first time "Black and brown skin did not herald debasement and a divinely created inferiority" (16). During a journey to the African village of Keta, she believed she reconnected with her African heritage. She wept with the women of the village "for the lost people, their ancestors and mine. But [she] was also weeping with a curious joy. Despite the murders, rapes and suicides, we had survived. The middle passage and the auction block had not erased us" (207). Angelou discovers that, like her ancestors uprooted by slavery, she, too, could keep Africa a part of her spirit despite physical separation from the Motherland. No matter how much she loved Africa and its connection to her ancestral roots, Angelou realized that America was now her true home. She decided in 1965 to return home to America with the belief that there was still the hope and promise of equality yet to be fulfilled in America. Angelou reiterates this hope at the conclusion of *All God's Children Need Traveling Shoes*: "Through the centuries of despair and dislocation, we had been creative, because we faced down death by daring to hope" (207).

In 1968, Angelou wrote *Black, Blues, Black*, a series of ten one-hour programs for the National Educational Television highlighting the role of African culture in America. *I Know Why the Caged Bird Sings*, Angelou's evocative autobiography about her painful childhood growing up in Stamps, Arkansas, was published in 1970. The title of her memoir is taken from a favorite childhood poem titled "Sympathy" by Paul Laurence Dunbar. The book met with great critical acclaim due to its personal honesty dealing with the distressful issues of rejection, racism, and fear; and yet it is often sprinkled with humor, warmth, and love. In 1973, Maya Angelou married her third husband, English writer and cartoonist Paul de Feu.

The second volume of Angelou's autobiography, *Gather Together in My Name*, was published in 1974. The title was inspired by the Gospel of Mark (18:20) as "she asks her family and readers to gather around her and bear witness to her past" (Neubauer, "Self," in Bloom, *Maya Angelou* 199). Revealing these painful events from her past was difficult for Angelou, but she hoped that by doing so others might benefit from her message: "You may encounter many defeats, but you must not be defeated" (*Contemporary Literary Criticism* 12:9).

Singin' and Swingin' and Gettin' Merry Like Christmas, volume three of her autobiography, was published in 1976 and highlights Angelou's stage career and her European tour with the opera *Porgy and Bess*. The title was derived from the African American tradition of spending Saturday night and Sunday evening socializing, attending church services, and enjoying a Sunday meal in order to sustain them through the rest of the arduous workweek (Lisandrelli 97).

In addition to the publication of three volumes of her autobiography, the decade of the 1970s was also enhanced by other literary contributions from Angelou. Her first volume of poetry, *Just Give Me a Cool Drink of Water 'Fore I Diiie*, published in 1971, was nominated for a Pulitzer Prize, and she wrote the screen play for *Georgia, Georgia* in 1972. Two other collections of poetry, *Oh Pray My Wings Are Gonna Fit Me Well* and *And Still I Rise*, appeared in 1975 and 1978, respectively. Along with her poetry, Angelou was involved in writing the teleplay for the television version of *I Know Why the Caged Bird Sings*, which premiered on CBS in 1979. Besides her literary endeavors, Angelou was also involved in directing two plays, *Ajax* and *And Still I Rise*. She earned a Tony nomination for her Broadway debut in the play *Look Away* in 1973 and an Emmy nomination for her performance of Kunta Kinte's grandmother in the television miniseries *Roots*. Academically, Angelou has been a distinguished visiting professor at Wake Forest University, Wichita State University, and California State University. She was selected as a Rockefeller Foundation Scholar in Italy in 1975 and that same year was appointed a member of the American Revolution Bicentennial Council by President Gerald R. Ford.

In 1981, *The Heart of a Woman*, volume four of Angelou's autobiography, was published. The title was inspired by a poem written by Georgia Douglas Johnson, "a poet who wrote with emotion about gender" (Lupton, *Maya Angelou* 49). In this inspiring personal narrative, Angelou chronicles her experiences in New York City where she explores her literary and dramatic talents, her commitment to the civil rights struggle, and her often turbulent relationship with her teenage son Guy. That same year, her marriage to Paul de Feu ended in divorce, and she relocated to Winston-Salem, North Carolina, where in 1982 she was appointed the lifetime Reynolds Chair in American Studies at Wake Forest University, where she lectures on literature and popular culture.

Angelou's fifth and final autobiography to date, *All God's Children Need Traveling Shoes*, was published in 1986. This memoir recounts Angelou's quest for identity by reconnecting with the homeland of her African ancestors. In returning to the Mother continent of Africa she not only finds "the roots of [her] beginning" (206), but she is inspired and strengthened by her search "for it brought [her] closer to understanding [herself] and other human beings" (196). Nonetheless, she also discovers that although part of her soul belongs to Africa, as an African American, America is now her true home. All of Maya Angelou's autobiographies convey the struggles and triumphs of her life with style, grace, and a strong sense of self-affirmation. Angelou told an interviewer in 1973 that she was not only interested in survival but "survival with some style, some faith" (qtd. in Shapiro 17). Therefore, her narratives convey a message of survival for African American people to rise above poverty, prejudice, and lack of power.

More collections of poetry followed with the 1983 publication of *Shaker, Why Don't You Sing; I Shall Not Be Moved* in 1990; *My Painted House, My Friendly Chicken and Me* and *The Complete Collected Poems of Maya Angelou in 1994*; and *Phenomenal Woman: Four Poems Celebrating Women* in 1994. Chosen by President-elect Bill Clinton to compose a poem for his inauguration, she delivered her poem "On the Pulse of Morning" to the nation at his inauguration in 1993. The 665 words of the poem described "a dark vision of American history . . . but one suffused nonetheless with hope" (Shapiro 17). The essence of the poem parallels "the poet's own history . . . [of] poverty and racial oppression" and survival "to reach a point where she could look with optimism toward the future" (17). In 1993, a selection of essays titled *Wouldn't Take Nothing for My Journey Now* was published, followed in 1997 by *Even the Stars Look Lonesome*, another selection of essays.

Besides her many literary and dramatic accomplishments, Maya Angelou speaks six languages and has been honored by the academic world, receiving the Yale University Fellowship in 1970. Although Angelou has not earned a college degree, she has been granted Honorary Doctorates from Smith College and Mills College and now holds more than fifty other honorary degrees. She is often referred to as Dr. Maya Angelou. Other awards include a National Book Award nomination for *I Know Why the Caged Bird Sings* in 1970, *Essence* magazine's 1992 Woman of the Year, the Horatio Alger Award for 1992, and the Frank G. Wells Award at the American Teachers Awards ceremony in 1995. Angelou is also a member of several prominent organizations, such as the Directors Guild of America, the American Film Institute, and the Harlem Writers Guild. She has served on several commissions and is a highly sought-after lecturer. She has composed musical scores and has written, directed, and acted in several plays and films. Maya Angelou became the first black woman to have an original script produced with the film *Georgia, Georgia* in 1972. Recently, she coauthored and cohosted a series of documentaries with her son Guy Johnson, titled *Maya Angelou's America: A Journey of the Heart*.

Maya Angelou has received great critical acclaim for her narrative skills because she blends honesty with dignity. For future generations, her literary contributions will remain an eloquent reminder that "we are more alike . . . than we are unalike" (Angelou, *Wouldn't Take Nothing for My Journey Now* 124).

AUTOBIOGRAPHICAL WORKS AND THEMES

Angelou is considered a major contemporary author and contributor to the black autobiographical tradition whose literary reputation is based on her five-volume autobiographical series and her poetry. The titles of the autobiographies are, in the order of publication, *I Know Why the Caged Bird Sings* (1970), *Gather Together in My Name* (1974), *Singin' and Swingin' and Gettin' Merry Like Christmas* (1976), *The Heart of a Woman* (1981), and *All God's Children Need Traveling Shoes* (1986). Her storytelling abilities are marked with wisdom and humor as she reveals herself to the scrutiny of the reader with an often painful but honest candor. Angelou's memoirs inspire hope in the face of adversity and reveal the resiliency of the human spirit as she "leads her readers to recognize that the human spirit need not cave in to ignorance, hatred, and oppression" (Leone 14).

Angelou's narratives have been criticized for using devices identified with writing fiction rather than autobiographies, resulting in a number of critics classifying "Angelou's five volumes as autobiographical fiction and not autobiographies" (Lupton, *Maya Angelou* 29). Angelou employs "a rather personalized autobiographical style," according to Carol E. Neubauer, in that "she adapts elements from both fiction and fantasy" (Neubauer, "Displacement," in Bloom, *Maya Angelou* 27). Mary Jane Lupton writes in *Maya Angelou: A Critical Companion* that according to Eugenia Collier "the writing techniques Angelou uses in her autobiographies are the same devices used in writing fiction: vividly conceived characters and careful development of theme, setting, plot, and language" (30).

Another characteristic of Angelou's work is the employment of the serial autobiography to convey her story. Lupton contends that "the five volumes [in] Angelou's series far exceed the standard number of volumes in an autobiography . . . so that they are in a sub-genre known as 'serial autobiographies'" (*Maya Angelou* 32). One of the foremost examples of serial autobiography in the black literary tradition is Frederick Douglass's* two-part autobiography: *The Narrative of the Life of Frederick Douglass* and *My Bondage and My Freedom*, published in 1845 and 1855, respectively. There is a freedom, a continuous fluctuation, in the serial form of autobiographical writing that the single form does not allow, but there is also the increased need for transitions, cross-references, continuity, and discipline (Lupton, *Maya Angelou* 32). Angelou has been quoted as saying that she enjoys the "stretching" required in going from book to book (32).

The structure of Angelou's autobiographical text is that of a journey or an odyssey in a quest for self-knowledge, self-identity, and "home." The first volume, *I Know Why the Caged Bird Sings*, finds the child Maya crisscrossing the United States from place to place with no permanent sense of home. Therefore, Maya's literary journey begins with a literal journey as she travels from California to her Grandmother Henderson's home in Stamps, Arkansas, when she is three years old. The journey will continue eastward from California to New York, ending finally on the Mother Continent of Africa throughout the next four volumes of her autobiographical text. Angelou's linear journey, in search of home and self-definition, comes full circle when she realizes that no matter how much she loves Africa, the roots of her ancestry, it is not her true home, and she returns "home" to America.

Some of the major themes prevalent throughout the narratives are imprisonment, identity, displacement, and motherhood. Beginning with the first volume of Angelou's autobiography, the theme of imprisonment is implied in the title of the text, taken from Paul Laurence Dunbar's lyrical poem titled "Sympathy." Like the caged bird who beats his breast bloody against the bars of his prison, the sentiment behind the poem is a prayer of hope for an imprisoned people to transcend their restrictions and to break free from the cages of racism, oppression, and hatred. According to Joanne Braxton, "like the song of the caged bird, the autobiography [also] represents a prayer sent from . . . the depth of emotion and feeling . . . to fly free from the definitions and limitations imposed by a hostile world" (Braxton, "Song," in Bloom, *Maya Angelou* 129).

The themes of imprisonment and identity are interconnected and established in the way that Maya, as a young southern black girl, views herself. Her childhood self-image is diminished by a society whose standard of beauty rejects blackness and values whiteness. At the beginning of *Caged Bird*, Maya laments her blackness with a wish that she would "[wake] out of [her] black ugly dream, and [her] real hair, which was long and blond, would take the place of [her] kinky mass" because "[she] was really white" (2–3). Sidonie Ann Smith writes:

Maya Angelou's autobiography . . . opens with a primal childhood scene that brings into focus the nature of the imprisoning environment from which the self will seek escape. The black girl child is trapped within the cage of her own diminished self-image around which interlock the bars of natural and social forces. (in Bloom, *Maya Angelou* 6)

Angelou's self-critical vision of herself in childhood echoes the imprisoned nature of the black community as a whole. Smith continues to elaborate on the theme of a community imprisoned by racial prejudice and economic depression in her essay "The Song of a Caged Bird." Smith argues that "Maya Angelou's diminished sense of self is reflected in the entire black community's diminished self-image" since "the black community of Stamps is itself caged in the social reality of racial subordination and impotence" (8). Smith ties the themes of imprisonment and displacement together with the idea that within "this imprisoning environment there is no place for this black girl child. She becomes a displaced person whose pain is intensified by her consciousness of that displacement" (6). However, it is not just the black girl child and the community that is imprisoned but the black adult woman, too, who is also a victim of the "tripartite crossfire of masculine prejudice, white illogical hate and Black lack of power" (Angelou, Caged Bird 272).

The quest for identity, a related theme to imprisonment and displacement, threads its way through all the volumes of Angelou's narratives. Although there are many psychological and emotional setbacks for Maya in her quest for self, she does find self-affirmation along the journey. In Caged Bird, during Maya's time of voluntary muteness, it is Mrs. Flowers, a surrogate mother figure, through affirmation and acceptance of the child for herself, who helps Maya reevaluate her self-image. In Angelou's words: "I was liked, and what a difference it made" (Caged Bird 101). Receiving respect and "unqualified acceptance allows her to experience the incipient power of her own self-worth" (Smith, in Bloom's Maya Angelou 9).

The theme of displacement is inherent in all five volumes of Angelou's autobiographies, beginning with the two young children being sent away from their parental home to the "home" of their grandmother in Arkansas. In her essay "Maya Angelou: Self and a Song of Freedom," Carol E. Neubauer notes that in Caged Bird "Maya Angelou calls displacement the most important loss in her childhood . . . and [she] never fully regains a sense of security and belonging" (in Bloom, Maya Angelou 194). Throughout Caged Bird, the frequent moves Maya makes between the homes of her parents and grandmother intensifies her loss of place, and the sense of displacement eventually becomes rejection. According to Smith, "Such rejection a child internalizes and translates as a rejection of self: ultimately the loss of home occasions the loss of self worth" (in Bloom, Maya Angelou 7). Therefore, displacement and rejection ultimately influence Maya's self-image and identity. The search for "home" continues to be the prevailing theme throughout Traveling Shoes as well. By threading the theme of displacement from Caged Bird through to the end of the narratives, Neubauer argues that in Traveling Shoes "Angelou continually reminds the reader that the quest for a place to call home is virtually endemic to the human condition" (in Bloom, Maya Angelou 206).

Throughout the five volumes of Angelou's narratives, motherhood remains a dominant theme and unifying element. According to Mary Jane Lupton in "Singing the Black Mother," "the mother-child configuration forms the basic pattern against which other relationships are measured" (Black American Literature Forum 260). Joanne M. Braxton advances the claim that "Maya Angelou celebrates black motherhood" in her "grandmother's feminine heroism, wisdom, and unselfishness" ("Song," in Bloom, *Maya Angelou* 127, 130). In the opinion of Paul Bailey, Maya's Grandmother Henderson "is an archetype of those noble, barely educated black women who inspired their children with a faith in themselves against the severest odds" (33). Both Annie Henderson and Vivian Baxter act as nurturers and protectors in their respective roles as grandmother and mother. In turn, Maya, who gives birth at the end of *Caged Bird*, learns to fulfill the role of nurturer and protector as a new mother. Braxton writes that Maya's relationship with Mrs. Bertha Flowers "represents another important turning point in the development of the autobiographer's consciousness" ("Song," in Bloom, *Maya Angelou* 136) when her maternal influence helps Maya tap into her creative resources and find self-healing. Mary Jane Lupton explores the theme of motherhood as a controlling element in *Gather Together in My Name*, stating that it "controls the plot. . . . Maya's motherhood is what keeps her connected to the world of responsibility" (*Maya Angelou* 86, 87). Likewise, the theme of motherhood evolves in the third volume, *Singin' and Swingin' and Gettin' Merry Like Christmas*. Lupton offers the argument that "the mother/son behavior pattern in *Singin' and Swingin'* shows . . . Maya as the mother in conflict over the need to love versus the need to be a fully realized person" (108). The theme of motherhood becomes more complex in *The Heart of a Woman* but is nonetheless at the heart of the narrative. It is a time of fluctuation between dependence and independence for mother and son, and between Maya and her own mother. At the end, a mature Maya finds herself alone: "Maya Angelou is at this moment simply herself" (131). Although the theme of motherhood does not consume the text of her last volume, *All God's Children Need Traveling Shoes*, it is developed as a positive way to close the series in that it "suggests liberation" (157). The theme of motherhood also aligns Angelou's quest for acceptance by Mother Africa with the theme of identity and displacement. Her quest for racial identity and "home," a place of belonging, are intricately interwoven within the context of those themes of motherhood and displacement.

CRITICAL RECEPTION

All five of Maya Angelou's autobiographical narratives have generated critical and popular interest. However, the first volume of her autobiographical series, *I Know Why the Caged Bird Sings*, is considered her most notable contribution to black literature, the work receiving the highest praise and critical acclaim. Generally, the other four volumes did not fulfill the literary promise of *Caged Bird* and have received mixed reviews. In his essay "Maya Angelou's *I Know Why the Caged Bird Sings* and Black Autobiographical Tradition," George E. Kent discusses how Angelou's later narratives lack "the feeling of the fully mastered experience [or] the full measure and imaginative penetration" found in her first narrative (in Andrews 163).

A comparative critical analysis of *Caged Bird* by Joanne M. Braxton, in her essay "A Song of Transcendence: Maya Angelou," likens Angelou's use of "rhyth-

mic language, lyrically suspended moments of consciousness, and detailed por-
traiture" to that of Zora Neale Hurston* and Era Bell Thompson, concluding
that "it is perhaps the most aesthetically satisfying autobiography written by a
black woman in this period" (in Bloom, *Maya Angelou* 128). Sondra O'Neale's
"Reconstruction of the Composite Self" discusses Angelou's examination of collective black identity and black female myths, crediting Angelou with being a
role model whose narrative subverts stereotypical myths about black women
through the autobiographical process in an attempt "to remold these perceptions
[and] whose message to all Black women is the reconstruction of her experiential
'self' " (in Bloom, *Maya Angelou* 42). Mary Vermillion's essay "Reembodying the
Self" offers an extended analysis of Angelou's representation of rape and the
"somatophobia that afflict[s] Maya and her race" in *Caged Bird* and concludes
that through the autobiographical process Angelou also "reconstructs her own
body" and "celebrat[es] the bodies of other black women" (*CLC* Vol. 77, 32).
Kent acknowledges the uniqueness of *Caged Bird* within black autobiographical
tradition "by its special stance toward the self, the community, and the universe,
and by a form exploiting the full measure of imagination necessary to acknowledge both beauty and absurdity" (in Andrews 170). A less-than-positive reading
of *Caged Bird* by Liliane K. Arensberg in "Death as Metaphor of Self" examines
Angelou's ironic style of writing about her youth, which "seems in counterpoint
to the meaning of her narrative. It is written with a humor and wry wit that
belies the personal and racial tragedies recorded" (in Leone, *Readings on Maya
Angelou* 116).

Angelou's second volume, *Gather Together in My Name*, garnered both negative
and positive reviews but generally fell short of her first critical success and has
been criticized as being episodic. Lynn Sukenick's review of *Gather Together* criticizes the book as an entertaining "chain of anecdotes" that places too much
importance on the tale and not the teller, therefore lacking the temperament
needed to "linger and infuse us long after the anecdotes are forgotten" (12). A
counterpoint argument can be found in the wide-ranging investigation of Angelou's works by Mary Jane Lupton titled *Maya Angelou: A Critical Companion*,
in which Lupton sees authenticity in the "episodic series of fragments that mirror
the kind of discord found in actual life" (in Bloom, *Maya Angelou* 78). In Selwyn
Cudjoe's 1984 essay "Maya Angelou and the Autobiographical Statement," he
contends, "Whereas [Angelou] presented herself as an integral part of the society
in *Caged Bird*, in *Gather Together* she separates herself . . . and projects a strikingly
individual ethos," which in his opinion weakens the work because it relies on
individual exploits rather than "traditional collective wisdom and/or suffering of
the group" (in Bloom, *Maya Angelou* 69–70). However, a positive review by
Annie Gottlieb praises Angelou's ability to write "like a song, and like the truth
. . . the product of a born writer's senses nourished on black church singing . . .
and on literature" (in Leone, *Readings on Maya Angelou* 129).

An optimistic reading of *Singin' and Swingin'* appears in Cudjoe's "Maya Angelou and the Autobiographical Statement" in which he explores some limita-

tions found in Angelou's first work, "a volume concerned with what it meant to be Black and female in America" (in Bloom, *Maya Angelou* 74), and argues that Angelou's concern for self evolves by *Singin' and Swingin'* to define herself "more centrally within the mainstream of the Black experience" (74). Cudjoe maintains that in *Singin' and Swingin'* Angelou now successfully addresses the question of "what it means to be Black and person in America" through the "writer work[ing] out her relationship with the white American world" (69–70).

According to David Levering Lewis, Angelou's success in *The Heart of a Woman* is due to her unique style of writing that yields "a rare compound of great emotional force and authenticity, undiluted by polemic" (*CLC* Vol. 35, 31). Bill Ott cites that although "Angelou's story of her adult life lacks [the] inherent drama or terrible poignancy of her childhood . . . it is nonetheless a stirring record of the complex fabric of a black woman's life" (*CLC* Vol. 35, 30). A negative critical reception from Daisy Alden cites Angelou's "venomous hostility to one and all of the white race [as] the epitome of stereotype and cliché" (*CLC* Vol. 35, 32) and adds that in spite of the book being skillfully narrated "on the whole, [it] cannot be called a great artistic or literary achievement."

In Wanda Coleman's review of *All God's Children Need Traveling Shoes*, she notes the authenticity found in Angelou's narrative of her adventures as an African American expatriate in Ghana and views the book "as an important document drawing more much needed attention to the hidden history of a people both African and American" (*CLC* Vol. 64, 36). However, Sharron Freeman "was left cold by this rambling account [that fails] to recreate the experience . . . as fully as she has done in her past recreations" (*CLC* Vol. 64, 36).

Deborah E. McDowell critiques the whole collection of narratives as a positive "show of self that defies the rusted razor, a self that—true to the demands of the genre—survives and triumphs" (*CLC* Vol. 64, 37). Priscilla R. Ramsey contends that Angelou's "autobiographies . . . reveal a vital need to transform the elements of a stultifying and destructive personal, social, political and historical milieu into a sensual and physical refuge" (in Bloom, *Maya Angelou* 76). In an analysis of *Caged Bird, Gather Together,* and *Singin' and Swingin'*, Cudjoe cites Angelou's celebration of black womanhood throughout these texts by her presentation of "a powerful, authentic and profound signification of the condition of Afro-American womanhood in her quest for understanding and love rather than for bitterness and despair" ("Autobiographical Statement," in Bloom, *Maya Angelou* 60–61). Finally, analyzing all five volumes of the narrative in respect to the autobiographical tradition, Lupton's essay "Singing the Black Mother: Maya Angelou and Autobiographical Continuity" concludes:

[T]he volumes are intricately related through a number of essential elements: the ambivalent autobiographical voice, the flexibility of structure to echo the life process, the intertextual commentary on character and theme, and the use of certain recurring patterns to establish both continuity and continuation. (*Black American Literature Forum* 259)

BIBLIOGRAPHY

Autobiographical Works by Maya Angelou

I Know Why the Caged Bird Sings. New York: Random House, 1970.
Gather Together in My Name. New York: Random House, 1974.
Singin' and Swingin' and Gettin' Merry Like Christmas. New York: Random House, 1976.
The Heart of a Woman. New York: Random House, 1981.
All God's Children Need Traveling Shoes. New York: Random House, 1986.
Wouldn't Take Nothing for My Journey Now. New York: Bantam, 1993.

Studies of Maya Angelou's Autobiographical Works

Alden, Daisy. Rev. of *The Heart of a Woman*. *World Literature Today* 46.4 (1982): 697. Rpt. in *Contemporary Literary Criticism*. Vol. 35. Detroit: Gale, 1985. 32.

Andrews, William L., ed. *African American Autobiography: A Collection of Critical Essays*. Englewood Cliffs, NJ: Prentice-Hall, 1993.

Arensberg, Liliane K. "Death as Metaphor of Self in *I Know Why the Caged Bird Sings*." *College Language Association Journal* 20.2 (1976): 273–91. Rpt. in Leone et al., *Readings on Maya Angelou* 115–19.

Bailey, Hilary. "Growing Up Black." *Guardian Weekly* 130.6 (1984): 21.

Bailey, Paul. "Black Ordeal." *The Observer* (April 1984): 22. Rpt. in *Contemporary Literary Criticism*. Vol. 35. Detroit: Gale, 1985. 33.

Benson, Carol. "Out of the Cage and Still Singing." *Writer's Digest* (January 1975): 18–20.

Bertolino, James. "Maya Angelou Is Three Writers: *I Know Why the Caged Bird Sings*." In *Maya Angelou's I Know Why the Caged Bird Sings*. Ed. Harold Bloom. Philadelphia: Chelsea House, 1998. 167–72.

Blackburn, Regina. "In Search of the Black Female Self: African American Women's Autobiographies and Ethnicity." In *Women's Autobiography: Essays in Criticism*. Ed. Estelle C. Jelinek. Bloomington: Indiana University Press, 1980. 133–48.

Bloom, Harold, ed. *Maya Angelou*. Philadelphia: Chelsea House, 1999.

Bloom, Lynn Z. "Heritages: Dimensions of Mother-Daughter Relationships in Women's Autobiographies." In *The Lost Tradition: Mothers and Daughters in Literature*. Ed. Cathy N. Davidson and E.M. Broner. New York: Ungar, 1980. 291–303.

Blundell, Janet Boyarin. Rev. of *The Heart of a Woman*. *Publishers Weekly* 106.17 (1981): 1919.

Braxton, Joanne. "Maya Angelou." In *Modern American Women Writers*. Ed. Elaine Showalter, Lea Baechler, and A. Walton Litz. New York: Charles Scribner's Sons, 1991. 1–7.

———. "A Song of Transcendence: Maya Angelou." In *Black Women Writing Autobiography: A Tradition within a Tradition*. Philadelphia: Temple University Press, 1989. Rpt. in Bloom, *Maya Angelou* 125–47.

Buss, Helen M. "Reading for the Doubled Discourse of American Women's Autobiography." *A/B: Auto/Biography Studies* 6.1 (Spring 1991): 95–108.

Butterfield, Stephen. *Black Autobiography in America*. Amherst: University of Massachusetts Press, 1974.

Casey, Ellen Miller. Rev. of *The Heart of a Woman*. *Best Sellers* (January 1982): 376–77.

Chamblee-Carpenter, Dana. "Searching for a Self in Maya Angelou's *I Know Why the Caged Bird Sings*." *Publications of the Mississippi Philological Association* (1996): 6–12.

Coleman, Wanda. Rev. of *All God's Children Need Traveling Shoes*. Rpt. in *Contemporary Literary Criticism*. Vol. 64. Detroit: Gale, 1991. 36.

Collier, Eugenia. "Maya Angelou: From 'Caged Bird' to 'All God's Children.'" *New Directions* (Howard University Publication) (October 1986): 22–27.

Cordell, Shirley J. "The Black Woman: A Focus on 'Strength of Character' in *I Know Why the Caged Bird Sings*." *Virginia English Bulletin* 36.2 (Winter 1986): 36–39.

Cudjoe, Selwyn R. "Maya Angelou and the Autobiographical Statement." In *Black Women Writers (1950–1980): A Critical Evaluation*. Ed. Mari Evans. Garden City: Anchor-Doubleday, 1984. 6–24. Rpt. in Bloom, *Maya Angelou* 55–74.

———. "Maya Angelou: The Autobiographical Statement Updated." In *Reading Black: Reading Feminist*. Ed. Henry Louis Gates Jr. New York: Meridian, 1990. 272–306.

Danahay, Martin A. "Breaking the Silence: Symbolic Violence and the Teaching of Contemporary 'Ethnic' Autobiography." *College Literature* 18.3 (October 1991): 64–79.

Davis, Mary. "Becoming: A Course in Autobiography." *English Journal* 74 (March 1985): 34–37.

Demetrakopoulos, Stephanie A. "The Metaphysics of Matrilinealism in Women's Autobiography: Studies of Mead's *Blackberry Winter*, Hellman's *Pentimento*, Angelou's *I Know Why the Caged Bird Sings*, and Kingston's *The Woman Warrior*." In *Women's Autobiography: Essays in Criticism*. Ed. Estelle Jelinek. Bloomington: Indiana University Press, 1980. 180–205.

Elliot, Jeffrey M. "Maya Angelou: In Search of Self." *Negro History Bulletin* 40 (1977): 694–95.

———, ed. *Conversations with Maya Angelou*. Jackson: University Press of Mississippi, 1989.

Estes-Hicks, Onita. "The Way We Were: Precious Memories of the Black Segregated South." *African American Review* 27.1 (Spring 1993): 9–18.

Evans, Mari, ed. *Black Women Writers (1950–1980): A Critical Evaluation*. Garden City, NY: Anchor Press, 1984.

Fox-Genovese, Elizabeth. "Myth and History: Discourse of Origins in Zora Neale Hurston and Maya Angelou." *Black American Literature Forum* (20th-Century Autobiography Issue) 24.2 (Summer 1990): 221–36.

Freeman, Sharron. Rev. of *All God's Children Need Traveling Shoes*. *Voice of Youth Advocates* 9.3–4 (1986): 170–71. Rpt. in *Contemporary Literary Criticism*. Vol. 64. Detroit: Gale, 1991. 36.

Froula, Christine. "The Daughter's Seduction: Sexual Violence and Literary History." *Signs: Journal of Women in Culture and Society* 11.4 (Summer 1986): 621–44. Rpt. in Bloom, *Maya Angelou* 91–112.

Gaines-Carter, Patrice. "Home Is Where the Heart Is." *Book World—The Washington Post* (May 1986): 11–12.

Gates, Henry Louis, Jr. *Reading Black, Reading Feminist: A Critical Anthology*. New York: Meridian, 1990.

Gilbert, Susan. "Maya Angelou's *I Know Why the Caged Bird Sings*: Paths to Escape." *Mount Olive Review* 1.1 (Spring 1987): 39–50.

Goss, Linda, and Marian E. Barnes, ed. *Talk That Talk: An Anthology of African-American Storytelling*. New York: Simon and Schuster, 1989.

Gottlieb, Annie. Rev. of *Gather Together in My Name*. *New York Times Book Review* (June 16, 1974): 3. Rpt. in Leone, et al. *Readings on Maya Angelou* 128–29.

Gropman, Jackie. Rev. of *All God's Children Need Traveling Shoes*. *Southern Literary Journal* (August 1986): 113.

Gruesser, John C. "Afro-American Travel Literature and Africanist Discourse." *Black American Literature Forum* 24.1 (Spring 1990): 5–20.

Guiney, E.M. Rev. of *I Know Why the Caged Bird Sings*. *Library Journal* 16 (March 1970): 1018.

Hagen, Lyman B. *Heart of a Woman, Mind of a Writer, and Soul of a Poet: A Critical Analysis of the Writings of Maya Angelou*. Lanham, MD: University Press of America, 1997.

Henke, Suzette A. "Women's Life-Writing and the Minority Voice: Maya Angelou, Maxine Hong Kingston, and Alice Walker." In *Traditions, Voices, and Dreams: The American Novel Since the 1960s*. Ed. Melvin J. Friedman and Ben Siegel. Newark: University of Delaware Press, 1995. 210–33.

Hiers, John T. "Fatalism in Maya Angelou's *I Know Why the Caged Bird Sings*." *Notes on Contemporary Literature* 6.1 (1976): 5–7.

Hill-Lubin, Mildred A. "The African-American Grandmother in Autobiographical Works by Frederick Douglass, Langston Hughes, and Maya Angelou." *The International Journal of Aging and Human Development* 33.3 (1991): 172–75.

Holte, James Craig. *The Ethnic I: A Sourcebook for Ethnic-American Autobiography*. New York: Greenwood Press, 1988.

Hord, Fred Lee. "Someplace to Be a Black Girl." In *Reconstructing Memory: Black Literary Criticism*. Chicago: Third World Press, 1991. 75–85.

Inge, Tonette Bond, ed. *Southern Women Writers: The New Generation*. Tuscaloosa: University of Alabama Press, 1990.

Jelinek, Estelle C., ed. *Women's Autobiography: Essays in Criticism*. Bloomington: Indiana University Press, 1980.

Kelly, Ernece B. Rev. of *I Know Why the Caged Bird Sings*. *Harvard Educational Review* 40.4 (November 1970): 681–82.

Kent, George E. "Maya Angelou's *I Know Why the Caged Bird Sings* and Black Autobiographical Tradition." *Kansas Quarterly* 7.3 (1975): 72–78. Rpt. in Andrews, *African American Autobiography* 162–70.

Kinnamon, Keneth. "Call and Response: Intertextuality in Two Autobiographical Works by Richard Wright and Maya Angelou." In *Studies in Black American Literature, Vol. II: Belief vs. Theory in Black American Literary Criticism*. Ed. Joe Weixlmann and Chester J. Fontenot. Greenwood, FL: Penkevill Publishing, 1986. 121–34. Rpt. in Bloom, *Maya Angelou* 113–24.

Leone, Bruno, et al., eds. *Readings on Maya Angelou*. San Diego: Greenhaven Press, 1997.

Lewis, David Levering. "Maya Angelou: From Harlem to the Heart of a Woman." *Book World — The Washington Post* (October 4, 1981): 1–2.

Lionnet, Françoise. "Con Artists and Storytellers: Maya Angelou's Problematic Sense of Audience." In *Autobiographical Voices: Race, Gender, Self-Portraiture*. Ithaca, NY: Cornell University Press, 1989. Rpt. in Bloom, *Maya Angelou* 143–72.

Lisandrelli, Elaine Slivinski. *Maya Angelou: More Than a Poet*. Springfield, NJ: Enslow, 1996.

Lupton, Mary Jane. "Maya Angelou." In *American Writers Supplement IV, Part I*. New York: Scribner's, 1996. 1–19.

———. *Maya Angelou: A Critical Companion*. Westport, CT: Greenwood Press, 1998.

———. "Singing the Black Mother: Maya Angelou and Autobiographical Continuity." *Black American Literature Forum* 24.2 (Summer 1990): 257–77. Rpt. in Bloom, *Maya Angelou* 173–90.

MacKethan, Lucinda H. "Mother Wit: Humor in Afro-American Women's Autobiography." *Studies in American Humor* 4.1–2 (Spring–Summer 1985): 51–61.

Maddocks, Fiona. Rev. of *I Know Why the Caged Bird Sings*. *New Statesman* 107.2758 (1984): 26.

Magill, Frank N., ed. *Masterpieces of African-American Literature*. New York: HarperCollins, 1992.

Maya, D. "Self Revealed and Self-Mythified: The Autobiographies of Maya Angelou and Kamala Das." *Literary Criterion* 32.3 (1996): 61–68.

McDowell, Deborah E. "Traveling Hopefully." *Women's Review of Books* 4.1 (1986): 17. Rpt. in *Contemporary Literary Criticism* 64. Detroit: Gale, 1991. 37.

McMurry, Myra K. "Role-Playing as Art in Maya Angelou's *Caged Bird*." *South Atlantic Bulletin* 41.2 (May 1976): 106–11.

McPherson, Dolly A. "Defining the Self through Place and Culture: Maya Angelou's *I Know Why the Caged Bird Sings*." *MAWA Review* 5.1 (June 1990): 12–14.

———. *Order Out of Chaos: The Autobiographical Works of Maya Angelou*. New York: Peter Lang, 1990.

Megna-Wallace, Joanne. "Simone de Beauvoir and Maya Angelou: Birds of a Feather." *Simone de Beauvoir Studies* 6 (1989): 49–55.

Metzger, Linda, et al., eds. *Black Writers: A Selection of Sketches from Contemporary Authors*. Detroit: Gale Research, 1989.

Miller, David Adam. Rev. of *The Heart of a Woman*. *Black Scholar* 13.4–5 (1982): 48–49.

Moore, Opal. "Learning to Live: When the Bird Breaks from the Cage." In *Censored Books: Critical Viewpoints*. Ed. Nicholas J. Karolides, Lee Burress, and John M. Kean. Metuchen, NJ: Scarecrow Press, 1993. 306–16. Rpt. in Bloom, *Maya Angelou* 173–80.

Neubauer, Carol E. "Displacement and Autobiographical Style in Maya Angelou's *The Heart of a Woman*." *Black American Literature Forum* 17.3 (1983): 123–29. Rpt. in Bloom, *Maya Angelou* 25–40.

———. "Maya Angelou: Self and a Song of Freedom in the Southern Tradition." In *Southern Women Writers: The New Generation*. Ed. Tonette Inge and Doris Betts. Tuscaloosa: University of Alabama Press, 1990. 114–42. Rpt. in Bloom, *Maya Angelou* 191–218.

O'Neale, Sondra. "Reconstruction of the Composite Self: New Images of Black Women in Maya Angelou's Continuing Autobiography." In *Black Women Writers (1950–1980): A Critical Evaluation*. Ed. Mari Evans. Garden City: Anchor-Doubleday, 1984. 25–36. Rpt. in Bloom, *Maya Angelou* 41–54.

Ott, Bill. Rev. of *Heart of a Woman*. Rpt. in *Contemporary Literary Criticism*. Vol. 35. Detroit: Gale, 1985. 30.

Pascal, Sylvia. Rev. of *The Heart of a Woman*. *Southern Literary Journal* (December 1981): 88.

Phillips, Frank Lamont. Rev. of *Gather Together in My Name*. *Black World* 24.9 (July 1975): 52, 61.

Premo, Cassie. "When the Difference Becomes Too Great: Images of the Self and Survival in a Postmodern World." *Genre* 16 (1995): 183–91.

Ramsey, Priscilla R. "Transcendence: The Poetry of Maya Angelou." *A Current Bibliography on African Affairs* 17.2 (1985): 139–53. Rpt. in Bloom, *Maya Angelou* 75–90.

Saunders, James Robert. "Breaking Out of the Cage: The Autobiographical Writings of Maya Angelou." *The Hollins Critic* 28.4 (October 1991): 1–11.

Schmidt, Jan Zlotnik. "The Other: A Study of the Persona in Several Contemporary Women's Autobiographies." *CEA Critic: An Official Journal of the College English Association* 43.1 (1980): 24–31.

Schulz, Elizabeth. "To Be Black and Blue: The Blues Genre in Black American Autobiography." *Kansas Quarterly* 7.3 (1975): 81–96.

Shapiro, Miles. *Maya Angelou*. New York: Chelsea House, 1994.

Shelton, Austin J., ed. *The African Assertion: A Critical Anthology of African Literature*. Indianapolis, IN: Odyssey, 1968.

Showalter, Elaine, ed. *Modern American Women Writers*. New York: Charles Scribner's Sons, 1991.

Shuker, Nancy. *Maya Angelou*. Englewood Cliffs, NJ: Silver Burdett Press, 1990.

Smith, Sidonie Ann. "The Song of a Caged Bird: Maya Angelou's Quest after Self-Acceptance." *Southern Humanities Review* 7 (Fall 1973): 365–75. Rpt. in Bloom, *Maya Angelou* 3–14.

Sukenick, Lynn. Rev. of *Gather Together in My Name*. In *Contemporary Literary Criticism*. Vol. 12. Detroit: Gale, 1980. 12.

Tangum, Marion M., and Marjorie Smelstor. "Hurston's and Angelou's Visual Art: The Distancing Vision and the Beckoning Gaze." *Southern Literary Journal* 31.1 (Fall 1998): 80–96.

Tate, Claudia, ed. *Black Women Writers at Work*. New York: Continuum, 1983. 1–11.

Vermillion, Mary. "Reembodying the Self: Representations of Rape in *Incidents in the Life of a Slave Girl* and *I Know Why the Caged Bird Sings*." *Biography: An Interdisciplinary Quarterly* 15.3 (Summer 1992): 243–60. Rpt. in *Contemporary Literary Criticism*. Vol. 77. Detroit: Gale, 1993. 26–38.

Walker, Pierre A. "Racial Protest, Identity, Words and Form in Maya Angelou's *I Know Why the Caged Bird Sings*." *College Literature* 22.3 (October 1995): 91–108.

Wall, Cheryl. "Maya Angelou." In *Women Writers Talking*. Ed. Janet Todd. New York: Holmes & Meier, 1983. 59–67.

Washington, Carla. "Maya Angelou's Angelic Aura." *The Christian Century* 105.34 (November 1988): 1031–33.

Washington, Mary Helen. "Black Women Image Makers." *Black World* 23.10 (1974): 10–18.

Weller, Sheila. "Work in Progress: Maya Angelou." *Intellectual Digest* (June 1973): 18–21.

Interviews with Maya Angelou

Manegold, Catherine S. "A Wordsmith at Her Inaugural Anvil." *New York Times*, January 20, 1993, C1, C8.

Neubauer, Carol E. Interview with Maya Angelou in *The Massachusetts Review* 28.2 (1987): 286–92. Rpt. in *Contemporary Literary Criticism*. Vol. 64. Ed. Roger Matuz et al. Detroit: Gale, 1991. 23–41.

Plimpton, George. "The Art of Fiction CXIX: Maya Angelou." *The Paris Review* 32.116 (Fall 1990): 145–67.

JAMES BALDWIN
(1924–1987)

Barbara L.J. Griffin

BIOGRAPHY

James Arthur Baldwin, born on August 2, 1924, in Harlem, New York, is acclaimed today as one of the most important literary voices of the twentieth century. His accomplishments are broad and wide-ranging. During his lifetime, he achieved success in the novel, the short story, the essay, and the dramatic arts. Baldwin's short story collection titled *Going to Meet the Man* (1965), his play *The Amen Corner* (1968), and the powerful Broadway play *Blues for Mister Charlie* (1964) make substantive contributions to the African American literary canon. His published novels include *Go Tell It on the Mountain* (1953), *Giovanni's Room* (1956), *Another Country* (1962), *Tell Me How Long the Train's Been Gone* (1968), *If Beale Street Could Talk* (1974), and *Just Above My Head* (1979). His first novel, *Go Tell It on the Mountain*, however, is regarded as his best (Gates and McKay 1652). Baldwin's mature narrative control and sustained thematic unity merge to transform this story of a young man's initiation into "sin" and "salvation" into a masterpiece. Protagonist John Grimes's psychological and emotional struggle with his ascetic and embittered father reflects Baldwin's struggle with his stepfather David Baldwin, a stern fundamentalist minister. An important aspect of *Go Tell It on the Mountain* are the themes of identity and the redemptive power of love, which will continue to resonate in Baldwin's subsequent works.

Although *Go Tell It on the Mountain* is recognized today as a classic, critics agree that Baldwin did his finest work in the genre of the essay (Gates and McKay 1652). Nick Aaron Ford in "The Evolution of James Baldwin as Essayist" writes, "James Baldwin is one of the most talented American essayists since Ralph Waldo Emerson." Except for his 1953 classic *Go Tell It on the Mountain*, observes Ford, Baldwin's remaining novels, his volume of short stories, and two published plays are inferior to his most accomplished essays (85). In 1955, while living in Paris, Baldwin published his first collection of essays, *Notes of a Native Son*. Frustrated by American racism, he moved there in November 1948 (Baldwin, *Notes of a Native Son* 4). Included in the collection was an earlier controversial piece, "Everybody's Protest Novel," published in 1949 in *Zero*, in which he attacked friend and mentor Richard Wright* and the whole genre of protest novels (Gates and McKay 1651–52).

In his first collection, Baldwin established the themes and styles that would be a "hallmark" of his essay writing for the rest of his career—for example, his employment of his personal life to show the human condition or to illuminate what he regarded as "universal truths." He would also continue to explore relentlessly the psychic landscape of race relations and the inextricable ties that connect people to communities and to each other. Baldwin's appropriation of an Old Testament persona to deliver prophetic warnings and his use of vivid imagery to enhance the emotional involvement of the reader are also distinguishing features of his work (Ford 90).

Following *Notes of a Native Son* came *Nobody Knows My Name* in 1961, consisting of essays written between 1954 and 1961. In this collection of thirteen essays, Baldwin continued to examine the color problem introduced in *Notes of a Native Son*. The most memorable essay from the collection, "The Discovery of What It Means to Be an American," outlines Baldwin's motivation for his emigration to France. He needed, he says, liberation from the narrow identity of "negro writer" and wanted to forge a kinship with a wider representation of humanity (Ford 91). *Nobody Knows My Name* won Baldwin a place on the *New York Times'* bestseller list (Ford 91).

At the age of fourteen, Baldwin became an adolescent preacher in a Pentecostal church. Although he felt driven to this decision by his chaotic Harlem environment and pressure from his authoritarian stepfather, he was deeply overcome by the dramatic richness of the church and adopted its language in his own works. Not long after his ascension to the pulpit, a seventeen-year-old Baldwin abandoned the church and renounced his belief in fundamental Christianity, but he never wrote a line without its shaping influence (Gates and McKay 1651). In works such as *The Fire Next Time* (1963), widely regarded as his finest essay collection, Baldwin assumes the role of Old Testament Jeremiah as he warns of a second destruction if blacks and whites do not find a way to love one another. A biblical verse, inscribed on a blank page following the frontispiece, conveys the ominous tone that Baldwin wishes to establish: "God gave Noah the rainbow sign,/No more water, the fire next time!" With astounding skill, in *The Fire Next Time*, Baldwin uses his personal life as a lens through which to examine issues such as the integrity and viability of the church, the credibility of the Black Muslim religion, and the tangled web of race relations in the United States (Ford 99–100).

If *The Fire Next Time* constitutes a prophetic vision of what might be, *No Name in the Street* (1972), Baldwin's fourth volume of essays, confirms that the

worst has occurred regarding race relations in America and abroad. The assassination of Martin Luther King, Malcolm X,* and Medgar Evers has left the once
idealistic author disillusioned and bitter. "All of the Western nations have been
caught in a lie," Baldwin declares, "the lie of their pretended humanism" (Ford
102). In 1957, Baldwin returned to the United States to become one of the
principal interpreters of the civil rights movement of the 1950s and 1960s. He
traveled throughout the South, writing piercing commentaries for the nation's
most important journals such as *Commentary*, *Partisan Review*, and *Esquire* (Gates
and McKay 1652). Recognized nationally and internationally as a premier social
and literary critic, Baldwin exposed within his trenchant essays the disparity
between the promise of American justice and its failed deliverance. Baldwin's
contributions as a novelist and essayist leave an important legacy to American
and African American literature. In order to understand his works, one must
examine his autobiographical essays.

AUTOBIOGRAPHICAL WORK AND THEMES

Baldwin's *Notes of a Native Son* can only be considered an autobiographical
collection of essays, in its entirety, if one were to consider the narrative voice
that speaks throughout as a reification of Baldwin's own voice as he alternates
between personal self and the collective self throughout the book. As Lauren
Rusk observes, "Although only three of the ten essays . . . are explicitly autobiographical, the speaker emerges as a person more and more throughout the course
of the book" (369). It is in the opening essay, "Autobiographical Notes," that
Baldwin gropes for a way to establish his identity. He is a writer, a "bastard" child
of the West, and the son of a father whose iron will he has opposed. In this part
of the text, he wishes to establish his new literary voice as a "prologue" for the
themes that will dominate his first book of essays and guide him as a writer
throughout his career (Porter 23). In "The Problem of Identity in Selected Early
Essays of James Baldwin," critic Jocelyn Jackson interprets the opening "Auto-
biographic Notes" as Baldwin's "Credo" (253).

Notes of a Native Son is divided into three parts. Part One consists of two
examples of essays of literary criticism: "Everybody's Protest Novel" and "Many
Thousands Gone." In "Everybody's Protest Novel," first published in *Zero* Magazine and *Partisan Review* in 1949, Baldwin rejects protest fiction as a valid genre
for expressing the collective complexity of a people. His primary focus is the role
of the writer, which he contends is not to function as a social scientist. The
writer's role, he argues, is to reveal the depth of the human soul. Targeting
Richard Wright's *Native Son* and Harriet Beecher Stowe's *Uncle Tom's Cabin* as
examples of sociology parading as literature, Baldwin articulates his philosophy
that propaganda cannot substitute for good writing. What Stowe and Wright
have accomplished, according to Baldwin, is the solidification of stereotypes.
Both works, inverted mirrorlike images of each other, are based on a theology
that implies the inhumanity of black people (*Notes* 19). In "Many Thousands

Gone," Baldwin continues his argument, but this time he brings greater emphasis and specificity to his stand against Wright's *Native Son*, arguing that in creating Bigger, Wright leaves out the reality of black people in this country. "What this means for the novel," writes Baldwin, "is that a necessary dimension has been cut away" (*Notes* 35). "Carmen Jones: The Dark Is Light Enough" expresses Baldwin's contempt for the Hollywood production of *Carmen Jones*, which he feels exploited the black cast (*Notes* 46–54).

Part Two comprises the most autobiographical aspect of *Notes of a Native Son*. The opening essay "Harlem Ghetto" describes the chaos and futility of life in Harlem as Baldwin sarcastically alludes to the calculated plan to keep people relegated to their fates. In "Journey to Atlanta," the second essay, the reader is given a specific case of exploitation as a Harlem quartet (two members are Baldwin's brothers) makes a bid for fame. Although these two introductory essays in Part Two offer important insight into Baldwin's themes, they serve an especially important role in establishing the context for Baldwin's most important essay in the collection, the title essay "Notes of a Native Son."

Baldwin's father looms large in this piece as the author draws on the parable of the prodigal son to suggest the gravity of his decision to abandon his father and his father's house. Within the essay the family is portrayed as a microcosm of the universal condition. The father, a victim of society, is trapped by a theology that denies the possibility of compassion and love. His wife and children must bear the weight of his burdensome, life-denying philosophy and must subsequently work through a complex tapestry of ambivalences. These ambivalences translate into their relationship to society, the outside world. Baldwin's often fragmented speculations on race relations and his pattern of linking his personal reality with larger issues no doubt stem from his family dynamics. He would continue throughout his career to link his personal reality with the reality of all humanity (Porter 23–24).

The essay "Notes of a Native Son" is divided into three sections. Critic Horace Porter suggests that this breakdown parallels the sections "Fear," "Flight," and "Fate" of Wright's *Native Son* (24). Although the first section begins in linear time with the death of Baldwin's father amidst the apocalyptic images of the Harlem riot and the birth of his father's last child, the narrative structure is interrupted by a series of flashbacks skillfully employed to build a composite portrait of his father, who could be "chilling in the pulpit and indescribably cruel in his personal life" (*Notes* 87). Baldwin's description of his father oscillates between admiration for his awesome power and fear as he recounts incidents that reveal his father's attempts to force upon his children the unyielding asceticism and bitterness responsible for ruining his own life. Chiefly he rejects white people and the world and wishes his children to do the same. In one incident, David Baldwin attempted to discourage a white teacher from encouraging Baldwin's talent as a developing young writer (91–92). But despite being branded a traitor by his father, Baldwin reaches out beyond his stultifying environment to a world that he feels will nurture his intellectual hunger. To do this, he must leave home

JAMES BALDWIN   33

(Porter 24). Baldwin's year of living on his own, working in racist defense plants in Trenton, New Jersey, causes him to become more sympathetic and reflective of his father's distrust of whites. Indeed, the son has inherited the chronic illness that resides in the skulls of most Negroes, a fever that rages in the blood (*Notes* 94). This rage will emerge as a dualistic voice in Baldwin's canon: a love/hate dilemma inherent in many of his important works.

In Part Two of the essay, Baldwin returns home to see his dying father, clinging to life, while Harlem is caught up in the throes of wartime restlessness. In this section Baldwin evokes the Old Testament sense of warning in the air as he observes strange occurrences in Harlem, emblematic of the last days:

Seventh Day Adventists and Methodists and Spiritualists seemed to be hobnobbing with Holyrollers and they were all, alike, entangled with the most flagrant disbelievers; something heavy in their stance seemed to indicate that they had all, incredibly, seen a common vision, and on each face there seemed to be the same strange, bitter shadow. (*Notes* 100)

The dying father and apocalyptic foreshadowing are brought together as objective correlatives for Baldwin's sense of anxiety and despair.

In Part Three of the essay, Baldwin displays his narrative dexterity as he compresses disparate images to achieve a mosaic effect. Set against images of the funeral, mob unrest, and his unsuccessful attempt to celebrate his birthday, Baldwin explores the stages of his relationship with his father. He uses a lens of memory to visualize the two of them when he was a young man, then an adolescent, and finally a boy (Porter 23–24). There is the adumbration of admiration. But in the final analysis, Baldwin, the reflective mature thinker and writer, must reject his father's legacy. "Notes of a Native Son" concludes with a major theme that is continued in *The Fire Next Time*—that those who indulge in hatred destroy themselves. Justice will come only when black and white people acknowledge their commonality and work together to improve the human condition (*Notes* 113–14).

In the final section of *Notes of a Native Son*, Baldwin uses Europe as the backdrop for his ruminations concerning questions of culture and identity. The first two essays—"Encounter on the Seine: Black Meets Brown" and "A Question of Identity"—are written in the objective narrative voice. Only mildly autobiographical, both essays examine how the phenomenon of geographic displacement affects notions of race and identity. Black Americans, white Americans, Europeans, and Africans are brought together for Baldwin's reflections on the human dynamics of perceived racial differences (Rusk 365).

The last two essays, which examine the theme of the "other," are "explicitly" autobiographical in that Baldwin uses his personal experiences to draw broad philosophical conclusions about social realities. In "Equal in Paris," Baldwin's eight day imprisonment in a rotting, deteriorating cell becomes a microcosm for the position of the have nots who must endure peril and wretchedness at the bottom of society. Unlike those with means, they are not "safe." While color is not foregrounded in this piece, Baldwin uses his alien status as a way to forge a connection between the Parisian downtrodden and himself. As Baldwin awaits his case—a case that has dragged on unnecessarily for an extended length of time—he ponders the "indifference" practiced by large institutions and concludes that such complaisance is exercised by people safe from the wretches of the earth. His close encounter with French institutions enables him to better understand America (*Notes* 138–58).

In "A Stranger in the Village," Baldwin brings into sharp focus the psychological and emotional responses of the black individual caught within the glaring landscape of whiteness. In this essay, set in a remote Switzerland community, color is reified as the stranger (Baldwin) finds himself struggling with his own ambivalences as he speculates upon the uneasy relationship that blacks have with Western culture. The villagers, meant to epitomize the West, mostly Catholics and tourists seeking the healing waters of the hot springs, display an innocence of experience that permits them to subject Baldwin to humiliating incidents that make him feel "not quite human." Baldwin recounts the painful experience of being called "Neger" by the Swiss children (*Notes* 162). He gains, from these occurrences, however, insight into the dynamics of race relations in the United States. He concludes that people do not intend to be cruel. "[They] are trapped in history and history is trapped in them" (162). "A Stranger in the Village" is a finely crafted piece that offers one of the best interpretations of "the black-white dilemma that appear in American literature" (Ford 89).

CRITICAL RECEPTION

Richard Wright was personally devastated by Baldwin's "Everybody's Protest Novel," which later became the leading piece in *Notes of a Native Son*. Wright had helped Baldwin obtain a Eugene F. Saxton fellowship to complete his first novel *Go Tell It on the Mountain* and had encouraged his writing generally. Ironically, it was Wright who helped Baldwin publish "Everybody's Protest Novel" in *Zero* by introducing him to its editor. Wright biographer Michel Fabre reports in *The Unfinished Quest of Richard Wright* that after "Everybody's Protest Novel" Wright severed his ties with his young protégé (362–63).

Nevertheless, *Notes of a Native Son* was published to critical acclaim. The reviews were explosively positive, establishing the reputation of the brash, young writer who dared to attack the "protest novels" of Richard Wright and Harriet Beecher Stowe. In a February 1956 review that appeared in the *New York Herald Tribune Book Review*, Saunders Redding lauding Baldwin's mastery of language in the essay form, argues that the author evokes thought in the essay more effectively than he arouses emotion in fiction. Redding doubted that Baldwin's ability to "handle words" could be matched by many American writers (4). In the same year, a review in the *U.S. Quarterly Book Review* simply stated that Baldwin's essays in *Notes* were "marked by a literary style of complexity and power" (35). A review appearing in *Commonweal*, on January 13, 1956, calls Baldwin "the most perceptive" Negro writer of the day, whose eloquence quite possibly transcends that of Richard Wright and Ralph Ellison. The only weakness the politically incorrect reviewer can detect is Baldwin's lack of humor—so vital to the Negro's survival. He is earnest to a fault (Rainer 384).

After dismissing the literary criticism portion of *Notes of a Native Son*, the reviewer for the *Christian Science Monitor* praises the purely autobiographical section for its dynamic and precise writing. The immediacy of Baldwin's style, observes the reviewer, places the reader in "the shoes of a Negro living in a big American city" (Brunn 9). H. Orlando Patterson in "The Essays of James Baldwin" congratulates Baldwin for his technical brilliance throughout the autobiographical section of *Notes*. "Throughout, the narrative never wanes, the shifts in scene and mood never jar, which is all the more amazing when one considers that interspersed throughout is the death and funeral of his father" (36).

The critical success of *Notes of a Native Son* is confirmed by its consistent inclusion in anthologies of note since its 1955 publication. *Black Voices: An Anthology of Afro-American Literature*, published in 1968, contains "Many Thousands Gone," one of the major essays from *Notes of a Native Son*. In his introductory paragraph, editor Abraham Chapman concludes that *Notes of a Native Son*, along with other Baldwin essay collections, established him as a premier essayist rivaling the accomplishment of Ralph Ellison (316). More recent anthologies continue to publish selected essays from *Notes of a Native Son*. For example, *The Norton Anthology of African American Literature*, edited by Henry Louis Gates and Nellie McKay, contains "Everybody's Protest Novel," "Many Thousands Gone," "Stranger in the Village," and the title essay "Notes of a Native Son." *Call and Response: The Riverside Anthology of the African American Literary Tradition*, edited by Patricia Liggins Hill, includes "Everybody's Protest Novel."

The ultimate confirmation that a work of literary seriousness has met with critical success is its consistent listing on college and university course syllabi. *Notes of a Native Son* has enjoyed canon status for a number of years, ironically having a permanent place in discussions that center on the naturalistic novels of Richard Wright. The literary criticism essays on protest fiction indeed offer intelligent alternatives for exploring themes and concepts associated with the modern age. The explicitly autobiographical essays are equally significant in that they bear out Baldwin's skill and discipline as a writer and provide a context for understanding his works. *Notes of a Native Son* is the powerful expression of a sensitive, discerning writer's reaction to his complicated world.

BIBLIOGRAPHY

Autobiographical Work by James Baldwin

Notes of a Native Son. Boston: Beacon Press, 1955.

Studies of James Baldwin's Autobiographical Work

Brunn, R.R. Rev. of *Notes of a Native Son*. *Christian Science Monitor*, December 16, 1955, 9.

Chapman, Abraham. *Black Voices: An Anthology of Afro-American Literature*. New York: Macmillan, 1968.

Cunningham, James. "Public and Private Rhetorical Modes in the Essays of James Baldwin." In *Essays on the Essay: Redefining the Genre*. Ed. Alexander J. Butrym. Athens: University of Georgia Press, 1990. 192–203.

Ford, Nick Aaron. "The Evolution of James Baldwin as Essayist." In *James Baldwin: A Critical Evaluation*. Ed. Therman B. O'Daniel. Washington, DC: Howard University Press, 1977. 85–104.

Gates, Henry Louis, Jr., and Nellie M. McKay, eds. *The Norton Anthology of African American Literature*. New York: W.W. Norton, 1977.

Jackson, Jocelyn W. "The Problem of Identity in Selected Early Essays of James Baldwin." In *Critical Essays on James Baldwin*. Ed. Fred L. Standley and Nancy V. Burt. Boston: G.K. Hall, 1988. 250–66.

Patterson, Orlando. "The Essays of James Baldwin." *New Left Review* 26 (Summer 1964): 31–38.

Porter, Horace A. *Stealing the Fire: The Art and Protest of James Baldwin*. Middletown, CT: Wesleyan University Press, 1989.

Rainer, Dachine. "Rage into Order." Rev. of *Notes of a Native Son*. *Commonweal* (January 13, 1956): 384.

Redding, Saunders. Rev. of *Notes of a Native Son*. *New York Herald Tribune Book Review* (February 26, 1956): 4.

Rev. of *Notes of a Native Son*. *U.S. Quarterly Book Review* (March 1956): 35.

Rusk, Lauren. "Selfhood and Strategy in *Notes of a Native Son*." In *Re-Viewing James Baldwin & Things Not Seen*. Ed. D. Quentin Miller. Philadelphia: Temple University Press, 2000. 360–92.

AMIRI BARAKA (LEROI JONES)
(1934–   )

Tarshia L. Stanley

BIOGRAPHY

Poet, playwright, activist, novelist, musicologist, editor, journalist, director, and teacher, this founder of a distinctly ethnic aesthetic movement and a unique political form of resistance changed much more than his name on his way to becoming Amiri Baraka. Everett LeRoy Jones was born to middle-class parents in Newark, New Jersey, on October 7, 1934. He grew up in a strong family unit where his maternal grandparents stressed self-reliance and a knowledge of his cultural history. In 1952 Baraka matriculated to Howard University where the spelling of his name changed to *LeRoi*. He later left Howard to join the air force. Baraka's military service was terminated abruptly because of allegations made against him for possession of Communist tracts. By 1957 he had moved to Greenwich Village and began associating with a group of highly visible "Beatnik" artists and writers. During the next year Baraka married Hettie Cohen, a Jewish woman with whom he founded Totem Press and coedited *Yugen*. This avant-garde magazine garnered him critical attention, and with Cohen's encouragement, he began to publish both his poetry and prose.

In 1961 Baraka published his first volume of poetry, *Preface to a Twenty Volume Suicide Note*, and in the next few years works of prose and several plays followed. *The Baptism* (1961), *The Toilet* (1962), and *The Slave* (1962) indicate a shift in Baraka's work from Beat writer to social commentator. It was during this period that he journeyed to Cuba and began to be heavily influenced by revolutionary struggles in Black America and abroad. On March 24, 1964, *The Dutchman*, which established Baraka as a major playwright, debuted at the Cherry Lane Theater in New York. It won the Obie Award for best Off-Broadway Play 1963–1964, and in 1967 a film version was released. *The Dutchman* condemned blacks who assimilated into white society and prophesied their social, emotional, and inevitable physical destruction. When in *The Dutchman* the black character Clay is murdered by a white woman in a subway car, it signaled not only the beginning of a new sociopolitical consciousness in Baraka but the end of LeRoi Jones and his marriage to Hettie Cohen.

Malcolm X* was assassinated in 1965, and LeRoi Jones became Ameer Barakat (Blessed Prince), divorced his wife, and moved to Harlem. In *The Autobiography of LeRoi Jones* Baraka described his move to Harlem as a flight. He plunged headlong into the Black Consciousness and the Black Power movements. Baraka became affiliated with the National Black Political Assembly and founded the Congress of Afrikan People and the Black Arts Repertory Theater/School. Although BART/S was short-lived, it was the base from which Baraka became the father of the Black Arts Movement. According to Henry C. Lacey in *The Oxford Companion to African American Literature*, Baraka created a "race-conscious art" (50). At the Black Arts Repertory Theater/School he contrived a neo-expressionist form of theatrical production that he took directly to the black people on the streets. Many of his productions were dubbed "antiwhite" and for "black audiences only," and Baraka unapologetically forged a new way of melding black political consciousness and forms of black self-expression. He combined his poetry, his politics, his understanding of blues and jazz, and his desperate need to create for his people a Black Aesthetic. In keeping with the theories of Malcolm X, Aimé Césaire, and Frantz Fanon, Baraka called for a new purpose and awareness in black art. Art for black people was to be for, by, and about them and their struggle. Unlike the Harlem Renaissance the Black Arts Movement was strictly concerned with black audiences.

By 1968 Baraka had edited *Black Fire: An Anthology of African American Writing* with Larry Neal and been given the name Imamu (Spiritual Leader) Amiri Baraka by the founder of the organization US Maulana Karenga. He would later drop the *Imamu* as he embraced a more Marxist/Leninist worldview in the early 1970s. Baraka also married Sylvia Robinson (Amina) in Newark, New Jersey. There they were involved in the election of the first black mayor and the opening of Spirit House, a community theater in keeping with BART/S. Next he founded the Black Community Development and Defense Organization, and his play *Slave Ship: An Historical Pageant* received critical attention as "living" theater. The piece was performed among the audience on a variety of stages and levels and utilized smells and sounds in order to overwhelm the sensibilities of the audience and cause them to *be* inside the slave ship.

After the decline of the Black Power and the Black Arts Movements, Baraka adopted a Third World Marxist view and continues to be an activist today. He has lectured at Yale, Columbia, and the State University of New York at Stony Brook. Baraka has held many fellowships including the Guggenheim.

AUTOBIOGRAPHICAL WORKS AND THEMES

In the first release of *The Autobiography of LeRoi Jones* (1984) the publisher edited much of his writing in order to produce a more concise version of the book. In 1997 Baraka rereleased the book in its original form. It begins with an ordering of his earliest reality. The reader finds him a "brown boy," preoccupied with color and meaning, who struggles when his sense of blackness is both challenged and defined by enrollment in a white high school. This splitting of his identity before he can rightly articulate it is thematic throughout the early years of his life.

His subsequent endeavors to study at Rutgers and Howard Universities and his short term in the military are further indications that Baraka cannot find the place he belongs. Baraka allows the reader access to some of the specific incidences that prompted him in the direction of the Beatniks in the mid-1950s. His desire to emulate the writers and poets of the Beat community, and his realization that he could not express himself in exactly the same way because of his differing reality, drove Baraka to seek forms of authentic black expression. He also offers insights into his marriage to Hettie Cohen and the reasons for their subsequent breakup. As Baraka's political views began to take on a decidedly more ethnic stance, he found himself unwilling to stay married to Cohen.

Baraka gives an account of his immersion into the world of Black Power and the new black consciousness. He greatly admired the tenacious Malcolm X whose death was a catalyst for Baraka's name and lifestyle change. As he became a key figure in the Black Power movement, Baraka was targeted by the FBI and beaten by the local police. None of these tactics kept him from the path he had chosen. He worked tirelessly at the Black Arts Repertory Theater School until his funding evaporated. Baraka's autobiography is honest in its evaluation of his sexist behavior and the problems this entailed in his second marriage. Yet at times the narrative seems less like an autobiography and more like poetry. It still offers insights, but perhaps there is too much room for individual interpretation.

As informative as his autobiography is, Baraka's 1966 work *Home: Social Essays* also offers much insight into the ideology of this multifaceted man. The essays are a compilation of Baraka's struggle with the major issues of his life. Baraka grapples with the notion of the Black Aesthetic, according to Henry C. Lacey in *The Oxford Companion to African American Literature* (364–65). Several of his essays are an impassioned plea for the black artist to find an "authentic, morally engaged voice," and he also denounces the black literature produced outside of the movement for its "apologetic nature" (Lacey 364–65). *The LeRoi Jones/Amiri Baraka Reader*, a collection of his work, also yields evidence about the evolution of LeRoi Jones to Amiri Baraka. Both Baraka and William J. Harris as editors on the project chose and arranged the selections and commentaries in ways that yield more comprehensive views of Baraka the man.

Like the staging of one of his plays, Baraka's work frames a post-civil rights, militant black consciousness at a specific historical moment. Baraka's own life and experiences mimic for the reader the kind of frustration and angst that were prevalent among revolutionary black men during the time. Baraka's autobiography is most useful for its insights on the development of the Black Arts Movement. He conveys his commitment to empowering his people through art and his position as a self-appointed guide in the practice of a Black Aesthetic. Baraka details his conversion to Islam and his burgeoning international sociopolitical agenda.

CRITICAL RECEPTION

Much of the critical inquiry directed at Baraka's autobiographical texts seems suspect. In Henry Louis Gates's May 1984 *New York Times* review of Baraka's autobiography, he states that Baraka has failed to convince his audience that his " 'Marxism' is any more sophisticated than any of his other political theories" (11). Here Gates, like many other critics, has trouble with Baraka's interpretation of his move from a life typified by a white wife and Beat ideology to one filled with activism, art, a black family, and eventually a philosophy that embraces Marxism as an advancement in consciousness rather than just motion. While Baraka does not make excuses for the period in his life in which he believed his only means of truly breaking free from the confines of a white American definition of blackness was to hate whiteness itself, he does briefly explain his transition. He writes as if Marxism were the only logical result of a life that moved from fascination with white culture to a total embrace of blackness. For Gates, Baraka suffers from "undigested Marxist discourse" (11). William J. Harris's introduction to *The LeRoi Jones/Amiri Baraka Reader* reads Baraka's willingness to discuss his rebuff of White America and his shift toward Marxism as further evidence of his ability to change and grow (xxix).

Amiri Baraka joins the ranks of the most distinguished contributors to African American literature with the penning of his autobiography. The autobiography in African American literature represents one of the earliest forms of self-expression and self-definition embraced by black people in America. Baraka's contribution to African American literature in general and particularly his place as founder of the Black Arts Movement situate him firmly as one of the most influential members in the canon of African American literature.

BIBLIOGRAPHY

Autobiographical Works by Amiri Baraka (Leroi Jones)

Home: Social Essays. New York: William Morrow, 1966.
The Autobiography of LeRoi Jones/Amiri Baraka. New York: Freundlich Books, 1984.
The Autobiography of LeRoi Jones/Amiri Baraka. Chicago: Lawrence Hill Books, 1997. The first complete edition, with reinstated material by the author excised from the first edition and a new introduction by the author.
The LeRoi Jones/Amiri Baraka Reader. Ed. William J. Harris. New York: Avalon, 1999.

Studies of Amiri Baraka's (Leroi Jones's) Autobiographical Works

Andrews, William L., Frances Smith Foster, and Trudier Harris, eds. *The Oxford Companion to African American Literature*. New York: Oxford University Press, 1997.

Baker, Houston A. "These Are Songs If You Have the Music: An Essay on Imamu Amiri Baraka." *Minority Voices* 1.1 (Spring 1977): 1–18.

Benston, Kimberly. *Baraka: The Renegade and the Mask*. New Haven, CT: Yale University Press, 1976.

Brown, Lloyd W. *Amiri Baraka*. Boston: Twayne Publishers, 1980.

Elam, Harry J., Jr. *Taking It to the Streets: The Social Protest Theater of Luis Valdez and Amiri Baraka*. Ann Arbor: University of Michigan Press, 1997.

Gates, Henry Louis. Rev. of *The Autobiography of Amiri Baraka*. *New York Times Book Review* (May 11, 1984), CT: 11.

———. ed. *Bearing Witness: Selections from African American Autobiography in the Twentieth Century*. New York: Pantheon Books, 1991.

Gibson, Donald. *Five Black Writers*. New York: New York University Press, 1970.

Gilyard, Keith. *Spirit and Flame: An Anthology of Contemporary African American Poetry*. Syracuse: Syracuse University Press, 1997.

Gwynne, James B., ed. *Amiri Baraka: The Kaleidoscopic Torch*. New York: Steppingstones Press, 1985.

Hudson, Theodore. *From LeRoi Jones to Amiri Baraka: The Literary Works*. Durham, NC: Duke University Press, 1973.

Jones, Hettie. *How I Became Hettie Jones*. New York: E.P. Dutton, 1990.

Lacey, Henry C. "Amiri Baraka." In *The Oxford Companion to African American Literature*. Ed. William Andrews, et al. New York: Oxford University Press, 1997. 50.

Melhem, D.H. *Heroism in the New Black Poetry: Introductions and Interviews*. Lexington: University Press of Kentucky, 1989.

Pickney, Darryl. "The Changes of Amiri Baraka." *New York Times Book Review* (December 16, 1979): 9.

Reilly, Charlie. *Conversations with Amiri Baraka*. Jackson: University of Mississippi Press, 1994.

Sollers, Werner. *Amiri Baraka/LeRoi Jones: The Quest for a "Popular Modernism."* New York: Columbia University Press, 1978.

Woodard, Komozi. *A Nation within a Nation: Amiri Baraka (LeRoi Jones) & Black Power Politics*. Chapel Hill: University of North Carolina Press, 1999.

HENRY WALTON BIBB
(1815–1854)

Nanette Morton

BIOGRAPHY

Born in May 1815 in Shelby County, Kentucky, Henry Bibb was the son of Mildred Jackson, a slave belonging to David White, and a prominent white Kentuckian named James Bibb. The oldest of seven children, he was soon "hired out" to various employers. Frequently mistreated, he ran away, soon becoming a habitual truant. Although Bibb resolved to win his freedom early on, he later recalled that he was soon distracted by other matters: At eighteen he met and married Malinda, a young woman who was the property of William Gatewood. Bibb eventually became Gatewood's property and, soon after, the father of a daughter. He escaped Kentucky and got as far as Detroit before returning for his family. Betrayed, he was captured in Cincinnati. Another escape and attempted rescue of his family resulted in another betrayal and imprisonment in Louisville. Bibb and his family were then sent to Louisiana, where they were bought by "one of the basest hypocrites that I ever saw": a Baptist deacon named Francis Whit-field (Bibb 110). When they attempted to escape yet again, Bibb was sold to gamblers, while his wife became the slave and concubine of a white man. Even-tually, Bibb became the slave of a Native American, an experience he charac-terized as comparatively mild.

Bibb escaped when his master died and made his way to Ohio. He became an antislavery lecturer and traveled throughout Pennsylvania, Ohio, Michigan, and New England. In 1845 he learned of his wife's fate, and though he brought "no charge of guilt against her," her concubinage meant he "could no longer regard her as [his] wife" (189). In 1848, therefore, Bibb married Mary E. Miles, an abolitionist, Quaker, teacher, and free black Bostonian. Although he had only three weeks' formal schooling (he had learned to read during his incarceration),

Bibb wrote and published *Narrative of the Life and Adventures of Henry Bibb* in 1849.

The Fugitive Slave Law of 1850 prompted the Bibbs to settle in Canada. With Mary's help, Bibb became the founder and editor of *The Voice of the Fugitive*, a newspaper that became the mouthpiece for both his own separatist views and the Michigan-based Refugee Home Society (RHS), in which the Bibbs played a prominent role. The RHS, which acquired land in Canada to resell to black immigrants, provoked criticism, most notably from Mary Ann Shadd, teacher, abolitionist, and editor of rival newspaper *The Provincial Freeman*. Shadd condemned RHS fund-raising as "begging" and the society's dependence on whites; the society was also said to have misappropriated funds (Ripley et al. 2: 114; Winks 204–8). There is no evidence that the Bibbs were involved in any misconduct.

Stung by this criticism and the loss of his newspaper office, which burned in 1853, Bibb died in 1854 at the age of thirty-nine. Although his premature death prevented him from reestablishing his newspaper, Bibb's influence on both African Canadian settlers and the abolitionist movement is undeniable.

AUTOBIOGRAPHICAL WORK AND THEMES

Published only four years after *Narrative of the Life of Frederick Douglass*, Bibb's *Narrative* clearly reflects the influence of the former. Douglass's* famous apostrophe to the ships on Chesapeake Bay, for example, is echoed in Bibb's own address to the Ohio River, which marked the boundary between the slave states and the free North. Douglass expresses a desire to fly to freedom while watching the ships' sails; Bibb wishes for "the wings of a dove, that I might soar away to where there is not slavery" (29). Both detail what they deemed to be the distracting dissipation of Christmas celebrations, and both resorted to "conjuration" as youths in an effort to escape punishment and, in Bibb's case, to attract feminine attention.

In spite of this apparent influence, Bibb's production is his own. Douglass focuses on his attempts to attain literacy—and, through it, freedom—in the face of his master's prohibition. The married Bibb focuses on his repeated escape attempts and the ways in which slavery hampers and eventually destroys his attempts to sustain family life. Bibb exposes the hypocrisy of the moral system that would condemn the slave's self-protecting deceptions even as it justified the destruction of African American familial ties, ties that, when formed between white Americans, were deemed sacred. Faced with such hypocrisy, Bibb had no choice but to defend himself with the only weapon he could safely use. "In fact, the only weapon of self defence that I could use successfully, was that of deception. It is useless for a poor helpless slave, to resist a white man in a slaveholding State" (17). In spite of his cunning, Bibb is unable to protect his wife and child from abuse. His love for his family, therefore, is heavily laden with regret: "If there was any one act of my life while a slave, that I have to lament over, it is that of being a father and a husband of slaves" (44). Although his daughter is "a pretty child . . . quiet, playful, bright and interesting," Bibb provides no information about her fate: He may not have known it, or just as likely, it may have been too horrible to contemplate.

CRITICAL RECEPTION

Bibb's narrative has received comparatively little attention. Although John Blassingame describes it as one of the most useful of its genre, very few critics have examined Bibb's narrative in detail (374). In *From Behind the Veil*, Robert Stepto argues that the supplementary documents collected to prove the authenticity of Bibb's narrative make it a first-phase, eclectic narrative. Unlike more sophisticated third-phase narratives, which subsume their authenticating documents, or second-phase narratives, which integrate them, first-phase narratives have authenticating documents and strategies appended to them. Stepto argues that, in Bibb's case, lengthy and elaborate authentication—including a publisher's preface, excerpts from a report by the Detroit Liberty Association, and a recommendation provided by a Michigan judge—all serve as "an intermediary between [Bibb's] text and his audience." Thus, Bibb "relinquishes control of the narrative. . . . [His] removal from the primary authenticating documents and strategy . . . relegates him to a posture of partial literacy" since he does not "control the imaginative forms which his personal history assumes in print" (8–10).

William Andrews writes that Bibb's effort to cast off his former slave identity is problematic: "As a family man in slavery, Bibb's quest for individual liberty was complicated psychologically and morally" since he was ultimately unable to save his wife and child (152). Andrews argues that while Bibb claims to "bring no charge of guilt" against his first wife, his description of her concubinage as "a state of adultery" and his assertion that Malinda is "dead to me as a wife" enable him to justify his remarriage (Bibb 189). "To brand Malinda as an adulteress was certainly to use a highly charged term of moral opprobrium. . . . Thus to escape the guilt of bigamy, by declaring himself a widower to slavery, Bibb wrote his autobiography as an elaborate bill of divorce intended to clinch his case for freedom from the wife of his youth" (Andrews 160).

Brief excerpts from Bibb's editorial writings can be found in the second volume of Ripley's *The Black Abolitionist Papers*. Bibb's separatist stance, which earned him the ire of Mary Shadd, is briefly described in both Litwack and Meier's *Black Leaders of the Nineteenth Century* and Wink's *The Blacks in Canada*. Scholarly interpretations of the possible connection between Bibb's autobiographical and editorial writings have yet to be done.

BIBLIOGRAPHY

Autobiographical Work by Henry Walton Bibb

Narrative of the Life and Adventures of Henry Bibb, an American Slave Written by Himself. New York: Henry Bibb, 1849. New York: Negro Universities Press, 1969. Also reprinted in *Puttin' on Ole Massa*. Ed. Gilbert Osofsky. New York: Harper Torch-books, 1969. 51–171 (page citations are to the Negro Universities Press edition).

Studies of Henry Walton Bibb's Autobiographical Work

Andrews, William L. *To Tell a Free Story: The First Century of Afro-American Autobiog-raphy. 1760–1865*. Urbana: University of Illinois Press, 1986.

Blassingame, John W. *The Slave Community: Plantation Life in the Antebellum South*. Rev. ed. New York: Oxford University Press, 1979.

Davis, Charles T. "The Slave Narrative: First Major Art Form in an Emerging Black Tradition." In *Black Is the Color of the Cosmos*. New York: Garland, 1982. 83–119.

Diedrich, Maria. "The Characterization of Native Americans in the Antebellum Slave Narrative." *CLA Journal* 31.4 (1988): 412–35.

Drew, Benjamin. *The Refugee: Narratives of Fugitive Slaves in Canada*. Boston: John P. Jewett & Co., 1856. Toronto: Prospero Books, 2000.

Foster, Frances Smith. *Witnessing Slavery: The Development of Ante-Bellum Slave Narratives*. Westport, CT: Greenwood Press, 1979.

Fulcher, James. "Deception and Detection: Some Epistemological Themes of Ethnic Americans in the Nineteenth Century." *Markham Review* 8 (979): 72–77.

Hill, Daniel. *The Freedom Seekers: Blacks in Early Canada*. Agincourt, Ontario: Book So-ciety of Canada, 1981.

Hite, Roger W. "Voice of a Fugitive: Henry Bibb and Antebellum Black Separatism." *Journal of Black Studies* 4.3 (1974): 269–84.

Howe, S.G. *The Refugees from Slavery in Canada West: Report to the Freedman's Inquiry Commission*. 1864. New York: Arno Press, 1969.

Jackson, Blyden. *A History of Afro-American Literature*. Vol. 1: *The Long Beginning, 1746–1895*. Baton Rouge: Louisiana State University Press, 1989. 141–42.

Koike, Sekio. "The Narrative of Henry Bibb." *Kyushu American Literature* 16 (1975): 21–33.

Landon, Fred. "Henry Bibb, a Colonizer." *Journal of Negro History* 5.4 (1920): 437–47.

Lowance, Mason I., Jr. "Bibb, Henry." In *The Oxford Companion to African American Literature*. Ed. William L. Andrews, Frances Smith Foster, and Trudier Harris. New York: Oxford University Press, 1997. 58–59.

Matlack, Lucius C. *Narrative of the Anti-Slavery Experience of a Minister in the Methodist E. Church. Who Was Twice Rejected by the Philadelphia Annual Conference, and Finally Deprived of Licence to Preach for Being an Abolitionist*. Philadelphia: Martin and Boden, 1845.

Mullen, Harryette. "African Signs and Spirit Writing." *Callaloo* 19.3 (1996): 670–89.

Osofsky, Gilbert. "Introduction: Puttin' on Ole Massa: The Significance of Slave Narra-tives." *Puttin' on Ole Massa*. New York: Torchbooks, 1969. 9–44.

Ripley, C. Peter, et al., eds. *The Black Abolitionist Papers*. 5 vols. Chapel Hill: University of North Carolina Press, 1985.

Salzman, Jack, David Lionel Smith, and Cornel West, eds. *The Encyclopedia of African American Culture and History*. 5 vols. New York: Macmillan, 1996.

Silverman, Jason H. "Mary Ann Shadd and the Search for Equality." In *Black Leaders of the Nineteenth Century*. Ed. Leon Litwack and August Meier. Urbana: University of Illinois Press, 1988. 87–100.

――――. *Unwelcome Guests: Canada's Response to American Fugitive Slaves, 1800–1865*. Millwood, NY: National University Publications, 1985.

Starling, Marion Wilson. *The Slave Narrative: Its Place in American History*. Washington, DC: Howard University Press, 1988. 147–52.

Stepto, Robert B. *From behind the Veil: A Study of Afro-American Narrative*. Urbana: University of Illinois Press, 1979.

———. "Sharing the Thunder: The Literary Exchanges of Harriet Beecher Stowe, Henry Bibb, and Frederick Douglass." In *New Essays on Uncle Tom's Cabin*. Ed. Eric J. Sundquist. Cambridge: Cambridge University Press, 1986. 135–54.

Winks, Robin W. *The Blacks in Canada: A History*. 2nd ed. Montreal: McGill-Queen University Press, 1997.

GWENDOLYN BROOKS
(1917–2000)

Emmanuel S. Nelson

BIOGRAPHY

Gwendolyn Brooks was born on June 7, 1917, in Topeka, Kansas. Her mother, Keziah Wims Brooks, was a schoolteacher who, when young, wanted to be a concert pianist. Her father, David Anderson Brooks, was a janitor. Son of a runaway slave, he had dreamed of becoming a doctor and even attended Fisk University for a year in pursuit of that dream. Although her parents' professional goals did not materialize, they offered Gwendolyn and her brother Raymond a secure and nurturing home environment. They encouraged her to develop her artistic talents and actively supported her ambition to become a poet. Brooks sensed in the ordinary lives of her parents a quiet heroism that she acknowledged later in her life as a source of enduring inspiration.

Brooks grew up in Chicago. In 1934 she graduated from Englewood High School and in 1936 from Wilson Junior College. By that time she had already published several poems in local magazines and newspapers. In the late 1930s she began to study formally the craft of poetry by attending numerous creative writing workshops. *A Street in Bronzeville*, her first collection of poems that appeared in 1945, reveals her fluent command of modernist techniques. In 1950 Brooks became the first African American to win the Pulitzer Prize for Literature. The Pulitzer, however, was only the first of many distinctions that marked her brilliant career. She later became the first citizen of the United States to receive the Society for Literature Award from the University of Thessaloniki, Greece. Recipient of over seventy honorary doctorates, she taught at numerous colleges and universities, conducted poetry workshops in prisons as well as on Ivy League campuses, became the National Endowment for the Humanities Jefferson Lecturer in 1994, served for a year as a Consultant in Poetry at the Library of

Congress, and received the National Endowment for the Arts Lifetime Achieve-ment Award. Until her death at age eighty-three she remained one of the most sought-after speakers in the United States and abroad.

AUTOBIOGRAPHICAL WORKS AND THEMES

Brooks's artistic reputation rests primarily on her achievements as a poet. One of the most distinguished bards of the twentieth century, her many volumes of poetry reveal her exceptional mastery of form, innovative style, and complexity of thought. Her two autobiographies—*Report from Part One* (1972) and *Report from Part Two* (1996)—offer glimpses into her personal life, her artistic credo, and her politics. However, neither text conforms to the format of conventional autobiographies. In both works Brooks emerges as an affable but private individ-ual who is determined to guard her privacy without appearing aloof.

Report from Part One begins with two prefatory statements: one by Don Lee, himself a poet of considerable talent; the other by George Kent, a distinguished African American scholar. Largely testimonials of the authors' affection and ad-miration for Brooks, the prefaces also contain some valuable insights into her poetic practice. "Report from Part One," the lengthy chapter that follows the prefaces, is an elegant essay in which Brooks comments on her childhood, the influence of her parents on the formation of her worldview, her marriage and motherhood, and the early stages of her career. What is particularly fascinating is her statement on her political transformation. After attending a raucous literary-political conference on the campus of Fisk University in 1967, Brooks says that she began to align herself with the new Black Consciousness movement. That conference, she points out, marked her transformation from "negro" to "black."

The third section of the book is titled "African Fragment." Here Brooks recalls her first visit to Africa. Her excitement is transparent, and she feels a deep sense of political and spiritual affinity with the people. Yet she also recognizes her profound cultural separation from the continent of her origins, and the Africans themselves sometimes remind her of her American identity. Nevertheless, ulti-mately, her African sojourn has the effect of strengthening her consciousness as a black woman and her ability to imagine herself as part of the African diaspora.

The fourth section of the autobiography contains a charming collection of photographs of Brooks and her family. The fifth section is particularly valuable: It has three interviews that she granted in 1967, 1969, and 1971. Here Brooks shares with her interviewers her thoughts on a variety of issues, particularly on her newly emerging political consciousness and her development as a poet. The final section is divided into two parts. The first part, titled "Marginalia," analyzes several of her own poems. Her comments are an invaluable guide to our under-standing of her often challenging texts. The second section, titled "Collage," is a short autobiographical essay that again focuses on her political radicalization.

The volume ends with an obituary for Fluffy, her family's pet dog, that died in 1971. The inclusion of this short statement is as playful as it is poignant.

Brooks's second autobiography, *Report from Part Two*, was published when she was nearing her eightieth birthday. Shorter and less substantial than the earlier autobiography, it is divided into seven chapters. In the opening section she identifies four sources of influence on her formation: her parents, books, church, and movies. It is followed by a moving tribute to her remarkable mother who died in 1978 at age ninety. In the next section, similar to the "African Fragment" in her first autobiography, she recalls her second visit to Africa, this time to West Africa, and she is accompanied by her husband, Henry Blakely. The essay titled "Black Woman in Russia," which follows her African reminiscences, contains a hilarious episode involving Susan Sontag, the distinguished Jewish American author and cultural theorist. When a Russian woman asks Brooks about what it means to be a black person in the United States, Sontag intrudes into the conversation with her own authoritative answer to the question. When Brooks points out that she (Brooks) is better qualified to respond to the query, Sontag becomes enraged. Sontag's hysterical outburst ends with a vulgar statement, "I turn my back upon you" (64), and crudely she shakes her buttocks before Brooks who is seated. Brooks, looking at Sontag's ample bottom, concludes the narrative with the observation that she was "ass-uredly impressed" (65) by the display!

In the next chapter Brooks remembers the year she spent in Washington, D.C. as a Consultant in Poetry at the Library of Congress. She completed the year with a lecture to a large audience. Among the guests who attended were many writers of distinction, and Brooks offers brief comments on several of them. "Family Pictures," the essay that follows, is a meditation on the concept of family. It is followed by an appendix that contains affectionate tributes to her husband, their son Henry Blakely III, and their daughter Nora Blakely. It is obvious that Brooks saw her children as her greatest legacy. Her public statements of her private affection also suggest, in part, that Brooks, aware that her long, productive, and eventful life was coming to an end, wanted to acknowledge the three individuals — her husband of more than five decades and their two children who had made her journey personally meaningful to her.

CRITICAL RECEPTION

Brooks's two lyrical autobiographies do not offer an intimate and elaborate portrait of the author. Neither is a sustained self-representational narrative. Her fragmentary recollections offer us only momentary glimpses into the life of a private woman who was very much a public figure as well. Her reticence disappointed some of her readers. Norman Lederer, in his review of *Report from Part One*, highlights Brooks's unwillingness to disclose personal information. He finds that even in "her accounts of meetings and encounters with black literary figures, she is uncritical and unrevealing" (9). Shaw finds the book "a series of unevenly written" pieces, although "the overall effect of the patchwork is an attractive presentation of a sensitive, intelligent, tough, shrewd, and humane poet, whose genuine humility contains veins of strong racial and personal pride" (535). Toni Cade Bambara, the fine African American novelist and short story writer, points out that Brooks's first autobiography "is not a sustained dramatic narrative for the nosey, being neither the confessions of a private woman/poet or the usual sort of mahogany-desk memoir public personages inflict upon the populace at the first sign of a cardiac" (1). For Bambara it is "an extremely valuable book" that "documents the growth of Gwen Brooks."

Brooks's second autobiography, a less substantial text than the first one, was largely unnoticed. There are no major reviews of it.

BIBLIOGRAPHY

Autobiographical Works by Gwendolyn Brooks

Report from Part One. Detroit: Broadside Press, 1972.
Report from Part Two. Chicago: Third World Press, 1996.

Studies of Gwendolyn Brooks's Autobiographical Works

Bambara, Tony Cade. Rev. of Report from Part One. New York Times Book Review (January 7, 1973): 1.
Lederer, Norman. Rev. of Report from Part One. Book Seller 33 (April 73): 9.
Shucard, A.R. Rev. of Report from Part One. Library Journal 98 (February 15, 1973): 535.

CLAUDE BROWN
(1937–   )

Emmanuel S. Nelson

BIOGRAPHY

Author, activist, and lecturer, Claude Brown was born in Harlem on February 23, 1937. His father, Henry Lee Brown, was a railroad worker; his mother, Ossie Brock Brown, was employed as a maid. Both his parents were migrants to New York City from South Carolina. Like many other rural Southerners of their generation, they had moved up North in search of employment and freedom from racist abuse. What they found in the North, however, was not the utopia of their dreams; instead, they lived out their lives in a cramped apartment in a violent, crime-ridden, drug-infested section of Harlem.

Brown was born two years after his parents' arrival in Harlem. Even as a child he began to steal, get into fights with the children in the neighborhood, and experiment with alcohol and other drugs. At age eleven he was sent to Wiltwyck School, a reformatory for troubled boys. When he was released two years later, he returned to Harlem and resumed his earlier lifestyle. He joined a notorious Harlem gang and became a burglar and drug dealer. His troubles with the law soon landed him in Warwick School, another correctional institution for young delinquents.

In the summer of 1953 Brown was released from Warwick. Rather than settle down in Harlem he decided to move to Greenwich Village, where he supported himself by doing a variety of legitimate jobs—he was at times a busboy, shipping clerk, and watch repairer—and started to attend night school. In 1959 he was awarded a grant by the Metropolitan Community Methodist Church in Harlem to attend Howard University in Washington, D.C.

Shortly thereafter, at the suggestion of Ernest Papanek, a counselor whom Brown had met while he was an inmate at Warwick School, he wrote an article about growing up in Harlem. It was subsequently published in *Dissent*, a leftist Jewish periodical. Impressed by the work, an editor at Macmillan Publishing Company offered Brown a contract and an advance to write an autobiography. In 1965, the year he received his B.A. from Howard University, his autobiography, *Manchild in the Promised Land*, was published.

During the 1970s Brown attended law schools at Stanford University as well as at Rutgers University. He currently lives in New York City. During his occasional public appearances, Brown tends to generate controversy by articulating views that place him at loggerheads with the mainstream African American leadership. For example, he advocates capital punishment, favors building of new prisons and expanding the police forces in urban centers, and supports legalization of drugs (Dudley 101).

AUTOBIOGRAPHICAL WORK AND THEMES

Perhaps *Manchild in the Promised Land* can be described best as an "autoethnography." It is not only the author's life story, but it is also the story of an ethnic community at a particular moment in its history. Brown's coming-of-age narrative is embedded in the larger narrative of life in Harlem during the 1940s and 1950s. His dual objective is explicit in the book's foreword. He says he wants "to talk about the first Northern urban generation of Negroes." He calls them a "misplaced generation": They are the "sons and daughters of former Southern sharecroppers . . . the poorest people of the South, who poured into New York City during the decade following the Great Depression." *Manchild in the Promised Land*, Brown insists, is "a story of their searching, their dreams, their sorrows, their small and futile rebellions, and their endless battle to establish their own place in America's greatest metropolis—and in America itself" (7).

The terrible disillusionment of his parents' generation provides a grim backdrop to his own story of growing up in Harlem. His father retreats into alcohol to cope with the bleak realities and disabling disappointments of his life. His mother, deeply injured by the racism that she had endured in the South, believes in black inferiority. Religious fundamentalism becomes her sanctuary. Brown grows up on the streets of Harlem, and at an early age he is introduced to drugs and sex. Crime becomes a way of life. The environment breeds a range of pathologies in the people; those pathologies, in turn, accelerate the deterioration of the environment. With chilling realism Brown documents the nightmarish lives of individuals caught in that vicious cycle.

Brown's depiction of Harlem in acute crisis is relentless and at times overwhelming. People live in fear and in suspicion of one another. The white world intrudes in the form of greedy merchants, extortionist landlords, and brutal police officers. People attempt to cope, but often in ways that are self-destructive. Brown talks extensively about the success of the Nation of Islam in converting a significant number of the Harlem residents to its politicized, African American version of Islam. But Brown sees those conversions as merely futile gestures against the white power structure and as desperate attempts to mask deep-rooted bitterness and alienation. By the end of the narrative, many of Brown's friends and accomplices are either dead or in prisons.

What remains unclear, however, is precisely how Brown extricates himself from the cycles of violence, crime, and drug abuse. How does his redemption come about? His discovery of music, especially jazz, and his own musical talent appears to be part of the explanation. But Brown does not explicitly link his music with his redemption. Certainly, his decision to leave Harlem at age sixteen and relocate in Greenwich Village is critical to the redirection of his life. However, his explanation for that decision is not entirely convincing: He says that one day he realized that he might have to murder an addict who had cheated him; that realization, he claims, frightened him into getting rid of his gun and moving to Greenwich Village. But such a realization hardly sounds like a life-altering epiphany. In the context of the many crimes he had committed with impunity, it is difficult to believe that the mere thought of murder could transform him in such a profound and dramatic manner.

One fact, nevertheless, is clear: Brown does change fundamentally. He learns to manage his anger and cope with racist rejection. When he goes to night school to complete his high school education, he proves to be a good student. The church scholarship he receives allows him to earn a university degree. By age twenty-five he is awarded a book contract by a major American publishing company. His achievements, when seen in the contexts of his deeply troubled childhood and disastrous early teen years, are spectacular. Brown's life story is a quintessential American success story. Like many other American autobiographies—from Benjamin Franklin's to Malcolm X's*—*Manchild in the Promised Land* gives substance to a central myth that animates American culture: the myth of the self-made individual who overcomes monumental obstacles to gain personal and material success through hard work, self-discipline, and sheer determination.

CRITICAL RECEPTION

Brown's provocative text has elicited a variety of critical responses. Houston A. Baker Jr. locates *Manchild in the Promised Land* in the context of American naturalistic writing and argues that Brown revises "the ideological rigidities of naturalistic conventions" (58). The early sections of the autobiography, according to Baker, substantiate the naturalistic precept that environment is destiny. However, toward the end of the narrative, Brown appears to suggest—by highlighting his own success—that the environment could indeed be transcended. By doing so, Brown avoids the nihilism that is at the core of the naturalistic worldview and points to the possibilities within ourselves (59).

R.F. Kugler considers *Manchild in the Promised Land* a "well written dramatic autobiography" that "tells the story of one man and, at the same time, that of the millions of slum-imprisoned Negroes." Romulus Linney praises Brown's narrative style:

[Brown's autobiography] is written with brutal and unvarnished honesty in the plain talk of the people, in language that is fierce, uproarious, obscene and tender, but always sensible and direct. And to its enormous credit, this youthful autobiography gives its devastating portrait of life without one cry of self-pity, outrage, or malice. Claude Brown speaks for himself—and the Harlem people to whom his life is bound—with open dignity, and the effect is both shattering and deeply satisfying. (3277)

However, not all readers are so enthusiastic. Albert Murray, the formidable African American critic and theorist, chastises Brown for adopting a sociological approach that fails to capture the intricacies and subtleties of African American life and reductively views black culture in pathological terms (143). Other critics, such as Martin Tucker, find Brown's artistic skills less than impressive. Tucker acknowledges that the autobiography "fascinates by its immediate power of honest statement and unadulterated speech," but he goes on to argue that the book "disappoints as an intellectual expression" (700). Warren Miller is far less restrained in his assault: He labels Brown's autobiography a "literary disaster."

It is perhaps reasonable to conclude that *Manchild in the Promised Land*, as a sociological document, is a valuable text. It offers a concerned insider's view of a community in crisis. As a work of art, however, it suffers from a lack of stylistic sophistication and aesthetic refinement.

BIBLIOGRAPHY

Autobiographical Work by Claude Brown

Manchild in the Promised Land. New York: Macmillan, 1965.

Studies of Claude Brown's Autobiographical Work

Baker, Houston A., Jr. "The Environment as Enemy in a Black Autobiography: *Manchild in the Promised Land.*" *Phylon* 32.1 (1971): 53–59.
Balliett, Whitney. "Please, Mr. Goldberg." Rev. of *Manchild in the Promised Land*. *The New Yorker* 41 (November 13, 1965): 242.
Daniels, Guy. Rev. of *Manchild in the Promised Land*. *New Republic* 153 (September 25, 1965): 26.
Dudley, David L. "Brown, Claude." In *The Oxford Companion to African American Literature*. Ed. William L. Andrews et al. New York: Oxford University Press, 1977. 101.
Kugler, R.F. Rev. of *Manchild in the Promised Land*. *Library Journal* 90 (August 1965): 3277.
Linney, Romulus. Rev. of *Manchild in the Promised Land*. *New York Times Book Review* (August 22, 1965): 1.
Lucy, Robin. "Claude Brown." *African American Authors, 1745–1945: A Bio-Bibliographical*

Critical Sourcebook. Ed. Emmanuel S. Nelson. Westport, CT: Greenwood Press, 2000. 50–56.

Miller, Warren. Rev. of *Manchild in the Promised Land*. *Saturday Review* 48 (August 1965): 49.

Murray, Albert. *The Omni-Americans: New Perspectives on Black Experience and American Culture*. New York: Discus-Avon, 1971.

Rosenblatt, Roger. *Black Fiction*. Cambridge: Harvard University Press, 1974.

Stone, Albert E. "After *Black Boy* and *Dusk of Dawn*: Patterns in Recent Black Autobiography." *Phylon* 39.1 (1978): 18–34. Rpt. in *African American Autobiography: A Collection of Critical Essays*. Ed. William L. Andrews. Englewood Cliffs, NJ: Prentice-Hall, 1993. 171–95.

Tucker, Martin. Rev. of *Manchild in the Promised Land*. *Commonweal* 82 (September 1965): 700.

WILLIAM WELLS BROWN
(1814–1884)

Linda M. Carter

BIOGRAPHY

William Wells Brown, son of a slave mother and a white father, was born near Lexington, Kentucky, in 1814. Brown, along with his mother, was moved by their owner to Missouri Territory in 1816. He was sold in 1827 to a slaveholder in St. Louis; the new owner forced Brown to work for various employers. His dream of fleeing to Canada with his mother and sister never became reality. However, Brown successfully escaped from slavery on January 1, 1834.

After residing in Cleveland for two years, Brown moved to Buffalo. He worked on Lake Erie steamboats where, for nine years, he ferried many slaves to freedom. Brown, who was self-educated, began lecturing for antislavery societies in 1843, moved to Boston in 1847, and became a professional writer. In 1849 he traveled to England and attended the International Peace Conference in Paris. After the Fugitive Slave Law was enacted in 1850, Brown remained in England until his British friends purchased his freedom in 1854, and he returned to America. Although Brown established a medical practice in the 1860s, he continued to lecture and write. Brown died at his Chelsea, Massachusetts, home on November 6, 1884. The first African American author of belles lettres was survived by his second wife, Annie, and two daughters from his marriage to the late Elizabeth Brown: Clarissa and Josephine, author of *Biography of an American Bondman, by His Daughter* (1856).

Brown's landmark publications include the first full-length African American novel, *Clotel, or the President's Daughter: A Narrative of Slave Life in the United States* (1853); the first African American drama, *The Escape, or A Leap for Freedom* (1858); one of the first volumes of African American history, *The Black*

Man: His Antecedents, His Genius, and His Rebellion (1863); and the first military history of African Americans, *The Negro in the American Rebellion* (1867).

AUTOBIOGRAPHICAL WORKS AND THEMES

Brown, during lectures, frequently narrated his life story. Publication of his autobiographies generated a wider audience. For example, 10,000 copies of his first autobiography were sold in two years in America. Brown, orating or writing, presented the same theme—slavery's dehumanizing effects. He authored several short autobiographies including the thirty-six-paged *Memoir of William Wells Brown, an American Bondman, Written by Himself* (1859). His book-length autobiographies are *Narrative of William W. Brown, A Fugitive Slave. Written by Himself* (1847); *The American Fugitive in Europe, Sketches of Places and People Abroad* (1855); and *My Southern Home: Or the South and Its People* (1880). Brown's autobiographies are potent antidotes for nineteenth-century works by Southern whites who romanticized antebellum life.

Narrative, Brown's account of his bondage and escape, is more than his story. Along with the autobiographies of Olaudah Equiano,* Frederick Douglass,* Henry Bibb,* Harriet Jacobs, and others, *Narrative* speaks for the silent, enslaved masses who experienced similar and even more brutal treatment. *Narrative's* succession of spirit-breaking incidents mirrors atrocities suffered by countless slaves. Brown audaciously cites the first cruel act in *Narrative's* second sentence; his master steals him immediately after his birth. Also in Chapter 1, Brown relives his horrendous boyhood memory of hearing his mother's cries as she receives ten lashes from an irate overseer because she is fifteen minutes late reporting to the fields. The remaining chapters do not spare readers from vicariously experiencing additional horrors including beatings, selling of families, "religion" used to abuse slaves, slave suicides, the sexual abuse of slave women, forced abandonment of a crying baby by its slave mother, slave auctions, slaves as murder victims, and slaves betraying one another in order to protect themselves. Undoubtedly for Brown, grieving after the final encounter with his sister before she is sold south, his nadir is bidding farewell to his mother, who is chained on a boat bound for New Orleans. Such devastating incidents are powerful testimonies against slavery.

Identity is paramount in Brown's autobiographies. In *Narrative*, he is stripped of his personhood at birth because his mother is a slave. Before his thirteenth birthday, William's name is changed to Sandford when his master's infant nephew, also named William, joins the household. Since Wells Brown, a Quaker, helps Sandford during his escape, he adopts the man's nomenclatures after reclaiming William as his first name. *Narrative's* ending is optimistic as Brown begins a new life as an abolitionist.

In the epistolary *American Fugitive*, the first travel book by an African American, Brown revels in his reception by Europeans. He writes, "But no sooner was

I on British soil, than I was recognized as a man, and an equal. The very dogs in the streets appeared conscious of my manhood" (40). Loggins states, "Being in Europe is to him a rebirth" (64). Jefferson adds that Brown is no longer "a humiliated slave"; instead he is "a racial ambassador and an eloquent man of letters" ("Introduction" 6). *Narrative* and *American Fugitive* combined are a case study that documents an extraordinary journey from slavery to freedom.

My Southern Home presents antebellum and postbellum images including selfish owners, slaves who laugh at whites, slaves who outwit their masters and each other, victims of miscegenation, slaves' reaction to the Emancipation Proclamation, a former slave who is reunited with his mother, and a father of 100 children. Brown, now the elder statesman, blames slavery for the moral and social degradation of postbellum blacks; he encourages them to practice self-denial (of luxuries and expensive clothes); to be self-reliant; to unite; to not rest on the accomplishments of famous blacks such as Phillis Wheatley and Benjamin Banneker; and to become educated.

CRITICAL RECEPTION

Ellison and Metcalf offer an annotated bibliography of criticism from 1844 to 1975 of Brown's works. Sekora's analysis reveals that Brown's writings were "in eclipse" between 1870 and 1900. From 1900 to 1945, "his memory was kept alive by only a few, mostly black, scholars." The "turning point" was the mid-1960s when more critics became aware of his work; and 1969 marked the "high point" with the publication of Farrison's definitive study (52).

Narrative (1847) remains Brown's most popular autobiography. Critics have generally appreciated its understated and unadorned writing style. Loggins views *Narrative* as "one of the most readable" slave narratives primarily because of its focus on incidents (161). According to Smith, the incidents interrupt Brown's narration of his bondage and escape. "The accumulated impact of the digressive material renders the grim reality of slavery inescapable" (8). Since its publication two years after *Narrative of the Life of Frederick Douglass, an American Slave* (1845), it has been overshadowed by Douglass's first autobiography. Redding describes Brown as "the most representative Negro of the age" (25) and Douglass as "too exceptional" (25). Farrison comments that Brown's "multifarious experiences as a slave familiarized him with many departments" of slavery ("William Wells Brown" 71). Douglass prior to his escape "was limited to Maryland's Eastern Shore and Baltimore. . . . [Thus Brown made] more sweeping statements about slavery" (Andrews, *To Tell* 107–8).

American Fugitive displays a "simplicity and fluency of style" (Farrison, *William Wells Brown* 209) as well as Brown's talent for describing landscapes, architecture (Reed 40), and people. He provides powerful, memorable images of intelligent, sophisticated African Americans in London and Paris. Jefferson remarks that *American Fugitive* "is best understood as an extended argument against slavery and the contrast between an ostensibly liberal Europe and a racist United States" ("The Autobiographical" 16).

Candela considers *My Southern Home*'s "commentary . . . on the growing despair and oppression of southern blacks, [as] a direct forerunner of W.E.B. Du Bois's* magnificent [1930] work, *The Souls of Black Folk*" (30–31). Andrews identifies *My Southern Home* "as a transitional text" (11) between slave narratives and works by Charles Chestnutt, James Weldon Johnson, and other early-twentieth-century authors. "When paired with the *Narrative* . . . these two autobiographies reveal . . . the African American narrative tradition . . . evolved out of the classic era of the fugitive slave narrative and moved into the first great period of fiction at the beginning of the twentieth century" (Andrews, "Introduction" 11–12).

As scholars add to the research on African American first-person narrative, they will continue to explore the works of William Wells Brown, a progenitor of African American autobiography.

BIBLIOGRAPHY

Autobiographical Works by William Wells Brown

Narrative of William W. Brown, a Fugitive Slave. Written by Himself. Boston: Anti-Slavery Office, 1847.
Three Years in Europe: Or Places I Have Seen and People I Have Met. London: Gilpin, 1852. Published as *The American Fugitive in Europe, Sketches of Places and People Abroad.* Boston: Jewett, 1855.
Memoir of William Wells Brown, an American Bondman, Written by Himself. Boston: Anti-Slavery Office, 1859.
My Southern Home: Or the South and Its People. Boston: Brown, 1880.

Studies of William Wells Brown's Autobiographical Works

Andrews, William L. "Introduction." *From Fugitive Slave to Free Man: The Autobiographies of William Wells Brown.* New York: Mentor, 1993. 1–12.
———. "Mark Twain, William Wells Brown, and the Problem of Authority in New South Writing." In *Southern Literature and Literary Theory.* Ed. Jefferson Humphries. Athens: University of Georgia Press, 1990. 1–21.
———. *To Tell a Free Story: The First Century of Afro-American Autobiography, 1760–1865.* Urbana: University of Illinois Press, 1986.
———. "William Wells Brown." In *The Oxford Companion to African American Literature.* Ed. William L. Andrews, Frances Smith Foster, and Trudier Harris. New York: Oxford University Press, 1997. 106–7.
Butterfield, Stephen. *Black Autobiography in America.* Amherst: University of Massachusetts Press, 1974.
Candela, Gregory L. "William Wells Brown." In *Dictionary of Literary Biography.* Vol. 50.

Afro-American Writers before the Harlem Renaissance. Ed. Trudier Harris and Thadious M. Davis. Detroit: Gale, 1986. 18–31.

Davis, Charles T., and Henry Louis Gates Jr., eds. *The Slave's Narrative.* New York: Oxford University Press, 1985.

Draper, James P., ed. "William Wells Brown." In *Black Literature Criticism: Excerpts from Criticism of the Most Significant Works of Black Authors over the Past 200 Years.* Vol. 1. Detroit: Gale, 1992. 292–306.

Ellison, Curtis W., and E.W. Metcalf Jr. *William Wells Brown and Martin R. Delany: A Reference Guide.* Boston: Hall, 1978.

Farrison, William Edward. "William Wells Brown." In *Dictionary of American Negro Biography.* Ed. Rayford W. Logan and Michael R. Winston. New York: Norton, 1982. 71–73.

———. *William Wells Brown: Author & Reformer.* Chicago: University of Chicago Press, 1969.

Foster, Frances Smith. *Witnessing Slavery: The Development of Ante-bellum Slave Narratives.* Westport, CT: Greenwood Press, 1979.

Heermance, J. Noel. *William Wells Brown and Clotelle: A Portrait of the Artist in the First Negro Novel.* Hamden, CT: Archon, 1969.

Jefferson, Paul. "The Autobiographical Writings of William Wells Brown." In *Masterpieces of African-American Literature.* Ed. Frank N. Magill. New York: HarperCollins, 1992. 13–17.

———. "Introduction." *The Travels of William Brown Including* Narrative of William Wells Brown, a Fugitive Slave *and* The American Fugitive in Europe, Sketches of Places and People Abroad. New York: Markus Weiner, 1991. 1–20.

Katopes, Peter J. "William Wells Brown." In *Dictionary of Literary Biography.* Vol. 3: *Antebellum Writers in New York and the South.* Ed. Joel Myerson. Detroit: Gale, 1979. 27–29.

Loggins, Vernon. *The Negro Author: His Development in America to 1900.* 1931. New York: New York University Press, 1971.

Osofsky, Gilbert, ed. "Introduction." *Puttin' on Ole Massa: The Slave Narratives of Henry Bibb, William Wells Brown, and Solomon Northup.* New York: Harper, 1969.

Redding, J. Saunders. *To Make a Poet Black.* Chapel Hill: University of North Carolina Press, 1939.

Reed, Brian D. "William Wells Brown." In *Dictionary of Literary Biography.* Vol. 183: *American Travel Writers, 1776–1864.* Ed. James Schramer and Donald Ross. Detroit: Gale, 1997. 35–42.

Sartwell, Crispin. *Act Like You Know: African-American Autobiography and White Identity.* Chicago: University of Chicago Press, 1998.

Sekora, John. "William Wells Brown." In *Fifty Southern Writers before 1900: A Bio—bibliographical Sourcebook.* Ed. Robert Bain and Joseph M. Flora. Westport, CT: Greenwood Press, 1987. 44–54.

Smith, Sidonie. *Where I'm Bound: Patterns of Slavery and Freedom in Black American Autobiography.* Westport, CT: Greenwood Press, 1974.

Steptoe, Robert B. *From Behind the Veil: A Study of Afro-American Narrative.* Urbana: University of Illinois Press, 1979.

Yellin, Jean Fagan. "William Wells Brown." In *The Intricate Knot: Black Figures in American Literature, 1776–1863.* New York: New York University Press, 1972. 154–81.

LEROY ELDRIDGE CLEAVER
(1935–1998)

David L. Dudley

BIOGRAPHY

Leroy Eldridge Cleaver was born on August 31, 1935, in Wabbaseka, Arizona. His family moved west in 1946, first to Phoenix and then to Los Angeles where Cleaver was soon arrested for bicycle theft. He later spent time in three reform schools and was finally imprisoned in 1954 for selling marijuana. Convicted in 1958 of assault with intent to murder, Cleaver was incarcerated again, serving time in San Quentin and Folsom. While imprisoned, Cleaver became a devotee of the Nation of Islam and Malcolm X,* to whom he stayed loyal after Malcolm's break with Elijah Muhammad. Also, he read extensively and began work on the essays that would later form the basis of his best-known work, *Soul on Ice*.

Released in 1966, Cleaver helped Huey Newton and Bobby Seale found the Black Panther Party in Oakland, California, becoming its Minister of Information. He married Kathleen Neal the following year.

The year 1968 brought Cleaver triumph and trouble. *Soul on Ice* was published, creating a sensation because of its revolutionary, prophetic tone. It sold a million copies, was chosen book of the year by the *New York Times*, and made Cleaver famous and financially secure. But on April 4, he and several other Black Panthers were involved in a shoot-out with Oakland police. Cleaver was arrested and then freed on bail. Fearing a return to prison, he jumped bail and fled the country, beginning a lengthy exile in Cuba, Algeria (where he founded a branch of the Panthers), and France. During these years, Cleaver gradually became disillusioned with Marxism as he saw it practiced by repressive regimes, and he also broke with Huey Newton and the mainline Black Panther leadership. Besides his involvement with revolutionary politics, Cleaver also created and promoted a line of men's pants that featured a cod piece designed to prominently display the male genitals.

Apparently bored, lonely, and depressed by the aimlessness of his expatriate life, Eldridge Cleaver returned to the United States on November 18, 1975, to face charges stemming from the events of April 6, 1968. He remained in jail until August 1976, when bail was finally raised. Upon his release, Cleaver announced that he had converted to Christianity. He renounced his former leftist positions and declared that the United States was the freest and most democratic nation on earth. His politics became right wing, and he endorsed the candidacy of Ronald Reagan for president in 1980. Cleaver soon joined himself to prominent Christian evangelists and organized his own ministry, Eldridge Cleaver Crusades. Many of his former associates were skeptical of his newfound faith and wondered if it was a ploy to regain the spotlight while making money. Cleaver wrote of his years in exile and his conversion in his second autobiography, *Soul on Fire*, published in 1978.

Eldridge Cleaver's spiritual journey did not end with his conversion in 1976. He briefly considered forming a new church combining elements of Christianity and Islam that he proposed calling "Christlam." He later drifted from evangelical Christianity and joined the Mormon Church.

By the mid-1980s, Cleaver had become addicted to crack cocaine. In 1988 he was put on probation after a conviction for burglary and cocaine possession. He was divorced that same year. A second arrest for cocaine possession occurred in 1993, but the case was thrown out of court by a judge who ruled that Cleaver had been improperly arrested. Then, in 1994, Cleaver almost died from a blow to the head inflicted by a fellow cocaine addict. He is said to have turned from drugs and reembraced Christianity at that time.

Eldridge Cleaver died on May 1, 1998, of undisclosed causes. At the time of his death, he was working as a diversity consultant for the University of La Verne, near Los Angeles. His critics could summarize his life as one of crime and opportunism and the man as an addictive personality forever seeking a rush from violence, from leadership in any convenient cause or movement, and later, from drugs. Others may see an individual troubled from his youth, searching for a center to give meaning and coherence to his chaotic life. Was Cleaver primarily a criminal hustler, seizing any opportunity for power and prestige? Or, like Malcolm X, whom he revered, was he first and last a sincere seeker after truth, a gifted writer born to best articulate the anger and demands of black Americans during the turmoil and political ferment of the late 1960s? It is difficult to decide.

AUTOBIOGRAPHICAL WORKS AND THEMES

Cleaver published two autobiographies: *Soul on Ice* (1968) and *Soul on Fire* (1978). The first, a collection of letters, vignettes, and essays—some of which are explicitly autobiographical—is the book that made Cleaver famous as the spokesman for radical, revolutionary Black America in the years following the death of Malcolm X. *Soul on Ice* is marked by its author's canny grasp of the cataclysmic convergence of political, social, and racial forces in America in the

1960s and by the angry passion with which he denounces the efforts of the white-dominated power structure to impose its will upon the world (epitomized by the war against North Vietnam) and the country (summarized by the "war" waged against the radical Left and black Americans in general). *Soul on Fire*, a more conventional autobiographical narrative, details Cleaver's childhood and youth leading up to his imprisonment, his involvement with the Panthers in the years between his release in 1966 and his flight from the country in 1968, his exile, and his return in 1975. Modeled on the spiritual conversion narrative, *Soul on Fire* traces Cleaver's growing disillusionment with the Panthers, with communism as practiced in various regimes such as Cuba and Algeria, and with the corruption of the radical Left in general. It is structured to culminate in its author's conversion, beginning with a vision he experienced in France and leading to his formal acceptance of Jesus Christ as personal Savior after his return to the United States. This second autobiography, despite its title, lacks the "fire" of its predecessor, not to mention the rhetorical and intellectual daring that made *Soul on Ice* a bestseller in its day and now a canonical document of the radical 1960s.

The first section of *Soul on Ice*, "Letters from Prison," gives the reader an "inside" view of black inmates' lives. Cleaver describes his daily routine, his reading, his encounters with prison psychiatrists and a saintly teacher. He also notes the inmates' delighted reaction to the riots in Watts in August 1965 and his agony over the assassination of Malcolm X, whom he chooses to follow even after Malcolm's expulsion from the Nation of Islam. Most important, however, in this section Cleaver introduces the sexual metaphor that he uses throughout the book as a way of describing the predicament of the black man in mid-twentieth century America.

Forbidden to have a pinup of a white woman in his cell, Cleaver meditates upon his desire for white women over black, a hunger shared by many of the other black inmates. He acknowledges this "sickness" in himself, knowing full well that the white woman is absolutely forbidden and that contact with her may mean his death. To Cleaver, she stands for everything that America denies the black man — wealth, opportunity, even his own masculine identity. Enraged at America's "look but don't touch" prohibitions, Cleaver had once used the rape of white women as a way of expressing his fury against the establishment. Although rape was, for him, an "insurrectionary act," he could not condone his own actions. Tormented by his own desires and actions, Cleaver began to write, he tells us, to save himself. But not even writing can prevent a further complication: Cleaver informs us that he has fallen in love with his lawyer, a woman. We learn later that she is white. Cleaver ends this first section by quoting from Ossie Davis's eulogy for Malcolm X. Davis asserted that Malcolm was the black man's manhood, "our living, black manhood!" Cleaver adds, ominously, "We shall have our manhood. We shall have it or the earth will be leveled by our attempts to gain it" (66).

The second section of *Soul on Ice*, "The Blood of the Beast," offers its most important social critique. Here Cleaver focuses on the spiritual and moral bank ruptcy of America. At home, the nation oppresses and emasculates black men, permitting them success only as entertainers and athletes. Abroad, America wages its colonialist war against people seeking independence, the people of North Vietnam. By linking the struggle of black Americans for freedom with the revolutionary struggles in the Third World against colonialist powers, Cleaver makes one of his most telling points. He predicts the eventual overthrow of the oppressors as black Americans organize, joined by a new generation of white youth who share their disillusionment and willingness to fight and die for freedom.

The third section, "Prelude to Love—Three Letters," is an exchange between Cleaver and Beverly Axelrod, his white lawyer. Cleaver's gratitude to this woman who took time to listen to him and help him is clear, but it is difficult to reconcile his lavish avowals of love—"ours is one for the books, for the poets to draw new inspiration from"—with what Cleaver writes elsewhere about the "sickness" and danger involved in the love of a black man for a white woman.

This theme is worked out at great length in the final section of the work, "White Woman, Black Man." Here Cleaver offers a detailed "allegory" of racial and sexual relations. The basic point seems to be that the effeminate white male, the "Omnipotent Administrator," has so arranged things in America that he is able to eternally repress the black man, the "Supermasculine Menial." The Omnipotent Administrator causes the black man to desire the white woman (the "Ultrafeminine") and despise the black woman (the "Amazon"). Only when the dominant white society is overthrown and a new, classless society, a new world order, takes its place, will the black man be freed of his sick desire for the Ultrafeminine, regain his own masculinity, and come together with the black woman, who will then be his "Queen." Together, they will build "a New City on these ruins."

Composed of seemingly disparate parts, *Soul on Ice* is held together by this theme of the physical and mental imprisonment of the black male. Confused in his sexuality, he wrongly desires the white woman, which is a sign of his psychic emasculation. Only when revolutions succeed around the world—for the freedom struggles in places like Vietnam are closely tied to the struggle within America—will the black man reclaim his masculinity and desire his rightful consort, the black woman. They—not the white couple—will rebuild the world.

Soul on Fire is an odd conversion narrative. It recounts Cleaver's troubled early life and briefly mentions the crimes for which he was sent to prison. More important, it details his involvement with the Black Panthers, the shootout of April 1968, and the escape to Cuba. Cleaver is candid about his criminal activities in Algeria and France, how he operated a business in forged documents in order to meet his expenses. Cleaver also explains his growing disillusionment with Marxism as practiced in Cuba and Algeria, noting particularly the racism of the Cuban authorities and the corruption of the Algerians. After his move to France, Cleaver notes his increasing sense of isolation and his depression. Back in America, things are improving with the end of the Nixon administration and gains in the civil rights struggle. But Cleaver feels excluded. The turning point in Cleaver's life occurs as he contemplates suicide. While looking at the moon, he sees in a vision a series of images, his "former heroes" such as Castro, Mao, and Marx. One by one the images pass and drop from sight, "like fallen heroes." The final image is that of Jesus. Cleaver finds a Bible, reads it, and then falls peacefully asleep. When he awakens, he knows that everything will be all right and that he can safely return to the United States.

The last part of *Soul on Fire* tell of Cleaver's return, his months in prison awaiting bail, and his coming to Christ through an act of personal surrender. The former Black Panther finds himself accepted by people he formerly hated, and the book ends as Cleaver contemplates a future evangelizing for God: "I am here to be used until I am used up. I praise the Lord."

Soul on Fire is an odd and unsatisfying performance. It has the trappings of the conversion narrative without the passion. On the one hand, Cleaver never seems regretful for his former life; in fact, he writes with more passion about his life as a Black Panther and expatriate revolutionary than he does about his "new life" as a convert to Christianity. He defends the original goals of the Black Panthers and tends to portray himself more as a victim than as a man responsible for any wrongdoing. The evangelical rhetoric sounds hollow and formulaic. The writing overall is flat and often dull, and Cleaver's portrait of himself as a "soul searching for redemption" offers little in the way of truly insightful self-analysis. Perhaps *Soul on Fire* was written to introduce evangelical readers to the "new" Eldridge Cleaver and to reassure them that he had changed. Perhaps it was written to make money. But given the vagaries of Cleaver's life in the years after 1978, it is hard to read the book unironically. Today, *Soul on Ice* rings more true as a testament to the real Eldridge Cleaver.

CRITICAL RECEPTION

The first critics of *Soul on Ice* united in praising its fresh and forceful style that served admirably as the vehicle for Cleaver's denunciation of a morally corrupt and racially repressive society. They hailed Cleaver as an important new talent, a writer of imperfectly refined skills who nevertheless already possessed an "innate gift of language" (Evanier 24) employed by a "formidably analytic mind" (Mayfield 638). Maxwell Geismar is unable to say enough about Cleaver, hailing him as "one of the best cultural critics now writing" (9), who describes his times with "the most astringent accuracy, the most ruthless irony, and the most insistent truthfulness" (11). Robert Coles sums up the critical consensus: "Eldridge Cleaver is a promising and powerful writer, an intelligent and turbulent and passionate and eloquent man" (107).

Richard Gilman, the most astute of Cleaver's earliest critics, admits that as a white man he is reluctant to judge *Soul on Ice* by the same standards he would apply to books by white or even other black writers. He says of *Soul on Ice* that "in its victories of understanding, its blindnesses and incompletions, its clean or inchoate energies, its internal motives and justifications, his writing remains in some profound sense not subject to correction or emendation, or most centrally, approval or rejection by those of us who are not black" ("White Standards" 25). For this reason, Gilman is reluctant to criticize any part of the book, although he confesses that he finds it "unsatisfying intellectually, schematic and unsubtle most of the time" (10). This is the strongest criticism one finds among the early major critics of *Soul on Ice*. Julian Mayfield thinks that Cleaver spends too much time on the black male/white female issue, while David Evanier complains that Cleaver does not probe the subject in sufficient depth. Evanier also faults Cleaver that in his insistence on seeing humans only as types, as players in political and social movements, he "too often excludes complexity, ambiguity, the variety of human beings" (24).

Despite these quibbles, most critics saw *Soul on Ice* as an important literary debut, a work as Richard Gilman notes, "unsparing, unaccommodating, tough and lyrical by turns, foolish at times, unconvincing in many of its specific ideas but extraordinarily convincing in the energy and hard moral of its thinking . . . a book for which we have to make room" (25–26).

The reviews of *Soul on Fire* expressed the deep disappointment of critics who found it a poorly written, spiritless book, especially when compared to *Soul on Ice*. Barbara Nauer commends Cleaver for writing of his years as a Black Panther with "excitement, enthusiasm, and, especially where the police and the F.B.I. are concerned, an impressive venom," but asserts that the account of Cleaver's conversion is too sketchy and is therefore "seriously disappointing" (458). Robins Masters, writing in *Library Journal*, agrees that the conversion, which ought to be the center of the book, "offers very little insight" and that overall the writing is "almost wholly without the gusto and strength that made its predecessor so outstanding" (1734).

The direst criticism, however, comes from Richard Gilman, who so highly praised *Soul on Ice* thirteen years earlier. He writes that Cleaver has apparently written the book to prove his sincerity in converting to Christianity but is distressed to find that religious conversion seems to mean for Cleaver what it too often means for those who would become religious in America: "If one gains faith one has to relinquish thought" (Rev. *Soul on Fire* 32). Gilman finds that *Soul on Fire* possesses "none of the sense of urgency of its predecessor, none of its intellectual participation in crucial issues of the mind and of politics" (29) and that Cleaver's once-eloquent style has become "filled with cliches and platitudes" (31). Adds Gilman, "When his writing isn't obvious and simpleminded, it's gnarled and pretentious" (31). Gilman's distress is obvious; like others, he had harbored high hopes for Cleaver as a writer and social critic but finds that the Cleaver who spent years in exile, converted to Christianity, and returned to America to write about it has ended up instead only "a footnote to the history of his times" (30).

BIBLIOGRAPHY

Autobiographical Works by Leroy Eldridge Cleaver

Soul on Ice. New York: McGraw-Hill, 1968. Reprint, New York: Dell, 1991.
Soul on Fire. Waco, TX: Word Books, 1978.

Studies of Leroy Eldridge Cleaver's Autobiographical Works

Anderson, Jervis. "Race, Rage, and Eldridge Cleaver." *Commentary* 46 (December 1968): 63–70.
Coles, Robert. "Black Anger." *Atlantic* (June 1968): 106–7.
Dudley, David L. *My Father's Shadow: Intergenerational Conflict in African-American Men's Autobiography.* Philadelphia: University of Pennsylvania Press, 1991.
Evanier, David. "Painting Black Cardboard Figures." *The New Leader* 51. 7 (March 25, 1968): 23–24.
Geismar, Maxwell. Introduction. *Soul on Ice.* New York: McGraw-Hill, 1968.
Gilman, Richard. Rev. of *Soul on Fire. New Republic* 180. 3 (January 20, 1979): 29–32.
———. "White Standards and Negro Writing." *New Republic* (March 9, 1968): 10–12, 25.
Masters, Robin. Rev. of *Soul on Fire. Library Journal* 103 (September 15, 1979): 1734.
Mayfield, Julian. "The New Mainstream." *The Nation* 206. 20 (May 13, 1968): 638–40.
Nauer, Barbara. Rev. of *Soul on Fire. America* 140 (June 2, 1979): 458.
Rout, Kathleen. *Eldridge Cleaver.* Boston: Twayne, 1991.

LUCILLE CLIFTON
(1936–   )

Edward Whitley

BIOGRAPHY

Poet Lucille Clifton was born Thelma Lucille Sayles on June 27, 1936, to Samuel L. Sayles Sr. and Thelma Moore in Depew, New York. At the time, the town on the outskirts of Buffalo that Clifton's parents migrated to from the South was home to a large Polish community where, according to Clifton, the Sayles "were maybe the only black family in town. . . . And we were poor'" (qtd. in Weeks C10). Clifton's father, who worked in the local steel mills, was the family griot, telling his children stories about their African and African American ancestors, especially his great-grandmother Caroline, who was captured from the Dahomey Republic of West Africa and sold into slavery. Clifton's mother, who worked in a laundry, was an amateur poet who read her poems to Clifton and her siblings until her husband, who opposed the idea of his wife becoming a poet, wouldn't allow her to publish in a magazine that had accepted her work. "One of the reasons I keep writing," Clifton says, is because "I wish to persist because she did not" (qtd. in Weeks C10). While neither of her parents finished elementary school, Clifton graduated from high school at sixteen and was awarded a full scholarship to Howard University in 1953. As a drama major at Howard, she met Leroi Jones (Amiri Baraka),* A.B. Spellman, Owen Dodson, and Sterling Brown and acted in the first performance of James Baldwin's* *The Amen Corner*. She left Howard after two years and attended Fredonia State Teachers College (now the State University of New York College at Fredonia) in 1955 where, as part of a group of African American intellectuals, writers, and dramatists, she met Ishmael Reed (who later introduced her to Langston Hughes*) and her husband Fred James Clifton (1935–1984), who was teaching philosophy at the nearby University of Buffalo. Fred and Lucille married in 1958 and had six children.

Clifton's distinguished career as a poet began in 1969 when, with the support of Robert Hayden and Carolyn Kizer, she published her first book of poetry, *Good Times*. The *New York Times* chose the book as one of the ten best of the year, and Clifton received the New York Young Women's and Young Men's Hebrew Association Poetry Center Discovery Award. Since then, she has received two fellowships from the National Endowment for the Arts (1970 and 1972), was a finalist for the Pulitzer Prize in poetry (1980 and 1988), served as the poet laureate of the state of Maryland from 1979 to 1985, and won a National Book Award in 2000 for *Blessing the Boats*, among other awards. She has written ten books of poetry, seventeen children's books, and a prose memoir. Although she never graduated from college, she has received honorary doctorates from Albright College in Pennsylvania, the University of Maryland, Towson State University, and Washington College (both in Maryland) and has taught literature and creative writing at Coppin State College in Baltimore, Columbia University, George Washington University, American University, the University of California at Santa Cruz, the University of Memphis, Duke University, and St. Mary's College of Maryland, where she is currently distinguished professor of humanities.

AUTOBIOGRAPHICAL WORK AND THEMES

In *Incidents in the Life of a Slave Girl*, Harriet Jacobs writes, "What tangled skeins are the genealogies of slavery!" (Harvard University Press, 1987, 78). In her one prose autobiographical work, *Generations: A Memoir* (1976), Clifton attempts to untangle these skeins by weaving together a narrative of the death and burial of her father with stories about the various generations of her family. Consisting mostly of brief, impressionist scenes, each of the five chapters of the memoir focuses on a different ancestor that connects Clifton to the African matriarch Caroline. The overarching theme of the memoir is expressed in her rewriting of Yeats's dire vision of the modern world: "Things don't fall apart. Things hold. Lines connect in thin ways that last and last and lives become generations made out of pictures and words just kept" (78). Jerry W. Ward writes, "*Generations* is a counterweight for Yeats's theory, because Mrs. Clifton wants to make a poetic argument for the possibility of having order, wholeness, affirmation and a sense of place" (369). The memoir's themes of connectivity, hope, and memory elaborate on this philosophy.

By allowing multiple voices into her memoir—her own, her father's, and Caroline's—and by blending the events of the past and the present, Clifton shortens the distance between the generations in a way that connects the individual with generations both past, present, and future. This sense of connectivity finds its fullest expression for Clifton in family: "When the colored people came to Depew they came to be a family. Everybody began to be related in thin ways that last and last and last. The generations of white folks are just people but the generations of colored folks are families" (64). Another voice Clifton allows into her memoir is Walt Whitman's, as quotes from "Song of Myself" are used to preface every chapter. Audrey T. McCluskey says that Clifton's use of "Walt Whitman as a literary model to suggest celebration and self-discovery . . . represents an ultimate attempt at reconciliation and synthesis of family, history, and the artist" (147). Accompanying each excerpt from "Song of Myself" are photographs of Clifton's ancestors, an effect that allows for multiple points of connection between Clifton's family and American culture. Joanne M. Braxton argues that this sense of connection places Clifton firmly in the tradition of African American women's autobiography in which "many streams converge, improvising, dancing, playing, together and with the rivers from which they emerge" (208).

When Clifton's father says to her, "We fooled em, Lue, slavery was terrible but we fooled them old people. We come out of it better than they did" (58), he expresses the theme of finding hope amid the tragedy of African American history. While Clifton never glosses over the horror of slavery (" 'Oh slavery, slavery,' my Daddy would say. 'It ain't something in a book, Lue. Even the good parts was awful' " [22]), she searches through her family history for moments of hope. In discussing her great-grandmother Lucy, the woman who was legally hanged for killing the white father of her child ("they didn't lynch her, Lue, cause she was Mammy Ca'line's child, and from Dahomey women" [34]), Clifton shows how this tragic family story could still be a source of hope and pride: "First Black woman legally hanged in the state of Virginia. He said Black like that, back then. And he would be looking proud" (27–28). This sense of hope fraught with tragedy is most fully expressed when Clifton's Aunt Lucille addresses the African matriarch Caroline at Clifton's father's grave, saying, "Mammy it's 1969, and we're still here" (59). The simultaneous sense of triumph and desperation at being "still here" despite the destructive influences of a racist culture resonates throughout the memoir.

When her father's coffin is lowered into the grave, Clifton says, "I wanted to tell him something, my insides screamed. I remember everything. I believe" (59), transforming the nadir of the narrative into an apotheosis of memory. Clifton identifies one of the reasons for writing the memoir as simply that "[s]omebody had to remember" (qtd. in Rowell 66). She reasons that "if the last person who remembers is gone, what is left? What will be left of my mother? I must stay alive so that in a way my mother stays alive" (qtd. in Rowell 58). Memory serves as a touchstone throughout the memoir to connect the generations of the past with those of the present and future.

CRITICAL RECEPTION

In the *New York Times Book Review*, Reynolds Price identifies *Generations* as an elegy, writing that Clifton "produced a short but eloquent eulogy of her parents. As with most elegists, her purpose is perpetuation and celebration, not judgment" (7). He calls attention to Clifton's substitution of conventional chronological narrative for "clusters of brief anecdote [that] gather around two poles, the deaths of father and mother" (7). In a further discussion of how the form of the memoir contributes to the focus on memory in African American families and communities, Price writes that "this seemingly random collection of memories becomes apparent only at the end (a funeral oration) in a modification of the style and language of America's great orators, Negro preachers" (8). *The New Yorker* review also calls attention to how the form of the memoir creates the effect of impressionistic memory: "It is as if the author were showing us a cherished family album . . . [and] as a result, we are left with some fairly mythical impressions of people, especially of her father" ("Generations" 139). Carol Muske writes in *Parnasus* that *Generations* "is not so much a memoir as a rocking-chair history, a tribute to a state of mind that survives. . . . The incidents recounted here, held together by a loose prose-poem mortar, swell with biblical intensity, tales of slavery and matriarchy" (113).

Given Clifton's insistence that "lives become generations made out of pictures and words just kept" (*Generations* 78), Cheryl Wall shows how the combination of the text of the memoir and the photographs of Clifton's ancestors that appear before every chapter serves as an imaginative reconstruction of Clifton's family legacy. She writes, "Representing a past that is largely unwritten, caught in photographs, and remembered only in fragments of music and memory demands of writers both a visionary spirit and the capacity for dramatic revisions of form" (552). As slavery has disrupted the traditional way that stories are passed down from generation to generation in African American families, Clifton's multiple revisions of form throughout the memoir—her combination of image and text, her inclusion of quotes from "Song of Myself" and the Book of Job, the modified family genealogies she offers at the end of the text, the multiple narrative voices, the silences kept and broken—create a new way of telling and preserving these stories. Wall also connects Clifton's memoir with the writing of other contemporary African American women, an important connection given that Toni Morrison was the editor of *Generations*.

Edward Whitley argues that *Generations* thematizes the two obstacles Clifton must overcome as an African American woman writer in order to, in Clifton's own words, "[bring] to American literature a long missing part of itself" (qtd. in Rowell 67): the tradition of male autobiography, which stresses the individual self over familial or communal connections, and the African American tradition of mourning stories, which, as Karla F.C. Holloway argues, replaces the conventional literary theme of an individual's quest for identity with the body's search for a safe harbor. Whitley shows that Clifton uses the "Song of Myself" epigraphs to signify the dual potential in Whitman for both individuality and collectivity and that she negotiates the tradition of mourning stories by making memory of the dead the site for, rather than an affront to, the possibility of identity.

BIBLIOGRAPHY

Autobiographical Work by Lucille Clifton

Generations: A Memoir. New York: Random House, 1976.

Studies of Lucille Clifton's Autobiographical Work

Braxton, Joanne M. *Black Women Writing Autobiography: A Tradition within a Tradition.* Philadelphia: Temple University Press, 1989.

Evans, Mari, ed. *Black Women Writers (1950–1980): A Critical Evaluation.* New York: Doubleday, 1984.

"Generations, by Lucille Clifton." *The New Yorker* (April 5, 1976): 138–39.

Holloway, Karla F.C. "Cultural Narratives Passed On: African American Mourning Stories." *College English* 59.1 (1997): 32–40.

Lazer, Hank. "Blackness Blessed: The Writings of Lucille Clifton." *The Southern Review* 25.3 (1989): 760–70.

McCluskey, Audrey T. "Tell the Good News: A View of the Works of Lucille Clifton." In *Black Women Writers (1950–1980): A Critical Evaluation.* Ed. Mari Evans. New York: Doubleday, 1989. 139–49.

Muske, Carol. "Ourselves as History." *Parnasus* 4.2 (1976): 111–21.

Plant, Deborah. "Good Woman: Poems and a Memoir, 1969–1980." *Praire Schooner* 62.1 (1989): 115–17.

Price, Reynolds. "A Daughter's Memories." *New York Times Book Review* (March 14, 1976): 7–8.

Rowell, Charles H. "An Interview with Lucille Clifton." *Callaloo* 22.1 (1999): 56–72.

Wall, Cheryl A. "Sifting Legacies in Lucille Clifton's *Generations.*" *Contemporary Literature* 40.4 (1999): 552–74

Ward, Jerry W. "*Generations: A Memoir,* by Lucille Clifton." *New Orleans Review* 5.4 (1977): 369–70.

Weeks, Linton. "Poetry's Persistent Listener: Lucille Clifton Pays Attention to the Voice of What Is True." *Washington Post,* November 18, 2000, C1+.

Whitley, Edward. " 'A Long Missing Part of Itself': Bringing Lucille Clifton's *Generations* into American Literature." *MELUS* 26.2 (Summer 2001): 47–64.

ANGELA YVONNE DAVIS
(1944–)

Emmanuel S. Nelson

BIOGRAPHY

Angela Yvonne Davis was born on January 26, 1944, in Birmingham, Alabama. Hers was a middle-class family: Her father, Frank Davis, and her mother, Sally Davis, were college graduates who taught at local high schools. Her father's business ventures augmented the family income, and she grew up in materially comfortable surroundings.

Frank Davis, an entirely fearless man, moved his family into an all-white suburb of Birmingham in 1948. Their arrival provoked hostility, but soon several black families began to purchase homes in the neighborhood. The white response turned violent. The homes of black families were routinely bombed; the bombings became so frequent that the neighborhood was nicknamed "Dynamite Hill." The anger and defiance that mark her later activist years no doubt stem at least partly from her childhood experiences in a violently racist Birmingham.

At age fourteen Davis won a scholarship from the American Friends Service Committee, a philanthropic organization set up to provide opportunities for black teenagers from the segregated South to attend integrated schools in the North. In 1961 she graduated from Elizabeth Irwin High School in Greenwich Village, New York City; later that year she enrolled at Brandeis University in Waltham, Massachusetts, on a full scholarship. She spent her junior year at the Sorbonne in Paris. A brilliant student, Davis graduated magna cum laude from Brandeis in 1965 and began graduate study at the University of Frankfurt, Germany, later that year. After two years she returned to the United States and enrolled at the University of California at San Diego. Within a year she received her master's degree and began to work toward a doctorate.

Before she completed her Ph.D. she accepted the offer of an assistant professorship in the Philosophy Department at the University of California campus at Los Angeles (UCLA). By then she had become a militant political activist, a vocal critic of the nation's domestic and international policies, and a member of the Black Panther Party as well as the American Communist Party. Despite her excellent record as a dynamic teacher and active scholar, she was fired from the university job at the end of her first year. Her membership in the Communist Party as well as her off-campus political activities, she was told, were incompatible with her academic appointment at a state-funded institution. The individual primarily responsible for the firing was Ronald Reagan, who was then the governor of California: The University Board of Regents, which voted to terminate Davis's employment on the UCLA campus, acted on Reagan's reactionary insistence.

Angela Davis's involvement in the movement to free the Solidad Brothers—three black inmates at the Solidad Prison in California who were accused of murdering a notoriously racist white prison guard in 1970—led to some of the most spectacular events of her life and made her an international figure. The movement culminated in violence at the Marin County Courthouse. Davis was not involved in the shootout, but a gun registered in her name was. Facing charges of "murder, kidnapping, and conspiracy" (Davis 15), she became a fugitive. Captured several weeks later by federal agents, Davis spent sixteen months in prison awaiting trial. The trial generated worldwide interest. On June 4, 1972, she was acquitted of all charges.

Angela Davis: An Autobiography was published in 1974. Davis's editor at Random House, which published the book, was Toni Morrison—the distinguished African American novelist who in 1993 won the Nobel Prize for Literature. In the last two decades Davis has authored and edited several volumes on issues of race, gender, and class. A cosmopolitan intellectual—Davis is fluent in English, French, German, and Spanish—she brings to her scholarship a clear political vision, strong grounding in Marxist and feminist theories, and impressive analytical sophistication.

From 1979 through 1991 Davis taught at San Francisco State University. In 1980 as well as in 1984 she was a Communist Party candidate for the office of the vice president of the United States. Currently she is a tenured professor in the History of Consciousness Program at the University of California campus at Santa Cruz. Although she is largely ignored by the mainstream media, she remains a fiercely committed activist. Prison reform is now one of the major items on her political agenda. She argues that the alarming growth in the number of prisons and prisoners in the United States during the last fifteen years or so has given rise to a prison-industrial complex sustained by an insidious collusion between punishment industry and corporate economy. And she works closely with a number of leftist organizations committed to political reform and progressive change.

AUTOBIOGRAPHICAL WORK AND THEMES

In the introduction to *Angela Davis: An Autobiography*, the author makes it clear that hers is not a conventional self-representational narrative. Her "instinctive reserve" (viii), she admits, would not allow her to write a thoroughly confessional text. As an intensely private, self-effacing individual and a very reluctant public figure, she does not want to "personalize and individualize" (viii) history; rather, she opts to use the autobiographical format to assess the public significance of her experiences. The result, therefore, is a political autobiography: The narrative focus is not on the personal but on the political dimensions of her dramatic and eventful life.

Davis's autobiography constitutes one of the boldest interventions in the American political discourse. Her narrative is a part of her larger emancipatory project. Her life story reflects her radical commitment to fundamental social transformation. The political vision inscribed in her text is shaped by a finely honed oppositional consciousness; she directs her resistant gaze at the founding myths of her nation and the social, judicial, political, and economic structures that help validate and legitimize those myths.

At the core of Davis's autobiography is an alleged crime. In February 1970 she had become actively involved in organizing the campaign to free the Solidad Brothers. One of them was George Jackson, with whom she soon developed a romantic friendship. On August 7, 1970, there was an armed revolt at the Marin County Courthouse initiated by Jonathan Jackson, George's seventeen-year-old brother. The shootout resulted in the deaths of the presiding judge, two black defendants, and Jonathan himself; several guards, attorneys, and spectators were wounded. One of the guns used by Jonathan Jackson was registered in Angela Davis's name. Although she was nowhere near the scene of the violence, she was implicated in the revolt and charged with murder, kidnapping, and conspiracy. She had been, for quite some time, under surveillance by local and federal law enforcement agencies because of her memberships in the Black Panther Party and the Communist Party. Jonathan Jackson's use of her gun therefore became a convenient basis to criminalize her and then attempt to silence her politically. The Federal Bureau of Investigation (FBI) placed her on its list of the Ten Most Wanted. Davis's autobiography is a detailed account of the events that led to the shootout, her flight and subsequent capture, her imprisonment while awaiting trial, the trial itself in which she eloquently defended herself, and her eventual acquittal. Woven into this gripping legal drama is the less public story of Davis's childhood, her education, and the formation of her radical political philosophy.

Written in forcefully clear and highly readable prose, *Angela Davis: An Autobiography* is divided into six parts. The opening section, titled "Nets," begins with a riveting account of her life as a fugitive. The events leading up to her capture make the early pages of the autobiography resemble a suspense thriller. The scene of her capture at a hotel in Manhattan by a large contingent of FBI agents seems almost scripted for a Hollywood movie. And there is high drama ahead. After weeks of incarceration in the roach- and rat-infested Women's House of Detention in Greenwich Village, she is driven to McGuire Air Force Base in New Jersey and flown on a U.S. military jet to California, where she is to stand trial. The routine intimidation and harassment that are a part of these events do not break her spirit. Davis remains defiant.

The next two sections of the autobiography, titled "Rocks" and "Water," respectively, focus on Davis's early years in a viciously racist Birmingham; her adolescent years at Elizabeth Irwin High School in New York City where teachers' political beliefs ranged from liberal to radical Left; her young adulthood on the campus of Brandeis University; and her epiphanic discovery of Utopian Socialism. *The Communist Manifesto* hits her "like a bolt of lightning"; she reads it "avidly, finding in it answers to many of the seemingly unanswerable dilemmas" that had haunted her (109). She begins "to see the problems of Black people within the context of a larger working-class movement" (110). "The emancipation of the proletariat," she begins to believe, could become the "foundation . . . for the emancipation of all oppressed groups in society" (110). Her intellectual curiosity about Marxism leads to her serious study of philosophy and political theory. At Brandeis University, she becomes a student of Professor Herbert Marcuse, the author of *Eros and Civilization* and a formidable Marxist scholar.

Davis spends the academic year 1963–1964 at the Sorbonne in Paris. Europe helps internationalize her perspective. To Europe she returns the following year, this time for graduate study at the University of Frankfurt, Germany. However, the images of the civil rights movement in the United States, which she sees on television screens and in newspapers, begin to haunt her. Intent on being part of the political scene, she decides to return to the United States in 1967.

Titled "Flames," the fourth section of the autobiography documents Davis's political activities while she continues her graduate studies at the University of California at San Diego and, subsequently, as an assistant professor at UCLA. Her increasing radicalism—manifested in her visit to Cuba and connections with the Black Panthers and the communists—soon makes her one of the most visible figures in the militant fringe of the civil rights movement. She becomes the target of appalling harassment by law enforcement agencies. Police officers routinely and often without any legitimate reason stop her on the streets; her critics infiltrate her classrooms posing as students to disrupt her lectures; and she receives death threats on a daily basis. Meanwhile, she mounts a legal challenge to Ronald Reagan's attempt to oust her from her teaching job and organizes a massive effort to free the Solidad Brothers. The fourth section ends with a concise account of the outbreak of violence in the Marin County Courthouse on August 7, 1970—an event that she learns from television reports. It precipitates her flight from California to evade the police, prompting the FBI to initiate a nationwide search for her.

The last two sections, titled "Walls" and "Bridges," respectively, chronicle Davis's suspiciously lengthy imprisonment at Marin County Jail awaiting trial and the trial itself. The autobiography ends on a note of legal triumph and personal vindication: An all-white jury returns a verdict of not guilty on all charges. Angela Davis is free.

Ever since Davis emerged as a political figure in the late 1960s, she has provoked a range of responses. Her detractors demonize her; her public image constructed and circulated by the mainstream media has led uninformed people to view her as a misguided, thuggish creature with an insane political agenda. Her supporters, both in the United States and around the world, see her as an iconic figure who is simultaneously a symbol of the institutional victimization of African Americans and an inspiring embodiment of black resistance. Her autobiography helps dismantle some of the myths and misconceptions that surround her. Given her decision to write a "*political* autobiography" (xvi), regrettably the narrative offers only a sketchy outline of her personal life. Her relentless foregrounding of the public events of her life blurs the private side of her personality. However, when we do get fleeting glimpses into her interior life, we find a highly complex individual vastly different from the monodimensional mythical character frozen in the public imagination. She is neither a demonic figure nor a flawless heroine.

In the pages of the autobiography, Davis emerges as immensely courageous and yet deeply vulnerable. Her intellectual sophistication is amply evident. We sense her instinctive identification with the most victimized members of society. In her articulate challenges to the various structures of oppression, we see her quiet decency. However, what is somewhat troubling is her willingness, at least at the time she composed her autobiography, to see Marxism as a panacea for all social malaise. Her narrative of her epiphanic discovery of Marxism and her conversion to that secular faith is startlingly similar to the descriptions of religious conversions so common in early African American autobiographies. However, there is a poignancy to her unassailable faith in her newly found "religion." It is apparent that the romantic streak in her draws her to a totalizing belief system that promises to create a heaven on earth. What frames her personal philosophy and political activism is her Utopian vision of a just and genuinely emancipated global community of human beings. The clarity of that vision is the foundation for her action. Her autobiography allows us to see, if only briefly, the woman behind the public activist persona: We see a visionary, a dreamer.

CRITICAL RECEPTION

Most reviewers were disappointed that Davis opted to write an essentially political autobiography that does not offer many details of her personal life. Elinor Langer articulates this general disappointment most clearly: "I wish she had chosen to present herself in a slightly more rounded way. Psychologizing can undercut the political argument, true, but political autobiography can be propaganda . . . I think she is too large to be confined in stereotypes, even heroic ones" (5). Walter Clemons echoes Langer's sentiments: "One can respect Angela Davis's austerity and self-effacement, but it's hard not to find her book a little dry"

Clemons concludes, "Instead of revealing herself, she has made an attempt to divest herself of individuality, and in that sacrificial effort she has pretty thoroughly succeeded" (97).

Jan Webster praises the autobiography for exposing the "horrors of the penal system"; that story, he points out, "needs telling, and [Davis] tells it powerfully and well" (31). But he wonders if Angela Davis should have written an autobiography at the young age of thirty. He finds the work too narrowly focused on her legal battles without providing a sense of the wider political history of the 1960s. Janet Burroway infers that Davis's autobiography "is not a good book" because it lacks literary merit, but that aesthetic judgment, she concedes, should not "undo the uncompromising courage" (594) of the author.

The best and most substantial discussion of Davis's book is in *Autobiography as Activism: Three Black Women of the Sixties*. The author, Margo Perkins, highlights the pedagogical content and uses of Davis's text along with those of Assata Shakur and Elaine Brown. She argues that these autobiographies are designed to further the objectives of liberatory pedagogy and that Davis, especially, is engaged in teaching her readers the need to foster critical literacy in order to understand the interlocking systems of oppression and to forge an activist sensibility geared toward effecting meaningful social transformation.

BIBLIOGRAPHY

Autobiographical Work by Angela Yvonne Davis

Angela Davis: An Autobiography. New York: Random House, 1974.

Studies of Angela Yvonne Davis's Autobiographical Work

Burroway, Janet. "All American." *New Statesman* 89.2302 (May 2, 1975): 593–94.

Carney, Francis. Rev. of *Angela Davis: An Autobiography*. *New York Review of Books* 21 (November 28, 1974): 17.

Clemons, Walter. "While Watts Burned." *Newsweek* (October 28, 1974): 97, 100.

Kent, George E. "The 1975 Black Literary Scene: Significant Developments." *Phylon* 37.1 (March 1976): 100–115.

Langer, Elinor. Rev. of *Angela Davis: An Autobiography*. *New York Times Book Review* (October 27, 1974): 5.

Lester, Julius. "Young, Female, Black and Revolutionary." *The Progressive* 39.2 (February 1975): 54–55.

Minogue, Kenneth. Rev. of *Angela Davis: An Autobiography*. *Times Literary Supplement* (November 7, 1975): 1318.

Perkins, Margo V. *Autobiography as Activism: Three Black Women of the Sixties*. Jackson: University of Mississippi Press 2000.

Webster, Jan. "Political Fury." *The New Republic* 171.20 (November 16, 1974): 30–31.

LUCY A. DELANEY
(c. 1830–c. 1890s?)

Loretta G. Woodard

BIOGRAPHY

Lucy A. Berry was born into slavery in St. Louis, Missouri, around 1830. Nancy, her only sibling, escaped to Toronto in the early 1840s, where she raised her own children in a world free from slavery. In 1832 their father, a mulatto servant, was torn from his wife and children and sold in the South. Polly Berry, their mother, who had been kidnapped as a child and sold into slavery, escaped to Chicago, Illinois, when Lucy was twelve. While there, she was arrested and then returned to St. Louis, where she secured her freedom in court owing to her freeborn status. For the next few years she would be preoccupied with obtaining the freedom of her second daughter, Lucy Ann Berry, who anxiously awaited her day of liberation.

At age twelve, Lucy refused to be whipped by her mistress, Mrs. Mitchell, and was ordered to be sold for insubordination, but she escaped to Chicago, where her mother was living. Since Lucy was the daughter of a freeborn and could not be held captive legally, her mother sued Mr. D.D. Mitchell for legal possession of her child, on September 8, 1842 (33). Although bond was set at $2,000, Lucy was put in jail, where she remained for seventeen months, pending resolution of her case (34).

Lucy's freedom began at age fourteen in February 1844. She and her mother supported themselves in Chicago with their trades. Lucy was an expert seamstress, and Polly was a first class laundress. Both were able to earn enough money for Polly to make a surprise visit to see her daughter Nancy in Toronto.

In 1845, Lucy married Frederick Turner, and her mother moved with the couple to Quincy, Illinois. Their union together was short lived, for Frederick died in an explosion aboard the steamboat *Edward Bates* on which he worked.

Soon after Frederick's death, Lucy and her mother returned to St. Louis and resumed their lives. In 1849, she married Zachariah Delaney of Cincinnati, a marriage that lasted for more than four decades. The couple had four children, three daughters and one son, two of whom died in childhood and the other two in their early twenties. As she reflects on their deaths, she writes, "[O]ne consolation was always mine! Our children were born free and died free! Their childhood and my maternity were never shadowed with a thought of separation" (58). Delaney's mother remained with her until her death. After forty-five years of separation, Delaney and her sister Nancy were briefly united with their father, who returned to more familiar surroundings when he learned of his wife's death.

For the next few decades, Lucy Ann Berry Turner Delaney led an active life. She joined the Methodist Episcopal Church in 1855. As an elected officer, she worked tirelessly to benefit others through several organizations, such as the Female Union, the Daughters of Zion, Daughters of the Tabernacle and Knights of Tabor, and the Shaw Woman's Relief Corps. Of her successes Delaney states, "Considering the limited advantages offered me, I have made the best use of my time . . . to benefit those for whom I live" (63). Delaney's autobiography, *From Darkness Cometh the Light; or, Struggles for Freedom*, which records her life as a slave and her desperate attempt to be a free black woman, was published in 1891. Delaney died sometime during the 1890s.

AUTOBIOGRAPHICAL WORK AND THEMES

Although Delaney's only literary work, *From Darkness Cometh the Light; or, Struggles for Freedom*, restates a number of the same themes explored by her literary predecessors, it is, nevertheless, a valuable contribution to the body of existing slave narratives, especially by women. By focusing on the dominant theme of the quest for freedom in her sixty-four-page autobiography, Delaney celebrates the mother's crucial role in the liberation of her children and, by extension, indicates the significance of strong mother-daughter relationships.

Recalling her "pathway" from slavery to freedom, Delaney states, "My pathway was thorny enough, and though there were no roses without thorns, I had thorns in plenty with no roses" (19). However, Delaney's "pathway" is made easier with the love, support, and determination of her mother, Polly Berry, who escaped to freedom when Delaney was twelve but had to prove that "she was a free woman" (24). Like Harriet Jacobs, her main concern, was to "save" her daughters from the exploitation of slavery. Polly had already successfully "instructed" her daughter Nancy to escape to Toronto. Delaney recalls her mother's jubilation: "She would dance, clap her hands, and, waving them above her head, would indulge in one of those weird negro melodies, which so charm and fascinate the listener" (19). From this moment on, Delaney is inspired by the power of her mother to manipulate the system. In her eyes and in the eyes of others, Polly is her hero, and Delaney becomes increasingly more optimistic of her flight. "I was beginning to plan for freedom, and was forever on the alert for a chance to escape and join my sister" (19). Delaney's plans for freedom, however, were abruptly interrupted when she was imprisoned for almost two years for escaping to Chicago. Of this sad state, she explains, "My only crime was seeking for that freedom which was my birthright!" (35).

Though "thorns," obstacles, and tragedies were still ahead for Delaney, her mother was continuously by her side. It was her mother's promise, "by the help of God and a good lawyer" (35), that won her daughter's freedom in a St. Louis court. Using the courtroom as the platform for justice, Delaney reveals how Polly cleverly and bravely takes on the judicial system, risking the possibility of her own exposure. But she is more than confident in the lawyer, Judge Edward Bates, "a distinguished statesman . . . of Quaker descent" (35), and must take the risk at any cost. Polly's heroic act shows the extent of a mother's unselfish love, support, sacrifice, and dedication, *repayable* only by a special "gaze" and moment. Delaney describes such a moment upon her mother's hearing the good news. She writes, "As soon as she heard of the result, she hurried to meet me, and hand in hand we gazed into each others eyes and saw the light of freedom there" (50).

The direct "gaze" further indicates the genuine respect they have for each other and the incredible bond they have developed as mother and daughter. It is a bond that develops into a lengthy and amicable relationship; according to the autobiography, Polly lived with her daughter until her death, an opportunity that many young slave or free daughters, such as Mary Prince, Harriet Jacobs, Mattie Jackson, Annie Burton, and Kate Drumgoold, did not have with their mothers. Consequently, when she recalls "that checkered time" (50), she pays a special tribute to her mother who had the "virtues of an honest woman!" (50) and praises her for being "steadfast." She writes, "Blessed mother! how she clung and fought for me. No work was too hard for her to undertake. . . . [S]he pursued her way, until my freedom was established by every right and without a questioning doubt!" (45).

In *From Darkness Cometh the Light*, Delaney's use of the journey motif and other common conventions of the slave narrative permits us to follow the path of a mother and daughter who refuse to allow the evil institution of slavery to keep them apart and to break their spirit. Their persistence, like that of Mary Seacole's,* ends in victory, and it is an inspiration to all readers. Hence, Delaney's autobiography is a remarkable testimony to how we can succeed, blacks "as well as whites, if given the same chance" (64). Inspired by her mother's tremendous impact on her life, Delaney dedicated the rest of her life to the service of others, employing "what few talents the Lord [had] bestowed on [her]" (63).

CRITICAL RECEPTION

Delaney's autobiography has received very favorable but limited critical attention. Upon close observation, historian and literary critic William Andrews notes in his introduction to the 1988 reprint of Delaney's narrative that it illustrates the continuing vitality of the slave narrative and extends considerably the black female literary tradition (xxix). Specifically, when compared to her literary predecessors, Andrews further observes that her story "extends beyond her family's reunion in freedom to record, in brief, the success she has made in the quarter-century since the end of the Civil War" (xxx).

Acknowledging that the art of writing African American autobiography is not only writing "from behind the veil," Lindon Barrett focuses on how Delaney "exposes the dual fictions of unity and autonomy in the autobiographical subject and its claim to self-identity" (123–124). In a more recent critical study, Verner Mitchell credits Delaney's work as far from being "a little tale," as she calls it. "Instead," he comments, "this modest description is merely the first instance of the narrative's fruitful use of 'masks' as a trope" (99).

With the 1988 reprint of the autobiography in *Six Women's Slave Narratives*, perhaps a wider readership will increase scholarly interest in Delaney's single work.

BIBLIOGRAPHY

Autobiographical Work by Lucy A. Delaney

From the Darkness Cometh the Light; or Struggles for Freedom. St. Louis: J. Smith, 1891. Rpt. in *Six Women's Slave Narratives*. Ed. William L. Andrews. New York: Oxford University Press, 1988.

Studies of Lucy A. Delaney's Autobiographical Work

Andrews, William L. Introduction. *Six Women's Slave Narratives*. New York: Oxford University Press, 1988. xxix–xli.

Barrett, Lindon. "Self-Knowledge, Law and African American Autobiography: Lucy A. Delaney's *From the Darkness Cometh the Light*." In *The Culture of Autobiography: Constructions of Self-Representation*. Ed. Robert Folkenflik. Stanford, CA: Stanford University Press, 1993. 104–24.

Mitchell, Verner D. "Lucy A. Delaney." In *African American Authors, 1745–1945: A Bio-Bibliographical Critical Sourcebook*. Ed. Emmanuel S. Nelson. Westport, CT: Greenwood Press, 2000. 98–100.

SAMUEL R. DELANY
(1942–   )

Karl L. Stenger

BIOGRAPHY

Samuel Ray Delany Jr., known as "Chip" to his friends, was born on April 1, 1942, in New York City as the oldest of two children of Samuel Ray Delany Sr., a funeral director, and Margaret Carey Boyd Delany, a librarian. Looking back at his youth, Delany stated in 1974: "I did not have a happy childhood. Nobody does. I did, however, have a privileged one" (*Longer Views* 308). Much of his unhappiness stemmed from Delany's strained relationship with his father, whom he experienced as a constantly angry and anxious man who was incapable of expressing love. A second reason for Delany's unhappiness was the alienation he felt at school as one of only a few black children in a mostly white environment. In addition, Delany was dyslexic, and because his condition remained undiagnosed, he was forced into remedial reading and spelling classes. Delany's unhappiness at home and at school resulted in rebellious behavior. On several occasions he ran away from home.

Because it was obvious that Delany was gifted and precocious, he was encouraged to explore the arts and the sciences. His parents were able to send their son to the private and progressive Dalton Elementary School in Midtown Manhattan and later to the prestigious Bronx High School of Science. From the age of six on, Delany spent his summers at camp where he was able to explore his interest in music, dance, and literature. He was exposed to folk music by Pete Seeger, learned to play the violin and guitar, and began reading science fiction stories. At camp he also realized that he was sexually more attracted to boys than girls. He secretly started to write down his erotic fantasies, discovering "a trade off between writing and desire" (*The Motion   1960 1965*, 54). When Delany's mother happened upon these homoerotic fantasies, which were based on sword-and-sorcery tales, she arranged biweekly therapy sessions with a psychiatrist.

The publication of an essay by one of Delany's female cousins in the high school's literary magazine caused a considerable stir in his family and made the boy aware of the power of writing. Throughout high school he wrote novels that were based on real characters and events. On the strength of his adolescent novel manuscripts Delany received a scholarship in 1960 to the Breadloaf Writers' Conference in Middlebury, Vermont, where Robert Frost advised him: "Do it your own way. Don't let anyone else tell you how to do it" (Peplow and Bravard, 18).

Shortly after Delany started attending the College of the City of New York, his father died of lung cancer. Delany left home and started a bohemian life in New York's East Village together with the prodigiously talented poet Marilyn Hacker, whom he had met in high school and whom he had married on August 24, 1961, after she had become pregnant during their second sexual experiment. Two months later Marilyn miscarried. When she was hired as an assistant editor at Ace Books, a small publishing company specializing in science fiction novels, Hacker complained to Delany about the dearth of quality science fiction. In response, he submitted his first science fiction novel *The Jewels of Aptor*, which was published December 1, 1962, in a severely truncated version. Delany dropped out of college and continued writing science fiction novels while eking out a meager living performing folk music in coffeehouses.

When his next novel was rejected, Delany decided to infuse his writing with more density and seriousness. His science fiction novels became stylistically and structurally more sophisticated, and Delany quickly gained the reputation of science fiction's newest "wunderkind." In 1967 he switched from Ace Books to the more prestigious Doubleday, and *Nova*, his first hardcover book, was published in 1968. Several Nebula and Hugo Awards followed, and Delany was occasionally, albeit mistakenly, associated with the "New Wave" group of science fiction writers.

Although Delany and his wife were living apart most of the time, they decided to have a child together. On January 14, 1974, Iva Alyxander Hacker-Delany was born in London, and both parents shared equally in her upbringing even after their divorce in 1980.

The publication of *Dhalgren* in 1975 signaled a new stage in Delany's career. This ambitious and experimental novel, which was informed by Delany's interest in poststructuralism and semiotics, stretched the limits of the genre to such a degree that some critics denied it was science fiction. Others, however, praised it as Delany's magnum opus. Never one to remain stagnant, Delany turned to the sword-and-sorcery subgenre and published the Neveryon cycle between 1979 and 1987. This series of four books constitutes, according to Michael J. Emery, "Delany's most sustained achievement as a gay writer" (105). Referring to his science fiction novel *Stars in My Pocket Like Grains of Sand* (1984), which featured gay characters and themes and which was supposed to be followed by the as-yet-unpublished sequel *The Splendor and Misery of Bodies, of Cities*, Delany stated in 1984: "[M]ore and more I'm coming to see my audience as gay and male" (216). For his lifetime contribution to gay and lesbian literature Delany received the fifth William Whitehead Memorial Award in 1993.

In the late 1970s Delany was embraced by the academy. He was invited by the State University of New York at Buffalo in 1975 to be Butler Professor of English, and in 1977 he became a senior fellow at the Center for Twentieth Century Studies at the University of Wisconsin at Milwaukee. He taught workshops at various writers' conferences, gave presentations during annual meetings of the Modern Language Association, and was a visiting fellow of Cornell University's Society for the Humanities in 1986. Since 1988 he has been a professor of comparative literature at the University of Massachusetts, Amherst, serving as acting department head for two terms.

As a consequence, Delany's literary output has shifted toward autobiographical and theoretical writings. He is now considered to be one of the most preeminent theoreticians of science fiction and an astute cultural critic. Since the fall of 1999 Delany has been on leave from the University of Massachusetts, rededicating himself to his writing, and his fans are eagerly awaiting future publications.

AUTOBIOGRAPHICAL WORKS AND THEMES

Many of Delany's fictional works contain autobiographical elements, such as direct quotations from his journals or fictionally transformed "fragments of Delany's own character and concerns and of actual episodes in his life" (Lunde 116). Delany has cautioned readers and interpreters of his novels not to ignore the fictional context in which his journal entries are embedded. While he admits that a quotation in "The Tale of Plagues and Carnivals" will always have the status of a journal account—in other words, that the text will always represent truth appropriate for that genre ("What I described, I saw.")—Delany insists that, as a piece of declared fiction, the journal entry is "just a text." He adds: "What is more, it is in the margin between claims of truth and the claims of textuality that all discursive structures . . . are formed" (*Shorter Views* 47 f.).

The fluid border between fictional and autobiographical text, which is so striking in Delany's fiction, can also be observed in his autobiographical writing. Whereas the publisher of *Heavenly Breakfast: An Essay on the Winter of Love* (1979) promises "[t]he real life story of a brilliant writer told as only he can tell it," the author himself stresses in the preface to his reflections that the text is not journalism, but rather that its relationship to reality is "peculiarly precarious" (x). Though based on actual journals and diaries, some incidents described in the essay have been displaced in terms of chronology and location. In addition, several characters have been combined into one, or one character has been split into several ones so that "all that was real, during the winter and spring of '67/'68 on Second Street, was the *Heavenly Breakfast*" (xi).

One of the reasons for Delany's manipulation of autobiographical elements is the focus of his reflections. By depicting life in a commune in a positive light, he questions existing and commonly accepted social structures and offers an alternative. Particular events in his own life are therefore of secondary importance. When Delany shows the manuscript of his essay to some of his friends five years after the commune and rock band called "Heavenly Breakfast" have disbanded, they agree: "You've left out an awful lot about yourself" (116). A second reason for his treatment of autobiographical material is Delany's attempt to question reality in general and autobiographical writing in particular. At one point, for example, he quotes his journal, offering two different versions of the fate of Judy, a young drug addict. In the first version she is found dead from an overdose. Delany reveals this to be a lie and offers a second version with a happy ending: Judy has gotten her life together: She is off drugs, taking art classes, and reading the works of Spinoza. This version, however, is immediately revealed to be fictitious as well. Delany admonishes the reader: "Recognize them for aesthetically manipulated lies when they occur in fiction. More important, recognize them for the same thing when they occur, as they do, in life. They are products of the same process that for so long reduced an American fiction in which all abortion ended in death, all female adultery in divorce" (101). Delany then proffers a third version to the by-now skeptical reader. Judy, who is still living in the commune, responds to the two versions of her life as follows before she continues reading Spinoza's *Tractatus*: "You haven't got it. . . . But you're getting there" (101).

Nine years after *Heavenly Breakfast* Delany again questions the reliability of memory and stresses the precarious nature of autobiographical writing in his introduction to *The Motion of Light in Water*. The realization that the erroneous statement "My father died of lung cancer in 1958 when I was seventeen" feels righter to Delany than the correct one ("My father died of lung cancer in 1960 when I was eighteen.") leads him to conclude: "[A] biography or a memoir that contained only the first sentence would *be* incorrect. But one that omitted it, or did not at least suggest its relation to the second on several informal levels, would be incomplete" (15). Consequently, Delany does not strive for the last word on event and evidential accuracy, and he purposely includes the displacements, disjunction, and elisions of his memory in his narrative. He is aware that "memory will make this only one possible fiction among the myriad—many in open conflict—anyone might write of any of us, as convinced as any other that what he or she wrote was the truth" (14).

Delany's favorite metaphor for the multiple levels of autobiographical reality are parallel columns that are at times complementary and at times contradictory: "[T]he second account . . . displaces the first . . . at once discrediting it and at the same time presumably revealing its truth" (68). The two imaginary columns can represent the public and the private, the legitimate and the illegitimate, the Marxist and the Freudian, the world of material and the world of desire. Delany also employs the metaphors of the bridge and the river to illustrate the multiple levels of his autobiography. In fact, its title is a direct reference to the split, the gap, the margin between columns: "Nothing there sustains the river dividing the two shores that allows all articulate passage, a river that is itself never constituted of anything more meaningful than blue lines (cut by a red marginal indicator) over white paper—or the motion of light in water" (208). The three major columns or strands that can easily be discerned in Delany's narrative deal with his development as a writer, as a gay man, and as a black man.

Delany's memoirs that represent his attempt to combine "the impressionistic flights of Mandelstam with . . . the analytic acuity you find in Barthes" (*1984* 204) and that consist of 343 numbered sections, 50 of which were left out of the first edition, begin with the death of Delany's father. We witness the young writer and his soon-to-be wife Marilyn move into a decrepit apartment in New York's East Village, where they struggle to make a living taking on part-time jobs while immersing themselves in the stimulating Bohemian atmosphere of the Village and trying to establish themselves as writers. Hacker encourages Delany to write and publish his first science fiction novel, and they make the acquaintance of the legendary British poet W.H. Auden and his lover Chester Kallman. Soon Delany's career is off and running, and he publishes ever more sophisticated science fiction novels in rapid succession. His emergence and empowerment as a gay man parallels the decline of his marriage. While he cruises the parks, docks, public bathrooms, baths, and movie theaters for copious and mostly anonymous sex, his relationship with Hacker turns into a "low-key nightmare" (120). Partially because of this emotional strain Delany comes close to a nervous breakdown and checks himself into Mount Sinai Hospital's psychiatric ward, where he spends several weeks coming to terms with his strained relationship with his father and his at times painful development as a gay, black writer.

When the ménage à trois dissolves into which Delany subsequently enters with his wife and Bob Folsom, a former hustler, and which he considers one of the happiest times of his life, he realizes that his marriage is over: "Bob had been the lynchpin holding us together; now we were very much apart" (500). Delany leaves for Europe with the awareness that a new phase of his life is about to begin. Compared to the detailed and at times deliberately shocking depiction of his emergence as a gay man, Delany's portrait of himself as a black man seems to be of secondary importance. In the predominantly egalitarian environment of the gay and Bohemian subculture, in which Delany lives, racial differences are to a certain degree suspended but never entirely abolished. Upon reading LeRoi Jones's (see Amiri Baraka*) novel *The System of Dante's Hell* (1965), Delany wonders "troubled, as now and again I had for so many years, if there was something wrong with me that so many of my friends were white, that so few were black" (344). Ross Posnock has shown in his book *Color & Culture* that Delany deliberately seeks "to frustrate and interrogate expectations about what *black intellectual* means" (261). By employing such innovative techniques as collage and fragmentation, Delany disturbs the conventions of black autobiography: "In Delany's book the generic expectations of black autobiography are subtly raised then left unfulfilled" (285). His deliberate fracturing of narrative and psyche initiates "a crisis in representation that decisively reconfigures the tradition" (293).

Since *The Motion of Light in Water* Delany has continued his autobiographical explorations. He has published his touching recollections of meeting his current partner, Dennis Ricketts, a homeless man who sells old books on the streets of New York, in the graphic novel or comic-strip *Bread & Wine: An Erotic Tale of New York*. The three tales in *Atlantis* are based on Delany's childhood and youth and on his father's move from North Carolina to New York. He has also infused more and more of his nonfiction works with autobiographical detail. The first part of *Times Square Red, Times Square Blue*, Delany's attack on the "Disneyfication" of New York's red light district, for example, consists of a detailed and graphic description of his sexual exploits in the adult movie theaters around Times Square and Forty-second Street. Delany's reminiscence is followed by an astute and provocative analysis of the deleterious economic and social impact of gentrification. It is to be hoped that Delany will continue to share the details of his fascinating life with the reading public.

CRITICAL RECEPTION

Although the uniqueness and importance of Delany's autobiography have generally been acknowledged, it has not yet received the critical attention it so clearly deserves. James Sallis regrets in his introduction to *Ash of Stars*, a recent collection of essays dealing with Delany's writing, that his landmark autobiography is not represented by a separate essay, "though it floats along alligatorlike throughout, head just above water, a constant presence" (xvii). Recently Hazel V. Carby (*Race Men*) and Ross Posnock (*Color & Culture*) have begun to assess the important role *The Motion of Light in Water* plays in the development of African American autobiography by comparing it to the autobiographies of Miles Davis and Adrienne Kennedy. Considering the complexity of Delany's autobiography, these critics have only been able to scratch its surface and it still awaits and deserves thorough analysis.

BIBLIOGRAPHY

Autobiographical Works by Samuel R. Delany

Heavenly Breakfast: An Essay on the Winter of Love. New York: Bantam Books, 1979. *The Motion of Light in Water: Sex and Science Fiction Writing in the East Village 1957– 1965*. New York: Arbor House/William Morrow, 1988.

The Motion of Light in Water: Sex and Science Fiction Writing in the East Village 1960–1965. London: Grafton, 1990. New York: Richard Kasak/Masquerade, 1993.

Atlantis: Three Tales. Hanover, NH: Wesleyan University Press, 1995.

Longer Views: Extended Essays. Hanover, NH: Wesleyan University Press, 1996.

Bread & Wine: An Erotic Tale of New York. New York: Juno, 1999.

Shorter Views: Queer Thoughts & The Politics of the Paraliterary. Hanover, NH: Wesleyan University Press, 1999.
Times Square Red, Times Square Blue. New York: New York University Press, 1999.
1984: Selected Letters. Rutherford, NJ: Voyant, 2000.

Studies of Samuel R. Delany's Autobiographical Works

Carby, Hazel V. *Race Men.* Cambridge, MA: Harvard University Press, 1998.

Emery, Michael R. "Samuel R. Delany." In *Contemporary Gay American Novelists. A Bio-Bibliographical Critical Sourcebook.* Ed. Emmanuel S. Nelson. Westport, CT: Greenwood Press, 1993. 101–9.

Lunde, David. "Black Man/Gay Man/Writer . . . Prodigy: The Quest for Identity in Delany's Early Work." *Review of Contemporary Fiction* 16.3 (Fall 1996): 116–24.

Peplow, Michael W. and Robert S. Bravard. *Samuel R. Delany: A Primary and Secondary Bibliography, 1962–1979.* Boston: G.K. Hall, 1980.

Posnock, Ross. *Color & Culture: Black Writers and the Making of the Modern Intellectual.* Cambridge, MA: Harvard University Press, 1998.

Sallis, James, ed. *Ash of Stars: On the Writing of Samuel R. Delany.* Jackson: University Press of Mississippi, 1996.

TOI DERRICOTTE
(1941–   )

Loretta G. Woodard

BIOGRAPHY

A poet, essayist, and educator, Toi Derricotte was born into a middle-class family on April 12, 1941, in Detroit, Michigan. Her father, Benjamin Sweeney Webster, was a mortician and salesperson, and her mother, Antonia Webster Cyrus, was a systems analyst. From the age of ten Derricotte found refuge and self-empowerment in poetry and journals, but it is not until the age of twenty-seven that she would share her poetry and later emerge as a nationally known poet whose work would draw much upon her Detroit childhood. Of her role as a writer of prose and poetry, Derricotte states, "I feel a need to represent what's not spoken. I discover a pocket in myself that hasn't been articulated, then I have to find a form to carry that . . . to make it have light and beauty and truth inside it" ("Contributor Spotlight" 209). Thus, Derricotte candidly articulates the unspeakable in her autobiographical collections.

In the 1950s, Derricotte attended Girls Catholic Central High School, which was staffed by the Sisters, Servants of the Immaculate Heart of Mary. When she graduated, she applied for admission into the order but ultimately decided against joining them. In 1960 she married Clarence Reese, an artist, had a son named Anthony, and obtained a divorce four years later.

Derricotte received a B.A. in special education from Wayne State University in 1965, after changing from a degree in psychology. She worked as a teacher in the Manpower program in Detroit until 1966, then as a teacher for the mentally retarded until 1968. She married Clarence Bruce Derricotte, a banking consultant, in 1967 and moved to New York City, where she participated in several writers' workshops. Eventually, Derricotte moved to Upper Montclair, New Jersey, where she continued to teach and was also actively involved in the Poet-in-the-Schools program sponsored by the New Jersey State Council on the Arts in 1974. She received the Pen and Brush Award from New School for Social Research for her untitled poetry manuscript in 1973 and was a member of the editorial staff of *New York Quarterly* from 1973 to 1977.

A year later, she published her first volume of poetry, *The Empress of the Death House*, followed by *Natural Birth* in 1983. While she was a graduate student at New York University, she was awarded first prize in the Academy of American Poets competition and a creative writing fellowship in poetry. She received her M.A. in English literature and creative writing in 1984. Five years later, *Captivity* was published. Of her first three volumes of poetry she claims, "Every book for me is about reclaiming something that had been extinguished, reclaiming emotions, memories, parts of self" ("Contributor Spotlight" 209).

Throughout the 1980s and 1990s, Derricotte received numerous awards and honors. They include fellowships from MacDowell Colony (1982), the National Endowment for the Arts (1985 and 1990), the Lucille Medwick Memorial Award from the Poetry Society of America (1985), the Arts Council Fellowship for the State of Maryland (1987), a Pushcart Prize (1989), the Folger Shakespeare Library Poetry Book Award (1990), and the Distinguished Pioneering of the Arts Award from the United Black Artists.

In June 1996, she, along with Cornelius Eady, cofounded Cave Canem, an intensive summer workshop and retreat for African American poets. As their brainchild, the nonprofit organization provides a safe haven for poets and writers, where, according to Derricotte, "like-minded people . . . can explore things that they can't explore in their regular communities" (Caudell 30).

While Derricotte is more famous for her poetry, Norton published *The Black Notebooks*, a literary memoir of poetry and prose, in 1997. A year later, it received both the Anisfield-Wolfe Award and Literary Award for Nonfiction from the American Library Association's Black Caucus and was chosen as a *New York Times* Notable Book of the Year. Her next volume of poetry, *Tender*, was also published in 1997 and won the Paterson Poetry Prize. The author of four volumes to date, her poems have appeared in a number of journals and anthologies.

For nearly two decades, Derricotte has been a guest poet and lecturer at numerous colleges and universities. She has taught in the graduate creative writing programs at New York University, George Mason University, and Old Dominion University. She currently is an associate professor of English in the Writing Program at the University of Pittsburgh.

AUTOBIOGRAPHICAL WORK AND THEMES

The Black Notebooks: An Interior Journey is Derricotte's autobiographical reflection on race as she recounts the shame and sadness at her memory of "escaping from blackness" and "passing" for white. A well-educated, light-skinned middle-class woman, she admits, "All my life I have passed invisibly into the white world, and all my life I have felt that sudden and alarming moment of consciousness when I remember I am black" (25). Written in journal form over the past twenty years, with both poetry and prose, Derricotte struggles to come to terms with her own racially constructed identity, an awareness that totally impacted her sense of self, motherhood, marriage, community, and work (Davis 105).

By revisiting her past, Derricotte examines and honestly reveals how racism drove her to make "imperfect choices." Several brief scenes recount her decision to "pass" and to accept the privileges intended for whites only. So that she could live in a more affluent neighborhood, while living in Upper Montclair, New Jersey, in the 1970s, Derricotte recalls leaving her dark-skinned husband behind. Another time she recalls passing in the local drugstore. "Slowly I began to bring myself into the store—my friendliness, my neighborly questions. . . . All the time I was charging, paying my bill on time, building bridges I walked on tentatively, holding my hat, watching the escape route" (155–156). Derricotte takes advantage of her "unaccustomed consumer rights and freedom" (DeMott 45), but she still experienced shame and fear of discovery. This happens largely because Derricotte allows people to "assume" she is white. Though she gets the home of her dreams, where she feels "safe" and "valued," her deep-ridden guilt and shame drove her into a suicidal depression, causing separation from her husband and at times a writer's block.

Derricotte's insightful memoir, like the works of Charles Chesnutt and Nella Larsen, forces us to examine our own "choices," to face the consequences, which will inevitably occur, and to ask and answer questions. The question Derricotte seeks to answer for herself is, Do I have a responsibility to claim racial identity, even if it means losing something? She does not offer us any "simple" answers but suggests that we must go on our own journey to answer this question for ourselves. Of her own journey she states, "I had to go back to those voices to find my way through and around them. The only difference was that this time I had words. It was language that saved my life" (22).

CRITICAL RECEPTION

Criticism of Derricotte's memoir is limited mostly to mixed reviews rather than scholarly articles. However, most critics note the value of such a work. A *Kirkus* reviewer acknowledges the work "as a very strong first prose offering on an always provocative subject" (1352). Stating that the memoir is both "instructive" and "introspective," Keith Gilyard, in *American Literary History*, observes how "[c]olor politics rendered her personal world perilously unstable" and credits her for "the insights that emerge from [her] diaries, [and for] her explication of things we cannot know" (194). Roger Gilbert of the *Michigan Quarterly Review* indicates that Derricotte writes with "remarkable honesty" and claims Derricotte's "special perspective allows her to write about race from both sides of the color line, with a painful awareness of her own complicity in it" (155).

While most critics note the work's strength, they also tend to focus on its weaknesses. Melanie Kaye-Kantrowitz writes in *The Women's Review of Books* that the "book is brilliant, devastating and uneven, occasionally vague or repetitive" and that the "interim genre, between journal and essays, can confuse" (6). In his critical appraisal Benjamin DeMott argues, "There are weak entries in this journal; the weakest of them are those in which Derricotte pretends momentarily to disbelieve in the distinctions that she elsewhere treats with appropriately intense seriousness" (45). He further notes that "for much of its length [it] is a sternly disciplined, unsentimental work" (45).

BIBLIOGRAPHY

Autobiographical Work by Toi Derricotte

The Black Notebooks: An Interior Journey. New York: Norton, 1997.

Studies of Toi Derricotte's Autobiographical Work

Burns, Ann. Rev. of *The Black Notebooks: An Interior Journey. Library Journal* (November 1, 1997): 100.

Caudell, Robin M. "Where Poets Explore Their Pain While Others Beware the Dog." *American Visions* (October–November 1999): 30–32.

"Contributor Spotlight: Toi Derricotte." *Ploughshares* 22.1 (Spring 1996): 208–11.

Davis, Thomas J. Rev. of *The Black Notebooks: An Interior Journey. Library Journal* (October 1, 1997): 105.

DeMott, Benjamin. "Passing: A Black Poet and Teacher Chronicles Life in a White World." *New York Times Book Review* 2 (November 2, 1997): 45.

Gilbert, Roger. "Dialogues of Self and Soul." *Michigan Quarterly Review* 39.1 (2000): 149–66.

Gilyard, Keith. "Kinship and Theory." *American Literary History* 11.1 (1999): 187–95.

Graeber, L. Rev. of *The Black Notebooks: An Interior Journey. New York Times Book Review* (August 8, 1999): 24.

Kaye-Kantrowitz, Melanie. "Opening a Vein." *The Women's Review of Books* 15.8 (1998): 4–6.

Lewis, Lillian. Rev. of *The Black Notebooks: An Interior Journey. Booklist* 94 (October 15, 1997): 380.

Olson, Ray. Rev. of *The Black Notebooks: An Interior Journey. Booklist* 94 (February 15, 1998): 978.

Peterson, V.R. "Word Star—Toi Derricotte: Making It Real." *Essence* (December 1997): 64.

Rev. of *The Black Notebooks: An Interior Journey. Kirkus Reviews* 65 (September 1, 1997): 1351–52.

Rev. of *The Black Notebooks: An Interior Journey. Library Journal* 122 (November 1, 1997): 100.

Rev. of *The Black Notebooks: An Interior Journey. New York Times Book Review* 102 (December 7, 1997): 67.

Rouse, Deborah L. "*Black Notebooks* Reveals Whiteness." *Emerge* 9.3 (1997): 78.

Rowell, Charles H. "Beyond Our Lives: An Interview with Toi Derricotte." *Callaloo* 14.3 (1991): 654–64.

"A Safe Space for African American Poets." *Black Issues Book Review* 2 (January–February 2000): 11.

Seaman, Donna. Rev. of *The Black Notebooks: An Interior Journey*. *Booklist* (February 15, 1999): 1025.

Stuttaford, Genevieve. Rev. of *The Black Notebooks: An Interior Journey*. *Publishers Weekly* (September 8, 1997): 69.

FREDERICK DOUGLASS
(1818–1895)

Harish Chander

BIOGRAPHY

Frederick Douglass, the renowned freedom fighter and civil rights champion of the nineteenth century, was born into slavery in February 1818 on a farm in Tuckahoe, Maryland. The date of his birth is not known because records of birth of slave children were seldom kept. His mother, Harriet Bailey, was a slave of Captain Aaron Anthony, and his father was probably a white man whose identity still remains a mystery and was rumored to be Captain Anthony himself. His mother was a literate woman. She had named him Frederick Augustus Washington Bailey, and it was only after his escape to freedom that he changed his name, first to Frederick Johnson, then to Frederick Douglass, the latter name after a character in Sir Walter Scott's *The Lady of the Lake*. Besides having a farm and slaves of his own, Captain Anthony worked as the chief manager for Colonel Lloyd V's estate of some 10,000 acres of land and more than 500 slaves.

While he was still an infant, Douglass was taken from his mother to be reared by his maternal grandmother, Betsey Bailey. Manumitted in 1797, Grandpa Isaac Bailey was a freeman who earned his living as a sawyer, but Grandma Bailey was Captain Anthony's slave who took care of slave children before they were ready for work. The Baileys lived in a log cabin on the banks of Tuckahoe Creek. Douglass lived with his grandparents till he was six, enjoying his grandma's love and kindness and without experiencing the harsher realities of slave life. However, this relatively comfortable life abruptly ended for Douglass when one day in 1824 Grandma Bailey took him to Captain Anthony's plantation house, twelve miles away, and then left after telling him to play with the other children there. Douglass did not see his grandmother again.

At Captain Anthony's plantation house, Douglass was assigned light house hold duties, such as cleaning the yard, keeping the chickens out of the garden, and running errands for Captain Anthony's daughter Lucretia. Lucretia had married Thomas Auld, the captain of Colonel Lloyd's sloop. Lucretia liked Douglass and often rewarded him with a piece of bread and water when he sang for her. He was then placed under the care of Aunt Katy, under whom he suffered for lack of sufficient food. In *Life and Times of Frederick Douglass* (1995 facsimile edition) Douglass complains: "I have often been so pinched with hunger as to dispute with old 'Nep,' the dog, for the crumbs which fell from the kitchen table" (34). However, Douglass was chosen to be the companion of twelve-year-old Daniel Lloyd, who took Douglass along when he went hunting and protected Douglass from harm from other whites. Though Douglass was himself spared physical abuse at that time, he witnessed the abuse suffered by other slaves. One night he was awakened from his sleep by a woman's screams and leapt out of bed to find Captain Anthony mercilessly whipping Aunt Hester. On another occasion, Douglass saw his badly beaten cousin Betsey imploring Captain Anthony in vain for protection from the sexual advances of a drunken overseer, one Mr. Plummer.

Douglass's mother could seldom see him because she worked on a farm that was miles away from the plantation house. His mother passed away when Douglass was just seven, and he was not allowed to attend her funeral. In *Life and Times*, he regrets, "I knew my mother so little, and have so few of her words treasured in my remembrance" (36).

In 1826, Douglass was sent to Baltimore to the home of Hugh and Sophia Auld to care for their two-year-old son, little Tommy. Hugh Auld was the brother of Thomas Auld, who upon Captain Anthony's death the same year had become Douglass's new owner. The new setting was rather congenial. He was no longer famished for lack of food. Sophia Auld, who had never before had a slave, treated Douglass kindly. She began to teach him to read, but when her husband came to know what she was doing, he forbade her from giving any further instruction. He said that "learning" would spoil even the best slave in the world, making him unfit to be a slave. In *Narrative of the Life of Frederick Douglass, an American Slave* (1845), Douglass says that Hugh Auld's objections to the education of slaves brought home to him the secret of the master's power, thereby revealing the "pathway from slavery to freedom" (78). Sophia followed Hugh's order and stopped teaching Douglass. The hunger for learning once aroused, Douglass sought other means of receiving instruction. When sent on errands, he would stuff his pockets with bread, which he would exchange for reading lessons from poor white children. Douglass spent seven years in Baltimore, except for a brief return to Talbot County in October 1827 during the settlement of Captain Anthony's estate. Soon after his return to Baltimore, Lucretia, Captain Anthony's daughter and Thomas Auld's wife, died.

In 1829, at the age of eleven, Douglass started working at the shipyard as a general assistant. His duties included beating and spinning oakum, stoking fires under pitch boilers, turning grindstones, and running errands. He learned to write by copying out letters written on lumber by carpenters to indicate their positions in the vessel. At night, he practiced writing by copying out words written by Sophia and Hugh Auld's son in the blank spaces left in their son's used copybooks. It was "after a long, tedious effort for years," says Douglass in his *Narrative*, "I finally succeeded in learning how to write" (87).

In 1831, at the age of thirteen, two important events deeply influenced Douglass. First, after experiencing a revelation, he accepted Jesus Christ as his Redeemer and Savior. He joined the Bethel African Methodist Episcopal Church in Baltimore and studied the Bible with Charles Lawson, a free black drayman. Later in life, however, Douglass became disillusioned with a religious establishment that not only tolerated but also supported slavery. Second, 1831 was the year he bought a used copy of *The Columbian Orator*, a collection of essays on liberty, for fifty cents he had earned by blacking boots. In one essay, a recaptured slave adroitly defends himself against his master's charge of ingratitude, convincing his master that it is wrong to hold a person in bondage. The speeches of Richard Brinsley Sheridan, Lord Chatham, and William Pitt, which Douglass read again and again, increased his knowledge and added to his vocabulary, enabling him to give "tongue" to his thoughts. As Douglass observes in *Life and Times of Frederick Douglass* (1995 facsimile edition) regarding Sheridan's Speeches on Catholic Emancipation in England: "[F]rom the speeches of Sheridan I got a bold and powerful denunciation of oppression and a most brilliant vindication of the rights of man" (85).

In 1833, Douglass returned to St. Michaels, Maryland, to his owner, Thomas Auld. Sophia and Hugh Auld, dissatisfied with the work of a crippled slave, Douglass's cousin Henny, had sent her back to her master Thomas Auld. This led to a quarrel between the two brothers, leading Thomas Auld to demand that Douglass be returned to him as well. In March, Douglass was sent to St. Michaels, Caroline County, where Thomas Auld then lived with his second wife Rowena. As Douglass describes in his *Narrative*, he found both Thomas and Rowena Auld to be "equally mean and cruel" (95). Douglass faced hunger, as well as whippings from Thomas Auld. As Douglass describes in *My Bondage and My Freedom*, Auld found biblical sanction for his cruelty. Finding Douglass too independent, Auld hired Douglass out as a field hand to the notorious Edward Covey "to be broken" (203). Covey proved to be a merciless tyrant, repeatedly beating Douglass until he felt broken in body and spirit. However, one day in August 1834, Covey pushed Douglass too far. Working at the wheat threshing machine in the oppressive heat, Douglass collapsed. After Douglass failed to get up, Covey bashed him on his head with a hickory board, leaving him bleeding. Douglass then trekked through seven miles to Auld's home to report Covey's assault, but Auld remained indifferent and sent him back to Covey. Upon Douglass's return, Covey tried to tie him up with a rope, but Douglass resisted. After a lengthy fight, Covey retreated. This fight set Douglass on the road to freedom. As Douglass puts it in his *Narrative*, "My long-crushed spirit rose . . . and I now resolved that, however long I might remain a slave in form, the day had passed forever when I could be a slave in fact" (113). In the five subsequent months he worked for Covey, he did not receive another beating. The battle with Covey thus proved to be the turning point in his life as a slave. Before the fight, Douglass believed that he was nothing, but after the fight he realized that he was "a man" (107).

In January 1835, Douglass was hired out to William Freeland, who gave him enough to eat and did not overwork him. Douglass secretly ran a Sabbath school where he taught his fellow slaves how to read. In the *Narrative*, Douglass calls Freeland "the best master I ever had, *till I became my own master*" (121; emphasis in original). During this time, he launched a plan to escape with five fellow slaves to the free state of Pennsylvania. However, the plan was betrayed and Douglass, the leader of the plot, was thrown into jail. After a week, Thomas Auld secured Douglass's release and sent Douglass back to his brother Hugh Auld in Baltimore. From 1836 to 1838, Douglass again worked in the shipyards, first as an apprentice, and then as a caulker, a job he was allowed to hold only because his wages went to a white man. On one occasion, four white workers attacked Douglass with stones and spikes, viciously beating him. Douglass could not seek legal redress because Maryland law did not permit a black person to offer evidence against a white person.

On September 3, 1838, Douglass escaped slavery. Dressed in a sailor's suit, and carrying a seaman's protection paper borrowed from a retired sailor, he boarded a train to New York City. There, he found the home of David Ruggles, a key figure in the Underground Railroad. From Ruggles's home, Douglass wrote his fiancée Anna Murray, a free black woman whom he had met in Baltimore and who had helped arrange his escape, about his safe arrival. After she joined him a few days later, they were married. At Ruggles's suggestion, the couple moved to New Bedford, Massachusetts. In order to hide his identity, Douglass changed his name, adopting the surname of Douglass. In Bedford, Massachusetts, Douglass found work as a general laborer after failing to find better-paid work as a caulker because of discrimination. Anna Douglass helped support the family by taking in washing and doing domestic work. They had five children—two daughters, Rosetta and Annie, and three sons, Lewis, Charles, and Frederick Jr.

Douglass's career as an abolitionist began in 1841 at a Massachusetts Anti-Slavery Society convention. Asked at the convention to tell of his experiences as a slave, Douglass delivered such a stirring and eloquent account of his life as a slave that he was offered a job as a lecturer for the Society, a position he accepted and held for four years. At the Society, he helped defeat a new Rhode Island constitution that would have extended the franchise to white men without property while denying the same right to blacks. Despite being heckled and beaten for being a black abolitionist, Douglass took a prominent part in the famous antislavery series of conventions held in a number of states, exposing the evils of slavery.

To silence skeptics, who doubted that anyone so articulate could have been a slave, Douglass published a narrative of his life as a slave in 1845. *Narrative of the Life of Frederick Douglass, an American Slave* proved an instant success, but its bold recital of the facts of his life as a slave put Douglass's life in jeopardy. Seeking to avoid recapture by his former owner, Douglass set sail for the United Kingdom and Ireland, where he spent two years lecturing against slavery. His oratory won the British people's support for the abolitionist cause, and two Quakers, Ellen and Anna Richardson, raised money to purchase his emancipation in December 1846 for 150 pounds sterling.

Douglass returned to the United States in 1847 with an international reputation of a representative African American, symbolizing the latent potentialities of the black people held in bondage. His English friends sent him off with a purse containing $2,175 to start a newspaper. Douglass moved to Rochester, New York, where he launched *The North Star* despite the opposition of the white abolitionist William Lloyd Garrison, who feared competition for his own paper, the *Liberator*, which had two-thirds of its readers in the black community. Douglass's paper sought "to attack slavery in all of its forms and aspects" and to "promote the moral and intellectual improvement of the Coloured people" (Quarles 81). With the assistance of Julia Griffiths, Douglass ran the paper successfully, himself writing most of the editorials and articles, and renaming it in 1851 as *Frederick Douglass's Paper* when it merged with the *Liberty Party Paper*. In 1858, Douglass also launched *Douglass's Monthly*, especially for British readers. It was in *Frederick Douglass's Paper* that Douglass in March 1853 first published his novella titled *The Heroic Slave*. Based on a historical slave uprising aboard the slave ship *Creole*, *The Heroic Slave* is considered the first work of prose fiction in African American literature. He continued publishing *Frederick Douglass's Paper* until 1860, and *Douglass's Monthly* until 1863, the year of the Emancipation Proclamation. During this time, Douglass's printing shop in Rochester served as a station on the Underground Railroad, helping over 400 slaves escape to Canada.

Douglass came to repudiate some central positions of Garrison's abolitionism. He rejected Garrison's "No Union with Slaveholders" doctrine, which argued for the dissolution of the Union. Arguing that slavery was incompatible with the noble goals set forth in the Constitution, he read that document as an antislavery charter and not the proslavery document Garrison saw. As indicated in *Life and Times* (1995 facsimile edition), Douglass sent a memorandum to the U.S. Senate in which he points out that the U.S. Constitution makes no mention of "color or race" as "a disqualification for the exercise of the right of suffrage" (386). Douglass believed in political action, along with moral suasion, to attack the institution of slavery. Douglass's differences with Garrison led him to write his second autobiography setting forth his positions, *My Bondage and My Freedom*, published in 1855. Douglass also opposed the 1859 raid on Harpers Ferry led by John Brown, the militant white abolitionist. Brown met with Douglass to enlist his support in a plot to seize the federal armory at Harpers Ferry, but Douglass rejected the plan as doomed to failure. After Douglass learned of Brown's capture, he fled to England via Canada, fearing that he would be implicated as an accomplice. After five months abroad, he returned home in May 1860 after learning of the death of his youngest child Annie.

Douglass's belief in human rights led him to take an active role in the women's rights movement. At the inaugural meeting of the Women's Rights Movement at Seneca Falls, New York, on July 19, 1848, he seconded Elizabeth Cady Stanton's suffrage resolution with the impassioned plea that "[t]he power to choose rulers and make laws is the right by which all others could be secured" (Douglass, *Frederick Douglass* 28). His paper *The North Star* carried the masthead "Right is of no sex—Truth is of no Color." He cautioned white feminists not to advance their cause without regard to slave women.

Douglass saw the outbreak of the Civil War as the final means of abolishing slavery. In his editorial "How to End the War" in the May 1861 issue of the *Douglass's Monthly*, Douglass proposed that President Lincoln should declare the emancipation of slaves as the primary war objective and permit slaves and free blacks to enlist for the Union forces. While the cautious president was not initially inclined to accept either proposal, Douglass's views gradually gained support among the Radical Republicans in Congress. Congress banned slavery in the District of Columbia in April 1862 and in the federal territories in June. Finally, in September 1862, Lincoln announced that, on January 1, 1863, he would issue a proclamation freeing all slaves in states in rebellion. The Emancipation Proclamation also permitted blacks to enter the U.S. military, and Douglass set about to recruit two regiments, the 54th and 55th Massachusetts colored regiments, with his own sons Charles and Lewis among the first to be recruited. In August 1863, Lincoln invited him for a private conference at which Douglass sought equal pay, equal promotion, and equal protection for black soldiers. After President Lincoln's assassination, Mrs. Lincoln sent Douglass President Lincoln's walking stick as a token of her husband's regard for Douglass.

After the war, Douglass led a black delegation in 1866 to discuss race relations with President Andrew Johnson. Johnson rejected the delegation's request for black suffrage on the grounds that such a step would increase racial tension and that it was the province of the states, not the federal government, to regulate suffrage. Douglass campaigned vigorously for the enactment of the Civil Rights Amendments to the Constitution.

In the 1870s and 1880s, Douglass's distinction as a national leader won him a number of political appointments. In 1871, President Ulysses Grant appointed him secretary of the commission on the annexation of Santo Domingo. In 1872, the Equal Rights Party nominated Douglass for the vice presidency on a ticket headed by Victoria Woodhull. Douglass nevertheless continued his efforts to support Grant's reelection. In 1872, a mysterious fire destroyed his Rochester home and newspaper files, and Douglass moved to Washington, D.C. In 1877, Douglass was appointed District of Columbia Marshall by President Rutherford Hayes, and in 1881, Recorder of Deeds of the District of Columbia by President James Garfield. In 1878, Douglass bought "Cedar Hill," a fifteen-acre estate with a twenty-room Victorian house commanding a view of the Capitol, which ironically once belonged to General Robert E. Lee. In 1889, President Benjamin Harrison appointed Douglass consul general to Haiti.

His first wife Anna died in 1882. Two years later, Douglass married Helen Pitts, a white woman, who had been his secretary in the Office of Record of Deeds. Some whites and blacks criticized him for his interracial marriage, but he calmly defended his right to marry the woman of his choice. Recently, Maria Diedrich, a German professor of English, has discovered Douglass's long romantic relationship with the German journalist Otillie Assing. Assing, who had read *My Bondage and My Freedom*, first met Douglass in 1856 in Rochester to interview him and was immediately attracted to him. She later translated *My Bondage and My Freedom* into German. She considered herself Douglass's "natural wife"—"his ideal mate in his intellectual and professional quests" (Diedrich 190). She spent every summer with Douglass as his houseguest till 1881 when she returned to Germany. She became utterly distraught when Douglass married Helen Pitts, and on August 21, 1884, she committed suicide by taking poison in Paris. Douglass twice updated his autobiography *Life and Times of Frederick Douglass*, first in 1881 and then in 1892. He died of cardiac arrest on February 20, 1895, having spent the day attending a meeting of the National Convention of Women.

AUTOBIOGRAPHICAL WORKS AND THEMES

Frederick Douglass devoted his life and writings to the cause of black emancipation, enfranchisement, and equal rights. Through his autobiographies, Douglass fought against slavery and racism, oppression, and exploitation. In *Life and Times* (1892), Douglass sets forth the purpose of his writings: "My part has been to tell the story of the slave. The story of the master never wanted for narrators" (479).

Narrative of the Life of Frederick Douglass, an American Slave (1845) is an American fugitive slave classic that merits an extended discussion. A subgenre of the black autobiography, the fugitive slave narrative describes, from the slave's own point of view, the trials and tribulations of a slave, as well as the slave's difficult journey from slavery to freedom. Its main objective is to show the horrors of slavery and their devastating impact upon the slave's life and personality, with the aim of ending slavery. Between 1830 and 1860, the antislavery movement produced some seventy book-length narratives, of which the following are among the most prominent: *Narrative of the Life of Moses Grandy* (1843); *Narrative of the Life of Frederick Douglass* (1845); *Narrative of William Wells Brown** (1847); *Narrative of the Life and Adventures of Henry Bibb** (1849); *Narrative of Henry Box Brown* (1849); *The Fugitive Blacksmith; or, Events in the Life of James W.C. Pennington* (1849); *Twelve Years a Slave: Narrative of Solomon Northrup** (1853); and *Running a Thousand Miles for Freedom; or, The Escape of William and Ellen Craft from Slavery* (1860). Slave narratives fall into three categories—those ghost written, those dictated by illiterate slaves, and those written by the slaves themselves. However, those written by the slaves themselves have greater authenticity than others because they tell slaves' experiences of slavery in their own words. They are the best testimony to the evils of slavery and the need for abolition of slavery.

Aside from *Running a Thousand Miles for Freedom*, all the above-mentioned narratives belong to the last category. Douglass's *Narrative* is, however, the crown jewel of all the slave narratives. Douglass wrote it in the winter of 1844–1845 when he still had vivid memories of his life as a slave.

In the *Narrative*, Douglass sets out as a truth teller and hero. Here, he gives an eyewitness account of the realities of the slave experience and slave system to hasten the demise of slavery and bring "the glad day of deliverance" to "millions of my brethren in bonds" (159). In this noble mission, he relies on "the power of truth, love, and justice" (159). Truth is his watchword: "I prefer to be true to myself, even at the hazard of incurring the ridicule of others, rather than to be false, and incur my own abhorrence" (75). To legitimize the reality of his slave experience, Douglass, like Benjamin Franklin in his autobiography, includes testimonials from friends. The abolitionist William Lloyd Garrison's "Preface" and Wendell Phillips' "Letter" vouchsafe to the authenticity of events and experiences described by Douglass in the *Narrative*. Garrison says that he is "confident" that Douglass's narrative shows "SLAVERY AS IT IS," without malice or exaggeration (38). And Phillips is equally "confident" that Douglass's narrative gives the "whole truth" about slavery, not a "one-sided portrait" (44).

Major themes of Douglass's *Narrative* include the horrors of slavery and the degrading influence of slavery not only on the slave but on the slaveholder as well. Douglass points out that "killing a slave, or any colored person, in Talbot county, Maryland, is not treated as a crime either by the courts or the community" (68). He gives many spectacular examples of slave masters' brutal behavior. He informs about Thomas Lanman's glorying in about his killing of two slaves, "one of whom he killed with a hatchet, by knocking his brains out" (68). Colonel Lloyd's giving the old stable keeper more than thirty lashes on his naked shoulders for no fault of his (61), Captain Anthony's whipping of Aunt Hester for visiting her lover Ned (52), and Thomas Auld's whipping of Henny, a crippled female slave, are cases in point (82). He also tells of the cruelty of Mrs. Hamilton who regularly whipped her two slaves—twenty-two-year-old Henrietta and fourteen-year-old Mary—with the cowhide. As a result of this cruel treatment, "[t]he head, neck, and shoulders of Mary were literally cut to pieces" (80). Sophia Auld's case perhaps best exemplifies the influence of slavery on slave owners. Douglass describes how the "lamblike" Sophia Auld, when instructed by her husband that she must treat Douglass like a slave and not as a fellow human being, is left with a "ston[y]" heart (82). Douglass's narrative also shows how slavery destroys the family, beginning with his own example as someone who never knew his father and barely knew his mother. Douglass is sad to write about his mother: "I do not recollect of ever seeing my mother by the light of the day" (48). Deprived of "her tender and watchful care," Douglass "received the tidings of her death with much the same emotions I should have probably felt at the death of a stranger" (49). Douglass also reveals that slave songs often voice slaves' grief: "[T]hey breathed the prayer and complaint of souls boiling over with the bitterest anguish" (57).

Another outstanding theme of the *Narrative* is that it debunks the myths of the moral and intellectual authority of the slaveholders. He employs the sentimental fiction device of pathos to excite pity in the hearts of the readers for the plight of the slaves, as well as black rhetorical strategies of signifying, inversion, and indirection to tear the slaveholders' pretensions apart. He shows the ingratitude of Master Thomas to his grandmother in his "virtually turning her out to die" in her old age (92). He describes her condition in a moving passage: "She stands—she sits—she staggers—she falls—she dies" (93). He shows the hollowness of the myth of slavery as a benevolent institution and the white slaveholder as the transmitter of civilization to the black people. On the contrary, he proves that under the slave system, slaveholders are corrupting the slaves morally by raping their women, denying them family life, and in general treating them as beasts. He wonders how a slaveholder like Edward Covey, who compelled his woman slave Caroline "to commit the sin of adultery," could deceive himself into believing that he was "a sincere worshipper of the most high God" (104). Douglass effectively shows an inversion of the roles in the slaveholder-slave relationship by demonstrating that it is the slaveholder, not the slave, who is the real cannibal. As Henry Louis Gates Jr. puts it, "[I]t is the human depriver who is the actual barbarian" (*Figures in Black* 93). Douglass uses the term "manhood" as a signifier for the realization of the true black male identity. Douglass in his search for a "feasible plan" for escape explains the meaning of this term: "I talked to them [his fellow slaves] of our want of manhood, if we submitted to our enslavement without at least one noble effort to be free" (122). Asserting one's manhood is also used in the *Narrative* for resolutely resisting and bravely fighting a tyrant. Master Thomas hires out Douglass for one year to the notorious Edward Covey, nicknamed "Snake," "to be broken" (100). Covey succeeds in breaking him, "body, soul, and spirit" (105), but for the epiphanic encounter Douglass gains strength—he does not know where it came from—resolves to stand up to the diabolical Covey and repulses his oppressor, once and for all. This is the moment when Douglass feels something that he has "never felt before," "a glorious resurrection, from the tomb of slavery, to the heaven of freedom" (113). This is also the moment when he regains his manhood. The ecstatic Douglass exclaims: "You have seen how a man was turned a slave, you shall see how a slave was made a man" (107).

The *Narrative* upbraids slaveholding Christians who profess faith but yet practice the fiercest cruelty. He uses both indirect and direct methods of attack on slaveholding Christians. Douglass attacks the Christians of the country indirectly when he observes: "[I]t is almost an unpardonable offence to teach slaves to read in this Christian country" (83). The statement makes one wonder how a Christian country can forbid the teaching of reading, and then reach the inference that the author is ironical in the use of the term "Christian," and he means the opposite of what he says. Douglass indirectly attacks Thomas Auld when he presents him as "one of the many pious slaveholders who hold slaves for the very charitable purpose of taking care of them" (99). Master Thomas found scriptural authority for his whipping of slaves. He would justify his cruelty by quoting the following lines: "He that knoweth his master's will, and doeth it not, shall be beaten with many stripes" (99). We also learn that the Reverend Rigby Hopkins "always managed to have one or more of his slaves to whip every Monday morning" (118). In the "Appendix" to the *Narrative*, Douglass is at pains to make it clear that he is only opposed to "the slaveholding religion of this land," not to "Christianity proper" (153). He loves "the pure, peacable, and impartial Christianity of Christ," while he hates the "corrupt, slaveholding, women whipping, cradle-plundering, partial and hypocritical Christianity of this land" (153). He quotes a number of passages from the Bible—Matthew 23:13–15, 23–28—invoking God's wrath on the self-righteous Christians who only observe the outer forms of Christianity (155–56).

Henry Louis Gates Jr. points out that black writers in their attempts to define themselves critique earlier texts (*Figures in Black* 242). Douglass's *Narrative* critiques both Benjamin Franklin's *The Autobiography* (1771, 1784) and Ralph Waldo Emerson's *Nature* (1836). The protagonists of both Douglass's and Franklin's works are self-made men; they teach themselves to read and write; they follow reason and strong work ethics; they believe in one Creator and his divine providence; they believe they are chosen persons; and they rise from humble beginnings to fame. However, whereas Douglass's protagonist believes in "equal rights and justice" for all people of America, Franklin's protagonist seems to believe in the "Manifest Destiny" doctrine of White America. As such, Franklin's protagonist hates native Indians and does not extend equal rights to them. He refers to Indians as "savages" and does not mind their extirpation through drinking rum to make room for white Americans, whom he calls "cultivators of the earth" (195). And the slaveholders in Douglass's narrative also treat slaves as savages and compel them to "drink to excess" during holidays (115–16). Also, unlike the Franklin's Protestant narrator, who believes in man's inherent depravity, Douglass's narrator seems to be subscribing to Rousseau's idea of goodness of the natural man and his gradual corruption by society, as exemplified by Sophia Auld's conduct before and after her husband's instructing her against teaching slaves. Furthermore, Douglass's persona does not believe in Emerson's idea of the transcendental self as put forth in *Nature*. Emerson's persona becomes a portion of divinity when he surrenders himself to the influence of nature: "I become a transparent eyeball; . . . I see all; the currents of the Universal Being circulate through me; I am part or parcel of God" (6). In lieu of experiencing the presence of God, Douglass's persona, when a white apprentice kicks him in the left eye, does not have a mystic experience and only feels as if his "eyeball" has "burst" (132). He perhaps believes that a person's self is a social construct, rather than a portion of "Oversoul."

Like the American Declaration of Independence, Douglass's *Narrative* is above all a political document, which tells of wrongs and injustices done to slaves, as well as sounds a warning to the nation that there will be a general uprising of slaves if slavery is not soon abolished.

In *My Bondage and My Freedom*, published in 1855, Douglass again seeks to reveal the "true nature, character, and tendency of the slave system" and to plead the cause of "my afflicted people" (vii). Appearing ten years after the *Narrative* and after his break with Garrison (who had written the preface to the *Narrative*), *My Bondage* offers more details about his experiences as a slave and also his work as an abolitionist, this time with an introduction by a black abolitionist and physician, Dr. James M'Cune Smith. In the book, Douglass rejects the Garrisonian abolitionist advice to stick to "the facts" and leave the "philosophy" to others: "It did not entirely satisfy me to *narrate* wrongs; I felt like *denouncing* them" (361–62). *My Bondage* tells some of the same stories he told in the *Narrative*, but with additional and often more horrifying details, as in, for example, the description of Captain Anthony's whipping of Aunt Esther: "Each blow vigorously laid on, brought screams as well as blood" (87). Douglass points out that a slave is not bound by social morality: "Make a man a slave, and you rob him of moral responsibility" (191). Thus, Douglass feels no qualms of conscience in stealing from Master Thomas or other slaveholders. Douglass returns to his theme of the toll that slavery has on the family, noting that "[m]y poor mother . . . had many children, but NO FAMILY!" (48). Douglass also describes the racism he experiences as a freeman. He is sometimes stoned or insulted with racist slurs at lectures; he must often sit in segregated train cars and is denied entrance to hotels and restaurants. In the "Appendix," Douglass includes the 1848 letter to Master Thomas in which Douglass tells him that he intends to make use of him as "a weapon with which to assail the system of slavery" (428).

In 1881, Douglass published his life story for the third time as *Life and Times of Frederick Douglass*. Nearly twice as long as *My Bondage and My Freedom* (which had itself been four times as long as the *Narrative*), *Life and Times* updates his autobiography to the year 1881. *Life and Times* offers only slight changes in the account of his years as a slave provided in *My Life and My Bondage*, except for the addition of the story of his escape from slavery. It adds a number of chapters describing his role in the Civil War and in the post–Civil War era, exposing particularly the problems facing blacks in the post-Reconstruction era. In 1892, Douglass updated *Life and Times*. Here, Douglass is primarily concerned with building his image for posterity. In his own words, "I like most men who give the world their autobiographies I wish my story to be told as favorably towards myself as it can be with a due regard to truth" (514). He would like to be remembered as a person who "endeavored to deliver [his people] from the power of superstition, bigotry, and priestcraft" and "urged upon them self reliance, self respect, industry, perseverance, and economy" (480). He sums up his contribution: "Forty years of my life have been given to the cause of my people, and if I had forty years more they should all be sacredly given to the same great cause" (480). In the final analysis, Douglass in his last autobiography presents himself as a Moses for his people, who not only delivered them from the jaws of slavery but also fought incessantly for their citizenship and equal rights.

Through his autobiographies, Douglass provides a black perspective that is not available in most works written by his contemporaries. These autobiographies also tell the story of Douglass's changing persona from that of a black hero to a black leader to a black messianic figure. However, the fact that Douglass tends to document rather than dramatize the conflicts, issues, and events by including numerous excerpts from his speeches and other writings makes his *Life and Times* (1881, 1892) much less interesting autobiography than the *Narrative* or *My Bondage and My Freedom*.

CRITICAL RECEPTION

Of Douglass's three autobiographies, the *Narrative* has received the most critical attention as well as highest critical acclaim. Most reviews of the *Narrative* were favorable. Margaret Fuller, reviewing the book for the June 10, 1845, issue of the *New York Tribune*, offers high praise: "Considered merely as narrative, we have never read one more simple, true, coherent and warm with genuine feeling" (2). Ephraim Peabody, however, in his July 1849 *Christian Examiner* article, finds Douglass prone to using "extravagance and passionate and rhetorical flourishes," indicating that he might be "thinking more of his speech than of the end for which he professes to make it," which makes Douglass's commitment to the antislavery cause suspect. (26). In 1969, the *Narrative* was included in Hennig Cohen's *Landmarks of American Writing*, signifying its acceptance into the American canon. In *Landmarks*, Benjamin Quarles calls the *Narrative* "a landmark in the literary crusade against slavery" (101). He adds that the *Narrative* owes its popularity to its "strong storyline," its believability, its "simple and direct prose," its power to evoke sympathy, and its "sharply etched portraits" (104–7).

Albert E. Stone, in a 1973 article in the *CLA Journal*, points out that the *Narrative* shows "the man revealed in the act of discovering and recreating his own identity in the face of slavery's denial of individuality and creativity" (65–66). In a 1978 essay, Henry Louis Gates Jr. points out that Douglass's narrative strategy employs "binary oppositions": "[B]y opposing two seemingly unrelated elements, such as the sheep, cattle, or horses on the plantation, and the specimen of life known as slave, Douglass's language is made to signify the presence and absence of some quality—in this case, humanity" (89).

Recent works have applied modern critical theories to the *Narrative*. Ann Kibbey in "Language in Slavery" (1983) deconstructs the *Narrative*: "The silence of the slave was not the silence of ignorance, much less of ineptitude, but the silence of a human being whose enslavement had forced on him an extraordinary knowledge of language use" (151). Valerie Smith in *Self-Discovery and Authority in Afro-American Narrative* (1987) says that "Douglass' *Narrative* celebrates both explicitly and symbolically a slave's capacity to achieve humanity in a system that conspires to reduce him to nothing" and suggests that "the plot of the narrative offers a profound endorsement of the fundamental American plot, the myth of the self-made man" (26–27). Fred Lee Hord in *Reconstructing Memory: Black Literary Criticism* (1991) argues that "Douglass' *Narrative* is a study of the 'power of truth' triumphing over 'irresponsible power' " and that the " 'power of truth' was necessary to the slaves to demystify their predicament and to resist the dehumanization of an alien identity and ethos" (45). Ann Kibbey and Michelle Stepto offer the Marxian perspective that alienation from the self and language is caused by the marketplace, and thus Douglass's awareness of the market's operation makes him "potentially free" (179). Deborah E. McDowell contends that the *Narrative* makes aggressive "manhood" identical with selfhood and points to Douglass's "complex and troubling relationship to slave women" (202–3).

Douglass's second autobiography, *My Bondage and Freedom*, according to Eric J. Sundquist, reveals that Douglass has thrown off the yoke of the "white father-figure," replacing him with "a self-fathered figure combining black and white ideals" (124). James Matlock in his March 1979 *Phylon* article finds *Life and Times* loose and rambling in design, as it is padded with excerpts from Douglass's "speeches, articles, and letters" and lacks in "excitement, anger and expectation" of the 1845 *Narrative* (26). Wilson J. Moses criticizes *Life and Times* as a "literary act of self-presentation . . . skillfully engineered to produce desired effects on certain sets of white liberals," and contends that in this book "Douglass became a stereotype, limited by the constraints of the myths . . . the myth of rags to riches and the myth of the heroic slave . . . to which he so successfully contributed" (68–69). And Jenny Franchot attacks Douglass for failing to give full due to the contributions of women to his struggle and reducing the description of the role of women to no more than a part of one chapter of his final autobiography, despite his advocacy of women's rights (149).

BIBLIOGRAPHY

Autobiographical Works by Frederick Douglass

Narrative of the Life of Frederick Douglass, an American Slave, Written by Himself. Boston, 1845. Ed. Houston A. Baker Jr. New York: Penguin, 1986.

My Bondage and My Freedom. Intro. Dr. James M'Cune Smith. New York, 1855. Rpt. with the original intro. and a new intro. by Philip S. Foner. 1856. New York: Dover, 1969.

Life and Times of Frederick Douglass, Written by Himself. Intro. George L. Ruffin. Hartford, CT: Park, 1881; Boston: De Wolfe and Fiske, 1892; reprint, with a new intro. by Rayford W. Logan. New York: Collier Books, 1962; facsimile, New York: Carol, 1995.

"My Escape from Slavery." *The Century Magazine* (November 1881): 125–31.

Frederick Douglass: Selected Speeches and Writings. Ed. Philip S. Foner. Abridged and adapted by Yuval Taylor. Chicago, IL: Lawrence Hill Books, 1999.

Studies of Frederick Douglass's Autobiographical Works

Cohen, Hennig, ed. *Landmarks of American Writing*. New York: Basic Books, 1969.

Franchot, Jenny. "The Punishment of Esther: Frederick Douglass and the Construction of the Feminine." In *Frederick Douglass: New Literary and Historical Essays.* Ed. Eric J. Sundquist. Cambridge: Cambridge University Press, 1990. 141–65.

Fuller, Margaret. Rev. of *Narrative of the Life of Frederick Douglass, an American Slave. New York Tribune,* June 10, 1845, 2.

Gates, Henry Louis, Jr. "Binary Oppositions in Chapter One of *Narrative of the Life of Frederick Douglass, an American Slave, Written by Himself.*" In *Afro-American Literature.* Ed. Dexter Fisher and Robert B. Stepto. New York: MLA, 1978. 212–32. Rpt. in *Figures in Black: Words, Signs and the "Racial" Self.* By Henry Louis Gates Jr. New York: Oxford University Press, 1987. 80–97.

Hord, Fred Lee. *Reconstructing Memory: Black Literary Criticism.* Chicago: Third World Press, 1991.

Kibbey, Ann. "Language in Slavery." *Prospects: The Annual of American Cultural Studies* 8 (1983). In *Frederick Douglass's Narrative of the Life of Frederick Douglass.* Ed. Harold Bloom. New York: Chelsea House, 1988. 131–52.

Kibbey, Ann, and Michelle Stepto. "The Antilanguage of Slavery: Frederick Douglass's 1845 *Narrative.*" In *Critical Essays on Frederick Douglass.* Ed. William L. Andrews. Boston: G.K. Hall, 1991. 166–91.

Matlock, James. "The Autobiographies of Frederick Douglass." *Phylon* 40 (March 1979): 15–27.

McDowell, Deborah E. "In the First Place: Making Frederick Douglass and the Afro-American Narrative Tradition." In *Critical Essays on Frederick Douglass.* Ed. William L. Andrews. Boston: G.K. Hall, 1991. 66–83.

Moses, Wilson J. "Writing Freely?: Frederick Douglass and the Constraints of Racialized Writing." In *Frederick Douglass: New Literary and Historical Essays.* Ed. Eric J. Sundquist. Cambridge: Cambridge University Press, 1990.

Peabody, Ephraim. Rev. of Douglass's *Narrative* in "Narratives of Fugitive Slaves." *Christian Examiner* 47 (July 1849): 61–93. In *Critical Essays on Frederick Douglass.* Ed. William L. Andrews. Boston: G.K. Hall, 1991.

Smith, Valerie. *Self-Discovery and Authority in Afro-American Narrative.* Cambridge: Harvard University Press, 1987.

Stone, Albert E. "Identity and Art in Frederick Douglass's *Narrative.*" *CLA Journal* 17 (1973): 192–213. In *Critical Essays on Frederick Douglass.* Ed. William L. Andrews. Boston: G.K. Hall, 1991. 62–78.

Sundquist, Eric J. "Frederick Douglass: Literacy and Paternalism." *Raritan* 2 (Fall 1986): 108–24. In *Critical Essays on Frederick Douglass.* Ed. William L. Andrews. Boston: G.K. Hall, 1991.

Biographical and Other Sources

Chesnutt, Charles W. *Frederick Douglass.* Boston: Houghton Mifflin, 1899.

Diedrich, Maria. *Love across Color Lines: Ottilie Assing & Frederick Douglass.* New York: Hill and Wang, 1999.

Emerson, Ralph Waldo. *The Complete Essays and Other Writings of Ralph Waldo Emerson.* Ed. Brooks Atkinson. New York: Modern Library, 1950.

Franklin, Benjamin. *The Autobiography of Benjamin Franklin.* Ed. Nathaniel Edward Griffin. Chicago, IL: Scott, Foresman, n.d.

McFeeley, William S. *Frederick Douglass.* New York: W.W. Norton, 1991.

Preston, Dickson J. *Young Frederick Douglass: The Maryland Years*. Baltimore: Johns Hopkins University Press, 1980.

Quarles, Benjamin. *Frederick Douglass*. Washington, DC: Associated Publishers, 1948. With revised intro. by James M. McPherson. New York: Da Capo Press, 1997.

Washington, Booker T. *Frederick Douglass*. Philadelphia: George W. Jacobs, 1907. New York: Greenwood, 1969.

W.E.B. DU BOIS
(1868–1963)

David L. Dudley

BIOGRAPHY

William Edward Burghardt Du Bois was born on February 23, 1868, in Great Barrington, Massachusetts. Before he was two, his father deserted the family, leaving Du Bois's mother to raise him alone. Du Bois's intellectual gifts were recognized while he was young, and with scholarship help, he was able to attend college, graduating from Fisk University in 1888. Studies at Harvard and the University of Berlin led to Du Bois earning the Ph.D. from Harvard in 1895; he was the first African American to do so.

In 1896, the University of Pennsylvania hired Du Bois to conduct a sociological study of the black population of Philadelphia. The result was *The Philadelphia Negro*, a groundbreaking work of urban sociology, published in 1899. Du Bois married Nina Gomer in 1896; they had two children, a son who died of diphtheria in 1899 and a daughter, Nina Yolande, who later was married briefly to African American poet Countee Cullen.

Denied a teaching job at Penn because of his race, Du Bois went to teach at Atlanta University in 1897. Under his direction, the university sponsored many yearly conferences in various areas of sociology, publishing them as Atlanta University Studies (1897–1914).

During his years at Atlanta, Du Bois became a leading opponent of Booker T. Washington's* philosophy of industrial education and the acceptance of social segregation. Believing that the nation would never willingly accept full equality for African Americans and stung by Washington's ongoing derogation of academic education, Du Bois first waged a paper war against the Tuskegee leader, highlighted by his 1903 essay "Of Mr. Booker T. Washington and Others," published as part of his superb *The Souls of Black Folk*. Then Du Bois joined others to act against Washington. He helped form the Niagara Movement in 1905 and became a founding member of the National Association for the Advancement of Colored People (NAACP) in 1910. As editor of the civil rights' organization's paper *Crisis*, Du Bois exerted profound influence on what black Americans read and thought for nearly twenty-five years.

Because of disputes with other leaders of the NAACP over control of *Crisis* and the philosophy of the organization, Du Bois resigned in 1934 and returned to Atlanta University as chair of its Department of Sociology. These were highly productive years for Du Bois: In 1935, he published what some consider his greatest work, *Black Reconstruction*. His first full-length autobiography, *Dusk of Dawn*, followed in 1940. Du Bois returned to the NAACP in 1944 as its director of special research. He continued his commitment to Pan-Africanism, an interest he had developed in the 1920s. Elected as chair of the Council on African Affairs in 1948, Du Bois found himself involved with an organization labeled subversive by the Office of the Attorney General. While serving as chair of the Peace Information Center, Du Bois was indicted by the federal government for associating with an organization considered an "agent of a foreign principal." At this time, he married Shirley Graham, his first wife having died in 1950.

Although Du Bois was acquitted of all charges, his indictment embittered him. When his passport was restored in 1958, he traveled extensively in communist countries; in 1961 he joined the American Communist Party and left the country for good, settling in Ghana, where he was received with honor. Du Bois had devoted his long life to fighting for African Americans, and he felt his own nation had betrayed his service as well as its promise of equality for all. He died on August 27, 1963, during the March on Washington that featured the Rev. Martin Luther King Jr.'s famous "I Have a Dream" speech. Du Bois had done much to move America toward that day and the realization of that dream. Sadly, he died a voluntary expatriate from the nation he had served so long and faithfully.

AUTOBIOGRAPHICAL WORKS AND THEMES

At Harvard, W.E.B. Du Bois was trained in a cluster of interrelated disciplines that he later identified as comprising the field of sociology. As a sociologist he did his life's work, drawing upon, as need demanded, his expertise in philosophy, psychology, history, and economics to solve the racial problems before him. He approached the autobiographical endeavor the same way.

In *Dusk of Dawn*, Du Bois writes, "[M]y autobiography is a digressive illustration and exemplification of what race has meant in the world in the nineteenth and twentieth centuries. It is for this reason that I have named and tried to make this book an autobiography of race rather than merely a personal reminiscence" (221). Indeed, the subtitle of the work is "An Essay toward an Autobiography of a Race Concept." But long before publishing *Dusk of Dawn* in 1940, Du Bois had been writing about incidents in his own life, not to record their intrinsic importance but because, as he writes in the "Apology" to *Dusk of Dawn*, "My life had its significance and its only deep significance because it was part of a Problem; but that problem was, as I continue to think the central problem of the greatest of the world's democracies and so the Problem of the future world" (vii–viii). The Problem, of course, is race.

In *The Souls of Black Folk* (1903), Du Bois writes autobiographically twice, linking personal experience with the dilemma facing all black Americans. In the first essay, "Of Our Spiritual Strivings," he recalls a question the world has asked his entire life: "How does it feel to be a problem?" Du Bois then recounts the experience that first made this problem real. The boys and girls in his school were buying and exchanging personalized visiting cards. A white girl refused Du Bois's card—because he was black. That made him realize he was different, separated from his classmates by a veil of color. The result was a double-consciousness Du Bois shares with other African Americans: "One ever feels his two-ness,—an American, a Negro; two souls, two thoughts, two unreconciled strivings, two warring ideals in one dark body, whose dogged strength alone keeps it from being torn asunder" (364–65).

In the chapter "Of the Passing of the First-Born," Du Bois writes for the only time of the death, from diphtheria, of his little son Burghardt in 1899. Du Bois finds consolation and meaning in the tragedy only by reflecting that the child was loved during his short life and died before he could experience the sting of race prejudice. The father admits to feeling "an awful gladness," telling himself that little Burghardt is "[n]ot dead, not dead, but escaped; not bond, but free" (510). He bids his son farewell: "Well sped, my boy, before the world had dubbed your ambition insolence, had held your ideals unattainable, and taught you to cringe and bow" (510). He adds, "[S]leep till I sleep and waken to a baby voice and the ceaseless patter of little feet—above the Veil" (511).

These two reminiscences, of being rejected as a schoolboy and losing a son, are instructive. Such glimpses into his personal life are rare; one reads *Dusk of Dawn* and *The Autobiography of W.E.B. Du Bois* without ever being told the name of Du Bois's wife (Nina Gomer Du Bois, to whom he was not very happily married for fifty-three years) or that he had a daughter, Yolande. Du Bois is not interested in detailing his private life, referring to it most often to illustrate the problems of racial prejudice.

In 1929, to observe his fiftieth year, Du Bois wrote *Darkwater*, a collection of essays, short fiction, and poetry. Like *The Souls of Black Folk*, which it resembles, it contains autobiographical elements. The opening essay, "The Shadow of Years," recalls the early period of Du Bois's life, a time also remembered with nostalgic affection and increasing detail in *Dusk of Dawn* and *The Autobiography*. The three versions of these early years make some things clear. Despite his father's desertion and the resulting poverty it brought him and his mother, Du Bois had a happy childhood and reveled in the beauty and freedom of growing up in small-town New England. He is proud of his family heritage, with its intermixing of African, Dutch, and French blood. Du Bois regards with wonder the series of events that took him, a poor black youth, out of rural obscurity into the larger world of Fisk University, Harvard, Europe, and study at the University of Berlin. Finally, in these reminiscences, one sees Du Bois's characteristic turn of mind. He always comments on racial conditions and how they affect him. He takes pride in Fisk, a self-contained world peopled with handsome black men and beautiful black women, taught by superb black scholars. The curriculum at Harvard is described to expose the racism inherent in its teaching of history and psychology. His European sojourn gives Du Bois opportunity to describe the relative lack of racism there, followed by the shock of his reentry into "nigger-hating America." Du Bois values most highly a handful of his early accomplishments—teaching at Wilberforce, despite difficulties with its ultraconservative administration, and pioneering work in urban sociology under the auspices of the University of Pennsylvania, resulting in the publication of *The Philadelphia Negro* (1899). And he knows the importance of helping found the Niagara Movement in 1905 and then the NAACP in 1909.

Du Bois ends his autobiographical essay in *Darkwater* by recounting a key moment of decision: While race-hatred and discrimination grew in America, would he continue his life as a sheltered academic or take a new course?: "What with all my dreaming, studying, and teaching was I going to *do* in this fierce fight?" (21). Despite his misgivings, Du Bois opts to become a leader in the war against racial injustice.

Du Bois had been in the forefront of the battle thirty years when he wrote *Dusk of Dawn.* He was seventy years old. The first four chapters are fairly standard autobiography, highlighting, as does "The Shadow of Years," his childhood, education, teaching, and publications. Du Bois discusses his conflict with Booker T. Washington and the founding of the Niagara Movement and the NAACP to counteract Washington's programs and policies. There is no mention of Du Bois's marriage, the births of his children, or the death of his son.

The heart of *Dusk of Dawn* is its middle third, the chapters "The Concept of Race," "The White World," and "The Colored World Within." Introducing them, Du Bois calls *race* his "main subject" and under this rubric discusses his own education, the racial mixing in his own family, and the meaning of his trip to Africa as "the sixth generation in descent from forefathers who left this land" (117). In contrast to Africa where free black people live with dignity and communal life nurtures the individual, America, asserts Du Bois, is a prison. African Americans, shut in a dark cave, have tried to speak reasonably to their white jailers, asking for seemingly simple things such as freedom of choice, expression, and education. But no one listens. The imprisoned eventually "may scream and hurl themselves against the barriers, hardly realizing in their bewilderment that they are screaming in a vacuum unheard and that their antics may actually seem funny to those outside looking in" (131). As a result, blacks tend to focus too narrowly only on the race issue at the expense of all other concerns and interests of life, see themselves more as members of a certain race than as individuals, or regard all whites as enemies. "This," writes Du Bois, "was the race concept which has dominated my life, and the history of which I have attempted to make the leading theme of this book" (132–33).

The chapter titled "The White World" centers on a lengthy conversation between Du Bois and an imaginary white man he names Roger Van Dieman, who speaks for the mass of white people of his time. Although he is not overtly hostile to Du Bois (and, by extension, to blacks), he carries within him all the knee-jerk prejudices of his race and class. Van Dieman and Du Bois spar over basic issues: whether blacks are by nature inferior to whites; which race is inherently the more beautiful; the supposed superiority of white technology, culture, and art over that of blacks—even over the definition of *race* itself. The conversation is doomed to end in failure; Du Bois, speaking reasonably for blacks, cannot penetrate the closed mind of Van Dieman, who at least is willing to talk with him over such matters. If *he* cannot be reached, how much less hope is their for changing the minds of hostile whites who will not even deign to discuss racial matters?

Why Roger Van Dieman cannot "hear" Du Bois is taken up in the rest of the chapter: Like most other whites, Van Dieman is hopelessly confused in his thinking. His training as a Christian and a Gentleman contradict what he's been taught as a White Man and as an American. How is the black man to communicate with such a conflicted, confused individual? As Du Bois puts it, "[W]hat can be done to make the attitudes rational and consistent and calculated to advance the best interests of the whole world of men?" (171). At one time Du Bois, trained in rational thought, had believed that education would be enough, telling the truth to the white world would be enough. But now he does not: "The present attitude and action of the white world is not based solely upon rational, deliberate intent. It is a matter of conditioned reflexes; of following long habits, customs, and folkways; of subconscious trains of reasoning and unconscious nervous reflexes" (172). Blacks, although victimized by these white attitudes, are nevertheless called to reach whites by a program of "carefully planned and scientific propaganda" (172). Du Bois sums it up: "The colored world therefore must be seen as existing not simply for itself but as a group whose insistent cry may yet become the warning which awakens the world to its truer self and its wider destiny" (172). To this task he devoted his own life.

Du Bois finishes *Dusk of Dawn*'s long meditation on race in the chapter "The Colored World Within." Here he discusses the dilemma the black world faces, especially blacks like himself—educated and aware of the race problem not only in America but also across the globe. Du Bois states three possible reactions or solutions: (1) Blacks can fight, constantly demanding equality of all sorts, in the workplace, in politics, and in society. (2) Blacks can follow the plan of Marcus Garvey and others and return to Africa, their native homeland. (This Du Bois finds eminently impractical.) (3) They can create within America a separate, independent economy centered in black enterprise. This plan, detailed at length, represents Du Bois's own solution to the racial problem at the time of his writing in 1940.

The remainder of *Dusk of Dawn* recounts Du Bois's life from 1910 until 1940. He describes the early years of the NAACP; the difficulties during the years of the Wilson administration, which was hostile to blacks; the reemergence of the Ku Klux Klan; and the victories achieved by African Americans in World War I, which, despite segregation within the armed forces, saw thousands of blacks serve with honor and the training and commissioning of hundreds of black officers. Nevertheless, the war years brought a rising tide of race hatred in America, exemplified by the many brutal lynchings in that time.

In the final chapters of *Dusk of Dawn*, Du Bois summarizes his work in the post–World War I era, noting particularly the dramatic social and political changes in Russia after the Revolution of 1917 and his own visit to the Soviet Union in 1927. Du Bois's later life was marked by an increasing interest in socialism and communism and by his eventual embracing of communism as the only solution to the problems of racist capitalism's exploitation of the colored peoples of the world. Writing of what he sees as the goals of the Russian Revolution, Du Bois states, "It made the assumption, long disputed, that out of the down-trodden mass of people, ability and character, sufficient to do this task effectively, could and would be found. I believed this dictum passionately. It was, in fact, the foundation stone of my fight for black folk; it explained me" (285).

As he had marked his fiftieth and seventieth years with autobiographical writing, so did Du Bois greet his ninetieth year with yet another life narrative. According to Herbert Aptheker, editor of *The Autobiography of W.E.B. Du Bois*, the manuscript of the work was taken by Du Bois to Ghana when he settled there in 1961, in an expatriation partly symbolic action and partly rooted in personal need. After Du Bois's death in 1963, the manuscript was published first in communist countries, where Du Bois was regarded as a hero, and in 1968 in America.

The *Autobiography* is not as important or original a work as is *Dusk of Dawn*. It does add new information from the years following *Dusk of Dawn*, especially the shameful episodes of Du Bois's indictment and trial for being an agent of a "foreign principal." But many of the earlier sections of the book repeat, with additional details, materials from the earlier autobiography. Sometimes the text of *Dusk of Dawn* is incorporated almost verbatim into the new book, but the added details usually add little to the reader's understanding of Du Bois's development as a thinker.

Readers today, living in the postcommunist world and noting particularly the economic ruin of Russia, may take a smug attitude toward Du Bois's extravagant praise of world communism. How could such a brilliant man be so wrong about the outcome of one of the greatest political conflicts of the twentieth century? But Du Bois died in 1963, when the victory of Western capitalism was far from assured. Uppermost in his mind was always how best to help African Americans and other peoples of color around the world. As his biographer David Levering Lewis notes, "W.E.B. Du Bois attempted virtually every possible solution to the problem of twentieth century racism — scholarship, propaganda, integration, cultural and economic separatism, politics, international communism, expatriation, third-world solidarity" (*Fight* 571). It was perhaps the greatest irony of his long, dedicated life that it was "the egregious failings of American democracy that drove him, decade by decade, to the paradox of defending totalitarianism in the service of a global ideal of economic and social justice" (571).

CRITICAL RECEPTION

Reviews of *The Souls of Black Folk* were mixed. It sold well and was praised for its eloquence, but according to David Levering Lewis, Booker T. Washington's "Tuskegee Machine" kept it from being reviewed in the black press (*Biography* 291–92). The white press in the South didn't like the book either, and various charges were leveled at Du Bois—everything from "inciting to rape" to not knowing anything about the Southern Negro, to his "impatience and impertinence" (293). Today, however, *Souls* is regarded as one of the most important milestones in twentieth-century American literature. It has been called "epochal" and "prophetic," a work that "redefined the terms of a three-hundred-year interaction between black and white people and influenced the cultural and political psychology of peoples of African descent throughout the Western hemisphere, as well as on the continent of Africa" (277).

Darkwater was widely hailed for the beauty and passion of its style; a writer for the *Socialist Review* also praises it for describing the plight not only of black Americans but also of all dark-skinned people subjugated by imperialist powers. Those who did not like the book faulted Du Bois for being too bitter and for incorrectly asserting his claims about the global domination of "coloured" peoples by whites. A reviewer in *The Nation* declares that *Darkwater* is "tinctured with hate, and the teaching of violence which often defeats [Du Bois's] own purpose" (Villard 726). Amazingly, the reviewer for the *New York Times* writes that the book focuses too much on one subject—race, presumably—a fault that leads its author to turn "general, universal wrongs into special negro wrongs" (19), thus taking a view opposite that of the *Socialist Review*. Widely divergent opinions of Du Bois's writing are often found among the critics, revealing much about their own racial beliefs.

Critics cited *Dusk of Dawn* for painting what Ernestine Rose calls "an unforgettable picture of the changing social life of our time" (707). They also agree that Du Bois's concern for the enormous problem of racism keeps him from the self-revelation usually associated with autobiography. The reviewer for *The Nation* laments that the book "provides but a dim portrait of that extraordinary man himself" but recognizes *Dusk of Dawn* as the manifesto it is: "His book is no petition; it is a personal bill of rights" (512). Lombard C. Jones, writing for the *New York Times Book Review*, notes that the book "traces sensitively and with vital force a progression of life and thought dedicated to what this great Negro leader believes is the central problem of our democracy and of the future world" (16). Jones asserts that the chapters "The White World" and "The Colored World Within" are central to the book and commends their frank discussing of

"[t]he Negroes' grievances and of proposals advocated for their correction" (16).
He goes on to note that any intellectuals who would like to believe that
America's racial problems are not serious should read *Dusk of Dawn*.

When *The Autobiography of W.E.B. Du Bois* was published in America, five
years after his death, critics used the opportunity to summarize not only the book
itself but also the extraordinary life of its author. Martin Duberman, writing in
the *New Republic*, gives both the book and the man a mixed review. He finds
the first third of the book, dealing with Du Bois's youth, the most compelling
but notes that the autobiography does not cause readers to reevaluate their assessment of African American history or of Du Bois but rather corroborates their
previous understanding. Duberman notes that *The Autobiography* confirms his
view of Du Bois's "own confusions and contradictions" and faults Du Bois's
"mindless defenses" of communism (what he calls the worst parts of the book).
On the other hand, Duberman hails Du Bois as a prophet who realized before
most other people how difficult it would be to implement the court-ordered
desegregation of public schools, who prefigured by five years the Black Panther
Party's call for blacks to undertake an "inner cooperative movement" in the
meantime, and who foresaw the African American fascination with African culture, clothes, and "black is beautiful" race pride of the 1970s.

As the title of his review in *Harper's* indicates, Irving Howe shares Martin
Duberman's ambivalent reaction to Du Bois and his autobiography. In "Remarkable Man, Ambiguous Legacy," Howe praises the early parts of *The Autobiography*
for its excellent prose style, calling it "a classic American narrative" (143). He
finds it interesting that Du Bois's life, which followed exactly the formula for
success mandated by the American Dream, was nevertheless doomed to be one
of frustration because of the race problem. Howe devotes considerable space to
the Du Bois–Booker T. Washington controversy, defending both men as posses-
sors of partial truth. He notes how Du Bois's views changed over a long life,
moving from a belief in complete integration to "a kind of segregated nationalism" (143). Like Duberman, Howe is troubled by Du Bois's defense of communism in the book, noting the irony that Du Bois, a victim of injustice at home,
came to be its apologist overseas and that his "final commitment was soiled both
morally and intellectually" (149).

While the critical literature on Du Bois's works has grown greatly over the
years, his autobiographies have received relatively little attention. When they
are written about, it is more for their sociological content, Du Bois's tireless
examination and reexamination of the myriad facets of the racial question. Now
that David Levering Lewis's monumental two-volume biography of Du Bois is
completed, readers have available an exhaustive study of the man's works as well
as of his public and private life, the truth of which is scarcely hinted at in the
autobiographies. Lewis gives ample time to *The Souls of Black Folk*, *Darkwater*,
and *Dusk of Dawn* but hardly mentions *The Autobiography*, which is perhaps his
tacit critical comment evaluation of that book. One of the most detailed analyses
of *Dusk of Dawn* is in my own book, *My Father's Shadow: Intergenerational Conflict
in African American Men's Autobiography*. I give particular attention to Du Bois's

treatment of his controversy with Booker T. Washington and how Du Bois creates an unusual autobiographical "I."

BIBLIOGRAPHY

Autobiographical Works by W.E.B. Du Bois

The Souls of Black Folk. Chicago: A.C. McClurg and Co., 1903. Rpt. in *W.E.B. Du Bois: Writings.* New York: Viking/Library of America, 1986.
Darkwater: Voices from Within the Veil. New York: Harcourt, Brace, and Howe, 1920. Rpt., New York: Schocken Books, 1969.
Dusk of Dawn: An Essay toward an Autobiography of a Race Concept. New York: Harcourt, Brace, and World, 1940. Rpt., New York: Schocken Books, 1968.
The Autobiography of W.E.B. Du Bois: A Soliloquy on Viewing My Life from the Last Decade of Its First Century. New York: International Books, 1968.

Studies of W.E.B. Du Bois's Autobiographical Works

Byerman, Keith. *Seizing the Word: History, Art, and Self in the Works of W.E.B. Du Bois.* Athens: University of Georgia Press, 1994.
De Marco, Joseph. *The Social Thought of W.E.B. Du Bois.* Lanham, MD: University Press of America, 1983.
Duberman, Martin. "Du Bois as Prophet." *New Republic* 158 (March 23, 1968): 36–39.
Dudley, David L. *My Father's Shadow: Intergenerational Conflict in African-American Men's Autobiography.* Philadelphia: University of Pennsylvania Press, 1991.
Horne, Gerald. *Black and Red: W.E.B. Du Bois and the Afro-American Response to the Cold War, 1944–1963.* Albany: State University of New York Press, 1986.
Howe, Irving. "Remarkable Man, Ambiguous Legacy." *Harper's* 236 (March 1968): 143–49.
Jones, Lombard C. "Fifty Years of Crusading for the Negro in America." *New York Times Book Review* (December 22, 1940): 16.
Lewis, David Levering. *W.E.B. Du Bois: Biography of a Race 1868–1919.* New York: Henry Holt, 1993.
———. *W.E.B. Du Bois: The Fight for Equality and the American Century, 1919–1963.* New York: Henry Holt, 2000.
Manning, Marable. *W.E.B. Du Bois: Black Radical Democrat.* Boston: Twayne, 1986.
Moore, Jack. *W.E.B. Du Bois.* Twayne's U.S. Authors Series. Boston: Twayne, 1981.
Rampersad, Arnold. *The Art and Imagination of W.E.B. Du Bois.* New York: Schocken Books, 1990.
Reed, Adolph, Jr. *W.E.B. Du Bois and American Political Thought: Fabianism and the Color Line.* New York: Oxford University Press, 1997.
Rev. of *Darkwater. New York Times Book Review* (August 8, 1920): 19.
Rev. of *Darkwater. Socialist Review* 8 (May 20, 1920): 381.
Rev. of *Dusk of Dawn. The Nation* 151 (November 23, 1940): 512.
Rose, Ernestine. Rev. of *Dusk of Dawn. Library Journal* 65 (September 1, 1940): 707.
Villard, Oswald Garrison. Rev. of *Darkwater. The Nation* 110 (May 29, 1920): 726.

ALICE MOORE DUNBAR-NELSON
(1875–1935)

Gwendolyn S. Jones

BIOGRAPHY

During the course of her life, Alice Moore Dunbar-Nelson participated in diverse activities, not all of which were related to writing. She also devoted her considerable talents, skills, and energy to pursuits where she excelled as teacher, lecturer, public speaker, administrator, editor, social activist, political activist, club woman, and scholar. A prolific writer, she produced poetry, short stories, drama, two unpublished novels, essays, newspaper columns, and magazine articles. Although she wrote more prose than poetry, she gained a reputation as a poet during the Harlem Renaissance.

Alice Ruth Moore was born in New Orleans on July 19, 1875, to parents with mixed African American, Native American, and European American backgrounds. She enjoyed an active professional and social life there until her family (mother, sister, and brother-in-law) moved to Medford, Massachusetts, when she was twenty-one years old. She was a well-educated woman, having received training in music, art, and drama; earned a teaching certificate from Straight College (now Dillard University); earned a master's degree from Cornell University; and pursued studies at the University of Pennsylvania, School of Industrial Art in Philadelphia, and Columbia University. She began teaching at age seventeen, a profession she followed for thirty-six years.

During her adult life, Alice Ruth Moore was to marry three times. In 1898, she secretly married poet Paul Laurence Dunbar in New York City. Shortly afterward, she announced the marriage, then moved to Washington, D.C., to join him. This marriage, alternately romantic and stormy, lasted four years. After their separation, Dunbar-Nelson and her family moved to Wilmington, Delaware, where she was a member of the faculty and administrative staff at Howard High

School during an eighteen-year period. She was released from her position because of her political activism. A second brief secret marriage from 1910 to 1911 was to Henry Arthur Callis. At the time, Callis, twelve years her junior, was a teacher at Howard High School. In 1916, she married journalist Robert Nelson, a widower with two small children. She remained with him until her death in 1935.

AUTOBIOGRAPHICAL WORK AND THEMES

The personal diary that Dunbar-Nelson kept in 1921 and again from 1926 to 1931 was edited by Gloria T. Hull and published with the title *Give Us Each Day: The Diary of Alice Dunbar-Nelson*. In the diary she records, reflects, and reacts to such personal topics as family, health, travel, friendships, occupations, recurring financial difficulties, lesbian relationships, and her writing. Contained also is information about contemporary social, political, religious, and civic organizations; and about prominent people in the arts, education, politics, and civic affairs.

Much information is available about Dunbar-Nelson's family, including her mother and her sister Leila, and her children, especially Pauline. Considerable information is also available regarding her husbands, Paul Dunbar, Arthur Callis, and Robert Nelson and his children.

The diary reveals the extent of camaraderie shared among professional black women. For example, Dunbar-Nelson talks about a visit to the home of Georgia Douglas Johnson in Washington, D.C. At one point "Georgia wanted to know how to put on hats, and I began to teach her. She really did not know how, and I had her practise and practise again and again" (87). On a visit to Daytona Beach, Florida, Dunbar-Nelson notes, "At home later, I tried to do something with this homemade head while Mrs. [Mary McLeod] Bethune had her feet pedicured and we gossiped in her room" (352). After a concert by Marian Anderson in Philadelphia, she "stood at the stage door to see her come out. . . . Pecked at Marian's cheek" (269).

A strong advocate for social and civil rights, Dunbar-Nelson fought for the rights of black people and for women. She was an active participant in the women's club movement. At a convention of the National Federation of Colored Women in Washington, D.C., she mentions an executive committee meeting: "I get the A.I.P.C. [American Inter-Racial Peace Committee] endorsed" (249–50).

Alice Dunbar-Nelson's appearance was that of an elegant, well-groomed, well-educated woman with regal bearing ("then I dolled up in my yellow percale and white shoes and stockings and big black hat—took brief case and sallied forth [63]"). At the same time, she was down to earth and loved to have fun. She admits to engaging in such unapproved activities as playing pinochle on Sunday. Once, while waiting in a dressing room to speak, and hearing a jazz group rehearsing, she "shimmies" and "let[s] go, hoarse voice and all; and shake[s] a shoulder and croak[s] a line or two to help on the jazz noise." (122).

Her use of the language is fluent, sophisticated, and descriptive in some entries but informal and colloquial in others. She refers to "Walkerized hair," describes an acquaintance as "Her Hugeness," and frequently evaluates her own performances as "I speak fine."

In addition to the diary, some of her writings are thought to be autobiographical. The assumption is that she uses herself and her experiences as material for some of her unpublished fiction. For example, in a letter (January 23, 1898) to her fiancé Paul Dunbar, some references are made to situations she encountered while teaching in a settlement area in New York City. Similar situations and events are incorporated in a set of stories, "The Annals of 'Steenth Street." The short story "Stones in the Village" treats racial passing, which she occasionally did. In the stories "The Decision" and "No Sacrifice," there are veiled accounts of her courtship and marriage to Paul Dunbar. An essay titled "Brass Ankles Speaks" addresses skin color. The pseudonymous speaker, often referred to as "light nigger," reveals her feelings about her racial status.

CRITICAL RECEPTION

Although her fiction and poetry are more valued than her diary and her journal essays, Alice Dunbar-Nelson's personal diary is a significant document because it provides considerable information and insight into the professional, social, and emotional life of an early-twentieth-century African American woman writer. However, very little critical attention has been devoted to the diary; critics focus instead on her short stories and poetry. In recent reviews of her life and works, critics simply mention the contents. Titus notes that the diary "details Dunbar-Nelson's professional labors, travels, friendships, and recurring financial difficulties and refers to her lesbian relationships" (242). She notes that the diary is significant because of the details it provides about Dunbar-Nelson's public and private life.

Roses and Randolph note, "The entries reveal that Dunbar-Nelson worked tirelessly against great odds to advance the cause of equality for Afro-Americans" (89). The diary also displays her complex emotional life, pointing out that she is devoted to her husband but also has strong romantic attachments to women.

While others see her poetry, short stories, and other genres as worthy of note, Hull sees her diary as "her strongest and most distinctive voice," where she reveals her "strength of mind, spirituality, and psychic power" ("Introduction" 28). Dunbar-Nelson uses the diary for her personal outpourings. It is frequently a place to make notes of daily activities. The entries vary in sentence style and intensity of reflection. Most significant about the diary is what it revels about being a black woman in early-twentieth-century America.

BIBLIOGRAPHY

Autobiographical Work by Alice Moore Dunbar-Nelson

Give Us Each Day: The Diary of Alice Dunbar-Nelson. Ed. Gloria T. Hull. New York: W.W. Norton, 1984.

Studies of Alice Moore Dunbar-Nelson's Autobiographical Work

Hull, Gloria T. "Alice Dunbar-Nelson (1875–1935)." In *Color, Sex, and Poetry: Three Women Writers of the Harlem Renaissance.* Bloomington: Indiana University Press, 1987. 33–104.

———, ed. *Give Us Each Day: The Diary of Alice Dunbar-Nelson.* New York: W.W. Norton, 1984.

———. "Introduction." In *The Works of Alice Dunbar-Nelson.* Vol. 1. New York: Oxford University Press, 1988. 3–13.

Metcalf, E.W., ed. *The Letters of Paul and Alice Dunbar: A Private History.* 3 vols. Berkeley: University of California Press, 1973.

Roses, Lorraine E., and Ruth E. Randolph, eds. "Dunbar-Nelson, Alice Ruth Moore (1875–1935)." In *Harlem Renaissance and Beyond: Literary Biography of 100 Black Women Writers 1900–1945.* Boston: G.K. Hall, 1990. 87–91.

Shockley, Ann Allen. "Alice Ruth Moore Dunbar-Nelson 1875–1935." In *Afro-American Women Writers, 1746–1933: An Anthology and Critical Guide.* New York: New American Library, 1988. 262–67.

Single, Lori Leathers. "Alice Moore Dunbar-Nelson (1875–1935)." In *African American Authors, 1745–1945: A Bio-Bibliographical Critical Sourcebook.* Ed. Emmanuel S. Nelson. Westport, CT: Greenwood Press, 2000. 139–146.

Smith, Jessie Carney, ed. "Alice Dunbar-Nelson (1875–1935)." In *Notable Black American Women.* Detroit: Gale Research, 1992. 293–96.

Titus, Mary. "Alice Moore Dunbar-Nelson." In *The Oxford Companion to African American Literature.* Ed. William L. Andrews, Frances Smith Foster, and Trudier Harris. New York: Oxford University Press, 1997. 241–42.

Williams, Ora. "Alice Moore Dunbar-Nelson." In *Dictionary of Literary Biography: Afro-American Writers before the Harlem Renaissance.* Vol. 50. Ed. Trudier Harris and Thadious M. Davis. Detroit: Gale Research, 1988. 225–32.

ZILPHA ELAW
(1790?–1846?)

Adenike Marie Davidson

BIOGRAPHY

An itinerant evangelist, Zilpha Elaw was born near Philadelphia, Pennsylvania, around 1790. Her parents were free and owned their own farm; she was one of only three surviving children. When Elaw was twelve, her mother died during childbirth, her twenty-second pregnancy. Elaw's oldest brother went to live with their grandfather; her younger sister was placed under the care of an aunt; and Elaw was placed in service to Pierson and Rebecca Mitchel, a Quaker family. Her father died a year and a half later, leaving her orphaned. She remained with them until the age of eighteen.

Elaw, under her parents, was raised in a pious home, but one with lively devotion. Thus the young servant girl found the silent and secretive religious exercises of the Quakers unsettling. In contrast, she was drawn to the emotional appeal and the active proselytizing of the Methodists in her region when she was in her midteens. It is also during this time that she began to have a series of visionary experiences. In her first vision, as she was milking a cow and singing, a figure of Jesus Christ appeared before her with open arms. In 1808, she was converted and joined the Methodist Episcopal Society in an outlying region of Philadelphia.

In 1810 she married Joseph Elaw, a fuller by trade. Their marriage was strained by differing attitudes and commitment to religion; his was a detached involvement with Christianity, while she had an increasingly growing interest in the work of the church. Yet her acceptance of the scriptures and biblical interpretations led her to accept, at first, a conventional role of wife. In 1811, the Elaws moved to Burlington, New Jersey, in response to job opportunities in clothing manufacturing. She gave birth to a daughter in 1812.

Elaw attended her first camp meeting and intense religious revival in 1817 where she fell into a "trance of ecstasy" and heard a voice declare now sanctified. During this meeting she made her first appearance as a public speaker, offering prayers for others at their requests. Also at this meeting, it was revealed to her that she must visit families and speak on the issue of salvation. Her desire and commitment to fulfill this ambition were strongly encouraged by other women. At a second camp meeting, she became an exhorter in the Burlington area, speaking to a congregation that included a large number of whites.

Joseph became quite hostile to her zealous commitment to religion and her enjoyment of and participation in camp meetings. Although her desire to preach was endorsed by the ministers of the Methodist Society, she initially was not supported by the African American Methodist community. Joseph was concerned that she would "become a laughingstock" and advised against the pursuit of public speaking. Despite lack of public consent, she found fortitude through the belief that her calling was divinely inspired.

In 1823, Joseph Elaw died of consumption. Her sudden widow status forced Elaw to work as a domestic; she also placed her daughter in service as a means of support and payment of debts. She also opened a school for African American children, combating the racist practice of refusing African American students into the public schools of Burlington. Yet within two years, Elaw closed the school, feeling these activities prevented her from pursuing the path she had been divinely instructed to follow. She left her daughter in 1827 to begin her career as an evangelical minister.

For seven months, beginning in Philadelphia and journeying to New York, led only by her inner guidance, Elaw's early itinerancy was entirely self-supported; her travels were financially successful, for upon her return she was able to pay her debts. She partnered on the ministry circuit with Jarena Lee* for a time in western Pennsylvania. Her travels were independent, never preaching under any religious denomination.

She returned home in April 1828 for a few days, only to be "called" to preach in the slaveholding states of Maryland and Virginia to racially mixed audiences. This mission lasted one and a half years, in spite of the danger to her personal freedom; upon the conclusion of her mission, she resumed and mostly confined her ministry to the northeastern and mid-Atlantic states until 1840.

In the summer of 1840, after a brief return to the Southern states, Elaw felt called to visit "a foreign shore." She left her native land to spread her message in England. In the next five years spent overseas, Elaw estimated that she preached over a thousand sermons. Details of her life after 1845—where she went and what she did—are unknown.

AUTOBIOGRAPHICAL WORK AND THEMES

Memoirs of the Life, Religious Experience, Ministerial Travels, and Labours of Mrs. Elaw, an American Female of Colour; Together with Some Account of the Great

Religious Revivals in America [Written by Herself], self-published in London in 1845, is Elaw's only known publication. Similar to the slave narrative, Elaw presents an individual transformation of herself and her attitude to her surroundings through knowledge—in the case of the spiritual narrative, it is a knowledge of God and thereby one's divine rights and responsibilities.

The love of God being now shed abroad in my heart by the Holy Spirit, and my soul transported with heavenly peace and joy in God, all the former hardships which pertained to my circumstances and situation vanished; the work and duties which had previously been hard and irksome were now become easy and pleasant; and the evil propensities of my disposition and temper were subdued beneath the softening and refining pressure of divine grace upon my heart. (57)

Despite the lack of an outward call against the institution of slavery, Elaw's memoir helps to fill the gap of knowledge of early African American women's activism, both with racial and gender struggles, fueled by a strong foundation of religious faith. By pursuing a call to public ministry, Elaw (and her contemporaries) radically challenged notions of respectable womanhood and proper female space as limited to the home. As a wife and mother, Elaw boldly places divine authority above patriarchal authority. In response to her husband's desire that she cease with her plans of public preaching, Elaw writes,

I was very sorry to see him so grieved about it; but my heavenly Father had informed me that he had a great work for me to do; I could not then descend down to the counsel of flesh and blood, but adhered faithfully to my commission. (84)

In addition to the challenging of prescribed gender roles, Elaw's narrative gives valuable insight into interdenominational and interracial relationships during the first half of the nineteenth century.

Her autobiography should be seen mostly as another part of her traveling ministry, although in her dedication she expresses concern over the negative influence of some written works, suggesting that she hoped her text may be viewed as a positive Christian contribution and influential in the transformation of others.

CRITICAL RECEPTION

Although Elaw's *Memoirs* was republished in 1986 in a collection of African American women's spiritual narratives (including Jarena Lee and Julia A. Foote*) titled *Sisters of the Spirit* and edited by William L. Andrews, critical examination of her autobiography remains sparse.

Elaw is usually credited as a pioneer in the genre of autobiography, but because little space is given to the details of her life outside of the manifestation of her need for spiritual enlightenment or the result of her commitment to fulfill the call for public speaking, most critics of autobiography do not take the discussion of Elaw's text further. Frances Smith Foster, in *Written by Herself*, gives a brief examination of Elaw's narrative; she argues that *Memoir* "demonstrates an important feature of African American women's literature by asserting the importance of race and gender to definitions and experiences even when neither of these is the focus of the work . . . [B]oth gender and race are assumed signifiers throughout the writing" (85–86).

To date Elaw's autobiography has not been examined fully outside the context of the spiritual narrative genre, nor without comparison and contrast with the narratives of Jarena Lee and either Rebecca Cox Jackson or Julia Foote. Andrews's introduction in *Sisters of the Spirit* gives a very thorough discussion of Elaw's heroic and feminist life in the face of seemingly insurmountable struggles. He sees her text as necessary foundation in the examination and understanding of the evolution of American feminism. Moreover, he sees her text as invaluable to understanding the camp meeting as a feminist space and "the importance of this kind of religious gathering to women who had never taken or felt justified in taking a leadership role in the more traditional religious institutions of the time" (7).

Critical examination of Elaw's autobiography is still greatly needed. As more attention is paid to early works by African Americans and African American women, perhaps Elaw will receive what is needed and deserved.

BIBLIOGRAPHY

Autobiographical Work by Zilpha Elaw

Memoirs of the Life, Religious Experience, Ministerial Travels, and Labours of Mrs. Elaw, an American Female of Colour; Together with Some Account of the Great Religious Revivals in America [Written by Herself]. 1845. Rpt. in *Sisters of the Spirit: Three Black Women's Autobiographies of the Nineteenth Century*. Ed. William L. Andrews. Bloomington: Indiana University Press, 1986. 49–160.

Studies of Zilpha Elaw's Autobiographical Work

Andrews, William L. Introduction. *Sisters of the Spirit: Three Black Women's Autobiographies of the Nineteenth Century*. Bloomington: Indiana University Press, 1986.

Foster, Frances Smith. *Written by Herself: Literary Production by African American Women, 1746–1892*. Bloomington: Indiana University Press, 1993.

Hunter, William R. "Do Not Be Conformed Unto This World: An Analysis of Religious Experience in the Nineteenth Century African American Spiritual Narrative." *Nineteenth Century Studies* 8 (1994): 75–88.

Laprade, Candis Anita. *Pens in the Hand of God: The Spiritual Autobiographies of Jarena*

Lee, Zilpha Elaw, and Rebecca Cox Jackson. Diss. University of North Carolina at Chapel Hill, 1995. Ann Arbor: UMI, 1996. 9538427.

Wharton, Martha Louise. *A Contour Portrait of My Regenerated Constitution: Reading Nineteenth-Century African American Women's Spiritual Autobiography*. Diss. University of Massachusetts, 1996. Ann Arbor: UMI, 1998. 9813652.

EDWARD KENNEDY "DUKE" ELLINGTON (1899–1974)

Joyce Russell-Robinson

BIOGRAPHY

Until 1915 when his sister Ruth was born, Edward Kennedy Ellington was the only child of Daisy Kennedy and James Edward Ellington. Growing up as an "only" for the first sixteen years of life amidst a large extended family of uncles, aunts, and cousins, from his earliest days, young Edward received an abundance of love, support, and nurturing. Starting the first grade at five years of age in Washington, D.C., where the Kennedys had always lived (James Ellington's family was from North Carolina), Edward was far less interested in academics and music than in baseball. As a result of his passion for the national pastime, his musical ability remained largely untapped during his childhood. Not until Ellington's sixteenth year did he really become interested in music. During a summer vacation in Philadelphia, Ellington heard a performance by pianist Harvey Brooks. The pianist with the "tremendous left hand" caused Ellington to say to himself, "Man, you're just going to *have* to do it" (*Mistress* 20). It was also around that time that he would be dubbed with the royal name by which he would always be identified.

A school chum, Edgar McEntree, simply announced at a party that "his friend 'The Duke' was a pianist who wouldn't object if asked to play" (20). Ellington's superb performance earned him the respect of his school friends and the enduring name of Duke.

In some ways that royal sobriquet was quite appropriate. First, Ellington's family—both the Kennedys and Ellingtons—belonged to what was perhaps the most elite African American social class of Washington, D.C. Ellington's father, known as J.E. by his intimate friends, always attempted to provide the royal treatment for his family. He, for example, "kept [the] house loaded with the best food obtainable, and because he was a caterer [the family] had the primest steaks and the finest terrapin" (10). Second, the family was cautious about associating with individuals whom they believed to be their social and economic inferiors. In his autobiography *Music Is My Mistress*, which was published in 1973 (just one year before his death), Ellington noted, for example, that during his childhood there had been talk of desegregating the schools of Washington. Strong objections were raised by his own family and other prominent African Americans who were worried that their children would mingle with white children who, in their minds, could only be socially and economically inferior to their own.

Although Ellington's family may indeed have been class conscious, and although they may have attempted to shelter the youngster from individuals whom they believed to be inferior, they were not altogether successful in avoiding class mingling. For Ellington notes that outsiders—many of whom were several rungs below his family on the socioeconomic ladder—had a great impact on his life. Specifically, he recalls Frank Holliday's pool room where black men of all ages, classes, and professions congregated: boys over and under sixteen, though legally no one under sixteen was allowed; college students; pool sharks; law school students; pickpockets; interns, who treated minor illnesses; and dining-car waiters and Pullman porters (23). Among others who frequented the pool room were Dr. Charles Drew (the doctor of blood plasma fame), Roscoe Lee (a pianist who became a dentist), and Doc Perry (a conservatory trained pianist who became an important mentor to Ellington).

Though Ellington would "collect" many musician-friends throughout his life, one of his longest friendships was with Sonny Greer, an excellent drummer who remained with the orchestra from 1920 until 1951. It is believed that the declining interest in Big Band music forced Greer and several other longtime band members to seek more lucrative employment. Greer and the others who left the band may have regretted doing so, for in 1956 a resurgence of interest in Ellington's music occurred after his band performed at a jazz festival in Rhode Island. Following that performance was an eighteen-year period of productivity for The Duke. His most significant compositions during those years were his three sacred concerts, the last one premiering at London's Westminster Abbey. Ellington's son, Mercer, assumed leadership of the band after his father's death in 1974.

AUTOBIOGRAPHICAL WORKS AND THEMES

Ellington's most important prose work is his autobiography *Music Is My Mistress*, although he also wrote more than a dozen articles and sketches, a few of which assume an autobiographical tone. And he wrote more than 2,000 musical compositions! *Mistress*, as one might expect, takes as its primary focus The Duke's musical journey; however, similar to many other memoirs and autobiographies, *Mistress* is dotted with the names of numerous individuals who were important in the autobiographer's personal and professional development. Ellington's inclusion of so many names—some well known, some obscure—is indeed a plus

He offers fascinating verbal portraits from jazz history. Of particular interest are the portraits of musicians who during the heyday of the Big Band were popular but now who have all but been forgotten. Ellington, for example, discusses the vocal talents of Betty Roche and Ivie Anderson and the composing talent of Maceo Pinkard, who wrote "Sweet Georgia Brown." Another important portrait is of Billy Strayhorn, who joined the Ellington band in 1939 and remained until his death in 1967. Strayhorn was a gifted composer who wrote "Take the 'A' Train," which became the theme for the orchestra.

In addition to its thematic focus on music, Ellington's *Mistress* takes as a secondary theme race and race pride. Rarely does the autobiographer miss an opportunity "to represent the Negro race." Race pride, he demonstrates in his portrait of violinist Will Marion Cook, may coexist with one's creative or professional abilities:

A reviewer said that Will Marion Cook was definitely "the world's greatest Negro violinist." Cook took his violin and went to see the reviewer at the newspaper office. "Thank you very much for the favorable review," he said. "You wrote that I was the world's greatest Negro violinist." "Yes, Mr. Cook," the man said, "and I meant it. You are definitely the world's greatest Negro violinist." With that Cook took out his violin and smashed it across the reviewer's desk. "I am not the world's greatest Negro violinist," he exclaimed. "I am the greatest violinist in the world." (97)

The theme of race pride and its intersection with professionalism and creativity is manifested in other writings by Ellington as well. In the essay "We, Too, Sing 'America,'" for instance, Ellington expounds on the creativity of black Americans and their cultural contributions to the nation and world.

CRITICAL RECEPTION

Although Ellington himself has remained a beloved person and musician through the years, his autobiography has drawn criticism from a number of reviewers. Comments that the 500-plus-page text reveals too little about the writer himself are fairly common. Other comments, like those of Don Rose of the *Chicago Daily News*, suggest that the work lacks a sharp critical opinion. Mark Tucker, an important Ellington scholar, notes that *Mistress* hardly contains a discouraging word about any person or event in Ellington's life (114).

Although artists, verbal and otherwise, may not always be capable of engaging in an objective evaluation of their own works, Ellington may have been an exception. He once told his son Mercer, "We've written the Good Book . . . and now let's write the Bad Book!" (Tucker 114).

Those who admire *Mistress* almost always offer praise on the basis of Ellington's musical contributions to the world and not on the aesthetics or readability of the text. John Widemann in the *New York Times Book Review* notes, for example, that "plenty of composers have taken pains to get their ideas down on paper, yet only this band and composer have succeeded in making great art on such a genuinely human scale" (6).

Although critics and scholars are divided in their views on the merits of Ellington's autobiography, there is near unanimity where his musical genius is concerned. More than twenty-five years after his death and Homegoing Service in New York—attended by numerous jazz greats like Count Basie, Buddy Rich, Ella Fitzgerald, Joe Williams, Mary Lou Williams—The Duke's fans, who are legion, continue to say of him what he always said to them at the close of his concerts: "We want you to know that we love you madly!"

BIBLIOGRAPHY

Autobiographical Works by Edward Kennedy "Duke" Ellington

"The Duke Steps Out." *Rhythm* (March 1931): 20–22.
"My Hunt for Song Titles." *Rhythm* (August 1933): 22–23.
"From Where I Lie." *The Negro Actor* (July 15, 1938): 4.
"We, Too, Sing 'America.' " Annual Lincoln Day Services: Scott Methodist Church, Los Angeles, February 9, 1941.
Music Is My Mistress. Garden City, NY: Doubleday, 1973.

Studies of Edward Kennedy "Duke" Ellington's Autobiographical Works

Collier, James Lincoln. *Duke Ellington.* New York: Oxford University Press, 1987.
Ellington, Mercer, and Stanley Dance. *Duke Ellington in Person.* New York: Houghton Mifflin, 1978.
Hasse, Edward, and Wynton Marsalis. *Beyond Category: The Life and Work of Duke Ellington.* New York: Da Capo, 1995.
Rose, Don. Review of *Music Is My Mistress. Chicago Daily News,* January 26, 1974, B24.
Steed, Janna Tull. *Duke Ellington, a Spiritual Biography.* New York: Crossroad, 1999.
Tucker, Mark, ed. *The Duke Ellington Reader.* New York: Oxford University Press, 1993.
Widemann, John. Review of *Music Is My Mistress. New York Times Book Review* (August 18, 1974): 6.

OLAUDAH EQUIANO
(1745?–1797)

Emmanuel S. Nelson

BIOGRAPHY

Olaudah Equiano, who was later renamed Gustavus Vassa, was born in West Africa most probably in the year 1745. At the age of twelve he was kidnapped and sold into slavery. Purchased by a group of Englishmen engaged in slave trade, Equiano was initially transported to the Caribbean and then to Virginia. There he was purchased by the owner of a small plantation who, after a few weeks, sold him to Michael Henry Pascal—an English sailor who commanded a trans-Atlantic merchant ship. Apparently, Pascal had purchased Equiano as a gift to some of his relatives in England; after becoming acquainted with the African child, however, Pascal decided to keep him as his personal servant and renamed him Gustavus Vassa. After a few years Pascal sold Equiano to the captain of another merchant ship who subsequently sold him to Robert King, a trader from Pennsylvania. By then Equiano was fluent in English and familiar with Western commercial practices. Recognizing his abilities, King placed him in a position of considerable responsibility in his trading company. In about four years Equiano had saved sufficient personal funds to purchase his freedom from his owner. Equiano became free on July 11, 1766.

Having become used to a life at sea, Equiano decided to seek employment aboard merchant ships. But after working briefly for William Phillips, commander of a North American merchant ship which was frequently involved in the transportation of slaves, Equiano decided to settle down in England where earlier, while a servant to Pascal, he had lived for a couple of years. There he worked for Charles Irving, an oceanographer, whom he accompanied once on a scientific expedition to the Arctic. Even while based in England, Equiano continued to travel to places as far as New York and Turkey.

By the 1780s, Equiano had become an active member of the antislavery movement in England. Notably, in 1789 he delivered a formal petition to end England's involvement in the practice of slavery to Queen Charlotte, the wife of
King George III. In 1972 he married Susanna Cullen, an Englishwoman, with
whom he had two daughters. Equiano died in London on March 31, 1797.

MAJOR WORK AND THEMES

African American scholars generally view Equiano as an African American
writer. That Equiano, a perennial traveler and long-time resident of England,
spent only a very small portion of his life in the United States does not seem to
discourage them from appropriating and integrating him into the African American literary tradition. Although he was certainly a part of the African diaspora
of the eighteenth century, he was primarily a rootless cosmopolitan adrift in
Europe and the Atlantic. Given his long periods of residence in England, and
his rather English attitudes and values, he could be placed more appropriately in
the Afro-British tradition in literature.

His largely non-American credentials notwithstanding, Equiano's impact on
the development of early African American written discourse is quite substantial.
His two-volume *The Interesting Narrative of the Life of Olaudah Equiano, or Gustavus Vassa, the African, Written by Himself*, published first in London in 1789
and then in New York in 1791, became "the prototype of the nineteenth-century
slave narrative" and "served to create a model that other ex-slaves would imitate"
(Gates 152). Moreover, the influence of Equiano's text was not limited to the
early self-representational narratives of newly freed slaves who created the
uniquely American genre of slave narrative. As Wilfred D. Samuels astutely
argues, "Equiano's narrative must, to a great degree, be perceived as the mold
from which much early black fiction was first cast" (129).

The Interesting Narrative of the Life of Olaudah Equiano is indeed a fascinating
work. Written in the abolitionist spirit, the book begins with an epistolary note
addressed to the members of the British Parliament, urging them to end Britain's
involvement in the international slave trade. At the end of the book appears his
petition to Queen Charlotte, which he gave her in 1788, pleading for her personal and political interventions in favor of the abolitionist cause. Between these
two epistolary statements Equiano, in twelve lucidly written chapters, narrates
the story of his extraordinary life.

The autobiographical narrative offers a detailed summation of Equiano's life
from his childhood in West Africa to his days as an antislavery crusader in
England in the 1780s. He recalls his abduction from his tribal village by some
local agents of the slavers and describes his subsequent transportation on a British
merchant ship to the West Indies. Equiano meticulously documents the horrors
of the Middle Passage and the appalling brutalities that he witnesses in Barbados,
where the ship unloads the bulk of its human cargo before sailing to Virginia.

Although the criminal abuse of the Africans aboard ships and on shores is a dominant theme in the autobiography, Equiano addresses a variety of other issues as well. At times the book reads like an anthropological text. In the opening chapter, for example, he offers a nearly ethnographic portrait of the tribal culture from which he was removed and sold into slavery. His reconstruction of various cultural practices is based partly on his own recollections but mostly on various African travel narratives published by European and North American explorers. His intense and almost anthropological curiosity about various human cultures he encounters becomes especially evident in his descriptions of his visits to Central America, Italy, and Turkey. He is fascinated by the Miskito Indians he meets on a voyage to Central America. The religious, musical, and architectural traditions of Europe amaze him. He records the sights and sounds of Turkey with wide-eyed wonder. Many aspects of British life charm him. Thus he becomes, in Geraldine Murphy's words, an "accidental tourist" (551). His postmanumission years, though not without challenges, are marked by his insatiable desire to travel and his immense curiosity about exotic peoples and places.

The quest for personal and political empowerment through literacy, a recurrent theme in African American autobiography, is a major feature of Equiano's narrative. During his first voyage to England, while in servitude to Michael Henry Pascal, Equiano notices that some of the white men aboard the ship, including Pascal, regularly read books. He senses that the books—and the ability to negotiate them—are at least partly responsible for the power that white men seem to possess and exercise. So when alone he picks up books at random and speaks to them in the hope that they will talk back to him. The resolute silence of the books saddens and perplexes him. During this time he becomes acquainted with Richard Baker, a young American sailor on board, who teaches him how to read and write. By the time Equiano arrives in England he is determined to master the English language. Some of his employers in England, sensing his academic inclinations, grant him access to formal education. By age fifteen he has fluent command of English. His literacy empowers him to enter the Western civilization in ways that his captors could not have anticipated. It lays the foundation for his own eventual emancipation and his later abolitionist activism.

Central to Equiano's autobiography is his search for spiritual enlightenment. He is intrigued by the diverse religious belief systems he encounters during his travels. Often he engages friends and strangers in elaborate discussions about religion. While there are records that indicate that he was probably baptized at age fourteen at St. Margaret's Church in London, it was not until 1773 that he formally declared his allegiance to the Methodist Church. His experience of spiritual conversion is pivotal to his sense of selfhood and his worldview. A profound religious sensibility informs the entire autobiography.

Thus, Equiano's text is located at the intersection of various discursive forms. It is an autobiography that maps the life of its narrator. It is also an exemplary slave narrative that documents the protagonist's journey from enslavement to emancipation. Equally significant is the book's religious content: it is a classic conversion narrative that records the author's epiphanic discovery of God and the ensuing spiritual transformation. With some justification, the book can be viewed as an anthropological text. Also evident in the work are various salient features of a typical eighteenth-century travel narrative. This textual hybridity is perhaps one of the major reasons for the substantial scholarly interest that Equiano's book has generated in the last decade or so.

CRITICAL RECEPTION

Equiano's *Narrative* was received with considerable enthusiasm at the time of its publication. In fact, the book was so popular in England that it was reprinted nine times. It was also translated into three European languages: Russian, Dutch, and German. In the United States the abolitionists ensured its popularity well into the early decades of the nineteenth century. The book subsequently slipped into obscurity until it was rediscovered in the late 1960s when new academic interest in African American writings began. Among the several editions of the text currently available, the two edited by Paul Edwards and Werner Sollors are especially useful. Both of these editions are accompanied by valuable introductory and secondary material.

Most major surveys of early African American writing include at least brief discussions of Equiano's *Narrative*. There are, however, several major scholarly articles that focus substantially on the work. The finest among them are the essays by Marion Rust and Geraldine Murphy. Both approach Equiano's text from a postcolonial perspective and engage some of the troubling aspects of his ideological self-positioning. Rust suggests that Equiano, who had internalized Western values and assumptions to a considerable extent, often adopts an imperialist attitude toward non-Western peoples and places. Murphy, too, examines what might be viewed as postcolonial ambivalence in Equiano's outlook; she uses a memorable expression, "dissident colonialism" (559), to characterize his advocacy of Western commercial and entrepreneurial expansions into Africa even as he argues against the trans-Atlantic slave trade. Gilbert N.M.O. Morris is one of very few critics to comment on an embarrassing irony in the book: the practice of slavery by Africans. Equiano himself came from a slave-owning aristocratic family; he freely acknowledges that his father owned a number of slaves. Oddly, he never calls for an end to the practice of slavery in Africa by Africans, although his autobiography is an eloquent plea to end the enslavement of Africans by non-Africans.

Charles Davis provides a useful commentary on the impact of Equiano's autobiography on the formation of early African American literature. Henry Louis Gates Jr. offers a superb analysis of the third chapter in the *Narrative* where Equiano chronicles his discovery of the power of literacy. The substantial introductory essays in Edwards' and Sollors' respective editions of the *Narrative* are also exceptionally fine commentaries on the text and its contexts.

BIBLIOGRAPHY

Autobiographical Work by Olaudah Equiano

The Life of Olaudah Equiano, or Gustavus Vassa, the African. Ed. Paul Edwards. London: Dawsons of Pall Mall, 1969.

The Interesting Narrative of the Life of Olaudah Equiano, or Gustavus Vassa, the African, Written by Himself. Ed. Werner Sollors. London: 1789.

Studies of Olaudah Equiano's Autobiographical Work

Acholonu, Catherine Obianju. "The Home of Olaudah Equiano—A Linguistic and Anthropological Search." *The Journal of Commonwealth Literature* 22.1 (1987): 5–16.

Andrew, Williams L. *To Tell a Free Story: The First Century of Afro-American Autobiography, 1760–1865.* Urbana: University of Illinois Press, 1986.

Caldwell, Tanya. " 'Talking Too Much English': Languages of Economy and Politics in Equiano's *The Interesting Narrative.*" *Early American Literature* 34.3 (1999): 263–82.

Carretta, Vincent. "Olaudah Equiano or Gustavus Vassa? New Light on an Eighteenth-Century Question of Identity." *Slavery and Abolition* 20.3 (1999): 96–105.

Costanzo, Angelo. *Surprizing Narrative: Olaudah Equiano and the Beginnings of Black Autobiography.* Westport, CT: Greenwood Press, 1987.

Dabydeen, David, ed. *The Black Presence in English Literature.* Manchester, England: Manchester University Press, 1985.

Davis, Charles T., and Henry Louis Gates Jr., eds. *The Slave's Narrative.* New York: Oxford UP, 1985.

Doherty, Thomas. "Olaudah Equiano's Journey: The Geography of a Slave Narrative." *Partisan Review* 64.4 (Fall 1997): 572–81.

Fichtelberg, Joseph. "Word Between Worlds: The Economy of Equiano's Narrative." *American Literary History* 5.3 (Fall 1993): 459–80.

Gates, Henry Louis, Jr. "The Trope of the Talking Book." In *The Signifying Monkey: A Theory of Afro-American Literary Criticism.* New York: Oxford University Press, 1988.

Hinds, Elizabeth Jane Wall. "The Spirit of Trade: Olaudah Equiano's Conversion, Legalism, and the Merchant's Life." *African American Review* 32.4 (Winter 1998): 635–47.

Marren, Susan M. "Between Slavery and Freedom: The Transgressive Self in Olaudah Equiano's Autobiography." *PMLA* 108 (1993): 94–105.

Morris, Gilbert N.M.O. "Olaudah Equiano." In *African American Authors, 1745–1945.* Ed. Emmanuel S. Nelson. Westport, CT: Greenwood Press, 2000. 141–54.

Murphy, Geraldine. "Olaudah Equiano, Accidental Tourist." *Eighteenth-Century Studies* 27 (1994): 551–68.

Ogude, S.E. "Olaudah Equiano and the Tradition of Defoe." *African Literature Today* 14 (1984): 77–91.

Orban, Katalin. "Dominant and Submerged Discourses in *The Life of Olaudah Equiano.*" *African American Review* 27 (1993): 655–64.

Potkay, Adam. "Olaudah Equiano and the Art of Spiritual Autobiography." *Eighteenth Century Studies* 27 (1994): 677–90.

Rust, Marion. "The Subaltern as Imperialist: Speaking of Olaudah Equiano." In *Passing and the Fictions of Identity*. Ed. Elaine K. Ginsberg. Durham, NC: Duke University Press, 1996. 21–36.

Samuels, Wilfred D. "Olaudah Equiano." *Dictionary of Literary Biography*. Vol. 50. Detroit: Gale, 1986. 123–29.

Sandiford, Keith A. *Measuring the Moment: Strategies of Protest in Eighteenth-Century Afro-English Writing*. London: Associated University Press, 1988.

Woodard, Helena. *African-British Writing in the Eighteenth-Century: The Politics of Race and Reason*. Westport, CT: Greenwood Press, 1999.

Zafar, Rafia. *We Wear the Mask: African Americans Write American Literature, 1760–1870*. New York: Columbia University Press, 1997.

JULIA A.J. FOOTE
(1823–1900)

Maxine Sample

BIOGRAPHY

Born free in Schenectady, New York, in 1823, the fourth child of former slaves, Julia Foote was a Methodist evangelist. Though stolen and enslaved, her father had managed to buy freedom for himself, her mother, and an older sister. Foote had little formal education, attending school for a very short time. She acquired literacy mostly through learning to read the Bible. After two years of indentured servitude starting at age ten, Foote returned home to her parents. The family moved to Albany, New York, where they joined the African Methodist Church. Then twelve years old, Foote began to develop a deeper appreciation for religion, resolving "to serve God whatever might happen" (*Brand* 28). Intensive Bible study and an interest in becoming sanctified followed Foote's conversion experience at age fifteen. Despite the discouragement of her parents and criticism from others, she sought spiritual advice from an elderly couple; through their teachings and prayers, Foote prepared spiritually for sanctification. Foote later married and moved with her husband to Boston, but she unhappily discovered that, like others, her husband George was not only unsupportive of his wife's religious fervor but also threatened to have her committed or returned to her parents. During his lengthy absence at sea, however, Foote was free to engage in religious activities in response to her calling.

Foote went from house to house holding prayer meetings when she was not permitted to exhort from the pulpit. When intimidation did not bring a cessation of her religious activities, she was excommunicated. Complaints to the Methodist Conference yielded no support. However, Foote remained steadfast against the criticism and continued to spread the gospel despite gender resistance to her activities. She traveled through New York, Ohio, New Jersey, Connecticut,

Rhode Island, Pennsylvania, and Maryland. Foote's autobiography shows that she was not just critical of gender discrimination in the church; she frequently took a stand on racial discrimination as well. For example, when a Methodist church to which she had been invited to speak would not allow blacks into the sanctuary, she declined the invitation. On another occasion, a church invited blacks in for the first time when she spoke there. Foote also traveled to Canada, visiting a number of churches there. She finally settled in Ohio in 1851. After a seven-year hiatus from preaching due to a throat ailment, Foote returned to preaching in the 1870s. Her activities after that are not documented. On May 20, 1894, she made history as the first ordained deacon in the A.M.E. Zion Church. She died on November 22, 1900, an ordained elder.

AUTOBIOGRAPHICAL WORK AND THEMES

A consistent theme in spiritual autobiography is the fate of the individual soul as one journeys from sin to salvation. Sanctification, the creation of a new self as the individual achieves spiritual perfection, shapes *A Brand Plucked from the Fire*. In the first ten chapters Foote depicts her early life through a series of incidents that document her escape from damnation, starting at the age of five when she gained access to a cabinet containing alcohol and got drunk. That she survived the experience was due in part to her being "plucked from the burning" (13). Similar incidents in the narrative suggest that Foote was divinely chosen to be a spiritual leader and are consistent with Foote's self-portrait as a devout child, uncharacteristically interested in religion and expressing concern about the fate of her soul and that of others. Through the use of the trope of the Christ-like child, Foote arouses sympathy in the reader and invokes feelings of anguish about their own souls (Moody 133–34). Like most adolescents, Foote had to contend with worldly distractions and temptations. She describes being stricken by a mysterious force while attempting to dance and being mocked by her peers when refusing to participate in "sinful" activities. Triumphing over such temptations, Foote was converted at age fifteen and studied the Bible at every opportunity. Chapter X marks the climax of her youthful spiritual quest and dramatizes the autobiography's theme of the quest for selfhood.

The next ten chapters narrate the challenges to Foote's authority as an evangelist. She establishes a divine authority to preach the gospel, arguing that "if the power to preach the Gospel is short-lived and spasmodic in the case of women, it must be equally so in that of men; and if women have lost the gift of prophecy, so have men" (78). In response to the notion that a woman's calling could be documented only by her performance of a miracle, she writes, "If it be necessary to prove one's right to preach the Gospel, I ask of my brethren to show me their credentials, or I can not believe in the propriety of their ministry" (79). Much of Chapter XX, "Women in the Gospel," defends her authority by citing the history of women in the gospel. *A Brand Plucked from the Fire* recounts numerous incidents where Foote verbally challenges the denial of her access to the pulpit. Speaking of the Methodist Conference's failure to address her complaint about being maligned and excommunicated, Foote reminds the reader, "It was only the grievance of a woman, and there was no justice meted out to women in those days. Even ministers of Christ did not feel that women had any rights which they were bound to respect" (76).

Another theme is women's self-definition and agency, addressed through Foote's attempt to move beyond the limits imposed by patriarchy. In charting her quest for egalitarian treatment in the church, *A Brand Plucked from the Fire* provides insight into the lives of religious women during the nineteenth century. Foote's autobiography displays a regard for women and a connection with her spiritual sisters that constitute what Joycelyn Moody refers to as a "matrifocal theology" that discloses the activities of black holy women and Foote's intention to project a "collective identity" (142–43).

Often having to deal with segregated accommodations Foote railed against racial prejudice, calling it a "cruel monster" (96). Once while traveling in Baltimore, she and her companions were examined upon arrival for marks on their bodies that could be used to identify them, should they turn out to be runaway slaves. On another occasion, dinner at the home of another guest was interrupted by a search for a runaway slave. Foote writes, "Thank the dear Lord we do not have to suffer such indignities now, though the monster, Slavery, is not yet dead in all its forms" (99).

The final chapters of the autobiography decry the worldliness in the church and call for sanctification, what Foote calls "Christian perfection—an extinction of every temper contrary to love" (120). The narrative culminates in Foote's triumph over bodily infirmities and the years of persecution she suffered, finding that she was able to "rejoice in persecution" and savor the gift of salvation. The death of her husband and later her mother dealt Foote an emotional blow, but she continued her traveling ministry. Despite the initial rejection of Foote's religious activities, her mother had come to respect her daughter's calling. Foote's final sermonic call to the reader is expressed as a prayer that the accounting of her life "will promote the cause of holiness in the Church" (124).

CRITICAL RECEPTION

William Andrews's *Sisters of the Spirit: Three Black Women's Autobiographies of the Nineteenth Century*, a collection of spiritual autobiographies by Julia Foote, Jarena Lee,* and Zilpha Elaw,* charted new territory in anthologizing this genre of African American autobiography. His introduction examines the tradition of African American spiritual autobiography and the social significance of the careers of these women. The appearance of the Schomburg Library's Nineteenth-Century Black Women Writers series generated additional scholarly interest in Julia Foote and her contemporaries, yielding both individual and collective exploration of these authors.

Susan Houchins writes in the introduction to *Spiritual Narratives*, which con-

tains the complete text of Foote's autobiography, that as African American female evangelical writers, Foote and her contemporaries staked their claim to
citizenship and selfhood while "initiating a dialogue . . . [about] the very existence of black folks' souls . . . [and] the possibility of their redemption" (xxix).
Houchins also comments briefly on other parallels among the narratives, including the motif of travel and journey, the body as a site of discourse, and the orality
of the texts.

While acknowledging that Foote's narrative and those of her contemporaries
emerge from the traditions of Christian conversion, slave narratives, and sentimentalism, Moody argues that more important is their emergence from "a tradition that privileges ecstatic, charismatic 'enthusiastic' religious expression and
power" (153); she reminds us that these narratives of African American women
evangelists "first and foremost assert a religious doctrine" (167). Jean M. Humez
treats this issue in "My Spirit Eye," noting in the parallel careers of Julia Foote,
Jarena Lee, Amanda Smith, Rebecca Jackson, and Elizabeth (last name unre-
corded) their use of "spiritual gifts and visionary experiences" such as prophetic
dreams, telepathic experience, voices, and divine intervention (136). Humez also
addresses the significance of female prayer bands in not only providing solidarity
for these evangelists but also helping these women hone their skills in "testimonial, prayer leading, and exhortation . . . ; [prayer bands] explain why so many
women emerged as itinerant preachers out of Methodism—especially Holiness
Methodism—over the nineteenth century" (140–41).

Jennifer Fleischner's *Mastering Slavery: Memory, Family, and Identity in
Women's Slave Narratives* examines *A Brand Plucked from the Fire* in the context
of how one generation transmits the memory of slavery to the next. Fleischner
proposes that Foote's identification with her mother, a former slave, expresses
itself as an attachment to the memory of slavery and that Foote's text "is the
linguistic manifestation of her desire to liberate herself from that maternal legacy
and to relocate herself beyond the reach of history: a brand plucked from the
fire" (154). The painful memories of slavery transmitted from mother to child
impact Foote's sense of self. In the autobiography "whipping reemerges as the
dominant metaphor for Foote's oratorical and rhetorical modes" (170). Foote
transforms the unjust whipping that her mother received at the hands of a cruel
slave master and that Foote herself received as a child after being falsely accused
by the Primes, her white employers, of stealing cakes. Through sanctification,
the love and benevolence of Foote's spiritual "master" supplants the abuse of the
predatory master and the Primes. Foote's self-conception as a preacher called by
God to use the gospel as a flail to thresh the devils out of sinners inverts the
experience of whipped victim. She achieves a position of authority as "a thresher
of human souls for the Lord" (171). Punishment becomes a symbol of spiritual
endurance as the narrative demonstrates the ability to transcend spiritually over
historical conditions (173). Moody sees the narrative as "a quest for the righting/
writing of her mother's victimization" (133). Through the trope of resistant orality, a form of verbal defense, Foote engages in a "matrilineal resistant discourse"

in response to religious patriarchal oppression as she "argues for a feminization of Christianity" (147, 148).

Moody's work takes the study of Foote and other spiritual autobiographers a step further to explore reasons why black feminist literary historians and womanist theoethicists have failed to address sufficiently "the intricacies of spirituality and sexuality" embodied in these texts (167). She attributes the glossing over of the theological significance of these women to the stereotype of the black church woman and to scholars' lack of comfort with the theological discourse in these writings (173). Moody argues that these women be read as "valiant and pious theologians" (166–67) and not just as literary figures or preachers.

BIBLIOGRAPHY

Autobiographical Work by Julia A.J. Foote

A *Brand Plucked from the Fire*. 1886. Rpt. in *Spiritual Narratives*. The Schomburg Library of Nineteenth-Century Black Women Writers. Intro. Susan Houchins. Ed. Henry Louis Gates. New York: Oxford University Press, 1988.

Studies of Julia A.J. Foote's Autobiographical Work

Andrews, William, ed. *Sisters of the Spirit: Three Black Women's Autobiographies of the Nineteenth Century*. Bloomington: Indiana University Press, 1986.

Fleischner, Jennifer. *Mastering Slavery: Memory, Family, and Identity in Women's Slave Narratives*. New York: New York University Press, 1996.

Humez, Jean M. " 'My Spirit Eye' ": Some Functions of Spiritual and Visionary Experience in the Lives of Five Black Women Preachers, 1810–1880." In *Women and the Structure of Society: Selected Research from the Fifth Berkshire Conference on the History of Women*. Durham: Duke University Press, 1984. 129–43.

Moody, Joycelyn. *Sentimental Confessions: Spiritual Narratives of Nineteenth-Century African American Women*. Athens: University of Georgia Press, 2001.

PATRICE GAINES
(1949–   )

Kelley A. Squazzo

BIOGRAPHY

Award-winning journalist and *Washington Post* reporter Patrice Gaines was born in 1949 to a homemaker mother and a marine father and spent her early childhood years on a military base in Quantico, Virginia. In 1954, the year the Supreme Court banned segregation in schools, she was a "five-year-old colored queen" to her white best friends and resided in a peaceful neighborhood (*Laughing in the Dark* 7). She had not yet been exposed to the racial tensions that were forming around her. However, when Gaines was in fifth grade her family moved to Beaufort, South Carolina, and racial prejudices began creating barriers, preventing cross-racial friendships. That year, a teacher made her clean the classroom while the white children listened to a story. This marked for her the beginning of a long struggle with racial discrimination. After graduating from high school in 1967 in a class of 63 blacks and 600 whites, Gaines's identity as a black woman became increasingly central to her life.

Throughout her adolescence and early adulthood, Gaines rebelled against her parents' values while struggling to define her own identity. She encountered numerous obstacles including rape, abortion, heroin use, imprisonment, and failed marriages; by the age of eighteen, Gaines had given birth to her daughter, Andrea. During this time, Gaines struggled to relate to both her family and her community. She craved the attention and love of her emotionally distant father: "When he was home, I could see and feel what he didn't do. No kisses. No hugs. No 'I love you' " (*Laughing in the Dark* 60). In attempt to fill these voids in her life, Gaines entered into self-destructive relationships with men. She endured both verbal and physical abuse, and one of her boyfriends introduced her to heroin. She struggled against an increasingly diminished sense of self-worth, find ing herself stealing from department stores and eventually being incarcerated on drug charges.

In the prologue to her autobiography *Laughing in the Dark: From Colored Girl to Woman of Color—A Journey from Prison to Power*, Gaines recalls a troubling memory that she observes as a pivotal moment in her life. While in prison, Gaines's two-year-old daughter was brought to visit her; sadly, Gaines realized that her daughter did not recognize her. From this point on, Gaines uses her love for her daughter to find inner strength and motivation. This relationship helped Gains to survive the deaths of many people who were close to her, including her father and her grandparents. She was also faced with the loss of seven friends who fell victim to AIDS. Struggling to deal with these hardships, Gaines began to identify writing as a therapeutic exercise: "I discovered that I thought differently when I wrote; I was smarter on paper" (175–76). She enjoyed writing poetry, short stories, and "matters of the heart" (174) and realized that a career in journalism would give her an opportunity to communicate these passions.

Gaines was first introduced to journalism as the only black secretary for the *Charlotte Observer*. She received her journalism training from the Maynard Institute for Journalism Education and landed her first professional job at the *Miami News*. She currently works as a staff writer for the *Washington Post* (since 1995). Having convinced the *Post* editors to overlook her drug conviction, Gaines marks this success as a significant milestone in both her personal and professional lives. Her contributions to the *Post* have been well received, including a Pulitzer Prize nomination for her reporting team.

Gaines resides in Fort Washington, Maryland, with her husband and is intimately involved with her community. She is a board member of Joseph's House, a home for men with AIDS, and she speaks around the country at schools and juvenile detention centers and for drug and domestic abuse programs. Her writing reflects on current social issues and has had a positive impact on her readers. Gaines has carved a niche for herself in the writing world and should be recognized as an important contributor to women's issues.

AUTOBIOGRAPHICAL WORKS AND THEMES

Laughing in the Dark, Gaines's first autobiographical work, spans the first forty years of her life. Her writing is bold, real, and honest, leaving out no details of her personal experiences. Her writing explores both racial and gender issues, focusing on the themes of racial discrimination, black consciousness, relationships, family values, and positive self-esteem. Most important, what comes forth most prominently in her prose is the survival of an African American woman in a racist and patriarchal society. Gaines's transformation from a submissive and impressionable girl to a courageous, successful, and autonomous woman gives her a distinct black feminist voice. Gaines's words offer inspiration for women. Her message encourages women not to define themselves in relation to the men in their lives. Gaines's text is one of survival. A strong voice emerges offering her life lesson: Self-esteem and self-worth come from within.

Gaines's second book, *Moments of Grace: Meeting the Challenge to Change*, is a compendium to *Laughing in the Dark* offering a prescription for personal change with the help of God's grace. She teaches her readers that "life is a lesson in perseverance. . . . Choose this day, this moment to change; by doing so, you will have already begun to" (201, 203). In *Moments of Grace*, Gaines recalls events from her own life story (many of which are chronicled in *Laughing in the Dark*) and couples them with testimonials of people from various backgrounds who have also survived painful life journeys and put faith in God.

CRITICAL RECEPTION

Laughing in the Dark, heralded as an "exhilarating memoir" (Joyce 189), was reviewed favorably in numerous journals. Gaines's text caught the eyes of young adults and was reviewed in *School Library Journal*, which found the book "an insightful story full of pain, anger, and emotional and mental growth" (Royal 238). The *New York Times Book Review* expressed gratitude to Gaines for sharing her "courageously frank memoir" (Brailsford 58). Gaines's book tour took her to various universities and bookstores where she was met with positive receptions. *Laughing in the Dark* can be easily assimilated into popular culture studies and is a book accessible to many audiences.

Gaines's freelance writing has appeared in many journals, including *Essence* and *Black Enterprise*. She won the National Association of Black Journalists Salute to Excellence Award in the "Best Commentary" category for her article "Tough Boyz and Trouble—Those Girls Waiting Outside D.C. Jail Remind Me of Myself." In this piece, which served as a building block for *Laughing in the Dark*, Gaines comments that many of the troubled lives she sees today remind her of her own tumultuous past.

Moments of Grace also received a positive reception, although not as striking as *Laughing in the Dark*. A *Booklist* reviewer acclaims that "Gaines' book may, because of the grittiness of her experience, reach a broader audience than that for most inspirational writings" (Whitney 908). Other critics had similar responses and felt that Gaines's nonpreaching approach in her writing remains powerful and offers encouraging words for readers to meet the challenge to change.

Gaines's autobiographical works capture a life of incredible triumph over odds that were clearly stacked against her.

BIBLIOGRAPHY

Autobiographical Works by Patrice Gaines

"Tough Boyz and Trouble—Those Girls Waiting Outside D.C. Jail Remind Me of Myself." In *Wild Women Don't Wear No Blues: Black Women Writers on Love, Men, and Sex*. Ed. Marita Golden. New York: Doubleday, 1993. 1–11.

Laughing in the Dark: From Colored Girl to Woman of Color—A Journey from Prison to Power. New York: Crown Publishers, 1994.
Moments of Grace: Meeting the Challenge to Change. New York: Crown Publishers, 1997.

Studies of Patrice Gaines's Autobiographical Works

Brailsford, Karen. Rev. of *Laughing in the Dark*. *New York Times Book Review* 144 (November 13, 1994): 58.
Cole, Anita L. Rev. of *Laughing in the Dark*. *Library Journal* 119 (October 1, 1994): 88.
Joyce, Alice. Rev. of *Laughing in the Dark*. *Booklist* 91 (October 1, 1994): 189.
Ladner, Joyce A. Rev. of *Laughing in the Dark*. *Book World* 24 (September 25, 1994): 11.
McGrath, Bernadette. Rev. of *Moments of Grace*. *Library Journal* 122 (January 1997): 106.
Pinckney, Darryl. Rev. of *Laughing in the Dark*. *New York Review of Books* 42 (April 20, 1995): 34.
Royal, Pat. "Book Review: Adult Books for Young Adults." *School Library Journal* 41 (March 1995): 238.
Smith, Dale Edwyna. "The Mother Tongue: Review of *Laughing in the Dark*." *Belles Lettres* 10 (Spring 1995): 68–70.
Stuttaford, Genevieve, and Marina Simson. "Forecasts: Nonfiction." *Publishers Weekly* 244 (January 13, 1997): 66.
Whitney, Scott. "Adult Books: Nonfiction." *Booklist* 93 (February 1, 1997): 908.

Interviews with Patrice Gaines

Interview. "Is the Color Gone?" By Ted Heck and Miriam D. Liggett. WTKR-TV, Norfolk, VA, May 6, 1986.
Interview with Lee Farbman. Sage Colleges, WAMC, Albany, NY, December 2, 1994.

HENRY LOUIS GATES JR.
(1950–   )

Emmanuel S. Nelson

BIOGRAPHY

A son of Henry Louis Gates Sr. and Pauline Augusta Coleman Gates, Gates was born on September 16, 1950, in Piedmont, West Virginia. He attended a segregated elementary school, graduated from an integrated high school, and attended Potomac State College of West Virginia for a year. He had intended to study medicine but decided to major in English after taking courses with Professor Duke Whitmore, an inspiring teacher of literature at Potomac State. In 1973 he graduated summa cum laude from Yale University with a B.A. in English. After working as a journalist for a short period of time, he enrolled at Cambridge University in England and obtained an M.A. and, subsequently in 1979, a Ph.D. in comparative literature.

Gates has taught at Haverford College and at Yale, Cornell, and Duke. One of the most distinguished contemporary literary scholars and public intellectuals, Gates is now a professor at Harvard University where he also chairs the Department of Afro-American Studies. Recipient of numerous awards and honorary degrees, he has held a MacArthur Prize Fellowship and won an American Book Award. Currently he lives in Cambridge, Massachusetts, with his wife Sharon Lynn Adams and their two daughters.

AUTOBIOGRAPHICAL WORK AND THEMES

Colored People: A Memoir begins with a poignant epistolary note from Gates to his daughters, Maggie and Liza. The letter makes it clear that the two young girls are the primary target audience for the autobiography. Gates tells them that he wants them to know the world that he came from — the world of the southern, small-town 1950s America that has all but vanished. He writes to them because he finds out that the concept of legalized racial segregation is so alien to them that they have difficulty imagining that such a system existed when their father was young. He wants them to know why he takes a "special pride in a Jessye Norman aria, a Mohammad Ali shuffle, a Spike Lee movie, a Thurgood Marshall opinion, a Toni Morrison novel, James Brown's Camel Walk" (xv). Above all, he wants them to know why sometimes—to the embarrassment of his children— he stops to chat with total strangers who happen to be African Americans. His friendliness, he wants his daughters to know, is a form of racial acknowledgment, an expression of cultural intimacy, that blacks of his generation growing up in the segregated South had developed as an antidote to the coldness and rejection of the white world.

Colored People is a typical *Bildungsroman*, a coming-of-age story, a work that maps the maturation of its young narrator–protagonist. In the chapters that follow his prefatory letter to his daughters, Gates chronicles his early childhood; the lives of some of his colorful friends, family members, and neighborhood characters; his awkward, unathletic, and overweight adolescence; his close emotional connection to his beloved mother; his sexual awakening; and his incremental politicization as he watches the civil rights movement explode on the television screen in the family living room.

But *Colored People* is more than a bittersweet remembrance of a childhood in a segregated small town in the South. It memorializes a way of life, a self-contained world that African Americans had constructed in response to segregation. It is a world of functional, nurturing, intact families that demand excellence from their children. It is a world of intimate friendships, church picnics, and self-confident men and women who refused to accept white definitions of their worth. Gates's near idealization of that world borders on nostalgia: He seems to long for the powerful sense of community that many African Americans in the South had forged in reaction to the rigidities of segregationist customs and conventions.

A figure who haunts the pages of *Colored People* is Pauline Augusta Coleman Gates, the narrator's mother. She is an embodiment of cultural pride, dignity, and decency. She occupies the emotional center of her son's life. The most moving scenes in the autobiography focus on her devastating mental illness that lasts, on and off, for almost twenty years until her death in 1986. The book is as much an elegy for his mother as it is an elegiac recollection of a vanished childhood and a way of life.

Despite the occasional power and poignancy of the narrative, *Colored People*, ultimately, is not an entirely convincing work. Gates's near-romanticization of the 1950s Piedmont at times reeks of false sentimentality. It also raises some troubling questions. If he led such a charmed life during the days of segregation, why did he become a defiant black militant in the 1960s? If his ideological commitment, by the late 1960s, is to black nationalism, how does he explain his voracious appetite for white girls? Gates, to be sure, has answers to these questions, but his book fails to probe the transformations of his consciousness and the internal contradictions of his politics. In fact, Gates generally retreats from close scrutiny of his own assumptions and attitudes. The autobiography, therefore, is regrettably superficial.

Even more disappointing is Gates's curious reticence on some of the most remarkable experiences of his youth. For example, he fleetingly refers to the fact that at age nineteen he moved to Africa and spent a year living "in a socialist village in Tanzania" and later, with a friend from Harvard, hitchhiked across Africa "from the Indian Ocean to the Atlantic Ocean" (101). Oddly, Gates says nothing more about these extraordinary experiences or how they influenced his personal and political awareness.

CRITICAL RECEPTION

Gates's status as a leading African American scholar and intellectual ensured that his autobiography would be widely reviewed. Many of the reviews were polite, if not enthusiastic. Jack E. White states that Gates's memoir is vastly different "from the harrowing, up-from-the-ghetto autobiographies" that have proliferated in the recent years and that it is a "reminder that black mainstream is not a tangle of pathology." He adds that "Gates' graceful, sparsely written memoir" proves that he "has not only brains but also a whole lot of soul" (73) Ellis Cose concludes that Colored People "illuminates, in a touchingly personal way, the loss that often accompanies progress" (160). Louis D. Rubin finds Colored People an "intricate book" and "a splendidly told memoir" (10).

However, some other reviews were less than flattering. Jill Nelson wonders if autobiography is an appropriate forum for Gates, given his unwillingness to engage in "personal revelation and introspection." She finds his reticence irksome and concludes, "Even seen through rose-colored glasses, most of these 'colored people' are colorless" (794).

Much more devastating is Gerald Early's lengthy review of the book in the New Republic. Early, himself a distinguished African American scholar, professor of English, and director of the African American Studies Program at Washington University in St. Louis, challenges Gates's evocation of the black community in Piedmont before the advent of integration. Early characterizes such idealized representation as "the American equivalent of an Edenic Africa before the coming of the white man" and dismisses Gates's narrative as a false idyll (34). He even wonders if Gates should have written the book at all. He finds Colored People "too facile and cliché ridden" and asks:

How many more accounts of hair straightening and greasy soul food can we stand? How many more scenes of conversion in black evangelical churches? How many more accounts of older relatives who were convinced that whites were dirty and smelled like dogs when wet? (35)

Early is also annoyed by Gates's abandonment of the formal, elegant prose that he is capable of writing and his decision instead to use the "vernacular street-smart style" (35). Like Jill Nelson, Early notes that his autobiographer is "coy and unforthcoming," which renders the narrative shallow and lacking in analytical vigor (35).

These weaknesses that Early catalogs, perhaps, explain why Colored People—despite the author's prominence—has received little serious academic attention.

BIBLIOGRAPHY

Autobiographical Work by Henry Louis Gates Jr.

Colored People: A Memoir. New York: Knopf, 1994.

Studies of Henry Louis Gates Jr.'s Autobiographical Work

Cose, Ellis. Rev. of Colored People. Newsweek (May 23, 1994): 160.
Early, Gerald. "Speak, Memory." New Republic (July 4, 1994): 33–36.
Nelson, Jill. Rev. of Colored People. Nation (June 6, 1994): 794.
Oates, Joyce Carol. Rev. of Colored People. London Review of Books (January 12, 1997): 14.
Rubin, Louis D. Rev. of Colored People. New York Times Book Review (June 19, 1994): 10.
Smith, David Lionel. Rev. of Colored People. America 171 (December 1994): 24.
Toledano, Ben C. Rev. of Colored People. National Review (August 29, 1994): 33.
White, Jack E. "Was the Picnic Ruined?" Time (May 23, 1994): 73.

NIKKI GIOVANNI
(1943–   )

Kathlene McDonald

BIOGRAPHY

The poet, essayist, activist, and educator Nikki Giovanni was born on June 7, 1943, in Knoxville, Tennessee. Although her parents named her Yolande Cornelia Giovanni Jr., her older sister's nickname of Nikki-Rosa was the name that stuck. While her family moved to Cincinnati, Ohio, shortly after her birth, Giovanni considers Knoxville her spiritual home. Her parents struggled financially in these early years, yet they taught Giovanni and her older sister, Gary, to love and respect themselves for who they were, not for what they had. From a young age, Giovanni developed a fierce sense of independence and determination, characteristics that manifest themselves throughout all her work. Although the family's financial situation improved by the time Giovanni was in elementary school, her father struggled emotionally, and he grew to be abusive. The situation became so bad that, at the age of fourteen, Giovanni moved to Knoxville to live with her maternal grandparents, Louvenia and John Brown "Book" Watson.

Giovanni formed a close bond with Louvenia during the three years she lived with her grandparents. The strong-minded Louvenia cultivated her granddaughter's independence and taught her the importance of commitment to her community; she regularly recruited Giovanni to help with various charitable and political activities. These experiences raised Giovanni's awareness of the plight of Black America and taught her the necessity of speaking out against racism and injustice. A high school teacher introduced her to African American writers and encouraged her to write. In 1960, she enrolled in Fisk University through the Early Entrants Program. However, she was unable to conform to institutional rules and expectations and was expelled after her first semester. She spent the next few years in Cincinnati, working in a retail store and taking classes. While she did not participate in any of the civil rights actions taking place around the country at the time, these events influenced her political thought and heightened her sense of social responsibility. In 1964, she persuaded Fisk to readmit her, and she quickly became a leader in civil rights activities on campus, reestablishing the Fisk chapter of the Student Nonviolent Coordinating Committee (SNCC), which the administration had banned a few years earlier. She also continued to develop her talent as a writer through her involvement with a student literary and political journal and exposure to Black Arts Movement writers such as John O. Killens and LeRoi Jones (Amini Baraka*).

Louvenia died two months after Giovanni graduated from Fisk, and Giovanni dealt with her grief by throwing herself into her writing and cultural work. She became the editor of *Conversation*, a revolutionary black journal, and organized the first-ever Cincinnati Black Arts Festival. She became acquainted with many of the major players in the Black Arts and Black Power movements, and although she adopted much of the rhetoric of both movements in her work, she maintained an independent stance. In 1967, she won a Ford Foundation fellowship to the University of Pennsylvania's School of Social Work. After one semester, she decided that she was not cut out for a career in social work and left school to devote time to her writing. In 1968, she moved to New York City and began pursuing an M.F.A. in creative writing at Columbia University's School of Fine Arts. After being told by white critics that she lacked literary talent, she quit the program. Within the next year, she published her first book of poetry, *Black Feeling, Black Talk*, a widely popular book that brought her immediate fame and helped launch her highly successful writing career.

Over the next three decades, Giovanni published fifteen volumes of poetry, nine spoken-word albums, dozens of articles, and three prose books, including her autobiography, *Gemini: An Extended Autobiographical Statement on My First Twenty-five Years of Being a Black Poet*. Although she has always been a controversial figure, her work is included in numerous anthologies, and she remains widely read and taught. She currently teaches in the English Department at Virginia Polytechnic Institute and State University, where she works to promote black culture and encourage young writers.

AUTOBIOGRAPHICAL WORK AND THEMES

Much of Giovanni's poetry and essays are autobiographical in nature; her work regularly blurs the line between the personal and the political. Her one autobiography, *Gemini: An Extended Autobiographical Statement on My First Twenty-five Years of Being a Black Poet*, is no exception. Rather than providing a chronological or detailed account of her life up until that point, Giovanni endeavors, in *Gemini*, to explain how and why she became a writer and an activist. She writes, "I was always just a little secreted away with the thought that one day I would be understood. This is probably a main reason any artist emerges" (140). And what Giovanni wants her readers to understand is the role that various people and experiences played in shaping her life, her work, and her beliefs. To that effect, *Gemini* consists of stories of her family and friends, interspersed with musings on society and culture. She balances these personal recollections with several chapters that focus entirely on social and political commentary, implying that to understand her involves knowledge of both her personal history and her political views. Inherent in that understanding, however, is an acceptance of the contradictions and conflicts in the artist's life; the apt title *Gemini* signifies the double realities, the simultaneous contradictions that define her work.

In the opening chapter of *Gemini*, Giovanni pays tribute to her hometown of Knoxville, describing her return there several years after her grandmother has died and all the old familiar landmarks—including her grandmother's house—have been razed to make way for highways and nightclubs. But she does not lapse into sentimental nostalgia for Knoxville or a way of life gone by; instead, she describes her connections to Knoxville in order to demonstrate that family and personal history cannot be destroyed. And her autobiography works, in part, to preserve this history; she writes, "I thought Tommy, my son, must know about this. He must know we come from somewhere. That we belong" (12). The next several chapters fill in this personal history by offering fragmentary sketches of the people who cultivated her sense of self. In addition to Louvenia, she provides glimpses into her relationships with her parents, her sister, her nephew, her son, and her friends. These stories offer some insight into various aspects of Giovanni's personality, temperament, career decisions, and political development. Yet while she attempts to construct a personal history, she omits or glosses over certain aspects, primarily the family's early years in poverty and her father's abuse.

In discussing how she became a writer, Giovanni situates her process of creative development within the larger framework of black culture. Rather than seeing herself as an individual writer influenced by a few people or events, she presents herself as an artist who has benefited from and been influenced by the generations of black writers before her. Her essays on the revolutionary nature of LeRoi Jones, Charles Chesnutt, James Baldwin,* Ralph Ellison, Lena Horne, and soul music underscore her overall belief that black people need "a collective historical memory" (12). However, she tends to essentialize blackness, making bizarre anthropological claims about the development of black spirituality and assuming a monolithic definition of blackness.

The chapters in which Giovanni discusses her political beliefs also contribute to a collective black history, combining stories of her political development with treatises on racism and black consciousness. In all of these essays, she holds fast to W.E.B. Du Bois's* belief that the problem of the twentieth century is the problem of the color line, and as in her early poetry, she calls for a revolution to combat white oppression. Yet the definition of revolution she espouses in *Gemini* differs greatly from the militant stance of her first volumes of poetry, which adopted the incendiary rhetoric of the Black Arts Movement. While these poems advocated violence and hatred, she writes in *Gemini*, "Nobody's trying to make the system Black; we're trying to make a system that's human so that Black folks can live in it" (50). In these essays, she embraces humanity and love to a much greater degree than she does in her early poetry.

While *Gemini* covers only the first twenty-five years of Giovanni's life, the main theme—her desire to explain how her life and her experiences shaped her worldview—is prevalent through many of her subsequent works. In her essay collections, *Sacred Cows and Other Edibles* (1988) and *Racism 101* (1994), she follows the pattern she establishes in *Gemini*: combining autobiographical reflections with social commentary. And she frequently draws on personal experiences in her poetry. Readers looking to learn more about Giovanni's early life will be disappointed with *Gemini*; those looking to understand Giovanni as a writer will gain insight into the forces that shaped her.

CRITICAL RECEPTION

While studies of Giovanni's poetry abound, few critics have addressed her prose work. Although *Gemini* garnered reviews in major publications such as the *New York Times Book Review, Time,* and *Newsweek*, it has been discussed rarely since its publication in 1971. Most reviewers found Giovanni's prose difficult and faulted her for the lack of autobiographical revelations. Even those who praised her essays on culture or politics were left wanting a greater understanding of the poet's life. June Jordan went as far as to claim that *Gemini* "is not an autobiography" and faults her for never revealing "any real trouble in her life" (6). Generally, critics seemed to agree that the book raised more questions than it answered about Giovanni's life, and after these initial reviews, *Gemini* has received almost no attention.

One exception to the dearth of criticism on *Gemini* is Elizabeth Fox-Genovese's essay "My Statue, Myself: Autobiographical Writings of Afro-American Women," which situates *Gemini* within a tradition of black women's autobiographies dating back to slave narratives. Fox-Genovese emphasizes the connections Giovanni makes between the personal and the political, noting that Giovanni "has, with special force, made the case for the relation of black women's autobiographies to changing political conditions" (69). She compares Giovanni's autobiography to those of her contemporaries Maya Angelou* and Gwendolyn Brooks,* claiming that all three use their personal stories as a way of bearing witness to the collective experience of African American women. She writes that, for writers of Giovanni's generation, "[t]he account of the black woman's self cannot be divorced from the history of that self or the history of the people among whom it took shape" (82–83). In placing *Gemini* within the context of a larger tradition that interweaves personal and collective history, Fox-Genovese legitimizes the form and methodology of Giovanni's autobiography.

BIBLIOGRAPHY

Autobiographical Work by Nikki Giovanni

Gemini: An Extended Autobiographical Statement on My First Twenty-five Years of Being a Black Poet. 1971. New York: Penguin, 1976.

Studies of Nikki Giovanni's Autobiographical Work

Bryant, Jerry H. Rev. of *Gemini*. *Saturday Review* (January 15, 1972): 34.

Duffy, Martha. Rev. of *Gemini*. *Time* (January 17, 1972): 63–64.

Fox-Genovese, Elizabeth. "My Statue, Myself: Autobiographical Writings of Afro-American Women." In *The Private Self: Theory and Practice of Women's Autobiographical Writings*. Ed. Shari Benstock. Chapel Hill: University of North Carolina Press, 1988. 63–89.

Giddings, Paula. Rev. of *Gemini*. *Black World* 21 (August 1972): 51–52.

Jordan, June. Rev. of *Gemini*. *New York Times Book Review* (February 13, 1972): 6, 26.

Prescott, Peter S. "Truth in Black and White." *Newsweek* (January 31, 1972): 80–81.

Interviews with Nikki Giovanni

Bonner, Carrington. "An Interview with Nikki Giovanni." *Black American Literature Forum* 18 (1984): 29–30.

Elder, Arlene. "A MELUS Interview: Nikki Giovanni." *MELUS* 9 (1982): 61–75.

Giovanni, Nikki. *A Dialogue: James Baldwin and Nikki Giovanni.* Philadelphia: Lippincott, 1973.

———. *A Poetic Equation: Conversations between Nikki Giovanni and Margaret Walker.* Washington, DC: Howard University Press, 1983.

"Nikki Giovanni: On Race, Age, & Sex." *The Black Collegian* 1 (1970–1971): 30–34.

"Nikki Giovanni: Three Decades of Writing on the Edge." *Publishers Weekly* 246.26 (1999): 46.

Reynolds, Barbara. "Interview with Nikki Giovanni." In *And Still I Rise: Interviews with 50 Black Role Models.* Washington, DC: Gannett, 1988. 93–96.

Tate, Claudia, ed. *Black Women Writers at Work.* New York: Continuum, 1983. 60–78.

MARITA GOLDEN
(1950–)

Emmanuel S. Nelson

Emmanuel S. Nelson

BIOGRAPHY

The only child of Francis Sherman Golden and Beatrice Lee Reid, Marita Golden
was born on April 28, 1950, in Washington, D.C. Coming of age in the 1960s,
she was profoundly influenced by the civil rights movement. Her commitment to
progressive politics and antiracism work remains central to her life and her art.

In 1968 she won a four-year scholarship to American University in Washington, D.C. Four years later she graduated from there with a degree in journalism.
After obtaining a master's degree in journalism from Columbia University in
1973, she began to establish a promising career in the publishing industry. In
1975, however, she gave up her career in the United States and moved to Lagos,
Nigeria, with Femi Ajayi, a Nigerian national whom she had met in New York
City. They eventually married, but the marriage failed and in 1979 Golden returned to the United States with her infant son.

For a few years she lived in the Boston area where she taught at some local
colleges. *Migrations of the Heart*, Golden's autobiography, was published in 1983.
The book was a critical success. Encouraged by the reception of her first published
book, Golden left her teaching career and moved to Washington, D.C. to pursue
creative writing on a full-time basis. She published her first two novels, *A
Woman's Place* and *Long Distance Life*, in 1986 and 1989, respectively. During
the 1990s she edited three nonfiction prose works. *The Edge of Heaven*, her most
recent novel, was published in 1998.

Winner of numerous awards and grants, Golden has taught creative writing at
George Mason University, Antioch College, Spelman College, and Wayne State
University. Currently she teaches in the Graduate Creative Writing Program at
Virginia Commonwealth University in Richmond.

AUTOBIOGRAPHICAL WORK AND THEMES

Written in exquisitely beautiful prose, *Migrations of the Heart* is a poignant chronicle of a young woman's search for home and wholeness. The autobiography is divided into three sections. The first part, titled "Beginnings," focuses on Golden's teenage years. She helplessly watches her parents' marriage disintegrate. Her father's habitual infidelity causes arguments and fights between her parents, and their marriage eventually ends in a disastrous divorce that leaves her mother homeless. The opening section also documents Golden's incremental politicization. Traumatized by the assassination of Martin Luther King Jr., Golden rededicates herself to political activism and to the civil rights movement. At least partly because of her awakening political and cultural awareness, she gravitates toward students and professionals from Africa whom she meets in Washington, D.C. and later in New York City. While she is a graduate student at Columbia University, she meets and falls in love with Femi Ajayi, a Nigerian architect. With him she moves to Africa.

In the second and longest section of the book, titled "Journeys," Golden offers a compelling account of her life in Lagos, Nigeria. Her romantic vision of Africa gradually collapses, but she makes a genuine effort to adjust to the new cultural surroundings. Even though she is fully aware of Nigeria's unstable politics and massive economic difficulties, she is willing to stake her future in that country. The growing incompatibility between Golden and her husband, however, precipitates an extended crisis. Pressured by her husband to have a child, she becomes pregnant; the pregnancy ends in miscarriage after six months, leaving her physically and emotionally exhausted. She becomes pregnant again—her African relatives insinuate that it is disgraceful for a woman to be childless—and this time gives birth to a baby boy. The arrival of the child rescues the marriage but only briefly. Ajayi grows increasingly frustrated by his inability to establish a lucrative career in Lagos. When Golden becomes a lecturer in English and journalism at a local university, his sense of his own professional failure intensifies. It leaves him angry. One afternoon the anger explodes in violence, and he brutally beats Golden.

Confused and helpless, Golden turns to Anita Okunwunmi, another black American woman married to a Nigerian. Anita, also a victim of her husband's violence, advises her to pamper Ajayi by cooking his favorite foods and eagerly catering to all his needs. Golden does precisely that. Her renewed attention makes Ajayi seem happy and at least prevents recurrence of further violence. Emotionally, however, their relationship remains tenuous at best. The distance between them grows dramatically when Golden begins to have a passionate affair with Lee Houston, an African American she meets in Lagos. Realizing that her marriage cannot be salvaged, Golden considers divorce. However, she is advised by her friends not to seek divorce in Nigeria if she wants custody of her son. The courts, she is told, would almost certainly hand over the child to his father. Determined to avoid such a loss, Golden, with the help of Anita Okunwunmi and Lee Houston, takes her son and, without her husband's knowledge, flees Nigeria and returns to the United States.

In the brief final section of the autobiography, titled "Coming Home," Golden relates her attempts to reestablish herself, personally and professionally. She makes a conscious effort to avoid relationships with men and undergoes therapy in search of greater self-understanding. Her close friendships with a few women sustain her, and motherhood gives her a sense of emotional fulfillment. At the end of the narrative Golden declares that "after a season of fitful migration" she had indeed come home. That home is "the bedrock inside" herself that has resulted from her newly forged sense of autonomy. She realizes that she will still wander; there will be other migrations, physical as well as emotional, in the future; but she knows that her sense of "home"—the strength and certainty of her newly found selfhood—will be with her wherever she goes (234).

Golden's autobiographical narrative pivots on the journey motif. As the title itself suggests, *Migrations of the Heart* is about a personal odyssey. The journey she embarks on is both literal and metaphorical: As she cuts across geographical boundaries, she also moves through new states of mind, new levels of consciousness. It is a voyage of self-discovery. Her illusions of romance—with her husband, with Africa—fade gradually even as she awakens to her potential and possibilities as a woman and as an artist. Having grown up in a troubled home with parents at odds with each other, she seeks the warmth and protectiveness of a home of her own. She frantically attempts to find that home in her often impulsive romantic relationships with men only to realize, after much pain and disappointment, that the home she seeks lies within herself.

Golden begins her autobiography with the declaration, "My father was the first man I ever loved" (3). She quickly adds that "he was a hard, nearly impossible man to love when love meant exclusive rights to his soul" (4–5). In her adult life she is often attracted to men much like her father: They are seemingly self-confident men who remain emotionally elusive and unattainable; they are unable or unwilling to grant her the intense love that she yearns for. Almost always her connections with men prove to be destructive. She is able to achieve her internal balance and stability only when she breaks the cycle of emotional dependency on men and resolves not to enter into potentially unhealthy relationships. It is this odyssey toward emotional independence that she charts eloquently in her autobiography.

A particularly interesting feature of *Migrations of the Heart* is Golden's representation of Nigeria, a gifted nation rich in human and natural resources but in an acute state of postcolonial crisis. Golden, a journalist, is a keen observer; everything, even the potholes on the roads in Lagos, registers on her mind. Yet, as a politically sophisticated African American woman, she writes about Africa in a restrained and measured manner. Even when she encounters cultural elements that are bafflingly alien to her—the complex family relationships and clan obligations, for example—Golden, remarkably, refuses to make any value judgments. While she frankly acknowledges the cultural differences between herself and her husband that ultimately end their marriage, she never questions the integrity of Nigerian cultural assumptions and practices. The tone remains resolutely nonaccusatory. Thus in *Migrations of the Heart* emerges a rare portrayal of Africa from an African American perspective. The image, finally, is not romantic or negative or even ambivalent. Instead, as the anthropologist Michael M.J. Fischer points out, Golden brings a "bifocal" (215) approach to her constructions of both Africa and America. She represents each cultural zone without letting her view of one place judgmentally distort her vision of the other.

Finally, perhaps what many readers are likely to remember most vividly about Golden's autobiography is her singular prose style. Her prose often borders on poetry. Hers is a supple style, full of elegantly chiseled sentences that are drenched in fresh metaphors and petalled with beautiful similes.

CRITICAL RECEPTION

Reviews of *Migrations of the Heart* have been almost unanimously favorable. Christine M. Hill, in the *Library Journal*, calls it an "engrossing, fiercely told story" of a woman's life. Malcolm Boyd calls it an "exquisitely written" narrative that is "filled with brilliance and promise." Michael M.J. Fischer offers a substantive interpretation of the text from an anthropological perspective. According to Fischer, Golden's work offers "a skillful portrait of the devastating dynamics of an intercultural marriage that does not work" (216). Simultaneously, he points out, the book reveals the consciousness of a woman "gradually freeing herself from dependencies and unexamined notions of identity" (217). He concludes that *Migrations of the Heart* ideally projects "a dialectical or two-directional journey examining the realities of both sides [Nigeria and the United States] of cultural differences so that they may mutually question each other, and thereby generate a realistic image of human possibilities and a self-confidence for the explorer grounded in comparative understanding rather than ethnocentrism" (217).

BIBLIOGRAPHY

Autobiographical Work by Marita Golden

Migrations of the Heart. New York: Anchor Doubleday, 1983.

Studies of Marita Golden's Autobiographical Work

Beerman, Jill. Rev. of *Migrations of the Heart. Antioch Review* 42 (Winter 1984): 117–18.

Bovoso, Carole. "Touchstones of Black Women's Experience." Rev. of *Migrations of the Heart. Ms* (June 1983): 37–38.

Boyd, Malcolm. "A Woman's Own Movement. Personal." Rev. of *Migrations of the Heart. Los Angeles Times Book Review* (April 17, 1983): 4.

Browne, Phiefer L. "Marita Golden." In *The Oxford Compendium to African American Literature*. Ed. William L. Andrews, Frances Smith Foster, and Trudier Harris. New York: Oxford University Press, 1997. 321–22.

Davies, Carole Boyce. "Long Distance and Moving Through Homes." In *Black Women, Writing, and Identity: Migrations on the Subject*. New York: Routledge, 1994. 147–48.

Fischer, Michael M.J. "Ethnicity and the Post-Modern Arts of Memory." In *Writing Culture: The Poetics and Politics of Memory*. Ed. James Clifford and George E. Marcus. Berkeley: University of California Press, 1986. 215–18.

Hill, Christine M. Rev. of *Migrations of the Heart*. *Library Journal* 108 (February 1, 1983): 202.

McWhorter, Diane. Rev. of *Migrations of the Heart*. *New York Times Book Review* (May 7, 1983): 16–17.

Trescott, Jacqueline. "Golden's Moments of the Soul: One Young Writer's Personal 'Migrations.'" *Washington Post*, May 22, 1983, K1–K2.

Woodard, Loretta G. "Marita Golden." In *Contemporary African American Novelists*. Ed. Emmanuel S. Nelson. Westport, CT: Greenwood Press, 2000. 177–84.

RICHARD "DICK" CLAXTON GREGORY
(1932–)

Nikolas Huot

BIOGRAPHY

Born the second of six children on October 12, 1932, Richard Gregory grew up on relief in St. Louis, Missouri. Ridiculed by teachers and by kids from his neighborhood because of his family's poverty and his father's constant absence, Gregory soon learned to counter the insults by telling jokes and making people laugh with him, not at him. While in high school, Gregory joined the track team for the sole purpose of taking a shower every evening after practice. Despite becoming one of the fastest one-mile runners in the country, his name, shortened to Dick Gregory by reporters, was left out of the Scholastic record book that year because it was reserved for white athletes only. Deeply upset at not seeing his name, Gregory decided to march on the Board of Education in order to integrate the high school cross-country program and to expose the poor learning conditions at his school. Unbeknownst to him, this march would mark the beginning of an extensive career as a civil rights advocate. With his athletic abilities and the help of his coach, Gregory earned a scholarship to attend Southern Illinois University in Carbondale. While at the university, Gregory performed his satire on stage during fraternities variety shows, integrated the local movie theater, and broke the color barrier by becoming the first African American to be elected Outstanding Athlete of the University. In 1954, he was drafted into the army, where he was forced to enter a talent show to avoid court martial (the commanding officers did not appreciate his humor nor his quick repartee). Gregory won the contest and later qualified for the All Army Show in 1955. After being discharged, Gregory settled in Chicago and started doing comedy acts in night clubs around the city. In the winter of 1959, Gregory rented his own nightclub and married Lillian Smith, the most important person in his life to this day.

Deeply in debt from the club and constantly borrowing money to support his growing family, Gregory finally got his big break in show business in 1961, when he was hired at the Playboy Club and appeared on the *Jack Paar Show*.

In 1962, after Medgar Evers invited him to Mississippi, he decided to do more for the civil rights movement than "writing checks and giving speeches" (*Nigger* 159). Deeply involved in the movement from that time on, Gregory marched alongside Evers, Martin Luther King Jr., Hosea Williams, John Lewis, Ralph Abernathy, Stokely Carmichael, and many others. As a famous entertainer, Gregory brought even more media attention to the movement and, by going to the South and being arrested countless times, indicated readily that "Black folks would always come first, even before [his] own children" and his developing career as a comedian (*Callus* 54). In 1964, expanding Martin Luther King's nonviolence tenant, Gregory stopped eating meat and started paying more attention to his diet. In 1967, Gregory ran for mayor of Chicago against Richard Daley and, a year later, was a write-in candidate for president of the United States, when he got in trouble with the Treasury Department for issuing dollar bills with his face replacing George Washington's.

From his first march as a teenager to the present day, Gregory has been protesting and demanding justice and equality for African Americans. Moreover, over the years, Gregory has been involved in fights against poverty, world hunger, violation of Native Americans' rights, apartheid, police brutality, and animal abuse. Starting in the mid-1970s, Gregory changed his means of protest from marching to running across the country and holding long fasts. This focus on health, nutrition, and fasting led him to concoct numerous nutritional supplements and, eventually, to market them through his company, Dick Gregory Health Enterprises. Despite being diagnosed with lymphoma in 1999, Gregory still performs his caustic satire on stage and continues fasting to protest against injustices. This happily married father of ten currently shares his time between Plymouth, Massachusetts and Washington, D.C.

AUTOBIOGRAPHICAL WORKS AND THEMES

Dick Gregory has cowritten three autobiographies: *Nigger: An Autobiography* (1964), which recounts his humble beginnings to his initiation into the civil rights movement; *Up from Nigger* (1976), which continues the story of his involvement in fighting for racial equality; and *Callus on My Soul: A Memoir* (2000), which sums up the previous autobiographies and focuses on his more recent fights and on his nutritional plans. Although cowritten by three different authors, the three autobiographies are fairly similar in their approaches to the history of racism in the United States, to the main figures of the civil rights movement, and to the black woman.

From a very early age, when he was kicked in the face for accidentally touching a white woman's leg while shining her shoes, Dick Gregory has been aware of the poor racial relations in the United States. In his autobiographies, Gregory is quite blunt in his depiction of a racist American system that keeps African Americans down. He discusses at great length the days when African Americans could not eat in certain restaurants, sleep in certain hotels, sit in certain parts of theaters, or vote in any elections. He also exposes some of the atrocities suffered by proud African Americans who tried to change the system and improve their lot. By telling the stories of Emmett Till, Clyde Kennard, and Jimmy Lee Jackson, Gregory puts faces and names on the victims and, at the same time, recounts a recent past too often forgotten and overlooked. Not only does he denounce injustices suffered before and during the civil rights movement, but he also condemns police brutality and racial discrimination in today's society. In his latest memoirs, Gregory talks about Rodney King, Abner Louima, and Amadou Diallo, as well as the Ron Brown controversy and the CIA's (Central Intelligence Agency) role in bringing "over one billion dollars' worth of cocaine into the inner cities" (*Callus* 281). Gregory exposes the inherent racism of America in his autobiographies because he wants "reparations for all the hurt that Black folks have suffered" and "will not let White America off the hook until it cashes that check Dr. King tried to cash at the March on Washington in 1963" (288).

Besides decrying the poor conditions of racial relations in the United States, Gregory also spends a lot of time praising people who supported him throughout the years and/or who were involved in the civil rights movement. In *Nigger*, and again in *Callus on My Soul*, Gregory pays a special tribute to Medgar Evers, whom he credits for his active involvement in the fight for civil rights. Gregory also lauds such important figures as Martin Luther King Jr., Muhammad Ali, Malcolm X,* Stevie Wonder, Al Sharpton, and Hosea Williams. More than simply commending their accomplishments, Gregory praises their generosity, their kindness, and their commitment in the fight for racial equality. Gregory also makes it a point to mention some unsung heroes who helped the movement every day and who gave up their lives for it. More than once, Gregory commends the courage and dedication of poor blacks in Mississippi and Alabama who protested and demonstrated even though their lives were in danger. Of those poor blacks, Gregory mentions especially the black women who worked behind the scenes by feeding, clothing, and sheltering protesters.

Indeed, in his three autobiographies, Gregory constantly extols black women, most notably his mother and his wife. Witnessing his mother's struggles, Gregory writes about her working sixteen hour days, receiving no respect from her employers, wearing hand me down clothes, raising a family by herself, and waiting every night in vain for her husband to come home. Despite all those difficulties, Gregory's mother, like so many other black women, is shown to be loving, beautiful, proud, and courageous. Gregory is quick to praise not only his mother's courage but also his wife's strength. For his entire married life, his wife has stood by him: "God and Lil are the only things in my life that have stayed the same through all these years" (*Callus* 234). No matter the difficulties (poverty, imprisonment, evictions, deaths), Lil has stood firm, raised the children, and "sorted out the problems" (234). Without her and her support, he readily admits that he could not have been as active in the fights he chose to embrace. Along with his wife and mother, Gregory also praises at great length Myrlie Evers-Williams, Coretta Scott King, and Dr. Betty Shabazz, who showed great perseverance following their husbands' deaths. In all three of his autobiographies, Gregory is quite adamant about the black woman's strength, courage, beauty, and vital role in the black community. This is why it is particularly shocking to him to see how today's stand-up comedy and gangster rap demean and disrespect black women.

CRITICAL RECEPTION

Despite (or because of) its controversial title, Gregory's first autobiography sold more than a million copies. Even though the other two did not fare as well, Gregory's memoirs have been usually well received by the public and the media. As a full-fledged member of the civil rights movement, Gregory's experiences and recollections are important for a better understanding of those momentous days. The appeal in Gregory's autobiographies lies not only in the interesting perspectives of an active witness to history but also in his honest and sincere portrayals of a racist society and of his difficult journey out of poverty. If all agree on Gregory's dedication and on the merit of his causes, his views on the murders of the Kennedys, Martin Luther King Jr., Malcolm X, and John Lennon are somewhat more controversial. As a great believer in government conspiracies, Gregory uses his memoirs as vehicles for denouncing the lies surrounding the deaths of some great men. Although expressed very convincingly, those conspiracy theories drive away some readers and make some critics uncomfortable or ambiguous about the rest of the book. Even his good friend Ossie Davis somewhat dismisses the conspiracy theories as "sublimated reactions to the fears he has been exposed to" (qtd. in Carlson C01). Of course, Dick Gregory has always been a controversial figure, so it should come as no surprise that his memoirs are as well.

If that controversy caused critics to downplay Gregory's memoirs, it also caused Gregory to lose some of the recognition he deserves for the sacrifices he made for his constant involvement in difficult causes. Southern Illinois University reversed that trend when, in 1987, it awarded Gregory with an Honorary Doctorate of Humane Letters. It would take thirteen years, the news of his illness to come out, and his third autobiography to be released before Gregory started to receive more acclaim for his lifelong activism. In October 2000, Gregory was honored at the Kennedy Center by such friends as Bill Cosby, Ossie Davis, Ruby Dee, and Stevie Wonder. One can only hope that as he continues to protest police brutality and institutional racism, Gregory will receive more attention from the media and from the masses for whose interests he is fighting.

BIBLIOGRAPHY

Autobiographical Works by Richard "Dick" Claxton Gregory

(With Robert Lipsyte). *Nigger: An Autobiography.* New York: Dutton, 1964.
(With James R. McGraw). *Up from Nigger.* New York: Stein and Day, 1976.
(With Shelia P. Moses). *Callus on My Soul: A Memoir.* Atlanta, GA: Longstreet Press, 2000.

Studies of Richard "Dick" Claxton Gregory's Autobiographical Works

Bergman, A.C.J. Rev. of *Up from Nigger*. *New York Times Book Review* (November 1, 1974): 3.
Carlson, Peter. "All-Vegans-Unite But Is Dick Gregory Still Vegetarian?" *Washington Post*, October 9, 2000, final ed., C01+.
"Comedian Dick Gregory." *Maclean's* 3 Dec. 1984: 8.
Dick Gregory: Keeping an Eye on the Globe. <http.www.dickgregory.com/dick/_TOC. html>.
Hefner, Hugh M. Introduction. *From the Back of the Bus.* New York: Avon, 1962. 11–18.
Hentoff, Nat. Rev. of *Nigger*. *Book Week* (November 1, 1964): 5.
Holland, Bill. " '50s Trailblazers Brought Social Satire to Masses." *Billboard* 108.39 (September 28, 1996): 1–2.
Millstein, Gilbert. Rev. of *Nigger*. *New York Times Book Review* (November 1, 1964): 3.
Muhammad, Charlene. "Revealing the Soul." *The Final Call Online* (January 23, 2001). < http://www.finalcall.com/perspectives/interviews/d_gregory01-23-2001.htm >.
Schenck, William. Rev. of *Up from Nigger*. *Library Journal* 102 (January 1, 1977): 96.
Wright, Mark H. "Sophistic Humor and Social Change: Overcoming Identification with the Aggressor." *JPCS: Journal for the Psychoanalysis of Culture & Society* 5.1 (Spring 2000): 57–64.

SUTTON ELBERT GRIGGS
(1872–1933)

Harish Chander

BIOGRAPHY

Sutton Elbert Griggs was born on June 19, 1872, in Chatfield, Texas, to Alan Ralph and Emma Hodge Griggs. Alan Griggs had been freed from slavery just seven years earlier. He became a highly respected Baptist minister and editor of *The Western Star* in Texas and served as the Texas delegate to the 1905 World's Baptist Congress in London, England. In *Paths of Progress* (1925), Sutton Griggs writes about his father's pioneer spirit demonstrated by his establishment of the first colored high school and colored newspaper in Texas (44). In the dedication to his novel *The Hindered Hand* (1905), he pays a tribute to his father as "preeminently a man of peace" and his mother, Emma Griggs, as "ever tender and serene of soul" (3). After finishing his high school education from the public schools in Dallas, Texas, Sutton Griggs attended Bishop College in Marshall, Texas, for his undergraduate studies and Richmond Theological Seminary (now the Virginia Union University) for his theological training. Griggs was graduated from the Seminary in 1893 and was appointed the pastor of the First Baptist Church at Berkeley, Virginia. While he was still in Virginia, Griggs met Emma Williams, a public school teacher of Portsmouth, Virginia. They were married on May 10, 1897. In his autobiography *The Story of My Struggles* (1914), Griggs refers to his wife as "the companion of my struggles, and my fellow sufferer" (14). They had one child, an adopted daughter named Eunice.

It was also in Virginia that Griggs wrote his first novel, *Imperio in Imperium* (first published in 1899), launching his literary career as the writer of racial protest novels. Between 1901 and 1908, Griggs wrote four more novels—*Overshadowed* (1901), *Unfettered* (1902), *The Hindered Hand* (1905), and *Pointing the Way* (1908). These novels depict the plight of the black people of the post-

Reconstruction era, when Southern states enacted codes to deny blacks the franchise and keep them "in place." They demonstrate the disastrous impact of white racism on black people's lives and minds and depict both nonviolent and militant means to reach equality.

From 1895 to 1906, Griggs served as pastor of the First Baptist Church in East Nashville, Tennessee, and the corresponding secretary of the National Baptist Convention (created in 1895 by the merger of the American Baptists and the Southern Baptist Convention). His leadership position in the National Baptist Convention gave Griggs an opportunity to seek interracial cooperation for the uplift of African Americans. He was also a major force in establishing the Nashville School for the training of African American clergymen. In 1901, Griggs set up the Orion Publishing Company, which published and distributed his own works. In 1905, he joined hands with college educated blacks, such as W.E.B. Du Bois,* Reverdy Ransom, William Monroe Trotter, and J. Milton Waldron, to launch a civil rights organization—the Niagara Movement. This movement evolved in 1910 into the popular organization called the National Association for the Advancement of Colored People (NAACP).

His 1907 work *One Great Question: A Study of Southern Conditions at Close Range* describes the deplorable conditions under which Southern blacks lived and argues that the solution to the race problem is racial equality, not further repression of blacks. Stung by his inability to sell his works to members of his own race and resultant financial failure, Griggs sought to seek white endorsement for his work. In his last novel, *Pointing the Way* (1908), therefore, Griggs seeks to solve the race problem by persuading a white attorney to run for the office of mayor on a platform pledging justice for all citizens. And in *Wisdom's Call* (1911), Griggs assembles a number of pamphlets in which he reasons that whites would advance their own interest by treating black people fairly. In this collection, he includes his arguments in support of the Fifteenth Amendment's assurance to African Americans of the right to vote (15).

In 1912, Griggs moved to Memphis where he served as the pastor of the Tabernacle Baptist Church for nineteen years. In 1914, he founded the Public Welfare League to help black talent and build black businesses and enterprises. His autobiography appeared that same year. *The Story of My Struggles* depicts his literary crusade in the cause of his race. During World War I, Griggs contributed to the war effort by inspiring people to buy Liberty Bonds (Fuller 266). In *Life's Demands or According to Law* (1916), Griggs focuses on cooperation, arguing that success comes "in proportion to the number and kind of people a man can inspire to lend him their aid" (12). He cites Booker T. Washington* as a leader who "attained his remarkable success and his great fame through co-operation" (101). In *Light on Racial Issues* (1921), Griggs emphasizes the need for blacks to exercise self-discipline, practice good morals, and support worthy enterprise (14). In *Guide to Racial Greatness or The Science of Collective Efficiency* (1923), Griggs enumerates personality traits that black Americans need to nurture to promote collective efficiency. He points out there the role that black churches can play in that process (209). In *Kingdom Builders' Manual: Companion Book to Guide to Racial Greatness* (1924), Griggs finds scriptural support for his quest for racial justice, emphasizing biblical passages that propound the personality traits he considers necessary for racial uplift.

Griggs served as president of the American Baptist Theological Seminary from 1925 to 1926. He continued to write social tracts that expound his theme of racial accommodation and cooperation, such as *Stepping-Stone to Higher Things* (1925), *Paths of Progress or Cooperation between the Races, a Series of Addresses, Articles, and Essays* (1925), and *The Winning Policy* (1927). *Triumph of the Simple Virtues; or The Life Story of John L. Webb* came out in 1926. In *Paths of Progress*, for example, Griggs declares that the race war is "over" (19), and the two races should seek closer cooperation for "our good and the good of the country at large" (65). However, this pro-white stance made Griggs increasingly unpopular with the less accommodating black Memphibians. With the 1929 stock market crash, Griggs lost white financial support. He was unable to make mortgage payments on the church building, resulting in the auctioning of the Tabernacle Baptist Church of Memphis in 1930. Griggs returned to Denison, Texas, to become the pastor of Hopewell Baptist Church. In 1932, he resigned this position and moved to Houston to start the National Religious and Civic Institute. Griggs died on January 2, 1933, in Denison, Texas.

AUTOBIOGRAPHICAL WORK AND THEMES

Griggs's single completely autobiographical work is *The Story of My Struggles* (1914). It is a slim, twenty-four-page booklet. It tells the story of his motivation and hardships as a writer and explains how Griggs the novelist became Griggs the pamphleteer. Here, he presents himself as the champion fighter for his people, as one who took up the pen to espouse their cause. Although disappointed and discouraged with lack of support, he continues the battle. He says that he has given much of his "time, energy and meager means" to help his people fight "the fierce winds of a hostile public sentiment" (6). Finding very little encouragement from his own people, Griggs is dismayed to see his novels as financial failures. Unable to bear the expenses of publishing long books, Griggs gives up writing novels; however, he continues to fight for equal rights and opportunities for black people through small pamphlets. To cite his own words, "I shall battle on as best as I can" (19), and "I have sought to obey the Biblical injunction to speak the truth in love" (21). If "failure should dog [his] footsteps to the end," he would like his epitaph to read: "Here lies one who was faithful to the cause. He lacked but one thing—support" (21).

In his autobiography, Griggs describes his inspiration for his works. In his fight for the rights of the black people, Griggs says that he was impelled by the high principle of the Declaration of Independence that "Governments derived their just powers from the consent of the governed" (7). To make a case for black participation in government, he wrote his first novel, *Imperium in Imperio*. Although favorably reviewed by Professor Kelly Miller, dean of the College of Arts and Science of Howard University, the book did not sell well. The few copies that were sold through Griggs's personal solicitations. Griggs's disappointment is obvious: "From the twenty copies sent to race leaders, four expressions were received" (19). Feeling that he has "somehow failed to deliver the right message" through *Imperium in Imperio*, Griggs wrote his second novel *Overshadowed*, determined to win the support of his people. *Overshadowed* met the same fate as its predecessor. At that time he thought, "Either I was wrong in expecting support from the race, did not deserve it, or else the race was doing wrong to withhold support" (10). To solve this puzzle, he wrote another book, *Unfettered*, putting forth "all that there was in me," but with the same disappointing results (10). He could now in good conscience lay the blame at the door of his race and "decided to abandon the field of literature" (11). Using a baseball analogy, he compares himself to a baseball player who knew "the right kind of play to make in every crisis that arose," but "the men behind him did not properly back him up." And this lack of support cost him the game (21).

His autobiography then turns to another event that inspired him to write another novel. The National Baptist Convention requested Griggs to write a novel to counteract Thomas Dixon's denigration of the black race in Dixon's infamous *The Leopard's Spots* (1902) and *The Clansman* (1905). Thus, he wrote *The Hindered Hand*, but the promised Baptist Convention support never came. Yet Griggs persevered, writing two additional books, *The One Great Question* and *Pointing the Way*, but they proved similarly commercially unsuccessful. Griggs turned to writing small pamphlets, vowing to persist in his writing efforts to help his people win their rights.

This autobiography contains a chapter titled "A Seeming Digression," in which Griggs apprises the reader of the "state of the public mind toward the Negro race" at the time of his writing (17). He quotes several authorities to show that racial prejudice and hatred are on the increase all over the country. This so-called digression falls into place, as Griggs once again points to the importance of literature as an instrument of social change. He suggests that members of "the Negro race [should] resolve to put literature in the hands of . . . the white race" to promote racial understanding (21).

Griggs's short autobiography ends on an affirmative note. Griggs informs the reader that he is starting a mutual aid organization—the Public Welfare League—to "fully cover our needs as a people" (23). He solicits his readers' support in "getting that organization before the people" (24).

Griggs's *The Story of My Struggles* passes the crucial test of an autobiography about the author's image building. As pointed out by Karl J. Weintraub in his 1978 book *The Value of the Individual: Self and Circumstance in Autobiography*, an autobiographical work is primarily concerned with its author's "self conception" and his efforts to remain true to it at all costs (xi). Griggs is in this regard eminently successful in projecting the self image of a lonely warrior who will continue his fight despite receiving very little encouragement from his people.

CRITICAL RECEPTION

While Griggs's works in general have received scanty critical attention, his autobiography has virtually been ignored by critics. It was perhaps disregarded partly because of its nonavailability. Only two critics—David M. Tucker and Wilson Jeremiah Moses—have taken note of *The Story of My Struggles*, but neither offers any judgment on its literary merits. In a chapter titled "Reverend Griggs and Black Social Efficiency" in his book *Black Pastors and Leaders*, Tucker repeats the autobiography's story of Griggs's disappointing book sales and financial failure for want of support from his own race (74, 76). In his book, *The Golden Age of Black Nationalism, 1850–1925*, Moses compares Griggs to Marcus Garvey in that he felt unappreciated by many of his own people. Moses comments on *The Story of My Struggles*: "In tones similar to those to be employed by Garvey a decade later, he [Griggs] called into question the racial pride of those who did not support him personally" (178).

BIBLIOGRAPHY

Autobiographical Work by Sutton Elbert Griggs

The Story of My Struggles. Memphis, TN: National Public Welfare League, 1914.

Studies of Sutton Elbert Griggs's Autobiographical Work

Moses, Wilson Jeremiah. *The Golden Age of Black Nationalism, 1850–1925*. New York: Oxford University Press, 1978.
———. "Literary Garveyism: The Novels of Reverend Sutton E. Griggs." *Phylon* 40.3 (Fall 1979): 203–16.
Tucker, David M. "Reverend Griggs and Black Social Efficiency." In *Black Pastors and Leaders: Memphis, 1819–1972*. Memphis, TN: Memphis State University Press, 1975. 71–86.

Biographical Sources

Byrd, James W., and David M. Tucker. "Griggs, Sutton Elbert." *The Handbook of Texas Online*. <http://www.tsha.utexas.edu/handbook/online/articles/view/GG/fgr85.html>.
Fuller, Thomas. *Pictorial History of the American Negro*. Memphis, TN: Hopkins Print, 1933.
Mather, Frank Lincoln, ed. "Griggs, Allen Ralph." In *Who's Who of the Colored Race*. Chicago, IL, 1915. Detroit, MI: Gale, 1915. 124–25.
———. "Griggs, Sutton E." In *Who's Who of the Colored Race*. Chicago, IL, 1915. Detroit, MI: Gale, 1915. 125.
"In Memoriam: Dr. Sutton E. Griggs." *The Mission Herald* 36 (February 1933): 9.

JAMES ALBERT UKAWSAW GRONNIOSAW
(1710?–?)

Terry Novak

BIOGRAPHY

James Albert Ukawsaw Gronniosaw was born around 1710 in Borno, located in what we now know as Nigeria. Nothing is known of Gronniosaw's childhood; however, it is known that at the age of fifteen or so a restless and bored Gronniosaw left his family to seek adventure. He set off for the Gold Coast with a trader who promised the boy intrigue and excitement. Instead, Gronniosaw met with hardship and genuine concern for his life, so much so that when he was sold into slavery, he experienced relief and gratitude.

Gronniosaw became a house slave for a Dutch family in New York City. In 1730 he was sold to a New Jersey Dutch Reformed minister named Theodorus Jacobus Frelinghuysen. Gronniosaw remained with the Frelinghuysen family some twenty years, during which time he learned to read and was exposed to an abundance of sermons and theological dialogue. After eighteen years with the Frelinghuysen family, Gronniosaw converted to Christianity amidst the fever of the Great Awakening. Shortly after Gronniosaw's conversion and following a long illness, Frelinghuysen died, although not before granting Gronniosaw his freedom.

Gronniosaw remained with the Frelinghuysen family for a few years after the minister's death and saw the remainder of the family die off. In order to alleviate debts he had incurred, Gronniosaw took a job as a cook on a privateer ship and experienced the action of the Seven Years' War. Once Gronniosaw paid off his debts, he enlisted in the British armed services in order to gain passage to the country he had read so much about and with which he had become so captivated. After battle stops in Martinique and Havana, Gronniosaw finally reached England. Shortly after his arrival, he paid an extensive visit to Holland, where he had more contact with Dutch Reformed ministers.

In 1763 Gronniosaw returned to England, was baptized by a Baptist minister, and married an Englishwoman named Betty, a widow with one child. The two had children together and faced tremendous hardships throughout their marriage. They experienced many employment difficulties and ongoing poverty. Throughout their trials, they looked to their Christian faith for strength. Eventually Gronniosaw dictated his story to an anonymous young woman who saw the book through seven publication editions, in the hopes that the book's revenue would help the struggling family. There is no evidence that the book sales helped the family through their trials. In addition, there is no indication of when or where Gronniosaw or his family members died.

AUTOBIOGRAPHICAL WORK AND THEMES

Gronniosaw's sole autobiographical work is titled *A Narrative of the Most Remarkable Particulars in the Life of James Albert Ukawsaw Gronniosaw, An African Prince, Written by Himself*. The work is unique in that it does not focus on many strictly autobiographical points. Gronniosaw brushes through the events of his life as if they were of little or passing importance, even down to points concerning his wife and children. Instead of focusing on himself per se, Gronniosaw chooses instead to focus on his faith, his faith experiences, and what he perceives as his faith failings. In the very beginning of his autobiography he asserts that he always wondered about God and questioned his parents about the existence of a higher being. According to Gronniosaw, his questions were met with hostility. Gronniosaw depicts himself as being far above his birth family in matters of spirituality, following a familiar religious thread that his faith makes him superior and makes him right.

Gronniosaw also focuses on his early fascination with books, describing his first encounter with books, expecting them to literally talk to him. It is clear that the author was drawn to intellectual pursuits. He passes rather quickly through his extensive time with Mr. "Freelandhouse," as he refers to Frelinghuysen, to the point of describing the man's death in the following manner:

The loss of Mr. Freelandhouse distressed me greatly, but I was rendered still more unhappy by the clouded and perplexed situation of my mind; the great enemy of my soul being ready to torment me, would present my own misery to me in such striking light, and distress me with doubts, fears, and such a deep sense of my own unworthiness, that after all the comfort and encouragement I had received, I was often tempted to believe that I should be a cast-away at last.—The more I saw of the beauty and glory of God, the more I was humbled under a sense of my own vileness. (40)

Much of Gronniosaw's autobiography reads in such a way. Indeed, there are sketches of his experience as a slave, but *Narrative* hardly falls into the standard

category of slave narrative. Likewise, there are perfunctory details of Gronniosaw's life, but not nearly enough to make the work a fetching take on the
particulars of eighteenth-century life in any way. What the *Narrative* does do
well is serve as a *spiritual* autobiography, which seems to have been the author's
primary intent. Gronniosaw even ends his text on a prayerful note: "As pilgrims,
and very poor pilgrims we are traveling through many difficulties towards our
heavenly home, and waiting patiently for his glorious call, when the Lord shall
deliver us out of the evils of this present world, and bring us to the everlasting
glories of the world to come.—To HIM be praise for ever and ever. Amen" (53).

One can also look to the text for its historical value, if one greatly limits that
history to a study of the Great Awakening and its effects on slaves and foreigners
to American soil. This is not to say that *Narrative* is not a valuable work, for it
is indeed a most valuable addition to the literary canon.

CRITICAL RECEPTION

As one would expect, scholars and critics have paid respectable attention to
Gronniosaw's *Narrative*, focusing to a large extent on the author's spiritual struggles and descriptions. Frank Lambert deals quite extensively with the spiritual
experiences of slaves, particularly during the Great Awakening, in an attempt,
as he puts it, to "understand the Christianization of American Africans through
their own eyes" (186). It is in this light that he sees Gronniosaw's work as most
valuable. Adam Potkay and Sandra Burr concur with this interest. They have
categorized Gronniosaw with other eighteenth-century writers such as Olaudah
Equiano in an attempt to correlate the slave experiences with the Great Awakening experiences.

Henry Louis Gates Jr. acknowledges the Great Awakening/Christianization
themes of Gronniosaw's *Narrative* but goes beyond discussions of religion and
salvation. Gates writes of Gronniosaw as fitting into a "Noble Negro" genre. As
Gates explains it,

Gronniosaw . . . represents himself as no mere common Negro slave, but as one nurtured,
indulged, and trained in the manner of royalty everywhere. Faced with what must have
seemed a deafening silence in black literary antecedents, Gronniosaw turned to the fictions
of the Noble Savage to ground his text with a tradition. He also turned to the tradition
of the Christian confession. (14)

Gates goes on to discuss the use of signifying in the work of Gronniosaw and
other early African American writers. He writes, "These narrators, linked by
revision of a trope into the very first black chain of signifiers, implicitly Signify
upon another 'chain,' the metaphorical Great Chain of Being." (24). Gates views
Gronniosaw's work as most important because of its inherent depiction of black
intellect and individuality of thought.

All available critical work on Gronniosaw's *Narrative* focuses on the positives of the autobiography. Many comparisons are made to Equiano's work, but even more comparisons are made to spiritual writings of the eighteenth century.

BIBLIOGRAPHY

Autobiographical Work by James Albert Ukawsaw Gronniosaw

A Narrative of the Most Remarkable Particulars in the Life of James Albert Ukawsaw Gronniosaw, an African Prince, Written by Himself. 1774. Rpt. in Black Atlantic Writers of the 18th Century: Living the New Exodus in England and the Americas. Ed. Adam Potkay and Sandra Burr. New York: St. Martin's Press, 1995. 27–63.

Studies of James Albert Ukawsaw Gronniosaw's Autobiographical Work

Costanzo, Angelo. "James A.U. Gronniosaw." In Oxford Companion to African American Literature. Ed. William L. Andrews et al. Oxford University Press, 1997. 330.

Gates, Henry Louis, Jr. "James Gronniosaw and the Trope of the Talking Book." In African American Autobiography: A Collection of Critical Essays. Ed. William L. Andrews. Englewood Cliffs, NJ: Prentice-Hall, 1993. 8–25.

Lambert, Frank. " 'I Saw the Book Talk': Slave Readings of the First Great Awakening." Journal of Negro History 77 (1992): 185–98.

Phillips, Caryl, ed. Extravagant Strangers: A Literature of Belonging. New York: Vintage Books, 1999.

JUANITA HARRISON
(c. 1891–?)

Kelley A. Squazzo

BIOGRAPHY

Male writers have traditionally dominated the field of travel writing. Juanita Harrison is not only a woman autobiographical travel writer but a black woman autobiographical travel writer who has a remarkable experience to tell about in her only publication *My Great, Wide, Beautiful World*. However, our knowledge of this intriguing woman is limited. She was born in Mississippi around 1891 to a family of modest means. The preface to her book written by her employer's daughter, Myra K. Dickinson, states Harrison "had only a few months of schooling before she was ten. Then began an endless round of cooking, washing, and ironing in an overburdened household, labour that might have daunted a grown person" (ix). Dickinson also tells us that Harrison had a small stature and an olive complexion, often appearing younger that she really was. Most of what else in known about this onetime writer can be derived from her work.

Harrison had a vision of her future, one that would include sailing "far away to strange places" (ix). At the age of sixteen her dream of traveling began when she found employment in Canada and Cuba. She took classes at the Young Women's Christian Association (YWCA) and learned conversational French and Spanish that assisted her in her journeys. Harrison dedicates her book to Myra K. Dickinson, who employed Harrison in Los Angeles and, with her husband, helped her invest money and save and earn interest. At age thirty-six, she took her savings and began her travels that lasted from June 1927 to April 1935, her passports show that she lived in twenty-two different countries. She was encouraged to write down her adventures by her employer in France, Mrs. Felix Morris, and her daughter Mildred arranged Harrison's book for Macmillan, the publisher.

AUTOBIOGRAPHICAL WORK AND THEMES

The *Time* review of *My Great, Wide, Beautiful World* states that readers will appreciate "Juanita's freedom from economic shackles" (83). Not only should we admire her determination to overcome her social status and acquire the financial means to travel, but we should also recognize that Harrison transcends race and gender barriers to accomplish her dream. She eludes problems of classism and racism throughout her travels and easily assimilates into various societies: "At Aleppo they though [*sic*] I was Chinese. Here they think I am Aribian" (65). She even is able to make herself "so native" in Egyptian costume that she is invited to wedding feasts (81). Harrison's joy of life, sense of humor, and appreciation of cultural differences allow her to make many friends. In Russia, she actually feels like she has discovered a new way of life: "Here are no cast, and class, no who's who. Here you are more free to do what you want to than any other country thats if its clean and honest" (279).

Harrison's goal is to forget the past and concentrate on the future. As Rebecca Barton remarks, Harrison is a woman "who is not concerned about all the whys and wherefores of her past live but who only wants to convey her immediate joys to her readers" (89). She enthusiastically celebrates life and enters seamlessly into new countries and new adventures. Harrison writes of Paris, "I think I love it best of all, but I can't help but love the last place best" (20). She loves to try new cuisine, experience the theater, and even attends a bullfight. If readers of Harrison only take away one lesson from her autobiography, it is to embrace life to the fullest.

Yet the theme that is most powerful throughout the work is that of women's autonomy. Mild feminist tones are present in Harrison's writing, thus giving the reader a sense of her convictions and identity as a black woman. Harrison often expresses her pride in being an unmarried woman. For example, she comments on the women washing clothes in Spain: "[I]f I was married I would be at home washing dirty clothes just as they are doing" (192). She is always observant of independent women doing what they please, especially the women of Rangoon: "[W]hat a joy to see the wide streets and the Women enjoying so much Freedom. and The Burma Women with their High Crown of black hair. I do not like their big cigars that are stuck in many of their mouths, but they say inside is as harmless as corn silk" (149).

Even in her relations with men throughout her travels, Harrison exhibits an air of independence. She turns down numerous male suitors who want to accompany her on her journeys and amuses herself by "keeping count of how many make love to me" (21). In Barcelona, she meets a German man and records, "I was to meet the German man at 9, but layd down to rest and went to sleep woke up at 11 so that was the ending of the German" (188). In fact, she waits until she is financially sound with the royalties from her *Atlantic Monthly* publications before allowing her new "sweatheart" to kiss her.

CRITICAL RECEPTION

My Great, Wide, Beautiful World was published in 1936, although selections of Harrison's travelogue appeared in the October and November 1935 editions of Atlantic Monthly. It is clear that the manuscript was not edited, and Harrison defends her illiteracy: "[I]f the mistekes are left out there'll be only blank" (243). Harrison is not constrained by rules of grammar, spelling, or punctuation, therefore marking another level of her personal freedom.

Despite its unedited state, the book was well received and reviewed in major journals including the New Republic and the Saturday Review of Literature as well as in reputable newspapers such as the New York Times. Reviewers were able to look past the lack of style in the writing and appreciate the realism of Harrison's personal record. The reviewer for the New Republic boasts, "This is a remarkable traveler, shrewd, intelligent, informal and wholeheartedly sympathetic, who adores gayety, loves good food, enjoys a trick and a joke, is moved by beauty, and is interested in everything" (111). Harrison's language obviously lacks the refinement of other writers like Zora Neale Hurston,* Alice Dunbar-Nelson,* and Frances Harper. Yet her writing is even poetic at times, and her narrative is readily understandable.

Harrison's book was out of print for sixty years, until Henry Louis Gates Jr. introduced the African American Women Writers 1910–1940 series and reprinted it in 1996 with a critical introduction by Adele Logan Alexander. Besides some flattering reviews, My Great, Wide, Beautiful World has not received the critical attention it deserves.

My Great, Wide, Beautiful World ends in 1936 on Waikiki Beach in Hawaii, where Harrison pitches a tent, concluding her long years of traveling. She expresses pure bliss in her decision to end her travels in "this lovely part of the World" (314). We do not know what became of Harrison or where and when she died. She never published another work and decided not to make writing her lifelong career. However, Saturday Review of Literature reviewer Katherine Woods comments, "There is nothing on our shelves, certainly, that is quite like this spontaneous, shrewd, and unselfconscious story of the Odyssey of an American Negress" (11). That Harrison lived the life she dreamed of is evident throughout her travelogue.

BIBLIOGRAPHY

Autobiographical Work by Juanita Harrison

My Great, Wide, Beautiful World. Arranged and with a preface by Mildred Morris. New York: Macmillan, 1936. First published in Atlantic Monthly (October and November 1935).

Studies of Juanita Harrison's Autobiographical Work

Alexander, Adele Logan. "Introduction." My Great, Wide, Beautiful World. New York: G.K. Hall, 1996. xv–xxviii.

Barton, Rebecca Chalmers. Witnesses for Freedom: Negro Americans in Autobiography. New York: Harper, 1948.

Rev. of My Great, Wide, Beautiful World. Booklist 32 (June 1936): 288.

Rev. of My Great, Wide, Beautiful World. Books 17 (May 1936): 19.

Rev. of My Great, Wide, Beautiful World. Christian Century 53 (June 10, 1936): 843.

Rev. of My Great, Wide, Beautiful World. Cleveland Open Shelf (July 1936): 16.

Rev. of My Great, Wide, Beautiful World. New Republic 87 (June 3, 1936): 111.

Rev. of My Great, Wide, Beautiful World. Springfield Republican (May 17, 1936): 7.

Rev. of My Great, Wide, Beautiful World. Time 27 (May 18, 1936): 83.

Rev. of My Great, Wide, Beautiful World. Wisconsin Library Bulletin 32 (July 1936): 85.

Rev. of My Great, Wide, Beautiful World. Yale Review 25 (Summer 1936): 839.

Roses, Lorraine E., and Ruth E. Randolph. Harlem Renaissance and Beyond: Literary Biographies of 100 Black Women Writers (1900–1945). Boston: G.K. Hall, 1990.

Woods, Katherine. "Juanita Harrison Has Known Twenty-Two Countries." Rev. of My Great, Wide, Beautiful World. New York Times, May 17, 1936, 4.

———. "Traveling for Adventure." Rev. of My Great, Wide, Beautiful World. Saturday Review of Literature 14 (June 20, 1936): 11.

JOSIAH HENSON
(1789–1883)

Rennie Simson

BIOGRAPHY

Most of what we know about Josiah Henson is what is revealed in his four autobiographies, *The Life of Josiah Henson* (1849), *Truth Stranger Than Fiction: Father Henson's Story of His Own Life* (1858), *Uncle Tom's Story of His Life* (1876), and *An Autobiography of Josiah Henson Mrs. Harriet Beecher Stowe's Uncle Tom* (1878). It is the designation of Henson as Stowe's Uncle Tom that has focused considerable attention on him. In her *Key to Uncle Tom's Cabin*, Stowe commented on the models she used in creating each of her major characters. When referring to the creation of Uncle Tom, she described a number of models, chief among them Josiah Henson. "A last instance parallel with that of Uncle Tom is to be found in the published memoirs of the venerable Josiah Henson" (42). She proceeded to include a detailed summary of his 1849 autobiography.

Henson was born in 1789, a slave on a farm in Charles County, Maryland. His most vivid recollection of his early childhood was seeing his father mutilated and severely beaten for daring to raise his hand against the overseer who had tried to assault his wife. The father, who had been a cheerful and amiable man prior to this event, became despondent, morose, and uncooperative thereafter. As a result he was sold to a planter in Alabama, and Henson never saw or heard of his father again. After the departure of his father, Henson lived with a series of owners, sometimes together with his mother, sometimes not. The most notable experiences of the young Henson during this period centered on dealing with the great cruelty of his masters who, among other things, temporarily separated him from his mother. As a child Henson had experienced no religious instruction, but as a young man he attended a revival meeting where he was introduced to Christianity. His conversion was immediate and complete, and he took on the role of evangelist and preacher among the slaves. His natural gift as a speaker and his charismatic personality made him a great success with his fellows. Although he could not read, he committed biblical passages to memory and used them freely in his sermons. His deep faith in his Christian principles led him to be reliable, steady, and honest, qualities that his master at the time, one Isaac Riley, regarded so highly that he made him the manager of his plantation in Montgomery County, Maryland. His fellow slaves respected him to such an extent that this arrangement worked well for a number of years. Perhaps the most noteworthy event during this period of Henson's life was his leading a group of Riley's slaves to Kentucky to Riley's brother Amos for safekeeping at a time when Riley had come upon hard times financially. On their journey they passed along the coastline of Ohio, and people on the shore shouted to them that they should all escape to freedom. Henson refused, feeling obligated to keep his pledge to his master, and continued marching his fellow slaves to further enslavement in Kentucky. Three years later all of these slaves were sold. When he wrote of this event, he expressed deep regret for his actions.

Harriet Beecher Stowe saw this act in a different light and referred to it in her *Key to Uncle Tom's Cabin* as a "most sublime act of self renunciation in obedience to its [the Bible's] commands" (43). Riley rewarded Henson's loyalty with an act of treachery. He sold Henson his freedom for $400, then tricked Henson into letting Riley hold on to Henson's freedom papers, later saying Henson owed him more than he had yet paid. After this duplicity, Riley decided to sell him in the New Orleans slave market and sent him there in the care of his son. In New Orleans the young master was taken very ill, and Henson nursed him back to health. Young Riley did not sell Henson but took him back to Kentucky, as he needed his services as a nurse. Once the young master was home, safe and well, little thanks was shown Henson by either father or son for all the care he had taken of the young man whose life all agreed he had saved. This ill treatment was the proverbial straw that broke the camel's back, and in 1830 Henson escaped with his wife (whom he had "married" when he was twenty-two) and four children to Canada. Henson's narrative includes the details of their difficult journey as well as the description of their joyful arrival in the northern states and finally in Canada.

His career in Canada flourished, and he was successful in numerous areas. He first became a Methodist preacher and was also a widely heralded abolitionist spokesman. In 1842 he attempted to establish an industrial school near Dawn, Canada. Although the school did not prosper, a sawmill established in connection with the school flourished for a time. Subsequent financial difficulties with the sawmill pressed Henson, who struggled hard to make his business a success. He went to England to raise money to cover the mill's debts. He was successful in this endeavor and was received by some of England's leading statesmen and awarded a bronze medal in recognition of his polished walnut lumber, which was exhibited at the World's Fair in 1851. He made two more trips to England, and on the final trip he and his second wife (the first died in 1852) were presented to Queen Victoria. On his return he and his wife were received by President Rutherford B. Hayes.

In his final years he encountered a number of problems, chief among them that in spite of all his efforts his sawmill failed. Additionally, he was charged with having violated the foreign enlistment act when he joined the second Essex Company of colored volunteers in the Canadian Rebellion (1837–1838). This charge was placed against him when he wished to participate in the Civil War, and he admitted his military involvement in Canada. He died in Dresden, Canada, on May 5, 1883, at the age of ninety-four.

AUTOBIOGRAPHICAL WORKS AND THEMES

Henson's only published works are the four versions of his autobiography alluded to earlier. These works belong in the category "slave narratives," a designation given to the autobiographies of former slaves, most of them published before the Civil War. From these narratives there emerges, according to Gilbert Osofsky in *Puttin on Ole Massa*, "a coherent picture of slave life" (14), striking in the similarities among people "who lived on widely separated plantations, in different states and in different decades" (14). These narratives give us excellent insights into what slaves endured in such areas as family structure, sex exploitation, physical brutality, housing, and religion. Henson's autobiography is no exception to this, and through his detailed account of his life in four different versions, he gives us much information about the time of enslavement.

"We have survived the middle passage and we have survived slavery. We have survived the deadly arbitrariness of Jim Crow and the hypocritical hatefulness of northern discrimination" (Bell 50). These words by historian William Strickland attest to the great strength of African Americans as survivors, and it is as a strong survivor that Henson gains our admiration. He struggled against enormous odds all of his ninety-four years. From sickly child he grew to a young man who wanted to "out-hoe, out-reap, out-husk, out-dance, out-everything every competitor" (Henson, *The Life* 19). His "pride and ambition made [him] master of every kind of farm work" (Henson, *The Life* 23), and he was eventually promoted to the position of superintendent of farmwork and as a result was "practically overseer" (Henson, *The Life* 23). When he saw, after many years of hard and successful labor, that his owners wished to sell him anyway, his survival instincts again came to the fore, and he masterminded not only his own escape to the North but the escape of his entire family. Throughout their two month journey North, he pushed himself and them beyond their physical and psychological hardships until they had all arrived safely in Canada on October 28, 1830. His exuberance at their survival was so great that he threw himself on the ground, "rolled in the sand, seized handfuls of it and kissed them and danced round till, in the eyes of several who were present [he] passed for a madman" (Henson, *The Life* 127). His joy at surviving his escape from slavery was rechanneled to focusing on survival in his new environment, and he did indeed succeed not merely in surviving but in becoming a leader of his fellow ex-slaves, both spiritually and economically. Although his financial endeavors were not always successful, his achievements brought him much recognition. He died in his ninety-fourth year, and the attendance at his funeral attests to the admiration many held for him. One of his biographers, Jessie Beattie, writes, "They buried him in one of his loved fields while thousands of white men and colored stood reverently by" (212).

His motivation to struggle for survival rested on a solid foundation of Christian faith, a faith often found among slaves. In the appendix to the 1845 narrative of his life, Frederick Douglass* wrote, "Between the Christianity of Christ and the Christianity of the land, I recognized the widest possible difference" (120). It was the Christianity of Christ that the young Henson heard preached one day by a white minister, John McKenny, noted for his detestation of slavery. McKenny stressed that Christ died for *everyone*, and after listening to his words, Henson concluded that "Jesus will be my dear refuge—he'll wipe away all tears from my eyes; nothing will seem hard after this" (29). Stowe, in her introduction to the 1858 version of Henson's autobiography, extols his Christian faith, which she deemed so great that the one sermon by McKenny made "him at once a believer from the heart and a preacher of Jesus" (iii). She states in her *Key to Uncle Tom's Cabin* that it was Henson's Christian faith that served as a model in her creation of Uncle Tom.

In spite of this claim by Stowe, one must note some major discrepancies between Tom and Henson. Tom was a very private person, not ambitious, not ever successful in a worldly sense, and escaped slavery only in death. His entire life was centered on a deep devotion to Christianity, and he emerges as an almost Christ-like figure.

Tom turned down Simon Legree's offer to become overseer of his plantation, and he paid for his decision with death by beating. On his deathbed he said to his former owner who had come to take him back, "O Mas'r George, ye're too late. The Lord's bought me and is going to take me home—and I long to go. Heaven is better than Kentuck" (Stowe, *Uncle Tom's* 426). Henson, on the other hand, was willing to take on the role of overseer, even to deny fellow slaves their chance at liberty. However much he regretted this decision later, he did make it, and he made if *after* his conversion to Christianity. The term "Uncle Tom" has come to mean a black man who is overly willing to accommodate the wishes of whites. The Uncle Tom of Harriet Beecher Stowe's novel certainly does not fall in this category, but the same cannot be said of Josiah Henson. Clearly the Christian faith Henson subscribed to was different than the Christian faith Tom subscribed to. Both saw Christ as their *personal* savior, but they differed in their interpretation of how God wished them to deal with their fellow man.

As narrations of enslavement, escape, personal struggle, and Christian faith, Josiah Henson's four autobiographies take their place beside the many narratives written by ex-slaves that give us an invaluable insight into the realities of the so-called peculiar institution.

CRITICAL RECEPTION

Henson's narratives have been commented on primarily in connection with his serving as the model for Harriet Beecher Stowe's Uncle Tom. Stowe herself in her *Key to Uncle Tom's Cabin* states that she created Tom based on the slave histories related to her that she claimed "would themselves made a small volume" (4). Among the models she includes in the *Key* is Josiah Henson whose strong Christian faith was his dominant contributing characteristic to her delineation of Uncle Tom. A number of scholars have described Henson as *the* model for Tom, implying that others were not nearly as relevant. Maurice Filler, editor of the Corner House edition (1973) of the 1858 version of Henson's autobiography, writes that "Henson's life story inspired Harriet Beecher Stowe's characterization of Uncle Tom" (dust jacket). In his pamphlet "The Story of Uncle Tom" William Chapple wrote that Henson's "early life provided much of the material for Harriet Beecher Stowe's *Uncle Tom's Cabin*" (1). Benjamin Quarles in *Black Abolitionists* refers to Henson as a reformer "destined for fame as the original Uncle Tom" (133). Not all historians share a conviction in the strength of this connection between Henson and Tom. J.C. Furnas in *Goodbye to Uncle Tom* calls it "dubious" (22), and Henson biographer Marie Stuart says Tom was only "loosely based on the life of Josiah Henson" (jacket).

Little has been written focusing on an analysis of either Henson's life or his works. Biographer Frances Cavanah writes that based on her research on Henson there emerged "a man of great charisma who proved that only in freedom can a gifted person realize his true potential" (10), and Dr. D.W. Bradwin (quoted in Beattie) called the Henson autobiographies "Canadian Classics" (x). Not all commentators were positive. Benjamin Brawley suggested that Henson cannot be said to have been a man of great character and "perhaps exploited himself unduly" (161), but even Brawley concluded "there was still something of the heroic about him, and some of the passages in his life story are of absorbing interest" (161).

The most meaningful analysis of Henson's faith and life's work appears in Sondra Millner's work in which she analyzes ex-slaves Henry Bibb,* Harriet Jacobs, and Josiah Henson as to their particular perception of land and space. She describes Henson as valuing education and landownership above all else, and she finds this valuation as "consistent with an African American aesthetic that holds the land as intrinsically valuable" (116). Henson combined this love of land with love of God and saw the migration of ex-slaves to Canada as "God's helping an enslaved people to their exodus to a free land" (117). This assistance of God in leading slaves out of the wilderness to freedom was also experienced by Henson on a personal level when he spent six harrowing weeks in the wilderness with his family while they were making their journey from slavery to freedom. Millner describes this period in Henson's life as a time "when he could begin to take care of his family as independent father and husband" (117).

In spite of the dearth of critical evaluations of Henson's life and work, the few comments that scholars and biographers have made give us some insight into his persona beyond that which is directly revealed in his autobiographies.

BIBLIOGRAPHY

Autobiographical Works by Josiah Henson

The Life of Josiah Henson, Formerly a Slave. Boston: Arthur D. Phelps, 1849.
Truth Stranger Than Fiction: Father Henson's Story of His Own Life. Boston: John P. Jewett, 1858.
Uncle Tom's Story of His Life. London: Christian Age Office, 1876.
An Autobiography of Josiah Henson—Mrs. Harriet Beecher Stowe's Uncle Tom, 1878.

Studies of Josiah Henson's Autobiographical Works

Beattie, Jessie. *Black Moses, the Real Uncle Tom.* Toronto: Ryerson Press, 1957.
Brawley, Benjamin. *Early Negro American Writers.* Chapel Hill: University of North Carolina Press, 1935.
Cavanah, Frances. *The Truth about the Man behind the Book That Sparked the War between the States.* Philadelphia: Westminster Press, 1975.
Chapple, William. *The Story of Uncle Tom.* Dresden, Ontario: Uncle Tom's Cabin and Museum, n.d.
Frances, Azra. *Josiah Henson: A Documentary Drama.* Windsor, Ontario: Windsor Italo-Canadian Culture Centre, 1988.
Furnas, J.C. *Goodbye to Uncle Tom.* New York: William Sloane Associates, 1956.
Gysen, Brion. *To Master—A Long Goodnight.* New York: Creative Age Press, 1946.
Hartgrove, W.B. "The Story of Josiah Henson." *Journal of Negro History* 3.1 (January 1918): 1–21.
Haynes, Elizabeth. *Unsung Heroes.* New York: Dubois and Dell, 1921.
Millner, Sondra. *Free Grace in the Wilderness: An Aesthetic Analysis of Land and Space in African American Culture, in the Narratives of Henry Bibb, Harriet Jacobs and Josiah Henson.* Philadelphia: Temple University Press, 1994.
Myers, Walter. *The Glory Field: With Connections.* Austin: Holt, Rinehart and Winston, 1999.
Quarles, Benjamin. *Black Abolitionists.* New York: Da Capo Press, 1969.
Sands, Diana. *Black Pioneers in American History.* New York: Caedmon, 1970.
Stowe, Harriet Beecher. *The Key to Uncle Tom's Cabin.* New York: Arno Press, 1968.
———. *Uncle Tom's Cabin.* Oxford: Oxford University Press, 1998.
Stuart, Marie. *Josiah Henson.* Bristol: Central Bristol Adult Education Centre, 1990.
Young, Mary, and Gerald Horne. *Testaments of Courage.* New York: Franklin Walts, 1995.

Related Materials

Bell, Janet. *Famous Black Quotations.* New York: Warner Books, 1995.
Douglass, Frederick. *Narrative of the Life of Frederick Douglass.* New York: New American Library, 1968.
Osofsky, Gilbert. *Puttin on Ole Massa.* New York: Harper, 1969.

CHESTER BOMAR HIMES
(1909–1984)

Robin Jane Lucy

BIOGRAPHY

Chester Bomar Himes was born in Jefferson City, Missouri, in 1909, the youngest of three boys born to Joseph Sandy and Estelle Bomar Himes. The marriage between his light-skinned mother and his dark-skinned father had, according to Himes, "the status of an interracial marriage with legal consent" (*Hurt* 16) and was fraught with tension. His father taught mechanical skills at various black colleges throughout the South. In 1922, Chester's brother Joseph Jr. was blinded while performing a chemistry experiment. The family spent two years in St. Louis, Missouri, seeking treatment for Joseph, then settled in Cleveland, Ohio, where Joseph Sr. took on a series of menial jobs.

Despite being seriously injured in a fall down an elevator shaft in the summer of 1926, Himes was able to enter Ohio State University that September; however, he was expelled in his second term because of a prank. Himes became increasingly involved in criminal activity and by 1927 was on probation. In the same year, his parents' marriage ended. In late 1928, Himes was arrested for the armed robbery of a wealthy white couple and, at nineteen years of age, was sentenced to from twenty to twenty five years in the Ohio State Penitentiary. In 1930 or 1931, while in prison, Himes began to write. In 1933 he began publishing in black magazines; between 1934 and 1936, he published exclusively in *Esquire*.

Himes was paroled in 1936, after serving seven and a half years in prison. In 1937, he married Jean Johnson and began work, first as a laborer and then as a writer, for the Work Projects Administration in Cleveland. He continued to publish short stories and began working on his prison novel, *Cast the First Stone* (1952), reprinted in a restored version as *Yesterday Will Make You Cry* (1998). When the Project ended in 1939, Himes was unable to find industrial work because of race prejudice; he described the inability to economically support his wife as a situation that meant "his hurt became violent" (*Hurt* 72). The couple moved to the Los Angeles area, where they lived until 1943; Himes had a series of low-skilled jobs, while his wife worked for the United Services Organizations. The city became the setting for his first two novels, *If He Hollers Let Him Go* (1945) and *Lonely Crusade* (1947), as well as several short stories; racial violence in the area during the war became the subject of several important essays. By 1944, he was also working on his most autobiographical novel, *The Third Generation* (1954).

Himes perceived the reception of his second novel to be so hurtful—"The left hated it, the right hated it, Jews hated it, blacks hated it" (*Hurt* 100)—that he began making plans to leave the United States. From 1946 to 1951, Himes worked in menial jobs in the New York area; by 1951, his marriage had ended. His affair with a white woman in 1952 became the basis of his novel *The Primitive* (1955). In April 1953, Himes left for Paris where he stayed for only a short time before leaving the city, living in London and in Spain with his white lover. When this relationship ended in 1954, he returned to Paris. He spent time in New York in 1955, and for most of 1956, in the company of another white woman and traveled across Europe while he worked on the satirical novel *Pinktoes* (1961). In 1956, Marcel Duhamel, the director of the French publishing company Gallimard's detective-story series, *La Série noire*, met with Himes and encouraged him to try writing detective fiction. Himes published his first detective story in 1957; in 1958, it was awarded Le Grand Prix du Roman Policier. Between 1958 and 1961, Himes published six more detective novels. *Une affaire de viol*, a fictional account of the persecution of a group of black men for rape, was published in 1963. Two more detective stories appeared, one in 1964 and the other in 1969, completing what is known as his Harlem Domestic Series. All but the first and last of these were published initially, in translation from Himes's English manuscripts, in France.

In 1959, he began a relationship with a white Englishwoman, Lesley Packard, who became his second wife in 1978. In the mid-1960s, American publishers became increasingly interested in Himes's work; several earlier novels were republished in the United States, and new work was published for the national market. Publishers' advances, and the option paid by Samuel Goldwyn Jr. for film rights to six of his detective stories, underwrote the house that Himes built in Moraira, Spain, in 1970; he and Lesley lived there for the rest of his life. In 1970, Goldwyn released *Cotton Comes to Harlem*, and in 1974, *Come Back, Charleston Blue* opened in theaters.

In the final years of his writing career, Himes published a self-selected anthology, *Black on Black* (1973), and his two-volume autobiography. In 1983, *Plan B* appeared. An account of a failed black revolution, it features the death of the two black detectives who are the central figures in his Harlem series. Its apocalyptic violence and its emphatically American locale make ironic Himes's statement that he "only felt at home" in his detective stories (*Absurdity* 381). Chester Himes died in Spain in 1984.

AUTOBIOGRAPHICAL WORKS AND THEMES

The *Quality of Hurt* covers the first forty-four years of Himes's life. The first forty-three of these, recorded in Book 1, comprise approximately one-third of the text's pages and, as Gilbert Muller writes, constitutes a type of personal "cosmology framed by the need of its creator to find an authentic voice through art" (7). Books 2 and 3 are an account of his first eighteen months of expatriation. In this and the subsequent volume of his autobiography, Himes establishes that the act of writing was a strategy for survival, both physical and psychological. While in prison, his literacy earned him the respect of his fellow inmates, and Himes believed that being a published author meant that the guards could not kill him. Outside of prison, writing was equally an act of fighting back, of claiming and creating an inviolable identity and, ultimately, of confronting the absurdity of racism: "The world can deny me all other employment, and stone me as an ex-convict, as a nigger. . . . But as long as I write, whether it is published or not, I'm a writer, and no one can take that away" (*Hurt* 117).

For Himes, prison life is a metaphor for the experience of living as an African American in a racist society. While angry at the judge who sentenced him to prison, he primarily directs his rage, and his autobiography, at a society that upon his release, "began punishing me for being black" (*Hurt* 61). Although the first page of his autobiography declares that much of his prison experience—and, by implication, the lived experience of racism—left "subconscious," and therefore invisible and unknowable hurts (*Hurt* 3), he describes his autobiographical writing as the articulate "record" of these "wounds and scars" (*Hurt* 132–33). In writing, Himes transforms what racism inscribes on body and soul, but often renders unseen and unspoken, into a personal, public, and political text. As Muller writes, Himes's recollections of experiences of hurt are "recurring metaphors of a self attempting to achieve liberation in a culture, a world, that would deny him authentic freedom" (9).

Himes's autobiographical works, however, largely deny a conscious desire for freedom to black women who are, in fact, significant figures only in Book 1 of *The Quality of Hurt*. With the notable exception of his mother and his first wife, black women are represented as purely sexual beings, ready to receive Himes's advances with "dumb passion" (*Hurt* 29); they are bodies that allay Himes's anxieties about his masculinity and what he describes as "color class" in the black community (15). While perhaps meant to shock an assumed white reader into an awareness of race prejudice with the graphic depiction of sexualized racial stereotypes, the representation of black women as embodied ciphers to be filled with the author's intentions is disturbing. After leaving Cleveland, Himes's continued frustration at being unable to economically support his wife in Los Angeles, while she has a well-paying job, is expressed in a sexualized metaphor that works to displace his economic fears onto his wife's body; under these circumstances, Himes is "her pimp" (75).

His relationships with white women dominate the rest of his autobiographical writing. While, as Margolies and Fabre write, Himes often identifies with them "as Negro-like victims" (x), they are also central to the construction of his own racial and gender identity. In *My Life of Absurdity*, Himes writes that sex and writing are conjoined "obsessions": Writing is his "profession" and "ambition," while sex is his "sword and shield against the hurts and frustrations of the other" (14). While his depiction of interracial sex, like that of relations with black women, is perhaps deliberately provocative and intended to illuminate racism— "the bare colors create a pornography of the [American] mind" (*Hurt* 285)—he also presents himself as a type of black hero, saving white women from defining and confining roles while he himself remains in a racial prison: "We can free the white man's women . . . but we cannot free ourselves" (219). Ironically, however, these relationships are violence filled, as are Himes's relationships with black women: "[T]he only way to make a white woman listen is to pop her in the eye, or any woman for that matter" (137). Himes consistently asserts a construction of masculinity that is predicated on control over the bodies of women. Many of the tensions and contradictions surrounding women, their bodies, and their relationships with black men are also present in Himes's fiction.

The power of violence, which Himes links to the assertion of masculinity and heterosexuality throughout his body of work, finds its expression in other aspects of his autobiography. At the age of seventeen, he begins carrying a gun and revels in the "glimmer of fear and caution in the eyes of most people I encountered" (*Hurt* 47). While in prison, his "violent seizures of rage" (62) keep him alive and protect him from sexual violence. Himes also links the personal to the political in his approach to violence, arguing that "[d]eep in the heart of every American black person is the knowledge that the only way to fight racism is with a gun" (*Absurdity* 27). As early as 1944, Himes expressed an interest in the forms of organized black revolution, whether violent or not. However, it is also clear from his autobiography that Himes understood writing to be a weapon, deciding in prison that he "was going to live as long as possible to aggravate the white race" (13). In his work, the obverse of this focus on the power of real or rhetorical violence is a fascination with its effects. The 1930 Ohio prison fire that killed over 300 inmates and that Himes barely escaped—the fire a rampant symbol of the violence of the penal system as a whole—profoundly affected his life and writing: "I have always been moved by the forced contemplation of death" (*Hurt* 326). These elements, added to the hurts of American racism, constitute the roots of an aesthetic of the absurd in Himes's writing, one that came to fruition in his detective stories: "Realism and absurdity are so similar in the lives of American blacks that one can not tell the difference" (*Absurdity* 109).

In *The Quality of Hurt*, Himes outlines his relationship to the expatriate African American community and its most prominent member, Richard Wright.* From his arrival in Paris, Himes distances, if not alienates, himself from his fellow black Americans. He accuses them, in an ironic and subversively self-reflexive gesture, of a new form of "Uncle-Toming" that necessitates the revelation of racial hurts "to get some sympathy . . . some white pussy and money, too" (224). He also subtly undercuts the literary and masculine authority of Richard Wright while simultaneously proclaiming his importance as the first black writer "to break into the big time" (211).

In *My Life of Absurdity*, Himes's assertion of an absurdist aesthetic in black cultural expression, one rooted in folklore and the blues, is also an attempt to create forms for black writing that express an alternative to the "Uncle-Toming" perspective of his peers: a declaration of an equally African American experience of "a tremendous love of life . . . of sex . . . of ourselves. We were absurd" (36). At the same time, this aesthetic works to displace Wright and his protest writing by "treat[ing] the American black as absurd instead of hurt" (158). He emphasizes his break with Wright by declaring William Faulkner's writing, in addition to black vernacular sources, as the source and inspiration for his experiments in form and content (106). Citing the positive critical reception of his first detective story, he writes that he had become "a person comparable to Richard Wright" (181). While the first volume of his autobiography records his struggle to convert a personal cosmology of racial hurt into a literary voice, his second asserts that this voice is capable of reshaping the black discursive universe.

CRITICAL RECEPTION

Several recent works, including the introduction to the Himes bibliography and Margolies and Fabre's biography, are concerned with further illuminating the facts of Himes's life. Most critics, however, have focused on the link between Himes's fiction and his autobiographical writing. Houston A. Baker Jr., writing on *The Quality of Hurt*, argues that "often it reads like a key to the creative works of Chester Himes" (90). Gilbert Muller's study of Himes's body of work takes as its premise the fact that the boundary between Himes's fiction and his life is permeable: His novels and short stories are themselves "a single autobiographical text" (7).

Both Baker and Gary Storhoff situate Himes's autobiographical writing within the African American tradition as a whole. Focusing on Himes's "signifying" critique of the black expatriate community, Baker declares that Himes does not break with the "quintessential component" of black autobiography, the reflexive movement between the individual and group consciousness (89); rather, he expresses both his own "deeply imbued" blackness (89) and "the manifold attenuations" of the collective consciousness (91). Storhoff argues that Himes's work is a repudiation of the political perspective and the "almost asexual" persona of Richard Wright's autobiographies, particularly *Black Boy* (1945), and that he consciously subverts that text's sense of triumphal closure (248). In turn, Storhoff sees this form of textual revolt as evidence of Himes's participation in a black male autobiographical tradition in which a writer signifies upon and tries to surpass his predecessors (248). As a whole, Storhoff argues, the black autobiographical tradition posits a white reader who must be "assaulted" by words in order to be confronted with the absurdity of racism (251). Muller, too, focuses on the power of Himes's representation and language, pointing out that he "represses nothing" (2). Baker invokes the "brutal unrestrainedness" (89) of *The Quality of Hurt* and its disruption of "*bourgeois* codes of 'decency' and classless formulas of sycophancy" as well as the "positive images of Black American experience" that, Baker argues, were championed by contemporary African American writers and critics (90).

Himes's refusal to conform to the conventions of a genre that assume the possibility of a completed self and a considered life, particularly in his second autobiography, has invoked a range of responses. Muller writes that the "interlacing of opposites, discontinuities, distortions, and deformities" (3) in Himes's texts are reflections of a life and aesthetic shaped by the absurdities of racism. Muller's book is the best single study of Himes's malleable concept of the absurd in black life and writing. Storhoff, who focuses on *My Life of Absurdity*'s numerous trivial details and its inclusion of seemingly irrelevant photographs, argues that they reflect "the comic absurdity of scrupulous concern for accurate representation" when the black writer is confronted by, and confronts the reader with, the effects of racism (249). In contrast, Nathan Huggins's review of *My Life of Absurdity* finds Himes perverse "in discussing the uninteresting, the petty and the mean" (32) and, as a result, finds "little indication of his growth and development . . . that might have given meaning to what has been a productive and eventful life" (5). The response of the black writer Julius Lester to Huggins's review asserts the value of the knowledge of experience that Himes offers young blacks and criticizes Huggins for "arrogantly decid[ing] how blacks should communicate the stories of their lives" (39). This claim to black representational freedom lies behind both Ishmael Reed's assertion that Himes is one of "our *griots*" (83) and Baker's characterization of Himes as "an *independent* Black author" (90, emphasis in original).

Reed is a staunch defender of Himes's autobiographical assertion of masculinity and heterosexuality and declares the author emblematic of tough, depression-era writers who were and are "[t]ruly robust, virile men" (32). Reed makes Himes a central figure in establishing an African American male literary tradition that, he argues, has been overlooked because of "fear [of] the heterosexual Black writer" (32). More recent work has critiqued Himes's masculinist representation. George Lipsitz, who focuses on Himes's fiction of the 1940s, turns to his autobiography to argue that the writer's need for "masculine self-affirmation" (37) was, in part, rooted in his wife's employability and in racialized conflict over women during the war, like that which provoked the Los Angeles zoot suit riots in 1943. He credits Himes with an astute awareness of how both "racist hierarchies and resentments became transposed onto issues of sexuality and gender" but points out that he was unable to attach this to a critique of the male "right" to possess women (37–38). Storhoff is less forgiving in his emphasis on Himes's construction of women as the "witnesses" and victims of his "ritualistic . . . gestures of manhood" (244) and, more generally, his "overly simplified social construction of [a] manhood that stresses brutality, dominance, and conflict" (242).

H. Bruce Franklin focuses on Himes's autobiographical depiction of prison life and argues that this experience is the impetus behind both his fiction and its absurd vision of "seething tension, appalling violence, macabre comedy . . . and agony relieved only by occasional hints of some future apocalyptic redemption" (212). In Himes's work, Franklin finds a representative voice of the African American experience of the related conditions of slavery, peonage, and imprisonment.

BIBLIOGRAPHY

Autobiographical Works by Chester Bomar Himes

The Quality of Hurt: The Autobiography of Chester Himes. Vol. 1. Garden City: Doubleday, 1972.
My Life of Absurdity: The Autobiography of Chester Himes. Vol. 2. Garden City: Doubleday, 1976.

Studies of Chester Bomar Himes's Autobiographical Works

Baker, Houston A., Jr. Rev. of *The Quality of Hurt: The Autobiography of Chester Himes.* *Black World* 21 (July 1972): 89–91.
Fabre, Michel, Robert E. Skinner, and Lester Sullivan, eds. *Chester Himes: An Annotated Primary and Secondary Bibliography.* Westport, CT: Greenwood Press, 1992.
Franklin, H. Bruce. *Prison Literature in America: The Victim as Criminal and Artist.* Expanded ed. New York: Oxford University Press, 1989.
Huggins, Nathan Irvin. "The Helpless Victim." Rev. of *The Quality of Hurt.* *New York Times Book Review* (March 12, 1972): 5, 32.
Lester, Julius. "*The Quality of Hurt.*" Reply to letter of Nathan Huggins. *New York Times Book Review* (April 30, 1972): 39–40.
Lipsitz, George. *Rainbow at Midnight: Labor and Culture in the 1940s.* Chicago: University of Illinois Press, 1994.
Margolies, Edward, and Michel Fabre. *The Several Lives of Chester Himes.* Jackson: University of Mississippi Press, 1997.
Milliken, Stephen F. *Chester Himes: A Critical Appraisal.* Columbia: University of Missouri Press, 1976.
Muller, Gilbert H. *Chester Himes.* Boston: Twayne/G.K. Hall, 1989.
Reed, Ishmael. "Chester Himes: Writer." *Black World* 21 (March 1972): 23–38, 83–86.
Storhoff, Gary. "Slaying the Fathers: The Autobiography of Chester Himes." In *The Critical Response to Chester Himes.* Ed. Charles L. P. Silet. Westport, CT: Greenwood Press, 1999. 241–55.

BELL HOOKS
(1952–)

Michael L. Cobb

BIOGRAPHY

Born on September 25, 1952, to Veodis and Rosa Bell Watkins, bell hooks, née Gloria Watkins, grew up to be one of the United States' most prolific feminist writers of the late twentieth century. hooks's childhood in Hopkinsville, Kentucky, was marked by the difficulties and pleasures of a black, poor, rural, and southern upbringing among six children. hooks describes her youth as "dysfunctional" yet still full of a kind of magic and mystery that taught her fundamental lessons about what it means to be racially, sexually, economically, and regionally disadvantaged in the United States. hooks graduated from Crispus Attucks High School in Hopkinsville before she attended Stanford University, graduating in 1973 with a degree in English. Her interest in literature continued as she received a master's degree from the University of Wisconsin, Madison, and as she began her long career in teaching courses in English literature, composition, writing, and African American literature at a variety of institutions including the University of California at Los Angeles and the University of California at Santa Cruz. While teaching at Santa Cruz, hooks completed a dissertation on Toni Morrison in 1983.

In the midst of so much intellectual work, feminism and activism fueled hooks's emotional and professional life, and in 1981 she published, under the name of her great-grandmother, her landmark book *Ain't I a Woman*, which indicted mainstream white feminism's exclusion of African American women's experiences and voices. Subsequent books such as *Feminist Theory: From Margin to Center, Talking Back: Thinking Feminist, Thinking Black; Yearning: Race, Gender, and Cultural Politics; Breaking Bread: Insurgent Black Intellectual Life* (with Cornell West); *Black Looks: Race and Representation*; and *Teaching to Transgress: Education* as the Practice of Freedom have firmly and irrevocably established hooks as a necessary thinker and teacher of African American feminist writing and politics and has led her to appointments to the faculties of Yale, Oberlin, and City College of New York. In 1994, she was made distinguished professor of English at City College, adding to her growing list of honors and awards that include the American Book Award before Columbus Foundation for *Yearning* and the Writer's Award from the Lila Wallace–Reader's Digest Fund. hooks continues her intellectual, teaching, and creative work at an exhaustive pace—in the year 2000 alone she published no fewer than three books that return to her persistent lines of inquiry about the way race, gender, sex, and class complicate and challenge the ways we conceive of the American cultural, political, and literary landscape.

AUTOBIOGRAPHICAL WORKS AND THEMES

Given such a highly visible, influential, and perpetually augmenting body of work, it is no wonder that interest in hooks's own life experiences motivated this feminist critic to write her life story. Although hooks's critical work has often included highly personal anecdotes and experiences about her past, her primary autobiographies, so far, are *Bone Black: Memories of Girlhood*, published in 1996, and *Wounds of Passion: A Writing Life*, published in 1997. hooks distinguishes these memoirs from her critical work because she innovates the more conventional form of life narratives that are obsessed with "telling a linear story" (*Wounds* xx), narratives that tend to be too commodity-driven in a literary marketplace that works in tandem with "white supremacist capitalist patriarchy" (xxi). Instead of narrating a coherent and chronological "tell all" tale of her rise as a public intellectual and expert feminist critic—a tale that would provide "the 'scoop' on bell hooks" (*Wounds* xx)—she experiments with the form of autobiography. hooks considers Audre Lorde's* *Zami: A New Spelling of My Name* a model for how one can write a different kind of life story, one that focuses on the ways dreams, fantasies, and feelings shape our views of ourselves. As a consequence, hooks, for instance, writes "imagistically" in *Bone Black* "to conjure a rich magical world of southern black culture that was sometimes paradisical and at other times terrifying" (*Bone Black* xi). She intends to give rich textures to her life experiences that explain and communicate their intellectual, emotional, and erotic significance rather than merely chronicle and reveal the various events of her past. Moreover, in both autobiographies, hooks transforms the genre further by switching between first-person and third-person narration to establish different vantage points on her experiences. She conceives of the third person as a way of distancing herself from the description of painful events, where she becomes "an observer—that bears witness" (*Wounds* xxii) to and lends critical insight into events that overwhelmingly shape hooks's life.

Significantly, both autobiographies do not give comprehensive accounts of hooks's past; instead, each focuses on particularly formative periods of the author's life that need significant and often rather poetic description capable of conveying the complex ways race, gender, and class shape one woman's life. In *Bone Black*, hooks offers glimpses into her rural and crowded upbringing in the Kentucky countryside. As is to be expected of any childhood narrative, hooks is in pursuit of deeper understandings into the world in which she belongs. Reading and writing offer the young hooks a method of organizing the different sensations and events of her youth into something understandable. For instance, she learns about poverty only through brief and instructive vignettes that reveal more complicated social problems: "We live in the country. We children do not understand that means we are among the poor" (4). There are no grandiose and systematic claims about what it means to be economically disadvantaged; instead, poverty is fleshed out in her narrative through the often underexplained flashes of experience of a child's more immediate perspective: "In the first grade the teacher gives tasting parties. She brings us different foods to taste so that we can know what they are like because we do not eat them in our homes" (6). Increasingly, hooks learns how to express these diverse sensations and responses through the more sophisticated means of literary expression that she acquires through vocabulary lessons, reading Dickinson and Whitman, and her own attempts at writing: "She eases her pain in poetry, using it to make the poems live, using the poems to keep living" (132). Thus, she finds a destiny in reading books and writing: "I tell myself stories, write poems, record my dreams. In my journal I write—I belong to this place of words. This is my home. This dark, bone black inner cave where I am making a world for myself" (183). Indeed, as hooks promises, "the events described as always less significant than the impressions they leave on the mind and the heart" (xv)—that is, the communication of such heart and head-felt impressions is the primary objective of her first unordinary autobiography.

Wounds of Passion is a grown-up version of the kinds of artistic testimony that help hooks understand the racially, economically, and sexually divisive world in which she lives. Instead of a more innocent and childlike perspective, this autobiography describes intellectual and sexual awakenings that forever change the way she engages with the politics and cultures of the United States. Her voice moves from a childlike quality to a more confident and sexual tone that corresponds with her movement away from her preoccupations with poetry into the writing of nonfiction that addresses the more politicized arenas of feminism, activism, and teaching that saturated her early adulthood. At age nineteen, she writes *Ain't I a Woman* and inaugurates a career of criticism that firmly establishes hooks as a major cultural critic. At the heart of this memoir is indeed hooks's own heart and the sexual and intellectual energies that a heterosexual partnership provided as she learned just how she could express her own experiences of sexism and racism through cultural criticism and teaching. hooks confesses, "I like to love a man who can teach me things. I read everything he reads" (116). Indeed, for hooks, "the desire for sex, the longing to reconcile these desires with a yearning to know love, were all part of my struggle to become a writer, to invent a writing life that could nurture and sustain a liberated woman" (*Wounds* xxiii).

Thus, her words about her life are often charged with her own heterosexuality, her own experiences with a supportive male partner who encouraged her to commit to the page her own frustrations with issues such as the neglect of African American women by mainstream, white feminism. For hooks, we learn, the fusion of writing and sexuality is a crucial in a more complete documentation of "the psychological and philosophical foundations of one woman's writing life" (xxiii). Issues around race, class, and gender have long been part of hooks's written repertoire, but concerns about passionate reading and relating have been more marginal to our understanding of hooks's intellectual and activist projects. Combined, both memoirs give hooks's critical work a more personal and intimate texture that illuminates and helps localize the reasons why hooks has become such an excellent reader and writer of culture. Because there is much more to tell, one can expect more autobiographies that will expound on the foundations hooks poetically captures in these first two books.

CRITICAL RECEPTION

Perhaps because of the sheer abundance of her very compelling and often controversial and personal critical work, and perhaps because of the relatively recent publication dates of her two life stories, very little critical response has been generated around hooks's purer autobiographies. This scarceness does not suggest that interest in hooks's life is not a priority. The influence of her work as cultural critic, as well as her very popular appeal, eclipses serious attention to the kinds of issues and kind of linguistic innovations she presents in her memoirs. Currently, most of the brief reception of her autobiographies tends to be laudatory and focused on the beauty of her language. Gloria Steinem notices a potential direction for placing these texts in critical context: "[W]ith the emotion of poetry, the narrative of a novel, and the truth of experience . . . ." hooks "takes us into the cave of self-creation" (*Bone Black* cover). hooks necessarily complicates the genre to describe the messiness of building a childhood and a writer's life. Confusions between reality and fantasy, autobiography and myth, make works like hooks's challenging documents that innovate language at the same time they innovate the critical landscape of feminism, African American studies, cultural studies, and transgressive teaching.

Discussions of the way hooks incorporates her life into her critical work, however, are more numerous and often investigate the significant issues for the kinds of authority of experience an autobiographical moment quickly lends to more activist and intellectual insights. Dwight McBride, for instance, critiques the way hooks's down-home anecdotes legitimize a dangerous speaking voice; in a discussion of her defense of openly homophobic utterances in a black community she has experienced, McBride asserts that "any understanding of black oppression that makes it possible, and worse permissable, to endorse any level sexism, elitism, or heterosexism is a vision of black culture that is finally not politically consummate with liberation" (367). Perhaps reading her autobiographies' own concerns with the complications of being heterosexual and black could explain such frustrating anecdotes that often serve as the evidence for her larger cultural claims. Nevertheless, it will be productive to see how reading her critical and autobiographical texts together will influence the response to hooks's impressive and numerous works.

BIBLIOGRAPHY

Autobiographical Works by bell hooks

Bone Black: Memories of Girlhood. New York: Henry Holt, 1996.
Wounds of Passion: A Writing Life. New York: Henry Holt, 1997.

Studies of bell hooks's Autobiographical Works

Adell, Sandra. "bell hooks, Sister of the Yam: Black Women and Self-Recovery." *African American Review* 29.3 (1995): 529–30.

Brown, L. "Politics, Theory, and the Role of the Black Intellectual: bell hooks and Patricia Williams." *Critical Survey* 9.2 (1997): 121.

Cheng, Cliff. "A Review Essay on the Books of bell hooks: Organizational Diversity Lessons from a Thoughtful Race and Gender Heretic." *Academy of Management Review* 22.2 (1997): 553–64.

Collins, Patricia Hill. "Breaking Bread: Insurgent Black Intellectual Life by bell hooks and Cornell West; Segregated Sisterhood: Racism and the Politics of American Feminism by Nancie Caraway." *Signs* 20.1 (Fall 1994): 176.

Fox, Tom. "Literacy and Activism: A Response to bell hooks." *Journal of Advanced Composition* 14.2 (Fall 1994): 564–70.

Jones, Lisa. "Rebel without a Pause." *Village Voice Literary Supplement* (October 1992): 43.

Leatherman, Courtney. "Gloria Watkins: The Real bell hooks." *Chronicle of Higher Education* 41.36 (May 19, 1995): A22.

McBride, Dwight. "Can the Queen Speak? Racial Essentialism, Sexuality and the Problem of Authority." *Callaloo* 21.2 (1998): 363–79.

Middleton, Joyce Irene. "bell hooks on Literacy and Teaching: A Response." *Journal of Advanced Composition* 14.2 (Fall 1994): 558–64.

Namulandah, Florence. *bell hooks' Engaged Pedagogy: A Transgressive Education for Critical Consciousness.* Westport, CT: Bergin and Garvey, 1998.

Olson, Gary, and Elizabeth Hirsh. "Feminist Praxis and the Politics of Literacy: A Conversation with bell hooks." In *Women Writing Culture.* Ed. Gary A. Olson and Elizabeth Hirsh. Albany: State University of New York Press, 1995. 105–37.

Thomson, Clive. "Culture, Identity, and the Dialogic: bell hooks and Gayatri Chakravorty Spivak." In *Dialogism and Culture Criticism.* Ed. Clive Thomson and Hans Raj Dua. London: Mestengo, 1995. 47–64.

LANGSTON HUGHES
(1902–1967)

Linda M. Carter

BIOGRAPHY

James Mercer Langston Hughes, one of the twentieth century's most eloquent, versatile, and prolific authors, was born on February 1, 1902, in Joplin, Missouri, to James and Carrie (née Langston) Hughes. His parents separated, and Hughes lived in various states during his formative years. Until the age of twelve, he lived with his maternal grandmother, Mary Langston. Hughes was proud of his ancestors. Mary Langston was a graduate of Oberlin College; her first husband, Sheridan Leary, died at Harpers Ferry during John Brown's raid; Charles Langston, her second husband (Hughes's grandfather), was an abolitionist. Charles's brother, John Mercer Langston, wrote his autobiography *From a Virginia Plantation to the Nation's Capital* (1894), was a U.S. congressman from Virginia, a U.S. minister to Haiti, and dean of the first Law School at Howard University.

John Langston was one of the most prominent African American men in the nineteenth century. However, Hughes's father, a successful attorney and businessman in Mexico, was not interested in prominence; he wanted his son to become wealthy. Hughes, who visited his father during the years immediately before and after his graduation from Cleveland's Central High School in 1920, listened as his father advised him to attend college in Switzerland and engineering school in Germany. The elder Hughes was unaware that his son had entertained thoughts of becoming a writer ever since he read a poem at his grammar school's graduation ceremony and received the audience's applause. His father, remembering the racial discrimination he encountered in the United States, wanted Hughes to earn enough money so he could live outside the United States and away from other African Americans. Yet Hughes's two career goals were set: to earn a living as an author and to write about black Americans. Adding to his father's chagrin was Hughes's keen interest in Harlem. He attended Columbia University (1921–1922) primarily because of its proximity to his cherished Harlem and spent three years traveling as a seaman to Africa and Europe before returning to the United States. By the time he received his degree from Lincoln University (1929), his literary career, with assistance from W.E.B. Du Bois,* Jessie Fauset, Vachel Lindsay, James Weldon Johnson, and Carl Van Vechten, among others, was well under way. Hughes enjoyed a highly successful career that spanned more than forty years (from the Harlem Renaissance to the Black Arts Movement). Although he was questioned by Senator Joseph McCarthy and other members of the House Committee on Un-American Activities in 1953 about some of his writings that were pro-Communist, Hughes left the hearings unscathed. While the careers of other artists were destroyed by the anticommunist hysteria, Hughes survived the controversy and continued as one of the first African American writers to have a profitable career.

Hughes, who frequently and eloquently combined social criticism with poetry and blended jazz, blues, and bebop with traditional verse, is best known for his seventeen volumes of poetry including *The Weary Blues* (1926), his first verse collection; *Fine Clothes to the Jew* (1927); *The Dream Keeper and Other Poems* (1932); *Shakespeare in Harlem* (1942); *Montage of a Dream Deferred* (1951); and the posthumous *The Panther and the Lash: Poems of Our Times* (1967). He created seven collections of short stories, including five that presented Harlem's Jesse B. Semple (also known as Simple), the fictitious character who is regarded as an African American Everyman. His essay "The Negro Artist and the Racial Mountain" (1926) quickly became a manifesto for many of his peers, the young Harlem Renaissance writers. Hughes created more than eighty works including novels, plays, autobiographies, anthologies, children's books, essays, newspaper columns, French and Spanish translations, histories, photo essays, lyrics for dramatic musicals, song lyrics, and screenplays as well as radio and television scripts.

Hughes, a world traveler, purchased a brownstone in Harlem in the 1940s and lived there until his death on May 22, 1967. Langston Hughes, who has been identified as African America's Poet Laureate and a Dean of African American Letters, remains one of America's most important writers.

AUTOBIOGRAPHICAL WORKS AND THEMES

Hughes's two autobiographies are *The Big Sea: An Autobiography* (1940) and *I Wonder as I Wander: An Autobiographical Journey* (1956). His first autobiography focuses on 1902 to 1931, the first twenty-nine years of Hughes's life, whereas the second covers 1931 to New Year's Day 1938. *I Wonder as I Wander* ends one month before Hughes's thirty-sixth birthday. Perhaps if Hughes had lived beyond 1967, readers would have gained additional insight into his later years. According to Emanuel, Hughes planned to write a third autobiography.

The titles of Hughes's autobiographies evoke thoughts of traveling. Indeed his "pattern of ceaseless wandering is dramatized" (Smith 75) in both narratives. In

The Big Sea, Hughes recalls living in Kansas, Illinois, Ohio, and Mexico before moving to New York and beginning his quest to see the world. Hughes, eager to travel, accepts a job as a mess boy before inquiring where the ship is sailing. Among the places he travels are Africa, "The great Africa of [his] dreams" (11); Paris, where he lives in a garret, has champagne for breakfast, writes poems, and falls in love with Mary, an English African; and Italy, where he is the first black in Dezenzano, is robbed on a train, and survives an earthquake in Genoa. When Hughes returns to the United States, he lives in Washington, D.C. before he matriculates at Lincoln University. The remainder of *The Big Sea* finds him in Harlem with side trips to such places as Tennessee, Texas, New Orleans, Cuba, Alabama, Georgia, Cleveland, and Haiti. *I Wonder as I Wander* documents Hughes's trips to Cuba, Haiti (only mentioned in *The Big Sea* yet detailed in the second autobiography), Mexico, Berlin, Finland, Helsinki, Moscow, Kiev, Odessa, Asian Russia, Korea, Japan, China, Spain, Paris, and elsewhere. During Hughes's travels in the Caribbean and the United States, he becomes aware of a Haitian class distinction based on individuals' ability to afford shoes and prefers those who are shoeless; travels with Mary McLeod Bethune and Zell Ingram from Daytona to Manhattan in a one-seat Ford coupe; meets a teenaged Margaret Walker and critiques her poems; leaves his imprint in a bathtub before he realizes it has been repainted in honor of his visit and is not completely dry; meets George Washington Carver at Tuskegee; and reads to the incarcerated Scottsboro boys. During his travels to Asia and Europe, Hughes is poisoned in Tashkent; becomes persona non grata in Japan after his trip to China; reports on the activities of African American soldiers during the Spanish Civil War for the *Baltimore Afro American*; stays at a hotel where machine guns are fired into; has several premonitions of death; receives a superficial wound while accompanying two American women on a tour of a clinic; and on his last night in Madrid, is the guest of honor at a farewell party hosted by Ernest Hemingway and others. Hughes also exposes various cultural differences pertaining to "the disappearance of the color line throughout Soviet Asia" (227), medical treatment, gender, relationships, working conditions, and food.

Hughes is not the first African American to write of his travels. He is following in the literary footsteps of William Wells Brown,* author of *The American Fugitive in Europe, Sketches of Places and People Abroad* (1855), the first travel book by an African American. Brown and Hughes provide images of sophisticated black men abroad, yet Hughes's travels are more extensive than Brown's. While Hughes's accounts of his travels are intriguing, both narratives' revelations of his mental journeys are of greater significance.

The Big Sea, an episodic record of Hughes's journey from boyhood to manhood, is a bildungsroman. Hughes's sixth book begins in medias res as a twenty-one-year-old Hughes, on board a ship, tosses his books into the Atlantic Ocean. During his first two decades, books are Hughes's haven; he "believed in books more than in people" (26). As a child, he endures his parents' divorce, moving to various residences, poverty, sometimes having only salt pork and wild dan delions to eat, and the frequent absences of his mother. One of his few childhood memories of his father is when the elder Hughes carries him (then six years old) in his arms during an earthquake in Mexico City. Yet until Hughes travels to Mexico when he is seventeen, James Hughes represents stability for him:

I had been in the States growing up while my grandmother died and the house went to the mortgage man, my mother traveled about the country looking for my step-father or for a better job, always moving from one house to another, where the rent was cheaper or there was at least a bathroom or a backyard to hang out clothes. And me growing up living with my grandmother, with aunts who were really no relation, with my mother in rented rooms, or alone trying to get through high school—always some kind of crisis in our lives. My father, permanently in Mexico during all those turbulent years, represented for me the one stable factor in my life. He at least stayed put. (35–36)

Hughes looks forward to being reunited with his father. However, during his visit to Mexico the summer before his high school graduation, he realizes that his father is obsessed with money, hates his family because they remain in the United States, hates other African Americans, and has contempt for the poor. Hughes dislikes and then hates his father. In a strange country and feeling sorry for himself, Hughes places a loaded pistol to his head and contemplates pulling the trigger before realizing, "But then, I began to think, if I do, I might miss something" (47). This epiphany is an early indication that Hughes has a tremendous curiosity about life.

Incidents such as the ones cited above compel Hughes to fling his books into the ocean. Hughes writes that as he tosses his books, he also wants to be rid of all the unhappiness from his past including memories of his father, his mother's problems, racism, fear of unemployment, the lack of a confidante, and the control exerted by his parents and employers (98). Hughes, eager to control his own life, no longer wants his life dominated by the actions of others. He asserts, "And I felt that nothing would ever happen to me again that I didn't want to happen. I felt grown, a man, inside and out. Twenty-one." (3). Emanuel comments that for Hughes, the sea is a "therapeutic" agent that "initiates" him into manhood (83–84).

To a certain extent "Twenty-one," *The Big Sea*'s first section, shares similarities with the slave narrative. Frances Smith Foster, in *Witnessing Slavery: The Development of Ante-bellum Slave Narratives* (Westport, CT: Greenwood Press, 1979), identifies "four chronological phases" of the slave autobiography: developing awareness, resolving to be free, escaping, and gaining freedom" (85). Hughes goes through the four phases in his narrative of childhood and maturity. At the autobiography's beginning, Hughes has already experienced the first two phases. He has realized that although he is twenty-one, he does not act like an adult. His parents and employers continue to exert too much influence over him. Thus he is determined to take charge of his life. Part One ends with Hughes in the third phase: escaping, as a member of the crew of the S.S. *Malone* as it sails to

Africa; and Part Two, "The Big Sea," finds him basking in his independence as he experiences life's highs and lows.

In addition to focusing on Hughes's progression from boy to man, *The Big Sea* traces the development of Hughes's career as a writer. Thus it is also, as Nelson points out, a *Kunstlerroman* (251), or a narrative that maps the protagonist's developing artistic consciousness. Hughes begins to take an interest in writing in grammar school, is inspired by the works of Paul Laurence Dunbar, Carl Sandburg, and Guy de Maupassant, and the summer after his high school graduation, he tells his father he intends to pursue a writing career. When James Hughes warns his son that black writers do not make money, his son reminds him of Alexandre Dumas's success. At this point in the autobiography, readers may remember lines from Hughes's poem "As I Grew Older": "And then the wall rose,/ Rose slowly,/ Slowly,/ Between me and my dream." Hughes's intimidating father represents the wall blocking his son's dream of a writing career. However, his dream does not die; the poem's final stanza begins, "My hands!/ My dark hands!/ Break through the wall!/ Find my dream!" Not only does Hughes defy his father by becoming a writer, he uses his "dark hands" to write what they reflect—African American life. In the first volume of *The Life of Langston Hughes*, Rampersad opines that Hughes, in addition to revealing his determination to become a writer, "establishes . . . his undying love of the black race. What his father detests, the son loves; thus Langston Hughes almost subliminally whispers to his black readers . . . that his life is completely devoted to their own. For them, he had 'killed' his own father. And killed his mother, too, who wished him to work and support her, instead of singing the black race at the price of poverty" (378).

The Big Sea mentions the publications of Hughes's earliest works such as "I've Known Rivers," *The Weary Blues*, *Fine Clothes to the Jew*, and *Not Without Laughter*. One of Hughes's most revealing observations about his writing is that the quantity and quality of his poems are proportionate to his happiness; he is more prolific and a better poet when he is sad. Also of interest is Hughes's reaction to Benjamin Brawley and other African American critics who want him to write about the black elite. Hughes responds, "Anyway, I didn't know the upper class Negroes well enough to write much about them. I knew only the people I had grown up with, and they weren't people whose shoes were always shined, who had been to Harvard, or who had heard of Bach. But they seemed to me good people, too" (268). Here Hughes is echoing what he wrote as a young member of the Harlem Renaissance in "The Negro Artist and the Racial Mountain" (1926); the priority is self-expression and not evaluation by black and white critics. While he encounters disapproval from black critics, his white patroness, Mrs. R. Osgood Mason, wants his writing to be "primitive" (325). Consequently Hughes severs all ties with her. Hughes does mention her name in *The Big Sea*, however, Zora Neale Hurston,* who is also a recipient of Mason's largess, identifies Mason in her autobiography *Dust Tracks on a Road* (1942). Regardless of the criticism and the odds, Hughes announces at the end of his narrative that he has decided to continue his career as a writer: "Literature is a big sea full of many fish. I let down my nets and pulled. I'm still pulling" (335).

In *I Wonder as I Wander*, the anecdotal sequel to *The Big Sea* and Hughes's twenty-first book, he continues to document his evolution as a writer. Readers immediately realize this when they peruse the last sentence of the opening paragraph: "This is the story of a Negro who wanted to make his living from poems and stories" (3). Seven paragraphs later, Hughes reveals his problem: "how to make a living from *the kind of writing I wanted to do*. I did not want to write for the pulps, or turn out fake 'true' stories to sell under anonymous names as Wallace Thurman did. . . . I wanted to write seriously and as well as I knew how about the Negro people, and make that kind of writing earn for me a living" (5). *I Wonder as I Wander* provides insight into Hughes's efforts to meet that challenge.

He begins "to turn poetry in to bread" (3) after he heeds Mary McLeod Bethune's advice to tour the South; she tells him, "People need poetry" (41). At first Hughes is reluctant: "I wanted to continue to be a poet. Yet sometimes I wondered if I was barking up the wrong tree. I determined to find out by taking poetry, my poetry, to my people. After all, I wrote about Negroes, and primarily *for* Negroes. Would they have me? Did they want me?" (41–42). Although Knopf has published two volumes of his poetry—*The Weary Blues* (1926) and *Fine Clothes to the Jew* (1927)—both volumes have received mixed reviews from African American literary critics. Now Hughes is anxious to learn how other blacks will react to his poems.

The narrative relives Hughes successful 1931 tour "into Dixie with poetry as a passport" (47). Indeed his tour is also extended to the West Coast before he joins twenty-one other young African Americans on a 1931 filmmaking trip to the Soviet Union; Hughes is contracted to write the film. Although the film about black life in America is never made, Hughes continues to create poetry and writes his first short stories while abroad. After returning to America, he spends an idyllic California interlude at Carmel-by-the-Sea writing. *The Big Sea* also includes Hughes's bittersweet memories of the transformation of *Mulatto*, his first play, from poetic tragedy to melodrama, at the producer's insistence, and a Broadway success. Hughes recalls that he and the African American members of the cast were not invited to the opening night party on Park Avenue. There is another incident of racism associated with *Mulatto*; although African Americans are eager to see the play, the theater attempts to avoid selling them orchestra tickets. An outraged Hughes protests, purchases as many center orchestra seats as he could afford, and gives them "to the darkest Negroes [he knows], including Claude McKay*" (313). In *I Wonder as I Wander*'s final chapter, Hughes reflects on his success as a writer:

For almost five years now I had earned a living from writing, so my dream was beginning to come true—to be a professional writer—and it had been my good fortune so far not to have to write anything I really did not want to write. Meanwhile, my interests had broadened from Harlem and the American Negro to include an interest in all the colored people of the world—in fact, in *all* the people of the world, as I related to them and they to me. (400)

Hughes, passionate about his career, is intensely ardent about Harlem. *The Big Sea*'s third section, "Black Renaissance," is Hughes's love song to Harlem. He is elated when he arrives in Harlem in 1921, sees black people everywhere he looks, and wishes he could shake hands with them. Hughes stays at the Harlem Y before moving into a dormitory at Columbia University and moves back to Harlem after dropping out of college at the end of his freshman year. After his travels abroad, Hughes returns when Harlem is still "in vogue" (227). He writes of the Cotton Club and its Jim Crow restrictions, cabarets, bars, the Savoy, white celebrities as guests at elite black dances and parties, house-rent parties, A'Lelia Walker (her parties and invitation only funeral), as well as the "spectacles" (the Hamilton Club Lodge Ball, Florence Mills's funeral, and the Yolande Du Bois–Countee Cullen wedding). He shares memories of Wallace Thurman, Zora Neale Hurston, Gwendolyn Bennett, Bruce Nugent, Countee Cullen, Rudolph Fisher, Jean Toomer, Arna Bontemps, Nella Larsen, and other writers. Harlem is still on Hughes's mind in *I Wonder as I Wander*. While at a coffee house in Berlin, a man who appears to be a slave from Cairo pours coffee for Hughes and his party, who assume that the man cannot speak English. To their surprise, they discover the man is from Harlem, and he inquires about Lenox Avenue happenings. Hughes also remembers meeting a young lady in Paris who claims her heritage is part Dutch and part Javanese; yet she speaks English and French with a Georgia accent. Later Hughes encounters the same girl on Lenox Avenue speaking Harlemese.

Near the end of *I Wonder as I Wander*, Hughes recalls a childhood incident in Kansas. When his grandmother gives him a bruised and spotted apple, he refuses to eat it. Mary Langston admonishes her grandson that he cannot expect every apple to be perfect and that he must refrain from throwing imperfect ones away. The self-portrait offered in *The Big Sea* and *I Wonder as I Wander* is a man who, after throwing the bad specks out of his apple of life, enjoys it, dares to dream what seems to be impossible, achieves the dream, and loves people, especially African Americans.

CRITICAL RECEPTION

Anyone interested in gaining further insight into *The Big Sea* and *I Wonder as I Wander* is advised to peruse the major studies on Hughes's life and works: James A. Emanuel's *Langston Hughes* (1967), Therman B. O'Daniel's *Langston Hughes, Black Genius: A Critical Evaluation* (1971), Richard Barksdale's *Langston Hughes: The Poet and His Critics* (1977), Faith Berry's *Langston Hughes: Before and Beyond Harlem* (1983), and Arnold Rampersad's *The Life of Langston Hughes*, Vol. 1 (1986) and Vol. 2 (1988). Also noteworthy are Donald C. Dickinson's *A Bio-Bibliography of Langston Hughes, 1902–1967* (1972), R. Baxter Miller's *Langston*

Hughes and Gwendolyn Brooks: A Reference Guide (1978) as well as *The Art and Imagination of Langston Hughes* (1989), Thomas Mikolyzk's *Langston Hughes: A Bio-Bibliography* (1990), and Tish Dace's *Langston Hughes: The Contemporary Reviews* (1997). An additional valuable source is *The Langston Hughes Review*, the official publication of the Langston Hughes Society.

Both autobiographies have received generally favorable reviews. *The Big Sea* has been described as candid (Herod; Lewis; Mullen; Villard; Woods), objective ([Richard]* Wright), realistic (Ellison; Wright), enthusiastic (Lewis), fascinating (Redding, Rev. of *I Wonder as I Wander*), exciting (Ellison), and humorous (Mullen; Wright). It has also been characterized as lacking bitterness (Rampersad, *Life*, Vol. 2; Woods), anger (Berry), and protest (Berry). Emanuel's analysis of the reviews reveals that the narrative is appreciated for its sociological and psychological value as well as its literary importance. *The Big Sea's* "Black Renaissance" section is acknowledged by literary critics and historians as the best eyewitness written account of the Harlem Renaissance. Another highlight of Hughes's first autobiography is the poet's artful prose that Rampersad, in the first volume of *The Life of Langston Hughes*, describes as "written by a man completely at ease with himself" (1: 378) and identifies as "astonishingly simple, water-clear prose, which certifies the integrity of Hughes' narrative. His sentences are utterly devoid of linguistic affectation, as pure and compelling as an innocent child's might be; Hughes wrote a quintessentially American prose" (1: 379). Bloom suggests that *The Big Sea* may be Hughes's "most lasting single book" (1). Mullen points out that the autobiography has been reevaluated by critics such as Miller, Rampersad, and others who view the narrative as a prerequisite to comprehending Hughes's life and other works (99); Nelson updates Mullen's comment by suggesting that both autobiographies are starting points for understanding Hughes and his works (251). *The Big Sea* and Richard Wright's first novel, *Native Son*, share the same publication year, and since then, *Native Son* has surpassed *The Big Sea* in critical acclaim and sales. Wright, reviewing *The Big Sea* for the *New Republic*, pays tribute to Hughes: "Hughes is tough; he bends but he never breaks, and he has carried on a manly tradition in literary expression when many of his fellow writers have gone to sleep at their posts" (601).

I Wonder as I Wander has been described as frank (Redding, "Travels"), amusing (Rampersad, *Life*, Vol. 2), humorous (Emanuel; Ford), and sympathetic (Emanuel). The autobiography "is a testimony to Hughes' irrepressible curiosity about other peoples and cultures and his ability to interpret and record his experiences in an engaging and unpretentious style" (Nelson 252). Hughes's writing style has been praised by an additional critic who proclaims, "He writes of his travels with reportorial objectivity, and with a sense of warm, human involvement whether recalling the soup and dirt of a Russian desert or the monthly ceremonial Tea at the Pan Pacific Club in Tokyo" (Emanuel 46). Records indicate that Hughes's second autobiography sold poorly during its first two years in print; Barksdale attributes the poor sales to a "particularly conservative segment" that may have resented Hughes's details of racial incidents during his poetry-reading tour of the South (9).

   Negative commentary on *The Big Sea* and *I Wonder as I Wander*, overshadowed by the positive reviews, is generally centered around three areas. First is Hughes's failure to analyze (Jackson; Locke). Ellison, reviewing *The Big Sea* comments, "For while the style . . . is charming in its simplicity, it is a style which depends upon understatement for its more important effects. . . . In the style of *The Big Sea* too much attention is apt to be given to the esthetic aspects of experience at the expense of its deeper meanings . . . but when Hughes avoids analysis and comment, and, in some instances, emotion, a deeper unity is lost" (21). Redding, critiquing *I Wonder as I Wander*, employs the pun, "Mr. Hughes, it seems, did more wandering than wondering" (6). Second is Hughes's failure to express his political views (Locke; Redding). Rampersad (*Life*, Vol. 1) writes that Hughes hides his radicalism in *The Big Sea* and omits his opinions as a radical socialist in *I Wonder as I Wander* (259). Third is Hughes's failure to allow readers less restricted glimpses into his life (Berry; Herod; Rampersad, *Life*, Vol. 1; Woods). Criticism of Hughes's reticence concerning his personal life calls to mind Wallace Thurman's description of a reserved Tony Crews (Hughes) in his novel *Infants of the Spring* (1932) published eight years before Hughes's first autobiography. Thurman concludes that his Harlem Renaissance colleague is a puzzling personality. More recently, a contemporary scholar updates Thurman's assessment; Nelson writes that Hughes "remains an enigma" (252).

   The aspect of Hughes's life that is a topic of controversy is his sexuality. Although in *The Big Sea*, he mentions falling in love with Mary, and in *I Wonder as I Wander*, he recalls being infatuated with Si-Lan as well as having an affair with Natasha, a married woman, Hughes's autobiographies do not elaborate on his relationships with women. Nelson concludes, "There is overwhelming circumstantial and anecdotal evidence that Hughes, who never married or forged any significant relationship with women, was primarily homosexual in his orientation" (250). Among the scholars who offer similar assertions are Berry and Watson, while among the critics who disagree with Nelson's statement are Rampersad (*Life*, Vols. 1-2) and Miller. It appears inevitable that scholars will continue to question Hughes's sexual status.

   Langston Hughes, eloquent poet, ingenious fiction writer, and powerful essayist, is also a master craftsman of autobiography. Unfortunately his autobiographies have received less critical attention than his poetry and other major prose works. His first person narratives are influential additions to African American autobiography. Thus additional scholarly attention to *The Big Sea* and *I Wonder as I Wander* is encouraged.

BIBLIOGRAPHY

Autobiographical Works by Langston Hughes

The Big Sea: An Autobiography. New York: Knopf, 1940.
I Wonder as I Wander: An Autobiographical Journey. New York: Rinehart, 1956.

Studies of Langston Hughes's Autobiographical Works

Baraka, Amiri. Foreword. *The Big Sea*. By Langston Hughes. New York: Thunder's Mouth, 1990. xv–xvii.

Barksdale, Richard. *Langston Hughes: The Poet and His Critics*. Chicago: American Library, 1977.

Barton, Rebecca Chalmers. *Witnesses for Freedom: Negro Americans in Autobiography*. New York: Harper, 1948.

Berry, Faith. *Langston Hughes: Before and Beyond Harlem*. 1983. New York: Wings, 1992.

Bloom, Harold, ed. *Modern Critical Views: Langston Hughes*. New York: Chelsea, 1989.

Butterfield, Stephen. *Black Autobiography in America*. Amherst: University of Massachusetts Press, 1974.

Dace, Tish, ed. *Langston Hughes: The Contemporary Reviews*. New York: Cambridge University Press, 1997.

Dickinson, Donald C. *A Bio-Bibliography of Langston Hughes: 1902–1967*. 2nd ed. Hamden, CT: Archon, 1972.

Ellison, Ralph. "Stormy Weather." Rev. of *The Big Sea*. *New Masses* (September 24, 1940): 20–21.

Emanuel, James A. *Langston Hughes*. New York: Twayne, 1967.

Embree, Edwin R. "A Poet's Story." Rev. of *The Big Sea*. *Survey Graphic* (March 1941): 96.

Ford, Nick Aaron. "Odyssey of a Literary Man." Rev. of *I Wonder as I Wander*. *Phylon* 18 (1957): 88–89.

Gates, Henry Louis, Jr., and K.A. Appiah, eds. *Langston Hughes: Critical Perspectives Past and Present*. New York: Amistad, 1993.

Herod, Henrietta. Rev. of *The Big Sea*. *Phylon* 2 (1941): 94–96.

Huggins, Nathan Irvin. *Harlem Renaissance*. New York: Oxford University Press, 1971.

Hurst, Catherine Daniels. "Langston Hughes." In *Dictionary of Literary Biography*. Vol. 7. Detroit: Gale, 1981. 314–24.

Jackson, Luther P., Jr. "Globe-trotting Bard." Rev. of *I Wonder as I Wander*. *Crisis* (February 1957): 119–20.

Kramer, Victor A., and Robert A. Russ, eds. *Harlem Renaissance Re-examined*. Rev. ed. Troy, NY: Whitston, 1997.

Lewis, Theophilus. "Adventurous Life." Rev. of *The Big Sea*. *Crisis*. (December 1940): 395–96.

Locke, Alain. "Of Native Sons: Real and Otherwise." Rev. of *The Big Sea*. *Opportunity* (January 1941): 4–9.

Mikolyzk, Thomas, comp. *Langston Hughes: A Bio-Bibliography*. Westport, CT: Greenwood Press, 1990.

Miller, R. Baxter. *The Art and Imagination of Langston Hughes*. Lexington: University Press of Kentucky, 1989.

———. " 'Even After I Was Dead': *The Big Sea*—Paradox, Preservation and Holistic Time." *Black American Literature Forum* 11 (1977): 39–45.

———. " 'For a Moment I Wondered': Theory and Symbolic Form in the Autobiographies of Langston Hughes." *Langston Hughes Review* 3.2 (1984): 1–6.

———. "Langston Hughes." In *Dictionary of Literary Biography*. Vol. 51. Detroit: Gale, 1987. 112–33.

————. *Langston Hughes and Gwendolyn Brooks: A Reference Guide*. Boston: Hall, 1978.

Mullen, Edward J. *Critical Essays on Langston Hughes*. Boston: Hall, 1986.

Nelson, Emmanuel S. "Langston Hughes." In *African American Authors, 1745–1945: A Bio-Bibliographical Critical Sourcebook*. Ed. Emmanuel S. Nelson. Westport, CT: Greenwood Press, 2000. 249–58.

O'Daniel, Therman B. *Langston Hughes, Black Genius: A Critical Evaluation*. New York: Morrow, 1971.

Ottley, Roi. "Politics, Poetry, and Peccadillos." Rev. of *I Wonder as I Wander*. *Saturday Review of Literature* (November 17, 1956): 35.

Rampersad, Arnold. "The Big Sea." In *The Oxford Companion to African American Literature*. Ed. William L. Andrews, Frances Smith Foster, and Trudier Harris. New York: Oxford University Press, 1997. 64.

————. Introduction. *I Wonder as I Wander*. By Langston Hughes. New York: Hill and Wang, 2000. xi–xxii.

————. "Langston Hughes." In *The Oxford Companion to African American Literature*. Ed. William L. Andrews, Frances Smith Foster, and Trudier Harris. New York: Oxford University Press, 1997. 368–70.

————. *The Life of Langston Hughes*. Vol. 1: 1902–1941: I, Too, Sing America. New York: Oxford University Press, 1986.

————. *The Life of Langston Hughes*. Vol. 2: 1941–1967: I Dream a World. New York: Oxford University Press, 1988.

Redding, J. Saunders. Rev. of *I Wonder as I Wander*. *Baltimore Afro-American Magazine* (January 12, 1957): 2.

————. "Travels of Langston Hughes as Seen in Passing." Rev. of *I Wonder as I Wander*. *New York Herald Tribune Book Review* (December 23, 1956): 6.

Rugoff, Milton. "Negro Writer's Heap of Living." Rev. of *The Big Sea*. *New York Herald Tribune Books* (August 25, 1940): 5.

Smith, Sidonie. *Where I'm Bound: Patterns of Slavery and Freedom in Black American Autobiography*. Westport, CT: Greenwood Press, 1974.

Villard, Oswald Garrison. "The Negro Intellectual." Rev. of *The Big Sea*. *Saturday Review* 31 (August 1940): 12.

Watson, Steven. *The Harlem Renaissance: Hub of African American Culture, 1920–1930*. New York: Pantheon, 1995.

Woods, Katherine. "A Negro Intellectual Tells His Life Story." Rev. of *The Big Sea*. *New York Times Book Review* (August 25, 1940): 5.

Woodson, Carter G. "Book Reviews." Rev. of *The Big Sea*. *Journal of Negro History* 25 (1940): 567–68.

Wright, Richard. "Forerunner and Ambassador." Rev. of *The Big Sea*. *New Republic* (October 28, 1940): 600–601.

ZORA NEALE HURSTON
(1891–1960)

Maxine Sample

BIOGRAPHY

Growing up in Eatonville, Florida, Zora Neale Hurston was one of eight children of Lucy and John Hurston, mayor of the all-black town that would serve not only as a setting for her well-renowned novel *Their Eyes Were Watching God* but also as a cultural reservoir that would shape much of her imaginative work. Her literary productivity for more than four decades charts her struggle through the Harlem Renaissance, depression years, World War II, and the postwar years to complete her mission of sharing the richness of the black folk tradition. At a time when neither her blackness nor her femininity was valued, Hurston sacrificed the comfort and security of traditional employment and domesticity to pursue a career as folklorist and writer. Traveling across the Western Hemisphere and often living where convenient or necessary, Hurston collected materials for her books and articles, totally immersing herself in the communities from which she extracted her material. Hurston claimed in her autobiography, "I discovered that geography was within me. It only needed time to reveal it" (85). From New York to Florida, to Haiti to Honduras, writing and working intermittently while fighting with poverty and illness, Hurston became an accomplished anthropologist and writer, establishing important links among African diasporan cultures. She authored four novels, two books of folklore, an autobiography, and over fifty short pieces of fiction and nonfiction.

Previous uncertainty about the date of Hurston's birth has been erased by information obtained from the Hurston family Bible. According to that document, she was born Zora Neal Lee Hurston [with no "e" on Neal] on January 15, 1891, the sixth child and second daughter of John Hurston and Lula Potts Hurston (Bordelon 7). Hurston was born in Notasulga, Alabama; shortly after her birth, the family moved to Eatonville, Florida. Both Hurston's maternal and paternal grandparents had been born as slaves in Georgia, though her parents were both born in Alabama. They were married in February 1882 and had nine children, one of whom died before Hurston's birth. A short time after settling in Florida, John Hurston, a carpenter by trade, began pastoring the Zion Hope Baptist Church in Sanford, Florida; Lula, known as Lucy, worked as a seamstress. Her death on September 19, 1904, was a turning point in young Zora's life. John Hurston's remarriage less than six months later to a twenty-year-old woman created tensions in the family. Zora, her sister, and a brother were sent to a school in Jacksonville for some time; later the four younger children, including Hurston, were dispersed among family members.

Hurston lived for an undetermined amount of time with her oldest brother, Hezekiah Robert (Bob) Hurston, who had established a medical practice in Memphis, Tennessee. However, she left to undertake a stint as a "lady's girl" with a traveling Gilbert and Sullivan repertoire theater company. By 1917 she would be in Baltimore, working as a waitress while attending night school at Morgan Academy (the high school division of what is now Morgan State University). She later enrolled in Morgan College and worked as a live-in "girl" to help pay her expenses. She was graduated from the high school division of Morgan College in Baltimore in 1918.

Hurston moved on to Howard University, first attending its Prep School from 1918 to 1919 and then attending the University from 1919 to 1924. She would receive an associate degree in 1920. Though still burdened with the responsibility of supporting herself, Hurston found time to write short stories, to participate in literary discussion groups, and to maintain membership in the Stylus, a literary club. She published her first short story, "John Redding Goes to Sea," in the club's magazine.

In 1925 Hurston arrived in New York City with only a dollar and fifty cents but abundant self-confidence and courage—at the height of the Harlem Renaissance. The black publications Crisis and Opportunity were encouraging young black writers such as Langston Hughes,* Countee Cullen, and other writers by sponsoring literary contests and awards dinners. Hurston would win prizes for "Spunk," an Eatonville story, and Color Struck, a drama of Florida folklife. Meanwhile, white intellectuals fascinated with the exoticism of the "New Negro" showcased newly discovered black artistic talent at private parties. Biographer Robert Hemenway writes that during the few years of Hurston's presence during the Harlem Renaissance, she was "a brilliant raconteur" known for her storytelling and personal anecdotes. Hurston attracted the attention of the writer Fannie Hurst, who offered Hurston a job as a personal secretary. Having also seen Hurston at her literary best, Annie Nathan Mayer offered Hurston a scholarship to Barnard College. The first black student at Barnard, Hurston studied under the eminent anthropologist Dr. Franz Boas, who helped her obtain a fellowship to travel south and collect Negro folklore. Barnard awarded Hurston the Bachelor of Arts degree in 1928.

On May 19, 1927, Hurston secretly married Herbert Sheen, whom she met at Howard University, but decided months later that she did not want to sacrifice her career for a domestic life. The couple divorced in 1931. From 1927 to 1931, sponsored by an elderly white patron whom she called "Godmother," Hurston traveled to parts of Florida, to New Orleans, and to the Bahamas, gathering material on folklore and hoodoo. Particularly moved by the beauty and drama of the folk culture, Hurston found that her creative and imaginative self urged her to abandon the scientific objectivity of the previous failed attempts to collect folklore and replace it with a subjectivity that selected the material and shaped it in a way that preserved the folk aesthetic. She began to think in terms of the creative productions that could emerge from this aesthetic. Writing up her field notes, Hurston created *Mules and Men* (1935), an ethnography of a small town. The first book of folklore by an African American, this collection of folktales, or "lies," was a success.

While waiting for the publication of *Mules and Men* Hurston collaborated with Langston Hughes to create the folk drama *Mule Bone: A Comedy of Negro Life* (1931), one casualty of which was the disintegration of their friendship. Hurston worked on a number of other short literary pieces, one of which became *Jonah's Gourd Vine*, a novel based on her father, a minister. No longer under the sponsorship of her patron and having exhausted her fellowship, a penniless Hurston had to borrow money to mail her novel to the publisher. It was published in 1934. Hurston worked in New York, Florida, and Chicago, creating folklore concerts and dramas. In 1935, *Mules and Men* was published, and Hurston found herself much in demand as scholars sought her assistance in collecting folklore. She continued to collect, not for scholarship but to fill her mission of communicating to the world the beauty, drama, and originality of the black folk aesthetic. She rejected pressure to purse academic scholarship and focused on writing. She produced folk concerts performed at such venues as Rollins College in Florida and the John Golden Theater in New York City.

A two-year Guggenheim Fellowship in 1936 enabled Hurston to travel to Jamaica and then to Haiti to collect folklore and voodoo. While in Haiti she wrote in seven weeks her second novel, *Their Eyes Were Watching God* (1937), capturing in it the beauty of a past love affair. She compiled the material gathered during her Haitian and Jamaican travels and published them in a volume called *Tell My Horse* (1938). The book was not received well in the United States but was quite successful in England. Though she had two more books to her credit, Hurston still had difficulty supporting herself. In 1938 she obtained employment with the Florida Works Progress Administration (WPA) writer's project to work for the book project *The Florida Negro*. Although she was hired to collect folklore, Hurston reportedly spent much of her time writing another novel.

In 1939 Hurston left the WPA and accepted a position as chairperson of the North Carolina College for Negroes Drama Department. On July 27 of that year she married Albert Price. Her fifth book, *Moses, Man of the Mountain*, also appeared in November to mixed reviews. Hurston's marriage to the twenty-three-year-old Albert Prince lasted only seven months. Divorce was granted in 1943.

In 1941 Hurston was employed as a story consultant at Paramount Studios and began working on her autobiography, finding that because of the nationalism she had to censor commentary critical of American society. Upon publication the autobiography received the Ansfield-Wolf Award from the *Saturday Evening Post*. With proceeds from that book, Hurston purchased a houseboat in Daytona Beach, Florida, and lived alone while traveling up and down the Halifa and Indian Rivers. Hurston became involved in the Florida Negro Defense Committee and addressed black GIs stationed in segregated units in Florida. She continued writing and published a few articles in several magazines. In 1945 when her money ran out, she traveled to New York to seek employment and financial support for a trip to Honduras.

An assortment of jobs occupied her time from 1945 to 1947. While in New York she accepted a position in Republican Grant Reynolds's congressional campaign against Adam Clayton Powell. After Reynolds's loss, Hurston retreated from friends and lived quietly in a basement apartment. In the spring of 1947 she received an advance from a publisher, sold her houseboat, and traveled to Honduras, where she spent most of her time in a hotel room writing a novel instead of out in the field collecting material. This novel, *Seraph on the Suwanee*, was published in 1948. A novel about white southerners, it was quite unlike her previous publications. To help promote her novel, Hurston returned to New York. While there, she was arrested for allegedly committing an "immoral act" with a ten-year-old boy. Despite her protestations of innocence and her assertions that she was in Honduras at the time of the crime, she was indicted solely on the testimony of the child. Although the indictment was dismissed, the newspaper coverage, particularly that of the black press, left her feeling betrayed. She returned to Florida a depressed woman.

Hurston spent her remaining years in Florida, writing much but publishing little. By 1950, in financial straits, she was working as a maid. When her employer discovered that Hurston was the author of an article in the *Saturday Evening Post*, Hurston explained that she was gathering research. She left the job, writing political essays as her career continued to flounder. She spent 1951 to 1956 seeking a peaceful existence in Eau Galie, Florida. Hurston came out publicly against the Supreme Court's landmark ruling in 1954 against segregation and was harshly criticized. From 1956 to 1957, Hurston worked as a librarian at the Patrick Air Force Base, after which she survived on unemployment benefits, welfare assistance, and substitute teaching.

During the last few years of her life, Hurston continued to work on a biography of King Herod the Great and continued unsuccessfully to seek a publisher for the manuscript. After 1958 her health continued to decline, and she suffered a stroke in 1959. Unable to care for herself, she was placed in the Saint Lucie County, Florida, Welfare Home. Hurston refused assistance from family members who inquired about her health and called upon her. She died of heart failure on

January 28, 1960, and was buried in Fort Pierce's segregated cemetery, the Garden of Heavenly Rest.

In her search for the talented writer, Alice Walker* traveled to Florida in 1973 and placed on an unmarked grave believed to be Hurston's final resting place a headstone that read: "Zora Neale Hurston, 'A Genius of the South,' 1901–1960, Novelist, Folklorist, Anthropologist." Since then Hurston's work has experienced a revival and considerable scholarly attention. The annual Zora Neale Hurston Festival of the Arts sponsored by the Association to Preserve the Eatonville Community began in 1990 in commemoration of Hurston's contributions in anthropology and literature and has continued to feature cultural activities along with an academic conference where scholarly papers on her works are presented.

AUTOBIOGRAPHICAL WORK AND THEMES

The restored text of *Dust Tracks on a Road* established by the Library of America for publication in 1995 affords a more complete look at Hurston's autobiography than the original 1942 edition, which omitted chapters containing content the publishers deemed irrelevant to the life story (and identity) of a black woman. Nontraditional and somewhat eclectic in form, *Dust Tracks* blends autobiographical narrative, essay, and folkloric elements to create a multidimensional and often conflicted identity that puzzles and frustrates most readers. Structured in sixteen chapters that characterize episodes in Hurston's life and philosophical musings on topics such as love, friendship, and race, *Dust Tracks* starts with a traditional linear narrative whose chronology is abandoned well into the text. An Appendix containing four other selections follows. Pierre Walker suggests that as an autobiography that focuses more on the life of Hurston's imagination than on an individualized self, *Dust Tracks* portrays "a person of many moods who is in tension with the world in which she moves" (388). Readers might also recognize in Hurston's discontinuous form the kind of fragmentation and interruption often associated with women's autobiography. Certainly the focus on interpersonal relationships and community characteristic of autobiographies by women and minorities appears in *Dust Tracks*.

The first chapter, "My Birthplace," provides background details about the all-black town of Hurston's childhood, situating her in a place and time of cultural and historical significance. Hurston warns the reader, "[Y]ou will have to know something about the time and place where I came from, in order that you may interpret the incidents and directions of my life" (1). What follows are the historical circumstances that gave birth to Eatonville, the legendary accomplishments of Joe Clarke, and in subsequent chapters, contrasting portraits of Hurston's parents and finally her birth. Hurston's father is away when her mother gives birth to young Zora, and a local white man stopping by to bring the family food assists with the delivery until the midwife arrives. This is the same man who later admonishes Hurston, "Snidlits, don't be a nigger," advice to which Hurston footnotes the following explanation: "The word Nigger used in this sense does not mean race. It means a weak, contemptible person of any race" (30). Chapter 4, "The Inside Search," depicts the world of an inquisitive youthful mind, giving the reader access to young Zora's vivid imagination, her dreams, and an account of a series of visions that would portend the break in the "comforting circle of family" (42). Chapter 5, "Figure and Fancy," is part ethnography, highlighting the folk culture of Joe Clarke's storefront porch with its "lying sessions" and sexually coded "men talk"; the other part shares artistic creations of Hurston's own imagination and fantasy. Readers learn much about the dynamics of the oral traditions that shaped the aesthetic that drives Hurston's art.

Certainly the quest or journey theme is evident from the title of the work. References to horizons, journeys, and the hunger to travel become the language of movement that prepares the reader for Hurston's later flight from Eatonville. Early in the narrative she writes, "[O]nce I found the use of my feet, they took to wandering. I always wanted to go. I would wander off in the woods all alone, following some inside urge to go places. . . . [My mother] believed a woman who was an enemy of hers had sprinkled 'travel dust' around the doorstep the day I was born" (23). A kind of wanderlust is expressed in her early exposure to that other world made accessible through the gateway of books. Hurston writes, "[E]arly reading gave me great anguish through all my childhood and adolescence. My soul was with the gods and my body in the village. . . . I wanted to be away from drabness and to stretch my limbs in some mighty struggle" (41).

Chapter 6, "Wandering," is appropriately titled as it presents a moving account of the death of Hurston's mother, an event that signals the end of the protected nurturing world of Hurston's youth and precipitates the picaresque existence that would characterize Hurston's later life. Lucy Hurston had raised her daughter according to the "universal female gospel," encouraging her to "jump at de sun" (13); she defended Zora against every effort to "squinch" her spirit. She encouraged her daughter to speak up rather than heed her father's caution to adapt a demeanor appropriate to avoid the fate of "sassy" Negroes. The four youngest children were dispersed among friends and relatives following her mother's death. Hurston attended boarding school in Jacksonville for a while; when her father advised the school to adopt Hurston after her fees remained delinquent, she was sent home. Chapter 7 recounts Hurston's dramatic fight with a stepmother whose appearance six months after Lucy Hurston's death created tension in the family. Hurston leaves, spends some time with an older brother in Memphis, and from there, strikes out on her own, forever on the move, experiencing one adventure after another.

Most of Chapters 7 through 10 describe Hurston's struggle to live independently of family, to educate herself, and to pursue her creative interests. Chapter 10, "Research," is one of the most colorful chapters, describing the highs and lows of a Barnard-educated Hurston's return to the South to collect folklore. Jook songs and work songs of Polk County accompany descriptions of the guardianship of "Big Sweet" and Hurston's initiation to hoodoo while in New Orleans. Bahamian songs liven up her accounts of her efforts to introduce folk material to New York audiences. Readers hear the story of Cudjo Lewis, a former West Indian slave interviewed by Hurston, learn of his Dahomean culture, and witness Hurston's outrage at discovering that some Africans actually sold their own people into slavery. The relationship between Hurston and her white patrons, particularly Mrs. Osgood Mason, helps the reader understand the paradoxical circumstances under which Hurston sought to authenticate African American culture and maintain authorial control of material presented to an audience interested primarily in exoticism. "Books and Things," Chapter 11, describes Hurston's undertaking of published works—novels, collections of folklore, folk drama, and short stories. We see Hurston offering the reader her own literary biography, sharing the responses of the literary community, giving insight into what she tried to accomplish, describing the financial challenges in bringing a work to fruition, and the subsequent rewards that followed.

The remaining chapters of *Dust Tracks*, along with the previously unpublished chapters in the Appendix, are primarily personal essays addressing a range of topics. In Chapter 12, "My People, My People," Hurston gives conflicting views about race and race consciousness while criticizing the expectation that blacks be "race men/women." Her monkey parables ridicule those who, on one hand, serve as champions of racial pride yet, on the other hand, simultaneously express shame at how some members of the race behave. Rejecting the imposition of a racial identity, Hurston claims, "I saw no curse in being black, nor no extra flavor by being white" (191). Judith Robey suggests that Hurston's shift to the essay mode at this point in the autobiography "signals the author's attempt to recreate a self whose fate is not determined by patrons. The protagonist becomes the fictional 'author herself,' and the discourse takes on an authoritative, confrontational edge" (677–78). Pierre Walker notes as well that while appendices in contemporary autobiography are nontraditional—usually written by white supporters to vouch for the authenticity of the narrator—Hurston's appendices assert her own authenticity.

The final chapters offer Hurston's reflections on a variety of issues. Chapter 13, "Two Women in Particular," discusses Hurston's friendship with writer Fannie Hurst and singer Ethel Waters. The next two chapters share her viewpoints on love and religion. The last chapter, "Looking Things Over," examines political and international affairs, closing the narrative with the appeal "Let us all be kissing friends" (232). Though, as she tells her readers, "I have been in Sorrow's kitchen and licked out all the pots" (227), Hurston refuses to focus on victimization and be driven by bitterness about past racial injustice. She asserts, "I have no race prejudice of any kind" (231). These comments, along with a similar stance on race issues displayed in the Appendix, have led some readers to conclude that Hurston's intent here was to appease her white readers, to wear an accommodating mask. For example, Robey wonders if perhaps *Dust Tracks*' value as an autobiography "lies in the statement it makes about the debilitating influence [Hurston's] white readership has on the act of writing an autonomous self" (679). However, the legitimacy of the presumed autonomous self that readers

expect to be revealed in autobiography is itself a contentious point within autobiography scholarship.

CRITICAL RECEPTION

Upon release, *Dust Tracks* received mixed reviews, although it has been considered a commercial success. The black intellectual community tended to be
critical of Hurston's racial views and her omissions of serious aspects of black
life—segregation, for example—and the Harlem Renaissance, which is barely
mentioned. Arna Bontemps's "From Eatonville, Florida to Harlem" concludes
that the perspectives on race were designed not to offend Hurston's relationships
with whites. The *Journal of Negro History*'s W. Edward Farrison did not consider
Dust Tracks a great autobiography but praised Hurston's fresh use of old material.
White critics were more favorable, responding to Hurston's use of language, humor, and conciliatory tone on race matters. The *Saturday Review*'s Phil Strong
called it a delightful narrative "told in exactly the right manner" without the
"race-consciousness that spoils so much of Negro literature" (6–7), and the *Saturday Evening Post* awarded the book the $1,000 Anisfield-Wolf Award. The
contrasting responses along racial lines surely fueled the sentiment that Hurston
was writing to appeal to a white audience upon whose financial patronage she
depended.

Much of the negative reception surrounding *Dust Tracks* has to do with what
the text does not reveal; this preoccupation with the missing text—the absent
Hurston—characterized many of the responses as a new generation of readers
became acquainted with Hurston in the 1970s and 1980s. Of particular note are
Alice Walker's conclusion that Hurston's autobiography "rings false" (85) and
Mary Helen Washington's suggestion that in avoiding "real self-disclosure" Hurston engages in "the art of subterfuge" (20). Elizabeth Fox-Genovese finds in *Dust
Tracks* "crafted deception" necessitated by self-preservation (233). Robert Hemenway, however, accuses Hurston of deliberate self-concealment. Hemenway's
Zora Neale Hurston: A Literary Biography compares *Dust Tracks* with the genre of
black American autobiography as defined by Stephen Butterfield and determines
that Hurston's work as a whole does not fit the profile of traditional black autobiography: "political awareness, empathy for suffering, knowledge of oppression, and a sense of shared life, shared triumph, and communal responsibility"
(278). On the contrary, *Dust Tracks* appears "politically naive" (279) and fails
to offer "the definitive statement of her character" (280). Yet Hemenway cautions
that *Dust Tracks* is best assessed in the context of Hurston's total career and art,
for "it is an autobiography at war with itself" (277–78).

Pam Bordelon's "New Tracks on *Dust Tracks*" is a more recent examination
that raises the issue of the autobiography's veracity in light of access to the
Hurston family Bible and interviews conducted with Winifred Hurston Clark,
the oldest surviving niece of Zora Neale Hurston and a family member who lived
with Hurston for some time. Bordelon, whose research is on Hurston's experience

with the Florida Federal Writers' Project, is hopeful that access to additional family information will prompt a reevaluation of Hurston's life. Bordelon writes that the new information "prove[s] Hurston's autobiographical account even more fictionalized than previously acknowledged" (18). However, Bordelon urges a consideration of the political, social, and cultural factors that may have motivated Hurston to fabricate parts of her life and calls for a rewriting of Hurston's biography in an attempt to gain a deeper understanding of the author.

More recent scholarship has challenged these views about the lack of authenticity and truthfulness of Hurston's representation of self. Pierre A. Walker rejects this negative criticism surrounding *Dust Tracks*, the source of which is Cartesian and Enlightenment expectations of a coherent, homogeneous self that Hurston fails to deliver (388). Walker argues that there exists no "true" interior persona hidden behind an alleged false exterior, and readers who insist on a "homogeneous, unitary, and autonomous conventional autobiography" will continue to be frustrated by *Dust Tracks'* inconsistency (387). Instead, the representation of the self in Hurston's autobiography is densely textured and multilayered, giving the reader an "individual that poststructuralist theory would identify as the postmodern subject—a fragmented, heterogeneous individual, inextricably interconnected with the rest of the world and human society" (Walker 388). Walker adds that "the lack of consistency, coherence, and unity is the most important feature of her text" and sees in the much criticized five final chapters Hurston's way of signifying on conventions of African American autobiography (such as slave narratives) as she asserts her own authenticity.

These ideas are shared in Phillip A. Snyder's "Zora Neale Hurston's *Dust Tracks*: Autobiography and Artist Novel," which argues that the text is as much about Hurston's absence as it is about her presence. Snyder states, "*Dust Tracks* functions poorly when read as an equivalent (re)presentation of Hurston's self and life but functions well when read as a fictive narrative associated with that self and life, an autobiographical act that is as much production as product . . . as much convention as creation, and as much imagination as memory" (174). The multiplicity of speaking subjects invites multiple readings. Another approach toward understanding the "absent" Zora is offered in Françoise Lionnet-McCumber's notion of *Dust Tracks* as autoethnography, "the process of defining one's subjective ethnicity as mediated through language, history and ethnographical analysis," what Lionnet-McCumber considers an anthropology of the self (242). In this way we can approach the text not as an autobiography but as a self-portrait that emerges through a process of self-invention; the layering of disparate elements that go into that portrait and the multiple personae and voices that appear as part of that portrait are no longer problematic. The nexus between the anthropological and personal in Hurston is explored by Kathleen Hassall's "Text and Personality in Disguise and in the Open: Zora Neale Hurston's *Dust Tracks on a Road*," which claims that by deconstructing the borders between self and work, Hurston "disguised herself all her life" (167). Thus *Dust Tracks* is no more than a "text in disguise" containing an "encoded response to racism," an autobiography that is best viewed as a "series of performances by an actress trained in Eatonville" (160). As Hurston grew up in a community that fostered perform-ance, contends Hassall, "[P]retense, misdirection, secrecy, and deliberate, slip-pery, unpredictability—all venerable confrontational strategies, and all lessons Hurston learned in Eatonville—direct her performances in Dust Tracks" (160).

Judith Robey's "Generic Strategies in Zora Neale Hurston's Dust Tracks on a Road" takes a reader response approach to address the ambiguities of self in Hur-ston's work. Robey contends that Hurston's use of three generic modes—myth, picaresque travel, and the essay—is connected to her attempt to evade catego-rization and reification by the reader and to erect an independent, authoritative self. Each shift from one mode to the next is "a means of constructing a self independent of the categories and expectations her reader brings to the reading act" (669). The narrative is written on two levels, one representing actual ex-perience and a second submerged level representing the author's encounters with her readers—"the white patrons whose presence compels her either to reinscribe herself in myth or seek empowerment in a new genre or mask" (669).

The double-voiced nature of Dust Tracks has generated considerable interest as a means of grasping Hurston's self-representation in the text. Henry Louis Gates sees Hurston's usage of a "divided voice, a double voice unreconciled" as one of her greatest achievements. He writes:

Hurston's unresolved tension between her double voice signifies her full understanding of modernism. Hurston uses the two voices in her text to celebrate the psychological frag-mentation both of modernity and of the black American. . . . The "real" Zora Neale Hur-ston that we long to locate in this text, dwells in the silence that separates these two voices: she is both, and neither; bilingual, and mute. (240)

Susan Willis in Specifying: Black Women Writing the American Experience examines the subversive intent in the autobiography's language as evident in Hurston's employment of shifting pronouns as she mediates polarized worlds and other forms of language use. Susan Meisenhelder's Hitting a Straight Lick with a Crooked Stick traces the ambiguity in Hurston's narrative to the double talk on Eatonville's front porches. Dust Tracks takes the "indirect verbal route to survival . . . by cast-ing her story in the form of timeless myth, one shaped as a quest, grounded in visions, and filled with allusions to European myths . . . [that] function as both mask and vehicle for her racial analysis and for her treatment of specific whites in her life" (148–49). The text reveals the importance of black women's knowing how to negotiate power relationships—when to fight or compromise, when to specify or signify, and when to play the trickster (143).

Intertextual aspects of Dust Tracks are explored in Deborah Plant's Every Tub Must Sit on Its Own Bottom, which considers parallels between Hurston's Dust Tracks and Booker T. Washington's* Up from Slavery. Both autobiographies re-ject collective pity and reflect an orientation toward individualism, achievement, and empowerment (49). Critical of Hemenway's assessment that the visions Hurston records in *Dust Tracks* serve merely to structure the autobiography, Plant argues that they are "an authenticating feature that further illustrates the narrative's resemblance to the sermon" (102). Through the "evangelical voice" of the folk preacher Hurston renders a narrative cast in biblical expression, images, allusion, proverbs, and folk expression. Plant calls *Dust Tracks* "a transforming, mythic narrative, a discourse of resistance to stereotypical, controlling images of Black womanhood" (96). Lynn Domina's "Protection in My Mouf" argues that *Dust Tracks* makes liberal use of folklore; in the autobiography Hurston "relates a lore of the self as well as a lore of the folk," resisting a subjectivity that has been "previously constructed through the orality of folklore" (197).

Finally, Claudine Raynaud's " 'Rubbing a Paragraph with a Soft Cloth'? Muted Voices and Editorial Constraints in *Dust Tracks on a Road*" examines the autobiography in the context of excised material and pressures exerted on Hurston by her publishers; restoring the omitted material enables the reader to appreciate Hurston's position as a black woman writer struggling for authorial voice.

BIBLIOGRAPHY

Autobiographical Works by Zora Neale Hurston

"How It Feels to Be Colored Me." *World Tomorrow* 11 (May 1928): 215–16.

Dust Tracks on a Road. Philadelphia: Lippincott, 1942. Rpt. with introduction by Larry P. Neal, 1971. 2nd ed., edited and with introduction by Robert Hemenway, Urbana: University of Illinois Press, 1984; New York: Library of America Restored Edition, 1995.

Studies of Zora Neale Hurston's Autobiographical Works

Bontemps, Arna. "From Eatonville, Florida to Harlem." *New York Herald Tribune* (November 22, 1943): 3.

Bordelon, Pam. "New Tracks on *Dust Tracks*. Toward a Reassessment of the Life of Zora Neale Hurston." *African American Review* 31.1 (Spring 1997): 5–21.

Domina, Lynn. " 'Protection in My Mouf': Self, Voice, and Community in Zora Neale Hurston's *Dust Tracks on a Road* and *Mules and Men*." *African American Review* 32.2 (Summer 1997): 197–209.

Farrison, W. Edward. Rev. of *Dust Tracks on a Road*, by Zora Neale Hurston. *Journal of Negro History* 28.3 (July 1943): 352–55.

Fox-Genovese, Elizabeth. "Myth and History: Discourse of Origins in Zora Neale Hurston and Maya Angelou." *Black American Literature Forum* 24.2 (Summer 1990): 221–35.

Gates, Henry L. "Zora Neale Hurston: 'A Negro Way of Saying' " (Afterword). In *Their Eyes Were Watching God*. 1937. New York: Perennial, 1990.

Hassall, Kathleen. "Text and Personality in Disguise and in the Open: Zora Neale Hurston's *Dust Tracks on a Road*." In *Zora in Florida*. Ed. Steve Glassman and Kathryn Lee Seidel. Orlando: University of Central Florida Press, 1991. 139–73.

Hemenway, Robert. *Zora Neale Hurston: A Literary Biography*. Urbana: University of Illinois Press, 1977.

Lionnett, McCumber. Françoise. "Autoethnography: The An-Archic Style of *Dust Tracks on a Road*." In *Zora Neale Hurston: Critical Perspectives Past and Present*. Ed. Henry L. Gates and Anthony Appiah. New York: Amistad, 1993. 241–66.

Lyons, Mary E. *Sorrow's Kitchen: The Life and Folklore of Zora Neale Hurston*. New York: Scribner's Sons, 1990. [Juvenile biography]

Meisenhelder, Susan Edwards. *Hitting a Straight Lick with a Crooked Stick: Race and Gender in the Work of Zora Neale Hurston*. Tuscaloosa: University of Alabama Press, 1999.

Plant, Deborah. *Every Tub Must Sit on Its Own Bottom: The Philosophy and Politics of Zora Neale Hurston*. Urbana: University of Illinois Press, 1995.

Raynaud, Claudine. " 'Rubbing a Paragraph with a Soft Cloth': Muted Voices and Editorial Constraints in *Dust Tracks on a Road*." In *De/Colonizing the Subject: The Politics of Gender in Women's Autobiography*. Ed. Sidonie Smith and Julia Watson. Minneapolis: University of Minnesota Press. 34–64.

Robey, Judith. "Generic Strategies in Zora Neale Hurston's *Dust Tracks on a Road*." *Black American Literature Forum* 24.4 (1990): 667–82.

Snyder, Phillip A. "Zora Neale Hurston's *Dust Tracks*: Autobiography and Artist Novel." In *Critical Essays on Zora Neale Hurston*. Ed. Gloria L. Cronin. New York: G.K. Hall, 1998. 173–89.

Strong, Phil. "Zora Hurston Sums Up." Rev. of *Dust Tracks on a Road*. *Saturday Review* (November 28, 1942): 6–7.

Walker, Alice. "In Search of Zora Neale Hurston." *Ms. Magazine* (March 1975): 74–79, 85–89.

Walker, Pierre A. "Zora Neale Hurston and the Post-Modern Self in *Dust Tracks on a Road*." *African American Review* 32.3 (Fall 1998): 387–99. Rpt. in *Critical Essays on Zora Neale Hurston*. Ed. Gloria L. Cronin. New York: G.K. Hall, 1998. 170–72.

Wall, Cheryl A. "Zora Neale Hurston." In *African American Writers*. New York: Scribner's Sons, 1991. 205–18.

Washington, Mary Helen. Introduction. In *I Love Myself When I Am Laughing . . . And Then Again When I Am Looking Mean and Impressive: A Zora Neale Hurston Reader*. Ed. Alice Walker. Old Westbury, NY: Feminist Press, 1979.

Willis, Susan. *Specifying: Black Women Writing the American Experience*. Madison: University of Wisconsin Press, 1987.

ELIZABETH KECKLEY
(1818–1907)

Adenike Marie Davidson

BIOGRAPHY

Businesswoman, activist, modiste, and confidante to Mary Todd Lincoln, Elizabeth Keckley was born Elizabeth Hobbs at Dinwiddie Court House in Virginia. She was the only child of devoted parents who were slaves on neighboring plantations. She was separated from her father, George Pleasant, when his owner decided to move west. She and her mother, Agnes Hobbs, remained together, both owned by Colonel A. Burwell.

Around the age of fourteen, Burwell sent Elizabeth to live with his eldest son, Robert; she relocated with the family to North Carolina. It was during this stay, and near the age of eighteen, that she gave birth to a son, George, conceived through a forced sexual relationship with a white man who remained unnamed. This was her only child.

Elizabeth eventually returned to Virginia to be in service to Ann Burwell, the colonel's daughter. Upon Ann's marriage to a Mr. Garland, Elizabeth and George relocated to St. Louis with the family. Mr. Garland soon found himself in poverty and proposed to place Elizabeth's mother out to service in order to remedy his financial situation. Elizabeth, who had developed a talent for dressmaking, supported her owners and their children by hiring herself out in order to save her mother the humiliation.

Elizabeth had met James Keckley, an African American man, in Virginia; he came to St. Louis during her time there and proposed marriage. Despite her misgivings—she did not want to support the institution of slavery by bringing more children into the world that would be considered property—she married him. Keckley proposed to buy herself and her son out of bondage; at first the Garlands flatly refused her offer of $1,200. Her persistence led to success and on

November 15, 1855, and at the age of thirty-seven, Keckley paid Ann Garland for her freedom and that of her son. Diligence, commitment, and a strong work ethic helped Keckley earn the money needed to repay her patrons who had loaned her the sum needed for her manumission.

In 1860, Keckley established her son in Wilberforce College in Ohio, announced to her husband that she was leaving him—he had become a drunkard and a poor husband—and left St. Louis for Baltimore and afterwards Washington, D.C., planning to support herself as a dressmaker. In the nation's capital, Keckley attracted an elite group of clients; her business grew so prosperous that at times she employed twenty other seamstresses to assist her. She became the seamstress for Mr. and Mrs. Jefferson Davis, until their return to the South. She was then recommended to Mary Todd Lincoln and quickly became the First Lady's dressmaker and confidante.

In 1862, after her son was killed in action while fighting for the Union, Keckley helped to found the "Contraband Relief Association," an organization of well-off free African Americans, especially women, formed for the purpose of providing assistance to former slaves in the D.C. area in making a smooth transition into independent, self-sufficient, and contributing citizens of the nation. Keckley served as president of the organization.

After President Lincoln's assassination, Keckley remained friend and comforter to Mrs. Lincoln and attempted to assist the First Lady in repaying her clothing debts. At first Keckley offered to arrange a fund-raiser, calling on the African American community to contribute out of loyalty to Lincoln; but such a proposal was at first refused by Mrs. Lincoln. Keckley then traveled with the widow to New York to assist in selling her wardrobe. The trip proved futile, causing more scandal than desired.

In 1868, Keckley published her autobiography, *Behind the Scenes; or, Thirty Years a Slave and Four Years in the White House*. Her motivation, she claimed, was to raise money to help her dear friend and to set the record straight regarding the scandal surrounding the infamous widow and her reputation. The book caused a permanent rift between the two women. Keckley was presented as betraying a confidence for personal gain, and her business suffered as a result.

By 1892, Keckley was teaching domestic arts at Wilberforce. Later, she dropped from public notice but worked for the Home for Destitute Women and Children in Washington, D.C. She lived on a small pension she received as the mother of a fallen Union soldier. She died from a stroke in 1907.

AUTOBIOGRAPHICAL WORK AND THEMES

Behind the Scenes, or, Thirty Years a Slave and Four Years in the White House is Elizabeth Keckley's only published work. Initially, her authorship of the text was contested, adding to the controversy. Her text is a hybrid of slave narrative, autobiography, and memoir. It defies strict definition and reveals parallels and contradictions between several American ideals and issues familiar to an American audience.

The title suggests a preponderance of discussion of the institute of slavery, yet these "thirty years" are condensed into three chapters. Moreover, she glosses over certain atrocities with comments such as, "Slavery had its dark side as well as its bright" (30). And in contrast to other female slave narrative, Keckley does not give the details of her sexual abuse or apologize for her lack of purity. Her rape is confined to two sentences: "I do not care to dwell upon this subject, for it is one that is fraught with pain. Suffice it to say, that he persecuted me for four years, and I—I—became a mother" (39). Instead of apology, Keckley suggests that George "must blame the edicts of that society which deemed it no crime to undermine the virtue of girls in my then position" (39).

The bulk of the text is devoted to a look "behind the scenes" of the White House with Abraham and Mary Todd Lincoln. Instead of exposing her own life up for scrutiny, as had been done during slavery (both physically and in antebellum literature), Keckley strips bare the ideals of democracy, liberty, womanhood, and the self-made man, thus suggesting revealing and critiquing the hypocrisy upon which middle- and upper-class White America is founded. She insists that "the veil of mystery must be drawn aside" (xiv), and this is achieved through publishing of Mrs. Lincoln's private letters and by contrasting the life of the First Lady with that of an ambitious and successful former slave.

CRITICAL RECEPTION

Upon first publication, *Behind the Scenes* received negative reviews, suggesting that Keckley had hit a snag in the delicate fabric of the nation. Robert Lincoln recalled the book, and Keckley was rebuked for publishing Mrs. Lincoln's letters. A review in the *New York Times* called it "grossly and shamelessly indecent," and *Putnam's Magazine* labeled it the "latest and decidedly weakest production of the sensational press." Soon after the appearance of Keckley's text, a vicious parody was published in New York by National News titled *Behind the Seams: By a Nigger Woman Who Took in Work from Mrs. Lincoln and Mrs. Davis* and signed with an X by "Betsey Kickley." The early reception succeeded in producing low sales and no income for Keckley.

Interest in Keckley and her text was resurrected first by historians and biographers of the Lincolns. In this field Keckley's text is viewed as an important and reliable historical source regarding the Lincolns and especially the First Lady.

The more recent attention to African American literature, especially that published in the nineteenth century, has propelled Keckley's text into the discussion of African American women's autobiographies and postbellum slave narratives. Unfortunately, until very recently, Keckley was usually overshadowed by Harriet Jacobs and Booker T. Washington* and rarely included in anthologies. *Behind the Scenes* had been dismissed as a problematic slave narrative because of the little attention spent on her enslavement and also questioned as an autobiography because of the vast amount of space spent on Mrs. Lincoln. But instead of forcing Keckley's text into a prescribed template, more recent critics have attempted to approach it on more varied terms. William L. Andrews and Frances Smith Foster include Keckley in examinations of postbellum slave narratives and autobiographies imagining the future of the nation more positively than antebellum texts and the inclusion of African Americans within that future. Michael Berthold moves beyond a condemnation of the distant narrator and suggests that Keckley resists constructing her life story as a romance (despite her defining it as such in the preface) and repudiates "a merely 'personal' self in favor of a deliberately public one" (105). Carolyn Sorisio gives a thorough and convincing argument of Keckley's text as a deliberate "unmasking [of] the genteel performer" (19); that is, Keckley's text can be interpreted as not passive but full of anger regarding the privileged and unearned position of white middle-class ladies. Lynn Domina and Ryan Simmons examine *Behind the Scenes* as a manifesto of American capitalism and patriotism. Jennifer Fleischner takes the economic argument further by showing how Keckley constructs Mrs. Lincoln as Other and "economic outcast" (102), both with her debt and with her inability to mourn respectfully. And Rafia Zafar pairs Keckley with another overlooked autobiography in a discussion of the necessity of veiling one's authority as author when exposing the shortcomings of White America.

It appears that *Behind the Scenes* is finally beginning to get the critical attention it deserves and will continue to offer readers and critics much to consider.

BIBLIOGRAPHY

Autobiographical Work by Elizabeth Keckley

Behind the Scenes; or, Thirty Years a Slave and Four Years in the White House. 1868. New York: Oxford University Press, 1988.

Studies of Elizabeth Keckley's Autobiographical Work

Andrews, William L. "Reunion in the Postbellum Slave Narrative: Frederick Douglass and Elizabeth Keckley." *Black American Literature Forum* 23.1 (Spring 1989): 5–16.

Berthold, Michael. "Not 'Altogether' the 'History of Myself': Autobiography Impersonality in Elizabeth Keckley's *Behind the Scenes, or, Thirty Years a Slave and Four Years in the White House.*" *American Transcendental Quarterly* 3 (June 1999): 105–19.

Domina, Lynn. "'I Was Re-Elected President': Elizabeth Keckley as Quintessential Patriot in *Behind the Scenes, or, Thirty Years a Slave and Four Years in the White House.*" In *Women's Life Writing: Finding Voice/Building Community.* Ed. Linda S. Coleman. Bowling Green, OH: Bowling Green State University Popular Press, 1997. 139–51.

Fleischner, Jennifer. *Mastering Slavery: Memory, Family, and Identity in Women's Slave Narratives.* New York: New York University Press, 1996.

Foster, Frances Smith. "Autobiography/after Emancipation: The Example of Elizabeth Keckley." In *Multi-Cultural Autobiography: American Lives*. Ed. James Robert Payne. Knoxville: University of Tennessee Press, 1992. 32–63.

———. "Romance and Scandal in a Postbellum Slave Narrative: Elizabeth Keckley's *Behind the Scenes*." In *Written by Herself: Literary Production by African American Women, 1746–1892*. Bloomington: Indiana University Press, 1993. 117–30.

Olney, James. Introduction. In *Behind the Scenes; or, Thirty Years a Slave and Four Years in the White House*. By Elizabeth Keckley. New York: Oxford University Press, 1988. xxvii–xxxvi.

Rev. of *Behind the Scenes*. *New York Times* (April 26, 1868): 3.

Rev. of *Behind the Scenes*. *Putnam's Magazine* (July 1868): 119.

Simmons, Ryan. "Naming Names: *Clotel* and *Behind the Scenes*." *CLA Journal* 43.1 (September 1999): 19–37.

Sorisio, Carolyn. "Unmasking the Genteel Performer: Elizabeth Keckley's *Behind the Scenes* and the Politics of Public Wrath." *African American Review* 34.1 (Spring 2000): 19–38.

Washington, John E. *They Knew Lincoln*. New York: Dutton, 1942.

Zafar, Rafia. *We Wear the Mask: African Americans Write American Literature, 1760–1870*. New York: Columbia University Press, 1997.

JAMAICA KINCAID
(1949–)

Suzanne Hotte Massa

BIOGRAPHY

Jamaica Kincaid—the writer—came to be in 1973 when she changed her name. It was a gesture that "she has described as a way of shucking family disapproval of her writing and gaining a sort of anonymity" (Simmons 5). Her name change was the crowning act of liberation for the West Indian girl raised under the strict thumb of British colonial rule. She was born Elaine Potter Richardson on May 25, 1949, on the island of Antigua. She never met her father and was raised by her mother and stepfather. Until the age of nine, she was an only child. The subsequent birth of her three brothers expelled Elaine from the "paradise" she had enjoyed with her mother. Around the same time, she became aware of her otherness as an Antiguan under British rule that made her feel as though her own identity had been erased.

Like most prolific writers, Kincaid became a voracious reader at an early age. This interest was viewed as subversive behavior by both her mother and school authorities. As a result, she was penalized for being a problem child. Her punishment was to memorize long passages of John Milton's *Paradise Lost*. Ironically, Milton's work provided one of her early inspirations by planting the "idea that one may rebel against even overwhelming power" (Simmons 4). This consciousness of self as a marginalized person set the tone for most of Kincaid's writing.

At the age of fifteen, Kincaid's mother withdrew her from school and sent her to the United States where she became a nanny in Scarsdale, New York. After becoming interested in photography, she enrolled in Franconia College in New Hampshire. However, that interest was short lived, so she returned to New York and found her first job in publishing at a magazine called *Art Direction*. She was almost immediately fired from that job for writing an article on black American advertising. Following unsuccessful attempts to land jobs at *Mademoiselle* and *Glamour*, she was successful at *Ingenue*, where she was assigned to interview Gloria Steinem. The success of that piece led her to a chance meeting with William Shawn, then the editor of *The New Yorker*. She published her first article for the magazine's "Talk of the Town" column in 1974 and began an association with the magazine that would last a decade.

Shawn's influence on Kincaid was far-reaching. In life, he was her mentor; in death, he remains a source of inspiration. He was also her father-in-law. In 1979, Kincaid married Allen Shawn, a composer who is on the faculty at Bennington College. The couple and their two children—Annie and Harold—live in Bennington, Vermont.

During her decade with *The New Yorker*, Kincaid blossomed as a writer. Her first short story collection, *At the Bottom of the River*, was published in 1983, making Kincaid a "literary star" (Simmons 7). Her short story "Girl" won the Morton Dauwen Zabel Award of the American Academy and Institute of Arts and Letters and was nominated for the PEN/Faulkner Award. In 1985, she published her first novel, *Annie John*, which was one of three finalists for the 1985 international Ritz Paris Hemingway Award. Following the success of her first novel, Kincaid went on to write *A Small Place*, a scathing essay about tourists and political corruption in postcolonial Antigua. The essay was originally intended for publication in *The New Yorker* but was rejected by the new editor, Robert Gottlieb. Two more novels, *Lucy* and *The Autobiography of My Mother*, were published in 1991 and 1996, respectively. Although most of Kincaid's works have a clear autobiographical tone, *My Brother* is her only text that falls neatly into that category. In all of Kincaid's works, the writer struggles with her fall from the paradise she remembers with her mother and the colonial domination that damaged her sense of self.

AUTOBIOGRAPHICAL WORK AND THEMES

Like most of Kincaid's fiction, *My Brother* also reveals her obsession with her paradoxical view of her mother: enmity and adoration. However, it is also the story of Kincaid's grieving process and the self-knowledge she gained during that process. Kincaid's memoir is less a conventional autobiography and more a catharsis for her grief. Writing has always been Kincaid's salvation, as she describes at the end of her memoir:

I became a writer out of desperation, so . . . I would write about his [my brother's] dying. When I was young, younger than I am now, I started to write about my own life and I came to see that this act saved my life. When I heard about my brother's illness and his dying, I knew, instinctively, that to understand it, or to make an attempt at understanding his dying, and not to die with him I would write about it. (196)

This book is a meditation of Kincaid's confrontation with and resolution of the memories her brother's death revived. Kincaid's pain is the fertile ground of her creativity.

The book is divided into two sections. In the first section, Kincaid announces that her brother, Devon, is lying in a hospital dying of AIDS. In the second section, we accompany Kincaid through her grieving process. However, the entire text is cyclical, a tribute to the cycles of healing Kincaid experienced before and during the writing of the book. She moves from resentment to joy and back again, sometimes in rapid succession and other times with indulgent leisure, reflecting her continual struggle between her past and her present. Emphasizing the cyclical motion, her prose is full of the refrains of her resentments, reminding us of the past's influence on the present: her anger toward her mother for acts of betrayal, her resentment of her brothers for disrupting her Edenic life, and her resentment toward the arrogance of British colonists who attempted to obliterate her identity. The second section is primarily a catalog of these resentments mingled with the joys and victories of her adult life.

Most important is the resentment she has toward her brother Devon for interrupting her life—her tidy, comfortable, contented life. One interruption occurred when he was born, the other when he died. But in each instance, her life was completely different. He forever marred the possibility of happiness in her first life, her late childhood and adolescence. Devon, however, was powerless to destroy her happiness in her adult life. Nonetheless, Kincaid resented being drawn away from her home with her husband and children to help care for her brother and face the demons that haunted her. She does not seem to be as sad about her brother's impending death as she is by the reconnection to her life that his illness necessitates. Nonetheless, she assumes some responsibility for his care. In her newly attained "privileged North American way," Kincaid is able to obtain and deliver the AZT that is unavailable in Antigua, where an AIDS patient is sequestered from society (125). The medication does ease his pain and discomfort as well as prolong his life temporarily. Kincaid describes the period during which Devon was sick and dying as a world of its own. "It was a really short time between the time that he became sick and the time he died, but that time became a world" (91–92). During that time, Kincaid was suspended between her two worlds, belonging to neither, but to the time of her brother's dying.

Her brother's tragic life stands in stark juxtaposition to her own, more satisfying, life. She managed to escape a fate similar to Devon's. Kincaid cannot help but wonder what her own life would have been like if she had never left Antigua, if her fate might have been similar to Devon's. "I shall never forget him because his life is the one I did not have, the life that, for reasons I hope shall never be too clear to me, I avoided or escaped" (176). Ironically, she claims that it was her mother's betrayal that led Kincaid to become a successful writer and self-assured adult woman. Therefore, the connection to her original home is ambiguous. She feels detached from, yet connected to, her Antiguan family: "I love the people I am from and I do not love the people I am from" (149). And she cherishes the physical beauty of both homes with lovingly rendered descriptions. However, her Antiguan home is spiritually hideous, while her Vermont home is a temple of comfort.

Ultimately, she speculates about the future her brother will not have. She says, "The plantsman in my bother will never be, and all the other things that he might have been in his life have died; but inside his body a death lives, flowering upon flowering with a voraciousness that nothing seems able to satisfy and stop" (19–20). Devon always wanted to be famous and, ironically, became so when Kincaid wrote this book. Her escape brought him posthumous fame, and his death brought her peace of mind.

CRITICAL RECEPTION

Anne P. Rice attributes Kincaid's obsession with her mother to "matrophobia" (25). She asserts that even when Kincaid tries to seek understanding of her brother's death that her "memory's landscape [is] always overwhelmed by her mother's powerful and threatening presence" (23). The events that created the chasm between mother and daughter—the birth of Kincaid's three brothers and, later, the intentional burning of Kincaid's beloved library books—is outlined in the first section and repeatedly revisited in the second. Rice points out that the "memory of her mother's double betrayal infects the entire narrative" (27). And Kincaid's inability to resolve this betrayal in her own psyche is even evident in her writing style: "This inability to achieve closure even at the sentence level is a delaying tactic typical of trauma recovery, with the witness buying the time needed to advance to the next difficult phase of memory. Kincaid cannot come to the point, and yet each parenthesis moves her closer to it" (28). This autobiography, then, is Kincaid's healing salve, for it "provides the perfect vehicle for talking back to her mother" (34). Indeed, facing her matrophobia is what helps Kincaid to transcend the demons of her past.

As a writer who is not afraid to voice an unpopular opinion, Kincaid is susceptible to suspicion and criticism. Although *Time* magazine's reviewer John Skow respects Kincaid's work as a whole, he considers *My Brother* to be "an irritating navel contemplation" that "repeats the pattern of familiar, well-written complaint[s]" (107). Most reviewers, however, found numerous positive aspects in the work despite the repetitious themes and resentful tone, namely, the candid approach with which Kincaid exposes the skeletons in her closet. As Deborah McDowell points out, "Kincaid does not aim to please," and she "dares to voice the unspeakable" (3). Anna Quindlen describes the text as "a rich, complex book . . . of a refugee who has never been able to forget where she came from" (7). Amy Boaz also celebrates the perfection of Kincaid's "stunning" narrative: "Reading novelist Kincaid's prose is like learning all over again why one writes: to sift endlessly, reorder, and distill one's raw, cluttered experience so that what emerges is, quite simply, perfect" (94). Donna Seaman is also undisturbed by Kincaid's candidness. She finds the book "[h]onest, unapologetic, and pure, . . . an eloquent and searching elegy for the dead and a prayer of thankfulness for the living" (5). Heather Caines asserts that it is a "gripping work in which Kincaid bares her soul and her family's history—revealing the pain, bitterness, defeat, and triumphs that make up life—conveying . . . that . . . her experiences . . . are . . . universal and timeless" (80). For the most part, critics are not only enchanted with Kincaid's storytelling; they empathize with the resolution that this text provides for her as well.

BIBLIOGRAPHY

Autobiographical Work by Jamaica Kincaid

My Brother. New York: Noonday Press, 1997.

Studies of Jamaica Kincaid's Autobiographical Work

Boaz, Amy. Rev. of My Brother. Library Journal (October 1, 1997): 94.
Caines, Heather. Rev. of My Brother. Multicultural Review (March 1998): 80.
Jayasundera, Ymitri. "Jamaica Kincaid." In Contemporary African American Novelists: A Bio-Bibliographical Critical Sourcebook. Ed. Emmanuel S. Nelson. Westport, CT: Greenwood Press, 1999. 260–66.
McDowell, Deborah E. "Darkness Visible." Rev. of My Brother. Women's Review of Books (January 1998): 1, 3–4.
Quindlen, Anna. "The Past Is Another Country." Rev. of My Brother. New York Times Book Review (October 19, 1997): 7.
Rice, Anne P. "Burning Connections: Maternal Betrayal in Jamaica Kincaid's My Brother." Autobiography Studies 14.1 (1999): 23–37.
Seaman, Donna. Rev. of My Brother. Booklist (September 1, 1997): 5.
Simmons, Diane. "Jamaica Kincaid." In Dictionary of Literary Biography. Vol. 227: American Novelists since World War II, Sixth Series. Ed. James R. Giles. Detroit: Gale Group, 2000. 23 pages. May 9, 2001. < http://www.galenet.com >.
Skow, John. Rev. of My Brother. Time (November 10, 1997): 107.
Wachman, Gay. Rev. of My Brother. Nation 265 (1997): 43.

JARENA LEE
(1783–?)

Maxine Sample

BIOGRAPHY

Born on February 11, 1783, in Cape May, New Jersey, into a family of free but poor blacks, Jarena Lee was an evangelist who traveled throughout the Middle Atlantic States spreading the Christian gospel. Lee was sent at the age of seven to live as a servant with a white family. Her autobiography recounts few details of her youth aside from her search for a church with which she could feel spiritually connected. Lee would later find that connection in the African Methodist Episcopal Church in Philadelphia. Once called to preach the gospel, Lee appealed to Rev. Richard Allen, the head minister, only to be told that women had no such place in the pulpit. Like other women, she was directed to the gender-appropriate activities of exhortation and prayer meetings. In 1811 she married Joseph Lee, pastor of a church in nearby Snow Hill. Reverend Lee's death after six years of marriage left her alone with two young children. Two years later, she appealed to Allen and received from him permission to hold prayer meetings in her "own hired house." One significant event Lee recounts in her autobiography is the time when she sprang to her feet after a male preacher in the church faltered and preached her own sermon on the same text. Expecting to be expelled from the church for such indecorous behavior, she instead found her talents acknowledged by Allen and others who recognized the seriousness of her calling.

From that point Lee continued to hold meetings at the homes of friends, relatives, and followers as well as at public venues. She traveled throughout the Northeast, sometimes on foot, delivering sermons and recording her travels in detail. For example, in her autobiography she records having traveled in one year 2,325 miles and preached 178 sermons. Lee supported the abolitionist movement,

attending the American Anti-Slavery Society Convention in New York. However, as a woman evangelist, Lee's most engaging challenge was the gender barriers that denied women equal access to the pulpit.

Lee financed the publication of the first edition of her religious journal in
1836. *The Life and Religious Experience of Jarena Lee, a Coloured Lady* would become the first published prose narrative by a black woman in America. An expanded edition was published in 1849 despite the African Methodist Episcopal
Church's book committee's rejection of the manuscript. Although Lee writes in
its final pages that she was "now something more than fifty years of age," she was
closer to sixty-six years old and still keeping a vigorous itinerary. Little is known
about Lee's life after the publication of her expanded autobiography.

AUTOBIOGRAPHICAL WORK AND THEMES

The most apparent theme in Lee's autobiography is the journey from sin to
salvation, the spiritual rebirth that accompanies sanctification. This quest motif,
symbolizing "multiple layers of spiritual evolution," is common to antebellum
black autobiography (Andrews, *To Tell a Free Story* 7). However, imbedded in
this and other black women's spiritual autobiographies are the issues of race and
gender oppression. Lee's narrative explores the theme of lack of women's self-
determination and agency. Joycelyn Moody's *Sentimental Confessions* argues that
these texts contain submerged subplots that "express a feminist resistance to racial
and religious oppression and to patriarchal obstructions to their work as sanctified
women" (125). Readers may also see in Lee's journal both spiritual autobiography
and travelogue in that her narrative not only shares her spiritual and visionary
experience in an attempt to exhort readers to conversion but also focuses on her
movement as an itinerant Methodist preacher. In fact, Katherine Clay Bassard
suggests in *Spiritual Interrogations* that through the emphasis on her physical
movement from place to place, Lee "is signaling her ownership of her body in
representing herself as an itinerant black and female subject" (92).

Typical of American spiritual autobiography, *The Life and Religious Experience*
follows the journey of the autobiographer as a wretched sinner who, amidst temptation and doubt, achieves sanctification. Lee's conversion came at the age of
twenty-one after being spiritually moved by a sermon by Reverend Richard Allen.
Her calling to preach about four or five years later expressed itself through a series
of dreams and visions, one of which included "the form and figure of a pulpit,
with a Bible lying thereon" and a dream in which she "took a text and preached"
(10). Lacking much formal education, Lee asserted her right to preach based on
spiritual inspiration and the belief in the possibility of attaining a perfect sin-
free life — sanctification or holiness. *The Life and Religious Experience* presents an
argument in defense of women's right to the pulpit, couching the argument in
scriptural terms. When her application to preach was rejected, Lee defended her
calling by asking, "If the man may preach, because the Savior died for him, why
not the woman? seeing he died for her also. Is he not a whole Savior, instead of

a half one? as those who hold it wrong for a woman to preach, would seem to make it appear" (11). She cites the case of Mary, who preached the resurrection of Jesus.

Lee's career as an itinerant preacher commenced after the death of her husband. Her travels took her throughout the Middle Atlantic States, to Canada, west to Ohio, and south to slaveholding counties of Maryland. During her travels she preached in private and public venues to racially and gender-mixed audiences of varied denominations. One of her travels even resulted in the reunion with a sister whom she had not seen in thirty-three years. The detailed chronicle of her travels is interspersed with narratives of souls saved or lost, accounts of challenges to her authority to preach, and bouts of illness and recovery.

The theme of suffering and the sentimental trope of the sick black woman's body are used by Lee to challenge religious skeptics and encourage Christian readers as they face death. Moody notes that Lee's use of the body involves an " 'incarnational theology' that inscribes a connection between 'the Word' and the flesh; readers therefore see a connection between physical well-being and spiritual health" (66). The "dis-eased" body depicted in the text reflects the body's spiritual condition; Moody explains, "Lee transforms her genuinely suffering self into the trope of the sick woman and exploits this trope in the representation of herself as an exemplary Christian" (67). Lee narrates numerous incidents throughout the text where physical maladies are caused by spiritual unrest, challenges to ministry, and her own sense of betrayal of her mission. As she emerges from these episodes even stronger spiritually, the text suggests that her "personal strength is a metaphor for collective Christian triumph over sin and flesh" (Moody 69).

Reoccurring passages of gender resistance include one account of a minister at a "colored meetinghouse" who "could not reconcile his mind to a woman preacher" and refused even to shake hands with her (24). Lee writes that in 1822, upon returning to Philadelphia, opposition was so strong that she considered withdrawing from the Methodist Church. In other cases she had to appeal to the Methodist Conference to register complaints against challenges to her authority to stand in the pulpit and preach. Though gender resistance was constant, Lee still was able to get support from several male clergy. One key supporter of Lee was Bishop Richard Allen, who helped her get appointments to preach in other AME (African Methodist Episcopal) churches in Philadelphia and raised her son for two and a half years during Lee's travels.

Lee closes her autobiography with a sense of accomplishment: "I have been instrumental in the hands of God of gaining many hundreds of dollars for the connexion [sic], by raising societies where there never had been any, since which time they have grown to such a mass as to build large churches, and that in different places" (88). Reportedly between its first appearance in 1836 and its second publication in 1849, about 3,000 copies of Lee's autobiography were in print.

CRITICAL RECEPTION

The appearance of Lee's autobiography as part of the Schomburg Library's Nineteenth-Century Black Women Writers series spawned tremendous scholarly activity about this marginalized writer and her work. Reproductions of the original texts (where possible), the series documents black women writers' pioneering roles in the African American literary tradition. Historical approaches to Lee's autobiography credit Lee as a literary foremother of later African American women's texts; thematic approaches have considered Lee's treatment of gender and race issues. Intertextuality, genre characteristics, and rhetorical strategies have been the subject of critical attention as well.

In her introduction to *Spiritual Narratives*, which includes the complete text of Lee's expanded autobiography, Susan Houchins comments on the orality of these texts, asserting that the spiritual autobiographies of these women are written extensions of their sermons, testimonies, and exhortations (xlii). Katherine Clay Bassard's *Spiritual Interrogations* pursues as well the nexus between the written text and performance, privileging the 1849 edition of Lee's autobiography (rather than the shorter earlier edition) as the ideal text for understanding the process of Lee's writing as religious ritual (89). Lee's autobiography functions as a preacherly text grounded in such African American religious oral cultural forms as preaching, singing, spirituals, shouting, and testifying, representing what Bassard calls a "narrative recontextualized as performance" (98).

In *Sisters of the Spirit: Three Black Women's Autobiographies of the Nineteenth Century*, William Andrews identifies Lee's autobiography as a pioneering text launching black women's autobiography in America and providing some of the earliest documentation of women's participation in organized religious life in the United States (2). Andrews adds that Lee's autobiography, like those of her contemporary evangelists Zilpha Elaw* and Nancy Prince,* "ground the tradition of Afro-American women's autobiography in feminist ideals sanctioned by evangelical Christianity's radical spiritual individualism" (3). In his *To Tell a Free Story: The First Century of Afro-American Autobiography, 1760–1865*, Andrews examines Lee in the tradition of black spiritual autobiography of the early nineteenth century. He contends that in their appropriation of scriptural texts to reveal the emergence of a new, empowered self, spiritual autobiographies transcend familiar narratives of conversion and become "preacherly texts" (64). He adds that Lee's autobiography claims "a spiritual essence that abolishes the privileging power of male over female" (70) and asserts a biblical right to be called preacher.

In *Written by Herself* Foster discusses Lee in the context of religious revivals during the Second Great Awakening and the social reform movements that subsequently emerged, noting the intersection of African American and Anglo-American women's activities and their texts. Foster argues that these texts "defied the social convention that women should not discuss theology and politics," responding instead to a higher authority and a ministry unrestricted to sex or gender (76). Yet Foster observes that although Lee's autobiography reflects the

characteristic form of Puritan and Quaker conversion narratives, Lee early identifies herself as an independent woman, "a pioneer breaking into the community
and developing a sense of selfhood" ("Auction Block" 127) in contrast to traditional female roles of the time.

Joycelyn Moody's *Sentimental Confessions: Spiritual Narratives of Nineteenth-
Century African American Women* is another genre study. However, Moody focuses on the hybridity of Lee's autobiography, exploring how the text revises the
early American spiritual autobiography and appropriates sentimentalism and
other literary conventions in refashioning black women's experiences, both sacred and secular (53). Moody identifies in Lee's autobiography the rhetorical
strategies of blending Christian Protestantism and sentimental tropes, particularly chattel slavery, the figure of the sick (black) woman's body, and the dying
or dead sinner (53). What makes these texts hybrid is the manner in which Lee
blends evangelism and theology with the mundane details of her travels as an
itinerant minister to create a text that speaks specifically to the experiences of
African American women evangelists. Personal religious experience showing the
journey toward sanctification is complemented by attention to issues of race,
gender, and nation. In this way the text departs from the genre of spiritual autobiography to assert a collective rather than individual identity. Moody also
acknowledges Lee's interdenominationalism, noting that Lee's attention to other
faiths and religious experiences of other people of color—in some cases Native
Americans—contributes to what Moody calls an "inclusive theology" (54).

Katherine Clay Bassard's *Spiritual Interrogations* points out that in recording
and publishing her journal, Lee follows a tradition urged on by Methodist founder
John Wesley, who encouraged the spiritual journal as a method of self-
examination. However, Bassard sees *The Life and Religious Experience* as a rein-
vention of the Anglo-Christian conversion narrative through Lee's search for a
culturally inscribed religious community.

BIBLIOGRAPHY

Autobiographical Work by Jarena Lee

The Life and Religious Experience of Jarena Lee, a Coloured Lady. Philadelphia: Privately
    Published, 1836. Rpt. in *Spiritual Narratives.* The Schomburg Library of
    Nineteenth-Century Black Women Writers. Ed. Susan Houchins. New York: Ox-
    ford University Press, 1988.

Studies of Jarena Lee's Autobiographical Work

Andrews, William, ed. *Sisters of the Spirit: Three Black Women's Autobiographies of the
    Nineteenth Century.* Bloomington: Indiana University Press, 1986.
———. *To Tell a Free Story: The First Century of Afro-American Autobiography, 1760–
    1865.* Urbana: University of Illinois Press, 1986.

Bassard, Katherine Clay. *Spiritual Interrogations: Culture, Gender, and Community in Early African American Women's Writing.* Princeton, NJ: Princeton University Press, 1999.

Foster, Francis Smith. "Neither Auction Block Nor Pedestal: 'The Life and Religious Experience of Jarena Lee, A Coloured Lady.'" In *The Female Autography.* Ed. Donna C. Stanton. 1984. Chicago: University of Chicago Press, 1987. 126–30.

———. *Written by Herself: Literary Production by African American Women, 1746–1892.* Bloomington: Indiana University Press, 1993.

Hardesty, Nancy, Lucille Sider Dayton, and Donald W. Dayton. "Women in the Holiness Movement: Feminism in the Evangelical Tradition." In *Women of Spirit.* Ed. Rosemary Reuther and Eleanor McLaughlin. New York: Simon and Schuster, 1979. 226–54.

Humez, Jean M. "'My Spirit Eye': Some Functions of Spiritual and Visionary Experience in the Lives of Five Black Women Preachers, 1810–1880." In *Women and the Structure of Society: Selected Research from the Fifth Berkshire Conference on the History of Women.* Ed. Barbara J. Harris and JoAnn K. McNamara. Durham, NC: Duke University Press, 1984. 129–43.

Moody, Joycelyn. *Sentimental Confessions: Spiritual Narratives of Nineteenth-Century African American Women.* Athens: University of Georgia Press, 2001.

AUDRE GERALDINE LORDE
(1934-1992)

Chandra Tyler Mountain

BIOGRAPHY

"I'd started as a coward, inarticulate, very shy" (Stief 32). Audre Lorde used these words in an interview with William Stief to describe her political debut. Although she is speaking of a very young Audre, it is still hard to believe that the warrior poet was once inarticulate or shy.

Lorde began her life as Audrey Geraldine Lorde and ended it as Gamba Adisa. Born in New York City to a Grenadan mother, Linda Belmar Lorde, and a Barbadian father, Frederic Byron Lorde, Lorde dropped the "y" from her name at four years of age in a subtle act of defiance that would foreshadow her acts of resistance and change to come later.

Lorde described herself as a lesbian-activist-warrior-poet-mother-cancer survivor. Her sense of "difference" and of obligation to her fellow human beings arises from not simply these various identities but from being "outcast" early in life. Lorde felt a sense of alienation within her family—her mother and father were a secretive West Indian pair who, while they could not afford to return to Grenada as they had planned when they first came to the United States, sought to shield their three daughters from the trauma of American racism; her sisters, older than her, exchanged stories and secrets that they felt the much younger sister could not fully appreciate.

Lorde started school ahead of others in her age group (having learned to read and write at four), was branded a discipline problem, and placed in a strict Catholic school by her mother. She developed into a brooding, sensitive teenager and formed alliances with other young women who, like her, were "branded" or cast out and reveled in this reality. She often recited poetry that she had memorized as a way of expressing her feelings, and when the learned poetry failed to express her feelings, she began to write her own. In fact, Lorde wrote her first poems during this period of outcast, in seventh and eighth grade, though she admits to always having written. Lorde spent much of her adolescence working through fundamental identity issues and questions of sexuality and purpose.

After completing her high school education at Hunter High School, Lorde moved out of her parents' home and began to support herself through a number of jobs—even working at a private hospital and a factory in Connecticut. While in Connecticut she had her first lesbian affair. After leaving there, she lived in and attended college in Mexico for one year. Returning to the United States, Lorde completed her Bachelor of Science degree at Hunter College in 1959. Lorde then pursued a master of library science degree at Columbia University and supported herself through various jobs—including the New York Public Library. Lorde completed her M.L.S. in 1961, worked as a librarian at Mount Vernon Public Library, and married attorney Edward Ashley Rollins; they later divorced in 1970 after having two children, Elizabeth and Johnathan. In 1966, Lorde became head librarian at Town School Library in New York where she remained until 1968.

Lorde experienced a number of turning points in her young life. The first occurred during her year in Mexico. It is in Mexico where her budding political and sexual awareness were affirmed, and she claimed two of her identities—poet and lesbian. The second turning point occurred in 1968 when she received a National Endowment for the Arts grant and became poet-in-residence at Tougaloo College, a historically black college in Tougaloo, Mississippi, where she met Frances Louise Clayton, who later became her partner of nineteen years. Her six-week tenure at Tougaloo gave her a greater appreciation for teaching and was followed by the publication of several books of poetry—*The First Cities* (1968), *Cables to Rage* (1970), *From a Land Where Other People Live* (1973), and *New York Head Shop and Museum* (1974). The publication of *Coal* (1976) and *The Black Unicorn* (1978) by W.W. Norton, a major publisher, introduced Lorde to a wider audience. These works were followed by publication of Lorde's first nonfiction works, *The Cancer Journals* (1980) and *Zami: A New Spelling of My Name*, published the same year as *Chosen Poems: Old and New* (1982). Ms. published Lorde's first lesbian poem in 1971.

Lorde's first bout of cancer occurred in 1978, breast cancer, a second bout, liver cancer, in 1984, and then a third with ovarian cancer in 1987. Even though struggling with her health, Lorde traveled extensively in the 1970s and 1980s to Africa, the Caribbean, Europe, and Russia, breaking silences and spreading her message of change in the treatment of women everywhere. She formed coalitions between Afro-German and Afro-Dutch women, founded a sisterhood in South Africa, established the St. Croix Women's Coalition, and began Women of Color Press. After discovering the ovarian cancer, she responded to an inward tug and moved to St. Croix, one of the U.S. Virgin Islands. She was named State Poet of New York for 1991–1993. Since her death in 1992, her words have been a guide and her life a standard for warriors fighting to change the status quo that gives privilege to those who fit into a constructed model of "the norm."

Lorde lived as an outsider, but this was not a precarious position that she simply accepted because it was assigned to her. The margins for her were a domain from which she could strategically propagate change. In a conversation with James Baldwin,* Lorde unapologetically maintains that she does not believe in the American Dream because she knew from a very young age as a black female that she was "out—*out*—by any construct wherever power lay" (*Essence* 73). Even though the dream was not hers, Lorde learned to use this "out"side position as a position of strength, claiming that from the outside you can see "both directions at once" (Stief 33). Her various identities suggest her outsider state, but Lorde insists that you can be all of these divergent things at once without conflict.

AUTOBIOGRAPHICAL WORKS AND THEMES

While most of Lorde's texts draw from her own lived experiences, her two autobiographical texts are *The Cancer Journals* and *Zami: A New Spelling of My Name*. Labeled an "autopathography," *The Cancer Journals*, first published by Spinsters Ink in 1980, chronicles the psychological, emotional and physical processes of Lorde's battle with breast cancer and mastectomy from 1977 to 1979, from a lesbian feminist perspective. The text is divided into three sections: "The Transformation of Silence into Language and Action," "Breast Cancer: A Black Lesbian Feminist Experience," and "Breast Cancer: Power and Prosthesis." The first section, originally given as a speech at the Lesbian and Literature Panel of the Modern Language Association, December 28, 1977, and written after a biopsy that reveals a benign tumor, examines the fears of exposure, visibility, and criticism that keep women entrenched in a silence that robs them of each other and themselves. Faced with her own mortality and "death . . . the final silence" (18), Lorde determines to speak all the words yet unspoken and challenges women to break through the silence and claim the visibility that speaking brings. She reminds, "Where the words of women are crying to be heard, we must each of us recognize our responsibility to seek those words out, to read them and share them and examine them in their pertinence to our lives" (21). The second section, like the first, originally appeared in *Sinister Wisdom*. Lorde speaks of her experience with what is now a malignant tumor and finds herself at a loss for role models, those who are black *and* lesbian *and* feminist with breast cancer. She speaks of her mastectomy and refusal to wear a prosthesis, emphasizing the psychical healing found in the network of womanfriends that keep her and her family whole, as she creates and becomes a black feminist lesbian cancer survivor model. In the last essay of the journals, Lorde uses her cancer and responses to her refusal to wear prosthesis as a metaphor for America's fixation with standards of beauty and definitions of "womanliness." She comments on the lack of sensitivity to the needs of women who are surviving cancer and on the treatment of women in society as ornamentation. She reviews various responses to her refusal that hon-

ored how she appeared physically over how she felt emotionally and psychologically. Lorde argues in this section that women with breast cancer are warriors
and the missing breast(s) is a casualty of war waged against American standards
of beauty. She asserts that she wished to affirm the difference rather than "cover
it up"; it is the covering up that makes women survivors absent to each other,
making cancer a private, personal matter, although the numbers of women afflicted with breast cancer clearly indicate that breast cancer is not a secret. She
decries the dollars spent on breast reconstruction research rather than cancer
prevention. In *A Burst of Light*, the sequel to *The Cancer Journals*, Lorde conveys
that the cancer has spread to her liver, and she shares her decision to treat the
cancer through homeopathic methods and meditation as opposed to surgery. Like
The Cancer Journals, this text becomes a weapon for fighting against injustice and
oppression.

The prequel to *The Cancer Journals*, Lorde describes *Zami* as a "biomythography," which suggests that this is a fictionalized account of her life, combining
both biography and myth. However, this is not myth in the sense that it is untrue
but in the sense that it points to an origin and explains Lorde's raison d'être.
Certainly, *Zami* takes us to the beginning of Lorde's life; it deals with only the
first nineteen or twenty years of her life and thus takes us to the beginning of
her awareness and involvement as a poet, a lesbian, and an activist. *Zami* is a
"Carriacou name for women who work together as friends and lovers" (*Zami* 255),
and Lorde's memoir of her youth pays tribute to the women, friends and lovers
included, who helped shape her identity as a black woman lesbian poet.

In the pages preceding the first section of the book, Lorde poses three questions: "1) To whom do I owe the power behind my voice, what strength I have
become, yeasting up like sudden blood under bruised skin's blister? 2) To whom
do I owe the symbols of my survival? 3) To whom do I owe the woman I have
become?" *Zami* is the story that evolves from the responses to these questions.
The autobiographical novel illuminates Audre's psychical and political development and her transformation from chubby, nearly legally blind black girl to a
woman with a pen and a purpose. It is divided into four sections: "Prologue,"
"How I Became a Poet," "The Last of My Childhood Nightmares," and the
"Epilogue."

The "Prologue," as she aptly names this section, represents the first years of a
child's life when the whole world to the child is a mixture of colors, words, and
sounds—and mother. So *Zami* begins as the story of a girl, stumbling through
her early childhood to get a hold of the big blurry world around her, especially
her mother. In this introductory section, Lorde pays homage to the women who
influenced her early development, especially those women of her bloodline, the
West Indian matrilineal relations that bond her to the earth and to her mother.
She primarily focuses on her mother and delineates her relationship to her
mother's homeland as well as her early connection to her mother, and her re-
membrances of her mother as a powerful woman, different from other women
she knew because she shared equal footing in her household and in her marriage,

strong in her poise and her physical appearance. The relationship between mother and child seems difficult and strained, but from child's perspective, the mother's strength is mysterious and overwhelming, a little too much for the child who wants free reign and freedom from restraint. In this section she also tells the story of her first year in school, which is also the story of her mother.

In the section, "How I Became a Poet," Lorde focuses on her years of discovery—the rhythms and cadences of the West Indian home, the colorful stories of her youth, the words that were always there, the euphemisms out of the mouths of adults that registered as something else to children, her mother's secret poetry. She speaks of the beginnings of her womanhood, of the early experiences that gave her the words, the poetry—the troubled adolescence, the death of her teenage best friend Gennie, the illegal abortion, the odd jobs here and there, her first lesbian experience with Ginger in Stamford, where she worked at a factory, her year in Mexico with Eudora her mentor, college, and the gay-girl scene of 1950s Greenwich Village. In this section, Lorde outlines the influences of other women, and though she fully embraces the lesbian world, her lovers and most of her friends are white—a reality that often leaves a racial void and yearning for sameness on that level at least.

Although Lorde is by now a young woman, she entitles the final section "The Last of My Childhood Nightmares," giving us the sense that with its conclusion she is now a grown woman, facing the world as a woman and not a child, and she is now capable of letting go of a haunting past. This section details the awful breakup with her lover Muriel, which leads to her self-mutilation, and her recovery. She shares with readers her lengthy rendezvous with Kitty/Afrekete, a black lesbian who marks the crowning act of her identification as a *black* lesbian. The two women discuss their experiences as black women who are lesbians and decry the politics that marginalize black women and inhibit women loving women.

Lorde closes *Zami* with a litany to the women, physical as well as spiritual, mythical, and natural, who have impacted her life, who have helped her become and have given her "substance: Ma-Liz, DeLois, Louise Briscoe, Aunt Anni, Linda, and Genevieve; MawuLisa, thunder, sky, sun, the great mother of us all; and Afrekete, her youngest daughter, the mischievous linguist, trickster, best-beloved, whom we must all become" (255).

In the journals as well as the biomythography, Lorde underlines themes that are germane to all of her writing—love, desire, displacement, alienation, racial and sexual oppression, survival, fear, silence, powerlessness, mother-daughter relationships, lesbianism. These themes are prevalent in the two texts—as well as Lorde's poetry and essays—because they are responses to, conversations with, and a working out of the separate selves that are one; they are very much a part of Lorde's politics of change.

CRITICAL RECEPTION

Responses to Lorde's texts have been animated and exciting. Although both *Zami* and *The Cancer Journals* were published nearly twenty years ago, discussion has not quelled. Lorde's texts have been essential in defining lesbian poetics, redirecting and revisioning feminist politics and theory, and complementing the body of African American culture and literature. Because of the open and unapologetic lesbianism in Lorde's texts, the African American community has been largely silent about Lorde's work. Lorde expected no more. In an interview with Claudia Tate, she muses, "Black writers of whatever quality, who step outside the pale of what black writers are supposed to write about, or who black writers are supposed to be, are condemned to silences in black literary circles that are as total and as destructive as any imposed by racism" (101). Nevertheless, there has been some criticism generated within African American literary circles. Most of the reactions to Lorde's texts have typically linked Lorde with other African American writers and have attempted to forge a dialogue on sexism and sexuality. Townsand Price-Spratlen's "Negotiating Legacies: Audre Lorde, W.E.B. Du Bois, Marlon Riggs, and Me," uses three "ancestor texts"—*The Cancer Journals*, *The Souls of Black Folks*, and *Tongues Untied*—to define his own praxis as a "queer scholar of African descent" (216). Lorde, like the other two, "challenged the perception of group affiliation by investigating the intersection of multiple selves within themselves" (217). In reading *The Cancer Journals*, Price-Spratlen recognizes the "reciprocity of power between author/artist and reader/observer—the power Lorde gained from documenting her post-mastectomy realization, the power he gained from reading her words, and the power her legacy gained from having inspired him" to challenge the "assumption of a disjuncture between his efforts" (218).

Other African American critics, such as Chinosole and Barbara Smith, examine Lorde's texts alongside other African American women's texts, linking her more specifically to the African American literary tradition. Barbara Smith's "Black Lesbians in Fiction of the 1980's," pointing out the homophobic exclusion and silencing of the lesbian writer and character, examines *Zami* alongside Gloria Naylor's *Women of Brewster Place* and Alice Walker's* *The Color Purple*, positing that Lorde, unlike the other two, has an overt consciousness about her lesbianism and does not define lesbianism as a problem in and of itself. "Lorde," she writes, "assumes that her Lesbianism, like her Blackness, is a given, a fact of life which she has neither to justify nor explain" (238). As such, *Zami* is clearly written for the lesbian reader but is still accessible to and applicable to the nonblack, non-lesbian reader. Smith declares, "Works like *Zami* which are based in the experiences . . . outside the mainstream provide vitally different perspectives on human experience and may even reveal new ways of thinking about supposedly settled questions" (239). In "Audre Lorde and Matrilineal Diaspora: Moving History Beyond Nightmare into Structures for the Future," Chinosole places Lorde in the same historical continuum as the runaway slave, a recent by-product of the Atlantic slave trade. She points out that Lorde characterizes herself as a "kind of maroon, a sister outsider, and a journeywoman" (381), thus linking her writing with the African American slave narrative and other narratives of movement and transition.

Other readings of Lorde's texts focus on the concepts of myth and revision in the texts. Yvonne Klein, comparing lesbian literature of the 1970s with that of the 1980s, asserts that "rather than projecting forward a vision of a new community of living Amazons, [lesbian novels of formation] reach back to reinvent a mythic history of female power out of the shards and scraps of their childhood and their culture" (331). Ann Louise Keating in "Myth Smashers, Myth Makers: (Re) Visionary Techniques in the Works of Paula Gunn Allen, Gloria Anzaldua, and Audre Lorde" argues that Lorde's revisionary mythmaking enables her to "externalize the inside ideas" (90), giving black women new ways to perceive themselves and act and enabling Lorde to speak both for herself and for other black women. Furthering the theme set forth by Keating, Kara Provost in "Becoming Afrekete: The Trickster in the Work of Audre Lorde" parallels Lorde's and Henry Louis Gates's* use of the trickster Eshu Elegba(ra) as a multivocal prankster, transmitter, and translator of languages between the gods. She points out that Lorde extends the analysis of the trickster by invoking Afrekete, "the [Afro-Caribbean] female manifestation of the trickster as supplement to the phallic Eshu" (46), emphasizing eroticism, fluidity, and unpredictability of gender and sexuality. Lorde's use of the trickster demonstrates once again that the margins can be a locus of power.

There are those critics who closely examine definitions of home as the locus of self-definition and power and as an integral part of home, the mother-daughter relationship. Chinosole does this in the essay cited early. So does Jennifer Gillan. She, using the mother-daughter bond temporarily forged the day Lorde gets her period, argues that *Zami* creates an empowering vision of home that lessens the alienation of marginality and exile. Because of her distance from "home"—her mother's Grenada—Lorde formulates a portable concept of home as everywhere. Gillan argues that for Lorde home is everywhere and nowhere—she is a journeywoman and *Zami* becomes a chronicle of intersecting meeting points and breaking points.

Continuing the theme of home in *Zami*, Cheryl Kader in "This Very House of Difference" argues that Lorde, through revealing the fluidity of lesbian identity and community, defines the lesbian body in her text as a paradigm for a new kind of writing, one that inhabits the very house of difference, a difference that is further explained in Barbara DiBernard's reading of *Zami* as the coming of age of the artist as a lesbian woman as opposed to the coming of age of a boy or a man. Regenia Gagnier in her psychoanalytic feminist reading of *Zami*, "Feminist Autobiography of the 1980's," discloses, "In *Zami* we see the historical process of those multiple identifications that would culminate in a feminist post-modern theory of the subject and its corresponding political agenda: coalition or unity by common goals rather than essence or sameness" (140).

Perhaps the most titillating commentary on Lorde's life and texts can be found in the documentary film of her life, *A Litany for Survival*. Filmmaker Ada Gay Griffin and codirector Michelle Parkerson capture the facets and textures of Lorde's life, personality, and contributions to various individuals as well as the worlds of activism, lesbianism, feminism, and literary study.

BIBLIOGRAPHY

Autobiographical Works by Audre Geraldine Lorde

The Cancer Journals. San Francisco: Spinsters/Aunt Lute, 1980.
Zami: A New Spelling of My Name. Freedom, CA: Crossing Press, 1982.
A Burst of Light. New York: Firebrand, 1988.

Studies of Audre Geraldine Lorde's Autobiographical Works

"Audre Lorde." In *Black Literature Criticism*. Vol. 2. Ed. James P. Draper. Detroit: Gale Research, 1992. 1275–89.
Carlston, Erin. "*Zami* and the Politics of Plural Identity." In *Sexual Practice, Textual Theory: Lesbian Cultural Criticism*. Ed. Susan J. Wolfe and Julia Penelope. Cambridge: Blackwell, 1993. 237–50.
Carr, Brenda. "'A Woman Speaks . . . I Am Woman and Not White': Politics of Voice, Tactical Essentialism, and Cultural Intervention in Audre Lorde's Activist Poetics and Practice." *College Literature* 20.2 (June 1993): 133–54.
Chinosole. "Audre Lorde and Matrilineal Diaspora: 'Moving History Beyond Nightmare into Structures for the Future.'" In *Wild Women in the Whirlwind: Afra-American Culture and the Contemporary Literary Renaissance*. Ed. Joanne M. Braxton and Andrée Nicola McLaughlin. New Brunswick, NJ: Rutgers University Press, 1990. 379–94.
Christian, Barbara. "No More Buried Lives: The Theme of Lesbianism in Audre Lorde's *Zami*, Gloria Naylor's *Women of Brewster Place*, Ntozake Shange's *Sassafras, Cypress and Indigo*, and Alice Walker's *The Color Purple*." In *Black Feminist Criticism: Perspectives on Black Women Writers*. Ed. Barbara Christian. New York: Pergamon Press, 1985. 187–203.
"Conversation Between James Baldwin and Audre Lorde." *Essence* (December 1984): 72–4.
Daly, Kathleen. "Class Race Gender: Sloganeering in Search of Meaning." *Social Justice* 20.1–2 (Spring–Summer 1993): 56–72.
Daniell, Rosemary. "The Poet Who Found Her Way." *New York Times*, December 19, 1982, late ed., sec. 7, 12.
DiBernard, Barbara. "*Zami*: A Portrait of the Artist as a Black Lesbian." *Kenyon Review* 13.4 (Fall 1991): 195–213.
Finney, Nikki. "Well Water: On Audre Lorde's *The Cancer Journals*." *Social Policy* 20.3 (Winter 1990): 66–68.
Gagnier, Regenia. "Feminist Autobiography in the 1980's." *Feminist Studies* 17.1 (Spring 1991): 135–45.

Gillan, Jennifer. "Relocating Home and Identity in *Zami: A New Spelling of My Name*." In *Homemaking: Women Writers and the Politics and Poetics of Home*. Ed. Catherine Wiley and Fiona R. Barnes. New York: Garland, 1996. 207–19.

Hammond, Karla. "An Interview with Audrey Lorde." *American Poetry Review* 9.2 (March–April 1980): 18–21.

———. "Audre Lorde: Interview." *Denver Quarterly* 16.1 (Spring 1981): 10–27.

Homans, Margaret. "Audre Lorde." In *Black Women in America*. Vol. 1. Ed. Darlene Clark Hine, Elsa Barkley Brown, and Rosalyn Terborg-Penn. Bloomington: Indiana University Press, 1993. 731–34.

Kader, Cheryl. " 'The Very House of Difference': *Zami*, Audre Lorde's Lesbian-Centered Text." In *Critical Essays: Gay and Lesbian Writers of Color*. Ed. Emmanuel S. Nelson. New York: Haworth Press, 1993. 181–94.

Keating, Ann Louise. "Audre Lorde." In *Contemporary African American Novelists: A Bio-Bibliographical Critical Sourcebook*. Ed. Emmanuel S. Nelson. Westport, CT: Greenwood Press, 1999. 284–88.

———. "Myth Smashers, Myth Makers: (Re) Visionary Techniques in the Works of Paula Gunn Allen, Gloria Anzaldua, and Audre Lorde." In *Critical Essays: Gay and Lesbian Writers of Color*. Ed. Emmanuel S. Nelson. New York: Haworth Press, 1993. 73–96.

King, Katie. "Audre Lorde's Lacquered Layerings: The Lesbian Bar as a Site of Literary Production." In *Lesbian Criticism: Literary and Cultural Readings*. Ed. Sally Munt. New York: Columbia University Press, 1992. 51–74.

Klein, Yvonne. "Myth and Community in Recent Lesbian Autobiographical Fiction." In *Lesbian Texts and Contexts: Radical Revisions*. Ed. Karla Jay and Joanne Glasgow. New York: New York University Press, 1990. 330–38.

Kulii, Beverly Threatt. "Audre Lorde." In *The Oxford Companion to African American Literature*. Ed. Williams Andrews, Frances Smith Foster, and Trudier Harris. New York: Oxford University Press, 1997.

Price-Spratlen, Townsand. "Negotiating Legacies: Audre Lorde, W.E.B. Du Bois, Marlon Riggs, and Me." *Harvard Education Review* 66.2 (Summer 1996): 216–31.

Provost, Kara. "Becoming Afrekete: The Trickster in the Works of Audre Lorde." *MELUS* 20.4 (Winter 1999): 45–60.

Smith, Barbara. "The Truth That Never Hurts: Black Lesbians in Fiction in the 1980's." In *Wild Women in the Whirlwind: Afra-American Culture and the Contemporary Literary Renaissance*. Ed. Joanne M. Braxton and Andrée Nicola McLaughlin. New Brunswick, NJ: Rutgers University Press, 1990. 213–45.

Stief, William. "Audre Lorde: 'I'm Angry about the Pretenses of America.' " *The Progressive* 55.1 (January 1991): 32–33.

Tate, Claudia. "Interview with Audre Lorde." In *Black Women Writers at Work*. Ed. Claudia Tate. New York: Continuum, 1983. 100–116.

Waldrep, Shelton. " 'Being Bridges': Cleaver/Baldwin/Lorde and African-American Sexism and Sexuality." In *Critical Essays: Gay and Lesbian Writers of Color*. Ed. Emmanuel S. Nelson. New York: Haworth Press, 1993. 167–83.

Wilson, Anna. "Audre Lorde and the African-American Tradition: When the Family Is Not Enough." In *Lesbian Criticism: Literary and Cultural Readings*. Ed. Sally Munt. New York: Columbia University Press, 1992. 75–94.

Zimmerman, Bonnie. *The Safe Sea of Women: Lesbian Fiction 1969–1989*. Boston: Beacon, 1990.

Film

A Litany for Survival. Dir. Ada Gay Griffin and Michelle Parkerson. Third World Newsreel, 1995.

MALCOLM X
(1925-1965)

Emmanuel S. Nelson

BIOGRAPHY

Malcolm Little, who later rechristened himself first as Malcolm X and then as El-Hajj Malik El-Shabazz, was born on May 19, 1925, in Omaha, Nebraska. His father, Earl Little, was a Baptist minister whose black nationalist philosophy was substantially influenced by the teachings of Marcus Garvey. Louise Little, Malcolm's mother, was born in Grenada, West Indies. When he was still an infant the family moved to East Lansing, Michigan; there, as in Omaha, his father's self-assertiveness and political militancy provoked white hostility. Later in his life Malcolm claimed that his father was killed by some members of the Black Legion, a racist organization related to the Ku Klux Klan. His father's body, he asserted, was placed on the railway tracks by his murderers and was crushed by a passing train. That version of Earl Little's death, however, is disputed by some of Malcolm X's biographers, but all agree that the reverend's death was a violent one.

Louise Little, soon after her husband's death, found herself increasingly unable to take care of her large family. Cheated by the insurance company that refused to compensate her for her husband's loss of life, harassed by various social workers from the state welfare agency, and overwhelmed by the burden of tending to eight children with her limited resources, she suffered a nervous breakdown. She remained in a psychiatric facility for the next twenty-five years. Her children were placed in different foster homes.

In 1941 Malcolm Little moved to Boston to live with Ella Little, his half sister. He held a variety of menial jobs before embarking on a career as a criminal, which, later in New York City, included gambling, pimping, using and selling drugs, and committing burglary. At age twenty-one he was imprisoned for armed robbery. The next six years he spent in jail proved crucial to his personal and political development. It was while in prison that he reeducated himself by using the prison library extensively, discovered the ideology of black nationalism, and formally converted to the politicized brand of Islam taught by Elijah Muhammad of the Detroit-based Nation of Islam. Upon his release from prison in 1952 Malcolm Little became Minister Malcolm X and soon emerged as a central figure in Elijah Muhammad's organization.

However, early in 1963, Malcolm X grew increasingly alienated from the Nation of Islam. Initially his estrangement was caused by internecine rivalries within the organization, but it later intensified when he discovered that Elijah Muhammad, whom he had trusted implicitly, was guilty of a variety of transgressions that included sexual misconduct.

Elijah Muhammad's betrayal shattered Malcolm X's faith in the Nation of Islam. Soon he left on a religious pilgrimage to Mecca, Saudi Arabia, to learn more about traditional Islam. The journey proved to be profoundly transformative; spiritually as well as politically he felt enlightened. To signify his newly found sense of selfhood he adopted an Arabic name: El-Hajj Malik El-Shabazz. Upon his return to the United States he broke all ties with the Nation of Islam and began to plan a new forum called the Organization of Afro-American Unity, "a non-religious, non-sectarian group organized to unite Afro-Americans for a constructive program toward attainment of human rights" (*Autobiography* 478). He began to travel internationally to establish firm personal and political ties with leaders in various countries in Africa and elsewhere. His rhetoric became less strident and his politics more flexible, but his adversaries, sensing his growing influence, began to find him increasingly more menacing. On February 21, 1965, as he began to speak before an audience at the Audubon Ballroom in Harlem, he was gunned down. Among the people who had gathered to listen to him were his wife and four young daughters. Who exactly was ultimately responsible for his death remains largely mysterious. It is unclear if his assassins, three African American men, were acting independently or as agents of the Nation of Islam. There are also some who suspect that the internal security apparatus of the U.S. government may have played a role in the violent death of El-Hajj Malik El-Shabazz, more widely known as Malcolm X.

AUTOBIOGRAPHICAL WORK AND THEMES

One of the central texts in the canon of African American lifewriting, *The Autobiography of Malcolm X*, as told to Alex Haley, was published late in 1965. The book reconstructs the life of a man who, even decades after his death, continues to provoke a myriad of emotions that range from uncritical adoration to irrational hostility. In the pages of the autobiography Malcolm X emerges as a fascinating and complex figure: immensely insightful yet at times oddly naive; often fearless but sometimes deeply vulnerable, apparently dogmatic and very sure of his beliefs yet surprisingly willing to learn, reassess, and change his views.

Like the autobiography of Angela Davis,* the life story of Malcolm X is a compelling intervention in the cultural productions of the twentieth-century United States. Malcolm X, like Davis, employs an oppositional logic to deconstruct the founding assumptions of American culture. Similar to Davis, he articulates a revolutionary consciousness, advocates militant resistance to injustice, and envisions radical social transformation.

The Autobiography of Malcolm X is the product of a collaborative effort. While Malcolm X acts as the informant, Alex Haley serves as the amanuensis: One provides the raw material; the other shapes the narrative. Gathering information from informal conversations, extended interviews, dictations, and diaries, Haley reconstructs the life of his subject. That the first-person narrative voice in the text belongs to Haley, and not to Malcolm X, does raise some troubling questions about authenticity and accuracy. Further concerns are prompted by the fact that Malcolm X died several months prior to the publication of the book and therefore did not authorize any alterations that Haley may have implemented independently. Nevertheless, one could argue that the collaboration, on the whole, probably enriched rather than diminished the text. Haley, after all, was a distinguished writer; his extensive journalistic background would have prompted him to ask probing questions and be alert to even minor details. Too, he had for the most part earned the trust of Malcolm X and therefore could tactfully elicit from him information that otherwise might have remained buried.

The Autobiography of Malcolm X presents a self in quest of wholeness. The search begins in chaos: Malcolm X's father has died a gruesome death; his mother has become mentally unstable; and the interventions of the welfare agency workers expedite the disintegration of the family. The autobiography maps the trajectory of Malcolm X's search for coherence and structure in his life that would grant him a sense of order and stability. The journey involves a series of metamorphoses, and each stage in the development is marked by a new name: Malcolm Little (during his younger days in Nebraska and Michigan); Homeboy (while he was in Boston and working as a shoeshine boy, soda fountain clerk, railway dining car attendant); Detroit Red (during his days as a hustler, pimp, numbers runner, drug dealer, and burglar in Harlem); Satan (while he was an angry and menacing prison inmate); Minister Malcolm X (from 1952 when he became a ministerial aide to Elijah Muhammad in the Nation of Islam, the letter X symbolizing the genealogical void caused by slavery); and finally, El-Hajj Malik El-Shabazz (the name he chose for himself in a healing gesture of self-naming to mark his conversion to what he believed to be the real Islam during his pilgrimage to Mecca in 1964).

This changing and evolving series of selves that the autobiography documents in detail offers an intriguing glimpse into Malcolm X's psychology. As he reveals the details of his multiple transformations, his postures remain defiant, and his rhetoric is laced with rage. He appears strikingly self-assured and projects an image of someone in command of himself and his circumstances. Underneath the veneer of such absolute self-confidence, however, lurks a deep sense of emo-

tional vulnerability. Beyond the rhetorical fireworks we see a vulnerable individual in search of a reassuring father-figure, an older, wiser man who can function
as a surrogate to the father whom he lost as a child.

For example, when Malcolm Little first arrives in Boston looking "countrified"
(47) and unfamiliar with big city life, he gravitates toward Shorty, an older and
more experienced man who offers "to school [him] to the happenings" (53).
Assuming the role of teacher and guide, he familiarizes young Malcolm with the
styles and forms of urban black life. Malcolm proves to be an eager learner. While
he is in prison, a stronger, older, and wiser inmate named Bimbi assumes the role
of a father to him. Bimbi recognizes Malcolm's exceptional intellect and advises
him to "take advantage of prison correspondence courses and the library" (178).
It is Bimbi's advice that becomes the foundation for a decisive change in Malcolm's personal and political outlook. When he gets out of prison he discovers
in Elijah Muhammad a powerful father-figure. In the presence of the leader of
the Nation of Islam, Malcolm X acts as a young son in awe of his father's immense
knowledge and authority. Even much later in Malcolm X's life, when he had
become an internationally known political figure, his emotional need for a father-
figure remains evident. During his visit to Mecca in 1964 he meets Dr. Abd-Al-
Rahman Azzam, an Arab diplomat and intellectual. The thirty-eight-year-old
Malcolm is vastly impressed by his intellect, wisdom, and experience; he writes
in his personal diary, "The elder Dr. Azzam [acted] as if he were my father. His
fatherly, scholarly speech. I *felt* like he was my father" (385). There is a certain
poignancy in this confession: Malcolm X, whose public persona is synonymous
with supreme self-confidence and emotional toughness, reveals a nearly adolescent longing for a strong father-figure who can guide him.

While the autobiography offers glimpses into Malcolm X's emotional life, it
reveals much more forcefully and elaborately his political transformations: *The
Autobiography of Malcolm X* is, in fact, one of the most significant documents in
the political history of the United States. Here he outlines the formation of his
radical subjectivity and articulates a programmatic approach to personal and
collective emancipation. During his youthful years on the streets of Boston and
Harlem, he appears not to have any coherent ideological outlook. Yet his experiences during those years are crucial to his political formation. It was during
that time he was able to observe, if not fully understand, from a subaltern perspective the various structures of oppression. He was able to see the coping mech-
anisms of the disenfranchised and to sense the depth of their alienation and
anger. However, only later when he was in prison, he gained the critical literacy
that enabled him to formulate his observations and ideas into a coherent political
philosophy. It was in prison that he became familiar with black nationalist
thought. His extensive readings in world history, philosophy, and anthropology
through the theoretical lens of black nationalism helped him fully understand
the extent to which he himself had been brainwashed by the dominant culture.
He was able to see how the educational, legal, political, and religious systems are
part of a larger apparatus that the dominant culture had established and insti-

tutionalized to validate and perpetuate its privileged position. He began to grasp how even the seemingly innocent school textbooks functioned as potent tools of ideological indoctrination.

Malcolm X's emerging political vision became considerably more sophisticated later in life when he traveled extensively in Africa and the Middle East. He was able to understand the fundamental links between racism, colonialism, and capitalist economic exploitation. His recognition of Black America as an internal colony within the United States prompted him to call for a separate homeland for African Americans. His alliances with many leaders and intellectuals of newly independent African nations allowed him to locate the predicament of African Americans in an international context and analyze the issues from a broad historical and global perspective.

Toward the end of his life, however, his politics began to assume a softer edge: His conversion to the traditional Islamic faith in 1963 tempered his militant nationalism with a utopian vision of a truly multicultural global community that he believed could be created by well-meaning people of all backgrounds. At the height of his nationalist phase, he denounced the "blond, pale-skinned, cold-blue-eyed devils" as the root of all evil on the planet. During the final year of his life, however, he conceded that white Americans were not inherently evil and incorrigibly racist beasts, but it was "the American political, economic, and social *environment* that automatically nourishe[d] a racist psychology" in them. The dramatic nature of his personal and political reassessment is evident in his declaration:

Since I learned the *truth* in Mecca, my dearest friends have come to include *all* kinds—some are Christians, Jews, Buddhists, Hindus, agnostics, and even atheists! I have friends who are called Capitalists, Socialists, and Communists! Some of my friends are moderates, conservatives, extremists—some are even Uncle Toms! My friends today are black, brown, red, yellow, and *white*! (432)

Such a changed political attitude, however, could not have occurred had it not been for the profound spiritual transformation that Malcolm X underwent near the end of his short life. In fact, his autobiography is as much a religious testimony as it is a political document. It is a classic conversion narrative in the tradition of spiritual autobiographies. It is a chronicle of his moral regeneration. As a child he was a member of a strict Baptist family. During his adolescent years, however, religion was conspicuously absent from his life. While Malcolm X was in prison his brother Reginald visited him and introduced him to the theopolitical vision of the Honorable Elijah Muhammad of the Nation of Islam. That vision captured Malcolm X's imagination; its unapologetic Afrocentricity appealed to his nationalist consciousness. At the heart of the theopolitical worldview advocated by the nation of Islam is the story that explains how the various "races" of human beings—black, brown, red, yellow, and white—came into existence. It is a poetic myth that privileges black people and declares them superior to all others. Clearly formulated as an enabling countermyth to challenge the entrenched myth of white superiority, its calculated political intent is to reha- bilitate the colonized minds of black people and empower them to reimagine the universe from an Afrocentric perspective. Its appeal is seductive. Malcolm X became an ardent member of the Nation of Islam and, after his release from prison, its most eloquent and charismatic spokesperson. However, nearly twelve years later, he left the organization after his devastating discovery that the Hon- orable Elijah Muhammad was quite a dishonorable character. His deep disap- pointment precipitated a profound spiritual crisis that prompted his journey to Mecca in search of the truth. His conversion to the traditional Islam while in Mecca filled the void caused by his separation from the Nation of Islam. His search for transcendence seems to have reached fruition in that moment of con- version.

Thus *The Autobiography of Malcolm X* is a map of his multiple quests and transformations. Given its many structural and thematic similarities to the an- tebellum autobiographical narratives by fugitive slaves, it can be viewed as a neoslave narrative—the story of a man who emancipates himself from mental slavery. For it is a record of his reeducation: how a colonized subject—through critical literacy, oppositional reasoning, and empowering knowledge—decolo- nizes his mind. Simultaneously the book brilliantly reveals the logic of rage in a racist society and advances an agenda for revolutionary resistance. It is a major cultural document that testifies to the mood of a segment of Black America at a particular moment in history.

However, our recognition of the enormous significance of Malcolm X's life and his impact on recent American history should not blind us to some of the troubling aspects of his life and views. His blind adoration of Elijah Muhammad for nearly twelve years, for example, borders on the bizarre. Why such a man of obviously superior intellect would surrender his will so totally to another indi- vidual is not entirely clear. Even the fact that he saw in Elijah Muhammad a strong father-figure does not adequately explain his subservience. That he would join and passionately defend the Nation of Islam—an authoritarian and cult-like organization that advocates some views that defy common sense—is not com- pletely unproblematic. His rejection of Christianity because of its culpability in slavery, segregation, and other racist practices is perfectly understandable, but his enthusiastic acceptance of Islam is not. Perhaps he was unaware that slavery was widely practiced in Africa and in the Islamic Arab world long before the Euro- peans became involved in international slave trade.

Malcolm X's astonishing naïveté becomes more evident on his first journey abroad. As a celebrity attending the *hajj*, the annual Islamic pilgrimage to Mecca, he is received with great respect and affection. The demonstrations of hospitality are overwhelming. He notices Muslims of various nationalities and ethnicities mingling freely. On the basis of these superficial impressions he arrives at the naïve conclusion that in Islamic societies there is no racism or color prejudice! When he explains to some of his fellow pilgrims how racist American society is, they seem appalled and he immediately infers, "As Muslims, they had a tender heart for all unfortunates, and very sensitive feelings for truth and justice" (389)! In moments such as these Malcolm X appears to be an innocent abroad, making romantic generalizations about exotic peoples he barely knows.

More unsettling than his naïveté in such matters is Malcolm X's regressive gender politics. While hustling and pimping on the streets of Harlem, he asserts his masculinity by abusing women. That the street culture fostered such sexism could hardly be a consolation for the women who were his victims. During his Harlem days he believes that "[a]ll women, by their nature, are fragile and weak" (108). As a minister in the Nation of Islam he asserts, "Islam has very strict laws and teachings about women, the core of them being that the true nature of man is to be strong, and the woman's true nature is to be weak . . . [and the man] needs to understand that he must control her if he expects to get her respect." He adds that his experiences with women only show that they are "tricky, deceitful, untrustworthy" (260). There is considerable evidence, however, that toward the end of his life Malcolm X abandoned many of his alarmingly crude sexist beliefs and began to emphasize the importance of women's participation in the liberation movement and the need for gender equality in society at large. The autobiography itself, regrettably, does not indicate any significant shifts in his gender politics.

CRITICAL RECEPTION

When *The Autobiography of Malcolm X* was published in 1965, most reviewers recognized in it the makings of a modern classic. Truman Nelson's statement in *Nation* sums up the general enthusiasm: "Viewed in its complete historical context, this is indeed a great book. Its dead-level honesty, its passion, its exalted purpose, even its manifold unresolved ambiguities will make it stand as a monument to the most painful of truths: that this country, this people, this Western world had practiced unspeakable cruelty against a race, an individual, who might have made its fraudulent humanism a reality" (336).

Since its publication, the autobiography has received extensive academic attention. An early article by Carol Ohmann, published in 1970, offers an intriguing comparative study of the autobiographies of Malcolm X and Benjamin Franklin. By locating Malcolm X in the Franklin tradition, Ohmann insists on the profoundly American nature of Malcolm X's self-creation. A more recent piece of scholarship by Maria Josefina Saldaña-Portillo, published in 1997, rearticulates Ohmann's idea with considerable poststructuralist theoretical sophistication. However, she not only exposes Malcolm X's "relentless deployment of the tropes of Americanness" (290) but also, from a specifically feminist perspective, critiques the masculinist construction of his very American revolutionary consciousness.

H. Porter Abbot offers a sensitive reading of the autobiography of Malcolm X as a classic text in the tradition of spiritual conversion narratives. A brilliant analysis of the crucial role of literacy in Malcolm X's intellectual and political formations is offered by Daniel Kempton. Paul John Eakin's "Malcolm X and the Limits of Autobiography" remains a classic piece of criticism. Joe Wood's collection of essays contains several outstanding assessments of Malcolm X's life and achievement. Maulana Karanga's superb article is a provocative analysis of Malcolm X's oppositional politics. Clenora Hudson-Weems and bell hooks address a long-neglected aspect of the autobiography: Malcolm X's sexism.

The best among the biographies of Malcolm X is Bruce Perry's controversial *Malcolm: The Life of a Man Who Changed America*. Although Perry's prose is less than engaging, his biography offers a detailed portrait of his subject. It serves as a useful companion text to *The Autobiography of Malcolm X*.

BIBLIOGRAPHY

Autobiographical Work by Malcolm X

The Autobiography of Malcolm X. 1965. New York: Ballantine, 1992.

Studies of Malcolm X's Autobiographical Work

Abbott, H. Porter. "Organic Form in the Autobiography of a Convert: The Example of Malcolm X." *CLA Journal* 23.2 (December 1979): 125–46.

Asante, Molefi. *Malcolm X as Cultural Hero*. Trenton, NJ: Africa World Press, 1993.

Benson, Thomas W. "Rhetoric and Autobiography: The Case of Malcolm X." *Quarterly Journal of Speech* 60.1 (1974): 1–13.

Berthoff, Warner. "Witness and Testament: Two Contemporary Classics." *New Literary History* 2 (1971): 311–27.

Breitman, George. *The Last Year of Malcolm X: The Evolution of a Revolutionary*. New York: Pathfinder Press, 1970.

Cineaste. Special Issue on Malcolm X. 19.4 (1993).

Dyson, Michael Eric. *Making Malcolm: The Myth and Meaning of Malcolm X*. New York: Oxford University Press, 1995.

Eakin, Paul John. "Malcolm X and the Limits of Autobiography." *Criticism* 18 (1976): 230–42.

Groppe, John D. "From Chaos to Cosmos: The Role of Trust in *The Autobiography of Malcolm X*." *Soundings* 66 (1983): 437–49.

Henry, Joseph. "The Public, Spiritual, and Humanistic Odyssey of Malcolm X: A Critical Bibliographical Debate." *Iowa Journal of Literary Studies* 4 (1983): 77–93.

hooks, bell. "Malcolm X: The Longed for Feminist Manhood." In *Essays in Context*. Ed. Sandra Trapp. New York: Oxford University Press, 2001.

Hudson-Weems, Clenora. "From Malcolm Little to El Hajj Malik El Shabazz: Malcolm's Evolving Attitude toward Africana Women." *Western Journal of Black Studies* 17.1 (1993): 26–31.

Karenga, Maulana. "The Oppositional Logic of Malcolm X: Differentiation, Engagement and Resistance." *Western Journal of Black Studies* 17.1 (1993): 6–15.

Kelley, Robin D.G. "House Negroes on the Loose: Malcolm X and the Black Bourgeoisie." *Callaloo* 21.2 (1998): 419–35.

Kempton, Daniel. "Writing the Dictionary: The Education of Malcolm X." *The Centennial Review* 37.2 (1992): 253–66.

Mandel, Barrett John. "The Didactic Achievement of Malcolm X's Autobiography." *Afro-American Studies* 2 (1972): 269–74.

Nelson, Truman. Rev. of *The Autobiography of Malcolm X*. *Nation* 201 (November 8, 1965): 336.

Ohmann, Carol. "*The Autobiography of Malcolm X*: The Revolutionary Use of the Franklin Tradition." *American Quarterly* 22 (1970): 131–49.

Perry, Bruce. *Malcolm: The Life of a Man Who Changed America*. New York: Talman Company, 1991.

Roark, Chris. "Hamlet, Malcolm X, and the Examined Education." *CEA Critic* 57.1 (Fall 1994): 111–22.

Rose, Shirley K. "Metaphors and Myths of Cross-Cultural Literacy: Autobiographical Narratives by Maxine Hong Kingston, Richard Rodriguez, and Malcolm X." *MELUS* 14.1 (Spring 1987): 3–15.

Rustin, Bayard. Rev. of *The Autobiography of Malcolm X*. *Book Week* (November 14, 1965): 1.

Saldaña-Portillo, Maria Josefina. "Consuming Malcolm X: Prophecy and Performative Masculinity." *Novel* 30.3 (1997): 289–308.

Smith, Sidonie. *Where I'm Bound: Patterns of Slavery and Freedom in Black American Autobiography*. Westport, CT: Greenwood Press, 1974.

Stewart, James B. "Malcolm X and the Economic Salvation of African Americans." *Western Journal of Black Studies* 17.1 (1993): 17–24.

Stone, Albert E. *Autobiographical Occasions and Original Acts*. Philadelphia: University of Pennsylvania Press, 1982.

Stull, Bradford T. *Amid the Fall, Dreaming of Eden: Du Bois, King, and Malcolm X, and Emancipating Composition*. Carbondale: Southern Illinois University Press, 1999.

Terrill, Robert E. "Colonizing the Borderlands: Shifting Circumference in the Rhetoric of Malcolm X." *Quarterly Journal of Speech* 86.1 (2000): 67–85.

Wood, Joe, ed. *Malcolm X: In Our Own Image*. New York: St. Martin's Press, 1992.

JOHN MARRANT
(1755–1791)

James L. Hill

BIOGRAPHY

One of the first African American ministers in North America, John Marrant was born of free parents on June 15, 1755, in New York City. After his father's death, when he was four years old, Marrant moved with his mother to St. Augustine, Florida. He was educated in the schools of Florida, Georgia, and South Carolina, although scholars are still disputing whether the Charleston cited in his *Narrative* is in South Carolina or Massachusetts. From his early years, however, Marrant exhibited a talent for music; and while in Charleston, he was apprenticed to study music and dance, soon learning to play the violin and the French horn and earning recognition as an accomplished musician. In his *Narrative*, he describes that fateful day of his conversion to Christianity. Intent on mischief, he was among a group of young boys who had gone to a camp meeting to disrupt the church service; but when he heard "Prepare to Meet Thy God, O Israel" preached by the renowned English Evangelist George Whitefield, Marrant was deeply stirred and converted to Christianity. From that time forward, he exhibited extraordinary sensitivity and compassion toward all he encountered.

Ridiculed by his family and friends for his Christian beliefs, Marrant ran away from home in search of spiritual guidance. In the wilderness, he encountered an Indian who befriended him, and they traveled to the local Cherokee village, where Marrant was subsequently jailed, tortured, and almost executed. When the Cherokee chief and his daughter overheard Marrant praying in their native tongue, however, they were surprised and spared his life. Later, Marrant converted both of them to Christianity and was set free. After his release, he lived among the Cherokee and undertook his first missionary journey among the Creeks, Catawars, and Howsaws. Six months later in 1772, he returned to

Charleston, where he engaged in fellowship for the next three years; and on one occasion, he witnessed the brutal whipping of thirty slaves who were attending the church school he had established. Although a freeman, Marrant did not escape the oppression of the Revolutionary War; for because of his musical abilities, he was impressed into British military service as a ship musician in 1781, serving first aboard the *Scorpion* and then the *Princess Amelia*. Despite being a musician, however, he participated in several battles and was eventually wounded so badly he could no longer serve.

From 1782 to 1785, discharged from the military, Marrant lived in London where he worked as a cotton merchant and studied for the ministry. Through his friendship with Reverend Thomas Wills, he was ordained into the ministry of the Countess of Huntington's Dissent Methodist Connection in England in 1785. That same year, he told the story written down by William Aldridge and published by the Countess as *A Narrative of the Lord's Wonderful Dealings with John Marrant, a Black*. Subsequently, Marrant's brother persuaded him to come to Nova Scotia to provide leadership for the Black Loyalists, and Countess Huntington aided Marrant in preparing for his missionary trip to Nova Scotia. On August 18, 1785, aboard the *Peggy*, therefore, Marrant sailed for Nova Scotia, where he served as a minister for the Black Loyalists and a missionary to Indians.

By 1787, Marrant had succumbed to the smallpox epidemic and suffered throughout the rest of his stay in Nova Scotia. Desperately poor and physically frail, he continued to try unsuccessfully to contact Countess Huntington for financial assistance. During a trip to the United States in 1789, he met Prince Hall, founder of the Black Masonic Lodges, who asked him to accept a position as chaplain. From 1789 to 1790, Marrant continued his ministry in Boston, became a freemason, and worked as a schoolteacher; however, cognizant of racism in America, he longed to return to England, which he thought more supportive of African freedom. Despite the pleas of Prince Hall, Richard Allen, and Absalom Jones, Marrant left for England on February 5, 1790. He arrived in London after March 7 and subsequently published *A Journal of the Rev. John Marrant, from August the 18th, 1785, to The 16th of March 1790*. The circumstances behind the publication of the *Journal*, however, were not solely celebratory. Based on rumors that he had squandered the Connection's money, Marrant published his missionary record to right public opinion. Although he was still a young man, his life in the wilderness had already taken its toll; and in 1791, less than a year later, Marrant died and received an honorable burial on Church Street in Islington, a small town outside London.

AUTOBIOGRAPHICAL WORKS AND THEMES

Written in the simple, eloquent, and measured prose characteristic of the eighteenth century, Marrant's two autobiographical works complement each other. His *Narrative* and *Journal* record most of what is known about his life and works. Though a popular work that has been considered both an Indian captivity narrative and a slave narrative, Marrant's *Narrative* is not a slave narrative. Since Marrant was a freeman, his recorded activities relate directly to his intense religious devotion and display no concern for slavery (Foster 41). Actually a precursor to the slave narrative, as Foster indicates, Marrant's *Narrative* in purpose and structure provides perhaps the best evidence that the slave narrative is a recognizable literary form created for a specific purpose (42). The *Narrative* and *Journal* are also providential texts, and as providential texts, they embody the themes of the spiritual journey and intervention of divine power.

In the *Narrative*, Marrant blends the themes, events, and structures of both the captivity and slave narratives, adhering strictly to the tenets of neither. He also explores several familiar themes: the heroic journey, appearance versus reality, and redemption through spiritual salvation. In contrast to the traditional Indian captivity narrative, however, Marrant's captivity is more than a test of faith; he becomes a missionary. He also manipulates events in the *Narrative*. There are, for example, numerous reversal situations in which spiritual belief is the only constant. Faced with the threat of death, he still feels compelled to spread Christian truth to the Indians. Further, Marrant's spiritual interpretation of life is prevalent throughout the work. As Costanzo observes, he incorporates "a wide variety of autobiographical elements, such as stating his intention to edify readers, depicting his fears of backsliding to a sinful life, describing his meditating in solitude and crediting Providence with protecting him from Indians and wild beasts" (99).

Perhaps the most extensive account of black evangelism and community life in the eighteenth century, Marrant's *Journal* was published for more than religious edification. The *Journal* carefully records the number of sermons preached, souls saved, and individuals baptized during Marrant's missionary travels. Structured around a series of dramatic moments when divine intervention prevails, the *Journal* is also a series of resurrection narratives that illustrate, as Marrant observes, that no "Preacher belonging to the Connection could have suffered more than I have" (v).

CRITICAL RECEPTION

A dramatic conversion and captivity story, Marrant's *Narrative* was well received in 1785, but not without suspicions. Some reviewers believed that Marrant had greatly embellished his *Narrative* or that William Aldridge had taken liberties in recording the story for religious or propaganda purposes. Recent literary criticism of the *Narrative*, however, has reassessed its literary and historical importance. Angelo Costanzo, Frances Foster, and William Andrews, among others, have appropriately classified it as an Indian captivity narrative, but they have also indicated that Marrant prefigures the slave narrative, more so than either Equiano or Hammon. Published five years after the *Narrative* and one year before Marrant's death, the *Journal* is a continuation of the *Narrative* and was published to quell suspicions about the author. Scholars are still reassessing the proper place of the *Journal* in African American and American literary history.

BIBLIOGRAPHY

Autobiographical Works by John Marrant

A Narrative of the Lord's Wonderful Dealings with John Marrant, a Black (Now Going to Preach the Gospel in Nova Scotia). 1785.
A Journal of the Rev. John Marrant, from August the 18th, 1785, to The 16th of March 1790. 1790.

Studies of John Marrant's Autobiographical Works

Costanzo, Angelo. *Surprising Narrative: Olaudah Equiano and the Beginnings of Black Autobiography.* New York: Greenwood Press, 1987. 96–104.
Foster, Frances Smith. *Witnessing Slavery: The Development of Ante-bellum Slave Narratives.* Westport, CT: Greenwood Press, 1979. 41–42.
"Marrant, John." *Call and Response: The Riverside Anthology of the African American Literary Tradition.* Ed. Patricia Hill. Boston: Houghton Mifflin, 1998. 191–94.
"Marrant, John." In *Oxford Companion to African American Literature.* Ed. William Andrews, Frances Foster, and Trudier Harris. New York: Oxford University Press, 1997. 477–78.
Montgomery, Benilde. "Recapturing John Marrant." In *A Mixed Race: Ethnicity in Early America.* Ed. Frank Shuffelton. Oxford: Oxford University Press, 1993. 105–15.
Schomburg, Authur. "Two Negro Missionaries to the American Indians, John Marrant and John Stewart." *Journal of Negro History* 21 (October 1936): 394–410.
"Three Black Ministers: John Marrant, John Chavis, Lemuel Haynes." In *The Black Presence in the Era of the American Revolution.* Ed. Sidney Kaplan and Emma Kaplan. Amherst: University of Massachusetts Press, 1989. 110–30.

JAMES McBRIDE
(1957–)

Harmony Nicole Booker

BIOGRAPHY

Born in 1957 to Ruth McBride, formally Ruth Shilsky, daughter of an Orthodox rabbi, James McBride grew up to become an acclaimed writer, journalist, and composer. After she married an African American man, Ruth Shilsky's Jewish family disowned her. Around 1938, she left home to get away from her father, a strong-willed man, because of his sexual and verbal abuse as well as adulterous behavior. Although Ruth did not want to, she left behind "her younger sister and beloved mother, who'd been disabled by polio and spoke no English" (Janis 2). For most of McBride's childhood, he was raised in the St. Albans section of Queens, New York. McBride's biological father, Andrew Dennis McBride, a Baptist minister, died of lung cancer while his mother was pregnant with him. Shortly after James was born, Ruth met and married Hunter Jordan. They had four additional children, adding to Ruth's eight children by her deceased husband.

James McBride grew up wondering why his mother's skin was lighter than his; as a child he continuously asked, though never succeeded in getting an answer, on the question if she was white. He and his eleven siblings all attended public schools that were predominately Jewish. Because there were no Jewish schools near McBride's largely African American neighborhood, "by age twelve" he "was traveling an hour and a half one way to junior high school" (McBride 88). As a teenager, McBride hit hard times and stopped attending school. He grew tired of seeing his mother, at this time raising twelve children on her own and struggling to make ends meet because her second husband, Hunter Jordan, had died. Daily he smoked marijuana and drank wine, occasionally trying LSD; he also began to shoplift and steal. During his rebellious teenage years, McBride began to play a variety of instruments with a street band. His mother, unable to cope with the loss of another husband and McBride's unruly behavior and continuous absence from summer school, sent James to live with his half sister in Louisville, Kentucky, during the summer months.

During this time, McBride received some of the best advice of his life from a street corner drunk named Chicken Man. He asked McBride, "Is that what you want for yourself?"—a life of drinking and smoking and inevitably jail (150). This sharp question helped McBride realize that he did not need to go down the road that he was and pushed him to get his life back on track. In the fall of 1973, he returned to Queens and began to "jump back into" his studies and "rebuild" himself (161). At the end of that school year, in June 1974, Ruth McBride Jordan moved her five remaining children at home—the others were away at college—to Delaware. For the first time, McBride entered an all-black public school. He devoted himself to schoolwork, and his love for music grew stronger. McBride had a background in music because in grade school he had taken up clarinet and piano. He joined the American Youth Jazz Band, and a white family, the Dawsons, funded his trip to Europe with the Band. At the end of the year, McBride graduated high school with good grades.

In the fall of 1975, McBride began attending Oberlin College in Ohio, later graduating from there with a bachelor's of arts degree. He went on to attend Columbia University, where he received a master's degree in Journalism. McBride's accomplishments have included being "a staff writer for the *Boston Globe,* the *Washington Post* and *People* magazine" ("Author" 1). "He also has contributed articles to *Rolling Stone,* the *Philadelphia Inquirer* and the *New York Times*" (1). McBride received "the 1997 Anisfield Wolf Book Award for his writing" ("James McBride" 1). Furthermore, he's an acclaimed saxophonist and has "composed for Anita Baker and Grover Washington Jr. and toured as a sideman for legendary jazz vocalist Jimmy Scott" (Janis 1). He received "the 1996 American Arts and Letters Richard Rogers Award, the American Music Theater Festival's 1993 Stephan Sondheim Award, and various other awards for music" ("James McBride" 1). Currently McBride is keeping up with his writing; he recently coauthored *The Autobiography of Quincy Jones* ("Author" 1). McBride lives in South Nyack, New York, with his wife and two children (McBride 293).

AUTOBIOGRAPHICAL WORKS AND THEMES

McBride's major work is a gripping and emotional autobiography, *The Color of Water.* Subtitled "A Black Man's Tribute to His White Mother," the work is a powerful look at the life of an African American male and his touching relationship with his mother. The memoir is told in counterpoint chapters, telling two life stories, one being McBride's, the other being his mother's. The major themes explore race and the search for identity.

Although the book narrates McBride's life story, it is the elaborate biographical account of Ruth McBride Jordan's life that helps best develop the themes of the narrative for the reader. Her story shows how one woman dared to cross racial

JAMES McBRIDE   261

and social barriers. Ruth McBride Jordan may have been a white Orthodox Jewish
woman, but she demonstrates how it was and is possible to shatter racial barriers
and become integrated into another culture. Many may believe that it is difficult
to date and marry interracially today, not realizing how much more difficult and
dangerous it was in the 1940s. Ruth tells that in 1940 "black and white didn't
do what me and Dennis were doing, walking around and such" (McBride 94).
As for her son James, his confusion over the difference between black and white
was most evident when he was a young child. One of the most powerful moments
of the narrative occurs when James is a child, and he asks his mother about the
color of God. Ruth responds, "God is the color of water" (51). The narrative
suggests that God has no color and, though unspoken, points to the absurdity of
racial categories.

Generally speaking, African American families accept outsiders into their family circle without much resistance. There is evidence of this in the memoir when
Ruth meets Andrew McBride's family for the first time. The family takes Ruth
in and accepts her. Though this happens, the narrative does not try falsely to
represent all interactions between African Americans and whites as smooth. The
narrative does show that not all African Americans were as welcoming to a white
person coming into their world, just as many whites were not accepting of blacks
crossing into theirs. Ruth did have unpleasant encounters with blacks. Once a
woman chased and yelled at her for living with a black, and there were other
African American women who would assert their racial pride in her presence
(231–32). Furthermore, the narrative goes on to show how Ruth McBride Jordan's children were affected growing up being African American during the civil
rights movement with a white mother. James's older sibling would advocate racial
pride and support the tidal wave pushing for equality that was sweeping across
America (73). The narrative displays the older children's self-awareness of the
revolution occurring by how they would discuss the issue; yet there is a sense of
discomfort because they knew they had a white mother.

The autobiography explores the theme of searching for identity. This theme
connects the lives of Ruth and James because they both look for a sense of
belonging and acceptance throughout the entire narrative. Ruth's search for acceptance begins in childhood. Her family moved around every few years because
her father was never able to keep a steady job as a rabbi. Ruth was never able to
get close to others or find others to identify herself with because she was moving
so often (39). When the Shilsky family finally settled in Suffolk, Virginia, Ruth
finally found comfort and happiness when she became friends with a girl named
Frances (81). Frances's openness helped Ruth become less ashamed of her Jewish
heritage. Although Frances was open-minded to Ruth's differences, other whites
in Suffolk were not. When Ruth had first arrived at Suffolk, other children were
cruel and malicious to her; they would ridicule her and make fun of her, calling
her "a dirty Jew" (80). She was embarrassed and jaded by their torment. Feeling
the need for greater social acceptance, Ruth Americanized her Yiddish birth
name of Ruchla to Ruth (80). Though changing her name did not work, her

decision to do so reveals her longing for an unproblematic social identity. Previously, Ruth's family had had its Yiddish surname of Zylaka Americanized to Shilsky.

Further in the narrative, Ruth does find a group with which to identify herself. This is after she meets Andrew McBride and decides to convert to Christianity. This tough decision to leave behind her heritage and accept Christianity shows Ruth's search for a nurturing sense of community. She converts because she wants to and not because she needs to, to fit in with others. Her husband Andrew never pushed her to convert; the decision was hers alone. This shows Ruth making judgments and decisions for herself, thus standing on her own.

McBride's search for identity begins fully when he is in adolescence. He goes through a period of rebellion and tries to identify himself with the local street gangs. James's feeling of invincibility kept him robbing, stealing, drinking, doing drugs, and cutting school. During this time, he did not aspire to become a professional. After his mother sent him to Louisville, Kentucky, a local man there helped him see that he was ruining his life and going down a path toward self-destruction. McBride sees the error of his ways and decides to get his life on the right track. He goes back to school and forges his sense of self through his writing and through his love for music.

CRITICAL RECEPTION

McBride's autobiography has received enthusiastic reviews. H. Jack Geiger of the *New York Times* wrote, "The triumph of the book—and of their lives—is that race and religion are transcended in these interwoven histories by family love" (16). Marina Budhos found that "McBride's memoir is not only a terrific story, it's a subtle contribution to the current debates on race and identity" (32). The American Library Association had McBride's memoir on its 1997 "Best" List, reviewing *The Color of Water* as an "absorbing, often hilarious dual memoir" (1285). The Association goes on to review the memoir as work that "upends conventional notions of racial identity as McBride retraces his white Jewish mother's odyssey toward marriage and unwavering allegiance to the black community" (1285). Most crucial is how McBride draws attention to the racial barriers apparent in society. Hugh Pearson admires McBride for "reminding us that we haven't yet reached such a point in dismantling the artificial construct of black vs. white" (A12). Pearson goes on to say, "*The Color of Water* exposes the essence of our racial problem" (A12). In addition, Alice Joyce praises the memoir, saying, "McBride composes a loving accolade to an extraordinary woman" (782). The complex and loving account of two individual lives led Jim Burns to write, "His mother's own story, juxtaposed with McBride's, helps make this book a standout. Recommended for all collections" (110). James McBride has shown readers how his mother, cofounder of New Brown Memorial Baptist Church with her first husband, defeated the odds of raising twelve biracial children on her own, all of whom became professionals. She decided to follow her children's example and go to college; at age sixty-five she received a degree in social work from Temple University (McBride 270). Ruth McBride Jordan has truly shown the world what it is to be a phenomenal woman. Her son's elegant autobiography is a fitting tribute to her defiantly unconventional and poignant life.

BIBLIOGRAPHY

Autobiographical Work by James McBride

The Color of Water: A Black Man's Tribute to His White Mother. New York: Riverhead Books, 1996.

Studies of James McBride's Autobiographical Work

"Author James McBride." Latest News Release. Greensboro: University News Service North Carolina. <http://www.uncg.edu/mcbride.htm>.
Budhos, Marina. "Black Man, Jewish Soul." *The Nation* (April 22, 1996): 32–34.
Burns, Jim. Rev. of *The Color of Water: A Black Man's Tribute to His White Mother. Library Journal* 121.1 (1996): 110.
Geiger, H. Jack. "Rachel and Her Children." *New York Times Book Review* (March 31, 1996): 16
"James McBride." Albany: New York State Writer's Institute, 1998. <http://www.edu/writers-inst/mcbride.html>.
Janis, Pam. "The Color of Love." *The Detroit News on the Web,* February 1, 1996. <http://detnews.com/menu/stones/34144.htm>.
Joyce, Alice. Rev. of *The Color of Water. Booklist* 92.9–10 (1996): 782.
Ott, Bill. "American Library Association's 'Best' List." *Booklist* 93.15 (1997): 1285.
Pearson, Hugh. "At the Center of Racial Dilemma." *Wall Street Journal,* February 9, 1996, A12.

NATHAN J. McCALL
(1954-   )

Susan Evans Pond

BIOGRAPHY

Nathan McCall, born in Portsmouth, Virginia, in 1954, was the third son of his eighteen-year-old mother Lenora and his father, identified only as J.L. The couple, having lied about Lenora's age, married when she was fourteen to legitimize the birth of their first son. They parted when McCall was two, after which J.L. was absent from their lives, even leaving his sons unmet at a bus station for a visit he had initiated in 1964. McCall and his brothers would not see him again until 1982.

McCall gained a stepfather when Lenora married Bonnie Alvin, a career navy man. After stints in North Africa and Florida, the family returned to Portsmouth, when McCall was nine, and took up residence in Cavalier Manor, a recently built black suburb. Their newly built home, set in a seeming paradise of crisp lawns and community lakes, soon became crowded by the birth of a new brother and the arrivals of Alvin's son from a previous marriage and Lenora's mother. Nonetheless, McCall recalls it as a carefree time, a "Huck Finn kind of existence" (7) that would change pivotally when he entered sixth grade in 1966.

Taking advantage of court-ordered, racially open enrollment, McCall's parents chose to enroll him in a white middle school across town. However, they failed to anticipate the barrage of racial harassment he endured daily in the classroom and on the long public bus ride. McCall receded into a private world of depression and fear. His parents finally recognized his pain and transferred him back to the neighborhood school.

Returned to a black environment, McCall recalls an intense awareness of the "solace of being around [his] own people" (22). His confidence fragile from the prior year, he rejected his studious label and sought the conferred status and protection of the in-crowd. Rituals of violence were endemic to gaining peer rank; McCall discovered he could let a numbing rage overcome his initial guilt and repulsion. The "Huck Finn" years evolved into an intensifying mix of demanding respect at the end of a fist, a stick, a knife, and by high school, a gun. From age twelve he and his friends shoplifted, engaged in rage-venting beatings of randomly picked white boys, and battled other gangs in the neighborhood and across the racial divide. At fourteen McCall joined in the first of many gang rapes ("trains"), a thirteen-year-old girl his victim. As fists escalated to guns, shoplifting shifted to robberies. Remarkably, amidst it all, he finished high school.

McCall's world was disintegrating around him. In short order he became a reluctant father, attended and dropped out of college, and shot a man over an insult to his son's mother. His victim escaped death, and McCall got by with eight days in jail, a $300 fine, and probation. However, in April 1975, his luck ran out, and he was sentenced to twelve years for an armed robbery.

Prison turned McCall's life around. Physical confinement enforced a certain level of discipline, and he began to educate himself, reading prodigiously, deriving particular insight from Richard Wright's* *Native Son* (1940). His conversion to Christianity changed aspects of his behavior, and he was paroled after three years.

Finding jobs denied due to his prison record, McCall reentered Norfolk State University, studying journalism and graduating with honors in 1981. Again, his criminal record produced numerous job rejections. Finally he began reporting for a hometown paper and later moved on to the *Atlanta Journal-Constitution*, choosing not to reveal his record. In 1987 a prestigious job offer from the *Washington Post* was withdrawn when the paper discovered his undisclosed prison record. Bill Coleman, the black assistant managing editor, told McCall the paper would likely approach him again and encouraged McCall to "trust [his] track record, tell the truth, and put the past behind" (361). Returning to Atlanta, McCall decided to reveal his past to his editor, Bill Kovach, and received a supportive, professional reaction. Two years later the *Washington Post* renewed its job offer, and McCall moved to Washington, D.C.

Now a respected journalist, McCall still struggled to manage his chaotic domestic life. A long-term relationship and two short marriages gave him three children but left him financially unstable and emotionally scarred. He missed the emotional sustenance of the friendships of his youth. In a *Post* article, he attempted to begin reconciling the ambivalence he felt toward both his new life and his old. The article spawned the book offer for his autobiography.

McCall left the *Washington Post* in 1999, joining the faculty at Emory University, in Atlanta, as a lecturer and writer in the budding Journalism Department, where he remains as of June 2001.

AUTOBIOGRAPHICAL WORK AND THEMES

McCall's autobiography, *Makes Me Wanna Holler: A Young Black Man in America*, is written as a memoir of himself and his peers, mostly male children of a primarily blue-collar segment of African American life, who are slipping back down the ladder their parents had so patiently climbed. Throughout the text, his triumphs are muted by the chronicles of friends still trapped as well as by the increasing dangers he perceives in their environment. Although McCall effects a major transformation of his intellectual and professional life, his emotional existence is troubled and unsatisfying, his frustrations with racism at times impairing his power to combat it. He wrestles with the duality of the emotional comforts as well as the dangers of his old neighborhood and his inability to find an entirely safe space in his new white surroundings. McCall's relationships with women are highly conflicted. However, in the public undressing of his life, he manages to produce a palpable image of the humanity, however tattered, of himself and his partners from the neighborhood. It is an unfinished examination, even by his estimation, with no easy recipe for the fix.

McCall's own story can be broken into four major periods: childhood through high school; prison; college; and his journalistic career. As a child he searches for an enabling sense of self, but his quest becomes a horribly misguided groping for esteem, power, and masculinity, tragically misdirected to the abuse of young African American women, his community, and ultimately, himself. Pursuing a common autobiographical theme, McCall's overarching motivation from prison forward is an attempt to weave the threads of his past into a meaningful and cohesive whole.

Although McCall frequently cites the constancy and support of his stepfather and mother, he explains how he turns to petty delinquency, largely unobserved: "My folks were typical of their generation . . . making sure we were clothed, fed, and protected . . . [but] not focusing on us unless we were sick or had done something wrong. . . . [V]alues [were] transmitted by example, not word of mouth" (38). It is a characterization that fits many families, black and white, in the American context of the 1950s and 1960s and is often cited in discussing the derailment of children from seemingly secure settings. McCall's parents are of a generation that trusts in eventual racial transformation and fails to recognize the mounting impatience of young black expectations or the growing influence of peer solidarity, manifested in gangs organized, in part, around racial antagonism. Into this vacuum, "hanging" buddies become the arbiters of social roles and mores.

In six quick years, torturing frogs and shoplifting candy give way to horrific beatings, gang rapes, and armed robberies. McCall identifies the motives: Robberies supply funds for fashionable clothing; beatings, gang warfare, and gang rape simultaneously vent and feed the pervasive rage while building status and bolstering vulnerable, ill-conceived notions of masculinity and self-esteem. Rising antiracist fervor connects squarely with their anger, at times shifting the target to whites and rationalizing criminal acts.

Yet despite their racialized rage, the gang primarily victimizes socially safer targets within the black community, reflecting a paradoxical self-hatred. McCall writes in a chapter titled "Nigger" of his generation's "enchantment with whiteness" (11), inadvertently fostered by his parents and grandmother. His mother, to control his public exuberance, hushes McCall by telling him to "stop acting like a nigger" (12). His beloved grandmother, a domestic, constantly holds up her two young white charges as symbols of good behavior. These children become iconic, in McCall's youthful mind, of everything good and right.

This is a subtler face of racism, less of cross-burnings and more of self-denigration and dead-ended social options. McCall and his brothers are ashamed and dispirited by watching their stepfather politely endure condescending familiarity exercised by his white clients on weekend gardening jobs or observing the dark faces of the men and women trudging up white, upper-class streets in the early hours to work as domestics and laborers. Legitimate jobs held by parents of the neighborhood are often poorly paying and menial. Hustling, on the other hand, holds the romantic appeal of offering an instant uplift in financial state and personal authority. Later on, McCall cannot help noticing the overly black face of prison and the whiteness of newsrooms.

As a journalist, McCall is initially deeply distrustful of interacting with white colleagues, anxiously and obsessively monitoring his every exchange for landmines that might set off the old rage. His self-consciousness stultifies his creativity. Eventually, several crucial events begin to relax his vigilance. A white reporter, Danny Baum, amazingly devoid of racial baggage, joins the *Atlanta Constitution-Journal*, becoming a close friend. Editor Bill Kovach, who had earlier worked for the *New York Times*, vastly opens up McCall's journalistic opportunities and advancement. And, during this period, McCall attends a multicultural management program, in which he discovers a sorely needed sense of collegiality.

McCall's examination of his attitudes toward women is insufficient, as is his self-control in interacting with them. In his youth, violence, defending or victimizing young girls, is mostly a matter of maintaining respect in the sensitive terrain of machismo and controlling one's possessions. Postprison, he has gained a vastly increased respect for women; yet with his energies consumed by his career, his marriages are ill conceived and children unplanned. He struggles to avoid the failures of his birth father. Only in his children is McCall able to find and foster an expressive, unequivocal, and enduring love.

The autobiographer's omissions are worth noting. Even while describing his troubled relationships, McCall rarely resorts to self-exculpating. When he makes it into "the big time" (387), at the *Washington Post*, there is no touting, indeed almost no mention of his reportage, just observations of the black leaders he covers and the day-to-day social dynamics of his survival in the newsroom. Nor are there remarkable transformative movements for his old friends. Most readers will be left without a sense of triumph or resolution for either McCall or the black and white worlds he and his friends pass through.

Although McCall's autobiography can be compared generically with Malcolm X's,* McCall's criminality and subsequent transformation are less easily heroicized. Despite periods of commitment to Christianity and Islam, his conversions ultimately are personal, not religious, nor does he achieve social redemption by rededicating his life to his people, as Malcolm does. But McCall has a way of relating the gritty stories of himself and his friends with unsparing plainness. The central value in his autobiographical reportage, beyond a personal analysis, is in giving face and compassionate dimension to men otherwise relegated to statistics.

CRITICAL RECEPTION

Makes Me Wanna Holler has received many thoughtful and scholarly reviews, considering that it is a relatively recent first book of midlevel prominence. Reviewers generally praise McCall's straightforward, unsparing writing style. Henry Louis Gates Jr., for example, comments that McCall never gives in to the temptation "to endow his earlier self with a consciousness beyond his years" (95). But there are disagreements over how McCall handles major issues, such as the conventional expectation of black autobiographies to serve as historical documents, the attribution of behaviors to the effects of racism or insufficient moral responsibility, the exposition of gender and class issues, and the completeness of his social vision.

Gates, Darryl Pinckney, and Sanford Pinsker provide in their reviews a foundational discussion of the African American autobiographical form, illuminating traditions, tracing the evolution of the style as well as the issues of transformation, and raising intertextual contrasts and comparisons. Gail Jardine, a self-acknowledged "white feminist scholar" (385), focuses on the substantial theme of masculine identity twined inextricably and influentially through McCall's story. Taken together, the four provide a thorough and provocative framework in which to view the text.

There is an inescapable expectation that the black memoirist will write history. Gates sees this as a "blessing and burden," an honorable opportunity for contributing to the vast project of Narrating the Negro, and a guarantee that "your tale is never completely your own" (94). This notion opens the door to a sometimes surprising narrowness of vision among reviewers, who in questioning inclusions, omissions, and slants seem almost to expect McCall to have lived a different life, in service to the correct historical image. Jill Nelson sees McCall as morbidly preoccupied with the pathology of black life and tags the book with categorical labels such as a "coming of rage" story (563). Pinsker also sees this genre of black autobiography as excessively caught up in a competitive chronicling of "the underbelly of black life, coupled with a craven refusal to apply the usual standards of human decency" (763). Pinckney points out that the black autobiography has moved from "historical document" to "sociological indictment," placing McCall's approach in the company of Richard Wright,* Malcolm X, and Claude Brown* (42). However, within the context of social diagnosis and indictment, reviewers are split over McCall's unwillingness to offer clear-cut answers to complex personal and social dilemmas, some calling it a conscious rejection of simplistic solutions, others, the mark of an unfinished or immature writing effort.

Regarding McCall's personal story, critics debate his weighting of racism against the acknowledgment of personal responsibility in causing his destructive behavior. Some reviewers suggest that McCall has somewhat ducked his personal accountability, others lament his politic glossing over of some of the harsher realities of growing up black. In the environment-versus-behavior debate, Gates perhaps best mirrors the balance that McCall intends to strike, saying, "Only at the price of relinquishing my own sense of humanity can I believe I had no hand in my own fate" (96).

Examining McCall's notable lack of success in transforming his relationships with women, Jardine presents the web of gender and class issues woven through the tragic riddle of his adolescence. Quoting James Baldwin's* statement "To be black and conscious in America is to be in a constant state of rage," she adds a third element, "masculinity in the American tableau," and suggests the synergy of the three "spawns the most formidable, unyielding rage of all" (386). Pinckney agrees, calling McCall a victim of the "demonization or hypersexualization of the black male," complicated by the "cult of macho," noting that McCall "could only express remorse after quieting the gut feeling that conscience is feminine, a chump's liability" (46). Nelson, looking at McCall's representations of the women with whom he gets personally involved, is deeply derisive of his understanding of black women and offended by his characteristically blunt and sometimes sexist descriptive style.

In the final analysis critics might characterize McCall as possessing one clear eye and one clouded. Many feel his poignant record of the lives of lost men is valuable for its honesty. Others fault what they see as an overreliance on the excessively sordid aspects of his experience as well as his insensitivity to the marginalization of black women. Few, however, can deny the acuity in his observation of an important segment of contemporary African American experience.

BIBLIOGRAPHY

Autobiographical Work by Nathan J. McCall

Makes Me Wanna Holler: A Young Black Man in America. New York: Random House, 1994.

Studies of Nathan J. McCall's Autobiographical Work

Gates, Henry Louis, Jr. "Bad Influence." The New Yorker 70 (March 7, 1994): 94–98.
Jardine, Gail. "To Be Black, Male, and Conscious: Race, Rage, and Manhood in America." American Quarterly 48 (June 1996): 385–93.
Nelson, Jill. "Hiding in Plain Sight." Nation (April 25, 1994): 562–65.
Pinckney, Darryl. "Promissory Notes." New York Review of Books (April 6, 1995): 41–46.
Pinsker, Sanford. "Home Boys between Hard Covers." Virginia Quarterly Review 70 (Autumn 1994): 757–72.
Toure. "Makes Me Wanna Holler." Village Voice (March 29, 1994): 64.
White, Jack E. "Between Two Worlds." Time (March 7, 1994): 68.

JANET McDONALD
(1953–)

Heather Rellihan

BIOGRAPHY

Janet McDonald, a writer best known for her critically acclaimed autobiography *Project Girl*, has struggled against the prevailing stereotypes around race, class, and gender in the United States. Coming to terms with the contesting realities of being poor, black, and female, and evidencing tremendous intelligence, McDonald uses her autobiography to make sense out of these seemingly disparate identities, all the while questioning their assumed dissonance. After many years of grappling with these identities, McDonald's text emerges as evidence of a certain self-understanding—one that successfully manipulates the American Dream while maintaining a critical recognition of its fiction. The larger text of *Project Girl*, then, serves to make meaning of the enigmatic words that mark the beginning of the first chapter: "I belong nowhere in particular anymore and feel comfortable most everywhere" (3).

Born in 1953, McDonald grew up in Brooklyn, New York, the middle child of a large working-class family. Her father and mother grew up against the background of the Great Depression—although McDonald jokes that they were too poor to notice it. McDonald describes her parents, both products of their time, as tireless workers: Her father, the uncontested head of their old-fashioned American family, an army veteran who retired from military service, moved north as a young adult to sort mail in a post office; her mother took care of the seven children—no easy task—while recreating the southern lifestyle of her youth in their northern home.

McDonald grew up in Brooklyn, in a government housing project, and was witness to the changing nature of, and attitudes toward, this community. McDonald was a self-described "Southern-style little Brooklyn girl" with a natural affinity for school, but once she was marked as "college-material," her future seemed at conflict with the realities of projects. From her early childhood, this identity created tension with her family, who alternately praised and mocked her book-learning, and the larger community who didn't see an immediate benefit from her academic focus. Later, the politics of the 1980s intensified her community discomfort by redefining what it meant to be a project girl: McDonald remembers that "with the eighties came the rigid notion of a permanent 'underclass.' . . . Much like India's untouchables, we came to be seen as a class of people destined to be poor, undereducated, and unemployable" (13).

McDonald was educated first at Erazmas, a well-known and well-established elite elementary school and, later, at Harlem Prep, a private but tuition-free high school that emerged in Harlem in the late 1970s to allow black students a quality education infused with the black consciousness of the time. She then made an awkward transition to Vassar College, where she felt ill-fitted to the white upper-class girls and even the other black students, whom she calls "Vassar's black Southern bourgeoisie" (59). Faced with these particular intersections of race and class, McDonald felt acutely alone—especially during her freshman year—and with this longing for community, she began to regret her too-ready retreat from the projects. She says, "I had left a unique subculture, a universe so distinct that we had our own mores, customs, style of dress, and even our own dialect. We were project people, a tribe apart. And I was apart from my tribe. It was terrifying" (64). As McDonald gradually adapted to the Vassar environment, she recognized that her opportunity to go to school with "rich white folk" divided her irreparably from the project community. She was caught in the crossfire of two inversely related variables: The more "white" she became, the less "black" she could be. And so, for McDonald, this period became marked by a dual endeavor: She strove to succeed at Vassar while attempting to reconnect with her Brooklyn community. In fact, McDonald began using heroin in efforts to belong, to make her "last stab at being truly *project* before [her] inevitable transformation into Straightback Sally" (69).

Although McDonald's education seemed to be upstaged by her identity crises, she notes that her English class in particular was important to her in that it exposed her to the works of writers like Virginia Woolf, Anne Sexton, and Sylvia Plath. She says that she identified with these writers, despite the obvious differences of race and class that divorced their experiences from her own. Outside of school, McDonald was supplementing these readings with Maya Angelou,* Zora Neale Hurston,* and Toni Morrison. These writers helped McDonald to push her identity search beyond the Vassar/projects binary. The lives and works of these women helped her to transcend these boundaries and therefore pave a way for her own consciousness.

McDonald spent her junior year in Paris, and this experience proves transformational. Here, she meets people from all over the world. She begins to understand that the particular construction of race that she was taught was unique to America. Abroad, she was identified simply as American, not African American, and this identity helps her to challenge the divisiveness she had grown accustomed to.

Unfortunately, McDonald's growth becomes stunted soon thereafter. As a Cornell University law student, she is raped by a classmate. Finding the atmosphere less than conducive to her healing process, McDonald breaks down and leaves Cornell. She is briefly institutionalized. When she returns to her studies, she transfers to New York University hoping to leave her demons behind her. Unfortunately, her anger escalates; McDonald lashes out and is arrested for setting fires to dorms on campus. McDonald eventually completes her law degree at the age of thirty-two. During this time she succumbs again to the insider/outsider dynamic that had plagued her youth. As a woman who has made it out of the projects, she yearns, somewhat ironically, to be a project girl again. Struggling to find community against ongoing disappointments, McDonald decides to leave New York and practice law in Paris, thereby giving up the race binary she finds inherent in, and peculiar to, American life.

AUTOBIOGRAPHICAL WORK AND THEMES

Project Girl is McDonald's only published autobiographical work, and it seems to have emerged as a therapeutic by-product of self-growth rather than as a conscious entrée into the literary world. Fittingly then, the major themes of the text center around the construction of identities—the various processes by which McDonald defines herself in and through the communities that claim her. In the process of working through her own individuality, McDonald presents an honest and angry critique of the rigid constructions that serve to characterize and contain communities. In contradistinction to her experiences in Paris, McDonald points to the particular burden of race and class constructions in the United States.

Project Girl is structured as a coming-of-age narrative, even as its content problematizes the traditional demarcations of this genre. That is to say, *Project Girl* tells the story of a woman who has tried to straddle different worlds in efforts to embrace two dueling communities, but the resolution of the text challenges and surpasses an identity contingent on community acceptance. McDonald finds herself, and eventually defines herself, in the conflict, not the resolution, of these two worlds. This story, then, is ostensibly a rags-to-riches tale that both supports and refutes the ideology that labels this success. McDonald stares down the American Dream, refusing to let it define her, and her narrative turns, thematically, on her need to invent a new template.

CRITICAL RECEPTION

Project Girl has met with a variety of criticism ranging from lukewarm praise to fervent applause. Most critics agree that McDonald's story is a powerful one—and one that offers both insight and motivation. The disagreement is around

McDonald's telling of her story: Some, like reviewer Sara Irvy, find the memoir "engrossing" and see her writing as a therapeutic response to the frustrations in her life, while other reviewers like Nora Harris find the book somewhat anticlimactic. Harris praises the first half of the book but finds that the memoir loses its momentum: "Unfortunately, the narrative bogs down [in the second half] . . . and the jumpy style . . . is difficult to read. While the ending finds McDonald successful at last in Paris, it seems hurried, leaving the reader unsatisfied" (97). Romesh Ratnesar, a reviewer for *Time*, praises McDonald for writing with "lucidity and drama" but argues that by the end of the book McDonald's "cynicism has become toxic." Ratnesar continues, "Her rise out of the underclass is, in many ways, testament to the resilience of American meritocracy. But McDonald refuses to see that, focusing instead on the injustices she suffered along the way. Her inspiring tale deserves more than it gets in this disheartening memoir" (81).

Popular reception seems to be a bit more consistently favorable. Certainly McDonald's story is appealing to many people who identify with various aspects of her struggle. McDonald has a Web site dedicated to *Project Girl* (<www.projectgirl.com>) displaying various photos of McDonald and her family as well as information about the book including various reviews. Certainly, McDonald's story is ripe for an American readership, even if her particular way of telling her story may not appeal to all readers.

BIBLIOGRAPHY

Autobiographical Work by Janet McDonald

Project Girl. New York: Farrar, Straus and Giroux, 1999.

Studies of Janet McDonald's Autobiographical Work

Bush, Vanessa, and Chris Sherman. Rev. of *Project Girl. Booklist* (December 1998): 649.
Harris, Nora. Rev. of *Project Girl. Library Journal* (November 1998): 97.
Irvy, Sara. Rev. of *Project Girl. New York Times Book Review* (February 1999): 17.
Ratnesar, Romesh. Rev. of *Project Girl. Time* (March 1999): 81.

CLAUDE McKAY
(1890-1948)

Barbara L.J. Griffin

BIOGRAPHY

Claude McKay, born in Jamaica in 1890, is considered by many scholars of African American literature to be the first significant writer of the Harlem Renaissance. In 1912, at the age of twenty-two, McKay left Jamaica for the United States. Before his departure, he firmly established himself as a poet by virtue of two acclaimed 1912 collections—*Songs of Jamaica* and *Constab Ballads*. In these poetic volumes, McKay planted the seeds for the development of modern Caribbean literature by employing the native dialect to probe the complexities of colonial existence under British imperialism. Throughout *Songs of Jamaica*, McKay speaks from the perspective of the Jamaican peasant who bemoans his inability to wrest a living from his impoverished lot. *Constab Ballads*, a smaller collection, reflects McKay's experiences as a police officer in the urban settings of Kingston and Spanish Town (Cooper 35–36). Five years after his arrival in the United States, McKay found himself in the vanguard of the new Negro Renaissance with the publication of two important poems, "Harlem Dancer" and "Invocation," published in the December issue of *The Seven Arts*, a highly regarded literary magazine. In 1922, he published his most important collection of poems, *Harlem Shadows*, bringing together thematic concerns that would figure prominently in his later works: the nostalgia for his Jamaican soil, the search for a valid black aesthetic, and the assertion of a rebellious spirit (164–66). McKay's most famous defiant poem, "If We Must Die," was included in this collection. For many African Americans, this rousing call for black resistance crystallized the spirit of a new generation.

McKay's publication in *Seven Arts*, a "mainstream" avant-garde journal edited by Waldo Frank and James Oppenheim, was typical of his pattern. Although he published in black journals such as the *Crisis* and *Opportunity*, from the beginning he sought recognition in white journals and aligned himself with white radical artists and intellectuals based around Greenwich Village (Gates 982). In 1922, McKay, whose inclination was toward socialism and the unconventional, trav-eled to Russia to witness the Bolshevik Revolution. His sojourn lasted for twelve years as his restless nature compelled him to experience life in Europe and North Africa. During his twelve-year odyssey, as an essayist and poet, he continued to contribute to important journals in the United States and created a great deal of controversy with the publication of his first novel *Home to Harlem*, published in 1928 (982–83). Written in the "primitivistic" style and achieving a place on the bestseller list, McKay celebrates the hedonistic, joy-loving world of subter-ranean Harlem (Singh 46). His focus on stevedores, prostitutes, and pimps and general lack of concern with writing a "respectable" tale ran counter to the aims of Renaissance leaders who regarded art as a means of advancing the race. W.E.B. Du Bois,* angered by McKay's book, pronounced in the *Crisis* that after reading *Home to Harlem* he felt a strong compulsion to take a bath (Du Bois 202). Most of the old guard of the Negro elite attacked McKay's book, while younger artists like Langston Hughes* celebrated its appearance (Cooper 243). In 1929, McKay published his second novel, *Banjo*, set in Marseilles and written in the loose, slice-of-life vein of *Home to Harlem*. Although McKay implies in both novels a Bohemian lack of regard for the conventions of Western society, he never con-vinces the reader that he is in total sympathy with the instinctual world he has created. *Banana Bottom*, his only novel set in Jamaica, was published in 1933. In this semiautobiographical work, McKay attempts to reconcile the ambivalences that marked his two earlier novels. His protagonist, Bita Plant, struggles to merge her two selves: Western and Jamaican.

Although Claude McKay was one of the most gifted writers of the early twen-tieth century, he was a complex man whose life and career reflected tensions and contradictions. He identified himself as a political and social radical, yet he held to strict conservative conventions when it came to matters of art, for example, favoring the sonnet even for his most revolutionary sentiments (LeSeur 297). His poetry aptly expressed the collective outrage of the masses, yet he frequently viewed himself as an outsider. And though generally celebrated as the first im-portant writer of the Harlem Renaissance, he ridiculed the movement and con-demned Harlem intellectuals for their bourgeoisie aspirations. McKay's autobiography provides a window through which readers can gain a clearer per-spective of his works (Ojo-Ade 65).

AUTOBIOGRAPHICAL WORKS AND THEMES

Although McKay's nostalgic memoir of his childhood, *My Green Hills of Ja-maica*, was published posthumously in 1979, his major autobiographical work *A Long Way from Home* appeared in 1937, three years after his arrival in the United States from a twelve-year absence. The Harlem Renaissance was over,

The depression had curtailed the interest in black books. Encouraged by a suggestion from his friend and mentor James Weldon Johnson and a generous grant from the Julius Rosenwald Fund, McKay began writing an account of his years abroad (Cooper 306). A *Long Way from Home* is written in an impressionistic style designed to carry the reader smoothly through the period of McKay's life when he was at the peak of his literary career—from 1918 to approximately 1932. Throughout the work, McKay focuses on his fantastic adventures and his acquaintances with celebrated people.

But despite its episodic structure, A *Long Way from Home* is bound together by a unifying theme of McKay's perception of himself as a "free-spirit," unfettered to any political organization or ideology (Cooper 307, 317). The first four chapters (part one) emphasize his association with whites and by implication provide insight into his sentiment regarding expected behavior vis-à-vis raced-based friendships and social organizations. Chapter One evokes McKay's memory of his meeting with Frank Harris, writer and editor of *Pearson's Magazine*, and Chapter Two recalls his initial encounter with Max Eastman, publisher of the left-wing journal *The Liberator* and radical biographer of Lenin. McKay paints a larger-than-life portrait of these two men as he unabashedly expresses his indebtedness to them as mentors. In 1918, Frank Harris published five of McKay's poems in *Pearson's*. McKay mentions that one of the poems, "The White Fiends," was rejected by *The Crisis*, "a Negro magazine" (McKay 26). In 1919, Max Eastman printed seven poems in a two-page spread that included "If We Must Die" (Cooper 99). For the next several years, McKay maintained a close association with *The Liberator*, serving as an associate editor from 1921 to 1922. McKay and Eastman developed a close relationship that lasted until McKay's death in 1948 (148–57).

One of the most satisfying chapters in A *Long Way from Home* deals with McKay's brief tenure (1921–1922) as an associate editor of *The Liberator*, where he met such luminaries as Charlie Chaplin, H.G. Wells, Carl Van Doren—one of the editors of *The Nation*—and poet Elinor Wylie (100–102). An incident involving poet e.e. cummings is particularly illuminating as an example of McKay's proclivity toward artistic independence. cummings had submitted some of his poems to *The Liberator*, and McKay wanted to feature a spread of his poetry, but coeditor Robert Minor objected because, according to him, the poems contained no political consciousness. A defender of the artist's right to pursue his own interests, McKay argued that "intrinsic beauty" was more important than "social significance." The poems did not appear in *The Liberator* (McKay 103).

McKay found himself constantly at loggerheads with the more hard-lined leftist members of *The Liberator's* editorial staff over the issue of art versus propaganda. After an especially bothersome quarrel with socialist writer Michael Gold, then sharing editorial duties with him, McKay resigned as an associate editor in July 1922 (Cooper 161–67). In the same year he published his groundbreaking collection of poems *Harlem Shadows* to rave reviews—in both the black press and the white press. But McKay felt no ties strong enough to keep him from

escaping to Russia and Europe (McKay 148–50). In 1922, he would leave America and the impending Harlem Renaissance behind him for twelve years.

In *A Long Way from Home*, McKay makes it clear that he visited Russia as an
independent writer with no affiliation with the American Communist Party than
attending the Fourth Congress of the Communist International. Despite his free-
agent status, the Bolsheviks and the Russian bourgeoisie embrace him with hearty
enthusiasm, regarding his black face as a good omen for the future (164, 170–
71). McKay visits literary gatherings and reads his poems in the presence of
luminaries of the Russian literary world, such as Chukovsky, Boris Pilnyak, Eugene Zamiatin, and Mayakovsky. In response to their criticism of the lack of
proletarian content in his work, McKay responds that his poetry expresses his
"feelings" (186). The high point of McKay's Russian visit is his introduction to
Trotsky, whom he calls "the most approachable of the big Bolsheviks." Trotsky
invites McKay to write a summary of his analysis of "the Negro problem." Mc-
Kay's ideas and Trotsky's response were published in *Izvestia* and *Pravda* (204).
Through Trotsky's influence McKay visits training schools for military forces,
meets military officers, and attends banquets. In Petrograd he witnesses the May
Day celebration on the reviewing stands with top party officials. Yet throughout
the Russian chapter, he insists upon his identity as only a poet (Cooper 183).

By way of Berlin, McKay travels to Paris, an atmosphere he finds more congenial than that of radical Greenwich Village or of propagandistic Russia. In his
Paris section, McKay offers his appraisal of the expatriate and modernist writers
just gaining recognition. For example, he states his preference for D.H. Lawrence
over James Joyce, whose *Ulysses* was published while McKay was in Paris. He
cites Lawrence's language and his ability to capture the "confusion," "sexual
inquietude," and "uncertainties" of the modern age as the determining factors
(247). Hemingway, too, receives praise for his brutal frankness and forthright
language. Unlike other expatriates, McKay saw nothing to admire in Gertrude
Stein. He found her treatment of Negroes in her short story "Melanctha" un-
original (248). The celebrated were all over Europe. McKay mentions meetings
with Edna St. Vincent Millay, Sinclair Lewis, the Paul Robesons, dancer Isadora
Duncan, and Louise Bryant, the widow of John Reed, the only American buried
in the Kremlin. Bryant was McKay's special friend (253–59). In Marseilles, Mc-
Kay finds a sense of negritude among the cross section of West Indians, African
Americans, North Africans, and West Africans. In this atmosphere he completes
his novel *Home to Harlem* (1928) and finds the inspiration to write his second
novel, *Banjo*, published in 1929 (283). *A Long Way from Home* is punctuated
with incidents that highlight McKay's perception of himself as a maverick spirit.
Conformity with any group is well nigh impossible, especially with the Negro
elites. In Morocco, his final pilgrimage, McKay observes the central role that
group life plays in the culture of the people and suggests how African Americans
might draw a lesson from this type of community design. He argues that racial
advancement is best served through group aggregation and not integration as
touted by the National Association for the Advancement of Colored People

(NAACP). But political advice aside, McKay ends his autobiography with the reiteration of his theme that he is just "a troubadour wanderer" passing through life, offering only "the distilled poetry of [his] experience" (354).

CRITICAL RECEPTION

A Long Way from Home received respectable reviews, but few critics were especially enthusiastic. The white press regarded McKay's book as well written and pleasant. Edwin Embree, director of the Julius Rosenwald Fund, was delighted with McKay's work for precisely its "cozy, companionable style" and "eclectic attitude." He also admired McKay's decision not to delve into "color and race consciousness" (Cooper 318–19). Horace Gregory of the New York Times called McKay's autobiography an unusual and very "readable book" (420). But the black press gave McKay's book a negative review, annoyed by his decision to fashion himself throughout as an independent, noncommitted persona. In "Spiritual Truant," published in New Challenge, Alain Locke accuses McKay of "a self-imposed impostasy," charging that throughout his life he has refused alignment with any racial group, political organization, or group of friends. McKay's apparent indifference to the plight of blacks bothered many critics who regarded his creation of the "troubadour" façade as a device calculated to evade commitment.

McKay's narrative is written in a vague and general style, certainly a disappointment for McKay scholars (Cooper 318–21). Yet in the final analysis A Long Way from Home fulfills the objectives that McKay had intended. It is a book-length sketch of his recollections, "the distilled poetry of his existence" (Long Way 354). In his autobiography, McKay provided a memorable impression of his experiences and the people he knew.

BIBLIOGRAPHY

Autobiographical Works by Claude McKay

A Long Way from Home. New York: Lee Furman, 1937.
My Green Hills of Jamaica and Five Jamaican Short Stories. Ed. Mervyn Morris. Kingston: Heinemann, 1979.

Studies of Claude McKay's Autobiographical Works

Chalmers, Rebecca Barton. Witnesses for Freedom: Negro Americans in Autobiography. Foreword by Alain Locke. New York: Harper & Brothers Publishers, 1948.
Cooper, Wayne. Claude McKay: Rebel Sojourner in the Harlem Renaissance. Baton Rouge: Louisiana State University Press, 1987.
Cruse, Harold. The Crisis of the Negro Intellectual from Its Origin to the Present Day. New York: William Morrow, 1967.

Du Bois, W.E.B. Rev. of *Home to Harlem*. *Crisis* 35 (June 1928): 202.

Gates, Henry Louis, Jr., and Nellie Y.: McKay, eds. *The Norton Anthology of African American Literature*. New York: W.W. Norton, 1977.

Gregory, Horace. Rev. of *A Long Way from Home*. *The Nation* (April 10, 1937): 414.

———. Rev. of *A Long Way from Home*. *New York Times* (March 28, 1937): 420.

LeSeur, Geta J. "Claude McKay's Romanticism." *CLA Journal* 32 (March 1989): 296–308.

Locke, Alain. "Spiritual Truant." *New Challenge* 2 (Fall 1937): 81, 83–84.

Ojo-Ade, Femi. "Claude McKay: The Tragic Solitude of an Exiled Son of Africa." In *Of Dreams Deferred, Dead or Alive: African Perspectives on African-American Writers*. Westport, CT: Greenwood Press, 1996. 65–81.

Singh, Amritjit. *The Novels of the Harlem Renaissance: Twelve Black Writers—1923–1933*. University Park: Pennsylvania State University Press, 1976.

ANNE MOODY
(1940–)

Emmanuel S. Nelson

BIOGRAPHY

Anne Moody was born on September 15, 1940, on a white-owned plantation in rural Mississippi. Her parents, Fred Moody and Elmira Williams Moody, were sharecroppers. After graduating from high school in 1959, she attended Natchez College in Natchez, Mississippi; in 1964 she graduated with a bachelor's degree from Tougaloo College, a historically black institution in her home state. During her two years at Tougaloo College she was an active member of the National Association for the Advancement of Colored People (NAACP) as well as an organizer and fund-raiser for the Congress of Racial Equality (CORE). After graduation she worked for a year as a civil rights project coordinator at Cornell University in Ithaca, New York. In 1967 she married Austin Straus; the marriage eventually ended in divorce. Moody was awarded a German Academic Exchange Service grant in 1972, and she spent a year as artist-in-residence in Berlin, Germany.

Moody was actively involved in the civil rights movement until the mid-1960s. By 1967, however, she had made a conscious decision to leave the struggle. The decision, she says, was prompted by her belief that racism was so deeply engrained in the minds of many southern whites that the legislative victories of the civil rights movement did little to change the attitudes of the people in any fundamental way. Deeply disillusioned by the slow pace of progress, Moody turned to writing. In 1969 she published her autobiography titled *Coming of Age in Mississippi*. The book received an enthusiastic reception. Six years later she published *Mr. Death*, a collection of short stories.

By the mid-1970s Moody had become increasingly reclusive. There are reports that she currently lives in New York City, but even her publishers are unable to confirm her whereabouts. She does not give public speeches, nor does she grant interviews.

AUTOBIOGRAPHICAL WORK AND THEMES

Comparable to Richard Wright's* *Black Boy* and Maya Angelou's* *I Know Why the Caged Bird Sings,* Moody's *Coming of Age in Mississippi* is one of the most compelling autobiographical narratives in the African American literary tradition. In a voice that is as subtle as it is insistent, as unpretentious as it is uncompromising, Moody maps her coming of age in Mississippi during the repressive 1940s and 1950s and the turbulent early years of the 1960s. Yet Moody's narrative is more than a poignant personal testimony; it is an immensely valuable cultural document that offers an insightful view of life in Mississippi during the middle decades of the twentieth century and the carefully orchestrated resistance to that way of life that the civil rights movement initiated during the 1960s.

The book is divided into four sections. In the first section, titled "Childhood," Moody remembers her early years amid the grinding poverty of rural Mississippi. Even though her parents labor in the cotton fields from dawn to dusk almost every day of the week, they are barely able to feed and clothe their children. At age nine Moody starts doing domestic work for white families. After her father abandons the family, she works several hours a day after school and on weekends to help feed her siblings. The opening section of the autobiography concludes with her recollection of her first calculated act of resistance to the southern racial codes. She begins to work for Mrs. Burke, a white woman. On her first day on the job Moody enters Mrs. Burke's house through the front door. The next day, when she knocks on the front door, Mrs. Burke directs her to the back entrance and Moody complies. However, the following morning, Moody knocks on the front door again. For about ten minutes Mrs. Burke ignores the knocks; finally Mrs. Crosby, Mrs. Burke's mother, opens the door and lets Moody in. Unsubdued by her employer's authoritarianism and meanness, Moody continues to knock on the front door every morning, and Mrs. Crosby, who waits for her, continues to open the door. Once Mrs. Burke realizes that she cannot dictate Moody's conduct, she lets her do the domestic chores without complaining. "Working for her," says Moody, "was a challenge," and Mrs. Burke would be the "first one of her type" that Moody would defy as she grows older (117).

Moody's minor revolt against Mrs. Burke foreshadows her later civil rights activism. Her political awakening begins during her teenage years, and Moody chronicles those years in the book's second section, titled "High School." During her first year in high school Emmett Till, a fourteen-year-old black boy visiting Mississippi from Chicago, is lynched for allegedly whistling at a white woman. His murder is a defining moment in Moody's life and in her political education. For the first time she realizes the barbaric extent to which many whites in Mississippi will go to protect their way of life and the appalling powerlessness of the blacks to challenge the existing arrangements. Their helplessness is manifest in their fear: When Moody asks black adults for information on the circumstances of Emmett Till's murder, she is told to shut up. When she asks her mother for the meaning of "NAACP" (127)—something she had overheard Mrs. Burke mention to a group of white women who regularly meet at her house—her mother angrily tells her never to mention that word in front of any white persons and orders her to complete her homework and go to sleep. Shortly thereafter Moody discovers that there is one adult in her life who could offer her the answers she seeks: Mrs. Rice, her homeroom teacher. Like Mrs. Bertha Flowers in Maya Angelou's *I Know Why the Caged Bird Sings*, Mrs. Rice plays a pivotal role in Moody's maturation. She not only answers Moody's questions about Emmett Till and the NAACP, but she volunteers a great deal more information about the state of race relations in Mississippi.

Moody's early curiosity about the NAACP resurfaces later when she attends Tougaloo College. Titled "College," the third section of the autobiography reveals Moody's increasing commitment to political activism. During her second year at Natchez College, she helps organize a successful boycott of the campus cafeteria when a student finds a maggot in her plate of grits. It is Moody's first experience in organizing a group of individuals to launch a structured revolt against the practices of an established institution. While a junior at Tougaloo College she joins the NAACP. The third section ends with Moody's recounting of a terrifying ordeal in Jackson, Mississippi. On a shopping trip there with Rose, a fellow student from Tougaloo College, Moody—without any planning or support mechanism in place—decides to go into the "Whites Only" section of the Trailways bus depot. Initially the whites in the waiting area react with shock, but soon a menacing white mob gathers around the two young women and threatens violence. Just before Rose and Moody are assaulted, a black minister, probably alerted by someone witnessing the event, arrives on the scene to rescue them and drive them away to safety.

The fourth and final section of the autobiography, titled "Movement," documents Moody's full-scale involvement in the struggle for civil rights. In the opening chapter of the final section Moody narrates her participation in a sit-in at a Woolworth's lunch counter in Jackson. She and three other civil rights workers—two of them white—take their seats at the lunch counter. They are, predictably, denied service, but the four continue to sit and wait. Soon a large number of white students from a local high school pour into Woolworth's. When the students realize that a sit-in is in progress, they crowd around Moody and her companions and begin to taunt them. The verbal abuse quickly turns physical. Moody, along with the other three, is beaten, kicked, and "dragged about thirty feet toward the door by [her] hair" (226). Then all four of them are "smeared with ketchup, mustard, sugar, pies and everything on the counter" (226). The abuse continues for almost three hours until they are rescued by Dr. Beittel, the president of Tougaloo College who arrives after being informed of the violence. When Moody is escorted out of Woolworth's by Dr. Beittel, she realizes that "about ninety white police officers had been standing outside the store; they had been watching the whole thing through the windows, but had not come in to stop the mob or do anything" (267).

This experience helps Moody understand "how sick Mississippi whites were" and how "their disease, an incurable disease," could prompt them even to kill to preserve "the segregated Southern way of life" (267). In the chapters that follow she comments on the impact of the assassinations of Medgar Evers and President John F. Kennedy on the civil rights movement, the escalating turmoil across the South, and her participation in the attempts to integrate white churches in Jackson on the Sunday after the murder of Martin Luther King Jr. The short final chapter ends with her joining a busload of civil rights workers on their way to Washington, D.C. As the bus moves through the Mississippi landscape, her fellow travelers sing the anthem of the civil rights movement: "We shall overcome" (384). As she listens to the words of the song, Moody wonders. The autobiography ends with two short sentences: I WONDER. I really WONDER" (384). The word *wonder*, in the context of the autobiography, lends itself to two different meanings. On the one hand, it suggests that Moody is skeptical if blacks in Mississippi will ever "overcome," as the anthem asserts. On the other hand, the word reveals her awe over her participation in a mass movement, her remarkable journey from her impoverished childhood on a plantation to her defiant participation as a young adult in a social rebellion that will shake the foundations of Mississippi, and the dignity and determination she sees on the faces of her fellow travelers on the bus to Washington, D.C.

Coming of Age in Mississippi is the story of a remarkable young woman's courageous battle against Mississippi's deep-rooted racist institutions and practices that remained largely unchallenged until the 1960s. Moody, however, is not entirely uncritical of the blacks in Mississippi. In fact, like Richard Wright's *Black Boy*, the autobiography of Anne Moody can be read as an articulate yet restrained critique of certain aspects of southern black folk culture. It is a culture of fear that attempts to stifle inquisitiveness. Many black adults actively discourage the children from asking probing questions about race relations. A curious black child, they are afraid, might grow up to be a rebellious adult, and rebellion, they knew, could be lethal in Mississippi. When Moody, as a child, wants to know why whiteness is a marker of privilege or when she asks questions about reports of racially motivated violence, she is faced with a wall of silence or sometimes even intimidation. Later when she becomes an activist, some of her relatives plead with her to abandon her activism; some, in fear of white retaliation, refuse to associate with her.

However, Moody's fiercest criticism is directed at the whites. She is relentless in her assault on the Mississippi way of life. While she freely acknowledges the decency of some individual whites, even contemplates the possibility of interracial unity, she carefully exposes how the politics of color informs every aspect of life in Mississippi. With appropriately sharp sarcasm, the title of her autobiography alludes to Margaret Mead's famous text *Coming of Age in Samoa*. Mead, an American anthropologist, examines in her work the social rituals and cultural codes that govern an individual's passage from childhood to young adulthood in a supposedly "primitive" Samoan culture. In *Coming of Age in Mississippi*, with nearly anthropological precision, Moody maps her initiatory journey from innocence to experience among the seemingly "primitive" whites of Mississippi.

CRITICAL RECEPTION

Reviews of *Coming of Age in Mississippi* at the time of its publication were overwhelmingly favorable. Shane Stevens, writing for *Book World*, calls it "quite simply, one of the very best" works to present the South from a black perspective. He calls it an "eloquent, moving testimonial" to Moody's personal courage, a narrative that "has the ring of authenticity and the spark of life" (28). E.M. Kennedy compares Moody's autobiography to Claude Brown's* *Manchild in a Promised Land* but concludes that Moody's narrative is considerably superior to Brown's. According to Kennedy, *Coming of Age in Mississippi* is "a history of our time, seen from the bottom up, through the eyes of someone who decided for herself that things had to be changed" (5). For C.N. Degler, "Anne Moody's candor and refusal to overdramatize create an air of verisimilitude that is the book's signal achievement" (83).

Although *Coming of Age in Mississippi* is not an infrequently taught text on American campuses, it has not received the serious scholarly attention it deserves. There is only one article devoted entirely to Moody's autobiography: Elease White's work that explores the impact of poverty on Moody's social maturation. The other four published articles on *Coming of Age in Mississippi* consider the text in the contexts of other fictional or autobiographical works. The best among those articles is William L. Andrews's study of Moody's text in relationship to Richard Wright's *Black Boy* and two white-authored southern autobiographies.

BIBLIOGRAPHY

Autobiographical Work by Anne Moody

Coming of Age in Mississippi. New York: Dell, 1976.

Studies of Anne Moody's Autobiographical Work

Anderson, Jace. "Re-writing Race: Subverting Language in Anne Moody's *Coming of Age in Mississippi* and Alice Walker's *Meridian*." *Auto/Biography Studies* 8.1 (Spring 1993): 33–49.
Andrews, William L. "In Search of a Common Identity: The Self and the South in Four Mississippi Autobiographies." *Southern Review* 24.1 (Winter 1988): 47–64.
Bloom, Lynn Z. "Coming of Age in the Segregated South: Autobiographies of Twentieth Century Childhoods, Black and White." *In Home Grounds: Southern Autobiography*. Ed. Bill J. Berry. Columbia: University of Missouri Press, 1991. 110–22.

Degler, C.N. Rev. of *Coming of Age in Mississippi. Saturday Review* 52 (January 1969): 83.
Ellmann, Mary. Rev. of *Coming of Age in Mississippi. Nation* 208 (January 6, 1969): 26.
Kennedy, E.M. Rev. of *Coming of Age in Mississippi. New York Times Book Review* (January 5, 1969): 5.
McKay, Nellie Y. "The Girls Who Became Women: Childhood Memories in Harriet Jacobs, Mary Church Terrell, and Anne Moody." In *Tradition and Talents of Women.* Ed. Florence Howe. Urbana: University of Illinois Press, 1991. 105–24.
Stevens, Shane. Rev. of *Coming of Age in Mississippi. Book World* (December 1, 1968): 28.
White, Elease. "Effects of Poverty on the Social Maturation of Anne Moody: A Commentary on Moody's *Coming of Age in Mississippi.*" *Journal of African Children's and Youth Literature* 6 (1994–1995): 43–55.

PAULI MURRAY
(1910–1985)

Leela Kapai

BIOGRAPHY

Born in Baltimore in 1910, Pauli Murray was brought to her maternal grandparents' home in Durham, North Carolina, at the age of three, after the death of her mother. Since her grandparents Robert and Cornelia Fitzgerald were in their seventies, the responsibility of raising her fell on her two maternal aunts, Pauline and Sallie.

Murray was an intelligent, precocious child who learned to read on her own before she was four as she sat in the classroom where her Aunt Pauline taught. Her grandfather, Robert Fitzgerald, was one of the educated, landowning "Free People of Color." Despite his Caucasian features, Robert Fitzgerald never disassociated himself from other African Americans; he fought for the Union army and helped open schools during the Reconstruction. Her grandmother, on the other hand, was born in slavery, the child of one of the sons of the plantation owner, and was brought up in the Smith family mansion by her father's sister. Though legally the property of the Smiths, Cornelia never considered herself a slave and talked proudly of her aristocratic relatives. The family lore of the Fitzgeralds and the Smiths made young Murray ambivalent toward her ancestry. While she admired her grandfather for his heroic efforts to fight for his race, she felt ashamed of her grandmother's kinship with the Smiths.

Murray's quest for higher education was fraught with obstacles. To escape the oppressive environment of the South, she decided to move to New York. However, in order to qualify for admission to Hunter College, she was required to complete an additional year of high school. Money was scarce and the depression years made the situation worse, yet her determination and diligence helped her to complete her undergraduate degree. She was rebuffed in her efforts to do

graduate studies at the University of North Carolina because of her race and was
next turned down for admission to Harvard Law School on account of her sex.
Undeterred, she went on to earn a law degree from Howard University in 1944
and then a Master's in Law degree from the University of California in 1945,
but circumstances thwarted her ambition to join the faculty at Howard. Her
experiences with discrimination based on race and gender made her into a lifelong activist fighting for justice. One of the founding members of the National
Organization for Women (NOW), she remained active in the work of the National Association for the Advancement of Colored People (NAACP). In between her many jobs and varied activities, she authored *Proud Shoes* (1956), a
biography of Robert Fitzgerald, a book of poems, *Dark Testament and Other Poems*
(1970), and numerous legal documents.

Murray had the honor of being the first African American to break several
barriers. She was the first African American deputy attorney general of California
in 1946, the first African American woman to be invited to the prestigious Mac-
Dowell Colony for artists in New Hampshire, the first African American woman
to earn a doctorate in Law from Yale University, the first African American
associate at the New York law firm of Paul, Weiss, Rifkind, Wharton, and Garrison, the first African American woman to teach law in Ghana, and above all,
the first ordained woman Episcopal priest in 1977. Such a checkered and distinguished career came to an end in 1985 when she died of cancer.

AUTOBIOGRAPHICAL WORKS AND THEMES

A study of Murray's autobiographical works cannot ignore *Proud Shoes*, her
biography of her maternal grandfather. Narrated from the perspective of Murray
as a child, the book reveals many significant details of her life. In the "Introduction" to the 1978 edition of the book, Murray explains that she wrote the book
during the period when "the country was gripped by the hysteria of McCarthy-
ism." She too had been victimized as Cornell University denied her fellowship
because of her past association with suspected communists. Enraged, she "found
it imperative" to declare her American heritage and suspended her fledgling law
practice to write the book. She observes, "The writing of *Proud Shoes* became for
me the resolution of a search for identity and the exorcism of ghosts of the past.
. . . I began to see myself in a new light—the product of a slowly evolving process
of biological and cultural integration, a process containing the character of many
cultures and many people, a New World experiment" (*Proud Shoes* xvi).

Murray's autobiography, *Song in a Weary Throat*, published posthumously almost three decades later, is an elaboration of her initial search for identity. The
epigraph to the book sheds light on the title; it comes from a line in one of her
poems, "Hope is a song in a weary throat." The subtitle *An American Pilgrimage*
suggests that it is an account of a purposeful journey. The narrative of her life,
arranged chronologically in thirty-five chapters, records her struggle to come to
terms with her multiracial heritage and reveals how the events shaped her to be

a rebel, an activist, and a feminist to fight for her rights as "a minority within minority." At the heart of the narrative lies a spiritual quest to seek the meaning of events and her own existence. It is remarkable to note how she repeatedly succeeds in channeling her anger into creative energy.

Jean Humez places Murray's autobiography squarely in the tradition of "women's spiritual awakening stories, particularly strong in Afro-American women's history" (317). She contends that it is "a journey to the core of self, a spiritual exercise in exploring her emotional depths, which we may see as part of her preparation for radical spiritual transformation" (322). However, Murray's portrayal of herself is devoid of any "emotional depth." She talks warmly of her friends and her family but provides no glimpses of her own emotional life. Her short-lived marriage when she was a sophomore at Hunter College is dismissed in a few sentences, and very little is mentioned of her relationship with her siblings or other members of her extended family. Her dry rational approach makes *Song in a Weary Throat* a valuable social document chronicling the battle for civil rights but tells little of the inner life of Murray.

CRITICAL RECEPTION

Song in a Weary Throat was widely acknowledged after its publication. However, most of the reviews stressed the achievements of Pauli Murray. Pat Williams, in the *New York Times Book Review*, echoed the view of many when she called the book "a rare self reflective social study of middle class blacks" (12). Jonathan Yardley, in the *Washington Post*, praised the "remarkable document," "smoothly written, good humored, passionate, thoughtful" (3). Susan McHenry, of the *Ms.* magazine, reminded the readers that Murray had been a civil rights leader boycotting lunch counters, arranging sit-ins, and protesting nonviolently thirty years before the civil rights movement of the 1960s. Enumerating Murray's "staggering range" of activities and accomplishments, she highlighted her "pilgrimage"—"her sense of her purposeful quest and . . . an expanding sense of identity" (14). Paula Giddings, in *The Nation*, also celebrated Murray's undiminished courage in the face of adversities.

Murray's autobiography, though generally acclaimed, has not received much critical attention as a literary work. Joanne Braxton, in her study *Black Women Writing Autobiography: A Tradition within a Tradition*, calls her autobiography "a testament to the vitality of autobiographical writing by black American women." She sums up, "Although her throat got weary, she never stopped singing. . . . She kept the vision and the song in front of her and she kept on moving" (207). Jean M. Humez's "Pauli Murray's Histories of Loyalty and Revolt" is a perceptive examination of her literary achievement. In her extensive discussion, Humez traces Murray's development as an autobiographer—from *Proud Shoes* to *Song in a Weary Throat*—and finds that in the latter work she "creates a strongly controlling intellectual, reflective, ethical, and politically liberal commentator's voice, through which she communicated an intense commitment to rationality and order" (316). As women's autobiographies continue to be examined at length, Murray's *Song in a Weary Throat* is likely to get the recognition it deserves.

BIBLIOGRAPHY

Autobiographical Works by Pauli Murray

Proud Shoes: The Story of an American Family. 1956. 2nd ed. New York: Harper, 1978.
Song in a Weary Throat: An American Pilgrimage. New York: Harper & Row, 1987. Rpt.
    as *The Autobiography of a Black Activist, Feminist, Lawyer, Priest, and Poet*. Knox-
    ville: University of Tennessee Press, 1989.

Studies of Pauli Murray's Autobiographical Works

Braxton, Joanne M. *Black Women Writing Autobiography: A Tradition within a Tradition*.
    Philadelphia: Temple University Press, 1989.
Giddings, Paula. "Fighting Jane Crow." *The Nation* (May 23, 1987): 689–90.
Humez, Jean M. "Pauli Murray's Histories of Loyalty and Revolt." *Black American Literature
    Forum* 24.2 (Summer 1990): 315–35.
McHenry, Susan. "The Unsinkable Pauli Murray." *Ms.* (May 1987): 14–17.
Williams, Pat. Review of *Song in a Weary Throat*. *New York Times Book Review* (March
    29, 1987): 12.
Williams, Shirley Anne. Review of *Song in a Weary Throat*. *Los Angeles Times Book Review*
    (May 24, 1987): 3.
Yardley, Jonathan. "Faith and True Grit: The Life of Pauli Murray." *Washington Post*,
    April 5, 1987, 3–4.

SOLOMON NORTHUP
(1808–1863?)

Elizabeth Marsden

BIOGRAPHY

Born in Minerva, Essex County, New York, in July 1808, after his father Mintus received his freedom, Solomon Northup and his elder brother Joseph were reared on a farm by loving parents who believed in education. In 1829, on Christmas, Northup married Anne Hampton of whom he wrote that "the blood of three races" flowed in her veins (Northup 21). Together, they had three children, Elizabeth, Margaret, and Alonzo. He used the money he earned repairing the Champlain Canal to purchase horses and hire hands to transfer timber from Lake Champlain to Troy, New York. Northup visited Canada during this time, broadening his knowledge. Changing jobs frequently, he farmed, cut lumber, worked as a carpenter, drove a cab, and played his fiddle. After happy years at Kingsbury, in March 1834, they moved to Saratoga Springs. When the family moved there, Northup's wife Anne worked in the United States Hotel. He met slaves with their masters who stayed in the hotel. The family lived for seven years in Saratoga Springs until 1841, when Northup ran out of jobs and money.

Kidnapped in Washington, D.C. in 1841 while seeking employment, Northup spent twelve years as a slave in Louisiana. After regaining his freedom in 1853, Northup published his autobiography. As an educated man, he presented accurate descriptions of his life both as a freeman and as a slave; thus, his account is unique. He was thirty-two when tricked into captivity and sold into slavery, three decades before the Civil War.

After twelve years of bodily harm and demeaning treatment, Northup was rescued. Encouraged to write his autobiography, he received $3,000 for the copyright of his book. He settled in Glens Falls, but no one knows what happened to him after 1863. Speculation suggested he was murdered by his former kidnappers. Some scholars doubt that Northup was murdered as an act of revenge; they believe his years of slavery took their toll on his injured body.

AUTOBIOGRAPHICAL WORK AND THEMES

The autobiography of Solomon Northup is well respected because it is written by someone who spent the first thirty-two years of his life as a free citizen of the United States, contrasting freedom with slavery, the educated man's perspective with that of the uneducated slave. Thinking of his family, this respectable husband and father made one naïve choice that led to twelve years of personal suffering and unbearable distress for his loved ones.

Alexander Merrill and Joseph Russell hired Northup and his violin for their circus at a dollar a day. Traveling to Washington, D.C., and pleased with his luck, he visited the Capitol and other sites. The men drugged Northup with belladonna, selling him into slavery. Handcuffed and fettered, robbed of his $43 and free papers, Northup was taken to Williams Slave Pen. James H. Birch bought Northup for $650 and planned to sell him in New Orleans. It took a few beatings before Northup realized he was indeed going to be sold. The more he told his story, the worse it was for him. Images of his wife and children nearly drove him to distraction, but he realized he must do as his kidnappers bid to survive.

In the middle of the night, the slaves were chained together and led to a steamboat headed for New Orleans. Trying to save himself, Northup convinced an English sailor to mail a letter alerting one of the white Northups. Although the letter reached Henry B. Northup, the nephew of Solomon's father's former master, Henry did not know where to search. After battling smallpox and almost dying, Northup was purchased by a kind and fair master, William Prince Ford. Unfortunately, Ford owed money to the cruel John M. Tibaut, who received Northup as partial payment while Ford held a mortgage on him worth more than the $400 debt.

Northup, who had never been beaten by Ford, soon discovered the delight with which Tibaut threatened his slaves. Once Northup retaliated. With others' help, Tibaut attempted to hang the slave; Ford's overseer, who knew Northup's value, stopped the hanging, but Tibaut sought revenge, and yet again Northup bested him. After almost killing Tibaut, Northup ran away through the swamps so the bloodhounds could not find him. Knowing how to swim saved his life; he returned to the home of Mr. and Mrs. Ford, who hid him for four days.

The worst was yet to come; Edwin Epps became Northup's new master. Northup was ordered to pick cotton, a backbreaking and finger-numbing task. While thus enslaved, he endured other suffering of the emotional kind. Northup met Patsey whom Epps raped repeatedly. Once, to punish Patsey for visiting another plantation, Epps forced Northup to lash Patsey. In spite of his strong distaste, he delivered forty-five lashes, then Epps took over. Eventually Northup was rescued when Epps ordered a new house built. A Canadian carpenter with a liberal mind set, Samuel Bass, worked side by side with Northup on the new house. When he felt it safe, Northup confided his identity and the tale of his kidnapping to Bass. Together, they sent a letter to the lawyer Northup hoped would rescue him. In January 1853, four months later, Henry B. Northup arrived to rescue Solomon.

Prominent themes that occur in Northup's account are varied. He examines life before and after slavery; slave life in Louisiana; the disparities between types of masters (Ford versus Tibaut and/or Epps); the separation of families sold into slavery; the use of music and dance to control slaves (Hartman 45); the use of the Bible to prove the natural order of slavery. Although Frederick Douglass's* slave narrative receives more attention than Northup's, it is the latter work that closely details themes only touched on by Douglass. Take, for instance, the time Northup whips Patsey, a fellow slave who incurs the wrath of Mistress Epps. As a rule, Douglass's account of brutal beatings, especially of his female relatives, distances the narrator from these types of extremely painful situations in ways that Northup's does not. Certainly his work is more accessible to younger readers (middle and high school) than Douglass's. One can use Northup in the classroom to demonstrate a mother's suffering when separated from her children (Eliza's story 29–32), the typical slave auction as described in New Orleans, or the process needed to rescue a free man from slavery (Henry Northup's efforts). In fact, Sue Eakin rewrote this slave narrative for children ages nine to thirteen in her work *Solomon Northup's Twelve Years a Slave*.

Northup gives information on whites who lived in both the North and the South; he reveals factors that contributed to the Civil War. The specific rituals and horrors of life on a cotton plantation support this. His editors praised his account as giving the most detailed history of life in the Gulf South (xi). Speaking of slave narratives in general, Polsky writes, "Primarily written as propaganda, the narratives served as important weapons in the warfare against slavery . . . pointing up the evils of slavery and combating the antebellum notion of black inferiority" (166). Northup's account falls into this category. Finally, Northup's book receives praise for handling such themes as power versus weakness, racism versus tolerance, and positive/negative responses to dehumanizing situations.

CRITICAL RECEPTION

In 1853, David Wilson helped Northup write *Twelve Years a Slave: Narrative of Solomon Northup, a Citizen of New-York, Kidnapped in Washington City in 1841*. The book sold 30,000 copies in three years. Northup received $3,000 and bought property near his daughter's house in Glens Falls, New York. Frederick Douglass wrote in his newspaper *The Liberator*, "Think of it: For thirty years a *man*, with all a man's hopes, fears, and aspirations . . . then for twelve years a thing, a chattel, classed with mules and horses. . . . Oh! It is horrible. It chills the blood to think that such are." Interviewed in Washington, Northup's story made the front page of the *New York Times*. The striking similarities of his story to the recent international sensation *Uncle Tom's Cabin* made him the news of the day. Of all the free blacks captured and sold into slavery (it is estimated that at least 300 kidnappings occurred), only Northup's appeared in book form. Although an important document, it was largely forgotten, according to Michelle Genz, writing in the *Washington Post*.

In recent years, Solomon Northup Day is celebrated in Saratoga Springs, New York, where his descendants from four states meet to promote remembrance of his remarkable life.

BIBLIOGRAPHY

Autobiographical Work by Solomon Northup

Twelve Years a Slave: Narrative of Solomon Northup, a Citizen of New-York, Kidnapped in Washington City in 1841, & Rescued in 1853, from a Cotton Plantation near the Red River, in Louisiana. 1853. Mineola, NY: Dover, 2000.

Studies of Solomon Northup's Autobiographical Work

Blassingame, John W. "Using the Testimony of Ex-Slaves: Approaches and Problems." *Journal of Southern History* 41.4 (1975): 473–92.

Cimbala, Paul A. "Black Musicians from Slavery to Freedom: An Exploration of an African American Folk Elite and Cultural Continuity in the Nineteenth Century Rural South." *Journal of Negro History* 80.1 (1995): 15–29.

Douglass, Frederick. Publisher's Advertisement. *The Liberator*, August 26, 1853.

Fleming, Dan B. "A Review of Slave Life in Fourteen United States History Textbooks." *Journal of Negro Education* 56.4 (1987): 550–56.

Genz, Michelle. "Solomon's Wisdom." *Washington Post*, March 7, 1999, F14.

Hanna, Fred J. "The Power of Perception: Toward a Model of Cultural Oppression and Liberation." *Journal of Counseling and Development* 78.4 (Fall 2000): 430–42.

Hartman, Saidiya V. *Scenes of Subjection: Terror, Slavery, & Self-Making in Nineteenth Century America.* New York: Oxford University Press, 1997.

Hay, Robert Pettus. "Writing History: Time and the Story of Slavery." *Mississippi Quarterly* 52.2 (Spring 1999) 329–35.

Hoganson, Kristin. "Garrisonian Abolitionists and the Rhetoric of Gender, 1850–1860." *American Quarterly* 45.4 (1993): 558–95.

Johnson, Walter. "The Slave Trader, the White Slave, and the Politics of Racial Determination in the 1850s." *Journal of American History* 87.1 (June 2000): 13–39.

McGary, Howard, and Bill E. Lawson. *Between Slavery and Freedom: Philosophy and American Slavery.* Bloomington: Indiana University Press, 1992.

Nichols, Charles H. *Many Thousand Gone: The Ex-Slaves' Account of Their Bondage and Freedom.* Bloomington: Indiana University Press, 1963. 167.

Olney, James. "'I Was Born': Slave Narratives, Their Status as Autobiography and as Literature." *Callaloo* 20 (Winter 1984): 46–73.

Polsky, Milton. "The American Slave Narrative: Dramatic Resource Material for the Classroom." *Journal of Negro Education* 45.2 (1977): 166–78.

Roback, Diane. "Bound for the North Star: True Stories of Fugitive Slaves." *Publishers Weekly* 247.47 (November 20, 2000): 69–71.

Roberts, Katherine. "Louisiana Sojourns: Travelers' Tales and Literary Journeys." *Journal of American Folklore* 113.449 (Summer, 2000): 347–51.

Solomon Northup's Odyssey. American Playhouse. Dir. Shep Morgan. Monterrey Movie Co., 1996. Videocassette.

Twelve Years a Slave: Solomon Northup Trailguide. Hamburg, LA: La Commission des Avoyelles, 1970.

Wyatt-Brown, Bertram. "The Mask of Obedience: Male Slave Psychology in the Old South." *American Historical Review* 93.5 (1988): 1228–52.

GWENDOLYN M. PARKER
(1950–   )

Loretta G. Woodard

BIOGRAPHY

Gwendolyn Parker was born on June 9, 1950, in Durham, North Carolina. Her father was "Yip" Judson Garrett Parker, a pharmacist who owned his own drugstore. Her mother was Arona Moore McDougald Parker, a mathematics teacher who taught at North Carolina Central University. Aaron McDuffie Moore, her great-grandfather, was cofounder of the North Carolina Mutual Life Insurance Company and founder of the Mechanics and Farmers Bank and North Carolina Central University. In 1959, a few weeks before Parker's ninth birthday, her family moved to Mount Vernon, New York, to seek better opportunities in the North. Thus began her painful journey through "the halls of privilege," which she would later recall in her memoir.

In 1964, by age fourteen, Parker had spent most of her formative years in advanced classes at Graham School in Mount Vernon. One of two blacks, she started high school at the Kent School in Connecticut in 1965. She entered Radcliffe College in the fall of 1968 and later received a B.A. While there, she writes that she straddled between two worlds, as a hippie and as a participant in the black liberation movement (134). She "acted in play . . . read treatises and tomes, debated tactics and methods of dissent . . . and went on strikes from classes" (134). She also read the works of Eldridge Cleaver,* Malcolm X,* LeRoi Jones (Imamu Amiri Baraka),* and Frantz Fanon (100).

In the spring of 1973, Parker moved from Boston to New York, where she worked briefly as a stage actress and as a substitute teacher in the summer. That fall, she entered New York University School of Law and later received a J.D. and LL.M. She was a tax attorney at Cadwalader, Wickersham and Taft from 1976 to 1978. In the fall of 1978, she began work at the American Express

Company as director of marketing and remained there for eight years. While in the Office of Strategic Planning, she was named a Black Achiever in Industry.

In 1986, after ten years of battling stereotypes on Wall Street, Parker left the corporate arena to pursue her first love, a career in writing. From the time she was five, writing was her passion (48), but she claims that it never seemed a "realistic option as [she] was growing up" (Carroll 197). She states, "Once I started writing the happiness I felt was overwhelming . . . [for it] . . . allows me to follow my own natural rhythms" (201). She credits such writers as Willa Cather, Dostoyevsky, and Toni Morrison for influencing her writing (203–4).

In 1994, Parker launched her literary career with the publication of her first novel *These Same Long Bones*. Woven in and through the Durham of her child-hood, the novel follows the lives of Sirus and Aileen McDougald as they expe-rience the death of their daughter Mattie and attempt to determine whether her death was an accident or whether it was the result of Sirus's refusal to allow local white businessmen to invest in his housing venture. Reviewers praised the work as a "thoughtful and generous-hearted novel" (Humphreys 19), with "its vivid multiplicity of detail . . . [and] exquisitely drawn characters" (Johnson 102).

Three years later, Parker published her memoir *Trespassing: My Sojourn in the Halls of Privilege*, which focuses on her personal journey in the corporate world and her abrupt decision to leave in order to become a writer. She has also written two screenplays, one of which is based on the slave narrative of Harriet Jacobs. Today Parker lives in Connecticut, where she enjoys her new life as a writer.

AUTOBIOGRAPHICAL WORK AND THEMES

As the title implies, *Trespassing: My Sojourn in the Halls of Privilege* depicts the growing tensions Parker experiences as a black female "intruder" in White Amer-ica. Consequently, she candidly addresses the triple oppressions of racism, sexism, and classism. Born and raised in a black middle-class family in the South, where she was nurtured and sheltered, Parker moves to the North. She states, "This is the real North, the North my father had talked so much about, a place of real opportunity and harmony" (64). Taught by her parents and grandparents that education and achievement were the pinnacles of success, Parker initially con-sidered her position as an attorney with a prestigious "old white-shoe firm" a mark of success (150). Ironically, but not surprisingly, she reveals how her Ivy League education and numerous accomplishments were never enough, for she was always viewed as a "trespasser" on private preserve.

The memoir is divided into six sections, but it is the last three—"Climbing the Ivy," "The Letter of the Law," and "Uppity Buppie"—that indicate Parker's isolation from a healthy environment. There were no women partners and no admittance at private clubs. She is one of two black attorneys and the only black woman in the firm, where people rarely spoke to her or addressed her directly. Some did not even believe she was a lawyer. Parker states that her biggest prob-lem was "to prove that you had what it took, in a system that was convinced it was impossible that you did" (161). Parker clearly has what it takes, but her invisibility ultimately causes psychological scars. Unable to make any real "human connections," she experiences anger and "rage over being rejected" (171). In this so-called privileged world, however, Parker learns that rage cannot sustain her. Finally, "caught up in the race to succeed" (167), she makes the difficult decision to walk away from the white community, which she so willingly embraced, to connect with a more loving and humane one.

Throughout *Trespassing*, including her first novel, *These Same Long Bones*, a sense of community is vital to Parker's work. Although far from a utopia, she realizes that it is the black community that she must reclaim to find acceptance and a true sense of self. Through the use of tropes, such as ancestors, storytelling, memories, food, music, and language, Parker finds various ways to reintegrate herself within the community that instilled lasting values and lessons in self-respect. When Parker reflects on her decision to eventually leave the boardroom, she writes, "And all of it—jockeying for power and position, the barriers I always met and the things that enabled me to smooth the way—fell behind. I was untethered, a balloon set loose, flying free on my way toward my past" (7). The image of flying suggests Parker's spiritual triumph and the rediscovery of self in a community rich in communal bonds. In the section of her memoir called "Epilogue: A Black Homecoming," Parker recalls what happens when she returned to the physical space of her childhood to celebrate the publication of her first book. She writes, "As I looked out at the faces looking up at mine—all of my family, so many friends—I realized that I had waited all my life to be here" (208). Such a recognition indicates that Parker has found a loving community—one that was always there waiting for her to reclaim.

CRITICAL RECEPTION

As a new writer, critical assessments of Parker's memoir have been confined largely to favoral reviews. In a *New York Times Book Review*, feminist critic Deborah McDowell praises the work for its "frank[ness], humor and compassion" and claims it "pleads a worthy case for the privileged few, who should not be expected to barter their dignity and self-respect for the pottage of wealth and position" (22–23). Identifying Parker's work as a "healing memoir," Patricia Bell-Scott, editor of *Life Notes*, claims *Trespassing* "offers comfort for anyone who has been wounded in the fray of race and gender politics" (Book Jacket).

Several critics acknowledge Parker's success as a writer. *Emerge* reviewer Lori Robinson notes that her autobiography "reflects the accomplished writer she becomes" (78). Praising her for her craft, Jill Smolowe observes how it is "carefully constructed . . . rendering . . . each moment with searing clarity" (75). A reviewer for *Publishers Weekly* notes that the memoir is "bittersweet and graceful" (392), while another from *Kirkus Review* states that it "grips the reader immediately" (1197) and holds the reader's attention.

Although Parker has written only two works, they are a welcome addition to the body of existing contemporary African American literature written by women. She joins the ranks with such writers as Tina McElroy Ansa, Marita Golden,* Bebe Moore Campbell, Jewell Parker Rhodes, and Jill Nelson. Now that writing is "a realistic option" for her, we eagerly await her next engaging work.

BIBLIOGRAPHY

Autobiographical Work by Gwendolyn M. Parker

Trespassing: My Sojourn in the Halls of Privilege. New York: Houghton Mifflin, 1997.

Studies of Gwendolyn M. Parker's Autobiographical Work

Bourne, Kay. "Writer Recalls Life in Corporate America." *Bay State Banner* 33 (March 26, 1998): 19–20.

Carroll, Rebecca. *I Know What the Red Clay Looks Like: The Voices and Visions of Black Women Writers.* New York: Carol Southern, 1994 194–214.

Humphreys, Josephine. "The Thing about White People." Rev. of *These Same Long Bones. New York Times Book Review* 43 (July 17, 1994): 12–19.

Johnson, Cynthia. Rev. of *These Same Long Bones. Library Journal* 119.5 (March 15, 1994): 102–7.

McDowell, Deborah E. "My Life as a Token." Rev. of *Trespassing: My Sojourn in the Halls of Privilege. New York Times Book Review* 147 (October 19, 1997): 22–23.

McHenry, Susan. "The Making of an 'Uppity' African American: An Interview with Gwendolyn Parker '72." *Radcliffe Quarterly* (Fall–Winter 1997): 34.

Rev. of *Trespassing: My Sojourn in the Halls of Privilege. Book World* 27 (October 5, 1997): 6.

Rev. of *Trespassing: My Sojourn in the Halls of Privilege. Kirkus Review* (August 1, 1997): 1197.

Rev. of *Trespassing: My Sojourn in the Halls of Privilege. Library Journal* 122 (November 1, 1997): 94.

Rev. of *Trespassing: My Sojourn in the Halls of Privilege. Publishers Weekly* 244 (August 11, 1997): 392.

Robinson, Lori S. "Memoir Peeks into 'Halls of Privilege.' " Rev. of *Trespassing: My Sojourn in the Halls of Privilege. Emerge* 9.1 (October 1997): 77–78.

Smolowe, Jill. "Finally Having Their Say." Rev. of *Trespassing: My Sojourn in the Halls of Privilege. Time* 150.9 (September 1, 1997): 75.

ELIZA C. POTTER
(1820–?)

Nikolas Huot

BIOGRAPHY

In 1859, the year that saw the appearance of *Our Nig*, the first novel written by an African American, Eliza Potter published anonymously her autobiography, *A Hairdresser's Experience in High Life*. As can be inferred by the title of her narrative, Eliza Potter, a hairdresser who learned her trade in France, was combing and styling the hair of ladies of wealthy and prominent families. Traveling across the United States and touring the trendy seasonal retreats of America's rich and famous, Potter would not only style the hair of her clients but also counsel them about personal matters. Quite open with her opinions and ever ready with her sharp tongue (some clients complained of her quarrelsomeness and pride), Potter put down on paper the same criticisms she presumably shared with her customers about unladylike attitudes, social climbers, *nouveau riches*, and white standards of beauty. Potter's temperament was so well known in Cincinnati and her personality was "so opinionated and extroverted that, when her autobiography was published, the public instantly recognized her as the author" (Dean, Introduction xlvii).

Although her later life was spent amidst high society, Eliza Potter had a very humble beginning in life. Born Eliza Johnson in Cincinnati, Ohio, in 1820, the future hairdresser followed her family to New York City at a very young age. Shortly after her arrival in New York, the freeborn Eliza Johnson found work as maid and governess for rich and respectable white families. Restricted by the color of her skin to domestic employment but not confined to a specific geographical place, Johnson traveled extensively in the northern states and in Canada. While in Buffalo, she "committed a weakness" and married (Potter 12). Her marital status, however, did not keep her from traveling. Occupied as a nurse,

Potter sailed to Europe in the early 1840s and spent more than a year in France and England. While in Paris, Potter increased her "marketability" by learning the arts of flower making, dressmaking, cooking, and hairdressing (27). Also in her European travels, she became fascinated with the higher social spheres, frequently traveling great distances to behold a royal procession, an aristocratic baptism, or a noble's funeral. This fascination with stylish and affluent people would not only shape her life and her employment choices but would also frame her one and only narrative. Although submitted as an autobiography, A Hairdresser's Experience in High Life presents mostly the author's opinions and reflections on white society. The author purposely shrouds the few biographical facts bestowed on the reader, either in an attempt to preserve the anonymity of the narrative or in order to expose the author's most important preoccupations. Little is known of Eliza Potter's life following the publication of her autobiography. After the 1860 census that lists Potter as living in her own house in Cincinnati with her two children, no further record is found about her.

MAJOR THEMES IN HER WORK

Despite her modest condition as a hairdresser (and as woman of color), Potter refuses to lower herself to the level of an indentured servant or to adopt a submissive stance. Even as a governess, she refused to call her "little charge" master: "I told him I would not do so, if he were as old as Methuselah. I will leave that word for the *South*, where it is exacted" (Potter 34). Distancing herself from slaves and poor free blacks, Potter uses her position as hairdresser and confidante to upper-class white women to redefine herself as the ultimate judge of standards of beauty and refinement. As such, Potter is able to criticize and condemn her white clients. Unwilling to lose the service of the best hairdresser in town, annoyed customers must endure Potter's biting remarks and personal advice.

Mostly preoccupied with high society balls, Potter constantly disregards relevant issues facing African Americans in general, and mulattos and women in particular, and rarely comments on slavery, abolition, racism, fugitive slave laws, or free blacks. When she does, however, her comments appear apologetic and "uncle tomish." About slavery, she contends that African Americans are the cruelest and worst masters, that not all slaves are mistreated, and that many slaves are quite satisfied with their situations. Instead of criticizing the institution of slavery as a whole, Potter criticizes individual behavior that, to her, is reprehensible and unbecoming. In her narrative, Potter relates stories illustrating the immorality of the slaveholder who keeps "his [black] mistress in the same house with his wife" (171), the lack of consideration of the master who forces freedom on his slaves (249), and the shameful behavior of those who lie to their slaves (254). However, for every deprecatory story about slavery, Potter recounts an anecdote where slaves are well treated by their owners (183), are reunited with family members through the intervention of a kind master (177), or are married by their good-hearted masters (254). Before one condemns such an attitude, one must remember the intended audience of the narrative. Potter was writing to a high society that included slaveholders; her goal was not to criticize the majority of her clientele, just those who acted in an undignified and immoral manner. As she says to an admitted abolitionist: "I like every person—slave-holders, free-holders, or any other kind of holders who treat all people right, regardless of nation, station or color; and all men and women who love their Redeemer" (249).

Potter's criticism of individuals is not restricted to attitudes toward slavery, however. The greater part of the narrative is spent denouncing social climbers, nouveau riches, and those guilty of immoral indiscretions. A strong believer in what should be an unchanging and steadfast hierarchy among classes, Potter contends that everyone should stay in their proper social spheres and not attempt to rise through them. Most contemptuous to her are those who try to make an entry into the higher social circles without the proper deportment or social credentials. Interspersed throughout her narrative are examples of belles who flaunt their wealth and, in the process, their lack of sophistication. Outmoded dresses and coiffures are also the subjects of Potter's ridicule. Not satisfied with gossiping about other people, Potter also freely admonishes her own clients for what she perceives as unladylike attitudes on their parts. If Potter is ever ready to criticize, she is also quite willing to counsel her customers on what constitutes true refinement and help debutantes to obtain invitations to important soirees. With her emphasis on white high society, it should be quite evident that Potter "has no interest in explaining black folks to white folks [;] her autobiography's premise rests upon a careful, unblinking critique of white standards of beauty" and of social structure (Dean, Introduction lviii).

CRITICAL RECEPTION

"Generally known to have been, in the words of a reviewer, the work of 'the bold, if not very polished pen of Mrs. Potter', [A *Hairdresser's Experience in High Life*] was a best seller" (Harlow 171). The success of Potter's narrative was largely due to curiosity and to the timeless popularity of gossip; in addition, many undoubtedly bought a copy of the tell-all to see if their names or their chatter appeared in its pages. Potter's autobiography was well received at its publication; however, its popularity soon waned. Local historians, concerned about pre-Civil War high society, occasionally relied on Potter's descriptions and insights, but no serious or exhaustive study of the autobiography appeared until the early 1990s.

In an attempt to correct omissions and bring out of anonymity important contributions to African American literary history, the Schomburg Library of Nineteenth Century Black Women Writers republished Eliza Potter's narrative in 1991. In the introduction to the republication, as well as in her entry for *The Oxford Companion to African American Literature*, Sharon Dean attempts to reinstate Eliza Potter's autobiography in the African American literary canon. Positioning the book as "the first of the genre of behind-the-scenes, tell-all autobiographies" written by an African American, Dean discusses how Potter's subservient role as an insider-outsider did not prevent her from achieving an assertive personality, which might be awed by her surrounding grandeur but refused to be debased by it ("Eliza Potter" 598). Moreover, by moving away from the traditional autobiographical genre, Potter's story becomes, Dean argues, "an affirmation of her artistry and her success, not merely of her survival" (Introduction lvii). Not only does she provide contextual information for Harriet E. Wilson's *Our Nig* and for Toni Morrison's *Beloved* but Eliza Potter also presents herself as a "full participant in her century, thus confirming absolutely her central status in the life of the nation" (Introduction lvii). According to Dean, Potter's spunk, as well as her ability to "control and dominate through language those who control her own social rise and that of her people," explains in part why *A Hairdresser's Experience in High Life* should be considered a significant work in the development of the African American literary tradition (Introduction lvii).

BIBLIOGRAPHY

Autobiographical Work by Eliza C. Potter

A Hairdresser's Experience in High Life. 1859. The Schomburg Library of Nineteenth-Century Black Women Writers. New York: Oxford University Press, 1991.

Studies of Eliza C. Potter's Autobiographical Work

Blassingame, John W. *Black New Orleans, 1860–1880*. Chicago: University of Chicago Press, 1973.

Dean, Sharon G. "Eliza Potter." *The Oxford Companion to African American Literature*. New York: Oxford University Press, 1997. 598.

———. Introduction. *A Hairdresser's Experience in High Life*. By Eliza Potter. New York: Oxford University Press, 1991. xxxiii–lix.

Graber, Susan P. "*A Hairdresser's Experience in High Life* by Mrs. Eliza Potter: Cincinnati in the Mid-Nineteenth Century." *Bulletin of the Historical and Philosophical Society of Ohio* 25.3 (1967): 215–24.

Harlow, Alvin Fay. *The Serene Cincinnatians*. New York: E.P. Dutton, 1950.

Huot, Nikolas. "Eliza C. Potter." *African American Authors, 1745–1945: A Bio-Bibliographical Sourcebook*. Ed. Emmanuel S. Nelson. Westport, CT: Greenwood Press, 2000. 353–56.

NANCY GARDNER PRINCE
(1799–?)

Yolanda Williams Page

BIOGRAPHY

Other than what is revealed in her narrative, little else is known about Nancy Gardner Prince. She was born in Newburyport, Massachusetts, on September 15, 1799, the second of her mother's eight children. Her father, Thomas Gardner, died when she was three months old, and her mother (whom she never names in the *Narrative*) suffered a mental disorder after the death of her second husband. Her mother's mental deterioration forced the young Prince to assume the role of caretaker of her younger brothers and sisters. She did this first by picking and selling berries and later by working as a servant for families in Essex, Salem, and Boston.

Prince was baptized in 1819 and shortly thereafter apprenticed herself to a seamstress. In 1824 she married Nero Prince who worked as a sentry for the Russian royal court. Soon after their marriage, the two left America for St. Petersburg, where they lived for ten years until her failing health forced her to return to America. She returned to America alone, however, for Nero Prince remained in Russia "to accumulate a little property, and then return" (45), but he died before he could rejoin his wife.

Upon her return to Boston, Prince helped to found an orphanage for poor children of color after seeing them turned away from other orphanages because of the color of their skin. However, the orphanage closed after three months because of inadequate funding. After the closing, she became active in the abolitionist movement, attending meetings of the Anti-Slavery Society.

In 1840, she departed for Jamaica to aid a Rev. Mr. Ingraham who had started a "station" in Kingston to aid the recently emancipated slaves. En route to Kingston, she stopped in St. Ann and stayed there after having been convinced by a

Mr. Abbott that her services were much more needed in St. Ann. She soon, however, became disillusioned with Mr. Abbott's mission after observing numerous instances where its teachers and leaders exploited the Jamaicans. She was threatened with dismissal for voicing her concerns about the exploitation, but left the mission because of failing health before Mr. Abbott could make good on his threat. After leaving St. Ann, she went to Kingston in hopes of working for Rev. Ingraham but learned that he had been dismissed upon her arrival.

In Kingston after observing the destitution of the area, Prince, along with some other friends, founded a home for destitute girls. In July 1841, she returned to America to raise funds for the school and, after having "collected in Boston and vicinity, in New York and Philadelphia" (60), returned to Jamaica in 1842. However, she never was able to see her plans for the school realized, for upon her return to Kingston, she found the entire country in upheaval in the aftermath of an insurrection. Fearing for her life, she left Jamaica for America.

She arrived in America in October 1842 after a voyage that put her in great physical danger. Because of a hurricane, the food and water supply were contaminated, and most of her personal belongings were stolen. Too, she narrowly missed being enslaved when the boat docked in Key West, which had recently passed a law "that every free colored person coming there, should be put in custody on their going ashore" (77).

She was able to work "with much success" (80) for the first twenty months after her return to America, but after that, her physical health dissipated, and she was no longer able to work and care for herself. By 1848, she was so destitute that she had to turn to friends for aid. In 1850 she published *A Narrative of the Life and Travels of Mrs. Nancy Prince* in the hope of generating enough money so as not to have to continue to rely on her friends for support.

Prince published two other editions of the *Narrative*, in 1853 and 1856. Of her life after the publication of the third edition of the *Narrative*, nothing is known.

AUTOBIOGRAPHICAL WORK AND THEMES

Prince's major work is her *A Narrative of the Life and Travels of Mrs. Nancy Prince*. Viewed by most as a travelogue as well as an autobiography, the *Narrative* contains concise descriptions of Prince's travel in Russia and Jamaica.

In the section detailing her life in Russia, Prince gives great detail about Russian life, including its geography, holidays, languages, and educational and religious practices. She also records several historical events that she witnessed while there: the flood of 1824, the cholera epidemic, and the Decembrist Revolt.

Prince provides just as much detail in the section detailing her travel to Jamaica. Similar to her portrayal of Russia, she also describes the social practices of the Jamaican people. In addition, she also includes a history of slavery in the West Indies and the Sierra Leone resettlement experiment; this information is part of a pamphlet on Jamaica she published in 1841.

Although primarily objective in nature, Prince does interject her personal beliefs into the text at times. Throughout the text she refers to religion and her belief in God and redemption. Too, she takes the opportunity to decry those who use religion as a justification of slavery. She also makes it clear that she considers slavery an abomination that should be abolished. In the section concerning Jamaica she denounces poverty, inhumanity, and the greed and corruption she observed there.

CRITICAL RECEPTION

Very little has been written about Prince's *Narrative*. Although mentioned summarily in several articles, no full-length study has been done of her work. Cheryl Fish compares Prince's *Narrative* to Mary Seacole's* *Wonderful Adventures of Mrs. Seacole in Many Lands*. In her comparison, she posits that in both works "the slave experience is presented and troped upon as a part of a dialectic with what it means to be a free and mobile subject with a complex relationship to nationality, class and public discourse" (476). In addition, she calls for the increased study and use of these works within the canon.

Cheryl Deborah Williams examines the *Narrative* as a work of self-discovery that leads to Prince's increased sense of identity. Similarly, Mary G. Mason espouses that travel becomes a metaphor for Afro-American women's life. Using Prince's *Narrative* as a springboard into a discussion of the autobiographies of Ida B. Wells* and Mary Church Terrell and the travel narrative of Eslanda Goode Robeson,* she describes it as a forerunner of those texts that used travel as the central metaphor to describe "the growth of authentic, individually authorized selfhood" (340). Indeed, much remains unsaid about Nancy Prince and her *Narrative*.

BIBLIOGRAPHY

Autobiographical Works by Nancy Gardner Prince

The West Indies: Being a Description of the Islands, Progress of Christianity, Education and Liberty among the Colored Population Generally. Boston: Dow and Jackson, 1841.
A Narrative of the Life and Travels of Mrs. Nancy Prince, Written by Herself. 1850. Rpt. in *Collected Black Women's Narratives*. Ed. Henry Louis Gates Jr. New York: Oxford/ Schomburg Library, 1988. Also rpt. in *A Black Woman's Odyssey through Russia and Jamaica*. Intro. Ronald G. Walters. New York: Markus Wiener Publishing, 1990.

Studies of Nancy Gardner Prince's Autobiographical Works

Fish, Cheryl. "Voices of Restless (Dis)continuity: The Significance of Travel for Free Black Women in the Antebellum Americas." *Women's Studies* 26 (1997): 475–95.

Mason, Mary G. "Travel as Metaphor and Reality in Afro-American Women's Autobi-ography, 1850–1972." *Black American Literature Forum* 24 (Summer 1990): 337–56.

McEwan, Dawn. "Nancy Gardner Prince." In *Notable Black American Women*. Ed. Jessie Carney Smith. Detroit: Gale Research, 1992. 882–84.

Williams, Cheryl Deborah. "Conceived in Transit, Delivered in Passage: Travel and Iden-tity in Nineteenth-Century African-American Women's Narrative." Diss. Uni-versity of Pennsylvania, 1999.

Winter, Kari J. "Nancy Prince." In *The Oxford Companion to African American Literature*. Ed. William L. Andrews, Frances Smith Foster, and Trudier Harris. New York: Oxford University Press, 1997. 600.

J. SAUNDERS REDDING
(1906–1988)

Geetha Ravi

Deriving his creative impetus and moral sustenance from the members of his race, Redding served the African Americans in various capacities. He was a scholar, the first serious black literary critic who contributed to the African American literature a canonical work, a reputed teacher with the highest honor of being the first African American to be a professor of literary criticism at an Ivy League university, an ardent advocate of the civil rights movement, a literary, cultural and social historian, and a prolific writer with the dual commitment of a serious writer to his people and to his art. His literary career spans the eventful decades of the Harlem Renaissance, the Great Depression, the two world wars, and the civil rights movement.

Redding was born on October 13, 1906, in Wilmington, Delaware, to educated, hardworking parents, Lewis Alfred and Mary Ann Holmes, who were neither rich nor poor. Both his parents graduated from Howard University. In *Twentieth Century Authors* (First Supplement, 1955) he admits that his father had to take up odd jobs after his regular working hours in his small government job. He served as a schoolteacher in a rural school in Maryland, but the family had its steady source of income only from his postal service. He was actively involved in the National Association for the Advancement of Colored People (NAACP) and was the secretary of the Wilmington branch and was also the founder of the first black YMCA there. Redding learned the need to be industrious to survive white racism, but he failed to be inspired by his father's "great and clear and unbending faith in God and Christianity" (Redding, *They Came in Chains* 141). His mother exerted tremendous influence on him during his childhood, instilling interest in literatures of both black and Western tradition, reading to him from famous authors such as Paul Laurence Dunbar, Longfellow, and Shakespeare, and teaching him the art of elocution, acquainting her children with the famous speeches of Greek and Roman orators. Redding's views on racism were fashioned with the influence of his parents.

Redding had the good fortune of being taught by the pioneering African American woman writer Alice Dunbar,* the widow of Paul Laurence Dunbar, who was then an English teacher in Wilmington's all-black Howard High School. Redding's rational views on religion find their source in the impact created by Dunbar, his drunken, "frustrated" anti-Negro black teacher who taught the black children the value of self-help. He admits that he held "both God and the Christian religion in some doubt" (Redding, *On Being Negro in America* 138). For the blacks, God was not an "abstraction" or a "spirit to be worshipped on Sundays" (139). Many were content with Jesus and never wanted the world: "He was a personal, intimate God with whom a 'little talk' could make things right" (Redding, *They Came in Chains* 141). Redding finds this religiosity the cause for the scorn of the whites and the very reason for being stamped as "inferior," (141). The early impressions of his father's hardship made the young Redding realize the need to prove the rugged strength of an individual to scale the steep barrier of racism, and Redding's relentless pursuits and laudable achievements did make the black community proud.

Redding finished high school in 1923 at the age of sixteen and attended Lincoln University in Pennsylvania for a year. It was a fruitful year, and he read the major classics of British and American literature. Then he enrolled at Brown University, where his older brother Louis received his law degree. Redding graduated with a bachelor's degree in 1928, immediately after which he worked for a short span at Morehouse College in Atlanta. He was fired from service from that black institution for expressing radical views on race in his honest admission that he feared and hated both the white and the black community and for supporting the radical W.E.B. Du Bois* rather than the conservative views of Booker T. Washington.* He married Esther Elizabeth James, a teacher, in 1929. He completed his M.A. at Brown University. The following year he joined Columbia as a graduate fellow and subsequently accepted lectureship in Louisville Municipal College, Kentucky, where he served till 1936. His first son was born in 1935 and was named Conway Holmes Redding. In 1936 he became the chairman of the English Department at Southern University in Baton Rouge, Louisiana.

His first book, *To Make a Poet Black*, was written at Southern and published in 1939. It was an attempt at presenting "certain factual material and critical opinion on American Negro literature in a sort of history of Negro thought in America" (xxix). Redding was keenly aware of the black literature's appeal to the "cognitive and the affective side of man's being" because it is a literature of "purpose and necessity" (xxix). In his introduction to the text, Henry Louis Gates Jr. calls him the "first eminent scholar critic" (xvi) among blacks and describes his work as "the first sophisticated book of literary criticism" (xvi) by an African American. In 1939 Redding received the Rockefeller Foundation fellowship. This gave him an opportunity to travel through the South and get an intimate understanding of his people. This experience took the shape of a unique autobiography, *No Day of Triumph*, in 1942. From Southern University he moved to Elizabeth City State Teachers College in North Carolina and served there till 1943. In 1943 Redding became the first Johnson Professor of English Literature and Creative Writing at Hampton Institute, Hampton, Virginia. From 1949 onward he was a visiting professor at Brown University, Providence, and lectured at a few other universities under the auspices of the American Friends Service Committee.

Redding's novel *Stranger and Alone* was published in 1950. The resources for this novel are found in his experience gained while teaching at various black colleges; the protagonist, Shelton Howden, a mulatto, exposes the ever quizzical plight of this new class of neither white nor black individuals whose only solution lies in accepting the strangeness and newness of their color and race. Redding's historical acumen is best mirrored in *They Came in Chains: Americans from Africa* (1950). The tragic twists that the black families experienced during slavery is poignantly rendered. Here he critiques black religiosity and maintains that "the Negro's religion was a withdrawal from reality" (141). In his 1951 volume *On Being Negro in America*, he addresses another sensitive topic: the color complex that exists within African American communities. This books unravels the complicated anatomy of racial prejudice.

In the early 1950s Redding visited India. This trip fulfilled his dream of addressing the Indians as an American. His passion to steer clear of the narrow path of race and his emerging consciousness of personal integration and the need for commitment to the human race made him address several issues on race relations in many Indian universities, where he strove to clear the mistaken notions many Indians had of America. His travel to India resulted in a volume titled *An American in India* in 1954. His *The Lonesome Road: The Story of the Negro's Part in America* (1958) pays tribute to the laudable achievements of the great black personalities. *The Negro* (1967) is a balanced survey of the contemporary America meant to educate the Americans and the world audience. Redding's tireless pursuits won him many laurels. He continuously published scholarly articles in numerous journals such as the *Survey Graphic*, *Nation*, and *Saturday Review*, to name a few. His struggle to draw the African American writers out of the literary ghetto has not been in vain, and his recognition bears testimony to this fact.

AUTOBIOGRAPHICAL WORK AND THEMES

Redding's *No Day of Triumph* is an autobiography with a difference. The writer turns into a "feller goin' round finding out about people" (185). He undertook the longest and the most tedious journey to get firsthand knowledge of his people. He did it at the risk of becoming "road weary and faint" (239), allowing his personality to be "shredded by too many contacts with others" (239). We accompany him into all areas of the American South and of the African American psyche as well. The narration seems a subversion or an externalization of the "stream of consciousness" technique that lets open the stream of disparate thoughts, memories, and a tangled bundle of emotions in the psyche. Redding has let the external world with its disparate places, motley of people of different races, rapid shifting of sights and sounds—in short, all that he saw, heard, and met down South—come alive before us. There is a photographic precision in his narration that gives it an effect of a motion picture on paper.

It is autobiographical insofar as it is a personal narration of his own journey. In the first few chapters in the first section—"Troubled in Mind"—he fullfils the requirement of an autobiography, sketching his family, his childhood, school, and college days. His family is also an "unwilling victim" (10) of their cultural complexes caught in a "tradition of ridicule and inferiority" (10). His father, clothed in humble attire, was no statesman but could quote from "Teddy Roosevelt and Fred Douglass" (3). To survive among the "merciless, argus-eyed spiritual enemies" (10) (i.e., the whites), he had to do a number of odd jobs including waiting at dinner tables and cutting corn on holidays. His handsome mother, a mulatto, equally well read, found it hard to mingle with the dark-skinned blacks. She, like many other mulattoes, found it hard to accept the pure-blooded blacks as her equal. Redding's family is composed of browns, and they maintained a respectable silence with regard to color and consciously avoided terms like "nigger." The most important distinction he learned was that blackness might be "uncomely" (28) but need not be associated with inferiority. He had an urge to learn everything from personal experience; after his graduation it was not just a safe refuge that he was looking for; he was looking for "people, for things, for something" (46). Weaving a few other details from his personal life, like his grandmother's story of the white master Caleb Wrightson and his visit to Cousin Christy, Redding gives the book a distinct autobiographical imprint.

But for this thin outline of his life, the "I" of the narration is the collective "I" of his race and the communal experience of a complex variety of the members of his race. When he meets his Cousin Christy, it was not just the "blood kinship" (234) that draws him closer but the awareness of "common flux of blood, of experience, of memory and heritage that made me one with many" (234). Once when he undertook a foolish venture of meeting the police commissioner in the riot-ridden South, he was stripped and checked under suspicion and for the first time experienced shame, humiliation, and "terrible impotence" (180). The hurt brought tears and along with it the "ancestral memory" (180).

No Day of Triumph is also a travelogue. It is a record of Redding's journey down the Black Belt in the South that he undertook with a mission to explode the mystery of what a "Negro" is in America. He left Washington not caring which road he took and without even consulting maps. The first stop was at Warrenton, then at Fredericksburg, where "abruptly the South began" (55). Lingering for a few days to get a deep knowledge of the complexities of the poor working blacks in the factory town on the "northwestern edge of the South's black belt" (69), he plunged further, deep into the South. During the trip through the mountainous Blue Ridge he has photographed the scenic beauty of the South:

"[T]he bald mountain top, with a dribble of sun upon it, rose above the mist and floated there like the escarpment of some fantastic aerial city hidden in the clouds" (94). The mining town from Kanawha Valley to Charleston is a "dismal succession of grim squalor" (95). Traveling through all the bylanes of West Virginia he lands in the "inhospitable flats of Arkansas" (139) from where he reaches the land that houses the typical southern white man, Memphis, Tennessee; and from there to Kentucky. Then he reaches the lands bordering the long, winding Mississippi, from where he sped across to the countryside of Louisiana. The journey concludes here with Redding announcing that he is to visit "Texas. Oklahoma" (342).

These places house the real men of his race who are of innumerable shades and hues of black and belong to different classes. Listening to the tales of these real-life characters, one gets the feeling of reading a novel. Every individual adds a new dimension to the author's understanding of his race. The travel makes it possible for Redding to project the microcosm of the black community. The common understanding of the oppressive impact of the white is echoed in the words of a young fellow, Leon, in a "shanty" hotel in Warrenton. Mike Chowan, a Negro intellectual, had to accept expulsion from college and from the job of a waiter, for he questioned the racist treatment. Becoming a worker he understood the need for unions and turned to communism. Even the uneducated miner's wife Virgle Mitchell found "Commanism" (112) the last resort.

Affluence and education drew the blacks close to the white snobs. The black physician who was supposed to be serving his folk was the embodiment of condescension toward the "dicktie niggers" and found no need for communism. The black schoolmen in West Virginia were cynical, "terrific snobs, the true bourgeoisie" (119). The black scholars were pedantic and were after "a puerile flight from reality" (121). If one was too black, getting a scholarship was difficult. Coe Harvis, the black lawyer in a mining town, led a life of liquor and lies and summed the black history as one of violence born of desperation. According to him, murder committed as an outcome of oppression was "clean killing" (108). In Hooten County he meets many angry young black men, and race relations are always dangerously tense. Indiscriminate killings born of suspicion often result in mob riots. Drunkard or bully, schooled or ignorant, dentist or worker, every single black man whom he happened to meet receives serious attention and a graphic portrayal. An orgy of prayer by the unlettered miners with the cymbals clanking and the preacher's sermon during a wake are carefully described.

Redding records the South's conception of the black: The Negro is "improvident, immoral and generally no good" (131). His travels among and contact with the southern white made him conclude that he was "a soulless creature of the devil, drooling blood and venom, ignorant beyond belief, but also cunning beyond belief, filthy, lecherous, murderous, cowardly, superstitious, and by God accursed" (169). Redding doesn't fail to see the simple faith in his people who always "do it, by God" (118). Their blood taught them to pray. The black man's wants are few: " 'That's three things a man's 'bliged to have: a dog, a plat o' land

somewhars, an' a woman' " (248). Some more prevailing notions have a prover-
bial quality: "[W]hite folks' shame ain't the same thing as niggers' shame" (195);
"Nigger was always wrong. White man was always right" (188); "Don' none de
white folks love no niggah noway" (315). And the one unanswered question
rings in every black man's heart: " '[I]f democracy's so good for white folks, why
ain't it good for niggers too?' " (259).

The nuances of the color problem do not escape Redding's microscopic vision.
The notion of color has been in a state of flux. The problem to the twentieth
century is not just the conflict between whites and blacks. Like Redding's mother,
many mulattoes could not accept the dark-skinned blacks. To be a mulatto and
have white blood was hailed by many as the respectable thing, and the change
in color helped many to pass for whites.

Very subtly Redding solves the mystery of the Negro by focussing on the image
of Menola, who, though classified as colored, had Cajun, Indian, Negro, and
white blood in her. America is indeed a land of people of all shades. The dance
party he attended with Menola had men and women of all hues who kept to the
rhythm of Louis Armstrong. Without much pretence at solving the jigsaw puzzle
of the so-called Negro problem, Redding concludes: "Negro is only an equation
in a problem of many equations, an equally important one of which is the white
man" (339). The salvation for America lies in treating everyone as a human
being, keeping alive human values such as "integrity of spirit, love of freedom,
courage, patience, hope" (340).

Quite typical of many writers of the Harlem Renaissance, Redding's experimentation with the autobiographical form is evident. The title of each chapter
is a line from a famous spiritual. The title No Day of Triumph expresses the
rational perception of the author about the status of the blacks. Individuals might
have experienced triumph but not the black race. But "There Is a Balm" (the
title of the last chapter) indicates that there is surely a balm for the pain felt by
the blacks. The book's language, which is often lyrical, is rich in striking metaphors.

CRITICAL RECEPTION

Redding received the Mayflower Award for distinguished writing for No Day
of Triumph. His own observations on how well the book was received are found
in his On Being Negro in America. He admits that the Communists had received
advance copies of it; the New Masses published an excerpt without even getting
permission from the author, and he "began to get letters from Communists all
over the country" (89). After publication, he was invited to New York for a party
with the popular writer Carl Van Vechten. It was announced that his book was
going to be a bestseller and he was going to become commercially successful like
some of his contemporaries, such as Richard Wright* and Langston Hughes.*

The detailed study in the Dictionary of Literary Biography by Thelma Barnaby
Thompson mentions the wide attention the author won and favorable reviews

his book received. John Vassilowitch Jr. argues that Ralph Ellison considered this work as "sociologically important" (109). Redding's unique contribution lies in his bringing to light the damage done to the black society by the so-called educated leaders of the black South. Ellison was so inspired by Wimbush, the college president in Redding's novel *Stranger and Alone*, and the black college president in *No Day of Triumph* that he created his Dr. Bledsoe in his *Invisible Man* based on them. In short, Redding's autobiography remains a highly readable, elegantly written work that offers a penetrating look at African American life during the first half of the twentieth century.

BIBLIOGRAPHY

Autobiographical Work by J. Saunders Redding

No Day of Triumph. New York: Harper, 1942.

Studies of J. Saunders Redding's Autobiographical Work

Gates, Henry Louis, Jr. Introduction. In *To Make a Poet Black*. By J. Saunders Redding. Ithaca, NY: Cornell University Press, 1988. vii–xxiv.
"J. Saunders Redding." In *Twentieth Century Authors*. Ed. Stanley Kunitz. New York: H.H. Wilson, 1955. 817–18.
Thompson, Thelma Barnaby. "J. Saunders Redding." In *Dictionary of Literary Biography*. Vol. 76. Ed. Trudier Harris and Thadious M. Davis. Detroit: Gale, 1989. 148–57.
Vassilowitch, John, Jr. "Ellison's Dr. Bledsoe: Two Literary Sources." *Essays in Literature* 8.1 (Spring 1981): 109–13.

SARAH RICE
(1909–?)

Terry Novak

BIOGRAPHY

Sarah Rice was born Sarah Lucille Webb on January 4, 1909, in Clio, Alabama, to Elizabeth (Lewis) and Willis Webb. The family largely made a living through sharecropping. Sarah's father was by vocation, however, a minister of the African Methodist Episcopal (AME) Church. Her mother was trained as a schoolteacher. Sarah was third of nine children, one of whom died at birth. Because of the size of the family, it was imperative that all of the children participate in working the land. That land constantly changed, as Reverend Webb found himself regularly reassigned churches and, therefore, regularly uprooting his family. At times the family stayed put, and Reverend Webb commuted from home to church.

Sarah took her family responsibilities quite seriously. She learned to plow, donning her brother's clothing so her parents would not discover that one of the girls was doing "boy's work." She knew she could do the work as well as or better than her brothers; the independent spirit that would continue to flower throughout her life led her to do as she saw right even in childhood. Sarah also took advantage of her fine mind and, with regular encouragement from her mother, worked her way through high school and into the field of teaching.

Sarah graduated from high school in 1925, the same year her father died, began teaching in 1926, and entered into an ill-fated marriage with Ernest Hayes in 1927. From that marriage came Sarah's son, James David Hayes. With personally characteristic strength, Sarah left her abusive and unfaithful husband in 1929. She continued her teaching career until 1933, when she moved to Florida to work as a domestic, making much more money than she could ever have made from teaching.

Sarah married for a second time in 1937, this time to James Myers. Once again, she had made a poor choice; the second marriage also quickly ended in divorce. Determined that she was done with marrying, Sarah concentrated on her work, on her son and other family members, and most important, on her own sense of independence. Fate had other things in store: In 1953, Sarah married Andrew Rice and remained happily married to him the remaining thirty years of his life; Andrew Rice died in 1983.

Some time after her husband's death, Rice's family members convinced her to write down her life story. Not quite trusting herself to the task, but evidently understanding the importance of such a task, Rice contacted Louise Westling, an English professor at the University of Oregon, for help. In 1986, Rice sat down with Westling and began to dictate her autobiography. Rice had worked for Westling's mother thirty years prior and trusted Westling to fashion an authentic autobiography out of their conversations. The collaborative work was published in 1989.

AUTOBIOGRAPHICAL WORK AND THEMES

Rice's sole autobiographical work is titled *He Included Me: The Autobiography of Sarah Rice*. The fact that this text was transcribed and edited by Louise Westling and is in fact a unique form of oral history is interesting in and of itself. One tends to place oral history in times gone by, not as late as 1989. One also tends to view the oral historian as one incapable of, for one reason or another, writing down his or her own story without the help of another person. Rice's autobiography, of course, was not produced in historically ancient times. And Rice herself seems a far cry from the person who cannot manage to write her own autobiography, independent of any transcriber or editor. Indeed, the reader is constantly reminded of Rice's fine mind and educational abilities throughout the reading of the text. Rice herself asserts that had she not made poor spouse choices in the early years of her life, she would surely have gone on with her education until she had reached a Ph.D. Yet something made this determined, intelligent woman believe she could not write her own story.

It is a story worthy of the telling and it does, as Westling points out in her preface, cover ground that has been previously ignored. Perhaps most important, it gives the reader pause for reflection. If one African American family in the rural South consisted of educated parents, if one poor mother worked to see her own children and those of her neighbors educated — at least to the point of being able to read — if one sharecropping family sent more than one daughter out in the world of the segregated South to teach in schools for African American children, were there not perhaps dozens more whose stories we simply do not yet know? Maybe. In any case, we do have Rice's story, and hers does begin as the story described above. And it goes way beyond those basics as well.

Rice tells about her older sister Beatrice obtaining a teaching position in a white school. Beatrice was immediately removed to another school once she was actually seen; it had been assumed by the school board that she was white because of her fine handwriting! Rice herself obtained her first teaching job at the age of seventeen, simply by lying and saying she was twenty-one! When Rice speaks of her teaching career, she speaks with a passion most sincere. She saw herself as successful if she could teach her students—many of whom were older than she— to read and write enough to fill out and understand a mail order form and to calculate enough math to not be cheated in financial dealings. This was a true vocation for Rice, one that she most probably should have continued. But, as she confides with regret, the necessities of life got in her way. She simply needed more money, more security. For that, an African American woman of the early twentieth century, in the South, turned to domestic work as a matter of course. If ever the reader had missed the message of history that many fine minds had been wasted on menial work, Rice gently but persistently gives that lesson again, this time in a way that is difficult to ignore. The reader is tempted to shout at Rice to go on with her teaching, with her education, but the reader also becomes fully and painfully aware that Rice has no real choice in the matter.

Rice has other lessons to teach as well. She very bluntly speaks of her failed marriages and her first two poor choices in husbands. She is very matter of fact when she tells of leaving her young son with her mother while she herself leaves the state to seek better work and better wages. She is again matter of fact when she speaks of bringing her ten-year-old son to live with her once again. Perhaps this is simply characteristic of the voice of the elder reminiscing, but it is probably more than that. The reader begins to learn that the matter-of-fact tone does not attest to a lack of emotion or regret but rather attests to reality as it very harshly existed for many African American women of Rice's time and place.

Rice goes beyond personal matters in parts of her autobiography. She often graces the reader with her view on social matters. For instance, she speaks of mulattoes and the building of the black middle class in the middle of her history:

There was a town called Abbeyville, Alabama, heavily populated with mulattoes. The white people built a Rosenwald school for them, because they wanted their mulatto children to have a good education. They called it a country training school, and it was better than some of the city schools. That way some of them were able to pull out of being poor. And because some of them had land, they were able to buy more. Some of them had black sisters and brothers. . . . One was just as smart mentally as the other one. They were sisters and brothers, and the light ones would help the black ones. Gradually a middle class would form that way. (73–74)

While one wishes in instances such as this to have Rice elaborate more on her own views, that wish is left unfulfilled, almost as if Rice is apprehensive about delving too deeply into sensitive social matters.

Rice provides the readers with messages that may be considered feminist as well. Once again, though, she draws back from speaking too deeply or too candidly. When she speaks of her aspirations, when she speaks of her choices and her regrets, she undoubtedly speaks to a younger generation, coaxing them in a grandmotherly fashion to think through their options carefully. One only hopes that they grasp her meaning.

Rice does indeed give us a peek into her life through her autobiography, but she goes far beyond that. She also treats the reader to a view of a time and a place that is often ignored, and she, so appropriately, teaches the reader things no history class has probably taught. One can only imagine the greater effect the autobiography would have had if Rice would have had the courage to write the book on her own, as she had the courage to do so many other things on her own.

CRITICAL RECEPTION

Serious scholarly studies of *He Included Me* have yet to be undertaken, perhaps because of the novel idea of the book's oral history format. Thus far, critical discussions have been limited to book review format and have been largely favorable. However, at least some of the reviewers find the oral history mode of the book suspect. Jacqueline Rouse of American University writes, "Just who is interpreting whose life? The lack of the proper historical, analytical, and cultural framework for the true significance of this activist who made it against all odds does a disservice to the legacy of all the Sarah Webb Rices in African-American history, regardless of the editor's statement of immunity" (361). Stephanie Shaw, of Ohio State University, also finds aspects of the book disturbing. Shaw questions the confusion that exists when Rice speaks of her domestic service in white homes and the lack of clarity as to which family is Louise Westerly's. Shaw writes, "The question raised . . . is ominous considering the editor's explanation of the origin of the book. The omission almost suggests that Rice was still, in a way, on the job" (358-59).

Other reviewers fail to look that deeply into the text. Susan Yates points out that the autobiography "seems one shaped less by history than by individuals" (110), although she does not see that as a fault. Herbert Mitgang finds the book to be "a moving story that reveals a hidden corner of American life" (C18).

It is important to note that all reviewers find value in the text and in the messages contained therein. However, those writing from a more academic perspective are apt to question, in one way or another, the format and/or the circumstances of the autobiography, whereas those writing from a more general point of view seem more eager to praise the book unconditionally.

BIBLIOGRAPHY

Autobiographical Work by Sarah Rice

He Included Me: The Autobiography of Sarah Rice. Transcribed and ed. Louise Westling. Athens: University of Georgia Press, 1989.

Studies of Sarah Rice's Autobiographical Work

Cain, Joy Duchett. Rev. of He Included Me: The Autobiography of Sarah Rice. New York Times Book Review (May 27, 1990): 715.

Leathem, Karen Trahan. Rev. of He Included Me: The Autobiography of Sarah Rice. Mississippi Quarterly 44 (1991): 518.

Mitgang, Herbert. "Learning to Wear Poverty Like a Crown." Rev. of He Included Me: The Autobiography of Sarah Rice. New York Times, November 22, 1989, C18.

Rouse, Jacqueline A. Rev. of He Included Me: The Autobiography of Sarah Rice. Journal of American History 78 (1991): 361.

Shaw, Stephanie. Rev. of He Included Me: The Autobiography of Sarah Rice. Journal of Southern History 57 (1991): 358–59.

Stuttaford, Genevieve. Rev. of He Included Me: The Autobiography of Sarah Rice. Publishers Weekly (September 1, 1989): 73.

Sullivan, Ann H. Rev. of He Included Me: The Autobiography of Sarah Rice. Library Journal 114 (1989): 118.

Weidman, Bette S. "Citizens of the Whole World." Rev. of He Included Me: The Autobiography of Sarah Rice. Commonweal 117 (1990): 297–99.

Westling, Louise, transcriber and ed. Preface. He Included Me: The Autobiography of Sarah Rice. By Sarah Rice. Athens: University of Georgia Press, 1989.

Yates, Susan. "Autobiography: He Included Me." Wilson Library Bulletin (April 1990): 110.

ESLANDA GOODE ROBESON
(1896–1965)

Bettye J. Williams

BIOGRAPHY

Called "Essie" by her two brothers, other kin, and familiars, Eslanda Cardozo Goode Robeson came from a Spanish-Jewish family of impressive lineage. Emigrating to the United States in the late eighteenth century, her great-grandfather, Isaac Nuñez Cardozo, married an octoroon slave in Charleston, South Carolina. Essie's grandfather, Francis Lewis Cardozo (a Reconstruction politician), who was one of six children, was cited after the Civil War by Henry Ward Beecher as "the most highly educated Negro in America" (Duberman 35). Daughter of educator John Goode and Eslanda Cardozo (known as "Ma Goode"), Essie was born on December 15, 1896, in Washington, D.C. She attended the University of Chicago and the Teachers College of Columbia University, where she earned a Bachelor of Science degree in chemistry in 1923. Wife of America's greatest concert and interpretative artist Paul Robeson, Essie was the single most influential person in launching and guiding his concert and film career. She handled much of his business-related contracts, travel itineraries, correspondence, and press briefs. Some few cohorts of Paul Robeson portrayed her as "bossy," pushy, and elitist. As a public speaker, she became actively involved in the political traffic that swirled around him.

Six years after marrying Paul Robeson, Essie gave birth to a son (Pauli), christened Paul Robeson Jr., on November 2, 1927. Occasionally domiciling with his celebrity parents in the United States (New York and Connecticut), England, Spain, and Russia, Pauli lived with and was reared by "Ma Goode," nicknamed "Queen Victoria" (Duberman 36). Beginning her scientist career in the early 1920s as the first African American analytical chemist working at Columbia Presbyterian Hospital, Essie later pursued anthropology, journalism, and world traveling. Possessed with a pioneer's spirit and in pursuit of a career independent of Robeson's in the early 1930s, Essie found herself at odds with society's definition of the proper place for a woman—especially an African American woman. With an "unquiet, tenacious spirit" and always ambitious, she took off with Pauli for Africa in 1936 (Duberman 538). Beginning in South Africa and for several months traveling through Mozambique, Swaziland, Kenya, Uganda, and Egypt, she explored African countries documenting their culture and languages in connection with her graduate studies in anthropology at the University of London and the London School of Economics. She continued her studies at the Hartford Seminary Foundation and received a Ph.D. in anthropology in 1945.

After World War II, Paul Robeson stood at the pinnacle of fame, fortune, and success as an international artist. In 1947, he spoke out on "Blacks being lynched in the South . . . Third World nations expressing their aspirations for independence from colonialism, and . . . for world peace" (Robeson, *Whole World* 171–72). The speech turned out to be the most controversial address of his entire career. He was subpoenaed by the California Legislative Committee on Un-American Activities, known as the Tenney Committee. Afterward, threats of violence followed the couple. Without passports, they became prisoners in the United States—accused of no crime. For eight years (1950–1958), the Federal Bureau of Investigation (FBI) relentlessly hounded them. Keeping a rumor-mongering, hostile press at arm's length during the anti-Robeson hysteria with the State Department and the FBI, Essie stood defiant and proud. Pursuing international issues, she became a correspondent at the United Nations and spent much of the 1950s observing world events through the insights of world leaders—Namide Azikiwe, Kwame Nhrumah, Jomo Kenyatta, Mao Zedong, Mohandas K. Gandhi, Jawaharlal Nehru, Nikita Khrushchev, and Fidel Castro. With a tremendous capacity for work and an unbending dedication to Paul Robeson's career, Essie died, after suffering bouts with terminal cancer, on December 12, 1965.

AUTOBIOGRAPHICAL WORKS AND THEMES

Becoming increasingly discomforted by the racial discrimination that she and Paul Robeson felt in the United States and England, Essie began to lecture on race relations and the plight of black Africans. With the encouragement of Carl Van Vechten (and Fania Marinoff, his actress wife), Essie wrote the first draft of a book that would feature Paul and the "Race Question." Signifying on Booker T. Washington's* *Up from Slavery* (1901), W.E.B. Du Bois's* *The Souls of Black Folk* (1903), and James Weldon Johnson's *The Autobiography of an Ex-Coloured Man* (1911), *Paul Robeson, Negro* (1930) profiled Paul as the representative person of his race, "wonderful, marvelous, great artist, great man . . . but who remain[ed] modest, simple, lovable" (170–71). Written dispassionately (except Chapter Ten, "Finding Himself"), *Paul Robeson, Negro* is a compendium of Essie's obtuseness, shrewdness, and ambition. The book met a hostile public. Essie quotes Paul, saying, "The whole trouble is . . . Essie thinks she knows me, and she really doesn't know me at all. She thinks I'm a little tin angel with no faults . . . of course the book is stupid, uninteresting, and untrue" (143).

In the early 1930s, Essie became fascinated with anthropology and challenged aloud the racism that permeated anthropology. Incorporating her anthropological interests with images from a 1936 African trip, the biographer published a second book that obliquely featured her. Originally called *African Material*, the travel book was entitled *African Journey* (1945). Illustrating it with some of the photographs taken during the sojourn, *African Journey* cataloged not only 1930s African rituals and customs but also the oppressive yoke under which millions of black Africans were living. In its thematic outlook, *African Journey* acclaimed the efficacy of African peoples and the African custom of leisure living (109). Describing Paul as "lazy," "everlastingly lazy," "lazy talk," "pathological laziness," "lazy life . . . leisurely lazy life suited him perfectly," and "lazy with a capital 'L' " in *Paul Robeson, Negro* (73–76, 80, 88, 156), Essie was made to realize during her six-month trek of the Continent that Africans philosophically did not waste nervous energy bewailing the unexpected or the unforeseen. On the aforementioned, Africans had tremendous ambition, energy, and capacity for work (*African Journey* 109). The preceding manifestation gave the biographer keener insights into the African behavior of her artist-husband.

CRITICAL RECEPTION

Failing to interest a publisher during the 1920s, *Paul Robeson, Negro* was published by Harper and Brothers in New York. Alfred Knopf had turned it down, and the London office of Doubleday and Doran had offered Essie an advance of a thousand pounds. "Miss Moody," Doubleday editor, found it "so fascinating that she read it straight thru without stopping." A draft of 25,000 words, the manuscript was "only half as long as was expected" by Doubleday (Duberman 121). Appearing the day after the opening of *Othello* without a preface, the book failed in terms of sales, but the reviews were amiable. Paul Robeson felt rekindled anger with the book's timing and content and did not "appreciate . . . being described as 'disloyal' to his friends (153–54), 'lazy' with a capital 'L' (154) and 'not in the least sensitive to racial slurs' " (100). Rose C. Field, a *New York Times* critic, says, "The book is compelling by its simplicity and naivete. Her technique . . . is almost childlike. [In] the light of literature, this book will not cast lengthy shadows, but as a homely picture of a colorful individual[,] it has much to recommend it" (5).

Originally bound in red cloth (later blue) by the John Day Company of New York and sold at $3.50 a copy, *African Journey* describes Essie's field trip from Capetown to Cairo. With 154 pages, of which 64 were contemporary photos of native life, *African Journey* was well received and quickly sold out its first printing. The *New York Times* review called it "an extremely attractive and natural book" (Duberman 293).

BIBLIOGRAPHY

Autobiographical Works by Eslanda Goode Robeson

Paul Robeson, Negro. London: Victor Gollancz, 1930. New York: Harper and Brothers, 1930.
African Journey. New York: John Day, 1945.

Studies of Eslanda Goode Robeson's Autobiographical Works

Brock, Euline W. "Thomas W. Cardozo: Fallible Black Reconstruction Leader." *Journal of Southern History* 57.2 (1981): 183–206.
Day, John. Rev. of *African Journey. Time* (August 13, 1945): 102, 104.
"Declaration of War." *Time* (July 25, 1949): 16.
"Double Play: Chaplin to Robeson to Malenkov." *Saturday Evening Post* (September 4, 1954): 10.
Duberman, Martin Bauml. *Paul Robeson.* New York: Alfred A. Knopf, 1988.
"Eslanda Goode Robeson." *Saturday Review of Literature* (February 5, 1949): 13.
"Eslanda Goode Robeson Is Dead; Writer and Wife of Singer, 68." *New York Times,* December 14, 1965, 43.
Field, Rose C. Rev. of *Paul Robeson, Negro.* "Paul Robeson Viewed by His Wife." *New York Times,* July 13, 1930, 5.
Graham, Shirley. *Paul Robeson: Citizen of the World.* New York: Julian Messner, 1946.
Hamburg, A.S. "Berkeley's Example." *Nation* (June 7, 1952): 536.
"Paul Robeson." *Time* (October 5, 1953): 42.
Perkins, Thelma Dale. "Tribute to Eslanda Robeson." In *Paul Robeson: The Great Forerunner.* Ed. Freedomways. New York: Dodd and Mead, 1965. 304–7.
Ransby, Barbara. "Eslanda Goode Robeson, Pan-Africanist." *Sage* 3 (1986): 2.
"Robeson, Eslanda (Cardoza) Goode." In *Current Biography: Who's News and Why 1945.* Ed. Anna Rothe. New York: H.W. Wilson, 1946. 505–6.
Robeson, Susan. *The Whole World in His Hands: A Pictorial Biography of Paul Robeson.* Secaucus, NJ: Citadel Press, 1981.
Smith, Anna Bustill. "The Bustill Family." *Journal of Negro History* 10.4 (1925): 638–44.
Stuckey, Sterling. *Here I Stand.* Boston: Beacon Press, 1958.

GEORGE SAMUEL SCHUYLER
(1895–1977)

Emmanuel S. Nelson

BIOGRAPHY

George Samuel Schuyler was born on February 25, 1895, in Providence, Rhode Island. While he was an infant his family moved to Syracuse, New York. His father, a chef, died when Schuyler was three; but his mother and stepfather, a determined and hardworking couple, provided him a stable, middle-class upbringing. He attended public schools in Syracuse until 1912, when he enlisted in the army. In 1919, when he left military service, he was a second lieutenant.

For the next three years Schuyler lived in New York City and supported himself by doing a variety of menial jobs. In 1922 he returned to Syracuse briefly and established a successful house-cleaning business. While in Syracuse he joined the Socialist Party of America; his fascination with the party, however, was short-lived, and his speedy disenchantment with socialism marked the beginning of his incremental move toward social and political conservatism.

In 1923 Schuyler moved back to New York City and began his controversial career as a journalist. Initially his essays and editorial pieces appeared in black-owned publications, such as *The Messenger*, *Opportunity*, and *The Crisis*. Eventually his work was widely published in a variety of American journals and newspapers, such as *The Nation* and *The Manchester Union Leader*. His satiric novel *Black No More* (1931) established his reputation as an artist of considerable talent. However, by the 1940s, Schuyler—through his increasingly provocative political pronouncements—began to alienate many members of the African American political establishment. By the 1960s, when he began to attack vociferously the tactics and objectives of the civil rights movement, he was seen by many black activists as a ranting Uncle Tom. His incendiary comments on Martin Luther King Jr., while they endeared him to conservative whites who were unsympathetic to the civil rights struggle, placed him on the lunatic fringe of the African American political opinion.

On May 9, 1967, Schuyler's only daughter, Philippa, died in a helicopter crash in Vietnam where she was on a journalistic assignment. A child prodigy, Philippa Schuyler had been an internationally renowned composer and concert pianist—in addition to being a journalist and author of two books. Her death at age thirty-seven devastated Schuyler and his wife, Josephine Cogdell. Two years later his wife died, apparently a suicide. Schuyler's final years were lonely. Although he knew many people, he had few friends. On August 31, 1977, he died in a New York hospital.

AUTOBIOGRAPHICAL WORK AND THEMES

Black and Conservative: The Autobiography of George S. Schuyler was published in 1966. As much a political dissertation as it is an autobiographical narrative, the book provides a fascinating portrait of its enigmatic author and an intriguing map of his political development. Written in crisp and lucid prose, *Black and Conservative* is also an immensely valuable cultural document. In the first few chapters, for example, Schuyler describes his childhood years in Syracuse. Those chapters also contain his astute assessment of the state of race relations in that northern town at the turn of the twentieth century. His compelling and at times hilarious account of his years in the U.S. Army—he was stationed mostly in Seattle and Hawaii—offers memorable glimpses into military life in the preintegration era. When he settled down in New York City in 1923, the Harlem Renaissance had begun, and he was a keen observer of that pivotal cultural phenomenon. Schuyler personally knew many of the artists and activists of the time, and his numerous colorful anecdotes capture the spirit and mood of the Renaissance. He briefly mentions his unconventional marriage to Josephine Cogdell, a white woman from Texas, whom he proudly describes as "blonde and shapely" (163), and with much enthusiasm he speaks of Philippa, their exceptionally gifted daughter.

In the second half of the autobiography, however, Schuyler's focus is less on his personal life and more on his political views. As he defiantly articulates his controversial political opinions, his tone becomes overtly self-congratulatory. He offers details of the favorable reactions many of his essays and editorial pieces elicited (almost always in right-wing political circles) and the friendly responses he received when he was invited to give lectures (to largely conservative audiences) in England and other European countries. But much more offensive than his self-congratulatory tone are his political opinions.

Schuyler's turn to the right of the political center seems to have begun at the time of his disappointment with the Socialist Party of America. He claims that soon after his brief flirtation with socialism he discovered that the differences between socialists and communists "were tactical and strategic, rather than fundamental" (149). He characterizes that discovery as a moment of profound political enlightenment. That epiphanic realization leads him to believe that there is a massive communist plot, spearheaded by the Soviet Union, to take over the world. His nearly hysterical anticommunism at least partly explains his bizarre political beliefs and behavior.

For example, Schuyler points out, with supreme contempt, that the National Association for the Advancement of Colored People (NAACP) was founded by a group of black and white socialists. Yet he fails to mention the monumental contributions of the NAACP to the struggle for social justice. He voices similar contempt for Marcus Garvey, the charismatic black nationalist who galvanized the political energies of millions of African Americans during the 1920s. Schuyler compares him to Adolf Hitler and, with faintly racist overtones, describes Garvey as "a short, smooth, black, pig-eyed, corpulent West Indian from Jamaica" who had brainwashed many black Americans "with his bull voice and his cry of Africa for Africans" (120). Schuyler's racist rhetoric becomes more blatant when he declares that Africans and Asians, whom he describes as "international retardates," are "victims of arrested development who, without European and American investment and direction, would have fallen farther behind each year until chaos and stagnation engulfed them" (338).

Just as alarming are some of Schuyler's comments on the American South. During the 1930s he spent a few months as a journalist in Mississippi where he, like other blacks, was subjected to the restrictions and humiliations of statutory segregation. Nevertheless, he arrives at an astonishing conclusion: He states that he "found Mississippi in many ways fascinating, the people kindly and cooperative, and the racial way of life not intolerable" (228). Furthermore, he argues that the sensational reports of racial violence in Mississippi printed in northern newspapers are often mere fabrications; he claims that he "checked on many of those stories of terror and persecution and found them to be entirely false" (229). Of course, he conveniently forgets to mention which specific stories he investigated, how he went about conducting those investigations, and who, precisely, were his witnesses and informants.

As a man and as a political thinker, Schuyler appears most loathsome when he launches his attack on the civil rights movement. In 1964 he endorsed Senator Barry Goldwater's presidential campaign. His endorsement was inspired at least in part because of Goldwater's virulent "opposition to the Civil Rights Act [of 1964] which he regarded as unconstitutional" (349). To Schuyler, the civil rights movement was nothing more than an elaborate communist plot to hoodwink blacks and destabilize the United States. His basic opposition to the civil rights struggle is based on a vulgar and thoroughly absurd premise: that black people in the United States, in contrast to black people in other parts of the world, "get the best schooling, the best living conditions, the best economic advantages, the best security, the greatest mobility and the best health" (121). In other words, black Americans should be grateful for what they have and not indulge in agitations that only "stir up desires and demands which cannot be realized for some time to come" (121).

Schuyler's solution to the problems African Americans face is quite simple. He is convinced of "the superiority of the free American civilization," which has the "capacity for change and adjustment" (321), and therefore progress can be achieved gradually through black self-help "in cooperation with willing whites" (160). In fact, Schuyler appears to have endless faith in white magnanimity and eagerly points out "the philanthropic contributions of middle- and upper-class whites to Negro education and welfare" (321). Progressive change, he seems convinced, can be eventually achieved through a merry alliance of compliant blacks and generous whites.

Why such an obviously intelligent man would forge such a grotesque political philosophy is not entirely clear. His anticommunism may partly explain his perspective, but the answer perhaps lies in his psychological makeup. At times his autobiography reveals some clues to his rather unusual reaction to racist abuse. For example, on his visit to London he is denied accommodation at twelve different hotels. He encounters similar rejections when he travels in Latin American countries. In cities such as Caracas and Buenos Aires he is ejected from hotel lobbies despite the fact he has confirmed reservations for accommodation. He realizes that he is being rejected because he is black. Oddly, however, he narrates these rejections without anger or bitterness and in a surprisingly matter-of-fact tone, as if he views racism—both on individual and institutional levels—as something he should simply accommodate rather than challenge.

Because he seems to react to racism unemotionally, perhaps he has difficulty comprehending why some others may, legitimately, react with rage. Since he has the ability as well as the willingness to accommodate racists without questioning their right to limit his options, maybe he expects others to do the same. One has to wonder if his political beliefs and behavior are a reflection of the extent to which he has internalized racism. One may, for instance, ask why he resorts to animal imagery while describing Marcus Garvey as a "pig-eyed" man "with a bull voice" (120). It is quite reasonable to question why a putative black intellectual would support the dangerous antics of Joseph McCarthy (which Schuyler enthusiastically did) or seek membership in the racist John Birch Society (which he joined in 1961). One may even ask why he mentions his marriage to a white woman—that "blonde and shapely" (163) creature—with obvious pride. It is in the answers to these questions we may have to seek an explanation for his puzzling retreat into far right-wing politics. His conservative cowardice may be rooted in his complicated attitude toward his own blackness; the autobiography hints at, but does not fully reveal, that psychological complexity.

CRITICAL RECEPTION

Responses to Schuyler's autobiography, predictably, are mixed. Michael Peplow, for example, calls it a "good autobiography" and states that "Schuyler's easy style, his anecdotes and character sketches, his organization from beginning to end, reveal a man at the height of his writing ability" (100). However, Peplow also points out that "Schuyler unsuccessfully mixes anecdotes and propaganda" (100), and what could have been a "highly readable autobiography" tends to become largely a "conservative manifesto" (101). In other words, the autobiographer's polemics are disruptive and distracting. Norma R. Jones, in her substantial chapter on Schuyler, declares that *Black and Conservative* "is a mine of information about black artists, intellectuals, and leaders from 1920s on" (246) but, oddly, has nothing else to say about the controversial book. Carleton L. Lee argues that Schuyler's impersonal tone is inappropriate for a self-representational narrative and dismisses the book as a work that lacks autobiographical substance (22). Ann Rayson offers the best and most judicious assessment of Schuyler's book. She concludes that at the heart of the autobiography is a "divided self" (106) and that the book presents the picture of a man in deep personal conflict over the conundrum of race.

BIBLIOGRAPHY

Autobiographical Work by George Samuel Schuyler

Black and Conservative: The Autobiography of George S. Schuyler. New Rochelle, NY: Arlington House, 1966.

Studies of George Samuel Schuyler's Autobiographical Work

Davis, Arthur P. "George Schuyler." In *From the Dark Tower.* Washington, D.C.: Howard University Press, 1974. 104–8.

Jones, Norma R. "George Samuel Schuyler." Vol. 51 of *Dictionary of Literary Biography*, edited by Trudier Harris and Thadious M. Davis. Detroit: Gale, 1987. 245–52.

Lee, Carleton L. Rev. of *Black and Conservative. Negro History Bulletin* 30 (January 1967): 22–23.

Peplow, Michael. *George Schuyler.* Boston: Twayne, 1980.

Rayson, Ann. "George Schuyler: Paradox among 'Assimilationist' Writers." *Black American Literature Forum* 12 (1978): 102–6.

MARY SEACOLE
(1805–1881)

Loretta G. Woodard

BIOGRAPHY

A nurse, a healer, and a heroine of the Crimean War, Mary Seacole was born Mary Jane Grant in Kingston, Jamaica, in 1805. Her father was a Scottish officer in the British army, and her mother was a free black woman and "an admirable doctress" (*Wonderful* 2) who operated Blundell Hall, a boardinghouse mainly for army officers and their families. Although Seacole lived with a relative for a short time at nearby Water Lane, she often visited her mother's house, observing the military surgeons at work. By the age of twelve, she was allowed to assist her mother with the patients, "learning a great deal of Creole medicinal art" (5). Seacole's own interest and love of nursing would later be of tremendous value to heal the sick and wounded during her extensive travels.

In 1836, Mary married Edward H. Seacole, a considerably older and sickly man who was a godson of British naval hero Admiral Horatio Nelson. Immediately after their marriage, they moved to Black River, where they owned and ran a small store. When her husband's health deteriorated, they returned to Kingston. Despite her efforts to nurse him back to health, he died within a few months. After her mother's death, Seacole assumed operation of Blundell Hall but left the managerial duties to her sister Louisa to embark upon her first love, the practice of medicine. Working with doctors as a nurse during the cholera epidemic in Jamaica in 1850, Seacole learned firsthand knowledge of the disease.

Seacole left Kingston to join her brother Edward in Cruces, Panama, where she used both her business and medical skills. After she helped Edward manage his hotel, she opened her own, the British Hotel, which she later relocated to offer meals and sell provisions to travelers. Since there was no doctor, she was able to eventually treat infectious and tropical diseases, using her own remedies of healing herbs and local plants, tend knife and gunshot wounds, as well as perform secret autopsies. In 1853, Seacole briefly returned to Jamaica to fight recurring yellow fever epidemics. After running stores in Navy Bay and Escribanos, she set sail for England to offer her services as a nurse to the British troops fighting in the Crimea.

Due to racial discrimination, Seacole was not granted an interview by the British officials and was denied a position in Florence Nightingale's nursing corps. This rejection fueled her desire to go to Crimea, with the assistance of Mr. Day, a distant relative of her late husband, who invested in her venture. On January 1855, Seacole reached Crimea aboard the steamship *Hollander* and opened up her own hotel, Spring Hill, which was two miles from Balaclava and a mile from the British headquarters. Known as "Mother Seacole" to the British soldiers, sometimes she risked her life on the battlefield for the soldiers she loved so loyally. Soon she became popular for her yellow dress and blue bonnet with red ribbons and her famous medical bag. After the war, in 1856, Seacole returned to London, bankrupt. The British press advertised appeals for donations on her behalf. To benefit her, the commander in chief Lord Rokeby and other prominent people organized the Seacole Festive, which was held for four nights at the Royal Surrey Gardens, featuring musical entertainment. After paying off her debts, the proceeds left were not enough to sustain her. In 1857, Seacole published her autobiography, *The Wonderful Adventures of Mrs. Seacole in Many Lands*, securing for herself a modest means of financial security.

Seacole spent her last years traveling between Jamaica and England, working with war heroes and orphans. On May 14, 1881, Seacole died and was buried in St. Mary's Roman Catholic Cemetery in Kensal Green. For all of her unselfish deeds and acts of heroism, she received numerous honors and awards after her death. In 1954, the nurses of Jamaica named their project headquarters "Mary Seacole House." Later she was awarded the Crimean Medal, the French Legion of Honour, and Turkish Medal. In 1980, her achievements were celebrated in "Roots in Britain," a touring exhibition. The Jamaican government awarded her posthumously with the country's highest honor, the Order of Merit, in 1990.

AUTOBIOGRAPHICAL WORK AND THEMES

Dedicated to those "noblemen and gentlemen" (199) soldiers, Seacole initially wrote her only literary work, *The Wonderful Adventures of Mrs. Seacole in Many Lands*, to earn an income after her bankruptcy at the end of the Crimean War. As it turns out, her 1857 autobiography, which was reprinted in 1984, was well received. The book chronicles the life of an exemplary woman, from her early childhood as a daughter of a Scottish army officer and free black boardinghouse keeper, from whom she learned the art of medicine, to her years as an owner of a British hotel, and her role as a nurse on the battlefield during the Crimean War. By positioning herself at the narrative center of both her culture and her text, Seacole provides valuable insight into her life and into the British culture.

Like Nancy Prince,* Seacole's key concern throughout her work is a quest for self-defining identity, a drive for public respect, and her desire to make a contribution to her country. Overall, however, the underlying subtext of her work is the widespread practice of racism and slavery in America, which directly impacted Seacole's life and profession.

Although Seacole was recognized for her skills as a nurse, she faced numerous obstacles as a "yaller" woman whose skin could not be bleached to make her acceptable (Davis 39). When Seacole offers her services as a nurse at the War Office, various military offices, and Florence Nightingale's organization, she was turned down on the basis of color. Gradually, as she ponders over her rejection, Mary writes in her autobiography: "Was it possible that American prejudices against colour had some root here? Did these ladies shrink from accepting my aid because my blood flowed beneath a somewhat duskier skin than theirs?" (126). Fueled by determination, Seacole's only mission or ambition, as she had professed earlier in her life, was to use her profession to save lives "wherever the need arises—on whatever distant shore" (78). During the Crimean War, she was forced to pay her own way to the battlefield, where she was "beloved" and "respected" by the entire army. It was her incredible loyalty, compassion, spirit, humor, and intellect that made her a favorite with the troops. Race or color was never an issue. Seacole refused to be treated like a second-class citizen, and her sheer willpower, like that of Lucy A. Delaney* and Harriet Jacobs, allows her to overcome defeat, even while remaining loyal to the empire that refuses to embrace her as its own native daughter.

Seacole's autobiography stands as a testimony to her life, her struggles, and her achievements, which went virtually unrecognized for almost a century after her death. A woman very much ahead of her time, she validates her own existence and exceeds the boundaries of race, gender, and class. As a free black independent woman of color, a nurse, a healer, an avid traveler, a "sutler," and writer, she emerges as a heroine or the black Florence Nightingale. Seacole does so at a critical historical moment because she claims that no one "could . . . shake my resolution" (84).

CRITICAL RECEPTION

Since the 1990s, Seacole's bestselling autobiography has garnered much critical attention with more in-depth scholarly studies. In the "Introduction" to the text, historian and literary critic William Andrews praises Seacole's work as "one of the most readable and rewarding black women's autobiographies in the nineteenth century" (xxviii). Sandra Pouchet Paquet carefully observes, in her engaging study, that "Seacole crafts her self-image in a journey from the perceived margins of civilization to its center" (652). Paquet's study further indicates Seacole's "desire to shape a life of personal, social, and cultural significance beyond Jamaica . . . as a woman of color" (652). However, Helen Cooper sees such a desire "problematic but powerful" and ultimately credits Seacole's work specifically with making an important contribution to England's increasingly complex sense of itself as an "imagined community" (130–31). According to Bernard McKenna, Seacole's autobiography "taps into a[n] intricate matrix of sometimes contradictory impressions and beliefs" (228). That is, "[b]y . . . alternatively valuing black culture and representing it in stereotypical form . . . Mrs. Seacole posits an alternative discourse that . . . undermines it" (228).

While a few other critics note some of the conflicts in Seacole's work, they also try to classify it. Amy Robinson sees the work as "a public manual of self-authorization" (537) as well as an "episodic autobiography that selectively chronicles Seacole's 'adventures' " (541). Evelyn Hawthorne claims, in her thorough article, it is "a rare cultural text that provides a key source of information . . . [but it] has also provoked conflicting readings" (311), which have been of interest to recent critics.

Noting her style of writing, Clive Davis observes that the memories are "recounted with a sharp tongue" (39) and further states, "A few veiled references suggest a certain bitterness, but Seacole is an optimist at heart" (39). Observing how Seacole espouses her views regarding "Western superiority and endorsement" (479), Cheryl Fish contends that sometimes in the autobiography "she ironically undercut[s] that flattery" (480). In her *Feminist Studies* review, Robinson sees it as "an entertaining and profitable account of a life" (537). Once a forgotten figure in British history, Seacole's scholars have now begun to give her the recognition she deserves.

BIBLIOGRAPHY

Autobiographical Work by Mary Seacole

The Wonderful Adventures of Mrs. Seacole in Many Lands. 1857. Schomburg Library of Nineteenth Century Black Women Writers Series. Ed. Henry Louis Gates Jr. New York: Oxford University Press, 1988.

Studies of Mary Seacole's Autobiographical Work

Alexander, Ziggi, and Audrey Dewjee. "Editor's Introduction." In *Wonderful Adventures of Mrs. Seacole in Many Lands*. 1857. Ed. Ziggi Alexander and Audrey Dewjee. Bristol: Falling Wall, 1984. 9–45.
———. "Mary Seacole." *History Today* 31 (September 1981): 45.
Andrews, William L. "Introduction." In *Wonderful Adventures of Mrs. Seacole in Many Lands*. 1857. Schomburg Library of Nineteenth Century Black Women Writers Series. Ed. Henry Louis Gates Jr. New York: Oxford University Press, 1988.
Ankomah, Baffour. "Mary Seacole—The Forgotten Nightingale. Part 2." *New African* (October 1, 2000): 34–38.
Bassett, C. "Mary Seacole: The Forgotten Founder." *Nursing Standard* 6 (1992): 44–45.
Carnegie, M.E. "Black Nurses at the Front." *American Journal of Nursing* 84 (1984): 1250–52.

Cooper, Helen M. "England: The Imagined Community of Aurora Leigh and Mrs. Seacole." *Studies in Browning and His Circle* (1993): 123–31.

Davis, Clive. "Mary Seacole." Rev. of *Wonderful Adventures of Mrs. Seacole in Many Lands*. *New Statesman* 107 (1984): 39.

Fish, Cheryl. "Voices of Restless (Dis) continuity: The Significance of Travel for Free Black Women in the Antebellum Americas." *Women's Studies* 26.2 (1997): 475–95.

Hawthorne, Evelyn J. "Self-Writing, Literary Traditions, and Post-Emancipation Identity: The Case of Mary Seacole." *Biography* 23.2 (Spring 2000): 309–31.

Iveson-Iveson, J. "The Forgotten Heroine." *Nursing Mirror* 157 (1983): 44–47.

Judd, Catherine. *Bedside Seductions. Nursing and the Victorian Imagination.* New York: St. Martin's, 1998. 101–21.

King, Anita. "Mary Seacole, Part I: A Matter of Life." *Essence* (1974): 4, 32.

"Mary Seacole." In *Larousse Dictionary of Women*. Ed. Melanie Parry. New York: Larousse, 1996. 590.

McKenna, Bernard. " 'Fancies of Exclusive Possession': Validation and Dissociation in Mary Seacole's England and Caribbean." *Philological Quarterly* 76.2 (Spring 1997): 219–39.

Mercer, Lorraine Susan Gallicchio. "Skirting Traditions: Travel Texts of Three Nineteenth-Century Women Writers (Anna Leonowens, Margaret Fuller, Mary Seacole, Narrative)." Diss. University of Oregon, 1966.

Moakler, Laura L. "Mary Seacole." In *African American Authors, 1745–1945: A Bio-Bibliographical Critical Sourcebook*. Ed. Emmanuel S. Nelson. Westport, CT: Greenwood Press, 2000. 371–74.

Paquet, Sandra Pouchet. "The Enigma of Arrival: *The Wonderful Adventures of Mrs. Seacole in Many Lands*." *African American Review* 26.4 (Winter 1992): 651–63.

Pollitt, N. "Forgotten Heroine." *Times Educational Supplement* 3965 (1992): 33.

Robinson, Amy. "Authority and Public Display of Identity: *Wonderful Adventures of Mrs. Seacole in Many Lands*." *Feminist Studies* 20.3 (Fall 1994): 537–57.

BRENT STAPLES
(1951–   )

Stacey L. Donohue

BIOGRAPHY

Born in 1951 into a large family, at times economically stable, at times not, due to an often absent and alcoholic father, Brent Staples recognized early on in life the value of individual responsibility. In his 1994 memoir *Parallel Time: Growing Up in Black and White*, Staples compares the individual choices he made and the opportunities he had growing up as a child and a young adult in the post-shipyard prosperity of Chester to those of his brother Blake: Staples is now a successful editorial writer for the *New York Times*, and an influential commentator on American politics and culture, while his brother was violently killed at a young age.

Chester, Pennsylvania, was once an economically prosperous center for ship-building before the plant closings of the 1960s. Melvin Staples, a truck driver, was gainfully employed, but his alcoholism soon led the once economically stable family into poverty. Despite a chaotic childhood, moving from one home to another, one step ahead of eviction, Staples was chosen to attend a special program for nontraditional students at Philadelphia Military College and Penn Morton College. With no previous expectations of ever attending college, this was Staples's opportunity. He earned a B.A. with honors from what is now called Widener University in 1973 and two graduate fellowships to the University of Chicago, where he earned a Ph.D. in psychology in 1977. He later worked as a reporter for the *Chicago Sun-Times* and then did some freelancing before being hired by the *New York Times* (*NYT*). Staples continues to work in the *NYT* editorial department; *Parallel Time* is his only full-length work to date.

AUTOBIOGRAPHICAL WORK AND THEMES

Staples's autobiography *Parallel Time* won the Anisfield Wolff Book Award, previously won by writers such as James Baldwin,* Ralph Ellison, and Zora Neale Hurston.* Although the book details Staples's childhood and young adult years, ending with his final year at the University of Chicago, the first and last chapters act as bookends, reflecting on his brother's life of crime and violent death. Staples's young adulthood is spent on the singular task of earning degrees, in places where he is a distinct minority due to his race and class, forcing him into the constant awareness of being a stranger in a predominantly white world. This tension is particularly apparent at the University of Chicago, where Staples at first felt physically uncomfortable and intellectually unprepared. Staples enjoyed walking the streets at night, and it took him a while to realize that he had been frightening other walkers by simply being a six-foot-one-inch-tall black man. So Staples accommodates: He whistles a classical tune in order to mollify the white pedestrians who fear a black man walking down the street at night. In another painful scene, Staples recalls the psychology professor—whom he initially mistakes for the daughter of Erich Fromm—who said he would take longer to finish the doctorate because he was black.

However, Staples does recognize one benefit of being one of the few black men in the University of Chicago's doctoral program in psychology: The black women secretaries went out of their way to help one of their own. He had the best office of all the graduate students, and the department secretary found a way to get him a large, sunny apartment in the married student housing building—even though he wasn't married.

Brent Staples's *Parallel Time* reads like an attempt to explain, or even justify, his singular success while his younger brother and older sister fall into trouble: Blake, his brother, was murdered in a drug underworld dispute at twenty-two. This murder opens the narrative, and Staples describes looking at the coroner's pictures of his dead brother (he did not attend the funeral): "I know his contours well. I bathed and diapered him when he was a baby and studied his features as he grew" (1).

The young Brent is determined to leave crime-ridden, working-class Chester, Pennsylvania, but it is an unexpected invitation to join a pilot remedial admission program for minorities at Widener College that offers him a way out. A key theme in the book is the idea that character, historical moment, and random luck determine our destiny, for better or worse.

Chester is depicted as a community where racism and lack of opportunity can destroy the individual and the family. Staples was the eldest of nine and painfully aware that his family was paralyzed by both his father's alcoholism and his mother's depression. But Staples avoids congratulating himself for his escape: This is not a simple retelling of the American Dream story. The parallels Staples makes between himself and his brother add a sadness that permeates the text even when we would want to celebrate Staples's successes.

Staples, however, refuses to act as a symbol of African American progress. In his memoir, he acknowledges the power of character and opportunity as forces that can control one's destiny. He refuses to see his work as emblematic of African American lives. In a 1994 interview, Staples told Paul Galloway of the *Chicago Tribune* that his book is on "universal themes—family and leaving home and developing your own identity."

CRITICAL RECEPTION

All of the critical responses to *Parallel Time* so far are in book reviews, and the memoir ultimately drew more praise than anger. David Nicholson writes in *American Visions* that Staples, unlike other black memoirists, doesn't place any blame on whites, depicting integrated settings as a place for personal growth, nor does he see Staples shy away from admitting his reluctance to fight, distinct from what he calls a "hallmark of writing by black men." Nicholson suggests that the reason for any negative responses to Staples's work is that it does not portray the black community as victims, a theme he says the media and publishing industry insist upon in writings by black men.

In the *New York Times Book Review*, Verlyn Klinkenborg's explanation of why people write memoirs also summarizes the overall theme of Staples's book: "Writing a memoir is almost always the privilege of those who have escaped their probable fates" (1). Klinkenborg goes beyond simply reviewing the book to analyzing it. According to the critic, "parallel" time refers to several different pairs of subjects: between black and white; between black Chester, Pennsylvania, and white Polish/Ukranian Chester; between Chester and Chicago; between black and white; and most important, between Blake and Brent. Klinkenborg describes Staples as an observer of all these parallels. He reminds us of three specific incidents where Staples observes the effect of the scene on himself: when his cousin is shooting heroin; when he sees a pimp beating up a john in Chicago; when he is waiting for Saul Bellow to pass by his street. Like his father Melvin, a man who returned to his family at his own convenience and who, Klinkenborg points out, is much more vividly portrayed than Geneva, Staples's mother, Staples recognizes that his first duty is to himself. Though he feared and hated his father, he is more like him than not. Klinkenborg concludes his review by referring to Staples's angry reaction to the interviewer who asked the writer if he grew up in a ghetto—if he was a "real" black man. According to Klinkenborg, Staples is angry at the question because he realizes, despite writing this memoir, that he still cannot answer the question either: Why did he succeed when so many others did not?

James N. Baker's review in *Newsweek* is more subdued, but positive nonetheless. He summarizes the book as a "memoir of what it felt like to be a bright black kid out of tune with his own large family," and he suggests that although it isn't as powerful as the autobiographical works of Richard Wright[*] or Lorraine Hansberry, *Parallel Time* does make an "eloquent" contribution to the genre. Baker also notes that the closing pages of the book contradict Staples's depiction of being an outsider from his own family: Staples's description of when his siblings had to rebury Blake (the original grave was too shallow) is a moving portrait of solidarity between Brent, his three brothers, and sister.

In an otherwise positive review, *Time*'s reviewer Jack White argues that Staples's memoir is a "horrifying catalog of the wasted lives and thwarted talents, misdirected rage and pitiful self-hatred" of the impoverished urban black experience. Yet he concludes by praising Staples's depiction of "contained fury" toward whites: Staples describes walking the dark streets of Chicago and playing a game he called "scatter the pigeons": scaring white folks walking on the street until the last moment when he shouts "good evening" at them. White recognizes that Staples honestly depicts, without oversimplifying, the struggles of a successful black man who fits in neither with his past world nor with his present. He concludes that the book seems to suggest that it is "nearly as difficult for young blacks to free themselves from bondage today as it was in [Frederick] Douglass's* time" (68).

Other reviewers did not see Staples's book as a tender or moving account but as distant, unemotional reportage. Sanford Pinsker, writing for the *Virginia Quarterly Review*, believes that the memoir doesn't gel because of the series of story lines that are only tangentially related. And unlike other critics, Pinsker claims that Staples does not deal honestly with his childhood because the writer assumes "a latter-day version of Hemingway's tight-lipped style": Staples's style is journalistic, refusing to get too emotionally involved in often painful subject matter. Jill Nelson, writing for the *Nation*, concurs. She complains about the exploitation of his brother's death in the admittedly "powerful" opening chapter and also of Staples's emotional detachment from both the death and his family. For Nelson, Staples's early recognition that he did not belong, that he was an "other," is not clearly explained: We never learn the reasons why he is so detached from his family. Despite the acknowledgment that Staples is a "gifted writer," Nelson notes that we never learn the reasons for many of Staples's observations. For an example, Nelson believes that Staples assumes the reader will understand why he wanted approval from strangers walking the streets rather than any approval from friends and family. Like Pinsker, the "reportorial distance" of the narrative at the expense of "brutal honesty" disturbs Nelson.

In an essay in *Contemporary Society*, Melvin Oliver's criticizes Staples's work not for stylistic reasons but because "like many of the new black middle-class autobiographies, it tells one story as if it were all stories" (605). He concedes, however, that *Parallel Time* does illustrate the unspoken influence and significance of racism on the black middle class.

BIBLIOGRAPHY

Autobiographical Work by Brent Staples

Parallel Time: Growing Up in Black and White. New York: Random House, 1994.

Studies of Brent Staples's Autobiographical Work

Baker, James N. "Together and Apart." Rev. of *Parallel Time: Growing Up Black and White*. *Newsweek* (March 14, 1994): 76. *Ebsco Academic Search Elite*. Online. November 2000.

Galloway, Paul. Rev. of *Parallel Time: Growing Up Black and White*. *Chicago Tribune*, March 7, 1994. *Ebsco Academic Search Elite*. Online. November 2000.

Klinkenborg, Verlyn. "An American Story." Rev. of *Parallel Time: Growing Up Black and White*. *New York Times Book Review* (February 20, 1994): 1, 26.

Nelson, Jill. "Hiding in Plain Sight." Rev. of *Parallel Time: Growing Up Black and White*. *Nation* 258 (1994): 562. *Ebsco Academic Search Elite*. Online. November 2000.

Nicholson, David. "Parallel Time, Divergent Paths." Rev. of *Parallel Time: Growing Up Black and White*. *American Visions* 9.2 (1994): 28. *Ebsco Academic Search Elite*. Online. November 2000.

Oliver, Melvin L. "Racial Formation Today." Rev. of *Parallel Time: Growing Up Black and White*. *Contemporary Society* 24.5 (1994): 603–5.

Pinckney, Darryl. "Promissory Notes." Rev. of *Parallel Time: Growing Up Black and White*. *New York Review of Books* 42.6 (1995): 41. *Ebsco Academic Search Elite*. Online. November 2000.

Pinsker, Sanford. "Home Boys between Hard Covers." Rev. of *Parallel Time: Growing Up Black and White*. *Virginia Quarterly Review* 70 (1994): 757 (16). *Ebsco Academic Search Elite*. Online. November 2000.

Thernstrom, Abigail. "The Futility of Black Rage." Rev. of *Parallel Time: Growing Up Black and White*. *Times Literary Supplement* (June 10, 1994): 14–15.

White, Jack E. "Between Two Worlds." Rev. of *Parallel Time: Growing Up Black and White*. *Time* (March 7, 1994): 68.

MARIA W. STEWART
(1803–1879)

Verner D. Mitchell

BIOGRAPHY

Born free in Hartford, Connecticut, in 1803, Maria W. Stewart is now remembered for two important firsts: She was the first American-born woman to speak in public and leave extant copies of her speeches, and she was the first to speak publicly on political matters before an audience composed of both men and women. Until recently, little was known of her early years, other than what she discloses in a brief introduction to her 1831 work *Religion and the Pure Principles of Morality*. There she states that she was "left an orphan at five years of age; was bound out in a clergyman's family; had the seeds of piety and virtue early sown in my mind, but was deprived of the advantages of education, though my soul thirsted for knowledge" (Richardson, "Introduction[s] 29). This statement has led many to believe that Stewart, "deprived of the advantages of education," first learned to read and to write as an adult. We now know, thanks to the rediscovery of her 1861 autobiographical narrative "The First Stage of Life" that this was not the case.

"*The First Stage*," published in Baltimore in the African Methodist Episcopal Church journal *Repository of Religion and Literature*, reveals that Stewart was initially raised by her mother and stepfather (no mention is made of her birth father). Her mother's death in 1808, when Stewart was age five, brought her halcyon days to an abrupt end. A year later, her stepfather died, and six-year-old Stewart was, in her words, "cast upon the cold charities of the world, with no one to care for [me] but [my] adopted aunt" (187). After this aunt deserted young Stewart, a kind family "took the little stranger under their charge" and "taught [her] about God, to read, [and] to pray" (188). Thus her formal education began as well as her religious life. She apparently left this family at age fifteen and began living on her own, supporting herself as a domestic servant and continuing her education in Sunday school classes.

By the early 1820s, Stewart had moved to Boston and become affiliated with the First African Baptist Church, then led by its founding minister, the Reverend Thomas Paul (1773–1831). He was the father of Stewart's friend, the abolitionist and educator Susan Paul (1809–1841). Much like Boston's other black clergymen, Paul used his pulpit to urge activism against Southern slavery and rampant racial discrimination in the North, issues Stewart would later address in her essays and lectures. The First African Baptist Church was also known as the African Meeting House; it was located on Beacon Hill—on Belknap Street (now Joy Street)—in the heart of Boston's antebellum black community. Stewart's decision to join this congregation proved key in her religious and intellectual development and even more so in spurring her heightened political activism. As a number of historians have noted, during Thomas Paul's pastorship at the African Meeting House, most of the city's black activists were members there.

On Thursday, August 10, 1826, church members gathered at the African Meeting House and watched as the Reverend Paul joined Maria Miller and James W. Stewart in marriage. No photographs have survived, but written accounts depict the groom as "tolerably stout" and "well built" and the bride, then twenty-three, as "in the flush and promise of a ripening womanhood, with a graceful form and pleasing countenance" (Richardson, "Introduction[s]" 89). City records show that the couple resided at 25 Belknap Street (close by the African Meeting House) and that James, a naval veteran of the War of 1812, was self-employed as a shipping agent, outfitting whaling and fishing vessels. He apparently asked his wife to use his middle initial, along with his surname, and she agreed. Their life together was happy but brief, for in December 1829, after only three years of marriage, James died.

This, as might be expected, was devastating for Mrs. Stewart. The following year she suffered two additional setbacks. First, as commonly occurred in nineteenth-century Boston, a group of white businessmen challenged her late husband's will, successfully defrauding her, thereby, of a sizable financial inheritance. Second, six months after her husband's demise, her close friend and Belknap Street neighbor David Walker was found dead, having been felled, many believed, by a Southern assassin. Four years earlier, in 1826, Walker and the Reverend Paul had helped organize the abolitionist Massachusetts General Colored Association. Subsequently, they served as the two Boston agents for the first African American newspaper, *Freedom's Journal*. Today, Walker is best known as the author of *Appeal to the Colored Citizens of the World* (1829), a candid, unapologetic work, notable for its denunciation of white supremacy, its strong anticolonization stand, and its insistence that blacks should rise up and overthrow slavery, by any means necessary. Walker and his *Appeal* had a profound influence on Stewart, as can be partially gleaned from an essay she penned in 1831 praising "the most noble, fearless, and undaunted David Walker" (Richardson, "Introduction[s]" 3).

After the deaths of her husband and Walker, Stewart underwent a religious conversion experience that initiated, among other things, her public speaking career. Hence between 1831 and 1834, when she left Boston for New York City, she delivered four public lectures, published a political pamphlet, and authored a collection of religious writings. She continued her life of public service and activism in New York, working for nearly a decade as a schoolteacher, lecturing, publishing, attending antislavery conventions, and participating in various women's organizations. She later taught school in Philadelphia, Baltimore, and Washington, D.C. At her death in December 1879, she was employed as Matron of the Freedmen's Hospital (now Howard University Hospital) in Washington.

AUTOBIOGRAPHICAL WORKS AND THEMES

Carla Peterson insightfully notes that Stewart's writings exude "a strong revolutionary note" (13). Indeed, religious fervor, urgent calls for black self-help, and a forceful critique of gender and racial oppression are prominent features of her autobiographical work. Stewart summarizes her Boston years in a September 1833 "Farewell Address to Her Friends in the City of Boston." She details, in particular, the backlash she faced in her own community once she heeded a spiritual interrogation, directing her to "go forward, and take off the reproach that is cast upon the people of color. 'Shall it be a woman?' And my heart made this reply—'If it is thy will, be it even so, Lord Jesus!' " (Richardson "Introduction[s]" 5). Stewart then went forth, advocating black unity, education, self-empowerment, religious virtue, and courage in the face of adversity. Earlier, she had watched black Bostonians warmly embrace David Walker when he voiced similar themes. Why then, she now ponders, was her message met with disdain and open hostility? We know that in addition to championing equal rights and privileges for black women ("How long shall the fair daughters of Africa be compelled to bury their minds and talents beneath a load of iron pots and kettles?"), Stewart had openly admonished black men (38). In one instance, she chides their "want of laudable ambition and requisite courage," a deficiency that, as she puts it, "causes my blood to boil within me" (58). In another, she asks that they turn less often to gambling and dancing and more frequently to opportunities for mental and moral improvement (60). In doing so, perhaps she miscalculated the extensiveness of sexism in Boston's black community, what she terms prejudice at home. The speech's most poignant moment comes when she laments, "Had experience more plainly shown me that it was the nature of man to crush his fellow, I should not have thought it so hard. Wherefore, my respected friends let us no longer talk of prejudice, till prejudice becomes extinct at home" (70). Convinced that further effort in Boston would be futile, she bids her "friends" farewell and—taking the high moral road—prepares to leave for New York City.

Stewart published her second autobiographical work, "The First Stage of Life," three decades later in April 1861. This, compared to the "Farewell Address," is a much more explicitly literary piece. She acknowledges that she has long desired to become a writer. However, like Zilpha Elaw,* Jarena Lee,* and most other early African American women writers, she repeatedly found herself hampered by material constraints: "In order to become a writer the mind must be stored with useful knowledge. It requires study, deep thought, nay more, it requires profound meditation, and fervent prayer. And how is this frame of mind to be acquired, this intellectual food obtained, amid the perplexing care of what shall I eat, and what shall I drink, and where withal shall I be clothed?" (84). Yet, as is evidenced by "The First Stage" itself, she did write. Such steadfast persistence in the face of adversity emerges, by the end of her story, as the work's primary theme.

Since "The First Stage" appeared in a church journal and was designed to impart religious lessons to young children, this goal necessarily informed Stewart's narrative choices. These choices—the work's narrative technique—are quite innovative, especially for the 1860s. After the opening frame, Stewart dispenses with the first-person narration, assumes a fictive guise, and uses a limited omniscient narrator to tell the life story of her heroine, "little Letitia." We receive valuable insight into Letitia's day-to-day activities and, through these, into her interiority. She enjoys, for example, knitting and making bouquets but also robbing birds' nests and rambling in the woods: play that challenges traditional gender roles and, as a result, earns her the label "so much of a boy girl" (188). The "boy girl" metaphor nicely forecasts Stewart's subsequent entrance in Boston into the "male" public sphere. As autobiographer, Stewart devotes a full third of the narrative to five-year-old Letitia painfully witnessing her mother's death, funeral, and burial. From this tragedy comes a key lesson learned. Although orphaned and in distress, "The first religious desire of Letitia was to be a good girl." Thus, with Letitia as guiding exemplar, the story makes plain its moral: "[T]he poorest little ragged boy may become an ambassador for Christ, and the pensive little maiden a mother in Israel" (188).

Seventeen years later, in 1878, federal legislation made Stewart and other widows of veterans of the War of 1812 eligible for a pension. With her first payments, she financed *Meditations from the Pen of Mrs. Maria W. Stewart* (1879), a reprint of her collected works from the 1830s, to which she added two newer pieces: a group of "Letters and Commendations" and the personal memoir "Sufferings during the War." The introductory letters function much like authenticating prefaces common in slave narratives. Accordingly, seventy-three-year-old William Lloyd Garrison writes from Boston, recalling their glory years during the antislavery struggle, as does Stewart's friend Louise C. Hatton. Letters from a group of ministers, including her pastor, the distinguished Episcopalian minister Alexander Crummell, attest to Stewart's "great piety and virtue" ("Letters" 11). With "Sufferings during the War," Stewart documents her travails in Baltimore and Washington during the Civil War. Perhaps because she composed this narrative during her final years, after she had begun her eighth decade, it evidences little of the passion and energy that animated her earlier work.

CRITICAL RECEPTION

Stewart was virtually forgotten until 1987, when Marilyn Richardson's *Maria W. Stewart, America's First Black Woman Political Writer: Essays and Speeches* rekindled interest in her life and thought. Her autobiographical work still has received little critical attention, but what it has received is decidedly favorable. For Richardson, "Stewart was a woman of profound religious faith, a pioneer black abolitionist, and a defiant champion of women's rights, and her message was unsparing and urgent" ("What If" 194). Paula Giddings similarly notes that "Stewart's assumptions—what would later become known as modernist thinking—gave Black women a freer rein to express and act upon ideas that liberated them from the oppression of both sex and race" (52). In *"Doers of the Word,"* an elegantly argued study of nineteenth-century black women activists, Carla Peterson lauds Stewart's autobiographical writing as "a hybrid discourse that reconfigures in interesting ways the genres of spiritual writing that form part of the Western literary tradition" (57).

BIBLIOGRAPHY

Autobiographical Works by Maria W. Stewart

"Mrs. Stewart's Farewell Address to her Friends in the City of Boston." 1833. In *Productions of Mrs. Maria W. Stewart*. Boston: Friends of Freedom and Virtue, 1835.
"The First Stage of Life." *Repository of Religion and Literature* (April 2, 1861): 84–86, 140–41, 187–88.
"Letters and Commendations" and "Sufferings during the War." In *Meditations from the Pen of Mrs. Maria W. Stewart*. Washington, D.C.: n.p., 1879.

Studies of Maria W. Stewart's Autobiographical Works

Bassard, Katherine Clay. *Spiritual Interrogations: Culture, Gender, and Community in Early African American Women's Writing*. Princeton, NJ: Princeton University Press, 1999.
Giddings, Paula. *When and Where I Enter: The Impact of Black Women on Race and Sex in America*. New York: William Morrow, 1984.
Peterson, Carla L. *"Doers of the Word": African-American Women Speakers & Writers in the North (1830–1880)*. New York: Oxford University Press, 1995.
Richardson, Marilyn. "Introduction[s]." In *Maria W. Stewart, America's First Black Woman Political Writer: Essays and Speeches*. Bloomington: Indiana University Press, 1987. 3–27, 79–86.
———. "'What If I Am a Woman?' Maria W. Stewart's Defense of Black Women's Political Activism." In *Courage and Conscience: Black & White Abolitionists in Boston*. Ed. Donald M. Jacobs. Bloomington: Indiana University Press, 1993. 191–206.

Ryan, Judylyn S. "Spirituality and/ as Ideology in Black Women's Literature: The Preaching of Maria W. Stewart and Baby Suggs, Holy." In *Women Preachers and Prophets through Two Millennia of Christianity*. Ed. Beverly Mayne Kienzle and Pamela J. Walker. Berkeley: University of California Press, 1998. 267–87.

SOJOURNER TRUTH
(c. 1797–1883)

Christine M. Lemchak

BIOGRAPHY

Hailed by many scholars as one of the first African American feminists, Sojourner Truth's eloquent speeches, despite her broken dialect and illiteracy, remain today a staple in the cause of the black woman's continued search for equality. Her orations were both thought-provoking and spiritually moving.

Because she was born into slavery, the date of Truth's birth is left uncertain. What has been determined, however, is that Truth, whose birth name was Isabella, was born sometime between 1797 and 1800, in Ulster County, New York. At the time, her parents, James "Bomefree" and Betsey "Mau-Mau Bett," were slaves owned by a Dutch family, the Ardinburghs. James and Betsey had ten or twelve children, with Truth being their second-to-last child. Given the evils of slavery, she knew barely half of her siblings; the others were sold away before she was born. Much of her childhood was spent with her parents and her younger brother Peter. Upon the death of her first master, of whom she knew little, she and her family were passed to his son, Colonel Ardinburgh, with whom she remained until approximately nine years of age. As was the practice at the time, she was then sold into slavery.

Treated no differently than common chattel, Truth was auctioned off several different times during her preadolescent years, preventing her from securing any sense of "roots." When she was nine, from which time her life's trials "may be dated" (Truth, *Narrative* (1997) 9), she was sold to John Nealy of Ulster County, New York, for $100. It was during her time with the Nealys that she received "the most cruel whipping she was ever tortured with" (10). She was then sold to a fisherman, Scriver, for $105; with him she lived for approximately a year and a half. She was then sold to John J. Dumont of New Paltz, New York, for £70.

It was with him that she remained until shortly before her state emancipation: 1810–1828.

During her time with the Dumonts, Truth fell in love with a slave from another farm—Robert. The relationship was short-lived, however; Robert's owner would not allow them to marry. He demanded that Robert marry from his own stock of female slaves to ensure, as with other farm chattel, that any offspring born of the union would be of benefit to *his* slave population (15). Given the unlikelihood of ever marrying someone of her choosing, she obediently married a fellow slave, Thomas. Over time, she and Thomas had four or five children, of whom one is thought to have died at birth. Not much is known of the marriages of slaves; since they were considered mere animals, their marriages were not recorded or recognized as anything other than a means of propagation. Children who were born into slavery immediately became property of the slave owner.

As her date for emancipation neared—1828—Truth began to realize that her owner, Dumont, had no intention of releasing her. In the mist of predawn hours, Truth left the only settlement she had known. The uncertainty as to the path of her journey did not sway her, however, as she determinedly walked toward her freedom. Her travels led her to the home of Isaac S. and Maria Van Wagener, who, not believing in "the practice of buying and selling slaves" (20), agreed to purchase Truth's remaining time with Dumont for $25. Because the Van Wageners did not consider Truth their property and because the time she spent with them was so vastly different from any other, Truth resolved to take their last name as her own.

Truth's religious teachings began with the humble instruction of her mother, Mau-Mau Bett. The faith and humility that her mother instilled in her remained with Truth throughout her years as a religious orator and preacher. Truth often turned to her belief in God to help her determine the best path for her life. It was her faith in God that led her to construct her own personal chapel in a quiet respite under a willow tree by a stream she frequented. As her faith deepened, she sought avenues in which to enrich it and share it with others. Upon moving to New York City, Truth found herself enlisted by some missionaries to help deliver the word of God to the morally weaker of society. She soon discovered that the sometimes riotous meetings were not for her and moved on. It was at this time, in 1832, that she met Robert "Matthias" Mathews, who was to become the worst "deception" of her religious education. Matthias was a loud, exploitive, religious fanatic who believed that "he was God upon earth" (53). Because of his deception and thievery, Truth lost most of her belongings and meager savings she had accumulated. However, as with many things, she turned her ignorant mistakes into lessons of truth, and from them, she realized what her life's work would be—a quest for, and "oration" of, the truth. It was at that time that she, born Isabella, made the life-altering decision to change her name to Sojourner Truth and journey north, lecturing for peace and equality for all.

To accomplish this task, Truth left New York City in 1843, with a small sack and two York shillings, and headed for New England. After brief stays at various places, Truth found a home with a "religious" commune called the Northampton Association in Northampton, Massachusetts. She continued to lecture and became known for her ability to influence people, bringing peace and solace to her listeners. By the time her collaborative *Narrative* was published in 1850, she was well known as an advocate for slaves' rights. When she arrived at the women's rights convention in Akron, Ohio, in 1851, a few of the participants worried that Truth's presence might deter the focus of their women's suffrage movement and raise too many issues concerning slavery. Squelching their selfish concerns, Truth took to the stage and delivered her poignant and powerful speech "Ain't I a Woman?" To support her travels, she sold her *Narrative* at every gathering she attended. Battle Creek, Michigan, became her final settlement in 1857. She continued her quest to help the downtrodden with her volunteer duties during the Civil War, fights for desegregated public transportation, and finally, her work "with the National Freedman's Relief Association counseling former slaves" (*Britannica Online*).

AUTOBIOGRAPHICAL WORKS AND THEMES

Because she was a slave with no formal education, Truth did not have the ability to transcribe her own life's story. With the help of Miss Olive Gilbert, Truth's courageous rise out of slavery—physically, emotionally, and spiritually— was recorded in a book titled *Narrative of Sojourner Truth*. It was published in 1850, and it documented the growth of Truth as a strong woman, a spiritual thinker, and an inspirational preacher. Despite the horrific, dehumanizing experiences of her youth as a slave, she was able to maintain her dignity. Truth's spiritual growth stemmed from her mother's first teachings of a Heavenly Father and continued with her own prolific wonderings. As a child, Truth was awed by her mother's stories of "the only Being that could effectually aid or protect" (1997, 4) her and inspired in a way she would only recognize later. Her mother's devotion to God struck Truth most deeply when she would hear her mother's tearful prayers at night for her many children that had been sold away from her (4). Although she did not foresee the strength she would receive from her faith in later years, she never forgot her mother's humble teachings and carried them as personal inspiration all the days of her life.

In her *Narrative*, we learn of Truth's years spent as a slave, with various masters. Her experiences are brought to the forefront, not to shock us but to familiarize us with the brutality of such practices and demonstrate the incredible inner strength of an entire race. Truth, as she did her entire life, put a human face on an evil, dehumanizing practice. But she did not do so for personal gain or to show one woman's rise from the devilry of slavery; she did so because she came to understand that it was not one person's triumph but a triumph for humanity that was needed. She "grew to understand that her personal quest for freedom was meaningful only as a moment in a larger struggle against the burden of injustice . . . her testament, shows how one resilient spirit can serve as a lever that helps to lift a whole world of oppression" (vi).

Although the *Narrative* catalogs Truth's life as a slave, its richness comes from the telling of her religious and awe-inspiring growth into one of the most prolific orators for the rights of slaves and women. In addition to the personal courage she demonstrated in her survival of slavery, we receive several dramatic looks at Truth's unyielding strength against monumental odds. Such strength becomes evident when she made a demand for her "promised" freedom. When she had been with her fifth owner, John J. Dumont, for a time, he promised to give her her freedom one year before "she was legally free by statute" (18) if she continued to carry on the work of more than one person, as she had been doing. According to a state law established in 1817, any blacks born before July 4, 1799, would be given their freedom when they reached twenty-five years of age for women and twenty-eight years of age for men. The law was to take effect on July 4, 1827. When that year came, however, Dumont reneged on his promise, claiming that an injury she had received a year before had kept her from her usual pace. Truth remained determined to make her owner keep his promise, and after a brief time period spent in prayer for guidance, the answer came: She would walk to her freedom; no violence or outbursts—she would simply use the mode of transportation God had graced her with and walk.

Truth's quest for her own freedom had been achieved; however, her most dramatic victory over slavery was yet to come: to get her son Peter back from an illegal slave sale. For Truth to win that battle, she would need to deal with people with formal educations—white people. The thoughts of going up against the very group that had enslaved her and her family never daunted her, however. She remained true to her faith and never doubted that, as she had told her prior owner Mrs. Dumont, she would have her child back one day (22). In her fight for her son's freedom, Truth's strength of character and unfailing persistence had once again been brought to the forefront. She not only retrieved her son; she developed a devotion to the Lord and a power to voice that devotion to all who would listen in the years to come. For as she stated, "I felt so *tall within*—I felt as if the *power of a nation* was within me!" (22).

Truth's passionate orations and awe-inspiring presence were never more recognized than when she single-handedly squelched a mob's uprising. During her stay with the Northampton Association, she attended several camp meetings, one of which was also attended by a group of young, white men whose rude behavior threatened to turn violent. Instead of avoiding or ignoring the bad situation, she marched up a small knoll and began to fill the air with her soulful voice. When she sang a hymn, it was said that few words could describe the sensations left by her verse, as was evident on that particular evening. The mob of hecklers listened to Truth as she delivered her words in her direct and humble manner. The charisma she possessed proved soothing, and the unruly group dispersed. But this was not to be the last time she caused a hush to come over a crowd; for Truth was to deliver many such orations, always leaving her audience with a sense of awe.

In addition to her *Narrative*, the story of Truth's life was compiled in another edition entitled *The Book of Life*. Entered according to Act of Congress in 1875 by Frances W. Titus, this particular addition, though much is directly from *The Narrative Truth* dictated to Olive Gilbert, contains over a dozen partial to full renditions of Truth's speeches, conversations, and comments. The appendix also features some comments about Truth from various newspapers of the time. Although the question of authenticity is always an issue, especially with apparent "snatches" of conversations, Truth's speeches, as much as can be determined, are documented to the fullest extent possible by historians. Most notable is her most famous speech "Ain't I a Woman?" which she delivered in 1851 at a women's rights convention in Akron, Ohio. The timeless political ideas conveyed in this speech gave it its power over generations of listeners and readers. In it, Truth pointed out many of the fallacies of such a gathering. Women *were* in need of equal rights and equal treatment; however, men were not willing to give these rights, and in Truth's opinion, women should then stand up and take them, not simply demand them (*The Book* 1–2). Moreover, the fundamental problem restricting the rights of white women versus black women was not entirely the same. True, both lacked certain inalienable rights, but the very humanity of black women was also at risk. The oppression of black women was based just as much on their color as on their gender. As many twentieth-century African American women writers would continue to state, the plight of the black woman is twofold: equal rights under the law and equal rights within society. It is difficult to be a woman in a man's world; however, it is far more difficult to be a black woman in a white man's world.

Sojourner Truth's life and work stand as a testament, both of one woman's courageous escape from the shackles of slavery and of one woman's quest to raise the consciousness of an entire nation. She continues to be regarded as an icon for the ongoing struggle of the oppressed. The hardships she endured and overcame were no less than horrifying, which makes her survival miraculous. But her relentless attempts to uplift an entire oppressed group make her accomplishments prophetic. As a New Jersey paper of the time was said to have reported, "She has uplifted her voice to two generations of mankind, and may yet become prophetess to a third" (qtd. in *The Book*). The only sentiment to be altered in this statement is the whisper of doubt of whether her words will touch another generation. Due to her wisdom and sagacity, Truth's words shall march on for generations to come.

CRITICAL RECEPTION

Given the time period in which *The Narrative* was first published, its critical reception is not well documented. The book did sell well when offered at gatherings where Truth spoke, and it was the profits from the sales that allowed Truth to keep up her travels and speaking engagements. In the last century, much has been written about slave narratives and whether narrative authenticity is a problem. Given that most slaves were illiterate, the question of how much of the content comes from the slave and how much comes from the transcriber is a major concern. Herman George Jr. in his review essay states that regardless of the question of authorial voice, in Truth's *Narrative*, "what is clear . . . is the courage and intelligence of this Afro-American woman, born a slave in New York, c. 1797. She refused to be paralyzed by enslavement, white supremacy, or patriarchy" (30).

In the preface to Margaret Washington's 1993 edition of the *Narrative*, she addresses the concerns of authorial voice in slave narratives. As was often the case, the compilers of such narratives would take advantage of the subject matter and the illiteracy of the slave and create an opportunity for "antislavery writers and activists to 'uplift' black women and present them favorably as 'moral' beings to a doubting public" (xxxi). Because of this practice, it is believed that some slave narratives contain more of the writer's voice than the slave's; therefore, a careful study is essential "whenever reading narratives of black women unable to write for themselves" (xxxi). Fortunately, the Truth and Gilbert collaboration has been found to be one of the more reliable historical pieces. Despite the sometimes confusing and inconsistent prose of the 1850 *Narrative*, it is not difficult for the careful reader to distinguish Truth's voice from Gilbert's.

In an article addressing the historical context and collaboration of Truth and Gilbert, Jean Humez states, "Although this text contains only the skeletal structure of the full spiritual autobiography that we might have had if Truth had had direct access to the pen, there is still plenty of rich material" (qtd. in Massa 422). Truth's voice, though her dialect is slightly broken at times, is heard stately throughout the *Narrative*. She describes her trials as an oppressed slave in a chillingly real manner. However, her sense of faith was founded in such a strong belief in God that nothing—neither strike of whip nor blow of hand—could cause her spirituality to falter. As Washington states:

It is ever both interesting and instructive to trace the exercises of a human mind, through the trials and mysteries of life; and especially a naturally powerful mind, left as hers was almost entirely to its own workings, and the chance influences it met on its way; and especially to note its reception of that divine "light, that lighteth every man that cometh into the world." (43)

The collaborative effort of Truth and Gilbert allows us a unique look into the windows of our pasts. This text gives us the rare opportunity to learn as much of ourselves as of Truth. She gives us more than a rendition of one woman's struggle out of oppression; she establishes a piece of historical commentary to be both studied and cherished.

BIBLIOGRAPHY

Autobiographical Works by Sojourner Truth

Narrative of Sojourner Truth. Comp. Olive Gilbert. 1850. New York: Dover, 1997.
The Book of Life. 1875. London: X Press, 1999.
Washington, Margaret, ed. *Narrative of Sojourner Truth.* New York: Vintage, 1993.

Studies of Sojourner Truth's Autobiographical Works

George, Herman, Jr. "Rediscovering Black Women's Literature." *The Black Scholar* 22.4 (1992): 29+.
Humez, Jean. "Reading the Narrative of Sojourner Truth as a Collaborative Text." *Frontiers: A Journal of Women's Studies* 16.1 (1996): 29–52.
Massa, Suzanne Hotte. "Sojourner Truth." In *African American Authors, 1745–1945: A Bio-Bibliographical Critical Sourcebook.* Ed. Emmanuel S. Nelson. Westport, CT: Greenwood Press, 2000. 418–23.

NAT TURNER
(1800–1831)

Joyce Russell-Robinson

BIOGRAPHY

Nat, who came to be known as Nat Turner, was born on October 2, 1800, in Southampton County, Virginia, and was hanged there on November 11, 1831, after being tried and convicted of murder. The year of his birth was also the year of fellow Virginian Gabriel Prosser's rebellion conspiracy and the year in which Denmark Vesy (planner of a South Carolina rebellion) won a lottery and purchased his own freedom. Nat was a precocious child who simply opened a book one day and, to the amazement of his family, began spelling the names of different objects (N. Turner 45).

He was the chattel of Benjamin Turner until 1810 when Benjamin died, at which time Nat became the property of Samuel Turner, a younger brother of Benjamin. Upon the death of Samuel in 1822, Nat was sold to Thomas Moore, and his wife Cherry Turner was sold to Giles Reese (Greenberg 13). Moore's death in 1828 meant that his nine-year-old son Putnam inherited Nat; however, the twenty-eight-year-old slave was actually supervised by Joseph Travis, whom the widow Moore had married.

Nat always thought himself great and capable of communing and communicating with the Holy Spirit. As he was ploughing one day, the Spirit said to him, "Seek ye the Kingdom of God and all things shall be added unto you" (N. Turner 46; see also Matthew 6: 33). From that time on, Nat believed himself "ordained for some great purpose in the hands of the Almighty" (46). The Spirit would visit the self-proclaimed preacher a number of times between 1828 and 1831. During that same period Nat frequently fasted and prayed, saw visions, and witnessed miracles. His *Confessions* reveals the following:

I looked and saw the forms of men in different attitudes—and there were lights in the sky. . . . [T]hey were the lights of the Savior's hands. . . . I discovered drops of blood on the corn as though it were dew from heaven—and I communicated it to many, both white and black, in the neighborhood—and I then found on the leaves in the woods hieroglyphic characters, and numbers, with the forms of men in different attitudes, portrayed in blood, and representing the figures I had seen in the heavens. And now the Holy Ghost had revealed itself to me, and made plain the *miracles* it had shown me. (47, emphasis added)

Miraculous it may have seemed when on August 13, 1831, the sun turned a bluish green. Believing that solar change to be a signal from the Spirit, Nat began to lay plans for what he considered to be God's work. (A solar eclipse on February 12, 1831, had been an earlier sign, but plans for the rebellion had to be aborted.) Meeting in the woods for a dinner on August 20, 1831, Nat and his fellow slaves Hark, Sam, Nelson, Will, and Jack finalized the plans for a massacre that would leave dead several white families and hundreds of other families throughout Virginia and the nation stricken with terror.

The Travis family, Nat's owners, were the first to be murdered, with Will delivering the initial blow of death. Joseph Travis was the victim. Nat himself had attempted to draw the first blood by murdering Travis, but the darkness of the night somehow prevented him from doing so. The group left after killing the adults and, presumably, all the children but quickly returned to kill an infant when it was realized that it had been left alive in its cradle. Before being quelled by a militia on August 23, 1831, almost two full days after the revolt began, Nat and his lieutenants had killed fifty-five European Americans, though some sources indicate more. What is amazing is that the "general" of this band avoided capture for two and a half months, being discovered on October 31, 1831, "under the top of a fallen tree" (53).

Shortly after being delivered to the Southampton County jail on the day of his capture, Nat was visited by slave owner and lawyer Thomas R. Gray. He began taking Nat's deposition, which would be published, widely circulated, and financially lucrative. On November 10, 1831, Gray procured a copyright for the deposition, which came to be known as *The Confessions of Nat Turner*. The next day, November 11, Nat was hanged. His body was skinned and grease made of his flesh (L. Turner 1141).

AUTOBIOGRAPHICAL WORK AND THEMES

Nat's autobiographical text, *The Confessions of Nat Turner*, poses an interesting set of authorial and thematic questions. Chief among them, May Nat be considered the true author of this text? And, if so, which portions of the autobiography most accurately represent his words, thoughts, and actions? In response to the first question, it is best to regard this text as one with a shared authorship. While Nat lived the life from which *The Confessions* was born, Thomas Gray recorded the narrative and gave shape to the final document. Hence, what exists today is a dually vocalized autobiography. More specifically, one hears the voice of Nat but also the voice of Gray. Because of the presence of two distinct voices, there is also the presence of two disparate themes. Gray's theme, on the one hand, is an admonition to bondsmen and bondswomen: Revolt will result in a sure death. Nat's theme, on the other hand, is a rallying cry to enslaved and free blacks: Resist the bonds of oppression—even if resistance means that one pays with one's own life.

What is stated in *The Confessions* certainly gives us some sort of impression of Nat, good or bad, martyr or madman. However, what is *not stated* should also be considered in an assessment of this autobiography. For one can never be certain that Nat revealed *all* in *The Confessions*. It can easily be imagined that some of the important matters surrounding the insurrection were withheld. Nor can one know what, if any, portions of *The Confessions* were fabricated by the "oral au thor" of this narrative. After all, Nat, from the inception of his plan, had taken great care to conceal information from most blacks and definitely from all whites. Hence, it is easy to imagine that withholding information or doctoring the details of the revolt might have been something that he chose to do. It is also easy to imagine that Gray, interested in depicting Nat as a coward, did not record Nat's true actions when he noted that the slave offered no resistance when captured. In a word, what is true and what is false in the text will never be known.

Because of the complex nature of the narrativity of *The Confessions*, and be cause of the shared authorship, competing voices will always be heard. Equally significant, competing themes will always be manifested. The first theme, Thomas Gray's, is a warning: Oppressed or enslaved people, if they choose to revolt, will be conquered; the second, Nat's (alias Nat Turner) is a rallying cry: Resist, resist, resist—even if in the end one must pay with one's own life.

CRITICAL RECEPTION

For scholars, critics, and students who read and study *The Confessions* the guiding word is—has always been—*caution*. Kenneth S. Greenberg, the editor of *The Confessions of Nat Turner and Related Documents*, stresses that Nat was not the author of what passes as *The Confessions*, at least, he says, not in the usual sense of the word "author" (8). According to Greenberg, it is certain that the writer of this autobiography, Gray, has given the reader some inaccurate infor mation. Gray, for example, appends to *The Confessions* a list of names identifying the insurrectionists, fifty four in all. His list does not agree with the number of names mentioned in the Southampton County court records, fifty in all (57 58, 91). Critic Lou Turner finds fault with Gray's suggestion that Nat's mother Nancy taught her son to read. Turner thinks it unlikely that the African born woman was herself literate.

It is quite difficult to find a critical perspective that does not question the veracity of the jailhouse deposition that Gray titled *The Confessions of Nat*

Turner. Perhaps more positive assessments are in the offing. However, at this time, few, if any, seem to exist. What is also worth mentioning is that not many literary critics have chosen to make *The Confessions* the subject of their work. One notable exception is Mary Kemp Davis. But even she, it seems, is interested in the autobiography only on a fictional level, as suggested by the title of her book: *Nat Turner before the Bar of Judgment: Fictional Treatments of the Southampton Insurrection.* Perhaps William Styron, a novelist whose 1967 *The Confessions of Nat Turner* was itself criticized for its inaccuracies, best sums up the scholars' concerns:

From the first word [*The Confessions*] poses serious questions of veracity. At a time when justice for slaves was at best a sham, and in the aftermath of a sensational trial in which the state's absolute authority must have prevailed, how reliable or authentic was anything Nat said, when filtered through the mind of this minion [Thomas Gray] of the state? (440)

BIBLIOGRAPHY

Autobiographical Work by Nat Turner

Turner, Nat. *The Confessions of Nat Turner.* Rpt. in *The Confessions of Nat Turner and Related Documents.* Ed. Kenneth S. Greenberg. New York: Bedford, 1996.

Studies of Nat Turner's Autobiographical Work

Addison, Bernard, Michael Collins, and Allen Gilmore. *America's Black Spartacus Remembered: The Confessions of Nat Turner.* New York: Audio Books, 1999. Audiobook.

Davis, Mary Kemp. *Nat Turner before the Bar of Judgment: Fictional Treatments of the Southampton Slave Insurrection.* Baton Rouge: Louisiana University Press, 1999.

From Revolution to Reconstruction. Dir. George Welling. February. 1996. The American Revolution—an HTML Project. February 26, 2001. <http://odur.let.rug.nl/~usa/D/1826–1850/slavery/confesxx.htm>.

Greenberg, Kenneth S. Introduction. In *The Confessions of Nat Turner and Related Documents.* New York: Bedford, 1996. 1–34.

Styron, William. Afterword. "Nat Turner Revisited." In *The Confessions of Nat Turner.* 1967. New York: Vintage, 1993. 431–55.

Turner, Lou. "Nat Turner." In *Notable Black American Men.* Ed. Jessie Carney Smith. Detroit: Gale, 1999. 1137–42.

GLORIA WADE-GAYLES
(1938–)

James L. Hill

BIOGRAPHY

Gloria Jean Wade-Gayles, poet, essayist, editor, literary critic, and educator, is an acclaimed writer and scholar of African American literature. Born on July 1, 1938, in Memphis, Tennessee, to Robert and Bertha Reese Willett Wade, she grew up in the 1940s in the segregated housing projects of Memphis. Gloria Wade graduated from high school in 1955 and received a scholarship from LeMoyne College, at that time the only college in Memphis that accepted African American students. Urged by a visiting scholar to pursue her writing, she decided to major in English. She graduated from LeMoyne College in 1959 and, because of her stellar academic record, received a Woodrow Wilson Fellowship to study for her masters's degree at Boston University. "In 1959," Wade-Gayles wrote, "Boston was a venomously racist city" (*Pushed* 122) "that failed every test on racial sensitivity and racial justice" (123). For Wade-Gayles, however, life in Boston became more tolerable because of the convergence of several events in her life, beginning what she has called her metamorphosis into a different woman. In 1959, she met Jimmy, whom she later married and with whom she became a civil rights activist. Viewing herself as an integrationist, she also joined the Unitarian Church in Boston. But perhaps the most catalytic event of this period was her discovery of the Congress of Racial Equality (CORE), which she joined in 1961. Wade-Gayles's experiences demonstrating and preparing leaflets in the 1960s, therefore, were seminal in her developing commitment to the civil rights movement (Adams 9).

In 1963, Wade-Gayles and Jimmy moved to Atlanta, Georgia, the city that would become her home off and on for the next three decades. She and Jimmy, however, separated in 1963 and were divorced a year later. From 1963 to 1964, she taught at Spelman College, but at the end of the year, she was dismissed from Spelman for being one of those "faculty at black colleges who were tampering with Atlanta's image" and "who risked losing their jobs" (*Pushed* 145). When the Confederation of Freedom Organizations (COFO) went to Mississippi in 1964, she joined them and taught that summer at the COFO Freedom School in Valley View, Mississippi. From 1965 to 1978, she taught at Howard University, Morehouse College, and Tougaloo College, respectively, and later in the 1990s, spent a year teaching at Bennett College on two different occasions. Concurrently and intermittently during her activist-educator life, she also continued her education, enrolling in the doctoral program at George Washington University from 1966 to 1967. While in Washington, D.C., she remarried, this time to Joseph Nathan Gayles. In August 1967, she and her husband moved to San Jose, California, and later had two children, Jonathan and Monica. From 1975 to 1981, Wade-Gayles studied at Emory University, receiving her doctorate in American Studies in 1981; and in 1984, she returned to Spelman College as assistant professor of English. A passionate and unorthodox educator, as she calls herself, Wade-Gayles earned the Faculty Award of the Year at Morehouse College in 1975 and the Spelman College Presidential Award for Scholarship in 1991. That same year, she was named Georgia's CASE Professor of the Year for Teaching Excellence, nominated for the CASE National Professor of the Year, and selected as a Research Fellow at the Du Bois* Institute at Harvard University. In 1994, Emory University presented her the Emory Medal, awarded to distinguished alumni.

Because of her personal commitments, Wade-Gayles began writing in her mid-forties. In 1984, she published *No Crystal Stair: Visions of Race and Sex in Black Women's Fiction, 1946–1976*, an interdisciplinary study of select contemporary novels by black women writers. Six years later, she published *Annointed to Fly*, a collection of poems, and then *Pushed Back to Strength: A Black Woman's Journey Home* (1993) and *Rooted Against the Wind: Personal Essays* (1996), two autobiographical works. A prolific writer and scholar, Wade-Gayles has also authored numerous scholarly articles, essays, and introductions and edited or written two additional books, all of which reflect her immersion in African American women's history and culture. An anthology that resists classification, *My Soul Is a Witness: African American Women's Spirituality* (1995) is a collection featuring major African American women writers, including Toni Morrison, Alice Walker,* and Maya Angelou.* And *Fathers and Sons: Testimonies by African American Sons and Daughters* (1998) presents true stories in which black men and women discuss their relationships with their fathers. Currently, Wade-Gayles is working on a book of personal essays about political issues facing African Americans and a novel about the sexuality of a black woman over fifty in a culture that narrowly defines feminism (Adams 11). In 1998, after thirty-five years in and out of Atlanta, Wade-Gayles left Spelman again, this time for Dillard University in New Orleans. At Dillard, she holds the RosaMary Eminent Scholar's Chair in Humanities/Fine Arts. "I have chosen to remain at historically black colleges," she says, "and that has meant that I'm outside of the mainstream" (11). Far from being outside of the mainstream, however, Wade-Gayles has earned an international reputation from her writings and scholarship.

AUTOBIOGRAPHICAL WORKS AND THEMES

Although most of her writings are in some ways autobiographical, Wade-Gayles's autobiographical memoirs are *Pushed Back to Strength* and *Rooted Against the Wind*. While the former chronicles her journey from childhood in Memphis, Tennessee, to adulthood, the latter is an exploration of critical moments in her adult life in the Atlanta community. Atypical of autobiographies, *Pushed Back to Strength* resists the traditional prescription of chronology and dates; for Wade-Gayles mostly eschews dates, moving back and forward and reconstructing and connecting events as she journeys through time. Her autobiography is, therefore, an intellectual and spiritual rendering of formative experiences in her life; it is, too, a remarkable revelation of didactic experiences in her life from which she, as the title suggests, gained strength, maturity, or wisdom. *Rooted Against the Wind*, like *Pushed Back to Strength*, is autobiographical but not chronological. Provocative and challenging, these essays are distinctly more feminist and political. Like other contemporary feminists, Wade-Gayles is unafraid of exploring the connections between the political and the personal.

Both *Pushed Back to Strength* and *Rooted Against the Wind* conjure up and employ metaphors that Wade-Gayles extends to convey her pervasive theme: the strength and importance of black people and the black community. The title "Pushed Back to Strength" comes from the wisdom of Wade-Gayles's grand mother. Responding to Wade-Gayles's constant complaints about white racism while growing up as a child, the grandmother told her: "They don't know it. They don't know it, but they're pushing you back to us, where you get strong. Get some strength" (*Pushed* 6).

Wade-Gayles extends this metaphor to explore various elements of black life and community in the South, focusing on her personal experiences as mirrors of the black community. In her 1993 memoir, therefore, Wade-Gayles writes about her coming of age in racially polarized Memphis and the lessons learned from her mother, family, and community. When she moves to Boston to pursue her master's degree, she encounters a profoundly racist city and becomes a courageous civil rights activist and poet. The second half of the memoir focuses on her return to the South to continue her activism and to teach. As the memoir ends, Wade-Gayles is passing her rememberings and history on to her children. She ends her narrative in this manner because, as she believes, African Americans are discon nected from their history, community, and ancestors. "They were our strength, they are our strength," she says. "We need to begin communicating with them and recognizing who they are. It's almost as if we've taken off our spiritual cloth ing, our cultural clothing, because we were uncomfortable wearing it" (Little 54).

In *Rooted Against the Wind*, Wade-Gayles also employs an extended metaphor to unify her essays. Fully defining the metaphor in the last essay of the volume, she says: "And as long as the racial waters in white America crash against the reality of my people with the force of hurricanes of hatred, I will hold on to my blackness with tenacity" (195). A personal odyssey, *Rooted Against the Wind* explores a wide variety of subjects, including aging, homophobia, interracial marriages, and the dilemma of young black intellectuals; and Wade-Gayles takes her readers with her as she probes uniquely contemporary issues and her own psyche. One of the six essays, for example, illustrates her terror and degradation when an intruder attempts to rape her, violating the sanctity of her home. In her "undressing herself, making herself naked to be safe" (*Rooted* x), Wade-Gayles often challenges her readers to face their own demons. While *Pushed Back to Strength* is a spiritual autobiography and *Rooted Against the Wind* is a collection of essays, both affirm again and again Wade-Gayles's belief that the black community is an indispensable source of strength for black people against the racism and injustices of our society.

CRITICAL RECEPTION

In both autobiographical works, Wade-Gayles extends her purpose beyond the mere events and experiences of her life; for with her readers in mind, she selectively presents formative experiences into which she can interweave and connect other aspects of her life. She extends the meaning of her experiences threefold: to her readers' lives, to contemporary political and social issues, and to memorable parallels in African American literature, especially writings by African American women. She "makes the reader believe in her mixture of rationalism and faith in the unseen" (Conway 19). As critics have observed, both *Pushed Back to Strength* and *Rooted Against the Wind* uniquely incorporate Wade-Gayles's poetic voice, humor, and effective use of dialogue to strengthen and enliven the texts. Further, as Conway concludes, "Her poetic voice makes her a powerful creator of images" (19). In actuality, *Pushed Back to Strength* is a celebration of mothers and maternal love and *Rooted Against the Wind* a provocative probing of important issues of race and gender. While most reviewers applauded the spirituality and boldness of both texts, one reviewer concluded that Wade-Gayles in *Rooted Against the Wind* is "prepared to challenge herself and her readers only up to a point" (Gunning 18).

Much of Wade-Gayles's success in these texts, however, rests not on her challenges to readers but on her willingness to defy conventions. "When you step outside the expectations of the academy," she believes, "you take a risk. But I can't breathe professionally without also breathing personally. My work is a reflection of my identity. It's about going to the art and hearing my own voice, my mother's voice, my grandmother's, my uncle's, my father's" (Adams 9). In both of her autobiographical works, Wade-Gayles has truly moved beyond the autobiographical to the representational.

BIBLIOGRAPHY

Autobiographical Works by Gloria Wade-Gayles

Pushed Back to Strength: A Black Woman's Journey Home. New York: Avon Books, 1993.
Rooted Against the Wind: Personal Essays. Boston: Beacon Press, 1996.

Studies of Gloria Wade-Gayles's Autobiographical Works

Adams, Allison O. "Coloring Outside the Circles." *Emory Magazine* 71 (1995): 8–11.
Bell, Janet Cheatham. "To Be Old, Female and Black." Rev. of *Rooted Against the Wind.*
    Black Issues in Higher Education (October 1998): 29.
Burns, Ann. Rev. of *Rooted Against the Wind. Library Journal* (October 1996): 80.
Conway, Jill Ker. "Mother Was Right After All." Rev. of *Pushed Back to Strength. New
    York Times Book Review* (April 7, 1994): 19.
Flanagan, Margaret. Rev. of *Pushed Back to Strength. Booklist* (October 1993): 416.
Gunning, Sandra. "The Roads Not Taken." Rev. of *Rooted Against the Wind. Women's
    Review of Books* 14 (1997): 18.
Hart, Jordana. Rev. of *Rooted Against the Wind. Ms.* (1996): 82.
Lewis, Lillian. Rev. of *Rooted Against the Wind. Booklist* (October 1996): 310.
Little, Benilde. "How Can You Bring Spirituality into Your Life?" *Essence* 27 (1996): 54.
Rev. of *Pushed Back to Strength. Essence* 24 (1993): 54.
"Wade-Gayles, Gloria." In *Who's Who among African Americans.* Ed. Ashyra Henderson.
    Detroit: Gale Research Group, 2000. 1363.
"Wade-Gayles, Gloria." In *Who's Who among Black Americans.* Ed. William C. Matney.
    Detroit: Gale Research, 1992. 1413.

ALICE WALKER
(1944–)

Paula C. Barnes

BIOGRAPHY

The eighth and last child of sharecroppers Willie Lee and Minnie Grant Walker, Alice Walker was born on February 9, 1944, in Eatonton, Georgia. When she was eight years old, an accident occurred that was to shape Walker's future: She lost sight in one eye as the result of being shot with a BB gun. This experience led to her becoming a loner; it also allowed her to attend Spelman College on a scholarship for the handicapped. After two and a half "uneasy" years there, she transferred to Sarah Lawrence College and spent the summer between her junior and senior years in Africa. When she returned to school, she was pregnant. While recuperating from an abortion (she also had contemplated suicide), Walker wrote the poems that comprise her first published volume *Once* (1969) and the short story "To Hell with Dying." These works were Walker's exploration into self-representational writing, as most of the poems are autobiographical, and Walker identifies this short story as one of the few that is autobiographical (*Living by the Word* [*LBW*] 37).

After receiving her B.A., Walker moved to New York City but left the summer of 1966 to work in the civil rights movement in Jackson, Mississippi. There she met Mel Leventhal, a Jewish law student, also a civil rights worker. After returning to New York, they lived together while he finished his last year of law school. They then married and moved to Mississippi. During the seven years there, Walker firmly established herself as a writer with a novel, a second collection of poetry, and a collection of short stories. Walker also gave birth to their only child, Rebecca.

After returning to New York and divorcing, Walker began working as an editor for *Ms.* magazine. She also completed a second novel and another volume of poetry, both of which reflect her experiences in Mississippi. In 1978, she relocated to San Francisco and four years later published the novel *The Color Purple*. This work placed Walker in the literary limelight, for in 1983, it won both the Pulitzer Prize for Fiction and the American Book Award. In 1984 Walker founded Wild Trees Press, which lasted only four years yet produced six books.

Since 1984, Walker has published three novels, *Possessing the Secret of Joy*, *The Temple of My Familiar*, and *By the Light of My Father's Smile*; two volumes of poetry, *Horses Make a Landscape Look More Beautiful* and *Her Blue Body: Everything We Know*; and *Warrior Marks: Female Genital Mutilation and the Sexual Blinding of Women* in addition to the five collections of essays, many of which are autobiographical.

AUTOBIOGRAPHICAL WORKS AND THEMES

Alice Walker has not written a book-length autobiography; however, she has revealed much about her life in her five collections of essays: *In Search of Our Mothers' Gardens* (1983); *Living by the Word: Selected Writings, 1973–1987* (1988); *The Same River Twice: Honoring the Difficult* (1996); *Anything We Love Can Be Saved: A Writer's Activism* (1997), and *The Way Forward Is with a Broken Heart* (2000). From these writings emerge the themes of "surviving whole," family/ancestry, spirituality, and love.

Walker's readers best understand her theme of "surviving whole" within the context of "womanism," the term she coined in *In Search of Our Mothers' Gardens*. In her definition of womanist, that is, "a woman who loves other women, sexually and/or nonsexually," Walker includes "[c]ommitted to survival and wholeness of entire people, male *and* female" (*In Search* [*IS*]). Walker explains that surviving whole is the antidote to violence, and she writes poignantly about violence against women—domestic violence, incest, and female genital mutilation. She explains that it was while viewing an incident of violence against a woman that she knew she would become a novelist. At age thirteen, she saw the newspaper stuck in a hole in the shoe of a woman whose face had been half shot off by her husband and determined at this "indelible moment" to "learn how to tell her story" (*Anything We Love* [*AWL*] 39). Claiming that "violence to others is soul abuse," Walker also writes about broader issues of violence, from man's inhumanity to man, as in the sale of weapons to Central America and killing in general to violence against animals and the earth itself (*Same River Twice* [*SRT*] 41).

Family and ancestry is a second theme that runs through Walker's autobiographical writing. A number of her essays reflect her coming to terms with her parents: with her father, whom she described as a "victim of sexist ideology," and with her mother as she admits that her early essays reveal how "deeply [she] was affected by her mother's life" (*AWL* 64). Walker writes not only about her parents but about being a parent (she admits that she saw motherhood as "a threat to her writing"), not only about her siblings but also her loves—and her bisexuality

(*IS* 224). In addition, Walker acknowledges the legacy of her triple heritage—African, European, and Native American—and pays homage to her ancestors. She explains that she keeps her maiden name in memory of the walk that her great-great-great-great grandmother, May Poole, undertook as a slave from Virginia to Georgia (*IS* 142; *AWL* xiii). She honors her mother's mother, Nettie, by naming a character in *The Color Purple* after her (*SRT* 29); she memorializes her "extremely misogynistic grandfather, whom [she] nonetheless adored," as the "much maligned character" Mister in *The Color Purple* (*SRT* 157, 34). Walker's notion of ancestor also extends beyond family lines. She writes extensively of the search for the gravesite of Zora Neale Hurston,* her literary ancestor, and of other ancestors, including Sojourner Truth,* and writers—Flannery O'Connor, Carl Jung—whose lives affected hers.

While the theme of spirituality appears in Walker's early works, it finds its fullest development in the essay "The Only Reason You Want to Go to Heaven" in *Anything We Love Can Be Saved*. In it, Walker, who rejected her Christian upbringing in college, traces her spiritual quest and identifies herself as a "born again pagan," a "person whose primary spiritual relationship is with Nature and the Earth" (17). In *The Same River Twice*, Walker explains her worship of the earth but also states that "what is holy is the whole thing" (35). This concept explains not only Walker's spirituality but also her "cultural, spiritual and political activism," for in order to protect the earth one must respect not only human lives but also the lives of animals and the earth itself (*AWL* xxii). This concept also makes apparent the interrelatedness of the themes in her writing: Whatever Walker is writing, she is ultimately writing about love. It alone is the key to "surviving whole," to maintaining family and honoring ancestors, for respecting the earth and the universe. Walker best summarizes her theme(s) when she states that her "religion is love" and her writings are "a prayer to and about the world" (*SRT* 33, 38).

CRITICAL RECEPTION

While the critics have differed greatly in their views on Walker's five collections of essays, they have generally been favorable toward the autobiographical essays in these works. They also make particular note of Walker's honesty and candor.

Of the collections, *In Search of Our Mothers' Gardens* has been the best received. It was listed in *Magill's Literary Annual* as one of the 200 outstanding books of 1983. As Jewell Parker Rhodes asserts, the collection is worthwhile simply for its autobiographical pieces (137). Two of its essays, "In Search of Our Mothers' Gardens" and "Beauty: When the Dancer Is the Self," have been greatly anthologized and are viewed as classics.

The Same River Twice, which records "Walker's experiences during and after the production and release of the film version" of *The Color Purple*, is clearly the collection that is the most autobiographical (Seaman). A reviewer's comment that "Walker's life and her interpretations of it are of continuing interest" seems to reflect the majority viewpoint (Seaman). However, the reviewers, like Walker, realize the difficulty of revisiting the past. With the exception of the journal entries Walker wrote while on the film set and her version of the script, which was not used by Spielberg, there is little in the collection that is new or surprising.

Responses to two of the collections are quite mixed. Using Walker's metaphors of a quilt or garden, some critics argue that *Living by the Word*, appearing five years after *In Search of Our Mothers' Gardens*, is unfinished or not carefully tended. Many reviewers identify the first essay in *Anything We Love Can Be Saved*, "The Only Reason You Want to Go to Heaven," as its most significant personal piece. However, there is the negative commentary that Walker's "writing about her spiritual development is simply of no interest" (Cummings 2).

The responses to Walker's latest collection, *The Way Forward Is with a Broken Heart*, are promising. Walker explains *The Way Forward* as "mostly fiction, but with a definite thread of having come out of a singular life" (Cleage 17). Its dustjacket explains that "it begins with a lyrical, autobiographical story of a marriage set in the violent and Deep South during the early years of the civil rights movement": That story is clearly Walker's own. The epilogue, subtitled "To the Husband of My Youth," clearly refers back to the initial story. While the works in between may indeed be fiction, most of the critics agree with the reviewer who subtitled her essay "New Stories Blend Autobiography with Spare Fiction" (Clark 15). One critic argues that the collection "reads less like fiction than personal testimony" (*Publishers Weekly*). But most agree that the stories are beautifully written. Whether more fiction than fact, these stories represent Walker's singular theme of the enduring power of love.

BIBLIOGRAPHY

Autobiographical Works by Alice Walker

In Search of Our Mothers' Gardens: Womanist Prose. San Diego: Harcourt Brace Jovanovich, 1983.

Living by the Word: Selected Writings, 1973–1987. San Diego: Harcourt Brace Jovanovich, 1988.

The Same River Twice: Honoring the Difficult. New York: Scribner, 1996.

Anything We Love Can Be Saved: A Writer's Activism. New York: Random, 1997.

The Way Forward Is with a Broken Heart. New York: Random, 2000.

Studies of Alice Walker's Autobiographical Works

Clark, Dorothy. "Walker Moves Forward: New Stories Blend Autobiography with Spare Fiction." Rev. of *The Way Forward Is with a Broken Heart*. *Daily Press* (Newport News, VA), December 12, 2000, 14, 15.

Cleage, Pearl. Rev. of *The Way Forward Is with a Broken Heart*. *Black Issues Book Review* (November–December 2000): 17.

Cummings, Charles. "No Regard for Fact." Rev. of *Anything We Love Can Be Saved: A Writer's Activism*. *New Statesman* (August 15, 1997): 2.

Rev. of *The Way Forward Is with a Broken Heart*. *Publishers Weekly* (September 11, 2000): 71.

Rhodes, Jewell Parker. Rev. of *In Search of Our Mothers' Gardens*. *America* (February 25, 1984): 137.

Royster, Philip M. "In Search of Our Fathers' Arms: Alice Walker's Persona of the Alienated Darling." *Black American Literature Forum* 20 (1986): 347–70.

Seaman, Donna. Rev. of *The Same River Twice: Honoring the Difficult*. *Hungry Mind Review*. Online. January 12, 2001. <http://bookwire.bowker.com/bookinfo/review. aspx?1696.>.

Smith, Pamela. "Green Lap, Brown Embrace, Blue Body: The Ecospirituality of Alice Walker." *Cross Currents* 48 (Winter 1998–1999): 471–88.

Tate, Claudia. "Alice Walker." In *Black Women Writers at Work*. New York: Continuum, 1983. 175–87.

Washington, Mary Helen. "An Essay on Alice Walker." In *Sturdy Black Bridges: Visions of Black Women in Literature*. Ed. Roseann P. Bell, Bettye J. Parker, and Beverly Guy-Sheftall. Garden City, NY: Anchor/Doubleday, 1979. 133–49.

———. " 'Sign My Mother's Name': Alice Walker, Dorothy West, Paule Marshall." In *Mothering and the Mind. Twelve Writers and Their Silent Partners*. Ed. Ruth Perry and Martine Watson Brownley. New York: Homes and Meier, 1984. 142–62.

BOOKER T. WASHINGTON
(1856–1915)

David L. Dudley

BIOGRAPHY

Booker Taliaferro Washington was born in 1856 on a tobacco farm in Franklin County, Virginia. His mother, Jane, was a slave, and his father a white man who may have been his master. At the end of the Civil War, Washington moved to Malden, West Virginia, where his stepfather had taken a job in a salt mine. Here Washington learned to read and write while also working in the salt furnace and later in a coal mine. Determined to further his education, he traveled to the Hampton Institute in Tidewater, Virginia, enrolling in 1872. While there, Washington came under the influence of the school's founder, General Samuel C. Armstrong, who had created Hampton to provide industrial education for African Americans. Washington later copied the Hampton model at Tuskegee and adopted Armstrong's philosophy of cleanliness, hard work, and self-reliance.

After graduating from Hampton in 1875, Washington spent three years teaching in Malden. A year studying at Wayland Seminary in Washington, D.C. showed him that ministry was not his calling. Disillusioned by urban life as lived by blacks untrained to perform any useful trades, Washington returned to Hampton Institute, where he taught for two years before being invited to Tuskegee by the Alabama legislature (at the recommendation of Samuel Armstrong) to create a new industrial school for blacks. The Tuskegee Institute was founded on July 4, 1881, and dedicated to training its students in "practical" trades such as brick making, dairying, carpentry, agriculture, and home economics. Tuskegee became Washington's true "ministry"; he devoted nearly thirty-five years of unflagging energy to raising money for its land, buildings, faculty salaries, and equipment. At the same time, he preached without stint his philosophy that African Americans would rise in the world and win their place in American society through

hard work and the mastery of practical skills that would make their talents indispensable to the white community. When blacks had pulled themselves up the
ladder of success, he asserted, they would be rewarded with the vote and other
civil rights.

The early years at Tuskegee were marked by unremitting toil and constant
anxiety about finances. Washington fathered three children and lost two wives
during those early years; by his own admission, his first wives virtually worked
themselves to death in the Tuskegee cause. A third marriage, to Margaret Murray,
in 1892, proved lasting and happy.

Washington's star, which had risen slowly since 1881, blazed to ascendancy
in 1895. In that year, Frederick Douglass,* the patriarchal leader of black Americans, died, leaving the way open for a successor. Washington took the mantle
of Elijah with one speech, his address at the Atlanta Cotton States and International Exposition on September 18, 1895. In this address, Washington urged
black and white southerners to pledge themselves to mutual support: He asked
whites to help blacks further their education in industry and the trades, trusting
in the ongoing goodwill of a people whose loyalty and character they knew.
Washington urged blacks to acquire skills needed by their communities, to save
their money, and to buy land. In time, whites would reward them with the vote
and social equality. Until then, Washington warned, agitation for equal rights
would prove "the extremest folly."

White America hailed the Cotton Exposition speech as the solution to the
nation's race problem. Money from northern philanthropists poured into Tuskegee; Harvard awarded Washington an honorary degree in 1896; President Mc-
Kinley visited the school in 1898; and Teddy Roosevelt had Washington to
dinner at the White House in 1901. To help cement his position as the anointed
leader of African Americans, Washington published his famous autobiography,
Up from Slavery, in 1901. The book restates its author's philosophy of hard work
and service to others, while offering its protagonist as a model of the success to
be derived from living those values.

Tuskegee and Washington's "gospel of Work and Money" were not without
their critics, even during the high tide of Washington's reign as the most famous
and influential black American. William Monroe Trotter, W.E.B. Du Bois,* and
other African Americans who comprised what Du Bois dubbed the "Talented
Tenth" challenged what they believed to be Washington's "accommodationist"
policies. They wondered who had given Washington the right to trade away
blacks' civil rights in exchange for Tuskegee's right to exist. Du Bois wrote that
blacks could not protect the property Washington urged them to acquire without
the vote, nor could blacks be expected to gain self-respect through labor while
being relegated to second-class citizenship through laws enforcing segregation.

Washington's opponents organized the Niagara Movement in 1905 to counteract his policies and then created the National Association for the Advancement of Colored People (NAACP) in 1909. Despite rising criticism, Washington
remained committed to his program and point of view, but secretly he supported

civil rights suits, combated the scourge of lynching, and worked for more public education for African Americans. He thus led a kind of double life: While publicly presenting the face of accommodation, counseling patience in the pursuit of civil rights, and promoting industrial training, Washington fought behind the scenes against racial violence and worked for the very rights he said blacks were willing to postpone to some indefinite future.

Washington died in 1915, worn out from decades of unremitting labor. With him died the "Tuskegee Machine" through which he had largely controlled the black press, assisted or prevented blacks from obtaining public office, and served as a clearinghouse for most decisions affecting national policy toward African Americans. Leadership fell to Du Bois and other like-minded people, who aggressively pressed for equality for blacks through a coordinated strategy based on winning courtroom decisions and public support through positive propaganda. Yet Washington left an enduring legacy: Tuskegee itself and a philosophy designed to help African Americans help themselves through hard work, acquisition of skills, and self-respect.

AUTOBIOGRAPHICAL WORKS AND THEMES

Shortly after his Atlanta Cotton Exposition speech, which established him as the new leader of black Americans, Washington began considering an autobiography. The project did not come about until four years later, but then Washington produced two works in two years. Both, according to Louis R. Harlan, were part of a larger plan to solidify Washington's place as "the possessor of the conventional wisdom in race relations" in turn-of-the-century America (*Making* 229).

Washington's first autobiography, *The Story of My Life and Work*, was published by J.L. Nichols and Company in 1900. Nichols sold books door to door by subscription, and this work seems to have been designed primarily for a black readership reachable by such direct marketing. Like *Up from Slavery*, *The Story of My Life and Work* was ghostwritten. The author was Edgar Webber, who did a poor job. Washington himself failed to oversee the project and was not even in the country to check the manuscript. The finished product, while containing most of the elements that made its successor so popular, is a shoddy piece of work, what Harlan condemns as "a thoroughly bad book" (*Making* 244). Its chief faults are two. First, it lacks an organizing principle and hence a coherent structure. Second, Webber relies heavily upon the complete texts of numerous Washington speeches and reviews from the national press to pad the work. The result is an overlong, bloated, and boring book. Nevertheless, perhaps because of its strong promotion by the Nichols company, it initially outsold *Up from Slavery*, chalking up sales figures of some 75,000 by 1903 (Harlan, *Making* 250).

Dissatisfied with *The Story of My Life and Work*, Washington immediately began a second autobiography. This time he involved himself much more in its writing, working closely with a new ghostwriter, Max Bennett Thrasher, a white man. Other expert editorial advice was obtained, and a Doubleday, Page, and Company, a leading publisher, helped assure a quality product.

First serialized in *Outlook* magazine, *Up from Slavery* was published in book form in 1901. Immediately hailed as an inspirational work expressing the best wisdom for solving the nation's "race problem," the autobiography did indeed attain its goal of making Washington the strongest African American leader of his time. *Up from Slavery* was soon translated into many languages and read throughout the world. Never out of print, it has inspired many readers throughout the generations even as it has dismayed and angered others.

Up from Slavery derives much of its appeal from Washington's canny use of the mythology of the American Dream. His account of his early life in slavery intentionally recalls the slave narratives of Frederick Douglass and others, while recasting their stories in a meliorist light. While detailing the poverty of his childhood, Washington downplays the abuses of slavery, daring even to state that "the black man got nearly as much out of slavery as the white man did" (17). This is what most of his readers, especially white ones, wanted to hear. Washington insists that he and most former slaves bear no bitterness toward whites for slavery and that, for himself at least, anger and race prejudice are things of his distant past.

As its title suggests, *Up from Slavery* is a tale of triumphant progress. Washington, like Douglass and Benjamin Franklin, whose *Autobiography* is another model for his work, describes how he attained an education. Hard physical labor first in a salt furnace and then in a coal mine does not keep the young Washington from learning to read and write. At sixteen, he departs West Virginia and makes his way to the Hampton Institute, where he meets Gen. Samuel C. Armstrong, whose personal values and philosophy of education for African Americans Washington adopts. Throughout this section of the work, Washington stresses repeatedly the importance of personal cleanliness, epitomized by what he calls "the gospel of the toothbrush"; determination to succeed through hard work (he labored as a janitor at Hampton to help meet his tuition costs); and the value of a practical education designed to give black Americans the skills needed by their community.

The heart of *Up from Slavery*, however, is the saga of the founding of Tuskegee Institute. Washington describes what even his most vehement critics must acknowledge as a singular achievement: the creation, virtually from nothing, of a school designed to instill in its students Washington's values of cleanliness, honest labor, and self-help. The measure of the school's success can be taken partly by its growth over twenty years so that at the time of the publication of *Up from Slavery*, Washington can boast that he heads a school of some 2,300 acres (700 tilled by students), forty buildings mostly erected by the students, twenty-eight industrial departments, property and buildings valued at nearly half a million dollars, and an endowment equally as large. Here is the American success story writ large.

Washington's autobiography is carefully structured toward two climactic moments. The first is his Atlanta Cotton Exposition Speech, delivered in September of 1895. Washington gives the text of the famous speech in full, with dramatic effect. After counseling white and black southerners to "cast down their buckets" in the South, to look to each other for aid in rebuilding the economy of the South, Washington makes the pledge that White America most wanted to hear. After assuring the nation that its black citizens are ready to lend their hands and backs to its industries and trades, he pledges, "In all things that are purely social we can be as separate as the fingers, yet one as the hand in all things essential to mutual progress" (221–22). Thus he seems to postpone to some indefinite future the demand for full civil equality. Despite criticism from some other black leaders, Washington's speech is hailed as the panacea for the nation's racial difficulties. Washington notes the accolades heaped upon him after the speech and details how he was congratulated by President Grover Cleveland, among other illustrious leaders.

The second climactic moment in *Up from Slavery* is the visit of President William McKinley to Tuskegee in 1898. On that day, while standing on the dais between the president and the governor of Alabama, Washington hears John D. Long, Secretary of the Navy, declare that America's problem had been solved. Long suggests that the image should be painted and displayed beside portraits of Washington and Lincoln, this "trinity" of president, white governor of a Deep South state, and "a representative of a race only a few years ago in bondage" (309).

In his chapter titled "Last Words," Washington sums up the philosophy that has guided him personally and that he has inculcated into his life work at Tuskegee:

In our industrial teaching we keep three things in mind: first, that the student shall be so educated that he shall be enabled to meet conditions as they exist now, in the part of the South where he lives—in a word, to be able to do the thing which the world wants done; second, that every student who graduates from the school shall have enough skill, coupled with intelligence and moral character, to enable him to make a living for himself and others; third, to send every graduate out feeling and knowing that labour is dignified and beautiful—to make each one love labour instead of trying to escape it. (312).

This is Washington's code. He presents his own life as one of success from living it himself, and he offers it as the only possible avenue of success for the African Americans of his time. The Washington model for success was what the nation wanted to hear, and it embraced his autobiography with the same enthusiasm it had already given to his career. If there were any doubt before *Up from Slavery* that Washington was the de facto leader of black Americans, that doubt was erased as the book found a large and adulatory audience. Readers were taken with Washington's simple, folksy eloquence; touched by his struggle and successful attainment of the American Dream; and inspired by his tale to make their own success through his formula of hard work and dauntless determination. If it is true, as Louis Harlan argues, that the popularity of *Up from Slavery* could be explained at least in part by its "principal fault . . . that it presented Washington's experience mythically rather than with candor, and thus gave an overly sunny view of black life in America" (*Making* 245), that fault was neither recognized nor openly acknowledged by any but a few readers. Today critics of autobiography recognize that autobiographers are naive or purposeless enough to tell their stories without an agenda; the rearrangement or omission of facts, not to mention a highly subjective "spin" on the author's account, is now regarded as an inevitable part of the autobiographical undertaking. Washington was not a naive man. Even W.E.B. Du Bois, his severest critic, acknowledges that Washington read the temper of his times with keen accuracy and molded his image and message to fit those times. While doing so in *Up from Slavery*, Washington also created a "minor classic" (245) of American autobiography featuring the mythology of the self-made individual who realizes the American Dream.

Washington published *My Larger Education: Being Chapters from My Experience* in 1911. Continuing to promote his philosophy of practical education, he structures the book around what he considers the most important sources of his ongoing education; not surprisingly, academics and "book learning" are not highlighted. Instead, Washington details what he has learned from "Men and Things," "Reporters and Newspapers," "Exceptional Men," and "Black Men." In his last chapter he discusses he views about the future of Negro education. While expressing his satisfaction about the rapid educational progress African Americans have made, Washington admits that blacks are not receiving educations equal to those of whites, and he calls for increased spending to bring black universities up to the level of white ones.

My Larger Education repeats the beliefs Washington had already been espousing for many years. New is the assertion of his own leadership by attacking his opponents such as W.E.B. Du Bois and other leaders of the "Talented Tenth," whom he derides for making their living by criticizing him and constantly calling attention to the problems of black Americans. But his overriding concern is to stress repeatedly the necessity for African Americans to base their education on hands-on learning experiences and to use the knowledge thus gained to "deal with the objects and situations of actual life" (134).

All of his autobiographical writings thus show that Washington remained forever faithful to the ideas upon which he had founded Tuskegee Institute and which he promoted unceasingly during the twenty years he was the de facto, if not undisputed, leader of African Americans.

CRITICAL RECEPTION

Critical response to Washington's autobiographies falls into two periods. The first occurred during the years the works were published, when most writers, as Louis Harlan notes, "followed the pattern of reviewing the life rather than the book" (*Making* 250). William Dean Howells's lengthy essay on *Up from Slavery*, published in the *North American Review* (August 1901), is typical of the praise-worthy evaluations of Washington's philosophy and program, as its title, "An Exemplary Citizen," suggests. Howells has much to say favoring the ideas propounded in the book and almost nothing to say about the autobiography as a literary creation. He does note how "touching" are the passages in which Washington portrays his devotion to his mother, but this is more to praise the man's character than the art with which he conveys it to his readers. Howells does note that Washington talks "simple prose" but "of sterling worth"; he notes that the writing is "interfused with a sweet, brave humor" (194), but that is nearly the extent of Howells's criticism of the autobiography *as literature*.

W.E.B. Du Bois, Washington's severest and most famous critic, takes a skeptical view of the Tuskegee program in his review in *The Dial* (July 16, 1901), which he later expanded into the famous essay "Of Mr. Booker T. Washington and Others" and published in *The Souls of Black Folk* in 1903. But like Howells, Du Bois is more interested in remarking on the life rather than the ways in which Washington fashions an autobiographical persona and structures its experiences.

The flourishing of interest in African American literature and autobiographical studies in the 1970s and 1980s led to critical studies of *Up from Slavery* and Washington's other autobiographies that explore these works as autobiographical art and take an objective stand toward Washington's philosophies. Sidonie Smith and Raymond Hedin were among the first to discuss the place of Washington's works within the traditions and tropes of the slave narrative. Houston Baker reveals how Washington artfully dons the "minstrel mask" to make his message palatable to white readers (*Modernism* 22 ff.) and discusses in another work (*Long Black Song*) how Washington negotiates his place in the African American literary tradition, especially how he comes to terms with his powerful predecessor, Frederick Douglass. James Olney and David Dudley pursue this same line; Olney discusses Washington's work in relation not only to Douglass but also to George Washington, Thomas Jefferson, and Benjamin Franklin, while Dudley focuses on how Washington sought autobiographical strategies by which to "tame" Douglass and claim this spiritual and literary "father's" place as undisputed leader of African Americans. More recently, Donald Gibson has explored ways Washington changed his self-representation in his various autobiographies.

BIBLIOGRAPHY

Autobiographical Works by Booker T. Washington

The Story of My Life and Work. Naperville, IL: J. L. Nichols, 1900.
Up from Slavery. New York: Doubleday, Page, 1901. Penguin Classics Reprint. New York: Penguin Group, 1986.
My Larger Education: Being Chapters from My Experience. New York: Doubleday, Page, 1911.

Studies of Booker T. Washington's Autobiographical Works

Andrews, William L. *To Tell a Free Story: The First Century of Afro-American Autobiography*. Urbana: University of Illinois Press, 1986.

Baker, Houston. *Long Black Song: Essays in Black American Literature and Culture*. Charlottesville: University of Virginia Press, 1972.

———. *Modernism and the Harlem Renaissance*. Chicago: University of Chicago Press, 1987.

Cox, James. "Autobiography and Washington." *Sewanee Review* 85 (1977): 235–61.

Du Bois, W.E.B. "The Evolution of Negro Leadership." *The Dial* 31 (July 16, 1901): 53–55.

———. "Of Mr. Booker T. Washington and Others." *The Souls of Black Folk*. In *W.E.B. Du Bois: Writings*. Ed. Nathan Huggins. New York: Viking/Library of America, 1986.

Dudley, David L. *My Father's Shadow: Intergenerational Conflict in African-American Men's Autobiography*. Philadelphia: University of Pennsylvania Press, 1991.

Gibson, Donald B. "Strategies and Revisions of Self-Representation in Booker T. Washington's Autobiographies." *American Quarterly* 45.3 (September 1993): 370–93.

Harlan, Louis R. *Booker T. Washington: The Making of a Black Leader, 1856–1901*. New York: Oxford University Press, 1972.

———. *Booker T. Washington: The Wizard of Tuskegee, 1901–1915*. New York: Oxford University Press, 1983.

Hedin, Raymond. "Paternal at Last: Booker T. Washington and the Slave Narrative Tradition." *Callaloo* 2 (October 1979): 95–102.

Howells, William Dean. "An Exemplary Citizen." *North American Review* 173 (August 1901): 280–88. Rpt. in *The Booker T. Washington Papers, Volume 6, 1901–02*. Ed. Louis R. Harlan and Raymond W. Smock. Urbana: University of Illinois Press, 1977. 191–200.

Olney, James. "The Founding Fathers—Frederick Douglass and Booker T. Washington." In *Slavery and the Literary Imagination*. Ed. Deborah McDowell and Arnold Rampersad. Baltimore: Johns Hopkins University Press, 1989. 1–24.

Smith, Sidonie. *Where I'm Bound: Patterns of Slavery and Freedom in Black American Autobiography*. Westport, CT: Greenwood Press, 1974.

Stepto, Robert B. "Lost in a Cause: Booker T. Washington's *Up from Slavery*." In *From behind the Veil: A Study of Afro-American Narrative*. Urbana: University of Illinois Press, 1979. 32–51.

Whitfield, Stephen J. "Three Masters of Impression Management: Benjamin Franklin, Booker T. Washington, and Malcolm X as Autobiographers." *South Atlantic Quarterly* 77 (1978): 399–417.

IDA B. WELLS-BARNETT
(1862–1931)

Lynn Domina

BIOGRAPHY

Ida B. Wells was born a slave in Holly Springs, Mississippi, on July 16, 1862. Her parents, Jim Wells and Elizabeth Warrenton Wells, had eight children, although only five survived to adulthood; Ida was the eldest daughter. As a child, Wells attended Shaw University, a school established by the Freedmen's Aid Society and later known as Rust College. She didn't graduate, however, for reasons that remain unknown but that were apparently linked to a scandal she later spoke of only obliquely. When Wells was sixteen, both of her parents and her infant brother died during a yellow fever epidemic. Wells was determined to provide support and nurturance for her siblings, so after passing the required examination, she began teaching in a rural district near Holly Springs. Four or five years later, an aunt, Fannie Butler, who lived in Memphis, suggested that Wells move there and secure a more lucrative position. She did, initially teaching in the rural district of Shelby County.

This position would provide one of the initial catalysts for Wells's activism. In May 1884, Wells was on a train commuting to her school in Woodstock, Tennessee, when the conductor informed her that she would have to move to the smoking car. Previously in Tennessee, an African American who could afford a first-class ticket had been permitted to ride in a first-class car; Wells did not consider a smoking car to be "first class" and refused to move. After the conductor and another railroad employee physically attempted to force her to move, Wells instead left the train. She sued the railroad and won damages of $500. The railroad appealed, however, and won when the appeal reached the Tennessee Supreme Court three years later.

She continued to teach in Tennessee throughout this time. During the fall of

1884, she obtained a position in Memphis, which was both more convenient and more lucrative, and she taught in Memphis for seven years. Although she was considered a competent teacher and constantly aimed to improve her own knowledge, by enrolling at Fisk University during the summers, for example, she never considered teaching her calling and generally found the profession less than rewarding.

During this period, Wells also began writing articles for church-sponsored periodicals and Negro weekly newspapers. Eventually, she became part owner and editor of the Memphis *Free Speech and Headlight*. As a result of an editorial she published in this newspaper criticizing the city's segregated school system, she was fired from her teaching job in 1891. Nevertheless, she continued writing about issues of racial justice as well as other controversial subjects. Then on March 9, 1892, three successful African American businessmen were lynched in Memphis, and Wells wrote an editorial condemning not only the lynching itself but also the attitudes of white citizens who silently permitted such acts. In response, a group of Memphis residents broke into her newspaper office and vandalized her equipment. Fortunately, Wells was attending a convention in Philadelphia at the time, and she took the advice of friends not to return. For decades, Wells would remain committed to eradicating lynching, and she would gain the reputation of an antilynching crusader by which she is still known.

Wells subsequently accepted a position writing for the *New York Age*, a similar newspaper in whose pages she continued her protests against lynching. She defined it as a terrorist activity aimed at African Americans. The primary justification for lynching had deemed it an appropriate response when African American men raped white women. Initially, Wells refused to believe that all lynchings had such rapes as their true motives; eventually, she suspected that very few such rapes had ever actually occurred. Over the next several years, Wells would argue that most interracial relationships were consensual and that many other factors contributed to a lynch mob's actions.

While writing for the *New York Age*, Wells also acquired speaking engagements in several northeastern cities. In 1893, she made her first trip to Britain, hoping that her speeches there would encourage the English to apply pressure on the United States to reform its system of racial inequalities and especially to eradicate the practice of lynching. In England, Wells was impressed by the popularity of organizations dedicated to civic causes, particularly among women. On her return to the United States, she urged American women to form clubs of their own; in response, the Women's Era Club, the first such club for African American women, was established in Boston. Similar clubs in several New England cities followed, as well as one later established in Chicago and named in honor of Wells. Although Wells's subsequent experience with these clubs was not entirely positive, much of her efficacy as a political leader occurred through her influence on women's organizations. In 1894, Wells made a second trip to England, this time writing regular articles describing her experience for the *Chicago Inter-Ocean*.

After she returned to the United States, she published *A Red Record*, which was a compilation of statistics on as well as an analysis of motivating factors behind lynching. This book elicited public outcries against the practice but also vociferous denials of Wells's interpretations and attacks on her character. For some people, these facts were too horrible to be true; for others, African Americans deserved the treatment they received.

To this point, Wells had lived as a single woman. Throughout her young adulthood, she had dated frequently, and several men had apparently been interested in a more serious relationship with her, but Wells had not reciprocated those feelings. In 1895, however, she married Ferdinand Barnett, a widower from Chicago with two young children. Barnett was a lawyer and the founder of the Chicago *Conservator*, a Negro newspaper. He was also active in several causes related to racial equality. After her marriage, Wells adopted the surname of Wells-Barnett. Contemporary references to her are inconsistent in the use of Wells and Wells-Barnett. Between 1896 and 1904, Wells-Barnett gave birth to four children. When her children were young, she spent the majority of her time as a homemaker, although she never completely relinquished her influence in civil rights causes.

Through her church in 1910, she organized the Negro Fellowship League, which provided lodging and employment services for young African American men. Wells-Barnett had hoped for significant financial support from middle-class African Americans for this venture, but her hopes were disappointed in part because she had located the organization in a disreputable neighborhood, where the men she intended to serve were likely to live. Middle-class and wealthier people, however, hesitated to venture into neighborhoods they interpreted as dangerous. The organization effectively closed in 1920.

Wells-Barnett continued to investigate injustice and write articles describing her findings. These articles were published in several Negro newspapers, including the *Defender* and *World*, as well as in pamphlets distributed through the Negro Fellowship League. She also organized African American men to vote and agitated for suffrage for women. After women gained the right to vote and hold political office, Wells-Barnett ran for state senate in 1930, though she finished a distant third.

Late in her life, Wells-Barnett realized that her contributions to American society were being forgotten or ignored, and she began her autobiography. This text, eventually published as *Crusade for Justice*, remained unfinished at her death. In late March 1931, Wells-Barnett became suddenly ill. After an illness of a few days, she died on March 25 in Chicago of uremic poisoning.

AUTOBIOGRAPHICAL WORKS AND THEMES

The writing Wells-Barnett published during her lifetime was not autobiographical in the conventional sense. Rather, this writing most often took the form of investigative reports or editorials published in religious or African American newspapers. These articles most often concerned issues of racial injustice, especially the epidemic of lynching that occurred throughout much of the country in the decades surrounding the turn of the twentieth century.

Two autobiographical texts, however, have been published posthumously. They are her incomplete autobiography, *Crusade for Justice*, edited by her younger daughter, Alfreda M. Duster, and *The Memphis Diary of Ida B. Wells*, edited by Miriam DeCosta-Willis. Both of these manuscripts had remained in the possession of Wells-Barnett's family and were published with the cooperation of family members. As readers might expect, the diary contains more intimate information and is less concerned with Wells-Barnett's public persona than does the autobiography, which had from its inception been written with the goal of publication in mind. Although the emphases in the two texts differ, both include substantial material on activism.

The Memphis Diary includes, obviously, material Wells wrote as a young single woman living in Memphis. The Beacon Press edition (currently the only edition) also includes a brief diary Wells kept when she was traveling in 1893, another brief diary she kept while living in Chicago in 1930, reprints of several articles she'd published in newspapers, and substantial critical commentary that contextualizes and identifies many references. Much of the material in the Memphis portion reveals Wells's concerns to be fairly typical of a young woman—she writes most often of her social life, her desires for new clothing, misunderstandings that occur with various acquaintances. She writes once or twice a week rather than daily, but she tends to summarize the events of intervening days. Most often at this point, her greatest anxieties are financial; despite her steady employment as a teacher, she frequently finds herself in debt, generally because of clothing purchases. This diary is not a site where she frequently interrogates her nature as an individual or a "self," nor does she express the acquisition of national influence as an overt goal.

Nevertheless, in this diary she does note several instances of racial injustice that come to her attention, including her own experience being denied first-class accommodations on a train and the lawsuit that followed. She critiques influential African Americans who seem to desire the personal approval of white people above the general good of African Americans. In this diary, too, Wells expresses her view that most interracial relationships are consensual, that sexual encounters between black men and white women, in other words, do not inevitably consist of rape and hence do not justify lynching. She speculates that these relationships incite white rage regardless of the presence or absence of force and that white desire for violence against blacks necessitates the accusation of rape rather than the reverse.

Wells began writing for publication during this period in Memphis, and several entries in the diary discuss or at least refer to articles she is working on. She devotes substantially more space to this work than she does to her work as a teacher, a clear sign that her teaching was a job, while her writing and activism were vocations. The diary ends abruptly in September of 1887, inviting speculation that Wells may have continued her diary in a new notebook that has subsequently been lost.

As might be expected, Wells's autobiography is much more substantial than her diary, though she may have used her diaries as sources—she clearly did rely on previously published articles and includes excerpts from some in the text of her autobiography. Among Wells's motives in writing this autobiography was to ensure that her accomplishments were not forgotten, as they seemed in danger of being near the end of her life. *Crusade for Justice* is the story of a woman's public life; while she mentions her family life and asserts that her greatest responsibility when her children were young was as their mother, she does not reveal much of an intimate nature. When she mentions her husband, for example, the context is most often his work as an attorney representing individuals whose rights have been violated. This autobiography, then, is not the story of the private development of an ordinary person but rather the story of the public development of an extraordinary person.

The title of the book is apt, for she reveals her obsession with justice on virtually every page. She chronicles her development as a journalist in these terms, and she describes her other activities—organizing women's clubs, assisting young men newly arrived from the South, traveling abroad—according to their effect on the lives of African Americans generally and on race relations in the United States. At the time she is writing her autobiography, she occasionally feels underappreciated, as evidenced by the number of times she describes feeling betrayed by friends or colleagues. The incidence of lynching—the issue for which Wells is primarily known—had diminished by this point, and other issues addressed by other personalities had risen to the fore. Simultaneously, Wells reveals herself to be a contentious, strong-willed, and not always patient woman, the type of person, perhaps, who can make an effective leader but not always a pleasant peer. Since Wells never completed her autobiography—the last events referred to occurred in 1927, four years before her death—it is impossible to know absolutely whether she intended to revise any of the portion we have. Nevertheless, *Crusade for Justice* provides significant insight into a period of African American and American history that is frequently overlooked as scholars leap from slave narratives to the Harlem Renaissance.

CRITICAL RECEPTION

Until recently, the work of Wells-Barnett was studied more often by historians than by literary critics. The fact that her autobiography was not published until nearly forty years after her death illustrates the extent to which she had been relegated to the margins of history—at least until the comparatively recent surge of interest in the writing of women and people of color. Compared to the writing of W.E.B. Du Bois* or Booker T. Washington,* for example, Wells-Barnett's work has received astonishingly little response. She is not viewed primarily as an autobiographer, and critics working primarily in the field of autobiography theory have yet to pay her much attention. Aside from a few reviews, most current critical work focuses on her rhetoric or reform work rather than on her autobiographical writing specifically. This is not surprising, though, since her autobiography itself serves to support her reform work.

However, Wells-Barnett's reception may be in the midst of a significant change. Even in the decade immediately following the publication of *Crusade for Justice*, scholars wrote very little about her. In the last decade, though, several books have been written about her life and work, sometimes in the context of other similar writers, and much of her journalism has been reprinted in new editions. Since the body of Wells-Barnett's work has become much more accessible, one could expect that the next decade will see more substantial attention paid to her.

BIBLIOGRAPHY

Autobiographical Works by Ida B. Wells-Barnett

Crusade for Justice: The Autobiography of Ida B. Wells. Ed. Alfreda M. Duster. Chicago: University of Chicago Press, 1970.
The Memphis Diary of Ida B. Wells: An Intimate Portrait of the Activist as a Young Woman. Ed. Miriam DeCosta-Willis. Boston: Beacon Press, 1995.

Studies of Ida B. Wells-Barnett's Autobiographical Works

Andrews, William L. *African American Autobiography: A Collection of Critical Essays.* Englewood Cliffs, NJ: Prentice-Hall, 1993.
Brundage, W. Fitzhugh. *Under Sentence of Death: Lynching in the South.* Chapel Hill: University of North Carolina Press, 1997.
Franklin, V.P. *Living Our Stories, Telling Our Truths: Autobiography and the Making of the African-American Intellectual Tradition.* New York: Scribner, 1995.
Goldsby, Jacqueline. "Checkered Career." *Women's Review of Books* (May 1999): 18–19.
Gunning, Sandra. *Race, Rape, and Lynching: The Red Record of American Literature, 1890–1912.* New York: Oxford University Press, 1996.
Jones, Suzanne Whitmore. *Crossing the Color Line: Readings in Black and White.* Columbia: University of South Carolina Press, 2000.
Lunsford, Andrea A. *Reclaiming Rhetorica: Women in the Rhetorical Tradition.* Pittsburgh: University of Pittsburgh Press, 1995.
McMurry, Linda O. *To Keep the Waters Troubled: The Life of Ida B. Wells.* New York: Oxford University Press, 2000.
Miller, Ericka M. *The Other Construction: Where Violence and Womanhood Meet in the Writings of Wells-Barnett, Grimke, and Larsen.* New York: Garland Publishing, 2000.
Moreau, Shannon. "Crusader for Justice." *American History* 35.6 (2001): 18.
Schechter, Patricia Ann. *Ida B. Wells-Barnett and American Reform, 1880–1930.* Chapel Hill: University of North Carolina Press, 2001.
Wilson, Francille Rusan. " 'This Past Was Waiting for Me When I Came': The Contextualization of Black Women's History." *Feminist Studies* 22.3 (1991): 3–9

JOHN EDGAR WIDEMAN
(1941–   )

Chris Roark

BIOGRAPHY

At the center of John Edgar Wideman's autobiography and fiction are his family and the Homewood section of Pittsburgh where he spent the first twelve years of his life. His fictional writing imaginatively transforms these subjects, and Wideman's two nonfiction books, *Brothers and Keepers* (1984) and *Fatheralong* (1994), are similarly sensitive to the complexities of moving people and places from life into words, the struggle to depict without imprisoning or exploiting those he writes of. In his nonfiction work this process hinges upon contrasts. For example, the stoicism of his father's world, where "you stand alone. . . . What counts is the doing, the discipline, the engagement with nothing on it's own terms" in contrast to the affection of his mother's: "My mother's first rule was love. She refused to believe she was alone" (*Fatheralong* 51). The intersections between these stark personal contrasts, as they take shape within the interwoven African American, African, and Western cultures, are among his habitual subjects.

Wideman was born in Washington, D.C. but moved to the Homewood neighborhood of Pittsburgh before his first birthday. His family moved from Homewood to Shadyside, a predominantly white section of Pittsburgh, when Wideman was about twelve, and at Peabody High School he was senior class president, valedictorian, and a basketball star. A scholarship student and English major at the University of Pennsylvania, Wideman was an all-Ivy League forward on the basketball team and graduated Phi Beta Kappa in 1963. He was the second African American to receive a Rhodes Scholarship, which was spent at Oxford University where Wideman studied the English novel. He married Judith Goldman in 1965, and from 1966 to 1967 Wideman was a Kent fellow at the University of Iowa's

Writer's Workshop. He next became the first black tenured professor at the University of Pennsylvania and helped create as well as chair the African-American Studies program there. From 1975 to 1986 he held a position in the English Department at the University of Wyoming, Laramie. He is a two-time Pen-Faulkner award winner (for *Sent for You Yesterday* and *Philadelphia Fire*) and a MacArthur Foundation Fellow. *Fatheralong* was a finalist for the National Book Award. In 1986 Wideman moved to his current position as professor and associate dean of Humanities and Fine Arts at the University of Massachusetts at Amherst, where he teaches primarily graduate courses in fiction writing.

Three tragedies have marked Wideman's life and writing career. In 1975, Robert Wideman, his younger brother by ten years, was part of an armed robbery that resulted in a homicide and a sentence of life without parole. This incident strongly influenced Wideman's Pittsburgh trilogy, three novels published in the early 1980s, and *Brothers and Keepers*, the 1984 nonfiction work that contrasts Wideman's life with Robby's. The second tragedy was a 1986 homicide by Wideman's second son Jacob. The focus of *Fatheralong* is Wideman's relationship with his father, but the book ends with a meditation addressed to Jacob. Finally, Wideman's most recent novel, *Two Cities*, was dedicated to the memory of Omar Wideman, his nephew and Robby's son, who was murdered in a 1992 gang-related homicide. While we should resist letting these tragic events subsume more substantial analysis of Wideman's complex art, *Two Cities*, the 1990 novel *Philadelphia Fire*, and the two autobiographical books seek through words, through family, and through love the strength to bear the weight of lives shattered by loss, the ability to shape rather than be shaped by experience.

AUTOBIOGRAPHICAL WORKS AND THEMES

While certainly autobiographical, it might be best to describe *Brothers and Keepers* and *Fatheralong* more broadly as nonfiction since both question and undermine many of the accepted notions of traditional autobiographical narrative. To Wideman, innovative writing, especially as it develops multiple voices, leads to fresh understandings and thus new dreams and new weapons to attack notions of race and culture that damage rather than enable communities and individuals. Wideman's nonfiction has debts to both slave narrative and conversion narrative. In *Brothers and Keepers* he writes, "Denying disruptive emotions was a survival mechanism I'd been forced to learn early in life" (11), and so both books chart the personal changes Wideman experiences as he confronts his past. Wideman pits incidents from his own life against larger social and political contexts and also works in the well-known African American autobiographical essay tradition that includes W.E.B. Du Bois,* Richard Wright,* and James Baldwin.* But Wideman's voice can be distinguished from these writers. He also writes in the tradition of Montaigne, exploring his own limitations to extremes, skeptically approaching himself and others, as well as the European or Western culture that he, by turns, both embraces and critiques. Indeed, one could argue that Wideman is working to free himself from a form of stoicism, defined in part as a need to appear self-contained (*Brothers and Keepers* 32), that Montaigne himself at first embraced and then outgrew. Among other distinguishing qualities is Wideman's ability to raise the most difficult questions about his relationship to himself and to others as son, brother, father, husband, and writer.

Wideman illustrates the flux of life with prose that leaps quickly between what seem to be disparate subjects, a practice more fully developed in his fiction and related to the collage style of the visual artist Romare Beardon, whose work Wideman refers to in his novel *Two Cities* (116). What appears at first to be a random juxtaposition of, for example, different voices can shift attention to how meaning is located as much in the tension between such different voices as in any individual perspective. *Brothers and Keepers* occasionally depends on the reader to identify the voice speaking, suggesting a collaboration between writer and reader that mirrors in some respects the collaboration between Wideman and Robby. Both books are infused with blues and jazz influences, especially as they reflect the struggle to listen deeply to others and locate meaning, again, between instead of within individuals as stories and different voices play off each other in a manner similar to different musicians responding to each other during a jazz performance. Sculpture is another influence, foremost the work of Alberto Giacommetti and his sense of the world as a moving target for an artist who works mostly through reconstructions of memory. Wideman's writing mediates between the worlds of inner-city poverty (including its folk culture) and academia, between mothers and fathers, between adults and the increasing abandoned young in America, and between people of color and the white population.

Similar to *The Autobiography of Malcolm X*, in the two books communication is bettered between conflicting groups and figures as much through the honest expression of anger and resentment toward, for example, racism as through "an attempt, among other things, to break out, displace, replace the paradigm of race" (*Fatheralong* xxv). Both books explore how Wideman's development as a writer enhances and complicates his relationship to his family, as well as the curious place of the artist compelled to leave home and then, for his own sake and for others, return. For example, Wideman asks,

Wasn't there something fundamental in my writing, in my capacity to function, that depended on flight, escape? Wasn't another person's skin a hiding place, a place to work out anxiety, to face threats too intimidating to handle in any other fashion? Wasn't writing about people a way of exploiting them? . . . If I can't be trusted with the story of my own life, how could I ask my brother to trust me with his? (*Brothers and Keepers* 77)

As the ambiguity of "keepers" suggests, Wideman asks what the difference is between the literal keepers of Robby, the white society and its prison guards who seek not just to punish but to stamp out his life and identity, and the brother as writer and keeper who risks losing his brother's unique humanity even in the process of recording his story. Wideman is acutely sensitive to how writing about others can be an exploitative evasion. Yet the primal language of his storytelling, arguably the source of Wideman's power as a writer/trickster in the signifying tradition described by Henry Louis Gates Jr., is drawn from Homewood. His books, among their many concerns, aim to honor that community and serve future generations by preserving and remaking it imaginatively.

Both books are a study of Wideman himself and the costs and evasions required to become a successful writer. Like his fiction, these books entertain important questions for those who would seek to document the lives of others. Double consciousness can be a two-edged sword, allowing Wideman to put his concerns aside one moment and thus enter and depict his brother's voice and yet at other times leading to near-crippling self-awareness. Wideman writes in *Brothers and Keepers* of the Pittsburgh trilogy and his attempt in fiction to reach his brother:

> Even as I manufactured fiction from the events of my brother's life, from the history of the family that had nurtured us both, I knew something of a different order remained to be extricated. The fiction writer was also a man with a real brother behind bars. I continued to feel caged by my bewilderment, by my inability to see clearly, accurately, not only the last visit with my brother, but the whole long skein of our lives together and apart. So this book. This attempt to break out, to knock down the walls. (18)

As suggested here, at the other extreme from these difficulties is the hope that words can become active forces. Wideman writes in a letter to Robby that opens *Damballah*, the first book of the trilogy that explores Wideman's Pittsburgh roots and Robby's story from a fictional perspective: "[T]hese stories are letters. Long overdue letters from me to you. I wish they could tear down the walls. I wish they could snatch you away from where you are" (1).

Brothers and Keepers is built on the contrast between John and Robby, but this is a variation, perhaps, of the contrast between the silent, inexpressive world of men that is depicted in *Fatheralong* and the magical aural world of Wideman's mother and aunts. These conflicting worlds can starkly battle, but occasionally the divisions are resolved and such worlds dance together. For example, in an interview we learn Wideman's father had a "beautiful singing voice" and that he sang "Farther Along," the gospel standard Wideman plays with for the book's title (*TuSmith* 158). Wideman works toward provisional understandings by an acute awareness of how much our thoughts can be constructions to evade knowing and yet enable survival, and that often these two forces are, by turns, locked in either awkward embrace or subtle dance. While he aims more toward questions than answers, some answers are clear: "If the stories dim or disappear altogether, a people's greatness diminishes, each of us becomes a solitary actor" (*Fatheralong* 63). Another key is the writer's ability to understand and remake time through stories, moving from punishing linear time to "Great Time," which can suggest how the past enfolds the present. Wideman is also attracted to the playful revolutionary time of Thelonius Monk, where, perhaps, "self merges with something greater than self" (*Fatheralong* xxi), where brothers find each other through their mutual stories and fathers through stories teach sons what it means to be human while continually relearning that lesson themselves.

Like his fiction, *Brothers and Keepers* and *Fatheralong* reward close reading and treatment as art over treatment as sociology or political tract, art in the sense of a self-conscious remaking of experience driven by images and metaphors, to reach the heart of their personal and social concerns. For example, an important reality and metaphor for both works is the prison: the literal and in some ways unthinkable prisons that contain a brother and a son, the prisons we construct for self-protection, circles that need to be broken down because they isolate us, and of course, the debilitating prison of race. On the other hand, his mother's language, like her love, is a circle or an "encompassing arc" or "thread spun finer than silk but steel strong, stronger, much stronger as it stretches, loops, weaves" (*Fatheralong* 52). In nearly all his work Wideman returns to the complementary images of the circle and the arc, which here suggests transcendence through a kind of musical free movement that connects people. Similar to much African art, which first and foremost serves a social function, Wideman's writing also works toward freedom for individuals by self-consciously depicting, exploring, and remaking strong familial and social connections. In this sense, it is not just the confrontation with painful conflicts that constitute *Brothers and Keepers* and *Fatheralong*, but it is, in the blues tradition, the artist's ability to reshape these confrontations as image and metaphor, as song that releases spiritual force.

CRITICAL RECEPTION

Wideman mentions in an interview that he sees less and less difference between fiction and nonfiction (*TuSmith* 120), and he makes it clear that writing nonfiction involves imagination and choice. Thus, perhaps the best critical perspective on Wideman's nonfiction is developed through a careful reading of his novels, especially the meditations concerning art found in the letters written by Mr. Mallory in *Two Cities*. While Wideman also expresses discomfort with the limitations of interviews, the collected interviews that range from 1963 to 1997, edited by Bonnie TuSmith, are also important. The most complete bibliography of Wideman's work, including fiction, nonfiction, journalism, critical writing, and secondary criticism, is found in *Callaloo* (22.3 [1999]), which also offers sixteen critical articles on Wideman's writing.

Ashraf Rushdy writes that "much of Wideman's career since the publication of his first three novels has been an attempt to acknowledge those factors limiting him from a better understanding of a whole Other community, in fact the one in which he grew up—Homewood" (312). Rushdy treats "The Homewood Trilogy," but his notion of a "blues mind" as a process and avenue of connection between people influenced by blues, jazz, and gospel is relevant to Wideman's nonfiction, especially as individuality is decentered and gives way to what Houston Baker calls "energizing intersubjectivity" (334). This sense is similarly rein-forced by Wideman's constant play with multiple forms of time. Heather Andrade writes:

[T]he text also embraces the notion that the formation and reformation of the past are dynamic processes enacted through synergistic acts of storytelling and listening. The form of *Brothers and Keepers* with its multiple shifts in narration, movement between past/present/future, blurring of the fiction/facts paradigm, problematization of that paradigm in relation to autobiography, and its multiple beginnings, causes the reader to literally experience the perplexity of writing a past reconstructed from memory. (364)

Wideman's writing asks the reader to learn the difficult art of listening to others as he himself has learned, by stops and starts, in the context of the tricky gym-nastics of memory and words.

Gender issues in both books are also intimately related to Wideman's play with narrative voice. Margot Hennessy writes of *Brothers and Keepers*:

We become aware of what is being said and of the way that it is being said. That act of reproduction of the author's experience allows us to consider gender within the text in very different ways. It is no longer simply a case of how the female is represented or not represented within the text, but more how the ways of telling enact a process which encodes gender within it. (305)

For Hennessy, Wideman's relationship to Robby suggests a kind of mothering that can break down aspects of hierarchal and patriarchal control, another way of challenging accepted notions of relationships, on the one hand, while helping us imagine new ways to see ourselves, on the other.

BIBLIOGRAPHY

Autobiographical Works by John Edgar Wideman

Brothers and Keepers. New York: Holt, Rinehart and Winston, 1984.
Fatheralong: A Meditation on Fathers, Sons, Race and Society. New York: Pantheon, 1994.

Studies of John Edgar Wideman's Autobiographical Works

Andrade, Heather. " 'Mosaic Memory': Auto/biographical Context(s) in John Edgar Wideman's *Brothers and Keepers*." *Massachusetts Review* 40 (1997): 342–66.
Berben-Masi, Jacqueline. "From *Brothers and Keepers* to *Two Cities*. Social and Cultural Consciousness, Art and Imagination: An Interview with John Edgar Wideman." *Callaloo* 22.3 (1999): 568–84.
———. "Prodigal and Prodigy: Fathers and Sons in Wideman's Work." *Callaloo* 22.3 (1999): 677–84.
Byerman, Keith. *John Edgar Wideman: A Study of the Short Fiction*. New York: Twayne Publishers, 1998.

Coleman, James W. *Blackness and Modernism: The Literary Career of John Edgar Wideman.* Jackson: University Press of Mississippi, 1989.

Feith, Michael. " 'The Benefit of the Doubt': Openness and Closure in *Brothers and Keepers.*" *Callaloo* 22.3 (1999): 665–75.

Grandjeat, Yves-Charles. "Brother Figures: The Rift and Riff in John E. Wideman's Fiction." *Callaloo* 22.3 (1999): 615–22.

Hennessy, C. Margot. "Listening to the Secret Mother: Reading John Edgar Wideman's *Brothers and Keepers.*" *American Women's Autobiography: Fea(s)ts of Memory.* Ed. Margot Culley. Madison: University of Wisconsin Press, 1992. 302–14.

Lucy, Robin. "John Edgar Wideman." In *Contemporary African American Novelists: A Bio-Bibliographic Critical Sourcebook.* Ed. Emmanuel S. Nelson. Westport, CT: Greenwood Press, 1999. 482–90.

Reed, Ishmael. "Of One Blood, Two Men." Rev. of *Brothers and Keepers. New York Times Book Review* (November 4, 1984): 1, 32–33.

Rushdy, Ashraf, "Fraternal Blues: John Edgar Wideman's Homewood Trilogy." *Contemporary Literature* 32 (1991): 312–43.

TuSmith, Bonnie. *Conversations with John Wideman.* Jackson: University of Mississippi Press, 1998.

HARRIET E. WILSON
(1828?–1863?)

Emma Waters Dawson

BIOGRAPHY

Relatively little is known about the identity or the biography of Harriet E. Wilson. Current biographical data stem from research germinated by Professor Henry Gates Jr., who discovered in 1982 that *Our Nig* (1859) was not only published in the United States by an African American but was written by an African American woman. Thus, this autobiographical text in the guise of fiction replaces *Clotel* (1864), by William Wells Brown,* and *Iola LeRoy* (1892), by Frances Watkins Harper, with the distinction of being the first novel written by an African American and an African American woman, respectively. Though there are obvious distinctions between the genres of the novel and the autobiography, novels can on occasion be autobiography in the guise of fiction. Such is the case with *Our Nig*, for it is the extended, organized narrative of the life of Harriet E. Wilson.

In the preface of Gates's 1983 edited version of the text, the reader is informed that the fate of Wilson remains uncertain, despite a search of legal documents that failed to ascertain the date of Wilson's death, for public records in New Hampshire and Massachusetts reveal the death of one Mrs. Wilson at the age of thirty-two and of another Mrs. Wilson at the age of fifty-two. Furthermore, because of the author's status in society as an indentured woman of color, Gates implies that the reader cannot be sure that either of the women is the author of *Our Nig*. However, we know that *a* Harriet E. Wilson was born as Harriet Adams in Milford, New Hampshire, around 1828. A marriage to Thomas Wilson from Virginia occurred in Milford on October 6, 1851, and a son was born in 1852. By the time of the text's publication in 1859, Wilson had moved to Boston. Both the research of Gates and Barbara A. White give credence to these essential details of Wilson's life. They also indicate that details in Wilson's autobiography in the guise of fiction may have originated from her employment in the Nehemiah Hayward household, where Wilson, the character of Frado in the text, suffered abuse, although the text itself was a result of Wilson's unsuccessful attempt to assist in her son's medical care. The son, George Mason Wilson, died in 1860, shortly after the publication of *Our Nig*. After Wilson's apparent return to New Hampshire in 1860, no record of her seems to exist.

AUTOBIOGRAPHICAL WORK AND THEMES

The work's genesis stemmed from Wilson's attempt to utilize the writing of a book as a means for sustenance for her and her son. It is the story of a free black woman who lives as an indentured servant in a white household, the Haywards/Bellmonts. In researching the text's history, White noted, "I uncovered information about Wilson and the Haywards by assuming the details of her story to be true" (23). Indeed, Wilson's self-portraiture presents much evidence that details in the narration are based on truth. Nehemiah Hayward/Mr. Bellmont inherited the family homestead from his parents. His sister Sally Hayward/Aunt Abby did own a "right in the homestead" (45). The youngest daughter Rebecca/Mary died in her teens on a visit to Baltimore. Lucretia Hayward/Jane married and settled in the West, and eldest son George/James worked in Baltimore and returned home to die and be buried in Milford. The lives of the Haywards correspond so closely to the presentation of the various sketches Wilson presents in *Our Nig* to leave little doubt that the text is autobiography in the guise of fiction.

The book's complete title is *Our Nig; or, Sketches from the Life of a Free Black, in a Two-Story White House, North. Showing That Slavery's Shadows Fall Even There*. Both the complete title and the fate of the central character are ironic. First, the title suggests that the oppression of slavery may extend to one who is free, and it dismisses the idea that the North is a free place for African Americans. Second, Wilson refers to Frado, the central character, as *Nig*, the demeaning name used by some of the characters in the text. Also, the story is about the *slavery of a free* black woman who refuses to grovel under the presence of assuming a subservient role. She rebels against the brutal beatings Mrs. Bellmont inflicts on her by shouting, " 'Stop! . . . strike me, and I'll never work a mite more for you" (105). Wilson's development of characterization and theme illustrates the social, psychological, and historical forces shaping Mrs. Bellmont's cruel and vindictive behavior toward Frado. Thus, Frado's/Wilson's decision to leave the Bellmont household asserts both character and author's sense of self in their refusal to conform to the dictates of others. In refusing to acquiesce, Frado/Wilson begins to search for some measure of success in her life, a theme that, within the context of black women's lives, connotes new meaning, for obstacles are three-fold: race, gender, and social class.

Initiating the theme of success, the author endeavors to save herself and her son despite being broken in body and spirit and having been deserted by her husband. Wilson relies on the emotions of the readers to guide them to perform the task she so eloquently requests of them in the last chapter, where the third-person point of view of the narrator and the first-person point of view of the author merge as one in Frado's plea for assistance:

Strange were some of her adventures. Watched by kidnappers, maltreated by professional abolitionists, who didn't want slaves at the South, nor niggers in their own houses, North. Faugh! To lodge one; to eat with one; to admit one through the front door; to sit next one; awful! Nothing turns her from her steadfast purpose of elevating herself. Reposing on God, she has thus far journeyed securely. Still an invalid, she asks your sympathy, gentle reader. Refuse not, because some part of her history is unknown, save by the Omniscient God. Enough has been unrolled to demand your sympathy and aid. (130)

In the introduction of the text, Gates informs the modern reader that an examination of public records indicates that Wilson's son died six months after the book's publication. Wilson's fate remains uncertain. Nevertheless, three letters in the appendix attest to the veracity of authorship and narrative of *Our Nig*. Allida writes, "Truth is stranger than fiction," and "whoever reads the narrative of Alfrado, will find the assertion verified" (133). Similarly, Margaretta Thorn states, "Having known the writer of the book for a number of years, and knowing the many privations and mortifications she has had to pass through, I the more willingly add my testimony to the truth of her assertions" (138). A final letter of authentication written by one who simply signs "C.D.S." captures the essence of its purpose: "Feeling a deep interest in the welfare of the writer of this book, and hoping that its circulation will be extensive, I wish to say a few words in her behalf" (140). Not one of the authenticators questions Wilson's authorship of *Our Nig*. Nevertheless, the text graphically depicts the emergence of an image of victory from the victimization of oppression for the African American female character unquestionably influenced by social conventions that denied the beauty of black women and the economic policy of slavery and its polemics that relegated them to the lowest stratum of the social and economic ladder.

CRITICAL RECEPTION

Wilson's contribution to African American fictional autobiography has received steady critical acclaim since its rediscovery by Gates in 1982 and its republication in 1983. Since that time, book articles, journal articles, and dissertations have added to the dialogue about *Our Nig*. Much of the critical attention identifies the connection between the autobiographical novel and the nineteenth-century tradition of the slave narrative and the sentimental novel. Included among this group are Beth Maclay Doriana, R.J. Ellis, Margaret Lindgren, Julia Stern, and Barbara White. While no full-length book has yet been written, contemporary scholars have debated many intriguing aspects about the text, including its satire as discussed by Elizabeth Breau; its publishing history as examined by Eric Gardner; and its analysis as a feminist text by Angelyn Mitchell, Debra Walker King, and Cynthia Davis, among others. Exploration of American racial dynamics and politics occurs in the discussions by Ronna Johnson and Katherine Clay Bassard. Elizabeth J. West examines the complexity of Wilson's adaptation of the conversion narrative in her discussion of Christian doctrines anchored by popular notions of womanhood and domesticity and yet limited by race and racial signifiers. Finally, Thomas B. Lovell and Gardner discuss both the social history and the politics of the economy as they operate in the text. Today scholars and critics continue to debate and engage in lively dialogue about *Our Nig* as it takes its place in the canon of African American autobiography.

BIBLIOGRAPHY

Autobiographical Work by Harriet E. Wilson

Our Nig; or, Sketches from the Life of a Free Black, in a Two-Story White House, North. Showing That Slavery's Shadows Fall Even There. Boston: G.C. Rand and Avery, 1859. Intro. and Notes by Henry Louis Gates Jr. New York: Random House, 1983.

Studies of Harriet E. Wilson's Autobiographical Work

Bassard, Katherine Clay. " 'Beyond Mortal Vision': Harriet E. Wilson's *Our Nig* and the American Racial Dream-Text." In *Female Subjects in Black and White: Race, Psychoanalysis, Feminism.* Ed. Elizabeth Abel. Berkeley: University of California Press, 1997. 187–200.

Breau, Elizabeth. "Identifying Satire: *Our Nig.*" *Callaloo* 16.2 (Spring 1993): 455–65.

Cole, Phyllis. "Stowe, Jacobs, Wilson: White Plots and Black Counterplots." In *New Perspectives on Gender, Race and Class in Society.* Ed. Audrey T. McCluskey. Bloomington: Indiana University Press, 1990. 23–45.

Davis, Cynthia. "Speaking the Body's Pain: Harriet Wilson's *Our Nig.*" *African American Review* 27.3 (Fall 1993): 391–404.

Doriana, Beth Maclay. "Black Womanhood in Nineteenth Century America: Subversion and Self Construction in Two Women's Autobiographies." *American Quarterly* 43.2 (June 1991): 199–222.

Ellis, R.J. "Body Politics and the Body Politic in William Wells Brown's *Clotel* and Harriet Wilson's *Our Nig.*" In *Soft Canons: American Women Writers and Masculine Tradition.* Ed. Karen L. Kilcup. Iowa City: University of Iowa Press, 2000. 99–122.

———. "Traps Slyly Laid: Professing Autobiography in Harriet Wilson's *Our Nig.*" In *Representing Lives: Women and Auto/Biography.* Ed. Pauline Polkey. New York: Macmillan St. Martin's, 2000. 65–76.

Ernest, John. "Economies of Identity: Harriet E. Wilson's *Our Nig.*" *PMLA* 109.3 (May 1994): 424–38.

Foreman, Gabrielle P. "The Spoken and the Silenced in *Incidents in the Life of a Slave Girl* and *Our Nig.*" *Callaloo* 13.2 (Spring 1990): 313–24.

Fox-Genovese, Elizabeth. " 'To Weave It into the Literature of the Country': Epic and the Fiction of African American Women." In *Poetics of the Americas: Race, Founding, and Textuality.* Ed. Bainard Cowan and Jefferson Humphrey. Baton Rouge: Louisiana State University Press, 1997. 31–45.

Gardner, Eric. " 'This Attempt of Their Sister': Harriet Wilson's *Our Nig* from Printer to Readers." *New England Quarterly: A Historical Review of New England Life and Letters* 66.2 (June 1993): 226–46.

Herndl, Diane Price, "The Invisible (Invalid) Woman: African-American Women, Illness, and Nineteenth-Century Narrative." *Women's Studies: An Interdisciplinary Journal* 24.6 (September 1995): 553–72.

Johnson, Ronna C. "Said But Not Spoken: Elision and the Representation of Rape, Race, and Gender in Harriet E. Wilson's *Our Nig*." In *Speaking the Other Self: American Women Writers.* Ed. Jeanne Campbell. Athens: University of Georgia Press, 1997. 96–116.

Jones, Jill. "The Disappearing 'I' in *Our Nig*." *Legacy: A Journal of American Women Writers* 13.1 (1996): 38–53.

King, Debra Walker. "Harriet Wilson's *Our Nig*." In *Recovered Writers/Recovered Texts.* Ed. Dolan Hubbard. Knoxville: University of Tennessee Press, 1997. 31–45.

Lindgren, Margaret. "Harriet Jacobs, Harriet Wilson and the Redoubled Voice in Black Autobiography." *Obsidian II* 8.1 (Spring–Summer 1993): 18–38.

Lovell, Thomas B. "By Dint of Labor and Economy: Harriet Jacobs, Harriet Wilson, and the Salutary View of Wage Labor." *Arizona Quarterly: A Journal of American Literature, Culture, and Theory* 52.3 (Autumn 1996): 1–32.

Mitchell, Angelyn. "Her Side of His Story: A Feminist Analysis of Two Nineteenth-Century Antebellum Novels: William Wells Brown's *Clotel* and Harriet E. Wilson's *Our Nig*." *American Literary Realism* 24.3 (Spring 1992): 7–21.

Mullen, Harryette. "Runaway Tongue: Resistant Orality in *Uncle Tom's Cabin, Our Nig, Incidents in the Life of a Slave Girl,* and *Beloved*." In *The Culture of Sentiment: Race, Gender, and Sentimentality in Nineteenth-Century America.* New York: Oxford University Press, 1992. 244–64.

Nelson, Emmanuel S. "Harriet E. Wilson." *African American Authors, 1745–1945.* Ed. Emmanuel S. Nelson. Westport, CT: Greenwood Press, 2000. 483–87.

Stern, Julia. "Excavating Genre in *Our Nig*." *American Literature: A Journal of Literary History, Criticism, and Bibliography* 67.3 (September 1995): 439–66.

Tate, Claudia. "Allegories of Black Female Desire: Or, Rereading Nineteenth-Century Sentimental Narratives of Black Female Authority." In *Changing Our Own Words: Essays on Criticism, Theory, and Writing by Black Women.* Ed. Cheryl A. Wall. New Brunswick, NJ: Rutgers University Press, 1989. 98–126.

West, Elizabeth J. "Reworking the Conversion Narrative: Race and Christianity in *Our Nig*." *MELUS: The Journal of the Society for the Study of the Multi-Ethnic Literature of the United States* 24.2 (Summer 1999): 3–27.

White, Barbara. " 'Our Nig' and the She-Devil: New Information about Harriet Wilson and the 'Belmont' Family." *American Literature: A Journal of Literary History, Criticism, and Bibliography* 65.1 (March 1993): 19–52.

RICHARD WRIGHT
(1908–1960)

H. Nigel Thomas

BIOGRAPHY

Richard Wright's biography could be structured around the places where he lived, inasmuch as those places seem to reflect radically new orientations in his life: The Deep South corresponds to his formative experiences, Memphis and Chicago to his writing apprenticeship, New York the apex of his writing success, and Paris the shift in his focus to existentialist and "Third World" issues.

Richard Nathaniel Wright was born on September 4, 1908, on the Rucker's Plantation in Adams County, Mississippi, about twenty-two miles from the city of Natchez. He was one of two children born to Ella Wilson Wright and Nathan Wright, the other being Leon Alan born in 1910. The name "Richard" was for his maternal grandfather, Richard Wilson, a slave, who, following Lincoln's Abolition Proclamation, joined the U.S. Navy. "Nathaniel" was for his paternal grandfather, Nathaniel Wright, who had been a freed slave at the time of emancipation and who, after emancipation, was given land that he managed to hold on to despite the ruthless violence against property-owning blacks in the post-Reconstruction period (Fabre 1). Wright's maternal grandmother, Margaret Bolton Wilson, was a white-looking woman, who was a blend of Native American, African American, Irish, and Scottish. Before emancipation, she had been a house slave; after emancipation, a midwife. In Wright's depiction of her she is a fearsome matriarch and fanatical Seventh Day Adventist. His paternal grandmother, Laura Calvin Wright, "was three fourths Choctaw" (Walker 14). Wright's father was an illiterate sharecropper, and his mother, before marriage, had been a schoolteacher (Fabre 5). According to *Black Boy*, two of his mother's siblings—Uncle Thomas, the oldest, and Aunt Addie, the youngest—were also schoolteachers. Margaret Walker reports that another sibling, Cleo, whom Wright mentions in the Chicago section of *Black Boy (American Hunger)*, had also been a schoolteacher (34). Apart from his father, Wright deliberately excludes any mention of his paternal family from his autobiography even though in 1916 his mother took him and Alan back to the Travelers' Rest plantation, where for three generations his forbears and then his uncle Solomon farmed: they remained there for almost a year as Wright's mother tried unsuccessfully to be rehired as a teacher (Walker 25).

In 1912, shortly after his parents gave up sharecropping and settled in Natchez. Wright in a fit of boredom burned down part of his maternal grandparents' house and was flogged to the point of being delirious for several days. A year later, his parents moved to Memphis, where his father deserted his family for another woman and left his children improvident. When his mother began working, Wright was left unsupervised and for a while spent his days in drinking saloons, where he recited obscenities in exchange for alcohol. Around this time he also learned, abetted by his mother, that he must counter violence with violence to prevent being bullied by his peers. Later, he would, however, learn never to hit white people even when they were the aggressors.

In September 1915, he began school, but his stay there was brief because his mother fell ill in 1916. Grandmother Wilson came to Memphis to take care of them, but when she left, Wright and his brother spent a short time in Settlement House, a Methodist orphanage; the experience traumatized Wright. That summer, while en route to Aunt Maggie's home in Elaine, Arkansas, Wright, his mother, and Alan stopped over in Jackson, Mississippi, where his maternal grandparents now lived. There, a schoolteacher boarding with Wright's grandmother told Richard the story of Bluebeard; she was accused of corrupting him with lies and was promptly evicted.

At Aunt Maggie's home, Wright became comfortable for the first time, but it ended abruptly when his aunt's husband was murdered by whites who coveted his saloon business. In terror, they fled back to Jackson, leaving behind whatever they could not carry, only to leave again within a few months and head back to Arkansas, this time to West Helena. Aunt Maggie soon fled again, with her lover after he murdered a white woman. But Ella and her children stayed on in West Helena, and Wright resumed his schooling. But his mother fell ill, and to stave off hunger, Wright left school and earned whatever money he could. Eventually Aunt Maggie took Alan with her to Detroit, and Wright and his mother returned to Jackson.

This time his stay in Jackson, after a brief, disastrous attempt to live with his Uncle Clark and his wife Jody in Greenwood, would be a long, agonizing one. Corporal punishment seemed to be the family's unique response to Wright's anxieties and need for affection. Wright resisted both corporal punishment and his relatives' attempts to transform him into a good southern "black boy." Such recalcitrance made him a pariah to his maternal uncles and aunts and grandparents.

At his grandparents' home, where his youngest Aunt Addie, who had been away at school, also lived (joined a little more than a year later by Uncle Thomas, his wife, and daughter after the death of Grandpa Wilson), Wright was subjected to his grandmother's Seventh-Day Adventist regimen. Since Seventh-Day Adventist doctrine proscribes working on Saturday and even exceeds the Levitical dietary laws (in urging a vegetarian diet), Wright was not only malnourished but was for a long time forbidden to earn much needed money on Saturdays. Initially he was forced to attend the Seventh-Day Adventist school where his Aunt Addie—they mutually hated each other—taught. In 1921, he attended Jim Hill, a public school. He was two years behind his peers. At school he was able to develop some lasting friendships (two, Essie Lee Ward's and Joe Brown's, would last a lifetime) and to derive some self-esteem from a good school performance. Working later as a newspaper delivery boy, he could read material Grandmother Wilson and Aunt Addie excluded from the household. In summer 1922, he traveled throughout the Mississippi Delta with an illiterate insurance salesman filling out insurance policies sold to mostly illiterate black sharecroppers.

Following his grandfather's death in 1922, Wright was allowed to work, running errands and doing odd jobs for whites. He was thus able to earn enough money to pay for his clothes and books and to supplement his meager home diet.

In the fall of 1923 he enrolled at Smith Robertson Junior High School. Around this time, too, he wrote his story "The Voodoo of Hell's Half-Acre," which the *Southern Register* published, and worked at the American Optical Company, where he was the target of race-motivated terror.

He graduated from Smith Robertson Junior High School as valedictorian in 1925 but refused to give a speech written by the principal despite pressure from his Uncle Thomas and blatant bribes and threats from the school's principal. For a very short while, he attended the newly opened Lanier High School. For the rest of 1925, he amassed as much money as he could legally and illegally in the hope of leaving Jackson, which he did, and went to live in Memphis in the fall of 1925.

The period of just over one year that Wright spent in Memphis was seminal to his literary development. There, using a system of subterfuge he had developed to combat Mississippi racism, he was able to borrow books from the Cossitt Public Library, which did not cater to blacks, and was thus able to discover the works of some of the giants of American literature.

In December 1927, Wright and his Aunt Maggie moved to Chicago, where another maternal aunt Cleo lived. Alan and his mother joined them in 1928. In Chicago he was struck by the overt absence of Jim Crow practices and racial taboos as well as by the extent to which his reactions to whites had been conditioned by his Mississippi upbringing. He supported himself with odd jobs, then with part time at the post office, before eventually, on the eve of the depression, attaining the body weight requirement for full time work. Throughout, he continued the literary education begun in Memphis. At the post office, he met others who shared his literary interests and who introduced him to Marxist ideas.

Lessened work at the post office, as the Great Depression worsened, gave

Wright more time for reading and writing. In 1931 he published "Superstition" in *Abbot's Monthly Magazine*, but the magazine went bankrupt before he was paid. Working first for a Republican politician and later for a Democratic politician, he received his first insights into the sordidness of politics. In 1932 he was a door-to-door salesman of insurance policies, an experience that, as Michel Fabre notes (87), provided him with the intimate details of African American living found in his book *12 Million Black Voices* (1941).

By the end of 1932, the depression forced Wright into a series of temporary jobs, culminating with his caring for laboratory animals at the Michael Reese Hospital. Here he had his best opportunity to observe white bigotry northern style as well as what he would probably call the stultifying effects of racism on some blacks.

Most significant was his joining the John Reed Club of Chicago, a literary club comprised primarily of white communists. He soon became its secretary-general. Moreover, the magazines directly and indirectly associated with the club and communism in general: *New Masses*, *International Literature*, *Left Front*, and *Anvil* not only spurred him to write but provided a publishing outlet for his writing. Although Wright found his relationships with the Chicago communists rife with conflict, 1933 through 1935 are the years in which several of his poems and his short story "Big Boy Leaves Home" were published. Moreover, by 1935, he had already written and sent out to publishers *Lawd Today* (posthumously published in 1963). He was employed by the Federal Writers' Project in 1935 as a writer. By 1937, it was clear in Wright's mind that he was a writer, for he turned down a $2,000 annual salary as a full-time postal worker and moved to New York, where he had no certitude of employment.

If Memphis represents Wright's literary awakening, and Chicago his literary apprenticeship, New York represents the fruit of his literary activities. The years 1938, 1939, 1940, and 1941 were almost breathless ones for Wright. In 1938 his short story "Fire and Cloud" won first prize in a *Story* magazine contest. Immediately following the announcement of the prize, Harper's accepted the four novellas that comprised the first version of *Uncle Tom's Children*. In 1939 "Fire and Cloud" also won second prize in the O. Henry Memorial Award. That year, too, Wright obtained a Guggenheim Fellowship and married his first wife, Dhimah Rose Meadman. On March 1, 1940, *Native Son* was published as a Book-of-the-Month Club selection; it received immediate superlative praise from the white and black critical establishments. In July 1940 Wright became the president of the League of American Writers and would use his position as its president, in 1941, to point out, in "Not My People's War," the irrelevance of World War II to the aspirations of black Americans, a position he reversed by year-end. In January 1941 he received the Spingarn Medal for *Uncle Tom's Children* and *Native Son*. In March 1941, the same month he married Ellen Poplar, having divorced his first wife, a stage adaptation of *Native Son* opened. Wright and Paul Green had collaborated on the script. In October 1941, *12 Million Black Voices*, a book he wrote in collaboration with photographer Edwin Rosskam, was published. Despite these seemingly superhuman literary tasks, Wright still found time to involve himself in social causes. He helped to obtain parole for Clinton Brewer, who had been in a New Jersey prison since he was eighteen and had already served eighteen years of a life sentence. When Brewer became a repeat offender within three months of his release, Wright became interested in the dynamics of the criminal mind, an issue he would explore in his novel *Savage Holiday*. During this period, he was an important mentor to Ralph Ellison.

Nor were the years 1942 to 1945 significantly less busy. His daughter Julia was born, and he quietly withdrew from the Communist Party. The year 1943 was crucial as regards the writing of *Black Boy*. In 1944, while the Wrights were visiting Quebec City, the *Atlantic Monthly* published "I Tried to Be a Communist," Wright's account of his experiences with the American Communist Party. In 1945 *Black Boy* was published as a Book-of-the-Month Club Selection and became an instant bestseller. He was in demand for interviews everywhere on every subject pertaining to his writing and to African American existence.

In 1946 Wright visited France as a guest of the government of France, and as an ad hoc cultural ambassador for the United States, but also with a view to living there. He met Gertrude Stein—they mutually admired each other's work—and several French intellectuals, including Jean-Paul Sartre, whom he had already met in New York earlier in the year, as well as the famous poet and cofounder of the Negritude movement Leopold Sedar Senghor.

The period 1947–1960, the years Wright lived in Paris, can be seen as a period in which he delved into existentialism and preoccupied himself with the process of African and Asian decolonization. The year 1948 was a busy year for Wright. He spent it getting to know the African American expatriate artistic community in Paris and the important intellectuals and literary figures in France, helping to organize the RDR Writers' Conference and to found *Présence Africaine*, the journal of the Negritude movement.

In 1949 his daughter Rachel was born. He worked on the film script of *Native Son* and on the manuscript of the novel that would eventually become *The Outsider*. That year he traveled to Chicago and Buenos Aires to film *Native Son*, in which he himself played the role of Bigger Thomas.

Between 1951 and 1953 Wright spent a great deal of time involved with establishing literary journals, giving lectures on literature, speaking out against the cold war, and writing his existential novel *The Outsider*, which was published in 1953.

Wright's deep interest in politics and the inexorable energy driving the pro-independence forces in the European colonies of Africa and Asia took him to the Gold Coast (Ghana) in 1953. This was essentially a journalistic exercise that resulted in the book *Black Power*, published in 1954. His novel *Savage Holiday*, which resulted in part from his interest in psychoanalysis and the backfiring of his attempt to help Clinton Brewer, was also published in 1954. As a travel writer, he visited Spain in 1954 and again in 1955. In 1955 he attended the Bandung Conference in Indonesia, an exclusive gathering of Asian and African heads of state, called to discuss the issues arising from decolonization and the West's hegemonic control of the nonwhite world. *The Color Curtain*, Wright's report on the conference, was published in 1956. His impressions of Spain, *Pagan Spain*, and four essays reworked from speeches he had given on politics and African American literature, *White Man, Listen*, were published in 1957.

The Long Dream, his last novel, was published in 1958. From then until 1960, he wrote several haikus, tried his hand at playwriting, and even had his adaptation of Louis Spain's *Pappa Bon Dieu* produced in Paris. But a Broadway adaptation of his novel *The Long Dream* was closed after one week. He died in 1960. However, his first novel, *Lawd Today*, was published posthumously, in 1963; as were the excised portion of *Black Boy (American Hunger)*, in 1977; and another manuscript, *Rite of Passage* (1994).

AUTOBIOGRAPHICAL WORKS AND THEMES

Even though there are autobiographical elements in all of Wright's nonfictional works, *Black Boy* (the unexpurgated text, published by the Library of America in 1991, in *Richard Wright: Later Works*, and available separately since 1993 as a HarperPerennial paperback under the title *Black Boy (American Hunger): A Record of Childhood and Youth*) is the only purely autobiographical book he wrote. Back in 1945 *American Hunger* was the title Wright had envisaged for the entire work; the section dealing with his years in the South was to be called "Southern Night," while that of the Chicago years was to be called "The Horror and the Glory."

Wright wrote this autobiography, he claimed, in response to the realization, following the reaction he received after a lecture he gave at Fisk University in 1943, that blacks were afraid to express publicly the effect of racism on their lives (Fabre 250–51). This may not have been the truth, since he had already published "The Ethics of Living Jim Crow" in the 1940 expanded edition of *Uncle Tom's Children*, an account of the terror white workers had subjected him to when they found out he was seeking to become skilled in the optical trade, which fell outside the menial jobs white southerners reserved for blacks. Perhaps the writing of *Black Boy* should be understood within the context of the success of *Native Son*, a success that instantly catapulted Wright into being a spokesperson for his race. Writing his autobiography, then, telling the "truth" about the impact of race on his life in particular, and on the lives of African Americans in general, would be his way of letting Euro-America and the world know of the destructive impact of white racism on African Americans.

Part I of Wright's autobiography, the section published in 1945 as *Black Boy: A Record of Childhood and Youth*, covers Wright's experiences for the first nineteen years of his life, the years spent primarily in Jackson, Mississippi, but with periods in Memphis, Tennessee, and Elaine and West Helena, Arkansas. If in *Black Boy* Wright employs his experiences to portray the total control white southern ra-

cism exerted on blacks and the ruthless brutality built into racist practices to
terrorize blacks into compliance, he also shows that racism forced blacks to be
liars, cheats, and tricksters—they must say what whites want to hear and do or
pretend to do what whites wanted them to do. Moreover, such terror kept blacks
childish; made many of them, including Wright's father, irresponsible parents;
so imbued black parents with anxiety for their own and their children's survival
that they became mere providers of food, shelter, and floggings; and encouraged
blacks to lose themselves in a fanatical, compensating, other-worldly religiosity.
In Wright's words, "The environment the South creates is too small to nourish
human beings, especially Negro human beings" (Kinnamon and Fabre 65). But
Wright also shows that if life for a child in a black southern family could be
oppressive, black survival for families like his own, which were always on the
brink of penury, would be impossible without the mutual assistance family members provide. Wright's depiction of his conscious negotiation of and resistance
to societal and familial oppression to minimize its impact on him invests his
autobiography with graphic drama, but it also has, as Isidor Schneider noted in
his *New Masses* review, the effect of telling the reader, "See what I have sur-
mounted!" (in Reilly, *Richard Wright* 149).

   "Part Two" of Wright's autobiography, subtitled "The Horror and the Glory,"
which was cut from the manuscript when *Black Boy* was published in 1945, was
posthumously published under the title *American Hunger* in 1977. But excerpts
from it, especially of Wright's portrayal of his experience with the Chicago
branch of the Communist Party, were published as essays, and a limited number
of offset copies of the actual manuscript seemed to have been in circulation
(George Breitman, in Reilly, *Richard Wright* 390). In its concrete aspects, *American Hunger* deals exclusively with Wright's experiences in Chicago.

   "The Horror and the Glory," (*American Hunger*), although continuing to explore Wright's apparent entrapment by his southern racial conditioning, is more
theoretically structured than "Southern Night." The text is rife with passages
like the following:

Hated by whites and being an organic part of the culture that hated him, the black man
grew in turn to hate in himself that which others hated in him. But pride would make
him hide his self hate, for he would not want whites to know that he was so thoroughly
conquered by them, that his total life was conditioned by their attitude; but in the act of
hiding his self hate he could not help but hate those who evoked the self hate in him.
So each part of his day would be consumed in a war with himself, a good part of his energy
would be spent in keeping control of his unruly emotions, emotions which he had not
wished to have but could not help having. (313)

Approximately one fifth of the text is occupied with such passages. They create
the impression that the concrete experiences Wright narrates subserve such theoretical constructs. Here, more so than in "Southern Night," Wright deliberately

instructs his readers on the impact of racism on African American existence. Nevertheless, "The Horror and the Glory" (*American Hunger*) is a convincing portrayal of Wright's quest to find salvation and speak to others through writing, of racism northern style and its blight on the lives of Chicago's ghetto blacks (a theme he had already explored in *12 Million Voices* [1941]; of the travail of the Great Depression on himself, his family, and others; of the disillusionment awaiting blacks who turn to organizations like the Communist Party for respite from and support against racism.

Other texts of autobiographical interest are: *12 Million Black Voices* (1941), *Black Power* (1954), *The Color Curtain* (1956), and *Pagan Spain* and *White Man, Listen!* (1957). These works, part journalism, part travelogue, contain Wright's personal opinions on the phenomena he was observing and, in the case of *12 Million Black Voices*, his description of conditions in which he himself had lived. Moreover, he narrates *12 Million Black Voices* using the first-person plural *we*, a clear indication that he wanted his audience to understand that the experience he was narrating was also his own.

As regards the autobiographical content in his essays, the following citation, for example, from "The Psychological Reactions of Oppressed Peoples" (in *White Man, Listen!*) reveals that the reason Wright gave for writing *Black Boy*—to tell the truth of the impact of racism on black lives—was expanded to incorporate his later assumed role as spokesperson for the colonized. After explaining that in the presence of whites American blacks spend all their lives acting, he writes:

In Asia and Africa this acting exists, but in a looser form. Not being as intimately related to the Western white man in their daily lives as the American Negro, the Asian and African do not need to practice this dissimulation to the degree that the American Negro does. Yet it is there. There are Asians and African who, when confronting whites will swear proudly that they have felt any racial feelings at all, that such feelings are beneath them, and will proceed to act in a Western manner. Yet, when alone or among themselves, they will confess their feelings freely and bitterly. I believe that it was only at Bandung that the full content Asian and African racial feelings were expressed publicly and for the first time in all their turgid passion. They were among themselves and could confess without shame.

. . . It is my conviction that the sooner all of these so-called secrets are out in the open, the sooner both sides, white and colored, realize the shadows that hem them in, the quicker sane and rational plans can be made. (19)

There are numerous other examples that link the controlling ideas in these works to those in Wright's autobiography. Wright's overconfidence in rationalism, for example, is patent in the advice he gives to Kwame Nkrumah at the end of *Black Power*: to militarize African life to "free minds from mumbo-jumbo" (347). John Reilly examines some of the more salient links between the ideas in the essays and travelogues and those in Wright's autobiography ("Richard Wright" 409–23).

CRITICAL RECEPTION

Wright's literary reputation was already well established when *Black Boy* (1945) was published, like *Native Son*, as a Book-of-the-Month Club selection in March 1945. Like *Native Son* it quickly made it to the top of the bestseller list. By May 10 Harper had sold 500,000 copies, and by August 1, the Book-of-the-Month Club had sold 325,000 copies (Fabre 283–84). The book, translated in ten languages, has sold "well over four million copies in hardcover and softcover" (Model 58). That, as of December 31, 2000, the Library of America edition (1991) has sold some 28,079 copies of *Richard Wright: Later Works* and the HarperCollins paperback edition of *Black Boy (American Hunger)* (1993) has sold 244,000 copies attests to the ongoing interest in Wright's autobiography (information provided by the Library of America).

Wright is now a seminal figure in African American literature, and *Black Boy (American Hunger)*, when the scholarly articles, book chapters, and M.A. and Ph.D. theses are counted, has elicited hundreds of scholarly works. In this sampling of the critical response to *Black Boy*, it is therefore a good idea to separate the reviews, written for general readers, from the articles and books written for scholars and students of literature.

Black Boy (1945) was widely reviewed. John Reilly's *Richard Wright: The Critical Reception* reprints sixty-one of these and lists seventy-six others (117–91); unless indicated otherwise, this and all subsequent page references for the reviews of *Black Boy* (1945) and *American Hunger* (1977) are to the pages in the Reilly text. Most reviewers praised the book, even if many of them wondered candidly or obliquely, How could someone subjected to such harrowing experiences emerge as a great writer? Some emphasized the discrepancies (Murphy 160–63); questioned the veracity of certain experiences (Flowers 148); saw it as important but superficial and naive (Mayer 153–54). Sinclair Lewis defended Wright's angry tone and charged the critics with using a double standard to assess Wright's work. Wright, he argued, could no more write generously about those who sought to deny him life than a concentration camp survivor could be expected to write a successful comedy about "the kindness and humor of warders in a German concentration camp" (167). But, as Wright had known, his candor and focus would elicit the harshest criticism from blacks and his former communist colleagues. Ben Burns, in *The Chicago Defender*, saw Wright "erring as he did in *Native Son* in his emphasis on the hopelessness of the Negro's lot. . . . In [Wright's] dread of life he has lost the zest of living" (128). W.E.B. Du Bois* emphasized the fictional aspect of the autobiography that literary critics of the 1970s, 1980s, and 1990s would focus on. But, unlike such critics, Du Bois considered *Black Boy* a failure as a work of art (132–33). Theophilus Lewis, one of African America's most respected critics, dismissed the work "as unexciting as the classified advertisements in your newspaper" (155); his review also accused Wright of intellectual dishonesty (155). But other African Americans such as James Ivy, in *The Crisis* (159), Patsy Graves, in *Opportunity* (174), and an unidentified reviewer in *Phylon*

(167) stoutly defended the vision of blacks that Wright portrays in *Black Boy*. But none of these, given the restricted length of book reviews, undertook the extensive, complex analysis of Ralph Ellison's "Richard Wright's Blues" (*Shadow and Act* 77–94).

American Hunger elicited less enthusiastic and less positive reviews than *Black Boy*. Wright's reputation as a writer of fiction had declined during the years he spent in France, and although he was enjoying a renaissance because his work appealed to the civil rights and cultural nationalist militants of the late 1960s and 1970s, it was with perspective and more rigorous aesthetic criteria that reviewers assessed the new book.

Frank Campenni's review for the *Milwaukee Journal* was typical of the positive reviews. It praised the book's publication for finally providing an account of Wright's experiences in the North and for bringing necessary balance to *Black Boy*, especially for modifying the Horatio Alger note on which *Black Boy* ends (386–87). The need for a single volume comprising both sections of the autobiography, expressed earlier by Lionel Trilling in his review of *Black Boy* for *The Nation* (151–53), was restated by Alden Whitman, who felt that the book, cut off from *Black Boy*, lacked the context that would have made it meaningful (375–78). He found, like Jay Thiemeyer, in the *Richmond News Leader Book Page* (378–79), that *American Hunger* was useful for the insights it gave us of Wright as a lonely, isolated, and egotistical outsider.

Two of the searing reviews are worth noting: The first is George Breitman's, in the *International Socialist Review* (389–92), for its correction of what he felt were deliberately false statements by Harper's publicist that the material in *American Hunger* had never before been published. He then drew attention to some of the inconsistencies in Wright's statements, to Wright's poor understanding of communist ideology and lack of interest in politics, as well as to the peculiarities of Wright's personality. He concluded that politically there wasn't much to be learned from *American Hunger*.

David Bradley (who, four years after writing this review, would become a famous novelist himself), in "Soul on Ice" for *Quest* (387–89), began his review by speculating that Harper and Row or the Book-of-the-Month Club manipulated Wright's material to make it conform to the myth of the American North as the Promised Land. The picture of the North painted by *American Hunger*, he argued, "was at variance with the North's liberal self-image; it would hardly have been popular" (387). In his denunciation of *American Hunger*, Bradley was, in 1977, as uncompromising as Theophilus Lewis had been in 1945. He granted that *American Hunger* was good protest literature, "but it is not autobiography" (388). Wright's "observations seem to reflect more than they illuminate; . . . they reveal a man horribly crippled, uneasy with emotion, unaccustomed to warmth" (388). (Margaret Walker, an ex-colleague of Wright and one of his biographers, will, in 1988, concur with Bradley.)

We now turn to the reviews of the Library of America edition of Wright's major works in two volumes in 1991. The reviews were several and laudatory.

Eleanor Blau's review for the *New York Times* (August 28, 1991), the *International Herald Tribune* (August 30, 1991), and the *Bremerton Sun* (September 12, 1991) praised the Library of America for restoring the cuts Wright had made to *Native Son* and *Black Boy* (*American Hunger*) at the insistence of the Book-of-the-Month Club and Arnold Rampersad for his superb work in annotating the texts. Alfred Kazin's review in the *New York Times Book Review* (December 29, 1991) was among the more outstanding. It praises Wright's honesty and defends his vision against those black writers today who discount it. Of all the reviewers, he stated best the problem that the reintegrated *Black Boy* (*American Hunger*) corrects:

The changes in *Black Boy* work to de-intellectualize Wright, to return him to his childhood and adolescence. Moreover, *Black Boy* as published, made the white South the only true villain of the text. In this way, Wright's broader criticism of the United States was blunted, as was his criticism of radical socialists. . . . Without the [earlier part of *Black Boy*] *American Hunger* is more memoir of a period than an integral part of a life story. Offering a limited vision of Wright, it sometimes makes him seem alternately quarrelsome and egotistical. (6)

Several of the giants of African American literature reviewed the restored works. Cyrus Colter, for the *Chicago Sun Times* (September 22, 1991), used his review to reminisce about his memories of Wright and to express his delight that the academic community has now recognized Wright's literary worth. John A. Williams, himself a Wright biographer, in his review for the *Washington Post*, drew on his extensive knowledge of Wright's work and letters to comment on the emendations the restored cuts bring. Charles Johnson's review for the *Chicago Tribune* (November 17, 1991) focused at length on each work and especially *Black Boy* before applauding the Library of America and Arnold Rampersad "for making available . . . a fuller vision of an artist . . . who gave us a 'new world' we are still trying to chart" (6).

Walter Mosley's review for *Fanfare* (December 8, 1991) resembles Johnson's in its argument for Wright's relevance. James Campbell's "The Wright Version?" in the *Times Literary Supplement* (*TLS*) (December 13, 1991) was the only controversial review. In essence he questioned whether Wright would have agreed to the new versions of his works published. Wright's widow, Ellen Wright, and daughter Julia Wright, replied to Campbell, arguing that the cuts reinserted into *Native Son* and *Black Boy* give the texts the shapes Wright desired for them (*TLS* January 31, 1992).

As stated earlier, the scholarly response to *Black Boy* has been abundant. The best place to begin is with Ralph Ellison's "Richard Wright Blues." In it Ellison raises most of the issues that would preoccupy future critics of *Black Boy*: Wright's models, Wright's aesthetic choices, Wright's folklore use, Wright's alteration of the truth, as well as the sociological conditions that created the brutal reality that Wright's Richard endures at the hands of whites and members of his own family. One area Ellison diplomatically avoids, no doubt because Wright was a friend and mentor, is the persona that Wright created of himself in *Black Boy*. Singly or combined, the foregoing preoccupations dominate the scholarship on *Black Boy (American Hunger)* (1945, 1977, 1991).

In all of the earliest studies of Wright's works—those that predate the publication of Michel Fabre's biography *The Unfinished Quest of Richard Wright* (1973)—especially the book-length ones, *Black Boy* is the key to explaining the environment out of which Wright's protagonists emerge. The book-length studies include Littlejohn's (1996), Bone's (1969), McCall's (1969), Brignano's (1970), and Bakish's (1973). Some of the early significant essays are collected in Donald Gibson's *Five Black Writers* (1970). At that point the only bona fide biography of Wright to appear was Constance Webb's (1968). It helped Wright scholars to understand some of the nuances that Wright had excised to make his environment starker than it had really been.

Later scholars of *Black Boy* have benefited from two events. The first is Yale's acquisition of the Richard Wright Papers, which made it easier for the later scholars to form a more complete picture of Wright. The second is the preoccupation with devising literary theory for the study of African American literature and to articulate the African American literary tradition that emerged in the late 1970s. These theorists of African American literature accorded a preeminent place to African American autobiography, and for them, *Black Boy* was a seminal text. It was quickly identified as a narrative of "ascent" following the tradition established by Frederick Douglas's* *Narrative*. In this regard Stephen Butterfield's analysis of *Black Boy*, in his *Black Autobiography in America* (1974), is significant even if it predates this ferment. Robert Stepto's "Literacy and Ascent: *Black Boy*" (1979) is the best of these essays. Some of the others include Abdul JanMohamed's, Lucinda Mackethan's, and David Dudley's.

Some of the studies stress the aesthetic benefits from Wright's careful (even if not altogether truthful) selection of his materials. These include Marjorie Smelstor's, which categorizes *Black Boy* as poetry and *American Hunger* as polemic; Yvonne Ochillo's; Carolyn Camp's, which treats the catalogs in *Black Boy* as poetry; Tamara Dennisova's, which explores blackness and hunger as central tropes in the creation of Richard's identity; and Herbert Leibowitz's, which evaluates the quality of Wright's prose as it relates to the issues Wright is depicting. Horace Porter's essay argues, contrary to most of the other critics, that the end of *American Hunger* effectively brings together the many themes Wright explores in *Black Boy*. A few of these essays, like Charles Davis's (one of the best essays on *Black Boy*, it argues that *Black Boy* employs three distinct voices), David Dudley's, and George Kent's, further probe the charge made in W.E.B. Du Bois's and Ben Burns's 1945 reviews of *Black Boy* and David Bradley's 1977 review of *American Hunger* that Wright's selection of his material distorted African American reality.

Studies that employ a sociological approach include Blyden Jackson's, George Kent's, John Hodges's, and Robert Butler's (Butler's is mythologic as well). Carla Cappetti's study focuses on the influence theories of urban sociology exerted on

Wright's structuring of *Black Boy* and *Native Son*. Yoshinobu Hakutani's study argues that what others find emotionally and aesthetically problematic in *Black Boy* results from Wright's deliberate sociological design.

Almost all of the studies mentioned above deal in some way with the psychological aspects of *Black Boy*. However, Elizabeth Ciner's Freudian reading and Sitamon Youssef's analysis of the recurring motifs of anger and violence as they relate to women stand out in this regard.

Some essays are especially insightful for their analysis of Wright's use of folklore in *Black Boy*. Timothy Adams's employs jazz as metaphor to analyze *Black Boy's* structure and rhetoric; Jay Mechling's argues that *Black Boy* resembles a blues performance but that ultimately Wright's use of folklore is aesthetically unsuccessful.

There are also the comparative studies. Keneth Kinnamon's compares *Black Boy* with Maya Angelou's* *I Know Why the Caged Bird Sings*. Other essays, like Roosevelt Williams's and Margaret Bass's, compare *Black Boy* with other autobiographies in Africa and the diaspora. Charles Nichols's compares *Black Boy* with several other African American autobiographies and shows their relationship to the picaresque in Spanish literature. William Andrews's compares *Black Boy* with three other autobiographies by Mississippi writers. William Profriedt's compares *Black Boy* with Euro-American immigrant autobiographies; and James Olney's proposes a theory for comparing African (which includes African American) autobiography with Western autobiography.

In conclusion, there are the biographies of Wright: Constance Webb's (1968), in large measure supplanted by Michel Fabre's (1973; rev. in 1993). Fabre's biography is complemented by Margaret Walker's (1988), in its exploration of Wright's psychology and Walker's analysis of her suspicion that Wright was self-hating and bisexual. These three biographies reveal the extent to which *Black Boy* is more fiction than autobiography. Addison Gayle's biography (1980) is limited by its cultural nationalist ideology, while John A. Williams's, as Houston Baker noted in 1972, is suited for a high school audience (8). There is also Madison Lacy's television documentary, *Richard Wright — Black Boy*, produced for the Mississippi Educational Television and the BBC (1994), which covers the significant periods of Wright's life and features discussions with Wright's biographers, critics, acquaintances, colleagues, school mates, and his daughter Julia.

BIBLIOGRAPHY

Autobiographical Works by Richard Wright

Black Boy: A Record of Childhood and Youth. New York and London: Harper & Brothers, Publishers, 1945. Rpt. as a Signet edition, 1963. Rpt. as a HarperPerennial edition, 1966.

American Hunger. With an afterword by Michel Fabre. New York: Harper & Row, Publishers, 1977. Rpt. as a Harper Colophon edition, 1983.

Black Boy (American Hunger). *Richard Wright: Later Works* (the reintegrated text annotated by Arnold Rampersad; without the five pages Wright added to the 1945 edition). New York: Library of America, 1991.

Black Boy (American Hunger). With an introduction by Jerry Ward. Annotated by Arnold Rampersad. New York: HarperPerennial, 1993.

Semiautobiographical Works by Richard Wright

(With photographer Edwin Rosskam). *12 Million Black Voices*. New York: Viking Press, 1941. Rpt. Thunder's Mouth Press, 1988.

Black Power: A Record of Reactions in a Land of Pathos. New York: Harper & Brothers, 1954. Rpt. Greenwood Press, 1974.

The Color Curtain: A Report on the Bandung Conference. New York: World Publishing, 1956. Rpt. University Press of Mississippi, 1994.

Pagan Spain. New York: Harper & Brothers, 1957.

White Man, Listen! Garden City, NY: Doubleday, 1957. Rpt. (with an introduction by John A. Williams) Anchor Books, 1964.

Studies of Richard Wright's Autobiographical Works

Adams, Timothy Dow. "I Believe Him Though I Know He Lies: Lying as a Genre in Richard Wright's *Black Boy*. In *Richard Wright: A Collection of Essays*. Ed. Arnold Rampersad. Englewood Cliffs, NJ: Prentice-Hall, 1995. 83–97.

Andrews, William L. "In Search of a Common Identity: The Self and the South in Four Mississippi Autobiographies." *Southern Review* (Baton Rouge, LA) 24.1 (1988): 47–64.

Baker, Houston A., ed. *Twentieth Century Interpretations of* Native Son. Englewood Cliffs, NJ: Prentice-Hall, 1972.

Bakish, David. *Richard Wright*. New York: Frederick Ungar, 1973.

Bass, Margaret Kent. "Whirling Out of the Dance: Three Autobiographies Written in Exile." *Griot* 13.2 (1994): 42–46.

Bone, Robert. *Richard Wright*. St. Paul: University of Minnesota Pamphlets, 1969.

Brignano, Russell C. *Richard Wright: An Introduction to the Man and His Works*. Pittsburgh: University of Pittsburgh Press, 1970.

Butler, Robert J. "The Quest for Pure Motion in Richard Wright's *Black Boy*." *MELUS* 10.3 (1983): 5–17.

Butterfield, Stephen. *Black Autobiography in America*. Amherst: University of Massachusetts Press, 1974.

Camp, Carolyn. "The Rhetoric of Catalogues in Richard Wright's *Black Boy*." *MELUS* 17.4 (Winter 1991–1992): 29–39.

Cappetti, Carla. "Sociology of an Existence: Richard Wright and the Chicago School." In *Richard Wright: Critical Perspectives Past and Present*. Ed. Henry Louis Gates and K.A. Appiah. New York: Amistad, 1993. 225–71.

Ciner, Elizabeth J. "Richard Wright's Struggles with Fathers." In *Richard Wright: Myths and Realities*. Ed. C. James Trotman. New York: Garland, 1988. 125–36.

Davis, Charles T. "From Experience to Eloquence: Richard Wright's *Black Boy* as Art."

In *African American Autobiography: A Collection of Critical Essays*. Ed. William L. Andrews. Englewood Cliffs, NJ: Prentice-Hall, 1993. 138–50.

Dennisova, Tamara. "Richard Wright: The Problem of Self-Identification." *Mississippi Quarterly* 50.2 (1997): 239–53.

Dudley, David L. *In My Father's Shadow: Intergenerational Conflict in African American Men's Autobiographies*. Philadelphia: University of Pennsylvania Press, 1991.

Ellison, Ralph. "Richard Wright's Blues." 1945. Rpt in *Shadow and Act*. New York: Vintage, 1972. 77–94.

Fabre, Michel. *The Unfinished Quest of Richard Wright*. New York: William Morrow, 1973. Rev. ed. University of Illinois Press, 1993.

Gayle, Addison, Jr. *Richard Wright: Ordeal of a Native Son*. Garden City, NY: Anchor Press, 1980.

Gibson, Donald. *Five Black Writers*. New York: New York University Press, 1970.

Hakutani, Yoshinobu. "Creation of the Self in Richard Wright's *Black Boy*." *Black American Literature Forum* 19.2 (1985): 70–75.

Hodges, John O. "An Apprenticeship to Life and Art: Narrative Design in *Black Boy*." *College Language Association Journal* 24.4 (June 1985): 415–33.

Jackson, Blyden. "Richard Wright: Black Boy from America's Black Belt and Urban Ghettos." *College Language Association Journal* 12.4 (1969): 287–309.

Kent, George E. "Richard Wright: Blackness and Adventure of Western Culture." In *Blackness and the Adventure of Western Culture*. Chicago: Third World Press, 1973. 76–97.

Kinnamon, Keneth. "Call and Response: Intertextuality in Two Autobiographical Works by Richard Wright and Maya Angelou." In *Studies in Black American Literature. Volume II: Belief vs. Theory in Black American Literature*. Ed. Joe Weixlmann and Chester J. Fotentot. Greenwood, FL: Penkevill Publishing, 1986. 121–34.

Kinnamon, Keneth, with Joseph Benson, Michel Fabre, and Craig Werner. *A Richard Wright Bibliography: Fifty Years of Criticism and Commentary, 1933–1982*. Westport, CT: Greenwood Press, 1988.

Kinnamon, Keneth, and Michel Fabre, eds. *Conversations with Richard Wright*. Jackson: University Press of Mississippi, 1993.

Lacy, Madison D., producer. *Richard Wright—Black Boy*. Television Documentary for Mississippi Educational Television and the BBC, 1994.

Leibowitz, Herbert. "'Arise Ye Pris'ners of Starvation': Richard Wright's *Black Boy* and *American Hunger*." In *Richard Wright: Critical Perspectives Past and Present*. Ed. Henry Louis Gates and K.A. Appiah. New York: Amistad, 1993. 328–58.

Littlejohn, David. *Black on White: A Critical Survey of Writing by American Negroes*. New York: Grossman Publishers, 1966.

Margolies, Edward. *The Art of Richard Wright*. Carbondale: Southern Illinois University Press, 1969.

McCall, Dan. *The Example of Richard Wright*. New York: Harcourt Brace Jovanovich, 1969.

Mechling, Jay. "The Failure of Folklore in Richard Wright's *Black Boy*." *Journal of American Folklore* 104 (Summer 1991): 275–94.

Model, F. Peter. "The Second Emancipation of Richard Wright." *Wilson Library Bulletin* (December 1991): 58–61.

Nichols, Charles H. "The Slave Narrators and the Picaresque Mode: Archetypes for Mod

ern Black Personae." In *The Slave's Narrative*. Ed. Charles T. Davis and Henry
    Louis Gates Jr. Oxford: Oxford University Press, 1985. 148–75.

Ochillo, Yvonne. "*Black Boy*: Structure and Meaning." *Griot* 6.1 (1987): 49–54.

Olney, James. "The Value of Autobiography for Comparative Studies: African vs. Western
    Autobiography." In *African American Autobiography: A Collection of Critical Essays*.
    Ed. William L. Andrews. Englewood Cliffs, NJ: Prentice-Hall, 1993. 138–50.

Porter, Horace A. "The Horror and the Glory: Richard Wright's Portrait of the Artist in
    Black Boy and *American Hunger*." In *Richard Wright: A Collection of Critical Essays*.
    Ed. Richard Macksey and Frank Moorer. Englewood Cliffs, NJ: Prentice-Hall,
    1984. 55–67.

Profriedt, William A. "The Immigrant or 'Outsider' Experience as Metaphor for Becoming
    an Educated Person in the Modern World: Mary Antin, Richard Wright and Eva
    Hoffman." *MELUS* 16.2 (1989): 77–89.

Reilly, John M., ed. *Richard Wright: The Critical Reception*. New York: B. Franklin, 1978.

———. "Richard Wright and the Art of Non-Fiction: Stepping Out on the Stage of the
    World." In *Richard Wright: Critical Perspectives Past and Present*. Ed. Henry Louis
    Gates and K.A. Appiah, New York: Amistad, 1993. 409–23.

Smelstor, Marjorie. "Richard Wright's Beckoning Descent and Ascent." In *Richard Wright:
    Myths and Realities*. Ed. C. James Trotman. New York: Garland, 1989. 89–109.

Stepto, Robert. "Literacy and Ascent: *Black Boy*." In *Richard Wright: Critical Perspectives
    Past and Present*. Ed. Henry Louis Gates and K.A. Appiah. New York: Amistad,
    1993. 226–54.

Walker, Margaret. *Richard Wright: Daemonic Genius*. New York: Warner, 1988.

Webb, Constance. *Richard Wright: A Biography*. New York: Putnam, 1968.

Williams, John A. *The Most Native of Sons: A Biography of Richard Wright*. Garden City,
    NY: Doubleday, 1970.

Williams, Roosevelt. "Mothers and Their Defining Role: The Autobiographies of Richard
    Wright, George Lamming and Camara Laye." *Griot* 13.2 (1994): 54–61.

Youssef, Sitamon Mbaraka. " 'Southern Night' and the Angry Voice of Richard Wright."
    The Marjorie Kinnan Rawlings Journal of Florida Literature 7 (1996): 85–98.

SELECTED BIBLIOGRAPHY

Andrew, William. *To Tell a Free Story: The First Century of Afro-American Autobiography, 1760–1865*. Urbana: University of Illinois Press, 1986.

———, ed. *African American Autobiography: A Collection of Critical Essays*. Englewood Cliffs, NJ: Prentice-Hall, 1993.

———, ed. *Critical Essays on Frederick Douglass*. Boston: G.K. Hall, 1991.

Barton, Rebecca Chalmers. *Witnesses for Freedom: Negro Americans in Autobiography*. New York: Harper, 1948.

Braxton, Joanne M. *Black Women Writing Autobiography: A Tradition within a Tradition*. Philadelphia: Temple University Press, 1989.

Brignano, Russell C. *Black Americans in Autobiography*. Durham, NC: Duke University Press, 1974.

Butterfield, Stephen. *Black Autobiography in America*. Amherst: University of Massachusetts Press, 1974.

Dudley, David L. *My Father's Shadow: Intergenerational Conflict in African American Men's Autobiography*. Philadelphia: University of Pennsylvania Press, 1991.

Fishburn, Katherine. *The Problem of Embodiment in Early African American Narrative*. Westport, CT: Greenwood Press, 1997.

Fleischner, Jennifer. *Mastering Slavery: Memory, Family, and Identity in Women's Slave Narratives*. New York: New York University Press, 1996.

Foster, Frances Smith. *Witnessing Slavery: The Development of Ante-bellum Slave Narratives*. 2nd ed. Madison: University of Wisconsin Press, 1994.

———. *Written by Herself: Literary Production by African American Women, 1746–1892*. Bloomington: Indiana University Press, 1993.

Lee, Robert A. *Designs of Blackness: Mappings in the Literature and Culture of America*. London: Sterling, 1998.

Mostern, Kenneth. *Autobiography and Black Identity Politics: Racialization in Twentieth-Century America*. New York: Cambridge University Press, 1999.

Perkins, Margo V. *Autobiography as Activism: Three Black Women of the Sixties*. Jackson: University of Mississippi Press, 2000.

Rampersad, Arnold, and Deborah McDowell, eds. *Slavery and Literary Imagination*. Baltimore: Johns Hopkins University Press, 1989.

Sekora, John, and Darwin T. Turner, eds. *The Art of Slave Narrative: Original Essays in Criticism and Theory*. Madison: University of Wisconsin Press, 1982.

Smith, Sidonie. *Where I'm Bound: Patterns of Slavery and Freedom in Black American Autobiography*. Westport, CT: Greenwood Press, 1974.

Smith, Valerie. *Self-Discovery and Authority in African American Narrative*. Cambridge, MA: Harvard University Press, 1987.

Sundquist, Eric J. *Frederick Douglass: New Literary and Historical Essays*. New York: Cambridge University Press, 1990.

INDEX

ABOUT THE EDITOR AND CONTRIBUTORS

PAULA C. BARNES is Associate Professor of English at Hampton University. She has published several scholarly articles on African American authors.

HARMONY NICOLE BOOKER is a graduate student in social studies and American history at the State University of New York, Cortland.

LINDA M. CARTER is Associate Professor of English at Morgan State University. She has coedited four books and authored over thirty articles on African American literature and culture.

HARISH CHANDER is Professor of English at Shaw University, North Carolina. He has contributed chapters to various reference volumes on African American and postcolonial literatures.

MICHAEL L. COBB is a doctoral candidate in English at Cornell University, where he is completing a dissertation on James Baldwin.

ADENIKE MARIE DAVIDSON, Assistant Professor of English at the University of Central Florida, holds a doctorate in African American literature from the University of Maryland, College Park.

EMMA WATERS DAWSON is Professor of English and Associate Dean, College of Arts and Sciences at Florida A&M University, Tallahassee.

LYNN DOMINA teaches in the Humanities Department at the State University of New York, Delhi. Author of the reference volume *Understanding a Raisin in the Sun* (Greenwood, 1999), she has published a collection of poems titled *Corporal Works* (1995).

STACEY L. DONOHUE teaches in the Humanities Department at Central Oregon Community College.

DAVID L. DUDLEY, author of *My Father's Shadow: Intergenerational Conflict in African American Men's Autobiography* (1991), is Associate Professor at Georgia Southern University.

BARBARA L.J. GRIFFIN is Associate Professor of English at Howard University. A specialist in African American literature, her articles have appeared in *MELUS, CLA Journal, Callaloo,* and *Black Scholar.*

JAMES L. HILL is Professor of English and Assistant Vice President for Academic Affairs at Albany State University, Georgia. He has published in a number of scholarly journals, including *Journal of Negro History, Resources for American Literary Studies,* and *Black Book Bulletin.*

NIKOLAS HUOT is a doctoral candidate in English at Georgia State University. He has contributed chapters to *African American Authors, 1745–1945* (Greenwood, 2000) and *Asian American Novelists* (Greenwood, 2000).

EILEEN O. JAQUIN recently graduated magna cum laude from the English Department at the State University of New York, Cortland.

GWENDOLYN S. JONES is Professor Emeritus of English at Tuskegee University. She has published extensively on the women writers of the Harlem Renaissance.

JACQUELINE C. JONES is Associate Professor of English at Washington College, Maryland.

LEELA KAPAI is Professor of English at Prince George's Community College in Maryland.

CHRISTINE M. LEMCHAK teaches in the Department of English at the State University of New York, Cortland.

ROBIN JANE LUCY, who has published on the works of Ann Petry, Claude Brown, and Ralph Ellison, received her Ph.D. in English from McMaster University, Canada.

ELIZABETH MARSDEN is Assistant Professor of English at Dillard University. A published poet, her scholarly interests include Gothic fiction and Native American literature.

SUZANNE HOTTE MASSA holds an M.A. in multicultural literature from the State University of New York, Cortland. Her scholarly work appears in *Contemporary African American Novelists* (Greenwood, 1999), *African American Authors, 1745–1945* (Greenwood, 2000), and *Asian American Novelists* (Greenwood, 2000).

KATHLENE McDONALD is a doctoral candidate in English at the University of Maryland, College Park.

VERNER D. MITCHELL is Associate Professor of English at the University of Memphis.

NANETTE MORTON teaches American literature at McMaster University, Canada, where she received her Ph.D. in English recently.

CHANDRA TYLER MOUNTAIN is Assistant Professor of English at Dillard University. The focus of her research is on women writers of the African diaspora.

EMMANUEL S. NELSON is Professor of English at the State University of New York, Cortland. Author of over forty articles on various international literatures in English, he has edited several reference volumes, including *Writers of the Indian Diaspora* (Greenwood, 1993), *Contemporary African American Novelists* (Greenwood, 1999), and *African American Authors, 1745–1945* (Greenwood, 2000).

TERRY NOVAK is Assistant Professor of English at Johnson & Wales University, Rhode Island.

YOLANDA WILLIAMS PAGE is a doctoral candidate in English at Louisiana State University and an instructor at Dillard University.

SUSAN EVANS POND is a recent graduate of the State University of New York, Cortland.

GEETHA RAVI is Reader in English at Fatima College in Madurai, India.

HEATHER RELLIHAN is a Ph.D. candidate in Women's Studies at the University of Maryland, College Park.

CHRIS ROARK is Associate Professor of English at John Carroll University, Ohio. He has published articles on a variety of writers ranging from Malcolm X to Shakespeare.

JOYCE RUSSELL ROBINSON, who holds a doctorate in English from Emory University, teaches at Fayetteville State University, North Carolina.

MAXINE SAMPLE is Associate Professor of English at the State University of West Georgia, Carrollton.

RENNIE SIMSON is Lecturer in the African American Studies Department at Syracuse University.

KELLEY A. SQUAZZO, recent recipient of an M.A. in English from the University of Maryland, is currently an editor for a nonprofit organization in Washington, D.C.

TARSHIA L. STANLEY is Assistant Professor of English at Spelman College, Atlanta.

KARL L. STENGER is Associate Professor of German at the University of South Carolina, Aiken.

H. NIGEL THOMAS is Professor of English at the University of Laval, Canada. Author of *From Folklore to Fiction: A Study of Folk Heroes and Rituals in the Black American Novel* (Greenwood, 1988), he has published a work of fiction titled *Spirits in the Dark* (1994).

EDWARD WHITLEY, author of scholarly articles on Ernest Hemingway, Lucille Clifton, and Walt Whitman, is a doctoral candidate in English at the University of Maryland, College Park.

BETTYE J. WILLIAMS is Associate Professor of English at the University of Arkansas, Pine Bluff. A specialist in African American literature, she has published widely in the field.

LORETTA G. WOODARD is Associate Professor of English at Marygrove College, Detroit.